DEFAMATION

COMPARATIVE LAW AND PRACTICE

UCL PRESS

DEFAMATION

COMPARATIVE LAW AND PRACTICE

ANDREW T KENYON

Director

CMCL – Centre for Media and Communications Law

Faculty of Law

University of Melbourne

Australia

UCL PRESS

First published 2006
by UCL Press

The name of University College London (UCL) is a registered trade mark
used by UCL Press with the consent of the owner

UCL Press is an imprint of the Taylor & Francis Group, an informa business

Taylor & Francis
2 Park Square, Milton Park, Abingdon, Oxon, OX14 4RN, UK

Published in the USA
by Routledge·Cavendish
270 Madison Ave, New York, NY 10016

Typeset in Palatino 9.5/11.5 by
Techbooks
Printed and bound in Great Britain

British Library Cataloguing in Publication Data
A catalogue record for this book is available from the British Library

Library of Congress Cataloging in Publication Data
A catalog record for this book has been requested

ISBN10: 1-84472-021-7 (pbk)
ISBN13: 978-1-84472—021-7 (pbk)

PREFACE

This book compares aspects of defamation law and litigation practice in three countries: the research for it could not have occurred without the assistance of many people. My first thanks go colleagues in the Faculty of Law at the University of Melbourne who have made the working environment so enjoyable and productive. The project benefited greatly through financial assistance from the University of Melbourne, from the Faculty of Law and its Centre for Media and Communications Law and, most substantially, from the Australian Research Council (DP0343258 'Defamation Law in Context'). Such funding is invaluable for empirical research and I thank all the sources of financial support and those who give their time to the funding process.

Many thanks go to all the legal practitioners, court officials and others who assisted with the empirical research. Several people were extremely helpful in organising interviews and access to court files: special thanks to Dave Heller, David Levine, Patrick Milmo, Matthew Nicklin, Richard Rampton and Sally Wiant. Early discussions about US law and practice with David Anderson, Brian Murchison and Rod Smolla were very valuable. This book has benefited greatly from my involvement in two research projects investigating defamation law and the media's news production practices: thanks to my co-researchers Tim Marjoribanks, David Partlett, Clive Walker and Russell Weaver.

Some of the aspects of defamation law and practice, and some of the jurisdictions, examined in this book originally were analysed in a PhD thesis at the University of Melbourne. Thanks to my supervisor, Michael Tilbury for his help during the candidature and to Richard Ingleby who acted as a co-supervisor during the first year of the research and provided valuable advice in its planning stages. Thanks also to the encouragement and advice of its examiners, Michael Chesterman and David Partlett. Some parts of the research have been published previously, as indicated in the book. But all the earlier work has been updated and substantially expanded here through further empirical research and doctrinal analysis. Colleagues at Melbourne and elsewhere provided specific help at various points of the project with research queries, and I thank particularly Camille Cameron and Belinda Fehlberg. Thanks also to all the staff of the Legal Resource Centre at the University of Melbourne and to Jason Bosland, Chris Dent, Peter Kenyon and Melissa Spencer for their outstanding research assistance. And many thanks to Amy Harrington, the Administrator of the Centre for Media and Communications Law.

Numerous people provided hospitality during the research: many thanks to Nan Manefield in Sydney, Eric Barendt in London, Shuli Sadé in New York, Monroe Price in New York, David Partlett and his colleagues in Virginia, Peter Jaszi and his colleagues in Washington, and the Farquharsons in San Francisco. And thanks to John Kelly for kindly providing *The mistrals* for the cover. I have been very fortunate that my family has long been supportive: I particularly thank Thais and Dick Kenyon and Ruth Boschen. Finally my greatest thanks go to Esther Milne, to whom this book is dedicated, for her great support throughout the enterprise.

The law is stated as at 31 May 2005.

TABLE OF CONTENTS

TABLE OF CASES

Given the comparative nature of this book, courts are listed in case citations in this Table unless the courts otherwise are identified by citations. Courts are listed by abbreviations; for example, HL (House of Lords), Eng CA (English Court of Appeal), HC (Australian High Court), NSW SC (NSW Supreme Court), Vic CA (Victorian Court of Appeal), and so forth. For simplicity, England is used to refer to the jurisdiction of England and Wales. In addition, it is noted in this Table where the year in which a judgment was delivered differs from its year of report.

TABLE OF STATUTES AND RULES

NEW ZEALAND

UNITED STATES

SHORT CITATIONS AND ABBREVIATIONS

References to articles and books in the footnotes use a short author-date citation. Full details for each item are listed in the bibliography. Cases are named in full in the first reference in the footnotes of each chapter. Subsequent references in that chapter generally use a shortened case name. The title of various Defamation Acts is abbreviated in the footnotes, with *DA* standing for *Defamation Act*.

– 1 –

INTRODUCTION

> Defamation actions are usually about words. The meaning of the words at issue is probably the most important single factor in a defamation case, since it is of cardinal significance at a great many stages.[1]

I OVERVIEW

This book combines a close analysis of defamation law with extensive empirical research into defamation litigation practice in England, Australia and the US.[2] It examines issues that are most often at stake in, and central to, defamation disputes in each country. Although some points related to remedies are considered – including aspects of mitigating damages in England and Australia – the book's analysis is focussed on two themes. The first examines the central role that a publication's meaning plays in defamation law and practice, especially in England and Australia. The second investigates the ways in which media speech is protected by qualified privilege in England and Australia, and by the US constitutional rules developed since *New York Times v Sullivan*.[3] The book provides legal analysis and empirical context for understanding important changes to defamation law, which have occurred in a number of commonwealth countries since the mid-1990s, and comparing them with the US law and practice that has experienced far longer constitutional influence.[4]

The book presents doctrinal and empirical material on the major elements of each party's case in England and the most significant Australian defamation jurisdictions, namely the country's two most populous states of New South Wales (NSW) and Victoria. In addition, defamation law elsewhere in Australia is noted at many points and the research's implications for Australian jurisdictions are

[1] Faulks Committee (1975) 22; also cited by Neill and Rampton (1983) 8.

[2] 'England' is used to refer to the jurisdiction of England and Wales.

[3] 376 US 254 (1964).

[4] A related matter should be noted, which is not examined in any detail because of the focus on defamation law and litigation. England's Press Complaints Commission and the Australian Press Council offer alternative avenues for complaints about content in mainstream print publications; see eg Weaver et al (2006) Chapter 4. Also note alternative legal remedies like malicious falsehood: see eg Price and Duodu (2004) Chapter 6.

discussed at length.[5] The issues examined concern each side's pleading practices; defences related to truth, opinion and privilege; and litigation practices at the pre-trial and trial stages. The book also uses doctrinal and empirical material to explain legal and procedural differences under US law. The central aims of these sections include enabling non-US readers to make more informed use of US law and commentary, and bringing the intricacies of English and Australian defamation law to US readers in an accessible manner.

In relation to each of its themes, defamatory meaning and privileges for media speech, the book suggests that the ways in which different jurisdictions regulate defamation litigation is a major influence on the way reputation and free speech are reconciled. In this the book builds on previous work that has reviewed how legal procedures affect the protection of speech,[6] and provides ample evidence of the ways in which the detail of practice matters for comparative legal analyses. The book has been completed when reforms to create uniform Australian defamation law appear reasonably likely to be enacted. They are discussed in detail in Chapter 10, and might be operating by the time the work is published. This makes it important to emphasise from the outset that almost every issue dicussed in this book related to meaning and privilege will have great relevance if the reforms occur. If the new provisions become law, Australian courts will need to make many decisions about their interpretation. In jurisdictions such as NSW, the research set out in the following chapters explains how some of the proposed changes should greatly influence the future operation of defamation law. Understanding how the existing law operates – especially in Australia and England – will be invaluable for working out how best to deal with uniform Australian defamation law. Similarly, those in non-Australian jurisdictions will need to take careful note of the current peculiarities in Australian defamation law, as discussed in later chapters, to appreciate how to draw on the Australian experience, both under its current and its proposed laws.

The focus on issues connected with the treatment of publications' meaning is worth examining a little further at the outset. The meaning of words is complex, and is central to defamation law, particularly in England and Australia. Yet this area of 'cardinal significance' has not been examined closely in the defamation literature. To do that is one of this book's central aims: it undertakes a comparative investigation of how meaning is dealt with in defamation law and litigation practice in England, Australia and the US. The most detailed examination is given to England, NSW and Victoria. The book addresses, in particular, the role of defence pleading of meaning under case law that has developed since the 1980s in England and Victoria, and the effects of the statutory cause of action and the limited role for the jury in NSW. Also examined are the very different ways in which issues of meaning arise in US law and practice. Meaning is a focus because it is almost inevitable that parties will differ as to what meaning is conveyed by a publication. This book explores how

5 For Australia-wide examination of the law, see eg Gillooly (1998); Butler and Rodrick (2004).

6 See eg Schauer (1978); Matheson (1987); Gilles (1998).

such a difference between the parties is dealt with in litigation, including the pleading and pre-trial practices that are open to each party and the arguments that can be presented at trial. The book investigates the various methods law can use for dealing with the word games that parties can play. It compares the law and litigation practice – concentrating on three significant English and Australian jurisdictions, while also explaining the very different US approach – to evaluate strengths and weaknesses in their differing approaches to meaning in defamation.

A Chapter outline

This chapter discusses existing empirical defamation research and other research into defamatory meaning and explains the project's sociolegal focus. (The appendix provides further background to the book's empirical research.) Addressing the book's first theme begins in Chapters 2 and 3, in which the law most relevant to defamatory meaning in England and Australia is analysed. The chapters raise four related aspects of the law, and address them purely in doctrinal terms:

(a) the way a party is bound to a pleaded meaning;

(b) the degree of specificity required in a pleaded meaning;

(c) whether, and how, defence meanings are pleaded and dealt with in litigation; and

(d) the stage of a dispute at which differences between the parties about meaning are dealt with, including pre-trial and trial determinations.

Three of these major aspects appear in Chapter 2: how parties are bound, the degree of specificity required, and the stage of a dispute at which differences are determined. How should defamation law deal with these aspects of pleading meaning? NSW requires great precision in defamation pleading. The reported cases suggest many interlocutory hearings occur about the capacity of a publication to convey the pleaded imputations. The common law approach, however, *may* no longer be very different. It also witnesses arguments about which meanings are capable of being conveyed. But the common law may have advantages in avoiding some of the NSW technicality, which has been criticised by some commentators. The fourth aspect, raised in Chapter 3, is to evaluate the Lucas-Box or Polly Peck style of defence pleading,[7] and the contextual truth defence under s 16 of the *Defamation Act 1974* (NSW). Does either approach arise often and how is it dealt with? Are there reasons of trial practice supporting either approach? This matter is timely after criticism of the Polly Peck approach in the Australian High Court and subsequent alteration of the law in many Australian states.[8] In short, defence pleading of meaning appears to be significant in practice and worthy of greater consideration.

---

[7] Named after *Lucas-Box v News Group Newspapers* [1986] 1 WLR 147 and *Polly Peck v Trelford* [1986] QB 1000.

[8] *Chakravarti v Advertiser Newspapers* (1998) 193 CLR 519, [8] (Brennan CJ and McHugh J); and see, in particular, Chapter 9.

In Chapters 4 to 6 the book moves to litigation practice in relation to these four aspects of the law. For defamatory meaning, examining practice is invaluable, as this chapter's opening quotation from the Faulks Committee in England suggests.[9] So, in these chapters, defamation practice from England, NSW and Victoria is investigated. By analysing court files and reporting on practitioners' understandings of litigation, the chapters examine the practices concerned with meaning in each jurisdiction in great detail, which provides the basis for many of the project's overall arguments about meaning in defamation.

The book then moves to its second theme: the treatment of media publications of political or public interest. While the approaches in each country do not necessarily apply to the media in particular, the media are a clear focus for their operation. Chapter 7 reviews the formal law – and evidence from practice – about English and Australian developments in qualified privilege under *Reynolds v Times Newspapers*,[10] *Lange v Australian Broadcasting Corporation*[11] and associated cases. The defences are analysed in terms of their scope, strength and practicality in litigation. Compared to the earlier chapter's examination of matters of pleading, truth and opinion, the consideration of qualified privilege in England and Australia remains somewhat tentative; while important issues about the defences are outlined, it also is made clear that much depends on further case law.

US defamation law and litigation practice is examined in Chapter 8 in relation to the twin themes of the book: matters connected with a publication's meaning and the protection of public interest speech. The chapter investigates issues such as a publication's meaning, substantial truth, opinion, mitigation, discovery and pre-trial motions. One aim in discussing the US position is to help readers from other common law jurisdictions better appreciate the US system: in particular, to place the US constitutional law affecting defamation in the context of state law and litigation practice. Appreciating the US situation beyond the federal constitutional influence would be important for more extended examinations of US law than has been common in English and Australian law reform reports.[12] Equally, Chapter 8 is addressed at US readers: the US law is described in light of the detailed consideration of English and Australian law in earlier chapters to give US readers a useful context in which to evaluate non-US defamation law and practice. In effect, Chapter 8 offers a common lawyer's snapshot of US defamation law and practice. Appreciating why the particular issues are addressed in the chapter – after the earlier exploration of the English and Australian law and practice – should help US readers gain a new perspective on their situation and on the issues that have importance when material is published in significant defamation jurisdictions outside the US.[13] In both instances, the intention is to support sophisticated

---

9 Also see eg Kirby (1977) 122.

10 [2001] 2 AC 127.

11 (1997) 189 CLR 520.

12 See eg Faulks Committee (1975); Australian Law Reform Commission (1979); Neill Committee (1991).

13 See eg *Berezovsky v Forbes* (as *Berezovsky v Michaels*) [2000] 1 WLR 1004; *Dow Jones v Jameel* [2005] EWCA Civ 75; *Dow Jones v Gutnick* (2002) 210 CLR 575.

comparative analysis by commentators and practitioners. Understanding central elements of litigation practice should only help comparative doctrinal analyses – especially when digital communications are increasing the risks of transnational liability for defamation, as well as transforming much legal practice.

The conclusions that are drawn from the doctrinal and empirical research are set out in Chapters 9 and 10. Chapter 9 examines defence pleading of meaning, especially for Australian jurisdictions. Investigating litigation practice suggests the jurisdictions display notable differences. These relate to the number of meanings that each side pleads; the frequency and type of pre-trial hearings about meaning; how often either party amends in relation to meaning; the number of defence pleas that respond to meanings alleged by the other side – for example, by arguing the meanings are true; the frequency and treatment of defence pleas about alternative meanings that are not argued for by the other side; and, in relation to NSW and Victoria, the rate at which proceedings end through settlement or trial. The chapter argues that legal changes since the High Court decision in *Chakravarti v Advertiser Newspapers*[14] increase attention on the plaintiff's pleaded imputations – in ways that are not warranted – and unnecessarily complicate defamation litigation. These Australian developments in relation to defence pleadings of alternative meanings are criticised, primarily because the evidence from practice suggests the changes will exacerbate a complex area of litigation. The chapter offers a detailed examination of the issues that, while centred on Australian developments, should underscore the benefits of the English approach for that jurisdiction and help explain to US lawyers what appears to be a significant difference in the protection of speech under the broadly similar defamation laws and litigation practices of England and Australia.

Chapter 10 then examines the implications suggested by the research for each of the jurisdictions. These relate to further aspects about the treatment of meaning and to privileges for media speech. A general point is that analysing doctrine and investigating practice shows that the treatment of meaning is an important area of difference between the jurisdictions, with significant implications for defamation litigation. For NSW, two possible changes relevant to meaning are examined in detail. They concern the statutory cause of action and the limited jury role under the *Defamation Act 1974* (NSW).[15] The chapter explores these possibilities for change in the NSW situation and argues for legislative reform that would bring the law on meaning closer to the common law. Close consideration of NSW law and practice also explains the need for common law courts to treat NSW precedents carefully. As well as issues about defence pleading of meaning, the chapter evaluates recent changes in case management, especially in England, and it considers proposed uniform defamation law in Australia.[16] In relation to Australian law reform, it is worth repeating that almost all the issues related to meaning and privilege will be very important if the reforms occur. Chapter 10 also evaluates English and Australian developments in qualified privilege and

[14] (1998) 193 CLR 519.

[15] Under ss 9 and 7A, respectively.

[16] See eg Defamation Bill 2005 (SA); and Chapter 10, Part I, E.

suggests areas that are likely to deserve future consideration. And it explores how Australian law, through drawing on *Reynolds*, could change in terms of the *Lange* and statutory defences,[17] and in terms of the uniform defamation proposals. Chapter 10 then draws out implications for future comparative analysis from the US doctrinal and empirical research. It aims to clarify key points in any comparisons for US and non-US readers and proceeds through these matters: the very different treatment of meaning in the US law; the common US procedural steps for media-related defamation cases; the relative defamation expertise of lawyers and judges; the law's focus on plaintiff status more than publication subject matter and the way in which much US defamation litigation may not be quite as complex as suggested in some of the prior research. While the material illustrates how simple comparisons are difficult, the aim is to help US readers appreciate how issues such as meaning, truth, opinion and privilege operate in England and Australia and help English and Australian readers remember how much more there is to the US situation than the *Sullivan* rules.

B Jurisdictional focus

The jurisdictions of England, NSW and Victoria have been chosen for closest doctrinal comparison – particularly in Chapters 2, 3, 7 and 9. Three reasons underlie this. First, cases from each jurisdiction commonly are considered in the others. This is true of appellate cases, and also of trial decisions, especially those of experienced defamation judges. Second, England and NSW offer interesting variations in defamation law, through the substantial statutory modification of common law defamation in NSW,[18] and the case law and statutory changes that have occurred in England since the mid-1980s.[19] In differing ways, each is trying to improve the operation of defamation law with regard to meaning. Third, London and Sydney have each been called the world's defamation capital owing to their volume of litigation,[20] although that appears to have changed markedly in England in recent years.[21] This suggests they may offer particularly good opportunities for research that seeks to add to doctrinal analysis by using information from litigation practice. And, in relation to the latter two reasons, Victoria offers a more traditional common law defamation jurisdiction, which should be useful in evaluating the other two.

The treatment of US law and practice is somewhat different, as Chapter 8 explains. While references to the First Amendment are common in non-American defamation writing,[22] comparing US and non-US defamation law is a more

---

[17] *Lange v Australian Broadcasting Corpn* (1997) 189 CLR 520; *DA 1974* (NSW) s 22.

[18] Under the *DA 1974* (NSW).

[19] Generally see *Polly Peck* [1986] QB 1000; *Lucas-Box* [1986] 1 WLR 147; Neill Committee (1991); *DA 1996* (UK).

[20] See eg Robertson and Nicol (2002) 71, who begin discussing defamation with 'London is the libel capital of the world'; see Brown (2002) for Sydney.

[21] See Chapter 4, Part II.

[22] Eg Loveland (1998); Chesterman (2000).

difficult task. But the comparative descriptions of central aspects of defamation law and practice in the US, England and Australia address these concerns to the extent possible in a study like this; in particular, the US law is considered in terms of state common law as well as federal and state constitutional law. The US is also important for this project because it has been a major site of empirical research into defamation law (generally focussed on the operations and content of the media more than detailed doctrinal comparisons[23]) and for the fact that *some* explorations of meaning and defamation law have been made there.[24]

C Procedure and terminology

The above outline indicates that matters of procedure are important for this book. The incidence and effectiveness of pre-trial procedures, which 'occupy an important position within the fabric of the law of defamation',[25] are significant matters for later chapters. Two general points need to be noted at the outset. First, English civil procedure has undergone substantial changes since the introduction of the *Civil Procedure Rules* on 26 April 1999.[26] The changes followed the Woolf Report on civil justice,[27] and have 'affected the management and conduct of defamation actions as much as any other branch of litigation.'[28] The rules' overriding objective is to deal justly with disputes and in a manner that is proportionate to the amount, importance and complexity of the issues and that take into account the parties' relative positions.[29] The changes also affect terminology; for example, plaintiffs have become claimants, writs are called claim forms, discovery is now disclosure, and pleadings have been renamed statements of case. In general, this book uses the terminology that applies in the relevant jurisdiction at the time in question, so older English cases are still described as

[23] Eg Soloski and Bezanson (1992a) provide an overview of US reform proposals, many drawn from empirical work; for the UK, see eg Barendt et al (1997), for a comparative investigation of the US, England and Australia, see Weaver et al (2006).

[24] Notably by Clay Calvert, some of which has been published in law reviews, having been drawn from his PhD thesis: (1996). Also see eg Tiersma (1987).

[25] Gillooly (1998) 52.

[26] See also the *Civil Procedure Act 1997* c 12, and the *Pre-action Protocol for Defamation* (in force from 2 October 2000). A specific Practice Direction was introduced for defamation from 28 February 2000: *Civil Procedure Rules 1998* (Eng) (*CPR*) Pt 53 PD, before which time the former *Rules of the Supreme Court 1965* (Eng) Ord 82 continued to apply. For an overview of the changes in relation to defamation (which predates the *Pre-action Protocol's* introduction), see Shillito and Barendt (2000) 391.

[27] Woolf (1996).

[28] Milmo and Rogers (2002) v. In relation to the *CPR's* general influence on defamation, see Price and Duodu (2004) Chapter 25. Note: the *Constitutional Reform Act 2005* (UK) creates a new Supreme Court instead of the House of Lords, but the changes appear unlikely to have immediate significance for comparative defamation law.

[29] *CPR* Pt 1, and see eg *Burstein v Times Newspapers* [2001] 1 WLR 579, [39]–[40] (May LJ, Sir Christopher Slade and Aldous LJ agreed); *Dow Jones v Jameel* [2005] EWCA Civ 75, [55]–[59] (Lord Phillips MR for Eng CA).

having plaintiffs and so forth.[30] But because the earlier terminology remains current in Australia and the US, it is sometimes used when comparing particular issues across jurisdictions; for example, what are now called statements of case in England may still be referred to as pleadings when the general issue of pleading is being considered. While not strictly accurate in relation to English procedure,[31] it simplifies the terminology needed for this book's comparative scope.

Second, NSW saw more recent changes to civil procedure under the *Civil Procedure Act 2005* (NSW), which introduced the *Uniform Civil Procedure Rules* across NSW courts. The Act sets out objectives for the management of litigation that bear some resemblance to the English reforms, although the rules made under the Act have not changed as much as the English rules. The effects that these changes could have on NSW defamation litigation are returned to briefly in Chapter 10. The short point is that the English experience under the *Civil Procedure Rules* offers important material that could be drawn on to improve NSW practice.[32] However, because this project's empirical research occurred under the older *Supreme Court Rules 1970* (NSW), those rules are referred to in subsequent chapters as well as the state's *Uniform Civil Procedure Rules*. It also should be noted that, at the time of writing, the newer rules in NSW did not contain specific provisions for defamation litigation. This means that Pt 67 of the *Supreme Court Rules 1970* remains a primary reference in later chapters.[33] (Broadly similar provisions were expected to be introduced in the *Uniform Civil Procedure Rules* in due course.)

Another point of terminology is noteworthy. In general, this book uses the concept of a publication's meaning rather than considering only the imputations that arise from a publication. The approach usefully distinguishes between defamation law's professed aim for a workable method of determining a publication's meaning, and the law's technical pursuit of that aim by requiring parties to plead imputations.[34] Using the general concept of meaning is also commonplace in England.[35] *Imputation*, however, has been seen as a preferable term in NSW because of the 'revolutionary change' wrought by s 9 of the *Defamation Act 1974* (NSW), which makes the imputation rather than the publication the cause of action.[36] The effect of this statutory cause of action is a major issue in later chapters and is examined in detail in Chapter 10.

---

30 The same approach has been taken elsewhere: eg Milmo and Rogers (2004) viii.

31 See eg Brennan and Blair (2004) [1-01].

32 The statutory basis for the NSW rules may encourage greater development than has yet appeared under some other Australian changes, eg Queensland's *Uniform Civil Procedure Rules 1999*.

33 But the *Uniform Civil Procedure Rules* take precedence over the *Supreme Court Rules 1970* (NSW) to the extent of any inconsistency: see *Civil Procedure Act 2005* (NSW) s 11 and definition of 'local rules' in s 3.

34 With regard to pleading requirements, see Chapter 2, Part III, G.

35 See eg *CPR* Pt 53 PD.

36 *New South Wales Aboriginal Land Council v Perkins* (1998) 45 NSWLR 340, 348 (Meagher JA).

II EMPIRICAL LEGAL RESEARCH INTO DEFAMATION

This book has several notable precursors in terms of *empirical* defamation research. Earlier work includes that done in the US by the Iowa Libel Research Project (Iowa Project), Marc Franklin and others; in Australia by Brendan Edgeworth and Michael Newcity, Tania Sourdin, Roy Baker, and as part of some law reform reports; in the UK by Eric Barendt and co-researchers (with similar methods being applied in New Zealand by Ursula Cheer)[37] as well as comparative and empirical research across the US, England and Australia by Russell Weaver and colleagues.[38] Here, some of the earlier work is outlined to illustrate how existing *empirical* defamation research has not focussed on issues of meaning, especially in relation to litigation practice, and comparative empirical research has not considered in detail the interaction of defamation doctrine and practice, addressing issues about defamation law and the media instead. In addition, the examples illustrate that existing research about *defamatory meaning* has not focussed on comparative law and practice.

A US research

The Iowa Project, conducted primarily during the 1980s, is the largest earlier research centred on the US. In a 1987 book about the study, *Libel Law and the Press: Myth and Reality*, Randall Bezanson, Gilbert Cranberg and John Soloski report on their extensive empirical research into defamation litigation.[39] The Iowa Project sought to study the entire litigation process, from a story's publication and initial discussions between potential plaintiffs and lawyers, to the determination or settlement of a case. The Iowa Project examined matters such as who sues for defamation, the role of lawyers and the media in decisions to sue, what plaintiffs seek when they sue, what legal arguments arise, who wins cases, and retrospective views of the litigation process from those involved. The researchers especially wanted to know why plaintiffs sued and what the media could do to prevent suits.

The report of the Iowa Project in *Libel Law and the Press* includes detailed information about its methodology. Various information sources were used. A major source was reported defamation cases from 1974 to 1984. The Iowa researchers could not select cases that would represent all US defamation litigation because they had no way to identify all trial-level cases. Reported cases involve a disproportionate number of appeals, and while it appears US media companies appeal most trials that they lose, comparative figures for plaintiffs are unknown.[40] Thus, the Iowa Project added other material including surveys and

[37] See eg Cheer (2005).

[38] Notable work also exists in Ireland, see eg McGonagle (1997); and for interview-based research focussed on US and Australian media, see Marjoribanks and Kenyon (2003); and comparing the US and England, see Weaver and Bennett (1993).

[39] See also Murchison et al (1994); Soloski and Bezanson (1992a); Bezanson (1988, 1986, 1985); Cranberg (1985); Soloski (1985).

[40] Bezanson et al (1987) 239.

interviews of plaintiffs and defendants,[41] and interviews of media professionals.[42] The researchers also examined more than 1,300 insurance files, surveyed more than 150 newspapers about rates of litigation and settlement, and interviewed lawyers.[43] In effect, the researchers were relying on ideas of triangulation through using these varied sources,[44] and they argued the research had a high degree of reliability.[45]

The researchers found that US defamation doctrine does not match its practice.

> [The US has] a legal system whose underlying assumptions about libel – that libel suits provide a reasonable opportunity to repair damage to reputation, that money is necessary to undo the harm to libel victims, that the constitutional privileges protect the press – bear little relationship to the real world of plaintiffs and media defendants.[46]

The Iowa researchers found plaintiffs almost always lose defamation cases and argue that defamation law does not offer claimants what they want: 'public vindication of the truth'.[47] Perhaps optimistically, they argue most plaintiffs in fact succeed on their own terms. That is, plaintiffs obtain a degree of vindication through the very act of suing.[48] The Iowa researchers also argue that media companies are troubled by defamation law and their speech is 'chilled' by fear of defamation litigation. These problems for both parties made libel reform critically important.[49] To address both parties' concerns, the Iowa Project developed a 'Libel Dispute Resolution Program'.[50] This voluntary program would inquire into a publication's truth or falsity and whether the claimant's reputation had suffered harm. Under this proposal the claimant would need to prove the publication was false.[51] The work also influenced other reform initiatives.[52]

Marc Franklin's work is another noteworthy body of US empirical defamation research. His research involved extracting quantitative information from hundreds

---

41 *Ibid* 247: the researchers estimate they interviewed plaintiffs from 30 to 40 per cent of cases issued against the media between 1980 and 1984.

42 *Ibid* 239–40.

43 *Ibid* 240.

44 Eg Burgess (1982) 165–66; cf appendix nn. 48–50 and accompanying text.

45 Bezanson et al (1987) 246. The researchers used a lower statistical confidence level than is common in such quantitative research: 0.1 not 0.05. But most variables they discuss meet the stricter standard. This approach allowed the researchers to report more findings, which they argued was justified because it was the first project of such a large scale: 247.

46 *Ibid* 3.

47 *Ibid* 177.

48 *Ibid* 181.

49 Soloski and Bezanson (1992b) 369, 374.

50 See Wissler et al (1992) 286.

51 *Ibid*. The proposal was considered in NSW Law Reform Commission (1993) 61–64.

52 Eg see Smolla and Gaertner (1989) 31.

of defamation case reports to examine whether there were differences between cases involving media and non-media defendants.[53] From this work, Franklin also proposed law reform: a declaratory judgment system for defamation.[54] Numerous other US projects exist, some from communications-related disciplines. Research analysing extensive numbers of defamation judgments includes work by Donald Gillmor and, more recently, Dennis Hale.[55] Research incorporating journalists' perspectives more directly includes work by David Barrett, who found publishers said they withheld stories because of legal concerns,[56] and by Richard Labrunski and John Pavlik, who suggested that most journalists believe some stories are not covered because of defamation concerns.[57] The Media Law Resource Center also should be noted. It is a non-profit information and research organisation funded primarily by media lawyers and media companies[58] that aims to promote the media's First Amendment interests and provides regular bulletins about US litigation trends and issues facing media defendants. Its work has been useful in academic writing – as seen in the discussion of Jeffrey Thomas's work below[59] – and it is drawn on further when examining the US situation in Chapter 8.

B Australian research

In Australia, 1980s empirical research into defamation litigation was based predominantly on NSW court records. The research examined who sues, about what matters and with what results. It also considered the apparent effect of defamation law on the media. Substantial work was carried out by Brendan Edgeworth and Michael Newcity,[60] who were concerned with freedom of political speech in Australia well before the case law developments of the 1990s, which are examined in Chapter 7.[61] They were keen to extend defamation research beyond

53 Eg see Franklin (1986, 1983, 1981, 1980). Through focussing on reported decisions, however, Franklin's cases are unlikely to have reflected general trials, which the Iowa researchers note: Bezanson et al (1987) 237–38.

54 See generally Franklin (1986); reprinted in Soloski and Bezanson (1992a) 68.

55 Gillmor (1992); Hale (2003).

56 Barrett (1986) 860.

57 Labrunski and Pavlik (1985) 15. See also Bow and Silver (1984); Bunker (1992). Further research is examined in Marshall and Gilles (1994).

58 See generally <www.medialaw.org>. Before 2003, it was known as the Libel Defense Resource Center.

59 Below fn 120 and accompanying text. Also see eg Newcity (1991) 9ff; Logan (2001); Weaver et al (2006).

60 Edgeworth and Newcity (1992). Other aspects of the same research are reported in Newcity (1991).

61 See particularly these High Court decisions: *Australian Capital Television v Commonwealth* (1992) 177 CLR 106; *Nationwide News v Wills* (1992) 177 CLR 1; *Theophanous v Herald & Weekly Times* (1994) 182 CLR 104; *Stephens v Western Australian Newspapers* (1994) 182 CLR 211; *Cunliffe v Commonwealth* (1994) 182 CLR 272;

reported cases,[62] and in the mid-1980s took limited quantitative information from NSW Supreme Court files. They examined defamation cases issued between February 1979 and June 1981, along with earlier writs that were listed for a pre-trial or trial hearing during this period. Their research shows that approximately 140 cases were commenced each year,[63] and provides detailed information on who sued about what material. They found many more men than women sued[64] and that business- or professional-related allegations were most prominent.[65] Edgeworth and Newcity considered the nature of the alleged defamatory publication, but did not examine issues of pleading or meaning in any detail.[66]

Edgeworth and Newcity's conclusions, however, may have exceeded their methodology. They only examined court records and found few politicians win defamation trials.[67] From this, they concluded there was no significant problem in airing political discussion in Australia. They concluded the 'surest way of minimising any chilling effect [on the media] is to recognise that in most cases, as our study has shown, public debate can proceed with impunity'.[68] But they seem to have made too simple a link between findings about who sued about what sorts of stories, to questions about what stories were initially written and published. That is not to criticise their argument about the 'different social distribution of investigative labour' between the US and Australia.[69] As they suggest, investigation of Australian political misconduct may enter the public arena initially through parliaments – to take advantage of the absolute privilege that exists there. In the US, investigations may use the media. The UK research, discussed below, perhaps used a more appropriate methodology for researching any chilling effect. And later projects such as those of Weaver and his co-researchers,[70] as well as my own work with Australian colleagues,[71] extend the methods in various ways for multiple-country studies.

Lange v Australian Broadcasting Corpn (1997) 189 CLR 520; *Levy v Victoria* (1997) 189 CLR 579; *Roberts v Bass* (2002) 212 CLR 1; *Coleman v Power* (2004) 209 ALR 182; *Mulholland v Australian Electoral Commission* (2004) 209 ALR 582; and eg Chesterman (2000) Chapter 2.

62 Edgeworth and Newcity (1992) 40.

63 318 writs were filed in the period February 1979 to June 1981: ibid 40.

64 Under 8 per cent suits by women in 1979–1982: Newcity (1991) 14–15.

65 Edgeworth and Newcity (1992) 43. Edgeworth and Newcity suggest politicians form the largest category of plaintiffs, but this is achieved after subdividing various groups of business and professional plaintiffs who more easily appear as the largest category.

66 See especially, Newcity (1991) 46–50. He classified subject matter in a similar way to Franklin (1980) 481 and (1981) 812.

67 They were the plaintiffs with the least success: Edgeworth and Newcity (1992) 54.

68 *Ibid* 62.

69 *Ibid* 59.

70 Weaver at al (2006).

71 Eg Dent and Kenyon (2004).

Tania Sourdin conducted another Australian study,[72] examining NSW court files for defamation cases commenced during 1987 and 1988. She extracted quantitative information from the files, focussed on the identities of parties and the sort of matters that were sued over, as well as settlement and costs details (where it was disclosed on the files). Among other things, she found the largest grouping of plaintiffs was business or professional people and corporations, and that just over half of all actions settled within 12 months.[73] Her research included some reference to pre-trial hearings and pleadings.[74] But Sourdin's concern was to see what general types of imputations were pleaded by and against different parties, not to investigate the role of pleading imputations in the process of determining meaning and its relation to other aspects of defamation law and litigation practice.

Australian law reform efforts also have referred to empirical research and conducted wide-ranging consultation with practitioners.[75] One law reform report is noteworthy for present purposes. Some empirical research into court files was carried out for the 1995 defamation report of the Community Law Reform Committee of the Australian Capital Territory.[76] The research mainly examined cases initiated between 1985 and 1988, but also included comparative cases from 1988 to 1993. In total, the Committee looked at 1,130 procedural steps in 133 actions and said defamation actions 'tend to get bogged down in interlocutory skirmishes'[77]:

> Anecdotal evidence tends to suggest that many of these are often frivolous or misconceived. Some may be deliberate ploys to 'wear down' the other party. This takes additional time and expense. Interlocutory applications are sometimes necessary but in some cases they become point-taking exercises to put the plaintiff or defendant to additional expense and frustration in the hope that he or she will abandon the action or else settle for a trivial amount.[78]

Again, the research was not focussed on defamatory meaning, although it had greater relevance to the interaction of law and procedure in defamation.

More recent Australian research includes the work of Roy Baker, who has extended US work about what is called the third-person effect through extensive interview and focus-group research.[79] (Some of that US research is reviewed below in Part II, D.) Baker's work, which is developed methodologically for legal research related to the media, raises questions about the relationship between the legal test for what is defamatory and what harms people's reputations for the

[72] Sourdin (1990); the research is also noted in NSW Law Reform Commission (1995) 11.

[73] Sourdin, *ibid* 7, 31.

[74] *Ibid* 31–33.

[75] Eg NSW Law Reform Commission (1995).

[76] Community Law Reform Committee of the ACT (1995).

[77] *Ibid* [167].

[78] *Ibid* and its note 111.

[79] See eg Baker (2004). For some of the relevant US research, see Calvert (1995b).

ordinary recipients of publications. On the basis of extensive Australian telephone surveys, focus groups and interviews, Baker argues that people misperceive how others will react to media publications. In general terms, people think that others will be affected by media publications more than they are affected themselves. If the harm caused by publications is 'consistently overestimated' in this way, it suggests the law 'unnecessarily silences harmless speech, or overcompensates for what harm is done'.[80] Although relevant to meaning, Baker's work differs from this book in being focussed more on media reception and the implications it might have for law, while certainly having some applicability to questions of comparative doctrine and litigation practice. (In particular, the third-person effect may mean that more damaging meanings are found to be conveyed.[81]) As discussed in later chapters, however, the question of whether meanings are defamatory appears to be side-stepped – at least to a fair degree – in litigation. That is, while the question of what is defamatory exists in every claimant's or plaintiff's case, in practice attention centres on what meaning is conveyed rather than whether it is defamatory.

C UK research

Substantial sociolegal research into UK defamation used more appropriate methods than Edgeworth and Newcity for examining whether media speech is chilled by defamation law. In their 1997 book, *Libel and the Media: The Chilling Effect*,[82] Eric Barendt and his co-reseachers examine the everyday work of defamation lawyers and journalists. The book is based on questionnaires, interviews and some documentary material.[83] The primary focus is defamation law's impact on the media – on decisions about what to publish and what stories to alter during production. *Libel and the Media* goes beyond the range of the Iowa Project's material, which was issued defamation cases.[84] And the work usefully compares different areas of the media, including national newspapers, regional

[80] Baker, *ibid* 2. Baker explores possible implications for increasing damages: 16–20. Further research may be warranted to investigate what links the third-person effect has to reputation. Eg if people believe others think less of a person (because the people overestimate a publication's effects) does that alter how people behave in relation to the person?

[81] *Ibid* 21–24. This is significant particularly in jurisdictions like NSW where the parties effectively are held to the plaintiff's pleaded imputations. See generally Chapters 9 and 10.

[82] Barendt et al (1997).

[83] Eg the then Lord Chancellor's Department's *Judicial Statistics;* see further Chapter 4, Part II, A. Barendt and his co-researchers intended to use questionnaires for all areas of media and supplement them with interviews. But they found subjects working in some media (such as national newspapers) did not want to reply to questionnaires because of limited time and confidentiality concerns. Instead, structured interviews were conducted: *ibid* 42–44; and cf eg 78–79 about regional newspapers where questionnaires were used.

[84] But plaintiffs are silent in *Libel and the Media,* unlike eg the Iowa Project.

newspapers, magazines, books and television news. The researchers found that defamation law has differential effects on these various media outlets, and it is notable that similar effects were found more recently in New Zealand by Ursula Cheer, with books and magazines altering or not publishing more material.[85] Barendt and his colleagues also found that particular categories of potential claimant affect publishing decisions. That is, media professionals check stories about the wealthy (or the financially supported) for libel risks more closely than other stories.[86] It seems this effect depends more on the *perception* of risk within media outlets than on whether lawsuits actually are more likely to be brought.

The researchers conclude that the British media may have an unrecognised form of self-censorship:

> [J]ournalists, particularly those with experience, are well aware of the libel regime in which they are working and, therefore, shape their research and their writing to meet its requirements. In this respect the observation that surprisingly few stories of public interest actually get suppressed or materially redrafted in light of legal advice may reflect the internalization of the restrictive norms of English libel law. This is the most effective form of censorship conceivable, one unrecognized by the writer.[87]

These findings suggest the value in conducting *comparative* and *empirical* research into defamation law and media production processes. Examples of such comparative work include that of Russell Weaver and co-researchers, who compared US, English and Australian law[88]: in particular, the changes since *New York Times v Sullivan*[89] in the US, *Reynolds v Times Newspapers*[90] in England and *Lange v Australian Broadcasting Corporation*[91] in Australia. The research – centred on law and the media as opposed to this book's focus on law and litigation – is valuable for investigating the changing defamation laws in each country related to political or public interest speech, with interviews in England and Australia spanning the years of great doctrinal change since the early 1990s. It is especially notable that, as the first three-country comparative study of defamation and the media, it tends to confirm earlier work arguing that traditional defamation law unduly chills the media. On the basis of a large amount of legal analysis and interview material, it supports doctrinal developments in Australia's *Lange* defence and probably also in the *Reynolds* defence in England. These points are broadly consistent with many of the comments in this book related to the

---

85 Cheer (2005). This also suggests Cheer's findings about a reasonably robust New Zealand media may relate to much of the media having a relatively strong financial position.

86 Eg interviewees in that study were most likely to mention entities like the Police Federation and the late Robert Maxwell: see Barendt et al (1997) 68.

87 *Ibid.*

88 Weaver et al (2006). See also the earlier Weaver and Bennett (1993).

89 376 US 254 (1964).

90 [2001] 2 AC 127.

91 (1997) 189 CLR 520.

research reported in Chapter 7. At the same time, the research acknowledges that English and Australian courts may be unlikely to defer to the media's own professional standards to the degree that appears to have occurred in the US. In this, it suggests that an element of First Amendment exceptionalism clearly needs to be considered in any comparative analysis.[92]

An alternative comparative and empirical approach to defamation and the media involves analysing the content of media products in various countries in relation to differing regimes of defamation law. Using content analysis is unremarkable within media studies and fields of social research,[94] and while some examples can be criticised for a too simple positivism of counting items,[93] content analysis very rarely focuses on legal issues. (And although there has been a great deal of sociological work done on factors that affect media content,[95] the literature has not paid substantial attention to roles that law may have.) Similarly, legal researchers have overlooked some of the possibilities content analysis offers for media law.[96] However, one recent defamation-related study into media content analysed more than 1,400 Australian and US newspaper articles.[97] The work suggests that in the US, where defamation plaintiffs face much heavier burdens than under the English and Australian law, defamatory allegations against political and corporate actors are published more frequently than in Australia.[98] The study's purposive sample was constructed to retrieve material that was likely to criticise political or corporate actors. It drew material from a similar number of mainstream newspapers in each country during periods in 2003 that were not dominated by any particular scandal. It probably also is worth noting that the US titles did not include the so-called supermarket tabloids – rather they were the sorts of titles that could be expected to be comparable to Australian newspapers. From this sample of general news articles and commentary, the US material was found to contain defamatory allegations at nearly three times the rate of the Australian articles. The Australian media appeared to be markedly less comfortable making allegations about corporate affairs than in the US, although the Australian media also appeared chilled in relation to political criticism.[99] While the

92 See eg Schauer (2005).

93 Young (1990) Chapters 5 and 6.

94 Eg approximately 20 per cent of dissertations and articles in 'mass communication research' use content analysis techniques: Riffe and Freitag (1997) 515–16. On media research methods, see eg Hansen et al (1998); Jensen (2002).

95 Eg Shoemaker and Reese (1996).

96 Exceptions from outside defamation could be drawn from extensive media effects research; see eg Barker and Petley (1997).

97 Dent and Kenyon (2004).

98 *Ibid* 106.

99 This aspect of the content analysis is consistent with Cheer's New Zealand findings that commercial reporting raises defamation concerns across all media forms: see Cheer (2005).

Australian study is only one analysis of media content, and there is more to develop in terms of the styles of analysis that can be supported through studying content, there are no obvious reasons to suggest its sample is atypical, at least with regard to ordinary newspaper reporting and commentary in these countries. Its results are also consistent with what could be expected in light of the interview-based research into defamation and journalism discussed above.[100]

While the volume of empirical research into defamation law has increased notably during the last decade, it is clear that the projects have not focussed on defamatory meaning specifically, nor on the relationship between doctrine and practice in defamation law more generally.

D Other research into defamatory meaning

In addition to empirical research into defamation law in general, there has been a small number of interdisciplinary investigations of *defamatory meaning*.[101] Given that a major focus of this book is the treatment of meaning in defamation law and practice, two areas of research are noteworthy: some communications research into media effects and linguistics research related to speech act theory and pragmatics.[102] First, communications research into the effects of media publications is relevant. Since the early 1980s, a strand of US communications research has investigated the 'third-person effect'.[103] This suggests that people assume the media affects other people more than it affects themselves. Jeremy Cohen and others have argued that the test for defamatory meaning is inappropriate because of the third-person effect.[104] The effect suggests that juries decide a publication's hypothetical reasonable recipient perceives more damaging defamatory meanings than the jury members themselves perceive. Cohen and his co-researchers argue the effect exists, having conducted empirical

[100] Eg studies such as Barendt et al (1997); Cheer (2005); and Weaver et al (2006) suggest altering content due to legal concerns is common under non-US defamation law. The results – if not the process – of any alterations are accessible through content analysis.

[101] Cohen and Gleason (1990) provide an overview of social research into law and communication. They consider defamation research and argue for further interdisciplinary work. Clay Calvert appears as one of the more prominent US researchers to take up their call: see (1998, 1996, 1995a, 1995b).

[102] A third area of research into defamatory meaning involves the 'awareness of meaning' standard, which is considered in Chapter 8, Part IV, B.

[103] Starting with Phillips Davison (1983). A useful overview of the research is provided by Baker (2004) 9–11; see also Calvert (1998). Debates within media studies on audience effects could be linked to these questions: see eg Jennings and Thompson (2002); Barker and Petley (1997).

[104] Cohen et al (1988). See also Price et al (1997); Rojas et al (1996); Mason (1995); Gunthier and Mundy (1993); Cohen and Gunthier (1987).

research involving mock jurors in a defamation dispute.[105] Their research has received limited attention within law journals. For example, David McGraw has argued for US defamation law to take a wider approach to a publication's context in determining the meaning it conveys, in part drawing on media effects research.[106] As mentioned above, Roy Baker has extended this work to Australia, where his work suggests the effect also exists.[107] A related interest in 'effects' is seen in research into the reputational harm caused by defamatory publication. Clay Calvert has called for greater consideration of the third-person effect, as well as suggesting that other communications studies research into reputational harm could assist defamation law.[108] Calvert notes that juries face a difficult issue in measuring harm,[109] and postulates that the task can be made less speculative through communications research. Calvert reports on a communications study which suggests that a publication containing a denial of a defamatory allegation reduces the harm to reputation. And publications with repeated denials appear to have this effect more strongly than those with a single denial.[110] From this, he argues for defamation law to direct more attention to denials within publications when assessing publications' effects.

Linguistics is the second noteworthy area, for present purposes, which has been drawn on in some writing about defamatory meaning. Speech act theory, derived from the work of John Austin[111] and John Searle,[112] is one example. Peter Tiersma has used speech act theory to suggest that law should recognise every utterance as having both an illocutionary (or intended) force and a perlocutionary (or perceived) effect.[113] Tiersma argues that defamation should be redefined to focus on a speech act's illocutionary force – and thus it should apply only to accusations. His argument is based partly on existing defamation doctrine and the ways in which it does consider illocutionary aspects of

---

[105] But their findings are inconclusive as to whether this effect is due to jury members' underestimating a publication's effect on themselves or overestimating its effect on others: Cohen et al (1988) 169–70. Baker notes non-legal research that tends to support the second option: (2004) 9–11. Difficulties with mock jury research also are significant: see eg NSW Law Reform Commission (2000) [2.55]–[2.68]; cf Chesterman et al (2001).

[106] McGraw (1991). McGraw is a journalism academic; he published this substantial article in a law review. See also Harkess (1998).

[107] See Baker (2004).

[108] Calvert (1995b).

[109] *Ibid* 935–36, discussing *Masson v New Yorker Magazine*, 832 F Supp 1350, 1354 (ND Cal, 1993) in which the first trial jury was deadlocked over the quantum of damages.

[110] *Ibid* 938. The effect of denying a defamatory allegation is particularly significant in US constitutional approaches to defamation. US doctrine assumes public officials and figures can access the media to put their side, with their denials reducing any reputational harm, as Calvert notes, *ibid* 941–42, 950.

[111] Austin (1975).

[112] Searle (1979, 1969).

[113] Tiersma (1987).

communication.[114] Tiersma argues US law is approaching a position that would require plaintiffs to prove a publication 'has the force of an accusation', which would help make a 'nebulous' area of law more rational.[115] 'Perhaps more important, this definition limits liability to those who accuse, excluding parties that inadvertently convey the accusations of others.'[116] While drawing in a sophisticated manner on theoretical work about the use of language, Tiersma's argument may have benefited from closer attention to law's operation. He does note that the examination of defamation law in the analysis is somewhat idealised,[117] and suggests the analysis is focussed on common law rather than US constitutional issues. But to a non-US reader it appears to rely on constitutionally derived doctrine fairly substantially in examining how defamation law does not consider speakers' intentions. Tiersma's concern to narrow what speech could be found defamatory has some similarities to Thomas Gibbons' suggestions in England. In an interesting analysis, Gibbons has argued that the basis of liability should be changed and defamation replaced with a legal (or administrative) remedy against publishing false information.[118]

Jeffrey Thomas has provided another linguistic approach to defamation law. Thomas has examined pragmatics and its consideration of meaning as depending on language usage.[119] Thomas draws on Paul Grice's arguments for the importance of context to meaning.[120] Thomas is wary of suggesting that these ideas from pragmatics should become part of defamation doctrine,[121] but he argues they could be drawn on to simplify existing common law approaches to meaning.[122] Within pragmatics, for example, the assumptions of speaker and hearer are seen to underlie how the hearer implies what he or she understands the speaker to mean.[123] This suggests law could focus more closely on how a recipient would interpret a publisher's intended meaning. Jason Harkess also has used linguistics in a broadly similar but less extensive investigation of defamation

[114] Eg the US ideas of actual malice (subjective knowledge of publication's falsity or reckless disregard to falsity) and the fact – opinion distinction, drawn from *New York Times v Sullivan*, 376 US 254 (1964) and subsequent cases, especially *Gertz v Robert Welch*, 418 US 323 (1974) and *Milkovich v Lorain Journal*, 497 US 1 (1990); see Chapter 8.

[115] Tiersma (1987) 306.

[116] *Ibid* 350.

[117] See *ibid* 304 and its note 6. Elsewhere, Tiersma has considered procedural and evidential aspects of language: eg Tiersma (1999) and its Chapter 9, 'Pleadings: Constructing the Legal Narrative'. But that book does not examine defamation, apart from two passing references to legal terminology.

[118] Gibbons (1996). For a somewhat similar more recent US proposal, see Stern (2004).

[119] Thomas (1999) 341–42.

[120] See Grice (1975).

[121] Thomas (1999) 350.

[122] The paper also examines US constitutional issues connected with defamatory meaning, for which Clay Calvert's work also is valuable.

[123] Thomas (1999) 348.

law. Harkess evaluated meaning in New Zealand defamation law in light of semantic and pragmatic linguistics.[124] Harkess's analysis is at the level of the formal rules within each disciplinary approach; for example, the legal ideas of natural and ordinary meaning and innuendo meaning are considered, as are linguistic ideas about denotative and connotative meaning.[125] With at least a degree of commonality to all this interdisciplinary research, it does not examine litigation practice nor does it address the practicality of adding to law's complexity by 'borrowing' linguistic tools.[126] That focus, of course, may be hard to expand without investigating litigation practice.

The above review shows that earlier *empirical* research into defamation has not focussed on meaning, apart from certain work investigating the third-person effect, which has some implications for issues of meaning. Nor has the research focussed closely on the interaction of defamation doctrine and litigation practice. And the examples in this section illustrate that research into *defamatory meaning* has not focussed on comparative doctrine and practice. Overall, the shape that the law relevant to defamatory meaning takes in practice has not been a closely researched area. The doctrinal analysis in Chapters 2 and 3 show the sorts of questions that could benefit from such research, which this project begins in subsequent chapters along with examining wider aspects of comparative law and practice, especially concerned with the treatment of public interest speech under English, Australian and US law.

III AN EMPIRICAL AND DOCTRINAL FOCUS

As a final introductory matter, this project's approach should be understood to arise within a long sociolegal tradition. There has been a recognised field of sociolegal research at least since the 1960s, with the US formation of the law and society association,[127] but it can be traced to far earlier legal realist concerns.[128] The field tends to be known as law and society in North America, sociolegal studies in the UK, sociology of law in Europe,[129] and by any of those terms internationally. The scope of the field has always been under debate,[130] but it commonly is taken to include empirical research. In one sense, this project takes a relatively traditional sociolegal approach: it focuses on legal practice. A long-standing interest of legal fieldwork has been legal actors, whether lawyers in

124 Harkess (1998).

125 *Ibid* 658–62.

126 Concerns exist about seeking to apply linguistics as some form of curative for law; see eg the general point raised by Pether when noting that such interdisciplinary approaches are commonplace: (1999) 55–57.

127 Cotterrell (1994) xi.

128 Ewick et al (1999) 1.

129 Cotterrell (1994) xii.

130 Eg *ibid* xi; Lacey (1994) 2–3.

courts[131] or regulatory officials outside courts.[132] This project does not follow an important recent trend in empirical legal research – namely, qualitative interview-based research into the experiences, understandings and attitudes of lay people about law – unlike some of the empirical research discussed above.[133] This shift in legal research can be seen to mirror general social research interests, which increasingly have turned to questions about culture and transnational comparison.[134] Empirical legal research displayed early concern with non-legal actors,[135] and the concern has resurfaced since the late 1980s. Significant northern hemisphere examples of this trend are provided by the work of Patricia Ewick and Susan Silbey,[136] Belinda Fehlberg,[137] Laura Beth Nielsen,[138] William O'Barr and John Conley,[139] and Austin Sarat and Thomas Kearns.[140] Australian-based use of similar methods exists in some areas, for example, in the work of Rosemary Hunter and Alice Leonard on sex discrimination[141] and Roger Magnusson on euthanasia.[142] But the bulk of Australian empirical legal research probably has focussed on legal actors.[143]

Although the project can be seen to take a traditional sociolegal approach, it may differ slightly in focus from some lawyer-centred sociolegal work. The project starts from the expectation that comparative *doctrinal* analysis can benefit from empirical research into litigation practice, at least for analysing laws that commonly are litigated. So the 'social' in this research is decidedly narrow: it is defamation litigation. And it is examined to understand the form that legal rules take in practice. The project's questions arise from legal discourse, and the position from which the questions are viewed is internal to law. The project is not focussed on questions of social power and access to law, although they appear to be acute with regard to defamation.[144] The project also leaves aside other significant sociological elements of defamation, notably media audiences and media practitioners. That is, the project's concern is not with how lay people think about defamation law and media publications;[145] nor with defamation law's

---

131 Eg McBarnett (1981); Ingleby (1992).

132 Eg Gunningham and Johnstone (1999).

133 Eg Barendt et al (1997); Weaver et al (2006).

134 See eg essays collected in Bonnell and Hunt (1999).

135 Macualay (1963).

136 Ewick and Silbey (1998).

137 Fehlberg (1997).

138 Nielsen (2004).

139 O'Barr and Conley (1988).

140 Sarat and Kearns (1993).

141 Hunter and Leonard (1995).

142 Magnusson (2002).

143 Eg Ingleby (1991); Dewar and Parker (1999).

144 Newcity (1991); Chesterman (2000) 173–74.

145 Eg in a non-defamation context Ewick and Silbey (1998).

effects on providers of media content[146] or potential litigants;[147] nor its role in influencing social discussion of contemporary issues.[148] Rather, the project studies legal doctrine and legal practice: the social that exists within – and under the influence of – the courtroom.

Thus, if the project seeks to develop legal methodology, it is to stretch the methods used in traditional doctrinal analysis. The aim is to provide an enriched comparison of English, Australian and US defamation law, to understand more about the different ways in which defamation law can process parties' disputes. This approach relates in part to the common sociolegal caution against comparisons that do not consider the differing legal cultures within which laws exist. As John Eekelaar and Mavis Maclean, for example, state:

> [O]ne of the major *points* of comparative socio-legal studies is precisely to sensitise researchers and policy makers to the fact that legal institutions and doctrine are embedded within particular cultures and therefore to caution in making facile inter-country comparisons.[149]

Of course, the book makes only small moves towards that point – focussed as it is on law and the litigation process. Much more could be investigated, for example, about the approaches taken by defamation lawyers in the processes of litigation in each country.[150] But, at a minimum and as the remaining chapters make clear, procedural rules and how they are enacted need to be considered as well as comparative defamation doctrine. So the project seeks to observe law in its particular, varied manifestations through empirical research in each jurisdiction. That research is outlined in Chapters 4 to 8. Next, the formal law most relevant to defamatory meaning in England, NSW and Victoria is examined.

---

146 Eg Barendt et al (1997); Weaver et al (2006).

147 In the US, see particularly Bezanson et al (1987).

148 Numerous examples include Donson (2000); and much of the work of Post, eg (1993).

149 Eekelaar and Maclean (1990) 623–24 (emphasis in original).

150 Outside defamation, see eg Abel and Lewis (1995) 281, 290–99.

– 2 –

IS A DEFAMATORY MEANING CONVEYED? ENGLISH AND AUSTRALIAN LAW

How do English and Australian defamation laws determine the meaning that a publication conveys? This chapter examines the issue in terms of legal doctrine. Part I outlines general aspects, Part II briefly considers what meanings are defamatory, while particular questions about meaning are raised in Part III. The three major concerns are as follows: how parties are bound by any meanings; the degree of specificity required in pleading meaning; and the stage of a trial for determining meaning. Part III also deals with subsidiary questions about interlocutory determination of meanings that are capable of being conveyed by a publication; differences between implications, inferences and speculation; the so-called single-meaning rule; the possible relevance of the publisher's apparent intention with regard to meaning; and meaning being said in law to involve general impressions rather than elaborate analysis.

I GENERAL ASPECTS OF MEANING

A Meanings are dealt with as imputations

Meanings conveyed by a publication are called imputations, both at common law and under NSW legislation.[1] An imputation is an 'act or condition asserted of or attributed to a person'.[2] The term *imputation* encompasses non-literal meanings and is useful to signify that a particular legal approach exists for meaning in defamation.[3] There are two types of imputation. Natural and ordinary meanings are one, and they can be conveyed directly or by inference. Such inferential meanings can be called popular[4] or false[5] innuendoes. The inferences depend only on general community knowledge, such as knowing a common slang

[1] Eg *Slim v Daily Telegraph* [1968] 2 QB 157, 172 (Diplock LJ); *Mirror Newspapers v Harrison* (1982) 149 CLR 293, 295 (Mason J); *DA 1974* (NSW) s 9.

[2] *Hall-Gibbs Mercantile Agency v Dun* (1910) 12 CLR 84, 91 (Griffith CJ); see also *Sungravure v Middle East Airlines Airliban SAL* (1975) 134 CLR 1, 10 (Gibbs J), 17 (Stephen J), 21 (Mason J).

[3] Eg Milmo and Rogers (2004) [2.1].

[4] Eg *Lewis v Daily Telegraph* [1964] AC 234, 280 (Lord Devlin).

[5] Eg *Grubb v Bristol United Press Holdings* [1963] 1 QB 309, 328 (Holroyd Pearce LJ).

expression. Legal innuendoes are the second type of imputation. They depend on facts outside the publication that are not within general community knowledge. These extrinsic facts, combined with the publication, convey a legal[6] or true[7] innuendo. For clarity, the terms *popular* and *legal innuendoes* are used in this book (with legal innuendoes being explained further below in Part I, K). But note that the *Civil Procedure Rules* terminology uses 'natural and ordinary meaning' to refer to both literal and popular innuendo meanings, and 'innuendo meaning' to refer to just a legal innuendo meaning.[8]

As well as the usual concept of conveyed *imputations*, cases discuss the *charges*, *allegations* or *statements* made by publications.[9] This distinguishes two crucial aspects about meaning for defamation law: an allegation that is raised by a publication and the meaning of that allegation. It is the meaning of an allegation that is distilled into one or more pleaded imputations. Consider this example. A newspaper article reports that the national taxation office is investigating the claimant or plaintiff over suspected non-filing of tax returns. It also reports that another person disappeared in mysterious circumstances and suggests the claimant or plaintiff had some involvement in that event. These two allegations – in almost all instances where one publication contained them both – would be separate and distinct allegations. However, disagreements easily could exist about just what meaning was conveyed in relation to each of the allegations: had the claimant or plaintiff actually not filed a tax return, was this merely suspected, or just being investigated? Was the claimant or plaintiff guilty of illegal conduct in relation to the disappearance and, if so, of what sort? This distinction between allegations and their meaning is significant and it is returned to below and in subsequent chapters.

B Determining meaning: the ordinary recipient

The test for determining meaning asks what an ordinary, reasonable recipient would understand from the material.[10] It is not a matter of evidence of the recipients' actual understanding. Similarly, the publisher's intention is not directly relevant to meaning[11] – unlike its relevance to issues of malice or damages. Courts often ascribe meaning to words, using particular rules of construction – for example, when interpreting contracts. Defamation law uses a

[6] Eg *Mirror Newspapers v World Hosts* (1979) 141 CLR 632, 642 (Mason and Jacobs JJ); Faulks Committee (1975) [97].

[7] Eg *Lewis* [1964] AC 234, 259 (Lord Reid, Lord Jenkins agreed); NSW Law Reform Commission (1995) [3.33].

[8] *Civil Procedure Rules 1998* (Eng) (*CPR*) Pt 53 PD 2.3.

[9] Eg *Gumina v Williams (No 2)* (1990) 3 WAR 351, 364 (Seaman J) 'charges'; *Khashoggi v IPC Magazines* [1986] 1 WLR 1412, 1417 (Sir John Donaldson MR, Slade LJ agreed) 'allegation'; *Polly Peck v Trelford* [1986] QB 1000, 1020 (O'Connor LJ, Robert Goff and Nourse LJJ agreed) 'statements'.

[10] Eg *Capital and Counties Bank v Henty* (1882) 7 App Cas 741, 745 (Selbourne LC).

[11] Eg *Slim* [1968] 2 QB 157, 172 (Diplock LJ); *Hepburn v TCN Channel Nine* [1983] 2 NSWLR 664, 667 (Hunt J).

different approach, and seeks to mimic the ordinary recipient's response. The test is primarily one of reasonableness.[12] There have been many case law descriptions of the ordinary recipient.[13] That person reads between the lines,[14] interprets publications in light of their general knowledge and experience,[15] is neither too suspicious nor naive and is not avid for scandal.[16] Courts accept some 'loose thinking', and ordinary people are said to have a greater capacity for implication than lawyers.[17] This capacity may now be tempered by increased levels of education, which improve recipients' powers of discrimination and interpretation.[18] In any event, general knowledge excludes outlandish meanings; for example, ordinary recipients do not believe in witchcraft.[19] Strained or forced meanings will not be perceived,[20] nor will the ordinary recipient interpret publications as conveying only the mildest imputations.[21]

C Manner, occasion and mode of publication

The general manner and occasion of publication are relevant to determining meaning.[22] Allegations that are prominent within a newspaper, for example, are more likely to convey a defamatory imputation. While publications must be taken as a whole, the prominence or style of some parts may affect meaning significantly:

> A headline, for example, expressed pithily and necessarily incompletely, but designed to catch the eye and give the reader a predisposition about what follows may well assume more importance than the latter.[23]

---

[12] *Amalgamated Television Services v Marsden* (1998) 43 NSWLR 158, 165 (Hunt CJ at CL; Mason P and Handley JA agreed).

[13] They are collected usefully in *Farquhar* [1980] 2 NSWLR 380, 386 (Hunt J); *Marsden* (1998) 43 NSWLR 158, 165-66 (Hunt CJ at CL; Mason P and Handley JA agreed); *Skuse v Granada Television* [1996] EMLR 278, 285 (Sir Thomas Bingham MR); *Hartt v Newspaper Publishing, The Times* (London) (9 November 1989); *John Fairfax Publications v Rivkin* (2003) 201 ALR 77, [23]–[28] (McHugh J), [181] (Callinan J, Glesson CJ agreed).

[14] *Jones v Skelton* [1963] 1 WLR 1362; *Chakravarti v Advertiser Newspapers* (1998) 193 CLR 519, [134] (Kirby J).

[15] *Lewis* [1964] AC 234, 259 (Lord Reid, Lord Jenkins agreed); *Harrison* (1982) 149 CLR 293, 301 (Mason J).

[16] *Lewis* [1964] AC 234, 259 (Lord Reid, Lord Jenkins agreed); *Chakravarti* (1998) 193 CLR 519, [134] (Kirby J).

[17] *Lewis* [1964] AC 234, 277 (Lord Devlin).

[18] *Lennon v Scottish Daily Record and Sunday Mail* [2004] EMLR 18, [39]–[40] (Tugendhat J) drawing on *Lukowiak v Unidad Editorial SA* [2001] EMLR 46, [47] (Eady J).

[19] *Loukas v Young* [1968] 3 NSWR 549, 550 (Taylor J); cf *Hughs v Farrer* (1628) Cro Car 141; 79 ER 724.

[20] *Jones* [1963] 1 WLR 1362, 1370 (Lord Morris).

[21] *Roberts v Camden* (1807) 9 East 93, 96; 103 ER 508, 509–10 (Lord Ellenborough CJ). The practice ended in England by the eighteenth century: Fleming (1998) 587.

[22] Eg *Morosi v Broadcasting Station 2GB* [1980] 2 NSWLR 418n, 419–20 (Samuels JA).

[23] *Rivkin* (2003) 201 ALR 77, [187] (Callinan J).

The mode of publication affects how carefully a recipient is thought to read, books being read with more care than newspapers.[24] Similarly, the ephemeral nature of electronic media is relevant to meaning.[25] Usually, broadcast publications are received only once, and recipients may not concentrate on them as continuously as on printed publications.[26] Application of these principles adapts with changing media technologies, products and audiences.[27]

D Role of evidence in determining meaning

No evidence of recipients' understandings is admissible on natural and ordinary meaning,[28] which is a 'curiosity of defamation law'.[29] Neither dictionary definitions[30] nor readership surveys are admissible. (Consideration has been given to surveys in the US.[31]) Evidence would usurp the jury function to use the objective test of the ordinary, reasonable recipient.[32] Evidence of recipients' understanding, however, may be admitted in relation to identification and damages, even if it may disclose a publishee's understanding.[33] Evidence also is admissible, but not determinative, where a legal innuendo is pleaded.[34]

E Considering the class of likely recipients

Although the meaning that recipients actually derived is generally not relevant, the class of likely recipients is an important part of a publication's context that can be relevant to meaning. As stated in the 1980s, the issue has 'received little attention in the decided cases'[35] – at least little express attention. But two references are particularly important. In *Sim v Stretch*, Lord Atkin noted: 'The question is complicated by having to consider the person or class of persons

[24] Eg *Farquhar v Bottom* [1980] 2 NSWLR 380, 386 (Hunt J).

[25] Eg *Gorton v Australian Broadcasting Commission* (1973) 1 ACTR 6, 10–13 (Fox J).

[26] *Marsden* (1998) 43 NSWLR 158, 166 (Hunt CJ at CL; Mason P and Handley JA agreed); see also *Skuse* [1996] EMLR 278; *Hinduja v Asia TV* [1998] EMLR 516.

[27] *Marsden* (1998) 43 NSWLR 158, 172 (Hunt CJ at CL; Mason P and Handley JA agreed); *Chakravarti* (1998) 193 CLR 519, [134] (Kirby J).

[28] *Hough v London Express Newspapers* [1940] 2 KB 507, 515 (Goddard LJ); *Reader's Digest Services v Lamb* (1982) 150 CLR 500, 506 (Brennan J).

[29] Baker (2004) 1.

[30] *Krahe v TCN Channel Nine* (1986) 4 NSWLR 536, 547 (Hunt J).

[31] See eg Calvert (1995b).

[32] Eg *Slim* [1968] 2 QB 157, 173 (Diplock LJ); *Reader's Digest* (1982) 150 CLR 500, 506 (Brennan J).

[33] *Hughes v Mirror Newspapers* (1985) 3 NSWLR 504, 509, 512 (Hunt J).

[34] Eg *Slatyer v Daily Telegraph Newspaper Co* (1908) 6 CLR 1, 9 (Griffith CJ); *Charleston v News Group Newspapers* [1995] 2 AC 65, 70 (Lord Bridge, Lords Goff, Jauncey and Mustill agreed).

[35] Neill and Rampton (1983) 13.

whose reaction to the publication is the test of the wrongful character of the words used.'[36] Equally, in *Drummond-Jackson v British Medical Association*, the class of recipients was held relevant in interpreting a medical article aimed at dental surgeons: the words should be understood 'by the sort of people likely to read . . . the *British Medical Journal*'.[37] Contemporary examples also exist, such as comments by Gray J in *Gillick v Brook Advisory Centres* that it is 'necessary to have in mind, in a suitable case, the kind of reader to whom the allegedly defamatory words were addressed.'[38] Similar statements have been made in Australia. In *Chakravarti v Advertiser Newspapers*, for example, Kirby J said the various descriptions of the ordinary recipient aim 'to conjure up an idea of the kind of person who will receive the communication in question'.[39]

F Roles of judge and jury

Judge and jury have distinct roles in determining meaning. The judge determines whether the published material is capable of conveying each imputation. Although commonly called a question of law, this question of 'capable meanings' may be better seen as one of fact reserved to the judge.[40] The jury, where there is one, determines if a meaning is actually conveyed.[41]

There has been some case law criticism as to whether judges can determine the question of what meanings are capable of being conveyed. Significant appellate decisions have shown differences between judges as to whether particular imputations can arise.[42] How can a meaning then be ruled incapable? The jury may agree with a dissenting judge, if given the opportunity. Thus Kirby P has commented:

> Some would consider it presumptuous for judges (many of whom lead narrow lives and some of whom may not even listen to the wireless) to assert that they know what reasonable fellow citizens will make of a broadcast. . . . Instead of indulging the charade of guessing what the ordinary reasonable listener would think, why not leave it to a tribunal more likely to reflect the response of such a listener – the jury?[43]

---

36 [1936] 2 All ER 1237, 1240.

37 [1970] 1 All ER 1094, 1099 (Lord Denning MR); and see 1106 (Sir Gordon Willmer). See also Faulks Committee (1975) [96].

38 (Unreported, QBD, Gray J, 12 March 2002) [13].

39 (1998) 193 CLR 519, [133]. See also *World Hosts* (1979) 141 CLR 632, 642 (Mason and Jacobs JJ, Gibbs and Stephens JJ agreed): reference to 'a reader of the class under consideration'.

40 *Slim* [1968] 2 QB 157, 174 (Diplock LJ); and see discussion in *Marsden* (1998) 43 NSWLR 158, 164 (Hunt CJ at CL; Mason P and Handley JA agreed).

41 *Jones* [1963] 1 WLR 1362; *Sungravure* (1975) 134 CLR 1, 7–8 (Gibbs J).

42 Eg *Capital and Counties* (1882) 7 App Cas 741; *Lewis* [1964] AC 234.

43 *Bond Corpn Holdings v Australian Broadcasting Commission* [1989] Aust Defamation Reports [50,050], 40,327 (Kirby P in dissent); see also *Slim* [1968] 2 QB 157, 187 (Salmon LJ).

This position, however, has not found general support. Judicial ruling on capability is not seen as usurping the jury's function, but as part of a long-standing 'partnership between judge and jury'.[44] This view is not expected to change, especially in England, with its increasing judicial willingness to supervise litigation actively under the *Civil Procedure Rules'* overriding objective to deal with disputes in proportion to importance and complexity of the issues they raise.[45]

Compared to its role in assessing damages, there has been little criticism of the jury's role as to meaning.[46] The jury is seen to have a special role,[47] usually traced to *Fox's Libel Act 1792*.[48] For example, in England, jury trials in defamation are regulated by s 69 of the *Supreme Court Act 1981*. It limits the non-use of a jury to cases where the court finds that trial would require 'prolonged examination of documents or accounts or any scientific or local investigation which cannot conveniently be made with a jury'.[49] The jury's importance is seen to continue even under moves to increase the judge's role – for example, in summary disposal provisions.[50]

In New South Wales (NSW), where the jury's role is now restricted, it still determines meaning. The NSW jury's limited role under s 7A of the *Defamation Act 1974* is important to note. For publications since 1 January 1995,[51] under the 7A process the judge determines whether a pleaded imputation is reasonably capable of being conveyed by the publication, and whether it is reasonably capable of being defamatory. These steps accord with the common law.[52] If these capacity hurdles are passed, s 7A then gives the jury very limited tasks: to determine whether the material was published[53] and whether any pleaded defamatory meaning was conveyed about the plaintiff. The judge determines whether any defence succeeds, sets the quantum of any damages, and determines all issues of fact relating to these questions. Section 86 of the *Supreme Court Act 1970* (NSW), which applies jury trial to actions for defamation, is

---

44 *Bond Corpn* [1989] Aust Defamation Reports [50,050], 40,336 (Samuels JA).

45 See Chapter 1, Part I, C.

46 In relation to damages, see, eg *John v MGN* [1997] QB 586; *Campbell v News Group Newspapers* [2002] EMLR 43, appendix; *Carson v John Fairfax & Sons* (1993) 178 CLR 44; Chesterman (2000) Chapter 4.

47 Eg Australian Law Reform Commission (1979) [288].

48 32 Geo 3, c 60.

49 See also eg *Supreme Court (General Rules of Procedure in Civil Proceedings) Rules 1996* (Vic) r 47.02(3) (*SCR* (Vic)); *Supreme Court Act 1970* (NSW) s 86; cf Chapter 7 re possible greater use of judge-alone trials under *Reynolds* qualified privilege.

50 Under *DA 1996* (UK) ss 8–10; see Chapter 10, Part I, D.

51 Section 7A was inserted by *Defamation (Amendment) Act 1994* (NSW).

52 See above fns 40 and 41 and accompanying text.

53 This is implicit in the wording of s 7A(3) and has been made clear by *Cinevest v Yirandi Productions* (2001) Aust Torts Reports ¶81–610. Amending s 7A to clarify and make explicit this role had earlier been suggested: see NSW Law Reform Commission (1995) [3.17]–[3.20] and recommendation 4.

subject to the 7A process.[54] Thus, the usual mode of jury trial for defamation damages in NSW has been altered by this 'stark, and indeed curious, bifurcation of roles'.[55] The changed process also means there may only be a theoretical possibility of arguing that a 7A jury should be dispensed with because of the need, for example, for prolonged examination of documents.[56] However, it appears that the jury role is not limited under 7A in relation to a cross-claim for contribution made by a defendant against another publisher.[57] Implications of such changes to the jury's role in NSW are explored in detail in Chapter 10.[58]

G Bane and antidote

This and the next three areas are sometimes seen as problematic, but they do not greatly add to the law's complexity. A publication may convey a bane and antidote;[59] that is, a possible defamatory meaning is removed by other parts of the publication. No defamatory 'sting' is conveyed by the publication overall.[60] Even an express disclaimer, however, will not necessarily amount to a sufficient antidote. Where the bane and antidote argument is open to be made, the antidote's effect usually remains a question for the tribunal of fact.[61]

H Rumour, repetition and meaning

Rumour can convey a substantial meaning,[62] and reports of hearsay are treated the same as direct assertions.[63] Given that point, the general approach to meaning still applies, and baseless rumours sometimes *can* be reported without conveying a defamatory meaning.[64] But repeating an allegation generally is treated as conveying a substantial meaning, under what is called the repetition rule:

> The repetition rule . . . is a rule of law specifically designed to prevent a jury from deciding that . . . a publication which conveys rumour, hearsay,

[54] *DA 1974* (NSW) s 7A(5); see *Smec Holdings v Boniface* [2004] NSWSC 526. Prior to 18 January 2002, the relevant provision applying jury trials to defamation claims was *SCA 1970* (NSW) s 88; see *Courts Legislation Amendment (Civil Juries) Act 2001* (NSW).

[55] *Tucker v Echo Publications* [2003] NSWSC 554, [38].

[56] See eg *Smec* [2004] NSWSC 526, [15].

[57] *Zunter v John Fairfax Publications* [2005] NSWSC 119.

[58] See Chapter 10, Part I, C.

[59] *Chalmers v Payne* (1835) 2 Cr M&R 156, 159; 150 ER 67, 68 (Anderson B).

[60] Eg *Bik v Mirror Newspapers* [1979] 2 NSWLR 679n, 682 (Herron CJ, Manning JA agreed), 683–84 (Taylor AJA).

[61] *Mitchell v Faber & Faber* [1998] EMLR 807, 815 (Hirst LJ, Sir Donald Nicholls VC and Waite LJ agreed); *Cruise v Express Newspapers* [1999] QB 931; *Sergi v Australian Broadcasting Commission* [1983] 2 NSWLR 669, 670 (Hutley JA), 673–74 (Glass JA).

[62] Eg *Chakravarti* (1996) 65 SASR 527, 541 (Doyle CJ).

[63] *Lewis* [1964] AC 234, 274–75 (Lord Hodson), 283–84 (Lord Devlin).

[64] Eg *Kennett v Nationwide News* (Unreported, Vic SC, Ashley J and jury, 11 March 1999).

> allegation, repetition . . . is true or alternatively bears a lesser defamatory meaning than would attach to the original allegation itself. . . .
>
> [T]he repetition rule is indeed a rule which, where it applies, dictates the meaning to be given to the words used.[65]

More recently, Simon Brown LJ has reiterated these statements from the English Court of Appeal in *Stern v Piper*[66] and emphasised, 'this is by no means to say that the meaning dictated is an artificial one. Rather the rule accords with reality.'[67] A differently constituted Court of Appeal has noted that it might be preferable to say the rule 'conditions' or 'qualifies' meaning.[68] The rule has withstood challenges drawing on case law from the European Court of Human Rights.[69] It seems such arguments will not influence the approach to a publication's meaning, but they do have significance for the common law defence of qualified privilege.[70]

I Jokes or vulgar abuse

A separate rule has been said to exist for jokes or vulgar abuse.[71] If the words were spoken in jest or as mere vulgar abuse, they may not have conveyed the relevant imputation. This should not be seen to exist as a separate defence; rather, it arises in relation to what meaning is conveyed.[72] The rule being limited to slander – which erroneously is suggested at times – would follow from a belief that written publications can always convey 'serious' meaning.[73] However, that should not mean satire's literal meaning must always be conveyed, even if English and Australian courts appear far more ready to hold that than US courts.[74]

---

65 *Stern v Piper* [1997] QB 123, 135–36 and 138 (Simon Brown LJ, Sir Ralph Gibson agreed).

66 *Ibid.*

67 *Mark v Associated Newspapers* [2002] EMLR 38, [29] (Simon Brown LJ, Mummery and Dyson LJJ agreed).

68 *Jameel v Times Newspapers* [2004] EMLR 31, [26] (Sedley LJ, Longmore LJ agreed with commentary, Maurice Kay LJ agreed with both judgments).

69 *Eg Thoma v Luxembourg* (2003) 36 EHRR 21 (ECHR).

70 *Mark* [2002] EMLR 38, [27]–[35] (Simon Brown LJ, Mummery and Dyson LJJ agreed); see *Al-Fagih v H H Saudi Research and Marketing (UK)* [2002] EMLR 13 and Chapter 7, Part II, C.

71 *Thorley v Lord Kerry* (1812) 4 Taunt 355, 365; 128 ER 367, 371; *Uren v Australian Consolidated Press* [1969] 1 NSWR 745, 752 (Sugerman JA).

72 *Mundey v Askin* (1982) NSWLR 369; *Ivory v Millett* (Unreported, WA SC, Anderson J, 29 January 1999). See also *Entienne v Festival City Broadcasters* (2001) 79 SASR 19; *Coleman v John Fairfax Publications* [2003] NSWSC 564.

73 It has not always explicitly been limited to slander: eg *Vander Zalm v Times Publishers* (1980) 109 DLR (3d) 531, 540 (Hinkson JA) suggesting it could apply to political cartoons in newspapers; *Coleman v Fairfax* [2003] NSWSC 564.

74 See Chapter 8, Part I, D in relation to the US; cf *Australian Broadcasting Corpn v Hanson* (Unreported, Qld CA, de Jersey CJ, McMurdo P, McPherson JA, 28 September 1998) and eg Fitzgerald (1999); Handsley and Davis (2001); Magnusson (2001).

J Reports of criminal charges, suspicions and allegations

Reports of criminal charges can give rise to various imputations. A report may convey only that a charge has been laid. It may convey that the person is suspected of being guilty, by the police, for example. Or it may convey that the person actually is guilty. Merely reporting that a person has been charged cannot convey guilt – this result often has been related to the ordinary recipient's awareness of the presumption of innocence.[75] Similarly, stating only that police are conducting inquiries cannot convey guilt, except to an unduly suspicious person.[76] Guilt, however, *can* be conveyed depending on the publication's content and context.[77] An imputation of guilt is conveyed if the charge is reported to be well founded.[78] English cases, in particular, have emphasised that reports of suspicions or allegations (not just those relating to criminal charges) may convey three different levels of defamatory meaning. First, a report may convey that someone is guilty of a defamatory charge. Second, it may convey that reasonable grounds exist to suspect a person of being guilty of the charge. Or third, it merely may mean there are grounds to investigate a person's conduct.[79] In Australia, the approach generally has not been commented on in cases where it could have been applied.[80] These three levels of meaning – guilt, reasonable suspicion, or grounds for an investigation – are particularly significant for the way that parties disagree about what meaning a publication conveys, and are explored further in Chapter 3.[81]

K Legal innuendo meanings

Legal innuendo meanings can arise where an unusual meaning is given to words, for example, by uncommon slang. Legal innuendos can also arise where facts,

---

[75] *Lewis* [1964] AC 234, 285 (Lord Devlin); *Harrison* (1982) 149 CLR 293, 300–301 (Mason J). But see discussion in *John Fairfax Publications v Obeid* [2005] NSWCA 60, [57]–[78] (McColl JA, Sheller JA and McClellan AJA agreed).

[76] *Lewis* [1964] AC 234, 258 and 260 (Lord Reid, Lord Jenkins agreed), 274 (Lord Hodson), 283 and 286 (Lord Devlin), but Lord Morris dissented on this: 267–69.

[77] Eg *Ainsworth Nominees v Hanrahan* [1982] 2 NSWLR 823.

[78] *Lewis* [1964] AC 234, 284 (Lord Devlin); *Harrison* (1982) 149 CLR 293, 303 (Mason J).

[79] Eg *Bennett v News Group Newspapers* [2002] EMLR 39, [36] (Robert Walker LJ for Eng CA); *Chase v News Group Newspapers* [2003] EMLR 11, [45] (Brooke LJ, Rix and Keene LJJ agreed); *Musa King v Telegraph Group* [2004] EMLR 23; *Jameel v Times* [2004] EMLR 31.

[80] Eg *Favell v Queensland Newspapers* [2004] QCA 135, [8]–[11] (Jerrard JA, Philippides J agreed). Note: the High Court granted leave to appeal in *Favell* in March 2005. In *Sands v Channel Seven Adelaide* [2005] SASC 182, [43]–[44] the 'three levels' approach was not adopted, although it appears to have been presented to the judge as a set approach. White J left open issues closely related to the English approach, such as justifying a 'reasonable grounds to suspect' meaning through circumstantial evidence: [42].

[81] See Chapter 3, Part I, E.

which are not included in publications, exist and result in the meanings being conveyed to recipients who know the facts. A common example is an imputation of hypocrisy being alleged when some recipients know of a relatively private stand taken by the claimant or plaintiff on the particular issue.[82] The question is what meaning would be conveyed to people with that knowledge. At least one recipient must be shown to have knowledge of the extrinsic facts.[83] That recipient need not interpret the publication in the defamatory sense.[84] The extrinsic facts must exist and be proved.[85] They cannot merely be believed to exist. A legal innuendo meaning gives rise to a separate cause of action.[86] This has been criticised,[87] and changed in NSW in that every imputation is a separate cause of action.[88]

II IS THE MEANING DEFAMATORY?

By the above legal rules, publications are understood to convey many meanings. Only some are defamatory. Although the literature on what meanings can be defamatory is extensive,[89] it largely is separate from this book's concerns with litigation practice. For example, one area of academic debate involves non-disparaging imputations and considers whether they could be capable of defaming. It is now fairly clear that such imputations can meet the 'ridiculous light' test of what is defamatory,[90] although insulting language will not necessarily amount to ridicule when a publication is taken as a whole.[91] But debate exists about how this approach fits with the idea that defamation protects *reputation*.[92] Such questions are separate to concerns about how differences between the parties over a publication's meaning are dealt with in law and

[82] Eg *Donovan v Logan and Wagadon (The Face magazine)* (Unreported, QBD, Drake J, 3 April 1992).

[83] *Capital and Counties* (1882) 7 App Cas 741, 748 (Selborne LC); *Lewis* [1964] AC 234; *Hughes* (1985) 3 NSWLR 504, 506 (Hunt J).

[84] *Hough* [1940] 2 KB 507, 514 (Slesser LJ), 515 (Goddard LJ); *Reader's Digest* (1982) 150 CLR 500, 505 (Brennan J).

[85] *Grubb* [1963] 1 QB 309, 328–29 (Holroyd Pearce LJ); *World Hosts* (1979) 141 CLR 632, 641–42 (Mason and Jacobs JJ).

[86] The *Common Law Procedure Act 1852*, 15 and 16 Vict, c 76, s 61 established this position; *Watkin v Hall* (1868) LR 3 QB 396; *Sim v Stretch* [1936] 2 All ER 1237; *Barclay v Cox* [1968] VR 664, 665; *Reader's Digest* (1982) 150 CLR 500, 505 (Brennan J).

[87] *Lewis* [1964] AC 234, 279 (Lord Devlin); Faulks Committee (1975) [104] recommended abolition; see also Australian Law Reform Commission (1979) [90].

[88] *DA 1974* (NSW) s 9(2); see also NSW Law Reform Commission (1971) [49]–[50].

[89] For a detailed Australian example, see McNamara (2001).

[90] Eg *Berkoff v Burchill* [1996] 4 All ER 1008; *Ettingshausen v Australian Consolidated Press* (1991) 23 NSWLR 443.

[91] Eg *Norman v Future Publishing* [1999] EMLR 325.

[92] See, eg Cottrell (1998); Harkess (1998); McNamara (2001); Watterson (1993); and more specifically with regard to reputation: Post (1986); Pound (1915).

litigation practice and to questions about qualified privilege and the US law since *New York Times v Sullivan*.[93] Even more than this, the research into litigation discussed in later chapters strongly suggests that whether a particular meaning is defamatory generally is not significant in practice.[94] The major recent exception has concerned NSW appeals against jury decisions in 7A hearings that particular imputations are conveyed but are not defamatory.[95] But, with the issue of whether conveyed meanings are defamatory being comparatively less significant in practice, the relevant law is outlined here only briefly.

A Common law tests of what is defamatory

In the English and Australian jurisdictions examined most closely in this book, the common law tests of what is defamatory apply. This is a notable area of difference from the Australian code states – Queensland and Tasmania have statutory definitions that, although similar to the common law, are broader in including material that is likely to injure the plaintiff in his or her profession or trade, without disparaging the plaintiff personally.[96] Elsewhere, case law provides no comprehensive definition,[97] but whether the publication is true or false is irrelevant to whether it is defamatory.[98] Instead, various judicial approaches are used, and satisfying any one of their descriptions is sufficient.

The earliest common reference is to Parke B in *Parmiter v Coupland*.[99] He said a publication is defamatory if it is likely 'to injure the reputation of another by exposing' the person 'to hatred, contempt or ridicule'.[100] The other frequent nineteenth-century reference is *Scott v Sampson*, in which Cave J said the law gives people 'a right to have the estimation in which [they stand] in the opinion of others unaffected by false statements to [their] discredit.'[101] Early twentieth-century cases also are relied on. In *Sim v Stretch*, Lord Atkin said,

> The conventional phrase exposing the plaintiff to hatred, ridicule or contempt is probably too narrow. . . . I do not intend to ask your Lordships to lay down a formal definition, but . . . I propose in the present case the test: would the words tend to lower the plaintiff in estimation of right-thinking members of society generally?[102]

---

[93] 376 US 254 (1964).

[94] *Gillick v Brook Advisory Centres* (Unreported, QBD, Gray J, 12 March 2002) offers a rare instance of a publication held incapable of being defamatory.

[95] The High Court and NSW courts have emphasised that challenging such jury decisions is difficult. See Chapter 10, Part I, C, 3; Rolph (2003).

[96] *DA* 1889 (Qld) s 4(1); *DA 1957* (Tas) s 5(1); see eg Gillooly (1998) 49–50.

[97] Eg *Sim* [1936] 2 All ER 1237, 1240 (Lord Atkin).

[98] Eg *Australian Consolidated Press v Uren* (1966) 117 CLR 185, 205 (Windeyer J).

[99] (1840) 6 M &W 105; 151 ER 340.

[100] *Ibid* 341. See also *Capital and Counties* (1882) 7 App Cas 471.

[101] (1882) 8 QBD 491, 503.

[102] [1936] 2 All ER 1237, 1240.

An Australian equivalent is found in *Gardiner v John Fairfax & Sons*, in which Jordan CJ used the formulation: 'anything which is likely to cause ordinary decent folk in the community, in general, to think less' of the plaintiff.[103] In addition, the idea of treating 'right-thinking' as equating to a person of ordinary intelligence rather than invoking any particular moral standard has been commonly approved in Australia.[104]

In *Youssoupoff v MGM Pictures*, an allegation that the plaintiff had been raped or seduced was held to be defamatory. It implied no moral fault on the plaintiff's part, but would lead people to shun or avoid her.[105] The imputation would be likely to exclude the plaintiff from society. This category traditionally has been applied to allegations of insanity, having a serious contagious disease, or of a woman having been raped – although the applicability of the test to allegations of rape has been doubted.[106]

The *general* effect of these tests is that material lowering the claimant or plaintiff in the estimation of others is defamatory – and that test usually is understood in England and Australia to relate to society in general.[107] The aim is to include material affecting 'any aspect' of reputation.[108] The Faulks Committee recommended a statutory definition of defamation to replace these common law tests:

> Defamation shall consist of the publication to a third party of matter which in all the circumstances would be likely to affect a person adversely in the estimation of reasonable people generally.[109]

The suggestion was not adopted in England.[110] The incrementalism of the common law has been preferred, but calls for a simpler 'lowering in the estimation' test remain.[111]

B Contemporary standards

The standard for what is defamatory is that existing at publication,[112] and can change over time.[113] John Fleming, for example, provides examples of imputations

[103] (1942) 42 SR (NSW) 171, 172. See also *World Hosts* (1979) 141 CLR 632, 638 (Mason and Jacobs JJ); *Slatyer* (1908) 6 CLR 1, 7 (Griffith CJ).

[104] Eg Law Reform Committee of South Australia (1972) 7–8.

[105] (1934) 50 TLR 581, 587.

[106] *Galea v Amalgamated Television Services* (Unreported, NSW SC, Levine J, 20 February 1998); see also *Sungravure* (1975) 134 CLR 1, 23–24 (Mason J).

[107] See Baker (2004) 2–5; cf US community-segment test: see Chapter 8, Part I.

[108] Milmo and Rogers (2004) [2.7]; citing eg *Sim* [1936] 2 All ER 1237; *O'Brien v Clement* (1846) 1 M&W 435; 153 ER 1141.

[109] Faulks Committee (1975) [65].

[110] Nor was it recommended by New Zealand, Committee on Defamation (1977) 20.

[111] Eg Cottrell (1998).

[112] Eg *Cairns v John Fairfax & Sons* [1983] 2 NSWLR 708, 721 (Mahoney JA).

[113] Eg *Harrison v Thornborough* (1714) 10 Mod Rep 196, 197; 88 ER 691, 691; *Krahe* (1986) 4 NSWLR 536, 545 (Hunt J).

that have been found defamatory, but would not necessarily still be found to defame.[114] These include allegations that the claimant or plaintiff is German,[115] communist,[116] anti-Semitic,[117] a scab,[118] or homosexual.[119] Changing social attitudes could be illustrated by the treatment of allegations of illegitimacy,[120] or ideas about the environment and corporate advertising.[121]

C Roles of judge and jury

The judge determines whether an imputation is capable of defaming the claimant or plaintiff. If doubts exist, the matter is for the jury. The jury usually determines whether a meaning was conveyed that was defamatory in a single step in England and Victoria.[122] That is, the jury is asked to decide whether the publication defames the plaintiff, without identifying a specific defamatory meaning. But in NSW the jury considers each issue separately because the NSW cause of action is the pleaded imputation. In any event, the jury determines the general community standard for what is defamatory without evidence.[123] (Evidence of a publication's adverse impact – and of its reputational harm – is admissible on damages.[124])

III QUESTIONS ABOUT MEANING

Several points complicate the legal approach to meaning in England and Australia. Two major aspects concern how parties are bound to the meanings they plead, and the degree of specificity required in pleading meanings. These aspects are significant at both interlocutory and trial stages. Six subsidiary issues provide useful context for these issues, and they are addressed here first in Sections A to F. Section G then provides a background to English and Australian legal requirements for pleading meaning in defamation before the two major questions are examined, in Sections H and I.

---

114 Fleming (1998) 526–27.

115 *Slazengers v Gibbs* (1916) 33 TLR 35.

116 *Braddock v Bevins* [1948] 1 KB 580; *Cross v Denley* (1952) 52 SR (NSW) 112.

117 *De Stempel v Dunkels* [1938] 1 All ER 238; *Templeton v Jones* [1984] 1 NZLR 448.

118 *Murphy v Plasterers Society* [1949] SASR 98.

119 *R v Bishop* [1975] QB 274, 281; cf Harkess (1998) 676–77; see eg *Kelly v John Fairfax Publications* [2003] NSWSC 586.

120 Milmo and Rogers (2004) [2.6] notes this, citing *Robson v News Group Newspapers* (Unreported, QBD, Previté QC, 9 October 1995).

121 Eg *Mount Cook Group v Johnstone Motors* [1990] 2 NZLR 488.

122 Eg *Capital and Counties* (1882) 7 App Cas 741, 772 (Lord Blackburn), 744 (Selborne LC); *Lewis* [1964] AC 234, 264 (Lord Morris), 271 (Lord Hodson).

123 Eg *Slim* [1968] 2 QB 157, 172 (Diplock LJ); *Reader's Digest* (1982) 150 CLR 500, 506–7 (Brennan J).

124 *Reader's Digest* (1982) 150 CLR 500, 507–8 (Brennan J).

A Interlocutory determination of 'capable meanings'

There can be separate preliminary determinations about whether pleaded meanings are capable of being conveyed.[125] A judge before trial may be in the same position as a trial judge to decide capacity. English provisions clearly allow for pre-trial determination of whether words are capable of conveying a pleaded meaning. In 1991, the English Court of Appeal approved the approach that had been used earlier in NSW,[126] and the Neill Committee supported this. Order 82 r 3A was added to the former English rules in 1994. Now, under the *Civil Procedure Rules'* Practice Direction 53, courts can determine possible meanings before trial.[127] Either party can seek a ruling on capacity. Defendants often argue the claimant's natural and ordinary meaning cannot be conveyed. The claimant could argue similarly about a meaning the defendant raises. A ruling even could be sought on the applicant's own meaning.[128] The *Civil Procedure Rules* state such applications should be made promptly.[129] The hearing is short and involves no evidence. If the meaning cannot arise, a lesser meaning often may be open,[130] and leave to amend will be given. The English Court of Appeal has sought to discourage appeals after such rulings,[131] but will be 'a little less reluctant to interfere' where a pleaded meaning has been held incapable of being conveyed.[132] Such rulings may have final effects, as a pleaded meaning will be removed from all future consideration in the litigation. However, an appeal sometimes will succeed against a first-instance order that a pleaded meaning is capable of arising.[133]

In Victoria, court rules allow for the separate trial of questions,[134] which can include 'capable meanings'. Rulings have been made, although there has been

---

[125] In England under CPR Pt 53 PD 4.1; formally under *Rules of the Supreme Court 1965* (Eng) Ord 82 r 3A (*RSC*); in Victoria under *SCR* (Vic) r 47.04 but see below fns 134 and 135; in NSW under *Supreme Court Rules 1970* (NSW) Pt 31 r 2 (*SCR* (NSW)) and now *Uniform Civil Procedure Rules* (NSW) r 28.2 (*UCPR* (NSW)).

[126] *Keays v Murdoch Magazines (UK)* [1991] 1 WLR 1184.

[127] *CPR* Pt 53 PD 4.1; see eg *Mapp v News Group Newspapers* [1998] QB 520. This has made redundant the earlier provisions for 'arguably capable meanings' under Ord 18 r 19, the availability of which had been ended by *DA 1996* (UK) s 7.

[128] Eg *Parry v Express Newspapers* (Unreported, Eng CA, McCowan, Saville and Ward JJ, 9 March 1995).

[129] *CPR* Pt 53 PD 4.2.

[130] *Skuse* [1996] EMLR 278, 286 (Sir Thomas MR).

[131] *Hinduja* [1998] EMLR 516.

[132] *Geenty v Channel Four Television Corpn* [1998] EMLR 524, 532 (Hirst LJ, Millett and Brooke LJJ agreed) explaining *Hinduja* [1998] EMLR 516; see also eg *Gillick v Brook Advisory Centres* [2001] EWCA Civ 1263; *Jameel v Wall Street Journal Europe SPRL* [2004] EMLR 6; *Jameel v Times* [2004] EMLR 31.

[133] Eg *Patterson v ICN Photonics* [2003] EWCA Civ 343, [17]–[18] (Kenne LJ, Rix, Schiemann LJJ agreed).

[134] *SCR* (Vic) r 47.04.

some question whether this is appropriate because the trial court has not been bound to any pleaded meanings under the traditional Victorian approach.[135] This position may have changed somewhat after the High Court *Chakravarti* decision[136] concerning how a plaintiff is bound to pleaded meanings at common law. This is discussed below in Section H and at length in Chapter 9. NSW also has a general provision in its rules.[137] It has been used frequently for almost as long as the state's Defamation List has existed.[138] Possible disadvantages in NSW interlocutory practice are mentioned below in Sections H and I, and investigated further in later chapters.[139]

A related option is an application to strike out the statement or particulars of claim. This is not limited to questions of meaning, but needs a plain and obvious case.[140] All or part of a pleading may be struck out under general provisions of court rules,[141] or the court's inherent jurisdiction. In addition, interlocutory rulings can be sought about whether a meaning can be defamatory. In England, the specific procedure of the former *RSC* Ord 82 r 3A generally was seen to concern only disputes about conveyed meanings, not whether those meanings were defamatory.[142] But other rules allowed questions beyond meaning to be dealt with in a similar manner at an early stage, including disputes as to whether particular meanings were capable of being defamatory.[143] Now the *Civil Procedure Rules'* general provisions about rulings on meaning extend to whether the statement

[135] *Roux v Australian Broadcasting Commission* [1992] 2 VR 577, 581–82 (Byrne J); cf *Carrey v ACP Publishing* (1998) [1999] 1 VR 875.

[136] *Chakravarti* (1998) 193 CLR 519.

[137] *SCR* (NSW) Pt 31 r 2 and now *UCPR* (NSW) r 28.2.

[138] The court's ability to decide capacity issues before trial is discussed in *Love v Mirror Newspapers* [1980] 2 NSWLR 112, 122 (Hunt J), referring to *Mirror Newspapers v Singleton* (Unreported, NSW CA, Hope, Reynolds and Mahoney JJA, 21 April 1980): see [1980] 2 NSWLR 129 note.

[139] There has been some Australian discussion as to whether the test on a capacity hearing is that the publication was not capable of conveying the imputation or a stricter test that, to be struck out, the claim must obviously be untenable; see eg *Nationwide News v Chapman* [2001] SASC 30; *Favell* [2004] QCA 135. Note: the High Court granted leave to appeal in *Favell* in March 2005.

[140] Eg *Hubbuck v Wilkinson* [1899] 1 QB 86, 91; *Monte v Mirror Newspapers* [1979] 2 NSWLR 663.

[141] In England under *CPR* r 3.4(2) and formally *RSC* (Eng) Ord 18 r 19; in Victoria under *SCR* (Vic) r 23.02; in NSW under *SCR* (NSW) Pt 15 r 26 (and Pt 13 r 5) and now *UCPR* (NSW) r 14.28.

[142] Cf *Aspro Travel v Owners Abroad* [1996] 1 WLR 132 where *RSC* (Eng) Ord 82 r 3A was used to rule whether a given meaning could be defamatory in law. Also, before the 1994 changes of adding Ord 82 r 3A in England, *Keays* [1991] 1 WLR 1184 held the court could rule whether a meaning is capable (not arguably capable) under Ord 33 r 3.

[143] *RSC* (Eng) Ord 14A provided for the disposal of a case on a point of law, while Ord 33 dealt with the place and mode of trial. Ord 14A was used this way in *Berkoff* [1996] 4 All ER 1008.

sued on or the meanings pleaded are capable of being defamatory.[144] Victoria corresponds to the English situation before the *Civil Procedure Rules*.[145] The NSW approach under Pt 31 r 2, however, explicitly includes disputes about whether meanings can be defamatory, and if a publication is incapable of defaming a plaintiff (eg a publication that is humorous and 'self-evidently absurd'), then judgment can be entered for the defendant on the pleaded imputations.[146]

These rules are interlocutory options for defamation litigants, but normal summary judgment procedures traditionally have not applied to defamation in these jurisdictions.[147] This differs from some other Australian states and territories where summary judgment can be sought in defamation, although it will be awarded only in rare cases.[148] In addition, England has extended summary judgment to defamation in some situations and introduced special summary disposal provisions in ss 8–10 of the *Defamation Act 1996* (UK).[149] The 2005 reforms to civil procedure in NSW apply summary judgment to defamation – subject to the jury trial provisions of *Supreme Court Act 1970* (NSW) s 86 and the 7A process.[150] Summary judgment – particularly English approaches under the *Civil Procedure Rules* – is discussed further in Chapter 10.[151]

---

[144] *CPR* Pt 53 PD 4.1.

[145] *SCR* (Vic) r 47.04 has provisions similar to England's former Ord 33 and provides for the separate trial of a question in the dispute, while r 13.02 specifically authorises a pleading to raise a point of law.

[146] Eg *Coleman v Fairfax* [2003] NSWSC 564.

[147] In England formally under *RSC* (Eng) Ord 14 r 1(2)(a); in Victoria still under *SCR* (Vic) r 22.02(2); in NSW under *SCR* (NSW) Pt 13 r 1 and the former *SCA 1970* (NSW) s 88, but see fn 150 below for details of the NSW position and the *UCPR* (NSW).

[148] See eg *Chapman v Australian Broadcasting Corporn* (2000) 77 SASR 181; *Wyss v Dobson* [2001] WASC 93; Cairns (2002) 385.

[149] *CPR* Pt 24; re *DA 1996* (UK) ss 8–10 see eg *James Gilbert v MGN* [2000] EMLR 680; *Loutchansky v Times Newspapers (No 2)* [2002] QB 783.

[150] It is worth explaining the NSW position further: in 2001, the *Courts Legislation Amendment (Civil Juries) Act 2001* repealed s 88 of the *SCA 1970*, which applied jury trial to claims such as fraud and defamation. The amendments also enacted s 86 of the *SCA*, which applies jury trials only to defamation claims (not claims involving fraud etc) and subjects them to the 7A process under *DA 1974* (NSW). Thus, the *SCA* provision for jury trials moved from ss 88 to 86. However, even after these amendments, *SCR* (NSW) Pt 13 r 1 continued to apply summary judgment to all proceedings except those affected by s 88 of the *SCA* (not s 86). The lack of reference to s 86 in the *SCR* (NSW) may well have been an oversight. In any event, the *UCPR* (NSW) rr 13.1 and 13.4 do not exclude defamation claims from summary judgment, and the *UCPR* will take precedence over the *SCR* (NSW) to the extent of any inconsistency: see *Civil Procedure Act (CPA) 2005* (NSW) s 11, and definition of 'local rules' in s 3. English experience, however, suggests summary judgment will be available only for issues the judge could properly decide in a defamation case: see *Safeway Stores v Tate* [2001] QB 1120 and Chapter 10, Part I, D. At the time of writing, leading commentary on NSW procedure still referred to s 88 of the *SCA 1970* (NSW) in relation to Pt 13 r 1 of the *SCR* (NSW), while also noting the *Safeway Stores* decision: Taylor (2005) [13.1.1].

[151] See Chapter 10, Part I, D.

B Implications, inferences and speculation

A great degree of technicality can arise in relation to whether meanings are capable of being conveyed, as is explored in detail in Chapters 4–6. In NSW, in particular, this has been discussed in terms of drawing distinctions between three concepts: a publication's implications; inferences drawn from a publication; and mere speculation.[152] This approach to the law either encourages clarity before trial – as statements in NSW case law suggest – or it is an example of unhelpful technicality. At this point, it is enough to examine the law. In *Lewis v Daily Telegraph*, media reports concerned an inquiry linked to possible corporate fraud. Lord Hailsham said the inquiry being held could imply suspicion, 'but to take the matter a further step and infer guilt, is in my view, wholly unreasonable. This is to draw an inference from an inference'.[153] Guilt apparently would only have been inferred by recipients who were avid for scandal. Later cases, particularly in NSW, have contrasted meanings that are implied by publications, inferred by recipients, or result from recipients' speculation.

The first distinction is between implications and inferences. Hunt CJ at CL has explained:

> An implication is included in and is part of that which is expressed by the publisher. It is something which the reader (or listener or viewer) understands the publisher as having intended to say. An inference is something which the reader . . . adds to what is stated by the publisher; it may reasonably or even irresistibly follow from what has been expressly or impliedly said, but it is nevertheless a conclusion drawn by the reader . . . from what has been expressly or impliedly said by the publisher.[154]

Thus, a recipient can add a conclusion to what the publisher has implied. This has been described as drawing an inference from an implication. A recipient, however, cannot go further and draw an 'inference on an inference', as discussed in *Lewis*, which is said to be quite a different process.

The second distinction separates a recipient's speculation from both implications and inferences. In *Jones v Skelton*, a letter to the editor criticised a local councillor who received building approval apparently against council policy. In the Privy Council, Lord Morris commented on the letter's questioning end, which read, 'It is beyond understanding. Or is it?'

> The reader, a jury might conclude, was invited to adopt a suspicious approach and so to be guided to the real explanation of what had taken place – an

152 *Marsden* (1998) 43 NSWLR 158, 167 (Hunt CJ at CL).

153 [1964] AC 234, 274.

154 *Marsden* (1998) 43 NSWLR 158, 167 (Hunt CJ at CL; Mason P and Handley JA agreed) (note omitted). See also *Bargold v Mirror Newspapers* [1981] 1 NSWLR 9, 12 (Hunt J); *Harrison v Mirror Newspapers* [1981] 1 NSWLR 620, 627 (Glass JA; Reynolds and Samuels JJA agreed) but the High Court did not discuss this point on appeal: *Harrison* (1982) 149 CLR 293, 300 (Mason J).

> explanation which the writer of the letter did not care or did not dare to express in direct terms.[155]

The effect of this comment was explained in *Amalgamated Television Services v Marsden*.[156] *Marsden* involved an 'in your face'[157] television report on homosexual paedophilia and youth prostitution. It made allegations concerning a prominent lawyer, who sued. In one part of the broadcast, a person's name was obviously deleted, by removing it from the audio track. Recipients could think the publisher did not dare to name the person directly. This would invite viewers to adopt a suspicious approach, but one that would still be limited by reasonableness. Merely removing a person's name would not be enough to invite untrammelled speculation as to who was referred to:

> [I]f the publisher invites the adoption of a suspicious approach, it is reasonable for [the publisher] to be responsible for at least some conclusions reached for which it would not otherwise have been reasonable. . . . A degree of conjecture or guesswork is therefore permitted which would not otherwise be permitted. However, the requirement of reasonableness still applies.[158]

The issue was significant in this interlocutory *Marsden* appeal because of comments at the Supreme Court level by Levine J.[159] He suggested the principles of earlier cases about this issue are 'apparently entrenched', but their application to modern media may need reconsideration. The earlier cases might be taken to suggest that it always is impossible to rely on any imputation that is an 'inference on an inference'. Such an imputation would be equivalent to unreasonable speculation and could not be conveyed. That traditional limit, however, may deny publications' capacity to convey meanings to contemporary recipients. What if material is likely to lead to speculation, if publications invite or even compel speculation? Is a recipient who then speculates 'avid for scandal'? Thus, Levine J commented:

> [T]he identification of the process of reasoning as inference upon inference, or indeed as speculation, should not automatically and finally preclude a plaintiff relying upon an imputation. . . .
>
> Where published material, by reason of its format, content, language, images, sound . . . can fairly be characterised as compelling conclusions that can be constituted as defamatory imputations, the publisher should not escape liability if those conclusions are reached by an inference drawing process or indeed by speculation when either . . . is clearly invited by the published material.[160]

---

155 [1963] 1 WLR 1362, 1372.

156 (1998) 43 NSWLR 158.

157 The description is used by Levine J: *Marsden v Amalgamated Television Services* [1996] Aust Defamation Reports [52,080].

158 *Marsden* (1998) 43 NSWLR 158, 169 (Hunt CJ at CL; Mason P and Handley JA agreed).

159 The case had a particularly lengthy, hard-fought history, with approximately 200 interlocutory judgments. The trial judgment provides an overview: *Marsden v Amalgamated Television Services* [2001] NSWSC 510, [21] (Levine J).

160 *Marsden v Amalgamated Television Services* [1996] Aust Defamation Reports [52,080] (Levine J). The first paragraph is quoted in the NSW CA: (1998) 43 NSWLR 158, 170.

It could be noted that Kirby J made somewhat similar comments in the *Chakravarti* decision about the *appropriate* dangers the media may face for 'loose language'.[161]

But on appeal in *Marsden*, Hunt CJ at CL explained that speculation should be seen as quite a separate interpretative activity to implication and inference, and that confusion could arise when they were discussed together. As well as his explanation of the *Jones v Skelton* style of speculation, described above, two points are important. One relates to jury directions, the other to inferences from inferences. First, where an imputation can result only from an inference on an inference, the judge will exclude it at, or before, trial. In most situations, however, there will be something to go to the jury. For example, a contested imputation *may* be capable of arising as an inference from what the publication implies, but also *may* be capable of arising as an inference from another inference.

> [I]t will usually be for the jury to determine whether the first step in the process of reasoning involves an implication or an inference. They must be directed that, if the imputation does arise, and if it does arise from drawing an inference upon an inference rather than upon an implication, it would not be reasonable for the defendant to be made responsible for that imputation, and the defendant is entitled to succeed in relation to it.[162]

One could wonder just what jury directions would make this sufficiently clear and useful to a jury.

Second, Levine J characterised the broadcast in *Marsden* as being 'likely to have the effect of, or can fairly be described as, an invitation to speculate to a given end or to draw an inference upon an inference', and the inference that the plaintiff was the person named 'readily can be identified by reason of the nature and quality of the program itself'.[163] Levine J said the publisher should be liable for that meaning, if it in fact was conveyed. That is, he suggested that some publications could invite drawing an inference from an inference, in circumstances where that process would be reasonable. On appeal, Hunt CJ at CL disagreed. He said if the contested imputation arose, it always would be implied by the publication, or be conveyed by only one inference.[164] The NSW Court of Appeal quickly affirmed the approach in decision in *TCN Channel 9 v Antoniadis*.[165] And the approach of Hunt CJ at CL has been cited without comment in the High Court.[166] The issue has not received substantial attention in English cases, although it has been noted in *Gatley* with some doubts being expressed. *Gatley* refers to the Australian Capital Territory (ACT) decision in *Kelson v David Syme*, where Crispin J does not accept that drawing a 'secondary

[161] *Chakravarti* (1998) 193 CLR 519, [133].

[162] *Marsden* (1998) 43 NSWLR 158, 171 (Hunt CJ at CL; Mason P and Handley JA agreed).

[163] [1996] Aust Defamation Reports [52,080] (Levine J).

[164] *Marsden* (1998) 43 NSWLR 158, 172 (Hunt CJ at CL; Mason P and Handley JA agreed), although he noted this may not be true in absolutely every case.

[165] (1998) 44 NSWLR 682, 687–88 (Handley, Beazley, Stein JJA).

[166] *Rivkin* (2003) 201 ALR 77, [54] (McHugh J in dissent).

inference' would always be unreasonable.[167] What the terms – implication, inference and speculation – add to the determination of meaning in the process of litigation is not entirely clear. Indeed, the NSW Court of Appeal has resisted arguments that particular imputations result from the impermissible inferences on inferences rather than from a process of implication, in a manner that suggests the allowed process of implication will be the more common situation facing courts.[168] Reviewing the NSW cases does not immediately suggest the approach should be adopted elsewhere. Instead, other jurisdictions may seek to adapt the comments of Hunt CJ at CL to the standard approach to meaning. In *John Fairfax Publications v ACP Publishing*, for example, the ACT Court of Appeal noted that the terminology of inference on inference 'is potentially misleading' and referred back to general Australian approaches to meaning.[169] However, the investigation of litigation practice in later chapters may alter this perception of the issue. It also is worth noting that, in a different sense to issues about inferences or speculation, imputations must be conveyed by the actual publication. It is not enough that a link is made, by the recipient, to previous defamatory publications.[170]

C The stage of a trial for determining meaning

Juries may assess conveyed meaning in a context particularly different to recipients. In a lengthy trial, the jury usually will consider the material on many occasions, and decide meaning after hearing extensive legal arguments and evidence about the case. Therefore, the stage at which meaning is determined has been made more flexible at law. In NSW, prior to the introduction of 7A hearings,[171] judicial statements suggested the jury could decide whether pleaded imputations were conveyed, and whether they were defamatory, at the trial's start.[172] The aim was to approximate the original recipients' position,[173] and to encourage settlement during trial.[174] This change moulds trial procedures so that meaning *is* more a matter of impression.[175] It has been extended from electronic to print publications.[176] A similar approach has been used in England. In *Marks &*

[167] Milmo and Rogers (2004) [3.16], referring to *Kelson v David Syme* [1998] ACTSC 60, [17]–[18] (Crispin J). See also Chapter 10, Part I, D.

[168] *Nationwide News v Warton* [2002] NSWCA 377, [42]–[45] (Heydon JA, Handley and Hodgson JJA agreed).

[169] [2005] ACTCA 12, [13] referring to *Harrison* (1982) 149 CLR 293.

[170] *Astaire v Campling* [1965] 3 All ER 666.

[171] Under *DA 1974* (NSW) s 7A; see above, fns 51–54, and accompanying text.

[172] *Radio 2UE Sydney v Parker* (1992) 29 NSWLR 448 and *TCN Channel 9 v Mahony* (1993) 32 NSWLR 397.

[173] Eg *Radio 2UE* (1992) 29 NSWLR 448, 473 (Clarke JA).

[174] NSW Law Reform Commission (1995) [3.33].

[175] *Radio 2UE* (1992) 29 NSWLR 448, 474 (Handley JA).

[176] *RZ Mines (Newcastle) v Newcastle Newspapers* (Unreported, NSW SC, 16 November 1994, Hunt J) cited in NSW Law Reform Commission (1995) [3.31].

Spencer v Granada Television,[177] a settlement was reached three days into a trial that was estimated to run six weeks. The trial judge asked the jury to decide the meaning after viewing the current affairs program and hearing brief submissions from counsel. The approach has not been commented on directly in relation to Victoria; for example, the Tobin and Sexton service makes no reference to Victoria and discusses only NSW on this issue.[178] Similarly, Neil Williams refers only to the NSW practice.[179] Although such changes to determining meaning appear to be quite straightforward, existing literature has not closely considered their effect and any complications that may exist; for example, in England the change entailed asking the jury what meaning was conveyed, which it answered by setting out its own version of the publication's meaning. The empirical research discussed in later chapters suggests the change could have significant implications for litigation practice.

D The single-meaning 'rule'

People vary in background, knowledge and temperament, so publications would usually convey different meanings to varied recipients.[180] But meaning for defamation law is taken to be uniform.[181] This is a major way that the legal meaning is 'artificial'.[182] Concern with the 'right' meaning does not entail a publication conveying only one meaning. It could convey several literal, inferential and legal innuendo meanings, but a publication cannot be found to convey inconsistent or contradictory meanings.[183] The House of Lords reaffirmed this single-meaning rule in *Charleston v News Group Newspapers*.[184] In that case, an article's headline and main photograph may have suggested that television actors were involved in making a pornographic computer game. The article's text said this was untrue. The parties agreed that the headline, photographs and text were

177 (Unreported, QBD, Popplewell J, 23 February 1998). The approach was approved in *Shah v Standard Chartered Bank* [1999] QB 241, 265.

178 Tobin and Sexton (2005) [26,600]. Earlier versions of the looseleaf service also noted the ACT precedent: *Gutman v Clouston* (Unreported, ACT SC, Gallop J, 15 February 1989).

179 Williams (2005) [I 49.01.250].

180 *Stubbs v Russell* [1913] AC 386, 398 (Lord Shaw); *Charleston* [1995] 2 AC 65, 71 (Lord Bridge, Lords Goff, Jauncey and Mustill agreed).

181 *Reader's Digest* (1982) 150 CLR 500, 506 (Brennan J); *Charleston* [1995] 2 AC 65, 71–72 (Lord Bridge, Lords Goff, Jauncey and Mustill agreed).

182 *Slim* [1968] 2 QB 157, 171 (Diplock LJ). The approach of Diplock LJ appears to have been mischaracterised as different to some Australian authority in *Entienne* (2001) 79 SASR 19, [39]–[42] (Olsson J, Willaims J agreed, Duggan J agreed with commentary).

183 There have been developments where the meaning believed by the publisher is not the conveyed meaning, particularly in relation to unintended meanings and qualified privilege; see Chapter 7, Part II, C.

184 [1995] 2 AC 65, 71–72 (Lord Bridge, Lords Goff, Jauncey and Mustill agreed), 73–74 (Lord Nicholls).

a single publication,[185] and the text neutralised any defamatory meaning in the other material.[186] But they disputed what meaning could arise; that is, they disagreed about the legal effect of some readers seeing only part of the publication. Lord Bridge, in the leading speech,[187] rejected the plaintiffs' claim in relation to 'limited readers' who did not peruse the text. Two basic defamation principles defeated the plaintiffs. Natural and ordinary meanings are those conveyed to the reasonable recipient, and the jury must determine the single meaning conveyed to that recipient.[188] Lord Bridge said many *unreasonable* readers could have done as the plaintiffs argued.[189] The Court of Appeal had held the same,[190] but perhaps with more disquiet owing to concerns about privacy.[191]

Meaning's uniform or singular quality in defamation was considered earlier by Diplock LJ in *Slim v Daily Telegraph*, when he provided a historical overview of defamation pleading and suggested a source for the rule.[192] Prior to 1792, judges determined meaning. From their legal training, they would have started with the 'unexpressed major premise that any particular combination of words has one meaning'.[193] *Fox's Libel Act* of 1792[194] transferred meaning to the jury in criminal libel. Subsequently, the jury was given that role in civil actions,[195] and the 'unexpressed major premise' could have been carried across to their role. Judges ruled out incapable meanings, but the jury still had to determine the conveyed meaning. In this way, Diplock LJ suggested that a general legal premise about meaning that was initially used by judges came to underlie how law understands jury determinations of meaning in defamation.

Such criticisms of 'artificial' meaning were acknowledged by the Faulks Committee. The approach, however, was thought unavoidable if meaning was tied to the ordinary recipient.[196] Change would be counterproductive,[197] as the expense and complexity of dealing with various meanings would be too great. In the early 1990s, the Neill Committee saw meaning as a key area for improving

185 *Ibid* 71 (Lord Bridge, Lords Goff, Jauncey and Mustill agreed).

186 *Ibid.*

187 Lords Goff, Jauncey and Mustill simply agreed with Lord Bridge. Lord Nicholls gave a separate, concurring speech.

188 *Charleston* [1995] 2 AC 65, 71 (Lord Bridge, Lords Goff, Jauncey and Mustill agreed).

189 *Ibid* 73. The US approach appears to be more flexible on this issue, as noted in Chapter 8, Part IV, B.

190 *Charleston v Newsgroup Newspapers, The Times* (London) (12 January 1994).

191 Shillito and Barendt (1996) 317, 334.

192 [1968] 2 QB 157, 171–75. For a more recent overview, see *Cruise* [1999] QB 931, 946–50 (Brooke LJ, Stuart-Smith LJ and Sir John Knox agreed).

193 [1968] 2 QB 157, 172.

194 32 Geo 3, c 60.

195 *Capital and Counties* (1882) 7 App Cas 741, 776 (Lord Blackburn).

196 Faulks Committee (1975) [102].

197 *Ibid* [103].

defamation practice,[198] but focused on the stage at which meaning is determined. It saw no need to comment on uniform or single meaning.

On this question, the Australian approach generally is seen as consistent with England. There has been some discussion, however, of a plural society in relation to whether conveyed meanings are defamatory.[199] Similarly, in 1995 the NSW Law Reform Commission alluded to social diversity when commenting on judge and jury roles. A jury, even of four people, as is usual in NSW defamation cases, is noted as better reflecting 'community values, perceptions and expectations' than a judge.[200] (In England, the usual civil jury numbers 12 in the High Court, while in Victoria it numbers six.[201]) There may be some tension between juries theoretically reflecting social diversity and this aspect of the law on meaning. The most prominent Australian criticism of uniform meaning has been that by Kirby J in *Chakravarti*. He strongly rejected *Charleston*'s approach that reasonable readers always consider the entire publication, whatever its form. It ignores how people receive communication, and changes in the media:

> Many people, including not a few judges and jurors, do not look beyond headlines and photographs. . . . To the extent that dicta in *Charleston* . . . suggest . . . courts should attribute to the recipients of matter published in the mass media a close and careful attention to the entirety of the item published, I would not follow that opinion. . . . To do so would be to defy common experience and, if I may say so, commonsense.[202]

Other High Court judges did not comment on *Charleston*, but Kirby J echoes an assertion that was long made by Fleming:

> [T]he quaint dogma prevails that the words must be understood in their 'natural and ordinary' meaning, in defiance of the plain semantic truth that it is futile to look for any single meaning as being the 'right' meaning.[203]

As is noted in Part IV of Chapter 8, at least some US cases take a more flexible approach to this issue.

E Possible relevance of the publisher's apparent intention

As mentioned earlier in Part I, the publisher's intended meaning is not directly relevant. But Hunt J, when he headed the NSW Defamation List, explored a distinct aspect of the need for imputations to be conveyed.[204] To determine

---

198 Neill Committee (1991) 8–9 and its Chapter II.

199 *Hepburn* [1983] 2 NSWLR 682, 694 (Glass JA); see generally Baker (2004) 2–5.

200 NSW Law Reform Commission (1995) [3.8].

201 For England see *Juries Act 1974* (s 17 allows some majority verdicts; s 16 does in more limited circumstances for serious crimes); for Victoria see *SCR* (Vic) r 47.02(4).

202 *Chakravarti* (1998) 193 CLR 519, [133].

203 Fleming (1998) 587; similar statements have been made since the fourth edition: eg (1971) 472; cf (1965) 509–10.

204 *Anderson v Mirror Newspapers (No 1)* (1986) 6 NSWLR 99; *Baltinos v Foreign Language Publications* (1986) 6 NSWLR 85; *Hepburn* [1983] 2 NSWLR 664.

conveyed meaning, he said one should ask what the ordinary recipient would think the publisher intended to mean. The apparent intention would be drawn from the publication.[205] The approach allows several significant cases about meaning to be criticised, which Hunt J has done. In *Anderson v Mirror Newspapers (No 1)*, he traced what was described as a fallacy in the binding authorities, and said,

> It is, in my view, a fundamental principle of the law of defamation that, in deciding what meaning was in fact conveyed by what the defendant published, the jury must determine how the reader would have understood *from what was published* what meaning the defendant had intended to convey.[206]

The principle can be seen in questions about identification.[207] Even if the claimant or plaintiff is unknown to the publisher, the ordinary recipient could believe the publisher intended to identify the claimant or plaintiff. The recipient would form this opinion from what was published. The problem Hunt J raised involved legal innuendo meanings and the *Cassidy* decision,[208] as well as its subsequent approval.[209] These English cases concerned the plaintiff women's marital status. In *Cassidy*, a newspaper published a photograph of the plaintiff's husband with another woman and identified them as one Corrigan and his fiancée. The plaintiff argued that she was defamed by a legal innuendo meaning of living with the pictured man outside marriage. That is, people who knew the plaintiff would have perceived this meaning. Contrary to some obiter English judicial comment,[210] Hunt J argued,

> [T]he matter published by the defendant did no more than provide a basis for such a reader to draw an inference that the plaintiff's own statements were false. The inference was not, however, drawn *from what the defendant had published*.[211]

In *Anderson*, Hunt J considered a case that would have been decided differently under this changed approach. An actor could leave the set of a film due to illness,

---

205 *Hepburn* [1983] 2 NSWLR 664, 667 on meaning; *Baltinos* (1986) 6 NSWLR 85, 90 on identification.

206 (1986) 6 NSWLR 99, 108 (emphasis added); see also *Hepburn* [1983] 2 NSWLR 664, 667.

207 *E Hulton & Co v Jones* [1910] AC 20.

208 *Cassidy v Daily Mirror Newspapers* [1929] 2 KB 331.

209 *Hough* [1940] 2 KB 507. Hunt J has noted the Eng CA, in a case on natural and ordinary meaning, has said the jury should determine what the recipient would think the defendant intended to convey from what was published: *Schild v Express Newspapers, The Times* (London) (5 October 1982); quoted in *Hepburn* [1983] 2 NSWLR 664, 667 (Hunt J).

210 *Morgan v Odhams Press* [1971] 1 WLR 1239, 1265 (Lord Donovan).

211 *Anderson (No 1)* (1986) 6 NSWLR 99, 110 (emphasis in original). Mitchell (1998) focuses on a somewhat different weakness in these English cases, namely, the way law came to presume malice for defamatory publications.

but be reported as attending a charity function.[212] That may not necessarily imply the actor left the set for convenience rather than illness. Hunt J suggests,

> The matter published by the defendant did no more than provide a basis for the reader who knew of the plaintiff's claim [of illness] to draw an inference that the plaintiff's own statements were false. That inference was not drawn *from what the defendant had published*, and it could not be said that the reader would have understood the defendant to have intended to convey such an imputation.[213]

Under traditional doctrine, this sort of legal innuendo arises because of special facts known to some recipients. These facts can be unknown to the publisher. The approach advocated by Hunt J, however, requires that the special facts appear to have been intended from what was published. A common example of a legal innuendo concerns a person being said to enter a particular address, which some recipients know to be premises used by prostitutes or drug dealers.[214] Readers *may* think the publisher intended to make that reference just from publishing the address. In many cases, however, it may not be so simple. The approach of Hunt J has been noted in passing in English commentary, but not engaged with.[215] It could be developed in light of comments in the English Court of Appeal that the apparent intention of the publisher has relevance for the tribunal of fact. For example, both *Berkoff v Burchill*[216] and *Norman v Future Publishing*[217] suggested the publisher's apparent intention was relevant to distinguish material that was merely insulting from material that was defamatory because it exposed the claimant to ridicule. But in *O'Shea v MGN*,[218] which concerned unintended identification, Morland J made no reference to the arguments of Hunt J and endorsed early case law such as *Cassidy v Daily Mirror Newspapers*.[219] Even so, in *O'Shea* the common law's strict liability approach was not applied to unintentional identification by publishing a look-alike photograph because the approach was not held to be necessary in a democratic society as required under the *European Convention on Human Rights and Fundamental Freedoms*.[220] As has been suggested, the judgment logically could have addressed strict liability for identification in general.[221]

---

212 The case is *Mirror Newspapers v Fitzpatrick* [1984] 1 NSWLR 643.

213 *Anderson (No 1)* (1986) 6 NSWLR 99, 111 (emphasis in original).

214 The prostitution example is from *Lewis* [1964] AC 234, 278 (Lord Devlin). It now may be unworldly: *Nicholson v Seidler* (1990) 5 BR 363, 365 (Hunt J). It was changed to a drug dealer in NSW Law Reform Commission (1995) [3.33].

215 Milmo and Rogers (2004) [3.13] and its note 43.

216 [1996] 4 All ER 1008.

217 [1999] EMLR 325.

218 [2001] EMLR 40.

219 [1929] 2 KB 331.

220 Opened for signature 4 November 1950, 213 UNTS 221 (entered into force 3 June 1952).

221 Coad (2001) 200–1.

F Meaning as general impression, not elaborate analysis

Some accounts of meaning in defamation may downplay how recipients' *general* impression is meant to be the focus. Each word should not be analysed.[222] Over-elaborate analysis should be avoided.[223] Defamation law, however, appears to analyse elaborately. Notable judgments lament the long and complex analysis that publications are subject to during pleading and trial. As just one example, which does not appear to be substantially outdated, Diplock LJ began his judgment in *Slim v Daily Telegraph*,

> In the spring of 1964 two short letters appeared in the correspondence columns of the 'Daily Telegraph'. . . . Neither letter can have taken a literate reader more than 60 seconds to read before passing on to some other, and perhaps more interesting, item. Any unfavourable inference . . . would have been one of first impression. *Yet in this court three lords justices and four counsel have spent the best part of three days upon a minute linguistic analysis of every phrase used in each of the letters.*[224]

Clearly, reconciling these concerns with present doctrine and practice on meaning poses some difficulties. The issue also underscores attempts to simplify the trial process by having meaning dealt with at the outset, discussed above in Section C.

G Legal requirements for pleading meaning

There has been a long-term trend toward both parties pleading meaning 'with as much clarity and openness as possible.'[225] In part, this returns to a much older approach for plaintiffs. The history of the plaintiff's position is examined here. England, Victoria and NSW are taken in turn, after a brief background to defamation pleading in general. The defendant's situation in pleading meaning in England and Australia is examined in Chapter 3, while aspects of US pleading are discussed in Chapter 8.

1 *Defamation pleading*

Defamatory meaning is intricately connected with pleading, so a general background to defamation pleading is provided here. Defamation pleadings 'have been described by no less an authority than Dr W Blake Odgers as more

---

[222] Eg *Lewis* [1964] AC 234, 260 (Lord Reid, Lord Jenkins agreed), 285 (Lord Devlin); *World Hosts* (1979) 141 CLR 632, 641 (Mason and Jacobs JJ).

[223] *Slim* [1968] 2 QB 157, 179 (Diplock LJ); *Norman* [1999] EMLR 325, 333 (Peter Gibson LJ, May LJ agreed).

[224] *Slim* [1968] 2 QB 157, 171 (emphasis added); Lord Denning MR made similar comments, 167. Other examples include *Boston v Bagshaw* [1966] 2 All ER 906, 912 (Diplock LJ); *Kelly v Special Broadcasting Service* [1990] VR 69, 71 (Murphy J); *Radio 2UE* (1992) 29 NSWLR 448, 474 (Handley JA).

[225] Milmo and Rogers (2004) [26.1] (notes omitted).

important, perhaps, than any other class of actions brought at common law'.[226] Defamation law's concern with meaning makes it not surprising that pleadings are more complex than in other actions.[227] This complexity may be a reason that interlocutory disputes, often about pleadings or statements of case, are more common in defamation than in other civil actions in England and Australia.[228] Specific court rules also appear to facilitate interlocutory hearings, as might some courts' separate defamation lists. England does not have a separate list for defamation cases, but interlocutory defamation matters go to the judge heading the jury list in the Queen's Bench Division of High Court of Justice, or to that judge's nominee.[229] Because few civil actions go to jury trial in England, the jury list operates as a defamation list in practice and specialist defamation judges deal with most matters.[230] The Victorian Supreme Court has a major torts list, on which all defamation matters must be listed for interlocutory management.[231] A significant amount of Victorian litigation also occurs at an intermediate court level, where the County Court operates a defamation division in its damages list.[232] The NSW Supreme Court has long operated a defamation list,[233] and there also is a list at the intermediate District Court level.[234]

Neither England nor Australia has seen a move towards US-style notice pleading (for US practice, see Chapter 8). Pleadings remain significant in English and Australian civil procedure, despite long-standing calls for a greater judicial role in settling issues in dispute pre-trial. For example, in 1978 Sir Gerard Brennan suggested markedly reducing the importance of written pleadings by making the court more involved in supervising all interlocutory aspects of disputes.[235] This would define issues earlier and encourage prompt settlement.

> The written pleading would lose the remnants of critical importance which it once had, but the process of understanding and defining the real issues may

---

[226] Eg *Ron Hodgson (Trading) v Belvedere Motors (Hurstville)* [1971] 1 NSWLR 472, 476 (Asprey J).

[227] Heerey (1987) 443.

[228] See eg Australian Law Reform Commission (1979) [276] and its fn 2; Neill Committee (1991) [I 4].

[229] See generally Neill Committee (1991) 137ff. Claims arising with other commercial matters might be brought in the High Court of Justice's Equity Division. A similar situation exists in Australia when defamation claims arise alongside allegedly misleading conduct under the *Trade Practices Act 1974* (Cth) and are brought in the Federal Court.

[230] In particular Eady, Gray and Tugendhat LJJ.

[231] See Victorian Supreme Court, *Practice Note* [1995] 2 VR 555.

[232] See Victorian County Court, *Consolidated Practice Note: Operation and Management of the County Court Civil Lists (Melbourne Registry)* (20 November 2002).

[233] See NSW Supreme Court, *Practice Note 14* (21 April 1978); later *Notes* on *Practice Note 14* (13 August 1979, 29 May 1978, 31 August 1979, and 14 September 1984); now *Practice Note 114* (25 July 2000).

[234] See NSW District Court, *Practice Note* 63 (31 October 2002).

[235] Brennan (1975).

> be improved. . . . The exigencies of modern practice may produce the final dispersal of the aura which has historically surrounded pleadings.[236]

Such changes would return matters toward the situation of oral pleadings under medieval English law. With no written pleading, parties were given wide leeway to define the matters in issue through debate before the judge.[237] While elements of such changes can be seen in civil procedure reforms such as the *Civil Procedure Rules*, the position remains markedly different to the US.

Pleadings – properly called 'statements of case' under the *Civil Procedure Rules* – also have remained significant while various forms of judicial case management have developed in the jurisdictions being examined here,[238] and while interlocutory disclosure of evidence has been made more open, for example, through the exchange of witness statements. Since 1988, statements could be ordered in all English High Court proceedings and they became part of the usual practice in defamation litigation.[239] Exchange of witness statements was ordered at the summons for directions heard after pleadings closed.[240] Witness statements are now required under *Civil Procedure Rules* Pt 32.[241] In Victoria, a list of witnesses and a synopsis of their intended evidence is usual and NSW has specific provisions.[242] But, even since the *Civil Procedure Rules*, statements of case remain central to the litigation process,[243] whether in terms of case preparation, disclosure or discovery and other interlocutory procedures, interlocutory hearings and the conduct of a trial, or in helping the parties agree to settle.

Statements of case or pleadings must provide a summary of all the material facts relied on for the cause of action or defence, but not the evidence that will be used to prove those facts.[244] Parties need not plead the legal result that follows from the pleaded facts. The legal result can be pleaded, for convenience, but a party is not bound to it.[245] Thus, in defamation the claimant or plaintiff must plead that defamatory material – an imputation in NSW because that is the NSW

---

[236] *Ibid* 47.

[237] Holdsworth (1937) vol ix, 635.

[238] See eg Woolf (1996); Hunter et al (2005) [1.8]–[1.20]. Also note the move to differential case management in NSW, various specialist Victorian lists, and the *CPA 2005* (NSW).

[239] *RSC* (Eng) Ord 38 r 2A and *RSC (Amendment No 2) 1988* (Eng).

[240] See eg Milmo and Rogers (1998) [30.135].

[241] See eg Price and Duodu (2004) [31.04].

[242] For Victoria, see *Practice Note* [1995] 2 VR 555; although there are no specific rules about witness statements, *SCR* (Vic) Ord 34 is the general rule for directions; for NSW see *Practice Note 114* (25 July 2000); *SCR* (NSW) Pt 36 r 4A and Pt 26 r 1 and now *UCPR* (NSW) rr 31.4 and 2.1.

[243] See Andrews (2003) 252–58.

[244] *CPR* r 16.4 and formally *RSC* (Eng) Ord 18 r 7(1); *SCR* (Vic) r 13.02; *SCR* (NSW) Pt 15 r 7(1) and now *UCPR* (NSW) r 14.7.

[245] *Re Vandervell's Trusts (No 2); White v Vanderwell Trustees* [1974] Ch 269.

cause of action[246] – was published that identified the claimant or plaintiff, and also must seek damages.[247] It is not necessary to plead that defendants published material 'falsely and maliciously', although the practice appears to persist in some jurisdictions.[248] It continues from forms of pleading scheduled to the *Common Law Procedure Act (CLPA) 1852*.[249] Such pleading is unnecessary[250] and is prohibited in NSW.[251]

Published words must be set out verbatim for a claim in libel. It is not sufficient to plead the words' substance and effect – they must be set out with reasonable certainty.[252] This differs from traditional pleading principles, under which the actual material would be a matter for particulars not pleading.[253] If the relevant words are contained in a longer publication, the claimant or plaintiff can set out the allegedly defamatory sections.[254] For claims in slander,[255] the words need to be set out as used in speech,[256] although the claimant or plaintiff can succeed if words substantially similar are proved to have been spoken.[257] For both actions, the actual published words are required to enable the court to judge the question of capacity to defame and the defendant to know the charge it faces.[258] Every passage from the published material that alters the imputation in a

---

246 *DA 1974* (NSW) s 9.

247 *CPR* Pt 16 and Pt 53 PD 2.3; formally *RSC* (Eng) Ord 18 r 15(1); *SCR* (Vic) r 13.02(1)(c); *SCR* (NSW) Pt 7 r 1 and now *UCPR* (NSW) r 6.12. For slander not actionable per se, actual loss must be pleaded: *Ward v Lewis* [1955] 1 WLR 9. General precedents for defamation pleading are in most practitioner defamation texts – eg Milmo and Rogers (2004) appendix 1; Price and Duodu (2004) appendix 1 – and general pleading texts: eg Brennan and Blair (2004) section 28.

248 See eg Tobin and Sexton (2005) [25,010]. The practice does not continue in England: eg Brennan and Blair (2004) [28–19].

249 15 and 16 Vict, c 76, sch B, 32 and 33. Bullen and Leake (1868) 304 notes the forms of pleading in the Act's schedule used the word maliciously and suggests 'it seems advisable to retain it'.

250 Eg Odgers and Odgers (1915) 343 and its note 'z'; but cf Bullen and Leake (1868) 304, which states plaintiffs must plead the material to be false, and that 'maliciously' is allowed but not necessary. See also Fachiri (1925) 380.

251 *SCR* (NSW) Pt 67 r 11(1); note, at the time of writing, the *UCPR* (NSW) did not contain specific provisions for defamation, although the *UCPR* take precedence over the *SCR* (NSW) to the extent of any inconsistency, see Chapter 1, Part I, C.

252 Brennan and Blair (2004) [28–14]–[28–15]; *Best v Charter Medical of England* [2002] EMLR 18; *Rubenstein v Truth & Sportsman* [1960] VR 473; *Ron Hodgson* [1971] 1 NSWLR 472, 476 (Asprey JA).

253 Eg NSW Law Reform Commission (1971) [54].

254 Eg *DDSA Pharmaceuticals v Times Newspapers* [1973] 1 QB 21.

255 Slander still exists as a separate action in England and Victoria. It has been assimilated under *DA 1974* (NSW) s 8.

256 *Collins v Jones* [1955] 1 QB 564 and see *CPR* Pt 53 PD 2.4.

257 *Tournier v National Provincial Bank* [1924] 1 KB 461, 488 (Atkin LJ).

258 *Eg Ron Hodgson* [1971] 1 NSWLR 472, 476 (Asprey JA).

material way must be pleaded.[259] Doctrinally, the meanings complained about are the basis for damages. Although a jury may not pay too much attention to pleaded meanings, an appellate court will examine them carefully (as will a judge using the offer of amends procedure, which is examined in Chapter 10).[260]

2 *Plaintiff pleading in England since the nineteenth century*

In England before 1852, if a publication allegedly conveyed a non-literal meaning, the plaintiff had to set out the circumstances creating that meaning in a prefatory averment. An innuendo meaning could only clarify matters already referred to in prefatory averments to the plaintiff's pleading.[261] If the jury found the innuendo meaning was conveyed but there was no supporting prefatory averment, the plaintiff would fail.[262] The approach was very technical, even within the formulary system then operating.[263] That technicality had developed in large part to reduce the number of defamation actions brought in the common law courts.[264] The technicality was continued in the need to give prefatory averments for any alleged non-literal meanings. Meaning and thus actionability were a 'lottery',[265] which is an early application of the word to defamation practice quite different to more recent use to describe the calculation of damages. Thus defamation was 'encumbered' by the 'perverse subtlety of special pleading'.[266]

The position changed in England after 1852, under s 61 of the *CLPA 1852*.[267] The provision was repealed in 1883, but the changed rule remained in force.[268] The change meant that a prefatory averment was no longer needed and the plaintiff did not need to plead extrinsic facts to support an innuendo meaning. Often highly 'rhetorical innuendoes' were pleaded with no supporting facts.[269] It

---

[259] *Ibid* 477; *Gordon v Amalgamated Television Services* [1980] 2 NSWLR 410, 413 (Hunt J). There have been unsuccessful suggestions to relax this approach under the *Uniform Civil Procedure Rules 1999* in Queensland (or to interpret it as a relic of pre-*Judicature Act* pleading): *Robinson v Australian Broadcasting Corpn* [2004] QCA 319.

[260] Eg Price and Duodu (2004) [28.06]; see Chapter 10, Part I, D.

[261] March (1647) 142.

[262] Eg *Holt v Scholefield* (1796) 6 TR 691; 101 ER 775.

[263] Before *CLPA 1852*, 15 and 16 Vict, c 76 and *CLPA 1854*, 17 and 18 Vict, c 125, and *Supreme Court of Judicature Act 1873–1875*, 36 and 37 Vict, c 66.

[264] Holdsworth (1937) vol viii, 333–78 discusses it generally.

[265] *Ibid* 359.

[266] Holdsworth (1937) vol viii, 356 citing Paine (1906) 563.

[267] 15 and 16 Vict, c 76. Lewis (1981) 49 and its note 78 discuss the history at length. Later editions refer back to this, see: Milmo and Rogers (1998) [3.17] and its note 64; (2004) [3.18] and its note 83.

[268] *Statute Law Revision and the Civil Procedure Act 1883*, 46 and 47 Vict, c 49; *Watkin* (1868) LR 3 QB 396.

[269] Eg *Lewis* [1964] AC 234, 278 (Lord Devlin).

seems that a claim without lengthily pleaded innuendoes was thought to understate the plaintiff's case.[270] Plaintiffs, however, still had to prove the necessary extrinsic facts at trial. This situation continued until the mid-twentieth century.

The Porter Committee recommended altering court rules to require plaintiffs to identify, in the pleadings, extrinsic facts to support innuendo meanings. The Committee noted that particulars were needed where extrinsic facts were used in relation to identification, but not for defamatory meaning. Defendants would be better informed if the meaning had to be pleaded.[271] Thus, since 1949, the English provisions required legal innuendo meanings to be particularised.[272] After these changes, there was a tendency for popular innuendoes not to be pleaded while legal innuendoes were pleaded. This could still leave matters unclear until trial. Lord Devlin in *Lewis v Daily Telegraph* suggested that popular innuendoes should be pleaded as well.[273] For nearly a decade, this was treated as persuasive dictum.[274] A series of Court of Appeal cases in the early 1970s held that plaintiffs should plead any popular innuendo meaning that was not clear from a publication's face.[275] The Faulks Committee supported this development.[276]

Therefore, before the *Civil Procedure Rules*, the plaintiff should have identified the meanings allegedly conveyed by the publication. Such pleading of the natural and ordinary meaning was seen as good practice.[277] It had to be followed whenever there could be any doubt as to the alleged meaning.[278] Now under the *Civil Procedure Rules*, claimants 'must specify in the particulars of claim the defamatory meaning' allegedly conveyed, whether natural and ordinary meaning or legal innuendo meaning.[279]

3 *Plaintiff pleading in Victoria and NSW*

Victoria followed the nineteenth-century English changes under the *CLPA 1852*.[280] Victorian court rules were not altered to follow English changes made after the

[270] Eg *Slim* [1968] 1 QB 157, 183–84 (Salmon LJ).

[271] Porter Committee (1948) [164]–[165].

[272] Under the former *RSC* (Eng) Ord 82 r 3(1). This aspect of Ord 82 r 3 was introduced in the former Ord 19 r 6(2) after the Porter Committee's report. It subsequently existed in Ord 82 r 3 in *RSC (Revised) 1962* (Eng).

[273] [1964] AC 234, 280–81.

[274] Eg *Slim* [1968] 1 QB 157, 184 (Salmon LJ).

[275] Eg *Allsop v Church of England Newspaper* [1972] 2 QB 161; *S&K Holdings v Throgmorton Publications* [1972] 1 WLR 1036; *DDSA Pharmaceuticals* [1973] 1 QB 21.

[276] Faulks Committee (1975) [114].

[277] Eg *Lewis* [1964] AC 234, 281 (Lord Devlin).

[278] Eg see *S&K Holdings* [1972] 1 WLR 1036; *Allsop* [1972] 2 QB 161.

[279] *CPR* Pt 53 PD 2.3(1). As noted above fn 8, the term 'innuendo' is used in the *CPR* to refer to legal innuendo meanings.

[280] *CLPA 1865* (Vic) 28 Vict No 274, s 6; *Dwyer v Macartney* (1877) 3 VLR 296.

Porter Committee about providing particulars of extrinsic facts.[281] By case law, however, legal innuendo meanings must be pleaded, and the plaintiff must particularise and prove the relevant extrinsic facts.[282] It also has become accepted that natural and ordinary meanings should be identified in the pleadings,[283] unless they are obvious from the face of the publication. In NSW, the *CLPA 1853* had an identical provision to the English Act,[284] and was construed similarly.[285] The Act was repealed in 1970,[286] and the court rules followed the English post-Porter wording.[287] But the *Defamation Act 1974* (NSW) changed the treatment of natural and ordinary meanings. It means that each imputation is a separate cause of action,[288] and must be pleaded.[289] Not surprisingly, defamation pleading in NSW is seen as even more important than in other common law jurisdictions.[290] It should be noted that, for more than 15 years before the *Defamation Act 1974*, NSW operated under a defamation code – the *Defamation Act 1958* – that largely was equivalent to the current law in Queensland and Tasmania.[291] For present purposes, however, the decisive change from the common law approach in NSW can be taken to be the 1974 defamation legislation.

H How parties are bound by pleaded meanings

In all jurisdictions, the claimant or plaintiff is bound by any pleaded *legal innuendo meaning*. If the jury finds a lesser meaning was conveyed, the claimant or plaintiff will fail.[292] *Truth (New Zealand) v Holloway* illustrates the principle. The plaintiff politician pleaded a legal innuendo meaning that he had acted dishonourably in connection with import licensing. The Privy Council noted that a *suspicion* of having acted dishonourably would not be enough.[293] The defendant did not argue for a 'suspicion' meaning, but for a lesser and different meaning; namely, calling for an inquiry because of existing public comment about the matter. As the defendant argued for a different meaning from the plaintiff's

---

281 Cf *RSC 1971* (WA) r 20.13A.2–3; *Supreme Court Rules 1987* (SA) r 46.19(1); *SCR* (NSW) Pt 67 r 12(c) (and see above, fn 251).

282 *Turner v The Bulletin Newspaper Co* (1974) 131 CLR 69, 80 (Barwick CJ).

283 *Kerney v Optimus Holdings* [1976] VR 399 applying *Allsop* [1972] 2 QB 161.

284 17 Vict No 21, s 56. It became s 72 in the *CLPA 1899* (NSW) 63 Vict No 21.

285 *Wilkinson v Bennett* (1921) 29 CLR 283.

286 *SCA 1970* (NSW) s 5 and sch 1.

287 *SCR* (NSW) Pt 67 r 2(c) (and see above, fn 251).

288 *DA 1974* (NSW) s 9(2); *Petritsis v Hellenic Herald* [1978] 2 NSWLR 174, 190 (Samuels JA).

289 *SCR* (NSW) Pt 67 r 11(2) (and see above, fn 251).

290 Eg NSW Law Reform Commission (1995) 8–9.

291 See, eg Gillooly (1998) 14–15.

292 *Ryan v Ross* (1916) 22 CLR 1, 27 (Isaacs and Gavan Duffy JJ); *Truth (New Zealand) v Holloway* [1961] NZLR 22, 24 (Lord Denning for PC).

293 [1961] NZLR 22, 24.

pleading, just how much *lesser* a meaning would disentitle the plaintiff to succeed was not commented on in detail.

It is less clear whether the claimant or plaintiff also is bound, or should be bound, by pleaded *natural and ordinary meanings*. As Gaudron and Gummow JJ noted in the Australian High Court: 'The consequences of a plaintiff pleading a specific meaning are far from settled.'[294] The whole issue is a major aspect of the research and analysis in this book. Here, the traditional approach is outlined, while litigation practice under the approach is considered in later chapters, and more recent developments, especially in Australian law, are evaluated in Chapter 9.

In England, it seems the court is not bound to either party's pleaded natural and ordinary meaning. In *Polly Peck v Trelford*, O'Connor J said that possible meanings *are confined* to those pleaded by the parties, at least where each pleads a different meaning.[295] In the later *Prager* decision,[296] however, Russell LJ said any possible meaning must be left to the jury: the court *is not confined* to pleaded meanings.[297] In any event, the statement of Diplock LJ in *Slim v Daily Telegraph*[298] is commonly approved that a plaintiff's pleaded meaning will be treated as the most injurious possible meaning.[299] It could be noted that *Gatley* suggests the claimant normally will be bound to a pleaded popular innuendo, at least as the most injurious possible meaning.[300] However, it cites largely Australian case law such as *Hadzel v de Waldorf*,[301] and notes that the claimant may be restricted in conducting its case, while the court could still be free to determine any conveyed meaning – which is the approach suggested in *Taylor v Jecks*.[302] The English decisions do not entirely clarify the allowed degree of variation, even if the claimant or plaintiff *is* bound to a pleaded meaning. In *Slim v Daily Telegraph*, Salmon LJ said a plaintiff should be bound, but not 'strictly':

> I am inclined to think that the plaintiff is bound by [the] pleading – otherwise it may prove to be nothing but a snare for the defendant. *I do not mean, of course, that the plaintiff is strictly confined to the very shade or nuance of meaning . . . pleaded* – but what [the plaintiff] sets up at trial must come broadly within the meaning . . . pleaded.[303]

---

[294] *Chakravarti* (1998) 193 CLR 519, [53].

[295] [1986] QB 1000, 1033.

[296] *Prager v Times Newspapers* [1988] 1 WLR 77, 93.

[297] See also *Lucas-Box v News Group Newspapers* [1986] 1 WLR 147, 153 (Ackner LJ for Eng CA).

[298] *Slim* [1968] 2 QB 157, 175.

[299] Eg *Skuse* [1996] EMLR 278, 285 (Sir Thomas MR for Eng CA).

[300] Milmo and Rogers (2004) [26.24].

[301] (1970) 16 FLR 174.

[302] (1993) 10 WAR 309.

[303] *Slim* [1968] 2 QB 157, 185 (Salmon LJ) (emphasis added).

The Faulks Committee supported that approach, which matches normal pleading principles.[304] The Committee noted that even late amendments would be allowed to avoid injustice to the plaintiff. It also thought precautions may be needed 'to prevent such pleading adding undue complications or unnecessary sub-issues to cases'.[305] Others have suggested that an entirely different meaning cannot be argued for.[306] That may still allow a substantially lesser though somewhat related meaning to be found, on the approach of Diplock LJ in *Slim*. Overall, the general English position would appear to be as stated by the Court of Appeal in *Lucas-Box*:

> We fully appreciate that where an action in defamation is tried with a jury, it is for the jury to decide what meaning or meanings the words in fact bear. They are not limited by the meanings which either the plaintiff or the defendant seeks to place upon the words.[307]

One caveat would be noting that the claimant's or plaintiff's meaning usually will be treated as the most serious possible meaning. Another caveat – which in Chapter 9 is argued to be a central aspect of how defamation law should deal with meaning – is that claimants or plaintiffs should be bound in terms of any distinct allegations raised by a publication: that is, if a distinct allegation has not been complained about, the claimant or plaintiff cannot succeed on that issue. (The issue is explained further at the end of this section.)

The Australian position about whether and how plaintiffs are bound occupied courts from the mid-1990s, notably in the *Chakravarti* litigation.[308] Before considering the High Court judgments in *Chakravarti*, it is worth examining the earlier situation. In some Australian common law defamation jurisdictions, the plaintiff appeared to be bound by any pleaded natural and ordinary meanings.[309] Those meanings, or lesser imputations that are not substantially different, must have been conveyed.[310] Otherwise, the plaintiff would fail. In Victoria, however,

---

304 Faulks Committee (1975) [113]; eg Jacob and Goldrein (1990) 2.

305 Faulks Committee (1975) [114].

306 Eg Jacob and Goldrein (1990) 624.

307 *Lucas-Box* [1986] 1 WLR 147, 153 (Ackner LJ for Eng CA).

308 *Chakravarti* (1996) 65 SASR 527; (1998) 193 CLR 519.

309 In the ACT: *Hadzel v De Waldorf* (1970) 16 FLR 174, 179 and 181–82 (Fox J); in South Australia, in most instances at least: *Prichard v Krantz* (1984) 37 SASR 379, 386 (King CJ); *Chakravarti* (1996) 65 SASR 527, 539–40 (Doyle CJ), 556 (Perry J), 559 (Williams J); but note *Jakudo v South Australian Telecasters* (1997) 69 SASR 440 in which the Full Court said common sting arguments would be open to defendants, and approved *Polly Peck* [1986] QB 1000 and *Khashoggi* [1986] 1 WLR 1412. But like *Khashoggi*, *Jakudo* was an interlocutory or interim injunction case. In *Jakudo*, there were no pleaded imputations and the first-instance judge agreed a number of imputations with counsel. Even so, *Jakudo* was approved in *Roberts v Bass* (2000) 78 SASR 302, 309 (Williams J).

310 Eg *Prichard* (1984) 37 SASR 379, 386 (King CJ); *Chakravarti* (1996) 65 SASR 527.

the plaintiff was not bound by pleaded meanings.[311] Conveyed meaning remained a factual jury question. Pleading a popular innuendo

> did not, and in our opinion could not, alter the position at law that the meaning of the words was ultimately a question for the jury, and that the jury must be at large in finding the true meaning amongst such possible meanings as were left to them by the trial judge, and that the judge was not bound to confine the jury to the false innuendoes asserted by the plaintiff.[312]

In NSW, the plaintiff was and is bound by pleaded imputations,[313] which is not greatly surprising because the imputation is the cause of action. The jury must find that at least one pleaded meaning was conveyed.[314] Each pleaded imputation, however, includes all meanings that are not different in substance,[315] such as imputations of slightly lesser seriousness.[316] For example, the plaintiff could not have an imputation of promiscuity removed from the jury by arguing the publication only 'bore imputations of sexual immorality of a slightly lesser degree'.[317] To rely on a substantially lesser imputation or an imputation different from any pleaded imputation, however, the plaintiff must amend its statement of claim.[318]

Chakravarti re-examined these questions, at least for Australian common law defamation jurisdictions. It was another of the 'guilt or suspicion' cases that have been significant in appellate case law.[319] Among other imputations, the plaintiff pleaded the meaning that he was involved in criminal or civil misconduct in relation to loans obtained as a financial executive. The defendant denied this meaning and pleaded that only a suspicion of misconduct arose. One issue for the High Court was whether the plaintiff could rely on non-pleaded meanings. All judges said the plaintiff could be bound to pleaded meanings, but could depart from them if the defendant would not be prejudiced. Brennan CJ and McHugh J strongly criticised Polly Peck[320] style pleading in relation to truth and opinion defences.[321] This issue is addressed later, particularly in Chapters 3 and 9.

---

311 *Barclay* [1968] VR 664, 666; *Kennett v Farmer* [1988] VR 991, 996 (Nathan J); *Kelly v SBS* [1990] VR 69, 72; *Curran v Herald and Weekly Times* [1993] Aust Defamation Reports [51,090], 42,882 (Gobbo J). The same applies in Western Australia: *Gumina* (1990) 3 WAR 351, 355 (Malcolm CJ), 364 (Seaman J, Pidgeon J agreed).

312 *National Mutual Life Association of Australasia v GTV Corpn* [1989] VR 747, 768.

313 Prior to *DA 1974* (NSW), plaintiffs were not bound by pleaded meanings: *Morris v Newcastle Newspapers* (1985) 1 NSWLR 260, 263 (Hunt J).

314 *SCR* (NSW) Pt 67 r 11(3) (and see above, fn 251).

315 Eg *Morosi v Mirror Newspapers* [1977] 2 NSWLR 749, 771.

316 *SCR* (NSW) Pt 67 r 11(3) (and see above, fn 251); eg *Anderson (No 2)* (1986) 5 NSWLR 735, 738 (Hunt J).

317 *Morosi* [1977] 2 NSWLR 749, 771.

318 Eg *Anderson (No 2)* (1986) 5 NSWLR 735, 738 (Hunt J).

319 Eg *Lewis* [1964] AC 234; *Harrison* (1982) 149 CLR 293; *Rigby v John Fairfax Group* (Unreported, NSW CA, Kirby P, Priestley and Meagher JJA, 1 February 1996).

320 Named after *Polly Peck* [1986] QB 1000.

321 *Chakravarti* (1998) 193 CLR 519, [8]–[13].

Their joint judgment – dealing with a closely related issue – also said that a plaintiff generally is confined to specified popular innuendo meanings.[322] Such pleadings or particulars can be needed to define issues and avoid prejudice to the defendant or the trial judge.[323] Nothing should be done to discourage plaintiffs pleading meanings and giving 'shape and focus to the cause of action'.[324]

Brennan CJ and McHugh J examined how plaintiffs are bound in some detail. They attempted to reconcile the comments of Diplock and Salmon LJJ in *Slim v Daily Telegraph* about the pleaded meaning being the most injurious possible meaning,[325] or the plaintiff being bound to a pleaded meaning.[326] Being bound could be too rigorous a requirement. It 'appears to sacrifice form over substance and to elevate minute differences from the meaning pleaded to the status of a substantial defence'.[327] Less injurious meanings, however, could be substantially different and could prejudice the defence. Brennan CJ and McHugh J suggested that 'a different nuance of meaning from the meaning pleaded' can go to the jury if that is not unfair to the defendant.[328] Support for the 'nuance of meaning' approach was found in English and Australian case law, including NSW decisions.[329] Thus, Brennan CJ and McHugh J described how a plaintiff was confined to pleaded meanings:

> A plaintiff who pleads a false innuendo thereby confines the meanings relied on. The plaintiff cannot then seek a verdict on a different meaning which so alters the substance of the meaning pleaded that the defendant would have been entitled to *plead a different issue*, to *adduce different evidence* or to *conduct the case on a different basis*.[330]

They concluded:

> If there be no unfair disadvantage to the defendant . . . as where the plaintiff seeks to rely on a different nuance of meaning or, oftentimes, merely a less serious defamation – the different defamatory meaning may be found by the jury.[331]

Gaudron and Gummow JJ, in another joint judgment in *Chakravarti*, considered the English and Australian authorities. They suggested the cases tend to

[322] *Ibid* [14]–[19].

[323] *Ibid* [16].

[324] *Ibid* [17].

[325] [1968] 1 QB 157, 175 (Diplock LJ).

[326] *Ibid* 185 (Salmon LJ). Previously, both statements had been referred to in the High Court: *Sungravure* (1975) 134 CLR 1, 14 (Stephen J).

[327] *Chakravarti* (1998) 193 CLR 519, [21].

[328] *Ibid*.

[329] Eg *Slim* [1968] 1 QB 157, 185 (Salmon LJ); *Hadzel* (1970) 16 FLR 174, 182 (Fox J); *Prichard* (1984) 37 SASR 379, 386 (King CJ, Millhouse and Prior JJ); *Taylor v Jecks* (1993) 10 WAR 309, 317–18 (WA FC); *Crampton v Nugawela* (1996) 41 NSWLR 176, 183 (Mahoney ACJ).

[330] *Chakravarti* (1998) 193 CLR 519, [19] (emphasis added).

[331] *Ibid* [24].

'translate into rules what are best seen as considerations going to fair and efficient practice'[332] – and practice should be flexible. They said changes could extend to meanings 'comprehended' in the statement of claim, less injurious meanings or simply variants of pleaded meanings.[333] Substantially different meanings, however, would usually be unavailable.

Kirby J commented at length on legal principles about meaning in defamation.[334] Encouraging parties to plead meanings merely aims to help determine disputes fairly. His judgment implied that greater change from pleaded meanings could be possible. Even if the plaintiff is bound, however, a pleaded meaning includes less serious meanings that are not substantially different. Kirby J also dealt simply with the concept of 'nuances' of meaning. 'No complaint can arise where additional imputations found represent nothing more than nuances or shades of meaning of those pleaded.'[335] He suggested that the NSW situation, where each imputation is a cause of action and must be pleaded with precision, should not be extended to common law jurisdictions.[336] It was seen to make interlocutory processes more complex, and create a danger that attention at trial 'will be deflected from the item actually said to have harmed the plaintiff's reputation' to debates about whether pleaded imputations arise.[337] Under the common law, courts should be flexible if conveyed meanings do not coincide exactly with pleaded meanings. Trial judges' discretion can protect defendants and prevent the trial being diverted from examining the publication in context to concentrating on the pleaded imputations.[338]

The Victorian position that pleaded meanings cannot restrict what meaning the court finds is conveyed appears to have been changed by *Chakravarti*. In *David Syme v Hore-Lacy*, the Victorian Court of Appeal said a plaintiff could only succeed on a meaning that is not substantially different from and not more serious or injurious than a pleaded popular innuendo meaning.[339] In Chapter 9, the significance and merit of this change and the varying judicial statements on the question – as well as the strong criticism by Kirby J of the NSW approach – is considered in light of evidence from litigation practice. Drawing on the empirical research – in particular the material discussed in Chapters 4 to 6 – and on case law analysis, it is argued that courts should not focus on plaintiff's being bound to pleaded *meanings*. Instead, attention should be placed on any separate

332 *Ibid* [56]. Brennan CJ and McHugh J agreed with Gaudron and Gummow JJ, except on two points they explored in their own judgment: first, the order of analysing the conveyed meaning and the availability of fair comment; and secondly, whether the defendant can justify meanings the plaintiff has not pleaded: *ibid* [1]–[2].

333 *Ibid* [60].

334 *Ibid* [139].

335 *Ibid*.

336 *Ibid* [144].

337 *Ibid* [139].

338 *Ibid*.

339 [2000] 1 VR 667, [17] (Ormiston J), [52[–[54] (Charles JA), [69] (Callaway JA).

and distinct *allegations* that are made in the publication, and a plaintiff should not be able to succeed on separate and distinct allegations about which the plaintiff has not complained. At trial, parties may be constrained from departing from pleaded meanings *if* such departure would prejudice the other side – that would be evaluated in light of all the circumstances at trial. That possible restriction on departure from pleading meanings, however, is a different issue to pre-trial battles about meanings and from at-trial determinations of conveyed meanings – both of these should focus on the publication, not on the pleaded imputations.

The issue can also be illustrated by returning to the example set out in Part I concerning allegations about tax returns and a person's disappearance. If the claimant or plaintiff only set out imputations related to the tax return issue, there could be no verdict in relation to the statements about disappearance. This is an obvious point, but is useful to bear in mind when considering how parties should be bound. The parties may well disagree about just what level of meaning is conveyed in relation to the tax return issue – does the publication convey that the claimant or plaintiff is guilty of tax offences (and exactly what offences) or does it merely raise suspicion? The parties will set out their positions about this in their statements of case or pleadings. But the empirical research and case analysis set out in later chapters strongly suggests that parties should not be bound closely to the level of any pleaded imputations about tax returns. At trial, the parties may be constrained in presenting their cases – if that is needed to avoid injustice to the other side – but the tribunal of fact is not restricted to the detail of the imputation. It should focus on the publication and the allegations that it contains which have been complained about.

I The degree of specificity required in pleaded meanings

The second major question this book poses about pleaded meaning concerns the degree of specificity needed in pleading. Under general principles, pleading alleged meanings serves good procedural aims in clarifying matters in dispute. The necessary degree of precision, however, would seem to be a matter of judgment. The issue has received considerable attention in NSW. In England, *Gatley* primarily refers to judicial comments on the NSW law.[340] Victorian references to the NSW position also exist.[341] Such statements suggest that NSW case law on this issue would be supported elsewhere, with only some awareness of the peculiar statutory basis to the cause of action in that state, which may not accord with the criticisms made by Kirby J in *Chakravarti*.[342] Those criticisms are not unprecedented. Encouraging – or requiring – parties to plead alleged meanings raises long-standing concerns about pleading. There is

[340] Milmo and Rogers (2004) [26.21] and its note 84, citing *Drummoyne Municipal Council v Australian Broadcasting Corporn* (1990) 21 NSWLR 135.

[341] Eg Williams (2005) [I 13.11.140].

[342] *Chakravarti* (1998) 193 CLR 519, [139]; above Part III, H.

a fear disputes can be diverted into arcane 'pleading points',[343] or simply lead to unnecessarily long and elaborate pleadings. When proposing change before the *Defamation Act 1974* (NSW), the NSW Law Reform Commission noted that making each imputation a separate cause of action could harm pleading practice and lead to prolix pleadings.[344] It suggested introducing the court rules that now exist to prevent separate imputations being pleaded unless they differ in substance.[345]

The NSW rules' detailed provisions relating to imputations place 'a premium on careful and accurate pleading'.[346] The apparent effect is to achieve greater precision in each party's case. The plaintiff must clearly and precisely specify each defamatory imputation.[347] The plaintiff must plead 'the precise act or condition asserted of, or attributed to' the plaintiff.[348] This reduces any confusion as to what meaning the plaintiff contends for. If the pleaded imputation is ambiguous, the jury should *not* be left to determine its meaning.[349] Precision in this area is described as a primary value in litigation.[350] *Drummoyne Municipal Council v Australian Broadcasting Corporation* is worth examining in more detail to consider possible weaknesses in the approach.[351] What is the appropriate degree of specificity when lack of clarity in an imputation follows more from the defendant's publication than from the plaintiff's pleading? *Drummoyne* is both a useful example of the general issue and an important case to review closely because it remains a leading decision on defamation pleading. For example, at least 30 Australian cases referred to *Drummoyne* between January 2002 and June 2004, overwhelmingly in relation to the issues of pleading and specificity that are explored here and in later chapters. The cases involved: the High Court hearing an appeal from NSW; the Supreme Courts in the ACT, NSW, Queensland, South Australia and Western Australia; and the Federal Court in its NSW registry.[352]

---

343 As Jacob and Goldrein (1990) 12 suggest it is misleading to refer to 'mere pleading points', citing *Farrell v Secretary of State for Defence* [1980] 1 WLR 172, 180 (Lord Edmund-Davies). English attitudes also may have changed under the *CPR*, see Chapter 10, Part I, D.

344 NSW Law Reform Commission (1971) [51]–[54]; see Chapter 10, Part I, B.

345 *Ibid* appendix C.

346 NSW Law Reform Commission (1995) [1.19]; see *SCR* (NSW) Pt 67 (and see above fn 251).

347 *SCR* (NSW) Pt 67 r 11(2) and (3) (and see above fn 251).

348 *Monte* [1979] 2 NSWLR 663, 678 (Hunt J).

349 *Singleton v Ffrench* (1986) 5 NSWLR 425, 427–30 (Mahoney JA), 435 (McHugh JA, Samuels JA agreed).

350 Eg *Monte* [1979] 2 NSWLR 663, 676 (Hunt J).

351 (1990) 21 NSWLR 135.

352 See, eg *Askew v Morris* [2004] WASC 43; *South Australian Water Corpn v Sullivan* [2004] SASC 42; *Griffith v John Fairfax Publications* [2004] NSWSC 66; *Magub v Hinchliffe* [2004] QSC 4; *Rivkin* (2003) 201 ALR 77; *Reading v Australian Broadcasting Corpn* [2003] NSWSC 716; *Byrnes v John Fairfax Publications* [2003] NSWSC 575; *Cashman v Hinchliffe* [2003] QCA 161; *NRMA v Nine Network Australia* [2002] ACTSC 37; *Stalyce Holdings (Aust) v Cetec* [2002] FCA 278; *Greek Herald v Nikolopoulos* (2002) 54 NSWLR 165.

Recent efforts to improve the treatment of these pleading battles in NSW – which are examined closely in Chapter 10[353] – are best understood in light of *Drummoyne*'s example of the longstanding NSW approach. *Drummoyne* was a strike-out application under court rules against pleadings tending to prejudice, embarrass or delay proceedings.[354] The plaintiff council allegedly failed to specify each imputation. (It should be noted that *Ballina Shire Council v Ringland* now prevents a council suing in defamation,[355] and *Lange v Australian Broadcasting Corporation* also could provide an extended form of common law qualified privilege defence for comments about a council.[356]) In *Drummoyne*, the council pleaded an imputation that it was corrupt without giving a particular meaning of corruption. Hunt J struck out the pleading.[357] He said 'corrupt' can convey at least three distinct meanings: being open to bribery, being dishonest, or lacking integrity. The plaintiff argued that it should not need to specify 'corruption', a word the defendant actually used. The plaintiff wanted to rely on all reasonable meanings of corruption as being included in its pleading. This was rejected: 'It is for the plaintiff to state its imputations with precision notwithstanding any imprecision of the matter complained of.'[358] The plaintiff, however, could replead and specify the sense of corruption intended. Or the plaintiff could argue that all three senses of the term arise, if each was separately pleaded.

The order to replead was supported on appeal, but through different reasoning. Priestley JA emphasised that corruption could have at least the three meanings mentioned by Hunt J, but also could have a very general defamatory meaning.[359] He agreed that a defendant is entitled to know the 'precise' meaning alleged *if* precise means 'sufficiently clear' to tell the defendant the case it must meet. 'Precision must always be a relative matter.'[360] This approach seems much closer to traditional pleading principles. It meant the plaintiff could replead and contend for any meaning of corruption – including a very general meaning – if it was clear which meaning each imputation alleged. In his judgment,[361] Priestley JA also dealt with his own earlier comments in *Hepburn v TCN Channel Nine* and those of Glass and Hutley JJA in that case.[362] In *Hepburn*, Glass JA differed on the appropriate degree of specificity. Glass JA said:

> I see no reason why the plaintiff should be compelled to define the sense in which the defendant employed a general expression. If the plaintiff is

---

353 See Chapter 10, Part I, A.

354 *SCR* (NSW) Pt 15 r 26(1)(b) and now *UCPR* (NSW) r 14.28.

355 (1994) 33 NSWLR 680.

356 (1997) 189 CLR 520.

357 The judgment of Hunt J is detailed on appeal: *Drummoyne* (1990) 21 NSWLR 135, 153–55 (Priestley JA).

358 Hunt J cited on appeal: *Drummoyne* (1990) 21 NSWLR 135, 154 (Priestley JA).

359 *Ibid* 155.

360 *Ibid*.

361 *Ibid* 156–57.

362 [1983] 2 NSWLR 682, 683–93 (Hutley JA), 693–94 (Glass JA), 694–96 (Priestley JA).

> castigated as a criminal, criminality is predicated of [the plaintiff] in all its amplitude. . . . The defendant is expected to know what [the defendant's] language conveyed and that, in adopting an epithet with a spread of meanings, [the defendant] will be understood as imputing them all.[363]

In *Drummoyne*, Priestley JA distinguished *Hepburn*. It was a case about capacity, while *Drummoyne* was purely a pleading case about whether the required specificity had been achieved.[364] He reasoned that the comments of Glass JA about specificity were obiter in *Hepburn*. In his own judgment in *Hepburn*, Priestley JA had not adopted the comments of Glass JA while the third appellate judge, Hutley JA, had not commented on them at all in *Hepburn*.[365]

In *Drummoyne*, Gleeson CJ agreed the court rules requiring specificity raised questions of degree, and suggested, 'If a problem arises, the solution will usually be found in considerations of practical justice rather than philology.'[366] As discussed in Chapter 10, this quotation increasingly has become a point of reference in NSW pleading decisions.[367] The degree of specificity should be decided in light of the published material, with reference to the appropriate test: whether confusion is likely about the plaintiff's alleged meaning.[368] Ambiguity may flow from the published material or from the defendant's own words or actions. For example, a placard labelled 'Corrupt Judges' could convey an allegation in those very terms, which would be specified enough for trial.[369] In that instance, it would be inappropriate to require the plaintiff to specify further the meaning of 'corrupt'. This seems equivalent to the 'general meaning of corruption' approach allowed by Priestley JA. The plaintiff must specify the meanings to be argued for, which may include quite general meanings, depending on just what was published. Thus, the *Drummoyne* majority was not requiring an extreme degree of specificity. The '*Drummoyne* point', however, has entered the lexicon of NSW cases when pleaded imputations are challenged on grounds of specificity or ambiguity. But *Drummoyne* also suggests that not all general meanings need be thought ambiguous.

In *Drummoyne*, Kirby P dissented. He viewed *Hepburn* differently to Priestley JA, and said that Hunt J had failed to follow the Court of Appeal in managing the Defamation List.[370] He also criticised the artificialities of defamation pleading.[371] In *Hepburn*, the plaintiff doctor pleaded an imputation that she was an abortionist,

---

[363] *Ibid* 693.

[364] *Drummoyne* (1990) 21 NSWLR 135, 156–57.

[365] *Hepburn* [1983] 2 NSWLR 682, 694–96 (Priestley JA).

[366] *Drummoyne* (1990) 21 NSWLR 135, 137.

[367] See Chapter 10, Part I, A.

[368] *Drummoyne* (1990) 21 NSWLR 135, 138 citing *Whelan v John Fairfax & Sons* (1988) 12 NSWLR 148, 155 (Hunt J).

[369] *Ibid* 137 citing *John Fairfax & Sons v Foord* (1988) 12 NSWLR 706, 726 (Clarke JA, Hope JA agreed).

[370] *Ibid* 142–48.

[371] *Ibid* 149.

which would not necessarily entail illegal conduct. Hunt J would not allow this imputation to go to the jury. Kirby P quoted Hutley JA in *Hepburn*:

> [I]t is strange to hear the suggestion that this defendant does not understand an imputation which is precisely in the words it has used, so that it is embarrassed in justifying it. This must mean it does not know what it is alleged an ordinary reasonable hearer would make of it.[372]

Kirby P noted criticisms that Hunt J made about these comments when he declined to follow the Court of Appeal in *Hepburn*.[373] Kirby P examined the various arguments for and against a high degree of specificity in pleaded meanings. He favoured a less strict approach, even though imputations 'ground' the statutory cause of action in NSW and the defendant may wish to plead differently to various alleged meanings.[374] He believed the approach of Hunt J creates an unduly complex procedure with unwarranted delays and costs, wrongly places the burden of pleading on the plaintiff (at least where published words' ordinary meaning can be defamatory), and may mean the plaintiff loses if its precisely pleaded imputation is found not to have been conveyed.[375] Three short quotes illustrate his view on the equities between the parties and the practical issues for jury trials:

> The plaintiff should not, in the laudable name of particularity, be forced to give meaning to the *nuances of the very words which the defendant itself used* and which the defendant must therefore be expected to defend.[376]
>
> An *excess of refinement* when a word with a pejorative meaning such as 'corruption' is used *is more likely to confuse than to assist the jury*.[377]
>
> Practical justice suggests that *those who use words ordinarily defamatory* in their imputation, and not those on the receiving end, *should bear the obligation of convincing the jury* of the innocence of the word in the particular context.[378]

The contentious point about specifying imputations illustrated by *Drummoyne* is more relevant for this book's investigation of law and practice than arguments about what *was* the precise holding in *Hepburn* and whether Hunt J failed to follow the Court of Appeal. Leave to replead was given in *Drummoyne*. The appellate court clarified that all meanings of corruption could be pleaded, including a general meaning. This might suggest the interlocutory dispute in *Drummoyne* was an expensive contest with little point. It may, however, highlight why some judges criticise the NSW approach. Kirby J has returned to the issue, notably in *Chakravarti*. There, he said the need for 'exact precision' in each

---

372 *Ibid* 144–45; quoting *Hepburn* [1983] 2 NSWLR 682, 688.

373 Eg *Tarkanyi v Mirror Newspapers* [1983] 2 NSWLR 698; *Hepburn* [1984] 1 NSWLR 386 when the case returned to the Supreme Court; *Morris* (1985) 1 NSWLR 260.

374 *Drummoyne* (1990) 21 NSWLR 135, 149–50.

375 *Ibid* 149–51.

376 *Ibid* 150 (emphasis added).

377 *Ibid* 151 (emphasis added).

378 *Ibid* (emphasis added).

imputation – clearly a matter of precedent in that state after *Drummoyne*[379] – may have disadvantages:

> It has led to many pre-trial applications, complex interlocutory proceedings and a potential for injustice, depending upon the ingenuity and skill of the pleader of the imputations. It enlarges judicial control over the consideration of the matter complained of by the tribunal of fact. . . . Because readers and viewers are not favoured with pleaded imputations when they receive the matter complained of, there is a risk that the attention at the trial will be deflected from the item actually said to have harmed the plaintiff's reputation to an evaluation of pleaded imputations and a debate about whether they truly arise.[380]

In *John Fairfax Publications v Rivkin,* Kirby J also noted the danger of the NSW approach 'diverting attention from the publication to the lawyer's pleading of the alleged imputations'.

> The problems that have arisen in the present case (as in others) are substantially the outcome of the replacement of what was formerly a comprehensive and intuitive process of jury assessment, taken to reflect community perception of a publication viewed as a whole, by a procedure whereby perception is substantially directed by lawyers towards formulae re-expressed by lawyers and ultimately, for the most part, evaluated and judged by lawyers.[381]

Suggestions that the approach increases the law's 'technicality' have been considered by the NSW Law Reform Commission,[382] but it has supported the state's method. It noted the contrast to other jurisdictions, saying that in common law jurisdictions a bargaining process often occurs between counsel and judge as to what meanings to leave the jury at the end of trial evidence.[383] 'In contrast . . . the NSW procedure emphasises precision and makes the issues clearer at trial, saving valuable court time.'[384] Any 'appearance' of technicality was far outweighed by precision.[385] The value of such an interpretation is evaluated in Chapter 10, and in light of evidence from litigation practice the Commission's statements are not supported.[386]

---

[379] It is 'well settled': *Rigby* (Unreported, NSW CA, Kirby P, Priestley and Meagher JJA, 1 February 1996), 12 (Priestley JA; Meagher JA agreed). See also *Marsden* (1998) 43 NSWLR 158, 162 (Hunt CJ at CL; Mason P and Handley JA agreed).

[380] *Chakravarti* (1998) 193 CLR 519, [139] suggesting a comparison be made with *Drummoyne* (1990) 21 NSWLR 135, 149–51 (Kirby P in dissent).

[381] (2003) 201 ALR 77, [84]; see also *Rigby* (Unreported, NSW CA, Kirby P, Priestley and Meagher JJA, 1 February 1996) 4–5 (Kirby P in dissent).

[382] Young Lawyers, *Submission* [to NSW Law Reform Commission] (1993) 13, cited in NSW Law Reform Commission (1995) [4.5].

[383] NSW Law Reform Commission (1995) [4.3].

[384] *Ibid* [4.5].

[385] *Ibid.*

[386] See Chapter 10, Part I, B.

IV CONCLUSION

This chapter has outlined the claimant's or plaintiff's case in relation to three of the most significant areas of debate about meaning in defamation, which should be central to understanding comparative approaches to defamation law and practice. They concern how parties are bound to pleaded meanings, the degree of specificity required in pleading, and the stage of a trial at which meaning is determined. How, if at all, does practice actually vary between England and Australia in relation to these matters? Is the detail required in NSW counterproductive? Some commentary, for example, implies that the specificity required in NSW is not a matter of great practical difference.[387] Research into litigation practice is one useful way of addressing these questions, and it is developed in later chapters of the book, after the next chapter examines the law that is most relevant to defences and meaning.

387 Eg Brown (1994) 1255–56. English and Victorian commentary also suggests the difference in practice is not great: see above, fns 340–341.

– 3 –

DEFENCES RELEVANT TO MEANING: ENGLISH AND AUSTRALIAN LAW

Defences excuse defamatory publications that would otherwise create liability. The defendant can plead inconsistent defences[1] and rely on a different defence for each imputation. Possible defences in England and Australia include justification, which is related to truth; comment or fair comment, which protect some opinion; absolute privilege, which, among other publications, protects statements made in judicial proceedings and parliaments; qualified privilege, which is examined in Chapter 7; innocent dissemination or secondary responsibility;[2] offer of amends after an unintentional defamation;[3] apology for publications in newspapers or other periodicals;[4] triviality or unlikelihood of harm, which has a narrow application and only applies in New South Wales (NSW), of the jurisdictions considered closely in this chapter;[5] and general law

[1] Eg *Casey v Australian Broadcasting Commission* [1981] 1 NSWLR 305.

[2] At common law innocent dissemination *may* survive in England; see eg Milmo and Rogers (2004) [6.26]; Collins (2001a) [16.06] (and see Collins 2005). Secondary responsibility is available in England under *DA 1996* (UK) s 1, and is wider than innocent dissemination.

[3] In England, complex and rarely used provisions in *DA 1952* (UK) s 4, were replaced from 28 February 2000 by *DA 1996* (UK) ss 2–4. see Chapter 10, Part I, D, and eg Milmo and Rogers (2004) [18.1]–[18.11]. See also *DA 1974* (NSW) ss 9A–9G; *Civil Law (Wrongs) Act 2002* (ACT) ss 116–122.

[4] In England, under Lord Campbell's Act, *Libel Act 1843*, 6 and 7 Vict, c 96, s 2. It is virtually never used. The provisions are reproduced in *Wrongs Act 1958* (Vic) s 7. An apology also could be relied on in mitigation of damages; *Libel Act 1843* s 1, *Wrongs Act 1958* (Vic) s 6, *Supreme Court Rules 1970* (NSW) Pt 67 r 18(2)(c) (*SCR* (NSW)); note, at the time of writing, the *Uniform Civil Procedure Rules* (NSW) (*UCPR* (NSW)) did not contain specific provisions for defamation, although they take precedence over the *SCR* (NSW) to the extent of any inconsistency: see Chapter 1, Part I, C. An apology could be combined with a payment into court (eg the former *Rules of the Supreme Court 1965* (Eng) Ord 22 (*RSC*)) or combined with an offer of compromise, which is available to both parties unlike the payment in procedure: *Supreme Court (General Rules of Procedure in Civil Proceedings) Rules 1996* (Vic) Ord 26 (*SCR* (Vic)); *SCR* (NSW) Pt 22 and now *UCPR* (NSW) rr 20.25–20.32. In England, see now *Civil Procedure Rules 1998* (Eng) (*CPR*) Pt 36, which is available to both parties, with claimants being likely to receive indemnity costs if they recover more than their offer: see eg *McPhilemy v Times Newspapers (No 2)* [2002] 1 WLR 934.

[5] *DA 1974* (NSW) s 13; see eg *Jones v Sutton* [2004] NSWCA 439. Elsewhere, damages may be less if harm was unlikely.

defences such as consent or time limits to taking action. Malice defeats some defences–such as fair comment and qualified privilege–and there are significant variations in the form these defences take in each jurisdiction, if they are available at all.

In England and Australia, two defences are most relevant to examining conveyed meaning: justification and fair comment.[6] A defamatory publication may be defensible if it is true, or if it is a matter of honest opinion, both of which are necessarily and intimately connected with the publication's meaning. While meaning also can arise in relation to other defences – for example, in relation to malice and qualified privilege[7] – truth and opinion defences provide a useful and practical focus for this chapter, particularly its concerns about defence pleading of meaning. English and Australian developments in qualified privilege under *Reynolds v Times Newspapers*,[8] *Lange v Australian Broadcasting Corporation*[9] and associated cases are turned to in Chapter 7, before the very different US approach to issues of truth, falsity and opinion are examined in Chapter 8.

Part I of this chapter examines justification defences as they relate to meaning. It provides an overview of law and procedure relevant to the book's third major question about meaning in defamation, which is to evaluate Polly Peck and Lucas-Box pleading for justification (the terminology is explained below in Part I, Section K) and the contextual truth defence under s 16 of the *Defamation Act 1974* (NSW). Do any of these defence approaches arise often? How are they dealt with in practice when they arise? Are there good reasons of trial practice for any of the approaches to be used? These issues also have significance for the opinion defences, which are examined in Part II. One subsidiary question in relation to the opinion defences is noted, which litigation research may help understand in more detail: defending unintended imputations.

I JUSTIFICATION

Meaning is especially important for justification.[10] At common law, defamatory publications are justified if shown to be true. Perhaps the defence should be renamed 'truth',[11] which is the term used under the statutory defence of ss 14–16

[6] See eg Faulks Committee (1975) 22.

[7] At common law the subjectively intended meaning can be significant for qualified privilege: see eg *Loveless v Earl* [1999] EMLR 530, 538–39 (Hirst LJ); in relation to NSW's statutory defence in *DA 1974* (NSW) s 22: *Morgan v John Fairfax and Sons (No 2)* (1991) 23 NSWLR 374. See also Chapter 7.

[8] [2001] 2 AC 127.

[9] (1997) 189 CLR 520.

[10] Eg Price and Duodu (2004) [8.04].

[11] Faulks Committee (1975) [129] recommended renaming it truth. New Zealand has made the change: *DA 1992* (NZ) s 8; as has NSW: *DA 1974* (NSW) s 15.

of the *Defamation Act 1974* (NSW), which replaces the common law defence in NSW. The common law terminology is 'unfortunate'[12] at the least. If a publication is true, harm to the claimant's or plaintiff's reputation may be thought to deserve no remedy. The reputation merely is brought down to its 'proper level'.[13]

These are the major points considered in Part I:

(a) An imputation may be narrow or general. An allegation may suggest a particular deed of misconduct rather than a general pattern of discreditable behaviour. In that event, only evidence relating to the particular deed may be used in justification. If an imputation is general, wider material can be referred to in a justification defence.

(b) Allegations may be distinct or non-distinct. Where allegations are distinct, the claimant or plaintiff may complain about only one distinct allegation. Then, the truth of another one cannot be used in justification. This means one imputation cannot be justified by proving a separate, distinct imputation to be true. Alternatively, the claimant or plaintiff may complain about several distinct imputations, some of which may remain undefended. The significance of undefended imputations can be reduced in several ways: the defendant may prove the truth of some imputations and rely on common law partial justification to reduce damages; in England, the defendant may rely on the extended form of justification under s 5 of the *Defamation Act 1952* (UK); and in NSW the statutory defence of contextual truth may be available under s 16 of the *Defamation Act 1974* (NSW).

(c) In some jurisdictions at least, the defendant may argue the claimant's or plaintiff's pleaded imputation is not conveyed at all. Instead, the publication may convey a different meaning. The defendant may seek to justify that meaning, if it is conveyed. This can be described as a Lucas-Box justification defence (which also is discussed below in Part I, K).

(d) In some jurisdictions at least, the defendant may argue that distinct imputations are not conveyed. Then, proving the truth of one aspect of the publication's 'common sting' will justify all the publication. This can be described as a Polly Peck justification defence (which is discussed below in Part I, K).

A General aspects of justification

Several general aspects of the approach to justification are noteworthy here. They concern the standard of proof and judge and jury roles; requirements in some jurisdictions for public interest (or public benefit) to be shown in addition to truth; the relationship of justification to comment defences; and malice.

---

[12] Milmo and Rogers (2004) [11.1].

[13] Eg *Rofe v Smith's Newspapers* (1924) 25 SR (NSW) 4, 21 (Street ACJ).

1 *Standard of proof; roles of judge and jury*

The defendant must prove justification on the balance of probabilities,[14] although it also is commonly noted that the 'more serious the allegation the more is the evidence required.'[15] The defendant can face a difficult task in proving all conveyed factual meanings to be true. Comparisons to the US approach are common.[16] As examined in Chapter 8, in the US, plaintiffs who are public officials or public figures must prove with clear and convincing evidence that a publication is false, and that the defendant knew of this falsity or was recklessly indifferent to it, to recover damages. In terms of English and Australian law, the US approach may be used to suggest that claimants or plaintiffs should have to prove falsity,[17] or to argue for a separate, wider defence for speech related to public or political matters. Developments to common law qualified privilege during the 1990s in England and Australia (discussed in Chapter 7) can be seen as responses to these public interest arguments. At common law, the judge decides whether there is evidence for a jury to find the publication true.[18] This is a similar supervisory role to judicial rulings on capable meanings, which are discussed in Chapter 2. If that evidential hurdle is met, the jury decides whether the publication or any part of it is true in substance and fact.[19] In NSW, however, the judge determines all issues of fact and law as to whether the defence has been established in the changed litigation practices under s 7A of the *Defamation Act 1974* (NSW).[20]

2 *Truth alone, or truth and public interest*

Truth is a complete defence at common law: the publication need not be of public interest.[21] Questions of privacy, therefore, are not relevant to common law defamation, in terms of doctrine at least.[22] In England and Victoria, common law justification is a complete defence. For the NSW statutory defences of truth and

[14] Eg *Sutherland v Stopes* [1925] AC 47; *Singleton v Ffrench* (1986) 5 NSWLR 425, 442 (McHugh JA).

[15] *Dellow's Will Trust, Re* [1964] 1 WLR 451; and eg *Hornal v Neuberger* [1957] 1 QB 247; *Abrahams v Catip* [1942] QWN 19; *Chase v News Group Newspapers* [2003] EMLR 11, [35] (Brooke LJ, Rix and Keene LJJ agreed); cf *Brown v McGrath* (1920) SALR 97.

[16] Eg NSW Law Reform Commission (1995) 75–85 and its Chapter 5.

[17] Eg *Ibid* 62–73.

[18] Eg *Sutherland* [1925] AC 47, 58 (Viscount Cave LC).

[19] Eg *ibid* 67 (Viscount Finlay); *McElhone v Bennett* (1885) 1 WN (NSW) 137.

[20] *DA 1974* (NSW) s 7A(4)(a), since 1 January 1995.

[21] Eg *Sutherland* [1925] AC 47, 62 (Viscount Finlay), 75 (Lord Shaw); *Allworth v John Fairfax Group* (1993) 113 FLR 254, 262 (Higgins J).

[22] Eg see discussion of the lack of a defamation remedy provided to the plaintiff actors in *Charleston v News Group Newspapers* [1995] 2 AC 65, 69 (Lord Bridge, Lords Goff, Jauncey and Mustill agreed); and commentary on the case: eg Shillito and Barendt (1996) 317, 333–35; Prescott (1995).

contextual truth,[23] the imputation must relate to a matter of 'public interest' or be published on a privileged occasion and be relevant to that occasion. The manner of publication then must be reasonable in the circumstances of the imputation and the occasion.[24]

Requiring public benefit or public interest has long been suggested. In the 1840s, a House of Lords Select Committee proposed requiring public benefit to be shown to justify criminal and civil libel. The proposal was adopted for criminal proceedings, but not in relation to civil proceedings.[25] Without a public interest element, justification can protect even malicious reference to old events. NSW adopted the Select Committee's suggestion in 1847.[26] It appears one reason for the change was to better protect the reputation of former convicts.[27] Victoria repealed the provision in 1856 after it became a separate colony to NSW.[28] More recently, the 'public benefit' requirement in NSW was changed to 'public interest'.[29] But introducing a public interest element has been opposed in Victoria, and this difference may have been a major obstacle to achieving uniform Australian defamation law during the 1980s and 1990s – contemporary Australian efforts towards uniformity are discussed in Chapter 10.[30]

3 *Justification and opinion*

Comment or opinion is normally understood as material that is not factual and so cannot be proved true.[31] In this way, justification and opinion defences are distinguished doctrinally. But there are two relevant points about how comment *can* be defended by justification. First, comment that is implicit within published facts that are proved true is said to come within justification.[32] Second, some

---

[23] *DA 1974* (NSW) ss 15 and 16.

[24] *Ibid* s 14.

[25] Lord Campbell's Act, *Libel Act 1843*, 6 and 7 Vict, c 96, s 6, which changed the prior position that truth was no defence to criminal defamation: eg Porter Committee (1948) [75].

[26] *DA 1847*, 11 Vict No 13, s 4, which is sometimes called the *Injuries to Character Act*, eg NSW Law Reform Commission (1968) [62]. The provision later existed in *DA 1958* (NSW) s 16.

[27] NSW Law Reform Commission (1971) 64, cf NSW Law Reform Commission (1968) 173.

[28] Community Law Reform Committee of the ACT (1995) [21].

[29] *DA 1974* (NSW) s 15. Public benefit remains required under *DA 1889* (Qld) s 15; *DA 1957* (Tas) s 15; and for the ACT: *Civil Law (Wrongs) Act 2002* (ACT) s 127, which was introduced from July 2002 in *DA 2001* (ACT) s 16. (The preceding ACT law existed under NSW's *DA 1901*.) The ACT provision aims to maintain the public benefit requirement, but it may allow the common law defence to operate as well: Collins (2001b) 336.

[30] See Chapter 10, Part I, E.

[31] Eg *O'Shaughnessy v Mirror Newspapers* (1970) 125 CLR 166.

[32] Eg *Gorton v Australian Broadcasting Commission* (1973) 1 ACTR 6, 19 (Fox J).

cases suggest an opinion that is shown to be 'correct' can be justified.[33] That is, if facts that are proved true warrant the opinion and make it one which should be drawn.[34] However, neither of these approaches appears to be significant in litigation practice.

4 *Malice*

Justification is not defeated by malice. Under English defamation law, an exception exists for 'spent convictions' that were incurred a substantial time before the publication. Justification fails if that type of old conviction is referred to maliciously.[35] The provision is a narrow response to arguments that public interest should be proved as well as truth, when compared to NSW's general requirement of public interest in its truth defence.

B Mitigation and justification

If some defamatory aspects of a publication are true, a claimant or plaintiff may deserve only reduced damages. There are limits, however, to the evidence admissible in mitigation.[36] In England and Victoria, truth is not in issue between the parties if justification is not pleaded. Then, evidence of truth cannot be given in mitigation.[37] Evidence otherwise before the court, however, can be considered in mitigation.[38] For example, a publisher may respond to allegations of malice with evidence of honestly believing the publication to be true. This evidence could be taken into account on damages. NSW legislation allows evidence to be given in mitigation, even if justification is not pleaded,[39] but that evidence is confined to the truth of the plaintiff's imputations because each pleaded imputation creates a cause of action in NSW. It is important to note that evidence of the truth of contextual imputations cannot be given in mitigation.[40] In all jurisdictions, if a justification plea fails, evidence before the court on justification can be considered in mitigation. The proved facts may not establish the publication's truth, but may well reduce damages. The damages may nearly

---

33 Eg *Howden v Truth and Sportsman* (1937) 58 CLR 416.

34 Eg *Hunt v Star Newspaper Co* [1908] 2 KB 309, 320.

35 *Rehabilitation of Offenders Act 1974* (UK) c 53, s 8. For detailed discussion of the Act and justification, see Milmo and Rogers (2004) Chapter 17.

36 For a discussion of mitigation and defamation generally, see Milmo and Rogers (2004) [33.28]–[33.59]; *Burstein v Times Newspapers* [2001] 1 WLR 579.

37 Eg *Hobbs v Tinling* [1929] 2 KB 1; *Plato Films v Speidel* [1961] AC 1090, 1133–34 (Lord Denning).

38 See eg *Peatling v Watson* [1909] VLR 198, 203 (Madden CJ).

39 *DA 1974* (NSW) s 47.

40 *NRMA Insurance v Amalgamated Television Services* (1989) Aust Defamation Reports [50,055]; *Hall v Hannaford* [1999] NSWSC 1197, [20] (Levine J); *Waters v John Fairfax Publications* [2005] NSWSC 394.

vanish.[41] In England, it is clear that defendants may seek to justify any meaning that words are reasonably capable of conveying.[42] Defendants can choose from any possible meaning in order to best present evidence for mitigation. Persisting in an improper justification plea in England or Australia, however, may aggravate damages because it is likely to increase the injury to the claimant or plaintiff.[43]

The role of mitigation will be seen to be an important aspect of practice related to meaning in England and Australia so it is worth describing a little more about the legal rules. There are various ways that damages may be mitigated,[44] but one noteworthy method is to show that claimants or plaintiffs have bad reputations in the relevant sector of their life.[45] The rule in *Scott v Sampson*[46] prevents evidence being given of specific acts to prove poor reputation, with an important aim being to prevent defamation claimants or plaintiffs being placed on trial for all their past life. One exception is for convictions relevant to the same sector of the claimant's or plaintiff's reputation, which can be proved. Traditionally this has concerned prior convictions, but it appears that convictions after publication also can be relevant[47] although the position in NSW at least remains undecided.[48] After *Burstein v Times Newspapers*, it is clear that another exception exists for matters of 'directly relevant background context' to the publication and the circumstances in which it came to be made.[49] While the NSW decision in *Australian Broadcasting Corporation v McBride* also suggests that a somewhat more flexible approach may be taken to the allowable evidence, the traditional approach has not been overruled in these cases. In *McBride*, Ipp AJA said,

> [T]he rule that evidence of bad reputation must be confined to the relevant *sector* of a plaintiff's reputation means merely that the evidence, to be admissible, must be relevant to that part of the plaintiff's reputation capable of being harmed by the defamatory material.[50]

---

[41] *Pamplin v Express Newspapers* [1988] 1 WLR 116 note, 120 (Neill LJ).

[42] See below, Part I, K.

[43] Eg *Sutcliffe v Pressdram* [1991] 1 QB 153, 184 (Nourse LJ).

[44] See eg Gillooly (1998) 292–300.

[45] Eg *Plato Films* [1961] AC 1090; *O'Hagan v Nationwide News* (2001) 53 NSWLR 89; *Australian Broadcasting Corpn v McBride* (2001) 53 NSWLR 430.

[46] (1882) 8 QBD 491, 504–505 (Cave J).

[47] Eg *Middendorp Electrical v Sonneveld* [2001] VSC 312, [338]–[339] (Gillard J); *Amalgamated Television Services v Marsden* [2002] NSWCA 419, [1403] (Beazley, Giles, Santow JJA); *McBride* (2001) 53 NSWLR 430, [64]–[75] (Ipp AJA, Beazley JA agreed), [91]–[98] (Fitzgerald AJA).

[48] See *El–Azzi v Nationwide News* [2004] NSWSC 1055, [25]–[31] (Levine J); *Nationwide News v El–Azzi* [2004] NSWCA 382.

[49] [2001] 1 WLR 579, [41]–[42] and [47] (May LJ, Sir Christopher Slade and Aldous LJ agreed).

[50] *McBride* (2001) 53 NSWLR 430, [28] (Beazley JA agreeing). See also *El–Azzi* [2004] NSWSC 1055, [32]–[37] (Levine J).

In NSW, the plaintiff's pleaded imputations must be given significant weight in determining what sector of the plaintiff's life is relevant.[51]

C Imputations must be proved true in substance

Conveyed imputations must be proved true, not just a publication's literal meaning.[52] Justification is pleaded to the imputations that are found to be conveyed.[53] Statements in certain cases that justification is pleaded to the entire publication[54] arose where only some distinct charges were justified. The statements underline how all the imputations that are complained about must be defended and, in that limited sense, it can be said that justification is pleaded to the entire publication. For justification, however, every detail need not be proved true. Rather, the imputations need to be true in substance.[55] Minor factual inaccuracies, not changing an imputation's character, are allowed.[56] But justification will fail if the publication omitted material facts that alter the imputation's substance.[57] The defamation's 'sting' must be true. Similarly, in NSW, substantial truth is described as not materially differing from the truth.[58]

D Justifying rumours

If a defamatory meaning is conveyed by repeating a rumour, the publisher must prove the rumour is true, or rely on some other defence. The fact that the rumour is in circulation is not a sufficient defence, and the publisher's belief (or disbelief) in the rumour's truth will not be decisive. In *Stern v Piper*, the English Court of Appeal adopted the orthodox position about this 'repetition rule' and the great weight of authority that supports it.[59] In *Stern v Piper*, a publisher repeated allegations made about the plaintiff in debt recovery proceedings. The publisher could not plead merely that the allegations had been made by way of justification. The differences in approach suggested by the earlier *Aspro Travel v*

---

51 *McBride* (2001) 53 NSWLR 430, [34].

52 Eg *Sutherland* [1925] AC 47, 75 and 78–79 (Lord Shaw); *Mirror Newspapers v Harrison* (1982) 149 CLR 293, 302–303 (Mason J).

53 Even at common law: eg *Sutherland* [1925] AC 47, 55 (Viscount Cave LC), 75 and 79 (Lord Shaw); *Hadzel v De Waldorf* (1970) 16 FLR 174, 177 (Fox J).

54 Notably *Allworth* (1993) 113 FLR 254, 265–66 (Higgins J).

55 Eg *Sutherland* [1925] AC 47, 55 (Viscount Cave LC), 62 (Viscount Finlay), 79 (Lord Shaw); *Kelly v Special Broadcasting Service* [1990] VR 69, 72 (Murphy J).

56 Eg *Speight v Syme* (1895) 21 VLR 672, 675 (Holroyd J); *Rofe* (1924) 25 SR (NSW) 4, 20 and 22 (Street ACJ).

57 *Howden* (1937) 58 CLR 416.

58 *DA 1974* (NSW) ss 7(2), 15.

59 [1997] QB 123; see notably: *Watkin v Hall* (1868) LR 3 QB 396; *Truth (New Zealand) v Holloway* [1961] NZLR 22; *Lewis v Daily Telegraph* [1964] AC 234.

Owners Abroad were not followed.[60] In *Aspro Travel*, potential customers were told a competitor was about to become bankrupt, or that there were 'reliable rumours' of this.[61] Particulars of justification were allowed even though they went to the rumours' existence rather than the allegations' truth. (Similarly, the much earlier decision of *Waters v Sunday Pictorial Newspapers*[62] is likely to be limited to reports of judicial statements in open court.[63] *Waters* involved a 'notorious dodgy operator of London slum properties' and the justification pleading relied on a previous judicial description of the plaintiff in those terms: the defence meaning was capable of arising and the particulars of justification were not struck out.) The subsequent statements in *Stern v Piper* apparently followed more substantial examination of the question and applicable precedents.[64] In any event, an issue to note from *Stern v Piper* is the emphasis Simon Brown LJ placed on the repetition rule affecting the normal test for the meaning of a publication.[65]

E Justifying three levels of meaning: guilt, suspicion or grounds to investigate

Although the approach can be seen in earlier decisions,[66] English cases since the late 1990s have focussed on the idea that there can be three different levels of meaning, as discussed in Part I of Chapter 2. Publications may convey that claimants or plaintiffs are guilty of discreditable conduct, or that they reasonably are suspected of that conduct, or merely that grounds exist for investigating them about possible wrongdoing. Australian cases have tended to differentiate between allegations of guilt and suspicion, but the same approach could be adopted in an appropriate case. If publications suggest the claimant or plaintiff is guilty of a crime, then the imputation of guilt needs to be defended.[67] Legislation

---

60 [1996] 1 WLR 132. See eg *Shah v Standard Chartered Bank* [1999] QB 241, 261–63 (Hirst LJ), 266–69 (May LJ) (Sir Brian Neill agreed with both judgments); *Chase* [2003] EMLR 11, [40] (Brooke LJ, Rix and Keene LJJ agreed). Similarly, the decision of *Waters v Sunday Pictorial Newspapers* [1961] 1 WLR 967 is likely to be limited to reports of judicial statements in open court: *Stern v Piper* [1997] QB 123, 134 (Hirst LJ, Simon Brown LJ agreed with commentary, Sir Ralph Gibson agreed with both judgments). *Waters* involved a 'notorious dodgy operator of London slum properties' and relied on earlier judicial description of the plaintiff in those terms. The defence meaning was capable of arising and the particulars of justification were not struck out.

61 *Aspro Travel v Owners Abroad Group* [1996] 1 WLR 132, 135 (Schiemann LJ, Stuart-Smith LJ agreed with commentary, Waite LJ agreed with both judgments).

62 [1961] 1 WLR 967.

63 *Stern* [1997] QB 123, 134 (Hirst LJ, Simon Brown LJ agreed with commentary, Sir Ralph Gibson agreed with both judgments).

64 The quality of counsels' arguments was noted: *Stern* [1997] QB 123, 134 (Hirst LJ), 135 (Simon Brown LJ).

65 See Chapter 2, Part I, J.

66 In particular *Lewis* [1964] AC 234, 282 (Lord Devlin).

67 Eg *Berezovsky v Forbes* [2001] EMLR 45.

has changed the common law rule preventing earlier convictions being used as evidence of crimes.[68] In addition, other imputations may arise through reference to a prior criminal offence. It may be imputed the claimant or plaintiff remains untrustworthy. That meaning could not be justified simply by proving the prior conviction.[69] Alternatively, a publication's meaning may be at the level of suspicion. Publishing that a person has been arrested and charged, for example, may impute a suspicion of guilt.[70] The defendant then must prove three matters: the arrest and charge occurred; the police had a suspicion of guilt, with reasonable cause; and (at least usually) that the claimant's or plaintiff's conduct giving rise to the suspicion occurred.[71] The common focus will be on the claimant's or plaintiff's conduct that gave rise to the suspicion.[72] But English decisions have acknowledged that circumstantial evidence, rather than direct evidence of conduct, could suffice in some situations,[73] and this has been left open in at least one Australian decision.[74] In any event, the defendant need not prove actual guilt where the meaning is one of suspicion.[75] The tribunal of fact decides whether the suspicion was held, and held on reasonable grounds.[76] A third option for a publication's meaning is merely that grounds exist for investigating the claimant of plaintiff's conduct. The English Court of Appeal has noted that, in certain circumstances, evidence of police holding suspicions or raiding premises, or the fact that numerous accusations had been made by others, for example, could be used in attempting to justify this level of allegation while it could not be used in relation to higher meanings.[77] But some doubts have been expressed about how the repetition rule operates in relation to this lowest level of meaning.[78] The approach to this question is likely to depend significantly on the precise circumstances involved with a given publication.

---

[68] In England, originally under *Civil Evidence Act 1968*, c 64, s 13. The provision has a narrower application under *DA 1996* (UK) s 12. In Australia, eg *Evidence Act 1995* (Cth) ss 91–93; *Evidence Act 1958* (Vic) ss 90, 91 (the sections apply to proceedings commenced since 1 January 1994); *DA 1974* (NSW) s 55 and see also *Evidence Act 1995* (NSW) ss 91–93.

[69] Eg *Sutherland* [1925] AC 47, 74 (Lord Shaw).

[70] See also Chapter 2, Part I, L.

[71] Eg *Harrison* (1982) 149 CLR 293, 302 (Mason J); *Gumina v Williams (No 2)* (1990) 3 WAR 351, 371 (Seaman J).

[72] *Shah* [1999] QB 240, 261 (Hirst LJ).

[73] Eg *Chase* [2003] EMLR 11; *Musa King v Telegraph Group* [2004] EMLR 23.

[74] *Sands v Channel Seven Adelaide* [2005] SASC 182, [42] (White J).

[75] Eg *Lewis* [1964] AC 234, 260 (Lord Reid), 274–75 (Lord Hodson).

[76] *Morris v Cash* (1993) 10 WAR 507, 516 (Owen J).

[77] *Musa King* [2004] EMLR 23, [21]–[35] (Brooke LJ, Jonathan Parker and Maurice Kay LJJ agreed); *Bennett v News Group Newspapers* [2002] EMLR 39, [38] (Robert Walker LJ for Eng CA).

[78] *Jameel v Times Newspapers* [2004] EMLR 31, [22]–[31] (Sedley LJ, Longmore LJ agreed with commentary, Maurice Kay LJ agreed with both judgments).

F Allegations may be narrow or general

A publication may convey a narrow or general meaning. If a publication conveys a general allegation of bad conduct, the defendant can justify by relying on facts not stated in the publication.[79] What may be referred to in this way is limited: the instances of conduct must not differ significantly in kind from the published allegation.[80] For example, if a publication suggests that a sports player infringed amateur status through a commercial book contract, it may convey a general meaning of 'shamateurism'. The publisher could justify this meaning with evidence of earlier product endorsements to which the publication does not refer.[81] If the publication only conveys a narrow meaning, however, the defendant cannot rely on such wider material.

G Allegations may be separate and distinct

A publication may convey separate and distinct allegations. Whether allegations are separate and distinct is a factual question and a matter of degree.[82] It is an issue of substance not form.[83] Is a particular meaning 'separate and self-contained' or just one ingredient in a whole that conveys a different meaning overall from that element?[84] An allegation of hating 'bureaucrats, civil servants, politicians, women, Jews and professionals' was held capable of conveying only distinct allegation in *Templeton v Jones*.[85] The publication also used a more general description, the 'politics of hatred', which apparently was intended to cover a more general attitude. That general meaning, however, was held incapable of arising. The decision that the allegations remained distinct has been criticised,[86] but the legal principle remains endorsed. The example set out in Chapter 2 about a publication raising allegations about not filing tax returns and having involvement in a person's disappearance, would be a clearer situation of separate and distinct allegations.[87] In almost every instance where a publication raised those matters, no ordinary recipient would interpret them to be part of one allegation that was being made by the publication.

---

[79] Eg *Maisel v Financial Times (No 1)* (1915) 84 LJKB 2145; *Williams v Reason* [1988] 1 WLR 96.

[80] Eg *Howden* (1937) 58 CLR 416, 420 (Dixon J).

[81] The example is *Williams* [1988] 1 WLR 96.

[82] Eg *Polly Peck v Trelford* [1986] QB 1000, 1032 (O'Connor LJ, Robert Goff and Nourse LJJ agreed).

[83] Eg *Howden (No 2)* (1938) 38 SR (NSW) 287, 290–1 (Jordan CJ).

[84] *Ibid*; *Cohen v Mirror Newspapers* [1971] 1 NSWLR 623, 627 (Jacobs and Manning JJA), 632 (Taylor AJA).

[85] [1984] 1 NZLR 448.

[86] Eg *Polly Peck* [1986] QB 1000, 1030 (O'Connor LJ, Robert Goff and Nourse LJJ agreed).

[87] See Chapter 2, Parts I, A, and III, H.

Where publications do convey distinct allegations, claimants or plaintiffs can choose to complain about only some of them.[88] If claimants or plaintiffs complain about only one allegation, defendants cannot justify by proving the truth of a different, separate allegation.[89] So in *Templeton v Jones*, a claim that was limited to the allegation of hating Jews could not be justified by proving the plaintiff did hate other people as listed in the publication.[90] As discussed below – in Section K – if the allegations had not been held to be distinct in *Templeton*, then proof that the plaintiff hated the other people listed in the publication could have been given.

Three other situations are relevant for distinct allegations when some may be justified, but others left undefended. At common law, this may mitigate damages by partial justification. In England, it also may establish a statutorily extended form of justification that operates as a complete defence. In NSW, the statutory defence of contextual truth may be available. In the next three sections, each situation is considered in turn.

H Distinct allegations and partial justification

If the claimant or plaintiff complains about several distinct allegations, they all must be defended. At common law, a defendant may justify some allegations and remain liable for other undefended allegations.[91] The defendant must specify which part of the publication is to be justified,[92] and this partial justification may mitigate damages.

I Distinct allegations and extended justification in England

Section 5 of the *Defamation Act 1952* (UK) extends the justification defence under English law. It can apply if unjustified allegations do not materially injure the claimant's reputation 'having regard to the truth of the remaining charges'. The seriousness of charges proved to be true is compared to the undefended imputations. Thus, comparatively minor errors need not defeat justification. If serious imputations are proved to be true, even significant errors may come within s 5 justification.[93] The section provides a full defence rather than mitigating damages. Claimants, however, can evade s 5 by suing only about distinct allegations that

---

[88] *Polly Peck* [1986] QB 1000, 1032 (O'Connor LJ, Robert Goff and Nourse LJJ agreed); *Hadzel* (1970) 16 FLR 174, 179 (Fox J).

[89] Eg *Plato Films* [1961] AC 1090, 1142 (Lord Denning); *Curran v Herald & Weekly Times* [1993] Aust Defamation Reports [51,090], 42,884 (Gobbo J); *Petritsis v Hellenic Herald* [1978] 2 NSWLR 174, 190–91 (Samuels JA).

[90] [1984] 1 NZLR 448.

[91] Eg *Sutherland* [1925] AC 47, 78 (Lord Shaw); *Plato Films* [1961] AC 1090, 1141–42 (Lord Denning).

[92] Eg *Goody v Odhams Press* [1967] 1 QB 333.

[93] For an example of the section's application, later upheld, see *Irving v Penguin Books* [2000] EWHC QB 115 and [2001] EWCA Civ 1197, [97]–[100] (Pill, Mantell, Buxton LJJ).

defendants are unable to justify – as the Australian Law Reform Commission commented about the equivalent Tasmanian version of the defence in s 18 of the *Defamation Act* 1957 (Tas).[94] If claimants do not sue about other allegations, defendants cannot prove them to be true. However, the jury still can see the entire publication sued on,[95] so the harmful but true material will be before the jury.

J Distinct allegations and contextual truth in NSW

In NSW, common law justification has been modified differently than in England, which follows in part from the plaintiff's pleaded imputation being the cause of action in NSW. Under the contextual truth defence in s 16 of the *Defamation Act 1974* (NSW), the defendant argues that another imputation is conveyed as well as the imputation sued on. This 'contextual imputation' must differ in substance from the imputation that is sued on, which the defence accepts is conveyed. Contextual truth can succeed if the imputation sued on causes no additional injury to the plaintiff's reputation compared to the injury that is caused by the facts and circumstances establishing the contextual imputation's truth.[96] The contextual imputation must relate to a matter of public interest or be published under qualified privilege, and it must be a matter of substantial truth.[97] Several contextual imputations in combination can be relied on, but not if they are inconsistent with each other or are just the same allegation put in differing degrees of seriousness.[98] There also are issues with contextual imputations that raise general allegations where plaintiffs' imputations are narrow.[99] The requirements largely mirror the plaintiff's position in pleading imputations in NSW, discussed in Chapter 2. It had been held that contextual imputations must be pleaded with the same precision as the plaintiff's imputations,[100] even though no cause of action is based on them. But the NSW Court of Appeal explained in *John Fairfax Publications v Blake*[101] that the detail required by 'considerations of

[94] Australian Law Reform Commission (1979) [121].

[95] Eg *Polly Peck* [1986] QB 1000, 1010 and 1020 (O'Connor LJ; Robert Goff and Nourse LJJ agreed); *United States Tobacco International v British Broadcasting Corpn* [1998] EMLR 816. See also Neill and Rampton (1983) 14.

[96] Eg *John Fairfax Publications v Blake* (2001) NSWLR 541. See also, generally, *Hepburn v TCN Channel Nine* [1984] 1 NSWLR 386, 405 (Hunt J); *Jackson v John Fairfax & Sons* [1981] 1 NSWLR 36 (Hunt J); *Waterhouse v Hickie* (1995) Aust Torts Reports ¶81–347, 62,488 (Priestley JA); *TCN Channel 9 v Antoniadis* (1998) 44 NSWLR 682, 691–2 (Handley JA, Beazley JA and Stein JA).

[97] *DA 1974* (NSW) s 16(2).

[98] See *Hepburn* [1984] 1 NSWLR 386, 397 and 399 (Hunt J); *Blake* (2001) NSWLR 541.

[99] See *John Fairfax Publications v Jones* [2004] NSWCA 205, [7]–[21] (Spigelman CJ), cf [57]–[67] (Hodgson JA), [107]–[114] (Ipp JA).

[100] *Marsden v Amalgamated Television Services* (Unreported, NSW SC, Levine J, 4 May 1998), explaining *Hansen v Border Morning Mail* (Unreported, NSW SC, Hunt J, 24 October 1986).

[101] (2001) NSWLR 541.

practical justice'[102] can be provided in particulars rather than in the contextual imputation itself.[103] The defence may appear similar to England's s 5 of the *Defamation Act 1952* (UK). Contextual truth, however, is more sophisticated. Under s 5, and at common law, defendants cannot justify distinct imputations that are not sued on. Thus, claimants or plaintiffs can narrow their complaints to exclude distinct harmful allegations, although juries may still see them in the full publications. Contextual truth does not have this limitation.[104] In this, the NSW approach follows the recommendations of the state's Law Reform Commission that aimed to improve on the Shawcross Report's proposal – a proposal that failed to be implemented in the Freedom of Publication Protection Bill 1966 (UK) cl 4(1).[105] Contextual truth could be compared with the possible US doctrine of 'incremental harm', which is examined briefly in Part IV of Chapter 8. It measures the reputational harm resulting from undefended parts of a publication in comparison with the harm flowing from the rest of the publication. The idea of incremental harm has been considered, but at times rejected in the US largely because it was not seen to distinguish between different areas of a person's reputation.[106] The NSW defence does differentiate in this way; it also is doctrinally distinct from Lucas-Box and Polly Peck pleading, which are discussed next.

K Non-distinct allegations and arguing about meaning: Lucas-Box and Polly Peck

The previous four sections have addressed justification when publications convey several distinct charges. The allegations, however, may not be distinct. Before exploring this, it is worth repeating that the parties in a defamation dispute may well argue about what meaning is conveyed. The claimant or plaintiff almost always will have pleaded the alleged natural and ordinary meanings. As discussed in Chapter 2, this either provides necessary information to the court and other party, in England and Victoria, or is necessary because the imputation is the cause of action, in NSW. The defence may seek to justify those pleaded meanings. Or, it may seek to justify a different meaning that the publication may be found to convey, in England and Victoria if not in NSW.

---

102 *Drummoyne Municipal Council v Australian Broadcasting Corpn* (1990) 21 NSWLR 135, 137 (Gleeson CJ).

103 *Blake* (2001) NSWLR 541, [19] (Spigelman CJ, Rolfe AJA agreed). But Hodgson JA ([54]–[61]) differed and held that the contextual imputation, rather than particulars, must state 'relevant facts, matters and circumstances fairly and precisely'. See also *Jones* [2004] NSWCA 205.

104 Eg *Jackson* [1981] 1 NSWLR 36, 39 (Hunt J).

105 See NSW Law Reform Commission (1971) [24], [177], and appendix D [73]–[74]; Shawcross Report (1965).

106 See *Masson v New Yorker Magazine*, 501 US 496 (1991), 960 F 2d 896 (9th Cir, 1992); *Liberty Lobby v Anderson*, 746 F 2d 1563, 1568 (Scalia J) (DC Cir, 1984); vacated on other grounds 477 US 242 (1986).

The defendant's 'different meaning' can be of two types. First, the defendant may deny that the claimant's or plaintiff's meaning is conveyed in any manner. Instead, a different meaning may be conveyed, which the defendant may seek to justify.[107] Most often, but not invariably, this is a less serious meaning. The situation can arise at common law in relation to natural and ordinary meanings, where the claimant or plaintiff may not be bound precisely to a pleaded meaning (see Part III of Chapter 2). These arguments about meaning should be distinguished from arguments over what words were published. If defendants believe that materially different words were published, they should deny publication.[108] Second, the defendant may argue that the claimant's or plaintiff's meaning is not distinct, but has a 'common sting' with other aspects of the publication. That is, a publication conveying multiple non-distinct imputations is said to have a common sting.[109] Then, even if the claimant or plaintiff does not complain about the other matters, the defendant can use them in justification. Proving one of the imputations true justifies all of them because they have a common sting. For example, allegations of separate acts of adultery may have a common sting of adulterous promiscuity. In *Khashoggi v IPC Magazines* this interpretation of a proposed publication was held to be arguable, so an injunction against publication was lifted.[110] If one allegation of adultery was false, but the common sting could be proved true, the publication could be defended. Another example is provided by *Carlton Communications v News Group Newspapers* about allegations of faking different television current affairs program – the allegations arguably raised a common sting meaning so evidence of faking one of the programs could be used in defence of the whole publication.[111] As Laurence Maher has explained,

> Thus, although the defendant is not entitled to select for justification a separate and distinct charge which the plaintiff has not pleaded, the defendant can, in respect of a distinct charge which the plaintiff has pleaded, justify that charge in a different meaning.[112]

English case law since the mid-1980s has been significant for the treatment of non-distinct allegations. The general approach was set out by the English Court of Appeal in *Lucas-Box v News Group Newspapers*[113] and *Polly Peck v*

---

[107] Eg *Polly Peck* [1986] QB 1000, 1023 (O'Connor LJ, Robert Goff and Nourse LJJ agreed); *Kelly v SBS* [1990] VR 69, 72 (Murphy J); *Woodger v Federal Capital Press of Australia* (1992) 107 ACTR 1, 23 (Miles CJ).

[108] Eg Milmo and Rogers (2004) [27.6].

[109] Eg *Polly Peck* [1986] QB 1000, 1032 (O'Connor LJ, Robert Goff and Nourse LJJ agreed); *Hart v Wrenn* (1995) 124 FLR 135, 152 (Mildren J).

[110] [1986] 1 WLR 1412. As to injunctions and defamation, see eg Gillooly (1998) 319–29; *Greene v Associated Newspapers* [2005] EMLR 10.

[111] [2002] EMLR 16.

[112] Maher (1993) 217.

[113] [1986] 1 WLR 147.

Trelford.[114] *Lucas-Box* involved an article about a suspected terrorist who was arrested outside the plaintiff's flat. The plaintiff's alleged meaning was that she knowingly assisted Italian terrorists, or was reasonably suspected of doing this. The defendants sought to offer particulars in justification about the plaintiff's association with various Italians. The Court of Appeal allowed this so long as the meaning being justified was made clear. Thus, in *Lucas-Box* it was decided that the defendant could plead the meaning it would seek to justify:

> It is axiomatic that the function of pleadings is to define the issues between the parties, so . . . everyone, counsel, judge and jury are able to focus upon the real nature of the dispute. Although to some it may seem a startling observation, we can see no reason why libel litigation should be immune from the ordinary pleading rules.[115]

That libel litigation may differ from ordinary pleading rules in other ways did not receive comment in *Lucas-Box*, which is ironic in light of Australian developments about defence meanings (in *Chakravarti v Advertiser Newspapers*[116] and subsequent cases), which are explored below and in later chapters.

The subsequent *Polly Peck* case in England appeared to say the defendant *must* plead the actual meaning it would seek to justify.[117] Although later Court of Appeal decisions took varying positions,[118] it has become accepted in England that the defendant must plead justification clearly, so as to inform the court and the claimant of its case:

> [I]t is still open to a defendant to plead so as to justify any reasonable meaning of the words published which a jury, properly directed, might find to be the real meaning. In doing this [the defence] does not have to identify the precise meaning for which [it] contends; but [the defence] must make clear to the plaintiff what case [it] proposes to make.[119]

Making the case clear, however, generally means the defendant must plead the actual meaning that it will seek to justify if that meaning is found to be conveyed. There is a somewhat subtle distinction here

> between (a) the meaning of the words complained of for which the defendant contends (. . . the defendant is not obliged to plead that meaning) and (b) the meaning of the words which, if it is the true meaning of those words, the

114 [1986] QB 1000. See also *Khashoggi v IPC Magazines* [1986] 1 WLR 1412; *Viscount de L'Isle v Times Newspapers* [1987] 3 All ER 499; *Prager v Times Newspapers* [1988] 1 WLR 77; *Morrell v International Thomson Publishing* [1989] 3 All ER 733; *Control Risks v New English Library* [1990] 1 WLR 183.

115 *Lucas-Box v News Group Newspapers* [1986] 1 WLR 147, 151 (Ackner LJ for Eng CA).

116 (1998) 193 CLR 519, [8] (Brennan CJ and McHugh J).

117 Eg see particularly the headnote to report of *Polly Peck* [1986] QB 1000, 1001, which has been referred to in later judgments.

118 Eg *Morrell* [1989] 3 All ER 733; *Control Risks* [1990] 1 WLR 183; *Viscount de L'Isle* [1987] 3 All ER 499; *Prager* [1988] 1 WLR 77.

119 *Prager* [1988] 1 WLR 77, 86 (Purchas LJ).

> defendant will seek to justify (that is the meaning which the defendant must now spell out sufficiently. . .).[120]

Similarly, Mustill LJ noted in *Viscount de L'Isle v Times Newspapers* that in the *Lucas-Box* case, even the 'radical amendments insisted upon by the court did not extend to any statement of the defendants' case about the true meaning of the articles'.[121]

Thus, a defendant who pleads justification must do so clearly, 'without circumlocution or obfuscation'.[122] If this is done in the particulars, the precise meaning may be lost. It certainly was lost when over 50 pages of particulars of justification were supplied where two pages would have done.[123] Lack of clarity about this issue appears to be purely tactical; for example in *Lucas-Box*, Ackner LJ noted the defence counsel 'frankly admits' the aim was to keep options open as to the meaning that would be justified 'until the last possible moment':

> [Counsel] contends that all that is required . . . is to state the particulars upon which [the defence] is going to rely, without in any way defining that which [the defence] is purporting to justify.[124]

However, there now appears no be no reason

> why the meaning or meanings should not be set out directly, briefly and at the start of the plea. That, in my opinion is the result of the authorities . . . and should be the practice followed in the future.[125]

Note the two situations that can exist here. The defendant must make clear the meaning it intends to justify in each. One situation exists when the defendant denies the claimant's or plaintiff's meaning but seeks to justify another meaning. The other situation exists when the publication is argued to have a common sting. Both types of defence meaning are sometimes known as the Polly Peck form of justification – in Australia the Polly Peck label has been almost ubiquitous – but the issue certainly did not start with that case.[126] Arguments about meaning are no recent development: much earlier case law on slander and contested meaning is just one illustration.[127] In England, the first type of defence meaning is called a Lucas-Box plea, and judgments commonly refer to Lucas-Box meanings or Lucas-Box lesser

120 *Ibid* 91 (Nicholls LJ).

121 [1988] 1 WLR 49, 60.

122 *Morrell* [1989] 3 All ER 733, 738 (May LJ).

123 *Ibid* 739 (Parker LJ).

124 *Lucas-Box* [1986] 1 WLR 147, 152.

125 *Morrell* [1989] 3 All ER 733, 738 (May LJ); see also *Prager* [1988] 1 WLR 77, 92 (Nicholls LJ).

126 *Khashoggi* [1986] 1 WLR 1412, 1417 (Sir John Donaldson MR).

127 Eg *Peacock v Wilkins* (1888) 15 VLR 23; *Mutual Assurance Society of Victoria v Abbott* (1893) 19 VLR 456. The defendant may admit words were spoken, but plead they are true without the plaintiff's alleged meaning. The defendant then cannot give particulars aimed only at the meaning it has denied: *Dorman v Good* [1918] VLR 269.

meanings.[128] The Lucas-Box plea should be distinguished from the second type of defence meaning – the common sting meaning – which can be called a Polly Peck plea. While the term Polly Peck pleading can be used for both styles of defence plea, it is useful to distinguish between the two situations by using the labels Lucas-Box and Polly Peck pleas: that distinction is adopted in this book. As is made clear through later chapters' investigation of litigation, the two types of defence plea arise with very different frequencies and pose distinct issues for practice. Distinguishing clearly between the two pleas is particularly significant because of the extremely high prevalence of Lucas-Box pleading in England and the great significance those pleas appear to have in promoting good litigation practices.

This makes it unfortunate that where Australian courts have applied the general approach of Lucas-Box and Polly Peck pleading,[129] they tend to have called it the Polly Peck defence.[130] Usefully, some courts have distinguished between the two pleas in terms of two Polly Peck 'principles' (drawing on the language of O'Connor LJ in *Polly Peck*). In *Woodger v Federal Capital Press of Australia*, for example, Miles CJ described a 'common sting' meaning as the first Polly Peck principle, and called a lesser meaning – or in the terminology of this book, a Lucas-Box meaning – the second Polly Peck principle.[131] Recently, Australian courts appear to be referring to Lucas-Box more frequently. In *Sands v Channel Seven Adelaide*, for example, White J noted that Polly Peck is used 'in Australia colloquially' to refer to Lucas Box.[132] For the purposes of comparative analysis, it is useful to use the distinct labels of Lucas-Box and Polly Peck.

In any event, there has been serious criticism of what the judgment called Polly Peck pleading by members of the Australian High Court in *Chakravarti v Advertiser Newspapers*.[133] In their joint judgment, Brennan CJ and McHugh J said pleading justification to a meaning that has not been raised by the plaintiff does not offer a good defence. They noted that justification is a plea of confession and avoidance, so raising a different meaning is inappropriate. In their view, the '*Polly Peck* defence or practice contravenes the fundamental principles of common law

[128] Eg *Jameel v Wall Street Journal Europe SPRL* [2004] EMLR 6, [13] (Simon Brown LJ); *Berezovsky* [2001] EMLR 45, [4] (Sedley LJ for Eng CA); *Burstein* [2001] 1 WLR 579, [22] (May LJ, Sir Christopher Slade and Aldous LJ agreed); *Carlton Communications v News Group Newspapers* [2002] EMLR 16, [1] (Latham LJ). They sometimes are described as '*Lucas-Box* particulars': eg *Control Risks* [1990] 1 WLR 183, 189 (Nicholls LJ, Dillon LJ and Sir George Waller agreed). But spelling out the meaning in particulars would not accord with comments that the meaning should be set out at the pleading's start, rather than in particulars: eg *Prager* [1988] 1 WLR 77, 92 (Nicholls LJ); *Morrell* [1989] 3 All ER 733, 738 (May LJ), and see below Part I, L.

[129] Eg *Kennett v Farmer* [1988] VR 991; *Gumina* (1990) 3 WAR 351; *Kelly v SBS* [1990] VR 69.

[130] Eg *Morris* (1993) 10 WAR 507, 510 (Owen J); *Grundmann v Georgeson* (1996) Aust Torts Reports ¶81–396, 63,513 (Dowsett J).

[131] (1992) 107 ACTR 1, 23–24.

[132] [2005] SASC 182, [58] (White J).

[133] *Chakravarti v Advertiser Newspapers* (1998) 193 CLR 519, [8] (Brennan CJ and McHugh J). In relation to New Zealand see: *Templeton v Jones* [1984] 1 NZLR 448; *Broadcasting Corpn of New Zealand v Crush* [1988] 2 NZLR 234.

pleadings' and must cause difficulties in practice by embarrassing a fair trial.[134] However, this view does not necessarily survive scrutiny, which is explored in detail in Part I of Chapter 9. Brennan CJ and McHugh J do not comment greatly on English case law since *Polly Peck* nor on the reasons for which it has developed. The apparent aim of the English approach is to deal effectively with a difference between the parties about meaning. Of course, if the plaintiff is held to any meaning that is pleaded, the issue may not arise in the same way in Australia. The plaintiff, however, is not held to the very nuance of any pleaded meaning. Australian cases state that a different nuance or less serious meaning can go to the jury if there is no unfair disadvantage to the defendant.[135] The defendant thus may need to plead to a *range* of meanings. And the overall analysis of law and practice in Chapter 9 suggests that Australian law should be wary of holding plaintiffs so closely to their pleaded meanings. In short, it appears likely to shift defamation law in the rest of Australia markedly towards the NSW approach, where each imputation is a separate cause of action. This is troubling for several reasons, which are explored at length through the rest of the book. These include the criticism in case law and commentary of the technicality that has developed under the NSW approach; the support that empirical research into litigation practice offers to that criticism; and a widespread recognition of the value in changing the NSW law.[136] It is argued in Chapter 9 that Australian courts should re-examine the way in which a plaintiff is said to be held to any pleaded meaning in defamation. In relation to pre-trial battles about meaning and the at-trial determination of meaning, the focus should remain on the publication and the allegations within it, not on the specifics of any imputations pleaded by the plaintiff. It is worth emphasising that this issue should become very significant Australia-wide if proposals for uniform defamation law are enacted. (The planned uniform Australian law is discussed in Chapter 10.) Then all Australian jurisdictions will have the opportunity to reinterpret the law on plaintiffs and defendants pleading meaning, with a more detailed understanding of the benefits to litigation practice that appear from well-managed Lucas-Box pleading.

It also should be noted that, in *Chakravarti*, Kirby J cited *Polly Peck* with no adverse comment when explaining the purpose of parties pleading meanings in defamation 'is, and is only, to facilitate the fair determination of the dispute which the parties bring to court'.[137] Gaudron and Gummow JJ made no directly relevant comment about *Polly Peck* in *Chakravarti*, but they appear to have assumed the defence is available.[138] Thus, the obiter comments of Brennan CJ and McHugh J do not represent an articulated majority view in the Australian High

[134] *Chakravarti* (1998) 193 CLR 519, [8].

[135] See generally Chapter 2, Part III, H, for a discussion of different meanings and prejudice under *Chakravarti* (1998) 193 CLR 519.

[136] See, particularly, state and commonwealth proposals for uniform defamation law: Chapter 10, Part I, E.

[137] *Chakravarti* (1998) 193 CLR 519, [139] citing *Polly Peck* [1986] QB 1000, 1021 (O'Connor LJ, Robert Goff and Nourse LJJ agreed).

[138] *Chakravarti* (1998) 193 CLR 519, [53]–[60].

Court. Trial level courts responded differently after *Chakravarti*. Great weight sometimes was given to the comments of Brennan CJ and McHugh J, with suggestions in the ACT that 'it would be courageous for any trial judge to ignore the dicta'[139] in *Chakravarti* and the rejection of Polly Peck pleas in Queensland.[140]

However, Hedigan J – who was then the most experienced defamation judge on the Victorian Supreme Court – would have allowed the 'firmly entrenched' practice of Polly Peck pleading to remain.[141] He saw good reasons of trial management for the English authorities that require parties to specify meanings. And he noted that overburdened courts 'have said on many occasions in the last decade that the practices of past times must yield to the necessities of prompt and frugal disposition of litigation.'[142] But in *David Syme v Hore-Lacy*,[143] the Victorian Court of Appeal held that defence meanings would be restricted to those that are not substantially different from, and not more injurious than, the plaintiff's meaning.[144] This followed from the court's consideration of the judgments in *Chakravarti*. As commentators have suggested, *Hore-Lacy* substantially narrows 'the avenues open to a defendant under *Polly Peck*' and its associated cases.[145] Victorian courts also have recognised that *Hore-Lacy* means the defence principles have been 'significantly qualified in [their] operation'.[146] The whole question of alternative defence meanings is returned to in Chapter 9, in light of litigation practices under the varying law in the English and Australian jurisdictions that are examined on this issue in Chapters 4 to 6.

A separate matter for Lucas-Box and Polly Peck pleas is more straightforward: namely, their relation to the contextual truth defence in NSW. Views differ as to whether the defences are coextensive. The better view is that contextual truth varies from the other pleas in its flexibility and width. Under Lucas-Box, the defendant may deny the claimant's or plaintiff's meaning and argue that another meaning can be justified. Under contextual truth, the defendant alleges a different meaning, but it is a meaning that is *additional to* the plaintiff's meaning. This approach is quite different in scope to the parties' disagreement about what meaning a publication conveys under Lucas-Box. Under Polly Peck, the defendant may argue that the imputations have a common sting, so justifying one defends all of them. In comparison to this, contextual truth is wider because under it the imputations can be distinct.[147] This interpretation of the contextual

139 Eg *Kelly v Nationwide News* (1998) 147 FLR 410, [33] (Gallop ACJ).

140 *Robinson v Laws* [2003] 1 Qd R 81.

141 *Carrey v ACP Publishing* [1999] 1 VR 875, 885.

142 *Hore-Lacy v David Syme* [1998] VSC 96, [8] (Hedigan J).

143 [2000] 1 VR 667.

144 *Ibid* [17] (Ormiston J), [52]–[54] (Charles JA), [69] (Callaway JA).

145 Tobin and Sexton (2005) [11,020].

146 *Dow Jones v Gutnick* (Unreported, Vic CA, Phillips, Buchanan JJA, 9 May 2003) [2] (Phillips JA for the CA) refusing leave to appeal from *Gutnick v Dow Jones (No 2)* [2003] VSC 79.

147 See generally *Hart* (1995) 124 FLR 135, 152 (Mildren J); *Jones* [2004] NSWCA 205, [88] (Hodgson JA), [1] (Spigelman CJ agreed on this point), [105] and [115] (Ipp JA agreed on this point).

truth defence differs from some Australian judicial comments that suggest Polly Peck is wider in application[148] – which may be more accurate to state in relation to Lucas-Box – or that there is no significant doctrinal difference.[149] Some Australian cases also contain passing references that equate contextual truth and the common law defences, without any substantial investigation of the issues; they should be understood merely as being decisions that the defence pleas fail in the particular situation in question.[150] These less than apt references have become more common because of the need to consider defences that are available under the law of other Australian states and territories where plaintiffs complain of multistate publication, since *John Pfeiffer v Rogerson*.[151] In short, however, the statutory and common law defences are not equivalent.

L Pleading and justification

Six relevant points about pleading justification are noted here. First, the pleading should make clear whether justification is pleaded to all of the publication or an identified allegation within it.[152] When a publication is capable of conveying two distinct meanings, the defence must make clear whether both will be justified.[153] Second, in England and Victoria the defendant must make clear the meaning sought to be justified.[154] Facts and matters that will be relied on to prove truth must be detailed, but not the evidence by which they will be proved.[155] The claimant or plaintiff needs to be informed of the defence case, including any acts that the defendant alleges in justification. For example, if a publication conveys a general defamatory imputation, then a justification defence must plead the specific acts that will be relied on in response. Under the traditional common law, this applies except in the rare case when the publication is so clear it does not

148 *TWT v Moore* [1991] Aust Defamation Reports [51,030], 42,032 (Higgins J); *Allworth* (1993) 113 FLR 254, 262 (Higgins J).

149 *Woodger* (1992) 107 ACTR 1, 23 and 26 (Miles CJ). ACT courts have persisted with *Woodger*'s idiosyncratic interpretation of the defences: see eg *Steiner Wilson & Webster t/as Abbey Bridal v Amalgamated Television Services* (1999) Aust Torts Reports ¶81–537, [199] where Crispin J states Miles CJ in *Woodger* did not extend the common law, but merely said the common sting Polly Peck defence 'is called a defence of contextual truth' in NSW. Investigation of the English law and practice suggests that interpretation is not correct.

150 Eg *Cotter v John Fairfax Publications* [2003] NSWSC 503, [127]–[131] (Simpson J).

151 (2000) 203 CLR 503; see Chapter 10, Part I, E.

152 Eg *Fleming v Dollar* (1889) 23 QBD 388; *Clarke v Norton* [1910] VLR 494; *Monte v Mirror Newspapers* [1979] 2 NSWLR 663, 676 (Hunt J); *SCR* (NSW) Pt 67 r 13 (and see above, fn 4).

153 Eg *Hennessy v Wright* (1888) 57 LJQB 594.

154 In England, see *CPR* Pt 53 PD 2.5.

155 *Ibid* and eg *Godman v Times Publishing Co* [1926] 2 KB 273, 280 (Bankes LJ); *Minchin and Church of the New Faith v Adamson* (1975) 10 SASR 119.

require particulars.[156] While that is still the situation in Victoria, in England court rules now require details to be given in all cases.[157] In NSW, court rules alter the position so particulars of truth need only be provided when ordered.[158] But particulars are delivered in almost every case,[159] to avoid plaintiffs being taken by surprise. Third, as discussed above in relation to Lucas-Box and Polly Peck pleas, there is a distinction between the meaning the defendant will justify *if* it is found to be conveyed, and the meaning the defendant believes was conveyed by the publication. Only details about the former are required. This accords with earlier case law that particulars of justification do not give a meaning to the published words. Instead, they limit the scope of evidence admissible to prove truth;[160] they are needed to define the issues.[161]

Fourth, for justification the defendant did need 'clear and sufficient evidence' when the plea was made.[162] In *McDonald's Corporation v Steel*, the English Court of Appeal held that requirement to be excessive.[163] This means that defendants in England can plead justification if they: believe the publication is true; intend to support the plea with evidence at trial; and either presently have that evidence or reasonably suppose sufficient evidence will be available before or at trial.[164] The older legal position required defendants to have facts on which to base a plea of justification when making the plea.[165] Defendants could not plead truth and then try to use disclosure or discovery to find something to support the plea.[166] *McDonald's* has little presence in Australian decisions – apart from some early references in Western Australia[167] – but Australian law would seem likely to follow the English developments.[168] Fifth, the claimant or plaintiff may wish to

---

[156] Eg *Marks v Wilson-Boyd* [1939] 2 All ER 605, 608 (Goddard LJ); *Sims v Wran* [1984] 1 NSWLR 317, 328 (Hunt J).

[157] *CPR* Pt 53 PD 2.5.

[158] *SCR* (NSW) Pt 67 r 18(5), (6) (and see above, fn 4). Particulars are needed of facts and matters showing public interest: Pt 67 r 18(1); *Roach v Truth and Sportsman* (1937) 54 WN (NSW) 172; *Johnston v Australian Broadcasting Commission* (1993) 113 FLR 307, 311 (Higgins J).

[159] Tobin and Sexton (2005) [25,135].

[160] Eg *Mutch v Sleeman* (1928) 29 SR (NSW) 125.

[161] Eg *Godman* [1926] 2 KB 273, 280 (Bankes LJ).

[162] Eg *Zierenberg v Labouchere* [1893] 2 QB 183, 188 (Esher MR), 189 (Kay LJ); *Associated Leisure v Associated Newspapers* [1970] QB 450, 456 (Lord Denning MR).

[163] [1995] 3 All ER 615, 620–23 (Neill LJ; Steyn and Peter Gibson LJJ agreed).

[164] *Ibid*.

[165] Eg *TCN Channel Nine v Berrigan* (1996) Australian Torts Reports ¶81–404.

[166] Eg *Sunday Times Newspaper Co v Sun Newspaper Co* (1919) 36 WN (NSW) 72, 73 (Ferguson J); *Associated Dominions Assurance Society v John Fairfax & Sons* (1952) 72 WN (NSW) 250, 254 (Owen J).

[167] Eg *McKechnie v Campbell* (Unreported, WA SC, Owen J, 21 December 1995).

[168] See eg Williams (2005) [I 13.07.55]. It also appears that *McDonald's Corpn v Steel* was not mentioned to the court in some Australian decisions: eg *Berrigan* (1996) Australian Torts Reports ¶81–404, 63,677. It was cited to the court in *Moir v Flint* [2001] WASC 183 but is not mentioned in the judgment.

challenge a justification plea at the interlocutory stage. The discussion of separate preliminary rulings about 'capable meanings' in Chapter 2, Part III should be noted in general in relation to defence meanings. Claimants or plaintiffs can seek rulings on meanings or seek to have pleadings struck out under court rules or a court's inherent jurisdiction. *Shah v Standard Chartered Bank* offers an example: the plaintiffs unsuccessfully sought a ruling under the former Ord 82 r 3A that the meanings pleaded in the defence were incapable of being conveyed and also sought a ruling under Ord 18 r 19 striking out the related particulars of justification.[169] Sixth, following the Neill Committee report in 1991, English plaintiffs – now claimants – have been required to reply and state whether any particulars of fact in the defence are admitted or denied, and state any fact or matter relied on in opposing the defence.[170] In any event, courts have power to require a reply to justification in appropriate cases.[171] In Victoria and NSW, replies are needed only if matters of defeasance such as malice are to be relied on (which are not relevant to justification but can be important for comment and qualified privilege defences).

II OPINION DEFENCES

Comment defences may defend defamatory opinion. In England and Victoria, the common law defence of fair comment applies,[172] although there appear to be increasingly prominent calls to rename the defence as comment, honest comment, or honest opinion.[173] In NSW, it has been replaced by a statutory defence of comment.[174] In doctrinal theory, they can be attractive defences because juries can find for defendants without condemning claimants or plaintiffs. A defendant can draw on free speech arguments while the other party is portrayed as a would-be censor.[175] The elements of common law fair comment can be categorised in various ways: it is a 'complex defence riddled with technicalities.'[176] The following elements are examined in the rest of Part II. The publication must be comment rather than fact, and it must be about a matter of public interest. It must be based on facts that are stated, or the factual subject matter must be indicated or

[169] [1999] QB 241; now for the *CPR*, see Chapter 2, Part III, A.

[170] See generally Neill Committee (1991). The requirement was introduced as *RSC* Ord 82 r 3(2A), subject to r 3(2B). Now see *CPR* Pt 53 PD 2.8.

[171] *Morrell* (Unreported, Neill, Glidewell and Ralph Gibson LJJ, Eng CA, 18 July 1990).

[172] *DA 1952* (UK) s 6 extends the common law defence: see below, Section D.

[173] Eg *Tse Wai Chun Paul v Albert Cheng* [2001] EMLR 31, ¶15 (Lord Nicholls); 2004 and 2005 Australian proposals for uniform defamation law (see Chapter 10, Part I, E). New Zealand has changed the defence to one of honest opinion: *DA 1992* (NZ) ss 9–12.

[174] *DA 1974* (NSW) ss 29–35.

[175] See eg *Human Rights Act 2004* (ACT) s 16 which has been mentioned in passing as 'further support[ing]' the defence: *Szuty v Smyth* [2004] ACTSC 77, [129] (Higgins CJ).

[176] Australian Law Reform Commission (1979) [127].

notorious. The facts must be true or privileged. The comment must be 'fair'; that is, objectively possible for a commentator to make. Malice defeats the defence.

Two issues about opinion defences are particularly relevant for defamation law's treatment of meaning. First, where Lucas-Box or Polly Peck pleading is available – discussed above in Part I, K – it applies to these defences. Second, there can be difficulties with the defence when unintended imputations are conveyed, particularly in NSW. The problems may suggest that opinion should not be actionable at all, or at least that opinion defences deserve reconsideration. These issues are discussed below in Sections H and J, during a brief examination of the opinion defences. As a final introductory matter, the roles of judge and jury are noted. In all jurisdictions dealt with closely here, judges rule on whether comment is on a matter of public interest.[177] In jury cases in England and Victoria, the jury decides whether the material is fact or opinion. However, if the material can only reasonably be understood as opinion or as fact, the judge removes the issue from the jury. In NSW, the judge decides whether all defences have been established, including factual questions for any defences.

A Opinion rather than fact

Case law distinguishes opinion from statements of fact, even if the division must be problematic. As Raymond Brown notes: 'Sorting out fact from opinion is a difficult and, occasionally, an impossible thing to do. They are not readily distinguishable.'[178] The cases can be 'somewhat tortuous'.[179] The approach in *Clarke v Norton* that comment is a deduction, inference, conclusion, criticism, judgment, remark or observation has been widely adopted.[180] Beginning with 'in my opinion' is not decisive.[181] The question is how recipients would be expected to regard the publication, as fact or opinion.[182] It can be asked whether the allegation is capable or incapable of proof.

On the question of fact or opinion, there are two common references. First, does the publication indicate both facts and opinion? If facts are indicated and a statement is inferred from them, it is more likely to be understood as opinion.[183] If facts are not indicated, an imputation is more likely to be understood as itself being factual.[184] For example, stating a person is guilty of disgraceful conduct without providing details of the conduct is likely to be treated as a factual

[177] This is so at common law: *Telnikoff v Matusevich* [1991] 1 QB 102, 109 (Lloyd LJ).

[178] Brown (1994) 964.

[179] Gillooly (1998) 125.

[180] [1910] VLR 494, 499 (Cussen J); see eg *Branson v Bower* [2001] EMLR 32; *Skrine v Euromoney Publications* [2002] EMLR 15.

[181] Eg *London Artists v Littler* [1969] 2 QB 375.

[182] Eg *Smith's Newspapers v Becker* (1932) 47 CLR 279, 302 (Evatt J); *Petritsis* [1978] 2 NSWLR 174, 182 (Reynolds JA).

[183] *Hunt* [1908] 2 KB 309.

[184] Eg *Gorton* (1973) 1 ACTR 6, 16 (Fox J).

allegation.[185] It may be better, however, to describe this as an opinion for which no facts are indicated. That is why it would be excluded from the defences. Similarly, critical comment that attacks the author of an earlier publication may be more likely to convey factual allegations, unless the earlier publication raises the aspect of the author's reputation that is attacked.[186]

The second common reference is that facts and opinion need to be indicated separately, not all mixed together.[187] If they are separate, the comment can be evaluated by a recipient. If facts and opinion are mixed together

> so that it is not reasonably clear what portion purports to be inference, [the recipient] will naturally suppose that the injurious statements are based on adequate grounds known to the writer.[188]

These two aspects of *indicating* facts *separately from* comment form a primary approach used by courts in distinguishing fact and opinion. They underline how the commentator's reputation is meant to be at stake in the operation of the defences. If the opinion is poor, publishers libel themselves rather than the object of the comment.[189]

B Comment on a matter of public interest

The comment must be on a matter of public interest, both at common law and under s 31 of the *Defamation Act 1974* (NSW). A matter of public interest invites comment or is of concern to the public. Artistic works, for example, invite comment.[190] Other matters need to be of concern to the public for the defences to be arguable. There must be a reasonable relationship between the public interest and the comment, and the public interest must be generated by an event apart from the comment itself.[191]

Courts have been reluctant to define public interest narrowly. A classic reference is to Lord Denning in *London Artists v Littler*:

> I would not myself confine it within narrow limits. Whenever a matter is such as to affect people at large, so that they may be legitimately interested in, or concerned at, what is going on; or what may happen to them or to others; then it is a matter of public interest on which everyone is entitled to make fair comment.[192]

---

[185] *Kemsley v Foot* [1952] AC 345, 356–57 (Lord Porter) quoting Odgers (1929) 166.

[186] Eg *Gardiner v John Fairfax & Sons* (1942) 42 SR (NSW) 171, 174 (Jordan CJ).

[187] Eg *ibid* 178 (Davidson J); *Hunt* [1908] 2 KB 309, 319 (Fletcher Moulton LJ).

[188] *Hunt* [1908] 2 KB 309, 319 (Fletcher Moulton LJ).

[189] *Popham v Pickburn* (1862) 7 H&N 891, 898; 158 ER 730, 733 (Wilde B). In addition, in NSW whether a 'fair-minded person' could have made the comment often is seen as part of the fact or opinion question, eg Gillooly (1998) 139.

[190] Eg *Gardiner* (1942) 42 SR (NSW) 171, 173–74 (Jordan CJ).

[191] *Loveday v Sun Newspapers* (1938) 59 CLR 503, 513 (Latham CJ).

[192] [1969] 2 QB 375, 391; cf apparently narrower comments in *Bellino v Australian Broadcasting Corpn* (1996) 185 CLR 183, 215 (Dawson, McHugh, Gummow JJ).

Public interest, however, is not everything the public may be interested in.[193] For example, the private life of a public figure *may* be of public interest, if it is relevant to the figure's suitability for a particular position or the figure has made it a matter of public interest. It seems most unlikely that saying a parliamentarian was 'nothing more nor less than a brutal wife-basher' would *not* be a matter of public interest today, unlike an Australian decision from the 1920s.[194]

C Comment based on stated, indicated or notorious facts

The opinion must be based on stated facts, or the subject matter that is true must be indicated or notorious. The basic position is the facts must be stated.[195] All the supporting facts, however, need not be set out where a work has been offered for public comment; for example, it is sufficient for artistic criticism to identify the criticised work's title. Similarly, the published comment may indicate the subject matter, or substratum, of underlying fact without referring to it expressly.[196] The facts may be notorious: they may be matters of 'contemporary history'.[197] For example, a political cartoon could show a controversial government minister, responsible for public welfare payments, happily taking wings off a fly. This would convey an opinion based on facts about the government's welfare policies that were already known to recipients.[198]

D Comment based on true facts

The opinion must be based on true or privileged facts. Comment on untrue facts cannot be 'fair', and misdescription means the defence will fail.[199] At common law, all facts stated in the publication must be proved true. Even errors in relatively insignificant facts can defeat the defence,[200] although this requirement has been criticised by many commentators.[201] In England, the defence has been extended, so it will not fail if comment is fair with regard to facts that have been proved

[193] Eg *Francome v Mirror Group Newspapers* [1984] 1 WLR 892; *Chappell v TCN Channel Nine* (1988) 14 NSWLR 153.

[194] Cf *Mutch* (1928) 29 SR (NSW) 125.

[195] Eg *Petritsis* [1978] 2 NSWLR 174, 181 (Reynolds JA).

[196] Eg *Kemsley* [1952] AC 345, 358–62 (Lord Porter); and see *Pervan v North Queensland Newspaper Co* (1993) 178 CLR 309, 340–47 (McHugh J).

[197] *Hawke v Tamworth Newspaper Co* [1983] 1 NSWLR 699, 704 (Hunt J).

[198] The example is *Vander Zalm v Times Publishers* (1980) 109 DLR (3d) 531, 545. The cartoon is reproduced at 554 (Aitkins JA).

[199] *Merivale v Carson* (1887) 20 QBD 275; *Christie v Robertson* (1889) 10 NSWLR 157, 161 (Windeyer J); *Newbury v Triad Magazine Ltd of Austral-Asia* (1921) 21 SR (NSW) 189, 198 (Wade J).

[200] Eg *Meckiff v Simpson* [1968] VR 62, 66; *Australian Broadcasting Corpn v Comalco* (1986) 12 FCR 510, but note 597–98 (Pincus J): substantial truth would suffice.

[201] Eg Porter Committee (1948) [89]–[90]; Faulks Committee (1975) [171]–[173]; NSW Law Reform Commission (1971) appendix D, [187]; Australian Law Reform Commission (1979) [130]; Chesterman (2000) 148.

true.[202] Somewhat similarly, in NSW the question is whether the comment is reasonable, given the stated facts that have been proved true.[203] A similar approach is proposed for the uniform Australian defamation law discussed in Chapter 10, Part I, E. The traditional defence takes a slightly different approach if facts are not stated in the publication; for example, the general subject matter is indicated instead. Then, every fact about that subject matter supplied in particulars need not be proved true.[204] The facts must exist *when* the comment is made.[205] The publisher, however, need not have had them specifically in mind when commenting, if they once were known about.[206] It has been suggested this should be extended so publishers need not know about the facts at all, if they existed and recipients knew about them.[207] It should be noted that, if the indicated facts themselves are defamatory, they need to be defended by something other than the opinion defences.[208]

E Comment based on privileged facts

The comment can be based on facts stated on a privileged occasion, such as during judicial or parliamentary proceedings.[209] The Australian High Court has left unresolved whether the protection is based on the truth of the facts or the occasion of privilege.[210] English authority is based on the occasion of privilege,[211] and the comment needs to be linked to a fair and accurate report of the privileged occasion. 'It would indeed be anomalous if a report lacking the qualities necessary to sustain a defence of privilege could nonetheless sustain a defence of fair comment.'[212] This still would leave some things undecided, such as whether a reasonable reply, which is required for some fair report defences, would also need to have been published.[213] The issue of misdescription also can arise at this point; for example, the defence would fail if the facts of a judicial decision were described inaccurately and then commented on.[214]

---

202 *DA 1952* (UK) s 6.

203 *DA 1974* (NSW) s 30(3). But the requirement that the comment is 'reasonable' can be a substantial requirement to meet and appears stricter than the English approach: see eg *John Fairfax Publications v O'Shane* [2005] NSWCA 164.

204 *Kemsley* [1952] AC 345, 357–58 (Lord Porter).

205 *Cohen v Daily Telegraph* [1968] 1 WLR 916.

206 *Australian Ocean Line v West Australian Newspapers* (1985) 58 ALR 549, 594 (Toohey J).

207 Brown (1994) 990 and its note 205, which also refers to Neill and Rampton (1983) 73.

208 Eg *Broadway Approvals v Odhams Press* [1964] 2 QB 683.

209 Eg *Mangena v Wright* [1909] 2 KB 958 (Phillimore J); *Sims* [1984] 1 NSWLR 317, 323 (Hunt J).

210 *Pervan* (1993) 178 CLR 309, 320–24 (Mason CJ, Brennan, Deane, Dawson, Toohey and Gaudron JJ); see generally Cassimatis (1994) 172–75.

211 Eg *Grech v Odhams Press* [1958] 2 QB 275, 285 (Jenkins LJ).

212 *Brent Walker Group v Time Out* [1991] 2 All ER 753, 760 (Bingham LJ); *Field v Local Sunday Newspapers (North)* [2002] EWHC 336, [158]–[159] (Gray J).

213 Brown (1994) 985 and its note 179.

214 Eg *Pryke v Advertiser Newspapers* (1984) 37 SASR 175; although the decision can be criticised strongly: Brown (1994) 987 and its note 190.

F Fairness: possible not reasonable opinion

Fair comment does not mean *reasonable* comment. The test has been expressed as whether it would be possible for a fair-minded person to express the opinion, even if it is exaggerated, prejudiced or obstinate.[215] But the term *fair-minded* probably should be avoided,[216] and honesty or genuineness is the 'cardinal test'.[217] This commonly is linked to fair comment's importance for free speech.[218] (The NSW legislation avoids these ambiguities by omitting entirely the term *fair*.[219]) Perhaps the common law test should refer to an honest person – rather than a fair-minded one – to make it clear that reasonableness is not required.[220] Thus, the test would ask whether an honest person would be capable of making the comment in question. A limit to criticism, however, has been suggested in the nineteenth-century *South Hetton Coal* decision:

> If a person undertakes to make such a criticism . . . he must do so with due moderation; and, if he can be shown to have made use of unfair exaggeration, then his criticism will go beyond the limits of fair comment on a matter of public interest.[221]

But 'unfair exaggeration' may be understood better as exaggeration beyond what 'can fairly be called criticism'.[222] It would be criticism beyond what is capable of being made by an honest person – or beyond possible opinion.

G No stricter test for comment imputing dishonest motives

For opinion that imputes dishonest motives, cases have suggested three alternatives. First, the defence may apply in the normal fashion.[223] Perhaps such comment would be examined more closely as to whether it was fair,[224] and it may be more likely to convey facts rather than opinion. Second, the defence may not

---

215 *Merivale* (1887) 20 QBD 275, 281 (Lord Esher MR), 283–84 (Bowen LJ).

216 *Branson* [2002] QB 737.

217 'Honesty' per *Slim v Daily Telegraph* [1968] 2 QB 157, 170 (Lord Denning MR); cf 'genuine' perhaps being preferable, Australian Law Reform Commission (1979) [130] and its note 39.

218 Eg *Pervan* (1993) 178 CLR 309, 328 (Mason CJ, Brennan, Deane, Dawson, Toohey and Gaudron JJ); and the jury direction of Diplock J in *Silkin v Beaverbrook Newspapers* [1958] 1 WLR 743, 745–46.

219 *DA 1974* (NSW) ss 32–34. The Faulks Committee recommended the defence be renamed 'comment': (1975) [6(b)].

220 Eg *Turner (otherwise Robertson) v Metro-Goldwyn-Mayer Pictures* [1950] 1 All ER 449, 461 (Lord Porter).

221 *South Hetton Coal v North-Eastern News Association* [1894] 1 QB 133, 140 (Lord Esher MR).

222 *McQuire v Western Morning News* [1903] 2 KB 100, 110 (Collins MR).

223 *Dakhyl v Labouchere* [1908] 2 KB 325 note, 326–27 (Loreburn LC); *Slim* [1968] 2 QB 157, 169 and 171 (Lord Denning MR); *Branson* [2002] QB 737.

224 Eg *Rocca v Manhire* (1992) 57 SASR 224, 230 (King CJ).

be available at all.[225] For example, some obiter English judicial statements note that mere invective cannot be comment.[226] Third, there may be an extra requirement for the defence to be available where comment attacks the claimant's or plaintiff's motives: the comment may need to be a reasonable or warranted one to make on the facts, rather than to be merely an objectively possible one.[227] On that approach, comment clearly is reasonable if the jury can find the imputation 'is a conclusion which ought to be drawn from those facts'.[228] However, the first approach is the better one – the defence should apply in the normal way, as it does in NSW and England.[229]

H Fairness: objective not subjective test for genuine opinion

Must the comment subjectively be the genuine opinion of the commentator, or need it only objectively be possible for a commentator to hold that opinion? The common law test for fairness had been unclear. The question arises starkly where publishers reproduce comment from strangers, for example, newspaper letters to the editor. The Canadian authority of *Cherneskey v Armadale Publishers* applied a subjective test.[230] It required the media to hold the opinions expressed in published letters, or at least it posed difficulties where the media did not believe the comment and there was no evidence from the original author. Raymond Brown notes the problems in determining exactly what the Supreme Court majority required in *Cherneskey*. It is important to note that no evidence was taken from the letter writers in the case, who were students from outside the jurisdiction.[231] The majority in *Cherneskey* claimed not to be restricting the media, but this has been criticised at length by Canadian writers and a strong dissent in the case explicitly considered policy issues about the media and free speech.[232] English courts have applied an objective test and expressly followed the Canadian minority.[233] An editor need not hold the views expressed in published letters. The test is whether any person 'however prejudiced and obstinate, could honestly hold the view expressed by the defendant'.[234] The Australian High Court

[225] Eg *Hunt* [1908] 2 KB 309, 319–22 (Fletcher Moulton LJ).

[226] *Telnikoff* [1991] 1 QB 102, 112–13 (Lloyd LJ); see also Milmo and Rogers (2002) [12.22].

[227] Eg *Kemsley* [1952] AC 345.

[228] *Hunt* [1908] 2 KB 309, 321 (Fletcher Moulton LJ).

[229] *DA 1974* (NSW) s 30(4); *Branson* [2002] QB 737; and eg Fleming (1998) 652–53; Faulks Committee (1975) [177(d)]; Australian Law Reform Commission (1979) [131]. New Zealand also has abolished the rule: *DA 1992* (NZ) s 12.

[230] *Cherneskey v Armadale Publishers* [1979] 1 SCR 1067, 1079–81 (Ritchie J; Laskin CJC, Pigeon and Pratte JJ agreed).

[231] Brown (1994) 994–95.

[232] Eg *ibid*, discussing Klar (1979); *Cherneskey* [1979] 1 SCR 1067, 1096–97 (Dickson J; Spence and Estey JJ agreed).

[233] *Telnikoff* [1992] 2 AC 343, 354–55 (Lord Keith; Lords Brandon and Oliver agreed) Lords Templeman and Ackner did not consider the point.

[234] *Ibid*.

approved the English approach in relation to the Queensland defamation code, and should apply the objective test to the common law defence for opinion.[235] The Victorian Court of Appeal has done the same in relation to fair comment: the test is objective.[236] (What now appears to be a historical anomaly also could be noted: Hunt J offered another approach while approving of the Canadian minority. In an addendum to a judgment,[237] he said the subjective test should apply, but also that the plaintiff would face the burden of showing the comment was not fair. As has been suggested, this appears to mix together fairness and malice.[238])

In NSW, if a stranger's comment is published – such as a letter to the editor – the comment defence is defeated if the plaintiff shows that the publication was not made in good faith for public information or advancing education.[239] But where the comment is that of the defendant, or its servant or agent, the NSW defence fails if the plaintiff shows it was not the commentator's opinion.[240] In any of these circumstances, there can be a problem if unintended imputations are conveyed in NSW.[241] This need not arise only in relation to comment, but usefully can be addressed here. Consider this situation – a publisher's comment is honestly made, but it conveys an unintended meaning. If the comment defence is directed to the imputations and an unintended imputation is conveyed, the defence fails.[242] This applies even if another commentator could have defended the same meaning as being comment, based on the stated and true facts. One commentator being liable while the other is not liable appears to be a more egregious example of the complexity that follows from the NSW statutory approach (and echoes the difficulties of *Cherneskey*). This position on unintended meanings may not arise at common law, but Australian cases relevant to the issue are explored in Chapters 9 and 10. A comparison also could be made to qualified privilege, as English cases have done: if an unintended meaning is conveyed, and the publisher has no honest belief in that meaning, malice is *not necessarily* established.[243] Honesty in the intended meaning is the important factor, so a plea

---

235 *Pervan* (1993) 178 CLR 309, 328–29 (Mason CJ, Brennan, Deane, Dawson, Toohey and Gaudron JJ).

236 *Herald & Weekly Times v Popovic* (2003) 9 VR 1, [254]–[265] (Gillard AJA), [1] (Winneke ACJ agreed), [453]–[454] (Warren AJA agreed).

237 *Hawke* [1983] 1 NSWLR 699, 714–20 (Hunt J).

238 Walker (1998b) [58].

239 *DA 1974* (NSW) s 34(2).

240 *Ibid* ss 32(2), 33(2).

241 Eg Rares (2002); Kenyon (1996), which discusses *Meskenas v Capon* (Unreported, NSW District Court, Christie DCJ and jury, 28 September 1993). Brown (1994) 999 and its note 235 mentions the problem and goes on to suggest all opinions should be immune in defamation.

242 *Austin v Mirror Newspapers* [1986] 1 AC 299, 315–16 (Lord Griffiths for PC); *Lloyd v David Syme* [1986] AC 350, 365 (Lord Keith for PC).

243 *Field* [2002] EWHC 336, [181] (Gray J); and see Chapter 7. In relation to the same issue for opinion defences, see *Next Magazine Publishing v Ma Ching Fat* [2003] HKLRD 75, [144]–[146] (Lord Cooke).

of malice against qualified privilege would be likely to fail where the publisher's intended meaning was honestly held.[244]

Some commentary suggests this sort of difficulty means that opinion should not be actionable at all.[245] Only defamatory facts, including those implied in statements of opinion, should be relevant. This basically follows the US position, which is examined in Chapter 8.[246] The approach might face difficulties in distinguishing fact and opinion, but that issue exists in any event. A variety of case law could be drawn on for such a development, including Bingham LJ in *Brent Walker Group v Time Out*. He stated the law is primarily aimed at defamatory factual publications:

> The law is not primarily concerned to provide redress for those who are the subject of disparaging expression of opinion, and freedom of opinion is . . . a basic democratic right.[247]

An approach that made opinion non-actionable could be based in the test of what can be defamatory. It would seem plausible for defamation law to state that it seeks to protect reputation based on facts, not opinion. That is, a publication's ordinary recipients should not think less of someone from a critical opinion, if the opinion does not convey a defamatory fact. Somewhat similarly, Thomas Gibbons, in exploring an alternative to defamation law, has suggested that statements of opinion 'should not be regarded as parts of the foundation for social appraisal', even if judgments may be influenced 'by persuasive comment'.[248]

I Malice

Once opinion is shown to be fair objectively – that is, comment that could be made by an honest person – the general view is that comment is presumed to be the publisher's honest opinion. Then malice defeats fair comment.[249] This makes malice a distinct element and gives the claimant or plaintiff the burden of proof. Malice in relation to fair comment has been described for many years as ill will or lack of honest belief, and must be the dominant motivation of the publisher.[250] It must actuate or distort the comment. If there is no honest belief, usually the

---

244 *Loveless* [1999] EMLR 530.

245 Eg Brown (1994) 999 and its note 235.

246 See *Milkovich v Lorain Journal*, 497 US 1 (1990); explaining *Gertz v Robert Welch*, 418 US 323 (1974).

247 [1991] 2 All ER 753, 760.

248 Gibbons (1996) 607–608.

249 *Telnikoff* [1992] 2 AC 343, 355 (Lord Keith; Lords Brandon and Oliver agreed), 357 (Lord Ackner); *Gardiner* (1942) 42 SR (NSW) 171, 173–74 (Jordan CJ); *Renouf v Federal Capital Press of Australia* (1977) 17 ACTR 35, 53–59 (Blackburn J).

250 See generally *Horrocks v Lowe* [1975] 1 AC 135, which considered malice for qualified privilege, but has relevance to fair comment: eg *Renouf* (1977) 17 ACTR 35, 54 (Blackburn J).

defence will be lost. The same applies if the publisher is reckless with regard to truth. Failing to inquire as to truth does not equal malice, but may indicate a lack of honest belief.[251] An honest belief arrived at carelessly, however, usually will allow the defence to stand.[252] The importance of honesty has been underlined by English case law since the end of the 1990s, which has emphasised that ill will is not relevant to malice in relation to fair comment (unlike in relation to qualified privilege) and that honesty of belief is the decisive issue.[253] Australian case law, however, has emphasised that the overriding test for malice – in relation to qualified privilege – is whether the publisher had an improper purpose. Lack of honest belief in the publication is not a distinct ground for malice to defeat qualified privilege under Australian law.[254]

J Pleading opinion defences

The general approach to pleading fair comment has similarities to justification. The plea and particulars should identify the comment, the facts on which it is based and its public interest subject matter.[255] Often the same particulars of facts relied on for justification will be relied on for comment, although facts arising after publication can only be used for justification.[256] Pleading justification and fair comment as an alternative to the same imputations is possible – and common – but it may weaken any argument that the words are opinion. Where Lucas-Box or Polly Peck pleading is available, it can be used for fair comment.[257] The issue has been explored doctrinally in relation to justification (above, in Part I) and it need not be repeated here. As with justification, English claimants must reply to any particulars of fact in the defence, and state any fact or matter that is relied on in opposing the defence.[258] In Victoria and NSW, a reply is needed only if matters of defeasance such as malice are to be relied on: particulars are needed of the facts and matters underlying malice.[259]

---

251 *Hansen* (1987) 9 NSWLR 44, 55 (Hunt J).

252 *Horrocks* [1975] AC 135, 150 (Lord Diplock; Lords Wilberforce, Hodson and Kilbrandon agreed).

253 Eg *Branson* [2002] QB 737 (Eady J) applying *Tse Wai Chun Paul* [2001] EMLR 31; see also *Field* [2002] EWHC 336, [177] (Gray J).

254 *Roberts v Bass* (2002) 212 CLR 1. The Australian reasoning is supported in Milmo and Rogers (2004) [16.4]; but cf eg *Halford v Chief Constable of Hampshire Constabulary* [2003] EWCA Civ 102.

255 See generally *Control Risks* [1990] 1 WLR 183 and now *CPR* Pt 53 PD 2.6. In NSW, court rules require defendants to distinguish fact and comment and specify the facts being relied on: *SCR* (NSW) Pt 67 rr 17, 18 (and see above, fn 4).

256 *Cohen* [1968] 1 WLR 926.

257 *Control Risks* [1990] 1 WLR 183.

258 *CPR* Pt 53 PD 2.8; formerly *RSC* Ord 82 r 3(2A), subject to r 3(2B).

259 *SCR* (Vic) r 13.10; *SCR* (NSW) Pt 67 r 19 (and see above fn 4); see eg *El-Azzi* [2004] NSWSC 1057.

III CONCLUSION

This chapter has set out the law on the defamation defences that are most relevant to a publication's meaning in England, NSW and Victoria. Two points are particularly noteworthy for the concerns of this book. First, justification and mitigation of damages appear to be connected in a significant manner (and the same could apply to the defence of fair comment). Second, defendants may seek to differ from claimants and plaintiffs about a publication's meaning in two distinct ways, which this book suggests should be distinguished as Lucas-Box and Polly Peck pleas. Understanding these two different ways in which the parties may disagree about meaning is important in relation to subsequent chapters' exploration of litigation practice, evaluating recent Australian changes to what defence pleading is possible in defamation litigation, and interpreting the options that will face Australian courts if proposed uniform law is enacted. Overall, the exposition of defamation law relevant to a publication's meaning in Chapters 2 and 3 has raised four central issues about defamatory meaning, namely:

- the *way a party is bound* to a pleaded meaning;[260]
- the *degree of specificity* required in a pleaded meaning;[261]
- whether, and how, *defence meanings* are pleaded and dealt with in litigation, which particularly raises Lucas-Box and Polly Peck pleading (and contextual imputations in NSW);[262] and
- the *stage of a dispute at which differences between the parties about meaning* are dealt with, including pre-trial and trial determinations.[263]

Next, evidence from practice about these issues is considered in relation to each of England, NSW and Victoria in Chapters 4 to 6. Then, after examining English and Australian law and practice on qualified privilege in Chapter 7 and US approaches to defamation in Chapter 8, lessons are drawn about the treatment of meaning in defamation law and litigation in Chapters 9 and 10.

---

[260] See Chapter 2, Part III, H.

[261] See Chapter 2, Part III, I.

[262] See Chapter 3, Part I, J and K.

[263] See Chapter 2, Part III, C.

– 4 –

MEANING: ENGLISH DEFAMATION PRACTICE

> You've got to look at what it is that those words truthfully mean, and there's no magic in it. *There's no magic in it at all.* It's what anybody would take, from a dustman to a professor, would understand these words to mean A, B and C. And yet, there is inevitably and always a degree of difference between the parties, at least a difference as expressed in the pleadings.[1]

> *Meaning is the most difficult thing* and you could ask very experienced defamation lawyers what something means and everybody is going to have slightly different views.[2]

Lawyers discuss the meaning of a publication as being both simple *and* complex.[3] They suggest everyone can agree on what a publication means, and yet lawyers will differ about its meaning in litigation. This chapter reports on fieldwork that investigated how a publication's meaning is dealt with in English practice. Earlier chapters raised four central issues about meaning in defamation law: namely, the way a party is bound to a pleaded meaning; the degree of specificity required in a pleaded meaning; whether, and how, defence meanings are pleaded and dealt with in litigation, which particularly raises Lucas-Box and Polly Peck pleading (and contextual imputations in NSW); and the stage of a dispute at which differences between the parties about meaning are dealt with, including pre-trial and trial determinations.

Here, material from practice is presented about these issues. Briefly, five themes emerge about English practice. First, each side tends to plead relatively few meanings,[4] partly because they are not strictly bound to their pleaded meanings. Second, the specificity of pleaded meanings is rarely an issue in litigation. Third, parties almost always argue that a publication conveys different meanings – claimants and defendants disagree about the publication's meaning. Practitioners see this as fundamentally important. It very often arises because defendants plead their own Lucas-Box meaning in response to the claimant's

---

[1] Interviewed lawyer 20S (emphasis in original). Interviewees are identified by number and role; see below, fn 13 and accompanying text.

[2] 25S (emphasis added).

[3] Generally, the term *meaning* is used in this chapter in preference to *imputation* to reflect the terminology common in interviews; see also Chapter 1, Part I.

[4] Cf NSW in particular. See Chapter 5, Part II, A.

pleading. That is, Lucas-Box pleading is the norm. Fourth, such justification pleas – and the use of justification evidence to mitigate damages – are where meaning becomes *central* in litigation. Fifth, jury determinations of meaning at the start of a trial are markedly atypical. It was done in *Marks & Spencer v Granada Television,*[5] but questions about mitigation have been important in preventing widespread use of the approach.

I INTERVIEW SAMPLE AND METHOD

A The sample of lawyers interviewed

Defamation litigation was the object of research and lawyers were the chosen source of information. To a far greater extent than in Australia, interviewing lawyers was the only viable empirical method.[6] During June 2000, interviews were conducted in London with 38 specialist defamation solicitors, barristers and judges (see Table 4.1; further interviews from 2003 are discussed below in Section B).[7] These interviewees represented a substantial cross-section of London lawyers with significant defamation involvement. They included two specialist defamation judges from the High Court of Justice, a retired Court of Appeal judge, 12 barristers from the two leading defamation chambers,[8] and a cross-section of solicitors from prominent London defamation firms, including some in-house lawyers for media companies.[9] Given this project's comparative scope, a particularly useful interviewee was one lawyer who had spent approximately six months in Sydney during 1998 working in defamation litigation. All the barristers and solicitors were approached after searching listing services such as *The Legal 500*[10] for prominent defamation lawyers.[11] The judges were contacted on the recommendation, and with the assistance, of the two leading defamation chambers.

---

5 (Unreported, Popplewell J, QBD, 23 February 1998).

6 See below, fn 15 and accompanying text. See the appendix for a more detailed discussion of empirical methodology used in this book.

7 Ten interviewees were women. See the appendix for a full list of people who assisted with the research. These interviewees were seen in pairs: 12S and 13S, 29S and 30S, 33S and 34S. These were seen in a group of three: 35S, 36S and 37B.

8 This comprised seven barristers from 1 Brick Court and five barristers from 5 Raymond Buildings, and included five QCs. Another barrister was interviewed from the prominent human rights and media law set, Doughty Street Chambers. (London barristers are organised into many specialised chambers, and 1 Brick Court and 5 Raymond Buildings account for a substantial majority of all London defamation work.)

9 Or lawyers with extensive previous in-house experience.

10 See <www.icclaw.com>.

11 During May 2000, 40 potential interviewees were contacted by letter or email. The vast majority agreed to be interviewed, and several suggested further contacts.

As Table 4.1 indicates, the sample included lawyers with very extensive experience. Defamation was the major part of almost every interviewee's practice, and in many cases it formed a sizeable majority of their work. For 22 interviewees, defamation law was more than 70 per cent of their practice, and for 33 interviewees it was more than 50 per cent. But it must be noted that these reports were given in the interviews conducted in 2000. As noted below, defamation litigation rates have fallen dramatically in England and these percentages should not be taken as accurate for more recent practice. The interviewees' experience with defamation law ranged from four to more than 30 years. There were nine to 15 interviewees in each of the categories of having practice experience of four to 10 years, 10–20 years, or 20–30 years. Many interviewees acted for both claimants and defendants, or had done at different stages of their careers. For 15 interviewees, however, the vast majority of their defamation work was for media defendants. Nine interviewees reported doing mainly claimant work, and the remainder (mainly barristers) did approximately equal amounts of work for claimants and defendants. It is worth noting not all defence work involved the media. One senior barrister, who was well known as a media law specialist, emphasised that 'about one-third about my libel cases have nothing whatsoever to do with the media. They are private, commercial, personal, letters of slander, and so forth.'[12]

B The interviews' style and content

Each interview lasted approximately one hour. Almost all interviews were audiotape recorded and later transcribed. For three interviews, handwritten notes were taken during meetings in accordance with the interviewees' preference. To protect the wishes of some interviewees who did not want to be identified directly with a particular statement, no quotation has been identified with a named interviewee. Instead, interviewees are referred to by number, along with their professional role: solicitor (S), barrister (B) or Queen's Counsel (QC).[13] Quotations that are used are direct transcriptions from interviews.[14]

The interviews were semi-structured and allowed for general comments to be offered by all interviewees. Interviews proceeded through five general areas: the interviewee's background; pleading meaning; defence pleading of meaning; the trial stage; and law reform. First, interviewees were asked about their background in defamation law, including the length of time they had worked in the field, the size of defamation within their practice, and the sorts of clients they acted for. Second, questions about pleading imputations were raised, including whether disputes about pleaded meanings were frequent; how they were resolved pre-trial and at trial; whether pleaded meanings were challenged for

[12] 26QC.

[13] The judges are referred to as QCs to avoid identifying particular respondents and to mirror their major prior experience.

[14] Gender-specific language used by interviewees has been retained in quotations, as the first of this chapter's opening quotations illustrates.

Table 4.1 – London Interviewee Sample

Interviewee	Subject	Libel over 50% work	Libel Over 70% work	5–10 years' libel work	10–20 years' libel work	20–30 years' libel work	>30 years' libel work	More claim ant work	More defendant work	Even claimant and defendant work
1	B		•	•						•
2	S	•			•				•	
3	S		•		•			•		
4	QC		•			•				•
5	S		•		•				•	
6	QC		•				•			•
7	QC	•				•		•		
8	QC		•			•				•
9	B		•	•					•	
10	S		•		•				•	
11	S					•		•		
12	S		•				•	•		
13	S		•		•			•		
14	B	•			•					•
15	B	•		•						•
16	B	•		•						•
17	S			•						•

18	S	•			•			•		
19	B		•	•					•	
20	S	•			•				•	
21	S		•		•				•	
22	S		•			•			•	
23	S					•			•	
24	QC		•				•			•
25	S		•		•				•	
26	QC		•			•				•
27	QC		•				•			•
28	QC		•				•			•
29	S				•				•	
30	S			•					•	
31	S		•	•						•
32	S	•			•			•		
33	S		•			•			•	
34	S		•	•					•	
35	S	•				•		•		
36	S	•			•			•		
37	B				•					•
38	B		•		•				•	

Note: S – Solicitor (any solicitor-advocate is identified here as S); B – Barrister; QC – Queen's Counsel. In a very few cases, the length of practice or proportion of work has been estimated from the interviewee's general comments about their practice.

imprecision; and whether interviewees had experience with other approaches to disputes about meaning such as mediation. Third, defence pleading of meaning was focussed on. Interviewees were asked about the frequency of Lucas-Box and Polly Peck pleading; the relationship of such pleading to justification and fair comment defences (including ss 5 and 6 of the *Defamation Act 1952)*; and the effect of such pleading before and at trial. Fourth, interviews explored defamation trials, in particular the stage at which meaning is determined and the approach adopted in *Marks & Spencer v Granada Television*.[15] Interviewees also were asked how the test for defamatory meaning is presented to the jury, and about their knowledge of (or initial response to) the NSW procedure under s 7A of the *Defamation Act 1974*.[16] Finally, 1990s reforms and future reform options were considered. This included the Neill Committee's report and introduction of Ord 82 r 3A (see now *Civil Procedure Rule* 53); summary disposal provisions in ss 8–10 of the *Defamation Act 1996* (UK); *Civil Procedure Rules (CPR)*, particularly Pts 24 and 36 and general effects of conditional fee agreements; possible roles for judge and jury; and the *Human Rights Act (HRA) 1998*.

In discussing these issues, some material in this chapter includes percentages, which need some explanation.[17] They were not created through *analysing* interview material, but come from the interviewees' own words. For example, an interviewee may have been asked how often a certain litigation step is made. Frequently, the reply was 'in one-third of cases' or 'about 30 per cent of the time'. The figures are not used for any direct statistical claim, but to indicate interviewees' opinions about practice in defamation litigation. It also should be noted that, in all the chapters reporting interviews, the aim is to treat the interview material comprehensively. This means atypical responses are included, which helps address concerns with anecdotalism that may arise in some reporting of qualitative research.[18] Extensive footnoting of responses allows readers to assess these issues, at least to some degree, by making the depth of response about particular issues more transparent. That is, the material reported in this book should be assessed with the understanding that where an issue receives many comments, practitioners see the issue as important; where many interviewees hold a particular view, that view is likely to be common among experienced practitioners; and where divergences of views appeared in interviews, they are noted in the reporting.

It is worth emphasising that a further 23 interviews were conducted in 2003 with London defamation specialists.[19] As well as discussing all the above matters about meaning, the later interviews examined issues concerned with qualified privilege. The findings about qualified privilege are discussed in Chapter 7 but,

[15] (Unreported, Popplewell J, QBD, 23 February 1998).

[16] See Chapter 1, Part I; and see generally Kenyon (2000) 100.

[17] For a discussion of criticisms of deriving numbers that appear statistical from qualitative research, see Eekelaar and Maclean (1990).

[18] See further the appendix.

[19] Eleven of the 2003 interviewees also had been interviewed in 2000.

for reasons of space and simplicity, the 2003 interviews are not drawn on in detail in this chapter. It is sufficient to note that the 2003 interviews supported the findings discussed in this chapter, although they did raise some matters about changing procedures (and reduced rates of litigation) under the *Civil Procedure Rules*, which are returned to in Chapter 10. But no meaningful changes appeared in the 2003 interviews in relation to this chapter's central concerns, such as the specificity of pleaded meanings and the use of defence meanings in litigation.

C Interviews provided the best information source

The number and length of interviews generated a very large amount of material.[20] The approach, however, was chosen because interviews offered almost the only source of empirical information about English defamation litigation. Two other common research methods were not suitable, namely, using documentary evidence and observing practice. Three points illustrate how useful documentary evidence was not available in any systematic form. First, at least before the *Civil Procedure Rules*, only the writ (and statement of claim where it was endorsed on the writ) was filed with the court. Thus, court files held almost no information about litigated cases, unlike in Australia. As well, files were not kept in any manner allowing easy identification of defamation claims.[21] Second, little information is published about defamation litigation, although the Department for Constitutional Affairs produces annual *Judicial Statistics*, which include some information about the number of defamation claims.[22] Third, interviewees suggested transcripts of in-court argument cost a great deal relative to total litigation costs.[23] It seems that lawyers rarely obtain transcripts and generally transcripts were not accessible for research. All these reasons mean documentary evidence, of the kind available in Australia, could not be obtained in England. Observing litigation might appear to be another useful source of information. But it would be impractical to attempt to observe a representative sample of hearings in such a specialist area as defamation. And in any event, observation would only reach activities that are visible within court, which is a small portion of the litigation process. Interviews, in comparison, can encompass material like letters before action, the *Civil Procedure Rules'* pre-action protocols, and other interlocutory steps. Thus interviews were used as the best available means of learning about practice.

---

[20] The transcriptions for the 38 interviewees that are the focus of this chapter exceeded 170,000 words.

[21] Although the situation changed somewhat with the *Civil Procedure Rules 1998* (Eng) (*CPR*), at the time of the fieldwork it seemed likely that access to files in defamation matters would remain sensitive: personal correspondence with Court Service, May 2000.

[22] See below, fn 25 and accompanying text.

[23] Eg 19B.

The interview sample represented a significant portion of London defamation practice. Interviewees were well aware of the small group of lawyers that dominated defamation litigation:

> An interesting question . . . is our situation with two specialist chambers and very few [barristers] outside the chambers who can genuinely say that they are . . . players. The extent to which we all know each other actually has a big impact on the way cases are run.[24]

At the least, the sample shows how a significant percentage of English practitioners discuss and understand their practice, which will allow comparisons to be made with the documentary and interview-based material from NSW and Victoria that is discussed in Chapters 5 and 6.

II GENERAL OBSERVATIONS ABOUT ENGLISH DEFAMATION LITIGATION

Three general points emerged from interviews, and other published material, which provide context to English defamation litigation. They concern the number of defamation claims that are brought, the types of parties involved, and the number of meanings that commonly are pleaded.

A The number of claims issued annually

A limited amount of empirical information already is available about the number of defamation claims issued in England. The Department for Constitutional Affairs publishes (and before 2003 the Lord Chancellor's Department published) annual *Judicial Statistics.* These show, for example, that in 1998 and 1999, 379 and 236 libel and slander writs were issued in the Royal Courts of Justice.[25] No information is available about the cases' outcomes. But it is notable the number does not appear high in comparison to the approximately 70 issued during 1998 in each of Sydney and Melbourne, given the population differences between England and Australia. More recent statistics, however, show that defamation claims have fallen markedly under the *Civil Procedure Rules*. Figures for the four most recent available years report that 190 defamation claims were issued in 2003, 128 claims in 2002, 220 claims in 2001 and 241 claims in 2000.[26] These figures suggest defamation claims have fallen meaningfully. This is a significant change but lower than the reduction in all civil claims in the Queen's Bench Division, which deals primarily with contract and tort claims. Claims in the Queen's Bench Division have fallen more than 85 per cent since 1998. If the last few years serve

---

[24] 19B; similar 11S, 16B, 18S, 20S.

[25] Lord Chancellor's Department (1999, 2000), Table 3.2 in each.

[26] Department for Constitutional Affairs (2004a, 2003) and Lord Chancellor's Department (2002, 2001), Table 3.2 in each. For further examination of litigation rates, see Weaver et al (2006) Chapter 9.

as a guide to current English litigation rates, approximately 160–180 defamation claims are issued annually. The higher of those figures suggests an annual rate of defamation suits of one claim per 295,000 people.[27]

The interviews clarified these published figures in that respondents *very* commonly suggested the number of claims had fallen.[28] Some interviewees linked this to the control of damages established by the *Elton John* decision in the Court of Appeal.[29] The *Civil Procedure Rules'* general effect in reducing the number of all civil claims also was mentioned.[30] And a change in media practices was raised. That is, the media *may* now be satisfying a higher percentage of potential litigants who complain about a publication. US research from the 1980s suggested the media's response to complaints plays an important role in the decision to sue.[31] One experienced media solicitor said in-house media lawyers have become 'much readier to publish speedy corrections'.[32] Not surprisingly, there still are many more letters before action than claims. For example, one claimant solicitor accurately estimated that hundreds of claims are issued each year and continued:

> What I see and write and receive [are] almost innumerable letters before action. But it's such a specialised area that if I receive a letter before action I generally have it dealt with and if I then receive a writ I tend to regard it as a bad result really. . . . As a plaintiff I would expect to get what I want from a letter before action. And increasingly that's what happens.[33]

B The types of parties in defamation claims

The second general point concerns the types of parties. Respondents reported a fall in celebrity actions,[34] and a rise in corporate claimants.[35] Several interviewees raised how corporate defamation actions can be used to protect a company's share price. This was seen as a growing sector and amounted to a significant minority of litigation. After the *McLibel* action of the 1990s, which finally concluded in the European Court of Human Rights in 2005,[36] some interviewees also raised the role of campaigning litigants, such as those who could be sued in response to their

---

[27] Using a population figure for England and Wales of 53 million people.

[28] Eg 8QC, 11S, 12S, 18S, 19B, 22S, 25S, 29S, 30S, 32S, 38B.

[29] *John v MGN* [1997] QB 586; eg 18S, 32S, 38B. Many interviews also noted that damages appear to have increased slightly after a mid-1990s drop: eg 20S, 21S, even though they may have reached a plateau: 32S.

[30] Eg 8QC.

[31] Eg Cranberg (1985).

[32] 25S; similar 22S.

[33] 11S.

[34] Eg 19B, 38B.

[35] 2S, 19B, 25S, 27QC, 38B.

[36] See generally *Steel v McDonald's* [1999] EWCA 1144; *Steel and Morris v UK* (Unreported, ECHR, 15 February 2005).

criticisms of corporate environmental policies.[37] The general impression from interviews was that a sizeable portion of all defamation claims was corporate.[38]

C The number of meanings pleaded by litigants

The third general issue concerns the number of meanings commonly pleaded by parties. During interviews, it became clear the number was not great,[39] and appeared to be lower than in Australia. Much depends on the actual publications sued over, and only a general impression can be gained through interviews (as opposed to being able to review a substantial number of pleadings, which was possible in Australia). But the statements of many interviewees were striking. While parties may plead multiple meanings where a publication makes distinct allegations, it is comparatively rare to plead a *range* of meanings:

> I mean certainly there are cases in which it's obviously debateable whether each defamatory meaning is conveyed, and there one would plead the higher meaning or if wrong about that . . . the lesser meaning. So far as I'm concerned that would be the end of it, without looking for half a dozen more variants, because it does have to be tried by a jury . . . My object would always be to plead one meaning which I consider the right meaning.[40]

> What often happens is that unless the article clearly raises several matters that are distinct, unless it's like that, *the claimant will tend to pick one meaning that's clear and sharp, damaging and memorable* and sue on it. And the defendant will tend to say well no, it means something else and defend it.[41]

The interviewee with recent NSW experience confirmed London practice was different. Fewer meanings are pleaded in London:

> Yes, absolutely. I would consider my pleading in need of serious revision if [it included lots of meanings]. The objective for me always is to run my meaning in one paragraph. And not to break it into paragraph 1, paragraph 2, paragraph 3 unless the matter complained of is amenable to making distinct allegations.[42]

In response to the idea that a NSW plaintiff might plead a range of meanings, one illustrative comment was: 'Attached to the same words?'[43] It might be suggested that NSW pleading responds to the statutory cause of action in that state in which each pleaded imputation is a cause of action.[44] But English practice also offers a

---

[37] Eg 19B.

[38] This also is illustrated by a barrister's comments, see above fn 12 and accompanying text.

[39] Eg 7QC, 16B, 19B, 20S, 21S, 23S, 24QC.

[40] 4QC.

[41] 23S (emphasis added).

[42] 16B.

[43] 21S.

[44] See Chapter 10, Part I, B; *DA 1974* (NSW) s 9.

strong contrast to Victorian pleading, where more imputations appear to be pleaded although the cause of action is the traditional common law one of the publication itself.[45] The possibility of a large number of meanings being pleaded was not unknown, however, as three points illustrate. First, pleading practice in Ireland was mentioned and criticised.[46] For example, a lawyer with extensive in-house experience suggested that in London where one or two meanings would be pleaded, in Ireland 14 would be set out.[47] Second, one claimant solicitor described, quite unprompted, the practice of pleading a range of meanings:

> As I'm sure you know . . . our usual practice in this jurisdiction is to . . . have a range of meanings starting with the highest meaning – you know, he's a murderer, whatever – and then at the bottom – he wasn't a terribly nice person. It's always been my practice to make sure that we actually set out the range of meanings from highest to lowest. You know, in the alternative, if it doesn't mean that, then it means this. And so you have things to fall back on.[48]

This description suggests the practice occurs, but other respondents indicated it is rare: the description was atypical.[49] The interviewee was a solicitor with most libel experience from the 1990s; that is, under Ord 82 r 3A (which is now *Civil Procedure Rule 53* PD 4.1).[50] This connects to the third point. It was suggested the Ord 82 procedure may have created a slight tendency towards pleading more meanings. Then if one meaning was ruled out at an interlocutory hearing, another meaning already would have been before the court.[51] But even where that *possible* effect was suggested, the interviewee continued: 'I think generally the approach isn't to put in lots of alternatives'.[52]

Why are few meanings pleaded? Interviewees suggested several reasons. They involve parties not being tied to pleaded meanings, s 5 of the *Defamation Act 1952*, and juries and the single-meaning rule. First, parties are not strictly tied to their pleaded meanings, which naturally allows less meanings to be pleaded.[53] Second, s 5 of the *Defamation Act 1952* allows for an extended justification defence, as discussed in Chapter 3, Part I. It can apply if multiple imputations are sued on, but only some are justified. If the undefended meanings do not materially injure the claimant's reputation, given what has been proved true, then s 5 provides a complete defence. The section appears to discourage pleading any meaning that can be proved true. The absence of an equivalent provision in Ireland was linked, at times, to their pleading practice.[54] There is more value in a claimant pleading

[45] See Chapter 6, Part II.

[46] 5S, 20S.

[47] 5S.

[48] 32S.

[49] See above, fn 39.

[50] See now *CPR* 53 PD 4.1. For an outline of the rule see Chapter 2, Part III, A.

[51] 7QC.

[52] *Ibid.*

[53] See further below, fn 104 and accompanying text.

[54] Eg 5S.

every possible meaning if s 5 is not available. This was an interesting suggestion about how there could be an important impact on practice from ss 5 and 6 (s 6 provides a similar defence for fair comment, see Chapter 3, Part II). The sections are pleaded frequently or invariably,[55] but rarely are an active issue at trial.[56] Third, lawyers expect meaning will be decided by juries, so lawyers want to keep claims simple.[57] Interviewees linked this to the single-meaning rule:

> The single-meaning theory here, which is that publication only bears one meaning and it is for the jury to decide . . . leads to self restraint in the sense that I will pitch my meaning high but simple because ultimately I'm going to be addressing my arguments to a jury and I don't want to bore them rigid with a list of imputations as if I can't make my mind up about what this means. The claimant wants to say 'members of the jury this article says nothing more and nothing less than my client [did X]'. *I want it to be memorable, quick and serious*. . . That's why plaintiffs are quite happy to read their meaning to the jury [from the pleading].[58]

In addition, the value of pleading a 'memorable' and 'serious' meaning would be enhanced by the rarity of jury questionnaires.[59]

III SEVEN LITIGATION ISSUES ABOUT MEANING

In the interviews, lawyers described seven aspects of litigation practice connected with meaning that are worth exploring in more detail. They concerned disputes about pleaded meanings, precision in pleaded meanings, the way a party is bound to a pleaded meaning, defence pleading of meaning, defence pleading in connection with particulars and evidence, the stage of a trial at which meaning is determined and presenting the test for defamatory meaning to the jury.

A Disputes about pleaded meanings

Disputes about meaning are common. In almost every case there will be a difference between the parties about a publication's meaning.[60] Meaning disputes 'have always been fundamental'[61] and meaning 'lies at the root of every

[55] Eg 7QC, 14B.

[56] 14B.

[57] See above, fn 40 and accompanying text. This also was raised by 4QC, 16B, 28QC, 20S.

[58] 16B (emphasis added). Some barristers (eg 19B) noted colleagues liked to read claimants' meanings to the jury, but said they would not follow that practice. The quoted description appears to differ slightly from Australia, where the single-meaning rule would be understood more in terms of preventing inconsistent meanings arising; see eg Fleming (1998) 586–88.

[59] See below, fn 170 and accompanying text.

[60] Eg 8QC, 9B, 14B, 20S, 23S, 25S.

[61] 14B.

defamation action.'[62] Meaning is the 'central' and 'often critical' issue.[63] Differences are clear even before a claim is commenced. Differences can be seen in letters before action and legal counsel frequently advise on their wording. To a large extent this is due to meaning's importance:

> It's very important even at that stage that the charge is formulated properly, because . . . if there's a gross discrepancy between the letter before action and the claim there's going to be great cross-examination.[64]

And by the stage of pleading, barristers nearly always are involved, particularly juniors.[65] At the pleading stage, the defence generally enters a Lucas-Box plea of a less damaging meaning than the claimant pleads. This is explored further below.[66] The difference between the parties may be customary, but it is not merely a matter of form.

> Genuine as opposed to formal disputes as to meaning arise in a great many cases. Very often it is the inability . . . of the parties to reach agreement on meaning that leads to an inability to settle the case and colours thereafter everything that happens.[67]

How often do these differences between the parties lead to pre-trial hearings? Estimates varied. A party can apply for a ruling about whether a pleaded meaning is capable of being conveyed, under *Civil Procedure Rule* 53 PD 4.1 (which is explained in Chapter 2, Part III). The most common suggestion by interviewees was that applications are made in about 30 per cent of cases,[68] or more frequently.[69] Some respondents, however, suggested that while differences about meaning would exist in most cases,[70] interlocutory applications would be made far less often:[71] the matter commonly would be left until trial. But those with experience from the 1980s or earlier tended to emphasise how the practice had altered. Disputes were 'dealt with atrociously' before Ord 82 r 3A (now *Civil Procedure Rule* 53 PD 4.1).[72] Rulings on capable meanings had been a '*huge* change'.[73] They had ended a common feature of defamation actions, namely, the

[62] 8QC.

[63] 25S.

[64] 15B.

[65] 16B, 6QC.

[66] See below, fn 109 and accompanying text.

[67] 26QC.

[68] Eg 3S, 15B (1/3 of cases), 21S (30–40 per cent), 26QC (about 25 per cent), 38B (25–30 per cent).

[69] 4QC, 6QC ('very frequent' under Ord 82 r 3A), 25S (about 50 per cent).

[70] 7QC.

[71] Eg 16B, 23S.

[72] 21S. Previously, the only pre-trial application on meaning involved meanings that were not 'arguably capable' of being conveyed, see Chapter 2, Part III, A.

[73] 38B.

way parties used to 'shadow box . . . sometimes for several years . . . about meaning'.[74]

The *Civil Procedure Rules* commonly were seen to have reduced further the number of applications: 'Before the *CPR*, effectively you would not have a case that went to trial without at least two applications on meanings.'[75] The *Civil Procedure Rules'* costs implications were raised by several interviewees as having changed pleading practice. It had made challenges less frequent and 'extreme' pleading of meaning less common.[76] Under the *Civil Procedure Rules'* costs regime, a judge at an interlocutory hearing can assess costs and order their immediate payment.[77] Now, an extreme pleading could lead to a successful challenge and immediate costs order of thousands of pounds:[78]

> Well nowadays I think that plaintiff counsel are rather more circumspect at what they plead the meaning to be because they recognise that if they are controversial they face an immediate application for a ruling which is going to have . . . undesirable immediate effects.[79]

It should be noted that several interviewees said it was still unclear how the courts would apply the new costs rule.[80] And some doubted the effect of such costs orders on media companies who use their 'financial muscle' against claimants.[81] Even with this apparent change in practice, parties continue to push meaning in differing directions. 'Extravagant' meanings will still be pleaded for tactical reasons, which is returned to below.[82] The overall impression was there may have been a slight tempering of pleading practice, but *evidential* considerations continue to push parties towards more extreme pleading.

What happens in interlocutory challenges to pleaded meanings? The hearing is quick, usually lasting an hour or two.[83] But judges may be overly cautious when determining what meanings are capable of being conveyed, even if there has been some change under the *Civil Procedure Rules* towards a more 'robust' approach.[84]

---

[74] 27QC.

[75] 5S; similar 6QC.

[76] Eg 18S, 19B.

[77] *CPR* 44.7 and *CPR* PD 13; and see eg Shillito and Barendt (2000) 391, 393–94.

[78] Estimates varied between £2,000–5,000 (6QC) and £15,000–20,000 (18S). Generally, defamation costs were seen as high: eg 14B, 22S, 38B. One cause was suggested to be that both sides will spend large sums (disproportionate to possible damages) to litigate points of principle: eg 14B, 22S. Greater case management under the *CPR*s may lessen that lack of proportion: see Chapter 10, Part I, D.

[79] 6QC; similar 10S; while 18S and 22S raised the serious effects immediate costs orders could have on litigants in person.

[80] Eg 10S.

[81] *Ibid*.

[82] Eg 21S, 27QC; and see below, fn 133 and accompanying text.

[83] 3S, 7QC.

[84] 26QC, 37B; similar 23S, 38B.

> Courts do sometimes produce rather curious decisions about what meanings words are capable of bearing. If I have a criticism it's that I think the courts are too feeble. I think they ought to be more interventionist. And I think they ought to be tougher because in truth I think the number of cases in which the meaning is genuinely ambiguous are much rarer than is sometimes thought.[85]

Several interviewees, however, said judges necessarily were limited by the jury's constitutional role.[86] As well, the test of what meanings are capable is not stringent.[87] So judges usually leave a wide range of meaning for trial.

Yet applications appear to occur in one-third of cases (and are considered far more frequently). This is because applications can dramatically alter the issues between the parties and 'fundamentally determine' how cases progress.[88] Part of a defence or claim can disappear if a meaning is ruled incapable. This can lead to substantial cost savings in preparing for trial, or even prompt an immediate settlement. But many applications will not see a meaning ruled out and the difference is often left until trial because both meanings are capable.[89]

B Precision in pleaded meanings

A second interview theme concerned the precision required in pleading meaning, and whether imprecise meanings were challenged. This appears to be a major issue in NSW.[90] But challenges to meanings, in terms of their form, appeared uncommon in London.[91] It was well known that, in theory, a pleaded meaning could be ambiguous or internally inconsistent. But challenges were rare:

> We are uncritical about the *form* of the defamatory meaning. . . . If it can't be potted on the basis that it's not defamatory or that it's not capable then it survives. Almost inevitably.[92]

Similarly, the concept of 'weasel words' does not appear to have the same currency.[93] The term came into use in NSW under Hunt J, and it has remained in common use.[94] It refers to words like *corrupt*, which on their own do not make a

[85] 8QC; similar 9B, 10S, 22S.

[86] Eg 16B, 24QC.

[87] 10S.

[88] 15B; similar 14B.

[89] Eg 20S.

[90] See Chapter 2, Part III, I, and Chapter 5, Part III, B.

[91] Eg 2S, 15B, 16B, 21S, 22S, 27QC, 28QC.

[92] 16B (emphasis added). Where such challenges were made, they were linked to the other side using non-specialist counsel: eg 15B, 16B.

[93] Eg 2S, 4QC, 6QC, 9B, 10S, 11S, 21S, 22S.

[94] Eg *Amalgamated Television Services v Marsden* (1998) 43 NSWLR 158, 163 (Hunt CJ at CL, Mason P and Handley JA agreed); *Vajda v John Fairfax Publications* [2001] NSWSC 306, [31] (David Kirby J); *Scott v Jones* [2002] NSWSC 210, [20] (Levine J); *Kermode v John Fairfax Publications* [2000] NSWSC 124, [6] (Studdert J).

party's case clear. A party must specify *in what way* the plaintiff was corrupt. In London, 'weasel words' is not a term that is used in reference to the pleading. Some interviewees used the term in reference to the contents of a publication; that is, a publication that uses a 'weasel word'.[95] In addition, the more recent NSW explication of the difference between inferences, implications and speculation (which is discussed in Chapter 2, Part III) was not in currency. (The NSW approach has been referred to subsequently in *Gatley*.[96]) When it was raised in interviews, an illustrative response was to ask why they worried about the different terms: 'Why do they do that? Inference is the term we always use.'[97] The word *corrupt*, for example, would be understood as an ordinary word that the jury could interpret,[98] and the claim would be understood by reference to the particulars.[99] In practice, the defence would welcome a general allegation from the claimant, because it would allow a very wide plea of justification.[100] As is explored below in Part III, justification (and the use of justification evidence to mitigate damages) appears to be the point at which meaning becomes central in litigation. In any event, the defence almost certainly will plead its own meaning, which could lessen its need to challenge the claimant's meaning.[101] But challenges for lack of precision then could arise in relation to *defence* meanings to narrow the scope of evidence the defence could adduce.[102]

C How a party is bound to a pleaded meaning

Respondents could add little to the leading case law about how parties are not *strictly* bound to pleaded meanings.[103] Basically, a lesser meaning can be found if it is within the same category of conduct as that pleaded. An example would be an accusation of stealing from a supermarket, which would include less serious conduct involving dishonesty such as reducing the items' prices and attempting to pay less for them.[104] As noted above,[105] it was suggested that this flexibility allows less meanings to be pleaded:

> You could hold the plaintiff to [the pleaded] meaning . . . but the net result would be that the plaintiff would then always plead the top meaning and the whole range of meaning. . . . You could also allow a jury to pick between the

[95] Eg 1B, 2S.

[96] Milmo and Rogers (2004) [3.16].

[97] IB.

[98] 3S.

[99] Eg 2S, 9B, 10S, 11S, 21S.

[100] Eg 6QC, 19B, 21S. A classic reference is to *Maisel v Financial Times (No 1)* (1915) 84 LJKB 2145.

[101] Eg 11S.

[102] Eg 18S.

[103] Eg *Slim v Daily Telegraph* [1968] 2 QB 157, 175 (Diplock LJ), 185 (Salmon LJ) and see Chapter 2, Part III, H.

[104] Eg 6QC; similar 7QC.

[105] See above, fn 53 and accompanying text.

> plaintiff's pleaded meaning and the defendant's pleaded meaning but being rigidly corralled into that. In my view, that is quite unrealistic because some journalism is . . . very ambiguous and so juries may well simply not think that either the plaintiff or the defendant has got it right.[106]

Respondents *also* were aware the jury may see the issue differently. The jury may be unconcerned with questions about whether parties are bound or not bound to pleaded meanings. Instead, respondents emphasised how pleaded meanings control what evidence is admissible, and evidence influences the jury far more than any question about the pleaded meanings themselves:

> The pleaded meanings define the issues in the case . . . and at trial affect what evidence gets in. But once . . . the jury goes back to give their verdict, meanings go out the window. They just say: 'This article accuses [the claimant] of being a "whatever". Is it right or not?' They don't sort of sit there and frantically go though [the] meanings.[107]

This would seem particularly likely when juries are asked for general verdicts, which is the usual English practice.[108]

D Defence pleading of meaning: Lucas-Box and Polly Peck

As discussed in Part I of Chapter 3, the cases of *Lucas-Box v News Group Newspapers*[109] and *Polly Peck v Trelford*[110] substantially changed the legal requirements for pleading meaning. Through Lucas-Box pleas, defendants must make clear the meanings they seek to justify (if the meanings are found to be conveyed). Polly Peck pleas can arise where publications make multiple allegations and claimants complain about only one. If the other allegations are distinct, defendants cannot raise them in defence. But if the allegations have a common sting, defendants can rely on their truth – that is, the truth of the common sting – in Polly Peck pleas. Important issues for the interviews concerned whether, in practice, Lucas-Box and Polly Peck pleas arise often and how they operate.

Lucas-Box pleas are very common.[111] That is, defendants do not accept *any* meaning pleaded by claimants, but plead their own meaning. Lucas-Box has 'revolutionised practice'[112] and it works well.[113] But some respondents did note the defendant *at times* would say the claimant's meaning is correct.[114] Often the difference between the parties is substantial (in terms of what evidence would be

---

[106] 8QC.

[107] 5S; similar 7QC. See also 20S, below fn 156 and accompanying text.

[108] See below, fn 170 and accompanying text.

[109] [1986] 1 WLR 147.

[110] [1986] QB 1000.

[111] Eg 6QC, 19B, or the pleas are made 'often': 32S.

[112] 4QC; similar 10S.

[113] Eg 1B, 3S, 6QC, 17S, 18S, 19B, 20S, 21S, 22S, 32S.

[114] Eg 8QC.

relevant under the pleas) and the Lucas-Box plea makes the difference more apparent.[115] Any problem with Lucas-Box lies in how defendants *still* try to avoid clarity[116] – the very thing the *Lucas-Box* decision sought to overcome.[117] Lawyers described Lucas-Box pleading as 'absolutely vital'[118] and 'so obvious, one wonders why it took so long to come in.'[119]

Polly Peck pleading is far less common.[120] The issue that respondents raised about Polly Peck concerned the degree of abstraction used to analyse a publication.[121] Because of the way in which this can vary, lawyers see Polly Peck as somewhat less straightforward to apply than Lucas-Box:

> Common sting? Well I think that's a difficult concept to apply because ultimately every libel has a common sting. In other words, someone . . . has acted in a way that is injurious to reputation. So there's always the problem of working out at what degree do you fix the common sting. And I don't think that in practice you can be ever quite sure where the judge or court is going to fix that line.[122]

Polly Peck, however, is supported by the profession.[123] This issue drew strong responses, and interviewees were *not* prompted by reference to Australian criticism in *Chakravarti v Advertiser Newspapers*.[124] The comments of Brennan CJ and McHugh J, described in Chapters 2 and 3, were raised only after respondents had commented on the English situation. There was no support for Australian doubts about Polly Peck's efficacy. In addition, the principles in Polly Peck and Lucas-Box are seen as being closely related in England. And the Australian comments are not *necessarily* limited to Polly Peck pleas – they have not been limited in that way in case law developments since *Chakravarti* that are discussed in Part I of Chapter 9. Respondents suggested the 'High Court comments sound very, very old fashioned'.[125] They would think it strange if Polly Peck pleading was removed from English law.[126] There is a danger of claimants 'picking and choosing' too much about what they sue on.[127] Polly Peck addresses this danger.

---

[115] Eg 4QC.

[116] Eg 4QC, 5S.

[117] *Lucas-Box v News Group Newspapers* [1986] 1 WLR 147, 152 (Ackner LJ for CA), and see Chapter 3, Part I, K.

[118] 24QC.

[119] 22S; similar 24QC.

[120] Eg 5S, 9B, 22S. It also appears to be a type of pleading point that solicitors may leave to counsel: eg 18S.

[121] This accords with the point made by Butler (2000).

[122] 6QC; similar 15B, 24QC, 25S.

[123] Eg 3S, 6QC, 7QC, 9B, 10S, 14B, 15B, 25S, 33S, 34S.

[124] (1998) 193 CLR 519.

[125] 9B.

[126] 1B, 2S, 6QC.

[127] 3S, similar 9B.

> What you're basically saying is, I've read the paper today and it said this, this and this about me . . . and I want some money. Now it seems to me eminently reasonable that you can look at the totality. . . . If you actually think about the tort and . . . the effect on reputation, people who've read those eight lines have also read the other eight lines. . . . I think [Polly Peck is] common sense.[128]

That is, there must be cases with a common sting, which defendants should be able to rely on.[129]

Although Polly Peck pleading is not litigated as often as Lucas-Box, it was seen to influence practice significantly because claims are rarely brought if they would allow Polly Peck pleas by defendants.[130] Finally, an English change may be important for handling Polly Peck and Lucas-Box claims, which is discussed further in Chapter 9. Under the *Civil Procedure Rules*, courts can exclude *relevant* evidence by citing the overriding interests of justice.[131] And proportionate methods must be adopted for dealing with disputes.[132] So even if defendants succeed in arguing that a wide meaning is capable of arising, for example under Polly Peck, the court has greater power to limit the admission of evidence to control potential misuse of such defence pleas.

E Particulars, evidence and defence meanings

Interlocutory challenges to Lucas-Box meanings are assessed in relation to the particulars of justification.[133] This means a defence meaning may be ruled out not because the article is incapable of bearing the meaning, but because the particulars of justification are incapable of *sustaining* the meaning.[134] The particulars determine the scope of evidence that can be adduced. And evidence is a very strong factor in Lucas-Box and Polly Peck pleading as well as in challenges to those meanings.[135] Defendants can seek to use a Lucas-Box meaning because they want to adduce damning evidence in justification,[136] and to affect the scope of disclosure.[137]

> When I get a claim, I would have a look at that article and do two things. One is I would form my own view [about its meaning], as any person in the world

[128] 10S; similar 7QC, 25S, 33S, 34S.

[129] Eg 6QC, 15B.

[130] 14B; similar 6QC, 20S.

[131] 21S; similar 26QC.

[132] 28QC.

[133] 26QC.

[134] Eg 21S emphasised this point.

[135] Eg 16B and 31S immediately linked the question of *any* interlocutory disputes about meaning to disputes about justification and fair comment; that is, to challenges to defence meanings.

[136] Eg 4QC, 5S, 7QC, 8QC, 16B, 20S.

[137] 5S, 18S.

> would. . . . And the second thing I'd do is [ask] what meaning can I extract out of it which is most helpful to my clients. The two things are often quite different.[138]

The situation follows from the limits on admissibility of evidence of bad reputation under *Scott v Sampson*[139] and *Pamplin v Express Newspapers*.[140] It is a 'grave reality' for defendants that meaning is affected by evidence.[141]

> Defendants will plead a lot wider but that's not because they think they need to establish those meanings for the meaning's sake. They're using it as a gateway to evidence. . . . So you get this contrast between [the] defendant's meaning, which tends to be a lot more verbose but only because it's the gateway to evidence, and the claimant's meaning, which is succinct, punchy and high in order to sell it to a jury.[142]

Thus a major reason lawyers differ about meaning may not be any complexity with meaning per se. At least within defamation law, the test for meaning is simple and refers to ordinary understandings, so important theoretical questions are bracketed out and play no explicit role in defamation doctrine. Instead, lawyers may differ about meaning because of their concern with justification. Claimants seek to plead a short, sharp and memorable meaning[143] that cannot be proved true – which may not be the most plausible meaning to arise from the publication. And defendants seek to plead a similar but broader and less damaging meaning that will allow them to adduce damaging evidence they have about the claimant. How the different jurisdictions deal with this sort of tension – and the tactical excesses of each side – is a central aspect of this book.

It should be noted that fair comment appeared to be far less significant in practice. A reasonably common suggestion was that juries do not understand the legal rules about fair comment, and focus instead on whether a publication's underlying facts are true.[144] That is, fair comment operates as a form of justification. A 'pure' fair comment case – one without a closely related justification defence – is rare.

F The trial stage for determining meaning: the Marks & Spencer approach

A settlement was reached early in the 1998 trial of *Marks & Spencer v Granada Television*.[145] At the start of the hearing, the judge asked the jury to decide the meaning that a current affairs program conveyed after viewing it and hearing

[138] 20S.

[139] (1882) 8 QBD 491.

[140] [1988] 1 WLR 116 note, and see Chapter 3, Part I, B.

[141] 21S.

[142] 16B.

[143] Eg see above, fns 41 and 58 and accompanying text.

[144] 1B, 3S, 10S, 18S, 19B; similar 21S.

[145] (Unreported, Popplewell J, QBD, 23 February 1998). See Chapter 2, Part III, C.

brief submissions from counsel. In *Marks & Spencer*, the claimant pleaded a meaning of *knowledge* of discreditable conduct involving child labour. The defence responded with a Lucas-Box meaning that the claimant *should have known* about the conduct *but did not know*. The *Marks & Spencer* approach of determining meaning early in a trial received relatively widespread coverage.[146] The case seems to have been praised by many lawyers then,[147] and some respondents still supported it.[148] They suggested that early determinations of meaning may prompt settlements as well as more closely mirror the legal test that seeks the impression of ordinary recipients of the publication. Under *Marks & Spencer*, the jury can 'decide on meaning as the original viewer or reader would', without hearing all the background evidence, which must be influential.[149]

But other respondents, and not only defendant lawyers, were pleased that *Marks & Spencer* had not been used frequently.[150] They could see good aspects to the approach, given how meaning was central to the case: 'the parties had a libel action because they didn't agree about what the program meant.'[151] These respondents, however, remained concerned for defendants under the *Marks & Spencer* approach. Three main reasons were suggested. First, a central weakness that respondents saw in *Marks & Spencer* was how it allowed the jury to respond with its own meaning.[152] In the actual case, the jury returned with a meaning somewhere between the two parties' pleaded meanings in content and seriousness, but that meaning appeared internally inconsistent to the lawyers.[153] This would have made the rest of trial very difficult to run. The case was 'embarrassing' and showed 'lay people can't draft defamation pleadings'.[154] Although a jury can determine for itself what meaning a publication conveys, under the traditional approach the meaning usually is not revealed because only a general verdict is sought from the jury. Second, *Marks & Spencer* was seen to alter the meaning that would be found by the jury. The jury would not hear all the defence evidence and it would decide meaning in a vacuum.

> You want to get all evidence in front of jury because they are affected by that in deciding meaning, you would never admit it but that's what happens.[155]

---

[146] See eg Shillito and Barendt (1999) 370, 371–73; Milmo (1998); Scott-Bayfield (1998) 231. The decision also was endorsed in obiter comments in *Shah v Standard Chartered Bank* [1999] QB 241, 265–66 (Hirst LJ).

[147] 13S, 25S (a media defence lawyer also suggested most lawyers approved at the time, but not the losing side), 27QC (only for cases with a clear conflict in meaning), 32S.

[148] 13S, 17S, 28QC (provided the competing meanings are clear), 31S.

[149] 31S.

[150] 20S, 23S, 24QC, 26QC, 32S, 38B.

[151] 38B.

[152] 16B, 19B, 26QC, 38B.

[153] The jury's meaning is reproduced in Shillito and Barendt (1999) 372.

[154] 26QC.

[155] 19B; similar 23S.

> One knows perfectly well conducting a case for the defence, that what you're really doing is battling for the jury's appreciation and sympathy. . . . If you've played it right and your evidence is good, you may have a difficulty about a particular meaning which the article could bear but . . . you gamble that the jury are not going to find that meaning because they don't like the claimant.[156]

Third, *Marks & Spencer* was seen to affect damages. At least, *Marks & Spencer* would affect damages if evidence in mitigation was not introduced in some other way.[157] Traditionally, the defence can adduce evidence to justify its Lucas-Box meaning. If the jury does not find the Lucas-Box meaning is conveyed, it can still take into account that evidence in relation to damages. The damages can be reduced dramatically by what the defence has proved true about the claimant. Under *Marks & Spencer*, the Lucas-Box evidence would be irrelevant if, at the outset, the jury had found for the claimant's meaning. Thus defendants dislike the idea of *Marks & Spencer* – it could exclude defence evidence significant for reducing damages.[158] In the *Marks & Spencer* case itself, however, it was agreed that the defence could have adduced the Lucas-Box style of evidence and the jury could have been instructed to consider it only in relation to damages. But if the defence adduced evidence on a meaning already rejected by the jury, it would run a great risk of aggravating damages. And in any event, admitting this type of evidence would remove any benefit that *Marks & Spencer* may offer in terms of shortening trials.[159] This was one area where the *HRA 1998* was predicted to affect questions relevant to meaning. Views varied about the Act's probable effects on defamation law in general. Some respondents doubted the *HRA 1998* would have any significant effect.[160] But the more common view supported two areas of change: privacy and defamation defences. That is, respondents correctly predicted that privacy-style remedies would develop in the general law,[161] and they suggested that defamation defences would develop from *Reynolds'* qualified privilege to a form of wider public interest defence.[162] One point, however, was indirectly important for meaning. It was suggested the rule in *Scott v Sampson* could breach provisions in the *European Convention on Human Rights and Fundamental Freedoms* for fair trials.[163] So defendants who were prevented from presenting evidence in mitigation of damages might successfully argue that their trial had not been fair under the *European Convention.*

It is worth noting that respondents generally and the lawyers involved in *Marks & Spencer* did not appear to have any knowledge of NSW practice from the

---

156 20S.

157 6QC, 8QC, 9B, 16B, 32S.

158 5S, 20S, 33S, 34S. Of course, if a justification defence fails and is determined to have been made improperly, it can aggravate damages.

159 6QC.

160 Eg 15B, 24QC, 38B.

161 See eg Kenyon and Richardson (2006).

162 Eg 1B, 5S, 10S, 23S, 25S, 26QC, 28QC, 31S, 38B.

163 Eg 8QC, 38B; see ECHR Art 6, opened for signature 4 November 1950, 213 UNTS 221 (entered into force 3 June 1952), and *Scott v Sampson* (1882) 8 QBD 491.

early 1990s (discussed in Part III of Chapter 2), which allowed a jury to determine meaning at a trial's outset.[164] Similarly, knowledge of its replacement by the s 7A procedure under the NSW *Defamation Act 1974* was very slight.[165] All that suggests the English development in *Marks & Spencer* occurred quite independently of NSW judgments and legislative reform.

G Presenting the test for defamatory meaning to the jury

Almost all respondents suggested the tests for what a publication means and whether it is defamatory are presented to the jury in a simple fashion.[166] For example, the approach of a case like *Mapp v News Group Newspapers*[167] would be used, but stripped of its legal language.[168] The presentation would be short and put in more general terms than the standard legal texts.[169] The jury would be told the parties' rival meanings and that they could determine their own meaning, provided it was within a similar subject area. Defamation jury questionnaires have long been avoided in England,[170] but they are less rare under the *Civil Procedure Rules*. Now the jury *may* be given questions to answer about what meaning was conveyed, whether it was defended, and what damages (if any) should be awarded,[171] but this is not normal practice.

Respondents varied about one aspect of the test for what is defamatory. That concerned how a jury would be directed if the claimant was accused of socially controversial action, for example, conducting legal abortions.[172] Would the test of 'right-thinking person'[173] be applied so the jury would have to arrive at society's supposed *singular* opinion about the question, when a jury would know that actual opinions about abortion varied? The question largely is academic: there very rarely is any real question about whether a pleaded meaning is defamatory.[174] This means interviewees could provide little relevant information about what

---

164 Eg 2S, 3S, 4QC, 24QC, 26QC, 38B. These interviewees included two lawyers involved in the case. Only one respondent, who was not involved in the case, had current knowledge of that NSW approach: 28QC.

165 Eg 2S, 10S, 33S, 34S, 35S had no knowledge of s 7A. Only 8QC had any relatively detailed knowledge of the s 7A approach.

166 Eg 1B, 7QC, 8QC, 14B, 16B, 23S. Only one respondent solicitor (21S) suggested a legalistic approach was used and that the tests were 'always presented very legalistically, they just trot out the tests' from the cases.

167 [1998] QB 520.

168 16B.

169 1B, 7QC.

170 Eg 19B.

171 3S; similar 7QC.

172 This example was raised in interviews, drawing on the NSW case of *Hepburn v TCN Channel Nine* [1983] 2 NSWLR 682. Another example, raised by most respondents, would concern an allegation of homosexuality; see below, fn 183.

173 *Sim v Stretch* [1936] 2 All ER 1237, 1240, and see Chapter 2, Part II, A.

174 Eg 8QC, 9B, 10S.

practice would be at trial, and their views varied about what jury direction would be likely. The more common response was that the test for what is defamatory does not allow for divided social opinion, and the jury would be told they must be unanimous.[175] The direction would indicate one moral view was required from the jury, namely, how would society react.[176] Respondents knew of no directions that had been given allowing for diverse opinions.[177] Some respondents recognised the law was happy to defer such problematic issues: juries are a 'life raft', enabling the law to avoid these judgments.[178] Other respondents went further and implicitly followed the US approach, which considers the views of a substantial (or respectable) section of society to be sufficient for an allegation to be defamatory.[179] For example, one very experienced litigator said:

> Cases in which there is a controversy and reasonable opinion is sharply split into two? I don't think I have any experience of such cases but abortion is an obvious one. I should have thought that the jury would be directed that if it was considered disreputable by a substantial section of reputable opinion then it is defamatory.[180]

The opposite conclusion, however, was suggested by other interviewees. That is, socially controversial subject matter should lead a judge to rule that meanings are incapable of being defamatory.[181] Or, for similar reasons, the jury would decide it is not defamatory.[182]

A general and important point can be made about the varied responses to this issue. Interviewees *agreed* the issue would be avoided in practice by pleading, for example, that the claimant was hypocritical in conducting abortions.[183] But interviewees *differed* about what would happen in the hypothetical case. There is little reason for this to be surprising, given the issue does not appear to arise in English practice. But significantly, the degree of diversity in interviewees' views greatly exceeded the diversity for most topics. It suggests that for most topics respondents did relate, reasonably accurately, how defamation litigation is practised. At the least, for most topics this group of interviewees displayed a similar understanding of practice.

Two other points about the jury are noteworthy. First, it was suggested that jury members hold different opinions about a publication's meaning and its

---

175 Eg 6QC, 14B, 19B.

176 19B.

177 Eg 14B.

178 23S.

179 See eg Lidsky (1996) for a discussion of the US 'community segment' approach.

180 8QC.

181 7QC.

182 23S.

183 14B, 16B. The equivalent claim in relation to homosexuality was famously pleaded by Jason Donovan in his legally successful claim against a magazine: *Donovan v Logan and Wagadon (The Face magazine)* (Unreported, QBD, Drake J, 3 April 1992) and see eg Price and Duodu (2004) 579.

truth, but practitioners commonly believe these differences are accommodated in the jury room through jury members bargaining over what damages to award.[184] Second, the jury may not be aware from a trial's start that an issue about meaning exists between the parties.[185] The claimant will open its case and tell the jury its own pleaded meaning before introducing the publication into evidence. Only sometimes can defendants reply in their own opening and clarify that the publication's meaning is in issue.

IV INTERVIEWEES' VIEWS ABOUT REFORMS

Recent and possible future reforms were addressed in all interviews. Here, three aspects particularly relevant to meaning are discussed: summary disposal provisions of the *Defamation Act 1996* (and *Civil Procedure Rules* Pt 24); the roles of judge and jury; and other approaches to dealing with meaning, such as mediation.[186]

A Summary disposal provisions of the *Defamation Act 1996*

Sections 8–10 of the *Defamation Act 1996* create a process for summary disposal of defamation cases, which is discussed further in Chapter 10.[187] The sections began operation in April 2000, which was only several weeks before the 2000 interviews were conducted. Even so, some respondents *did* have experience with a hearing involving them, or were considering arguments to be made in the near future. Not surprisingly, many respondents limited their remarks, saying it was too early to know much about the sections.[188] And it must be noted that the brief comments made here about the provisions are of less contemporary relevance than the rest of this chapter's material. There generally were divergent views as to whether the summary disposal provisions would be quick and cheap,[189] and whether they would be used often by claimants or defendants.[190] Several

[184] Eg 6QC, 7QC, 9B, 23S.

[185] Eg 9B.

[186] Other notable changes were *CPR* Pt 36, the *CPR*'s general effect on costs, and Conditional Fee Agreements; for contemporary comments on which see Shillito and Barendt (2000) 394–96.

[187] See Chapter 10, Part I, D.

[188] 10S, 11S, 19B, 24QC, 31S, 32S, 38B.

[189] Eg 1B suggested the provisions would not be quick or cheap because parties would fight against their use; 4QC supported this in terms of media defendants' opposition to court-ordered apologies under *DA 1996* (UK) s 9(1), or orders to publish summaries of courts' reasons under s 9(2); 2S suggested the procedure could become a mini-trial in itself. Others, eg 24QC, thought the provisions may reduce costs and in that way were a worthy reform attempt.

[190] Eg 38B, 4QC suggested claimants were not 'gold-diggers' and would welcome the speedy vindication the provisions offered. But others, eg 6QC, 11S, disagreed and said the £10,000 damages limit would deter claimants from using them. Similar variation existed for whether defendants would like the provision.

respondents noted the first case involving the provisions concerned a privilege dispute.[191] The argument in that case, *James Gilbert v MGN*,[192] concerned whether a newspaper article was privileged. Eady J held it was not privileged and the case was suitable for summary disposal because the defendant had no real prospect of success. It would seem the provisions were thought more likely to be used in these situations, than to resolve disputes about meaning.[193] That is, the provisions allow a judge to determine meaning, but it was unclear whether this would be done except where there was no substantial difference between the parties about meaning.

The interviews were conducted when both the summary disposal provisions and the *Civil Procedure Rules'* Pt 24 summary judgment provisions were thought to be available in defamation without any restriction.[194] While some doubts were expressed about how the two 'legislative juggernauts'[195] would work together, a reasonably common view was that Pt 24 would be used more often.[196] Unlike summary disposal, it did not limit damages to £10,000. For claimants at least, there seemed to be little attraction in summary disposal. In any event, a more activist role by judges was expected to develop under the *Civil Procedure Rules*.[197]

It also is notable that far more concerns were raised about conditional fee agreements in the 2003 interviews. Conditional fee agreements (CFAs) allow successful claimants' lawyers to recover up to double their usual legal fees.[198] Serious criticisms have been raised by media layers that this leaves defendants in an invidious position: they can choose to settle claims quickly, whatever they believe about the claims' merits, or risk facing very substantial legal fees.[199] Strong arguments, however, can be put about the importance of conditional fees in promoting access to law.[200] The issue is returned to in Chapter 10.[201]

---

191 Eg 3S, 32S, 7QC.

192 [2000] EMLR 680.

193 Eg 3S, 7QC, 27QC.

194 In December 2000, the Court of Appeal limited the use of Pt 24 in defamation to questions within the judge's role in *Safeway Stores v Tate* [2001] QB 1120; see also Chapter 10, Part I, D.

195 Several interviewees used the words of Eady J in *James Gilbert v MGN* [2000] EMLR 680, 685.

196 Eg 1B, 8QC, 26QC; cf 25S, who predicted the *DA 1996* (UK) provisions would end up being the only ones available to use where there were issues of fact to be determined.

197 Eg 26QC, 38B.

198 See *Courts and Legal Services Act 1990*, c 41, s 58, and *Access to Justice Act 1999*, c 22. They can be used by defendants, although this appears rare, see eg Price and Duodu (2004) [34.23].

199 For an overview see Shillito (2004).

200 See eg Price and Duodu (2004) [34.18] and [34.25]; Price (2005).

201 See Chapter 10, Part I, D.

B Possible roles of judge and jury

The jury's role in defamation is controversial: some respondents thought having defamation juries was 'utterly *absurd*',[202] while others said juries were 'best placed and most qualified to decide meaning'.[203] But respondents quite commonly suggested that juries find more serious meanings to be conveyed than judges would find.[204] Thus a move to judge-alone trials was thought to benefit defendants.[205] It was thought unlikely that juries *would* be removed entirely from defamation claims,[206] even if their role may be marginalised and limited.[207] That is, some respondents suggested there was a trend to judge-alone defamation hearings,[208] at least for less serious claims.

Changing the usual trial mode to judge-alone would allow determinations of meaning early in a dispute. It was thought that this would simplify trial preparation enormously and make it far less costly.[209] 'If there's no jury then the whole meaning issue becomes much more straightforward.'[210]

> Personally I think it would be a lot better if you simply had a judge deciding these cases and . . . especially if you had a judge assigned to the whole case, the judge could say what the meaning was. . . . You'd get your decision on meaning and then you could take the case further forward if you wanted to do so.[211]

This view was not without dissent, which did not only relate to the jury's constitutional role under *Fox's Libel Act*.[212] Some saw the jury as a key element in keeping defamation doctrine and practice as simple as possible. Juries avoid the law on meaning becoming even more complex,[213] because in the end everything will be presented to the jury. This issue will be returned to in Part I of Chapter 10, particularly in relation to lessons that can be drawn from the NSW situation, where meaning appears to be dealt with far less simply.

C Other approaches to dealing with meaning

Mediation or expert determinations of defamation disputes have been rare in London.[214] Some media companies, notably the *Times*, have schemes to encourage

---

[202] 20S (emphasis in original).

[203] 16B.

[204] 1B, 5S, 10S; similar 9B.

[205] 33S.

[206] 20S, 22S.

[207] 14B, 32S.

[208] Eg 16B, 32S, 38B.

[209] Eg 1B, 24QC, 28QC, 33S.

[210] 26QC.

[211] 7QC.

[212] 32 George 3 c 60; and see Chapter 2, Part I, H.

[213] 1B.

[214] Eg 25S had only one experience in defamation arbitration in a career dating from 1984.

such dispute settlement. But few interviewees had personal experience with alternative resolution methods. Some claimant lawyers were dubious about the value of pursuing these avenues: 'We'd be very loath to do mediation under any circumstances and to justify that paranoia is difficult. I just think we'd be against it.'[215] They saw the jury as independent, non-legalistic and responsive to all the shades of meaning that could arise from a publication: 'Meaning is so important, I would want someone independent' to determine it.[216] But one of the few lawyers with direct experience of mediation had an improved view of it after successfully using mediation, 'having been a person utterly opposed to it'.[217] Some media lawyers suggested this aversion to non-court resolution was really because claimants believed a jury would treat them more sympathetically. That is, juries' supposed aversion to media companies would help claimants. In any event, when mediation was pursued it was because of reasons quite separate to meaning, such as maintaining a litigant's privacy.[218]

V CONCLUSION

This chapter has reported on aspects of English defamation litigation that are particularly relevant to a publication's meaning. It has suggested that relatively few meanings are pleaded in England, but defence pleading of meaning is common. Interlocutory disputes about meaning may be more likely in relation to these defence meanings than for plaintiff meanings, but they do not appear to be particularly common (especially compared with the NSW practice explored in the next chapter). These defence meanings are important for determining the evidence that can be adduced by defendants and that evidence is a central issue in litigation. It appears to be the major reason that meaning can be understood by defamation lawyers as being both simple *and* complex. Evidence influences juries more than the precise words that have been used to plead the publication's meaning. This especially is true given the traditional use of general verdicts, rather than jury questionnaires in England. The approach, however, appears to sit awkwardly with that tried in *Marks & Spencer* – and evaluating it and the NSW approach under s 7A of the *Defamation Act 1974* will be an important topic for Chapter 10. Before then, Chapters 5 and 6 report on fieldwork research into defamation litigation in NSW and Victoria related to meaning, before qualified privilege is examined in Chapter 7 and the US situation investigated in Chapter 8.

---

215 18S.

216 7QC.

217 20S.

218 17S.

– 5 –

MEANING: NEW SOUTH WALES DEFAMATION PRACTICE

> [I]t must be borne in mind that the conduct of defamation litigation in this state is straight-jacketed by the undue technicality that attends the formulation of imputations.[1]

> I suspect that [s 7A of] the Act is part of an unstated culture which is not altogether easy for the uninitiated to appreciate.[2]

> The next thing [members of the jury] is to repeat the battle lines as they apply to each of the three articles. Shortly stated, the plaintiff says the articles say 'did it'. The defendant says the articles go no further than raise questions as to whether or not the plaintiff 'did it'. Substantially different concepts. Those arguments from each side apply to the three articles.[3]

This chapter reports on fieldwork conducted in Sydney that investigated how a publication's meaning is dealt with in NSW defamation litigation and examines the 'unstated culture' of NSW defamation practice. There is a common perception in the legal literature that the 7A trial procedure in NSW (outlined in Part I of Chapter 2) is unusual in its effects and approach. The opening quotations suggest the NSW system *is* different, but also allude to how the issue for the jury resembles the one that arises at common law. The first quotation underlines the perception that more difficulties exist in NSW, especially in pre-trial procedures, and comes from a judge with very extensive defamation experience. The second quotation is from a judge without extensive defamation experience who echoes the common perception that 7A trials are peculiar. But the third quotation is interesting for underlining how the task facing the jury has similarities to the task at common law – under each approach, parties tend to disagree about a publication's meaning and the jury must decide between them, even though the context in which it decides is very different in NSW.

The quotations also suggest two major legal differences from England and Victoria that underlie this investigation of NSW practice. The first concerns pre-trial

[1] *Hughes v Seven Network* (Unreported, NSW SC, Levine J, 13 November 1998) (also BC9806166, 6) (Cases identified by BC followed by a seven digit number are available on the subscription service LexisNexis Australia; see <www.lexisnexis.com.au>).

[2] *Cinivest v Yirandi Productions* [1999] Aust Defamation Reports [53,050] (Adams J).

[3] Transcript of Proceedings, *Whelan v John Fairfax Publications* (Unreported, NSW SC, Levine J and jury, 14 February 2001).

practice and especially the effect of s 9 of the *Defamation Act 1974* (NSW). The second is the 7A trial procedure, in which the jury determines questions about publication, identification, and defamatory meaning, while in a later hearing the judge determines everything else. This was a relatively recent development during the fieldwork and issues about 7A were prominent in practice. With these two differences in mind, this chapter discusses the matters that are central to meaning in defamation that have been raised in earlier chapters: namely, the way a party is bound to a pleaded meaning; the degree of specificity required in a pleaded meaning; whether, and how, defence meanings are pleaded and dealt with in litigation; and the stage of a dispute at which differences between the parties about meaning are dealt with. In the rest of the chapter, material from NSW practice is presented about these issues. The fieldwork included analysing court files for cases issued in 1998 and interviewing specialist defamation practitioners. Each area of research is outlined in Part I, before the court files are discussed in detail in Part II and the interviews are reported in Part III.

Briefly, six themes emerge about NSW practice. First, plaintiffs tend to plead a number of meanings, quite often at varied levels of seriousness. This is not surprising as the pleaded imputation is the cause of action under s 9 of the *Defamation Act 1974* (NSW). Second, the form of pleaded imputations is often an issue pre-trial: a high degree of specificity is required and challenges to the imputations' form appear routine. Third, the law says plaintiffs are held to their pleaded imputations, or to ones not different in substance. In practice this appears to operate so that plaintiffs are held to their imputations very closely. But the effect of this aspect of NSW law at trial remains unclear because there is little evidence about what juries make of the minimal instructions that are given to them about what 'not different in substance' means. Fourth, defendants virtually never agree with the plaintiff's imputations, but they very rarely plead contextual imputations (although this appears to have changed in the period since the fieldwork).[4] Defendants do not *plead* meaning at all, unlike the way that Lucas-Box pleas are commonplace in England and Victoria. So the field of dispute between the parties as regards meaning is not set out to the same degree in NSW pleadings. This is a surprising situation given the attention that pleading and imputations have received in NSW law, but it also can be seen to follow from s 9, which encourages the plaintiff to plead a range of meanings. Fifth, truth and comment appear to be rare defence pleas. Chapter 4 has suggested that pleading justification or fair comment, especially under a Lucas-Box plea, is the point at which meaning becomes *central* in English litigation because evidence to support the plea can be used to mitigate damages irrespective of whether the defence succeeds (so long as the plea did not improperly aggravate the harm). In NSW, the situation is different. Evidence of an imputation's truth can be used to mitigate damages,[5] but the imputation-centred approach in NSW means only

[4] See below, Part III, C.

[5] Unlike the situation at common law, this evidence is admissible whether or not justification is pleaded, see *DA 1974* (NSW) s 47, and *Singleton v Ffrench* (1986) 5 NSWLR 425, 443.

evidence of the truth of the *plaintiff's* imputation is admissible in relation to mitigation.[6] And NSW practice suggests little breadth is given to the concept of 'substantial truth'.[7] So evidence that might be used to mitigate damages is tightly contained, which in turn focusses the defence even more closely on the plaintiff's pleaded imputations and pre-trial battles to attack them. Sixth, the jury's confined role under the 7A procedure and splitting the tribunal of fact between jury on meaning and judge on defences has accentuated these peculiarities about NSW's imputation-centred approach.

Before examining these six themes more fully, it is important to note that developments in NSW law appear to have occurred since *Greek Herald v Nikolopoulos*.[8] In particular, challenges to the form of pleaded imputations could be expected to have reduced *marginally* in frequency and technicality under these developments. The developments appear to move NSW practice slightly from the imputation-centred approach described in this chapter. It is valuable to understand the long-standing earlier approach under the *Defamation Act 1974* (NSW) – both to appreciate the importance of these types of developments for NSW and to consider the lessons that should be drawn for other jurisdictions from its law and practice. The developments and possible lessons are explored in Chapter 10.[9] As discussed there, the lessons would have added Australian importance if proposed uniform defamation law is enacted. Then, NSW courts as well as other jurisdictions would have the opportunity to appreciate what can be gained under the broadly common law approach of the proposed uniform law. First, the detail of NSW practice as it relates to publication's meaning is described in this chapter.

I RESEARCH SAMPLES AND METHODS

A Court files for defamation claims

The NSW Supreme Court Registry is not open to the public.[10] Permission to access files was obtained from the court's Chief Executive Officer, but information about specifically named cases is included in this chapter only when it relates to material discussed in open court and available though public judgments. Registry records suggest that 68 defamation cases were issued in the NSW Supreme Court during 1998. Another six cases were identified through diaries for the Supreme Court's Defamation List, but these six cases' files showed they contained no defamation claims. These figures correspond closely with those supplied by the Supreme Court in a statistical summary of defamation

---

[6] Eg *Waters v John Fairfax Publications* [2005] NSWSC 394 and see Chapter 2, Part I.

[7] *DA 1974* (NSW) s 47 allows evidence to be given of an imputation's truth or substantial truth.

[8] (2002) 54 NSWLR 165.

[9] See Chapter 10, Part I, A.

[10] For the treatment of access to court files in various Australian jurisdictions see Butler and Rodrick (2004) 207–12; Walker (2000) 463–79.

filings during the years 1990–2000, which listed 74 files for 1998, that is, the total number identified through the court diaries.[11] Although 68 cases is less than might be expected in comparison to Victoria, it is thought that almost every case has been identified. The Registry's court diaries and computerised records were consulted for 1998 and 1999. Given the Defamation List's existence, it is very unlikely that cases would have commenced in 1998 and not have come before the List by the end of 1999, nor appeared on the Registry's computerised records. Practitioners suggested that in 1998 relatively few defamation cases were run in the NSW intermediate court, the District Court. That had changed somewhat by the time of the interviews, with the Supreme Court transferring more cases and the District Court's jurisdictional limit having become $750,000. The decision to concentrate here on the Supreme Court is similar to the conduct of the ACT's Community Law Reform Committee. It began its 1990s investigation into defamation by examining the procedural rules for the ACT Supreme Court, Magistrates' Court and Small Claims Court, but concentrated its research on the Supreme Court because most claims were issued there and the court had more detailed information available.[12] All this meant the District Court Registry was consulted only in relation to six cases that were issued in the Supreme Court during 1998 and later transferred to the District Court. Overall, the sample of 68 Supreme Court files is taken to illustrate relatively recent NSW practice. Interviews with practitioners conducted in 2000 and 2003, and discussion of doctrinal developments in Chapter 10, help to highlight subsequent changes in practice.

The court files for the 68 cases were consulted at length. The files were accessed primarily during 2000 and again briefly in 2001. Information was taken from the files for the period ending 31 December 2000. All cases had been issued two to three years earlier and had been through common interlocutory activity. Only 26 of the files remained open at the end of 2000, and the period under study was extended for these open files by referring to judgments delivered during 2001. Information from the files was extracted into word-processed documents, and photocopies were taken of relevant pleading documents. These records, combined with the extensive availability of judgments in digital form,[13] and transcripts of 7A hearings that were supplied by some lawyers, mean a detailed picture of pleading practices and challenges was built up.

B Interviews with specialist lawyers

To supplement the extensive court records, 10 interviews were conducted in Sydney with specialist defamation solicitors, barristers and one judge during

---

[11] Unpublished correspondence, on file.

[12] Community Law Reform Committee of the ACT (1995) [180].

[13] Through the NSW 'Lawlink' site <www.lawlink.nsw.gov.au>, the 'Australasian Legal Information Institute' site <www.austlii.edu.au>, and commercial services, eg see above fn 1.

Table 5.1 – Sydney Interviewee Sample

Interviewee	Subject	5–10 years' libel practice	10–20 years' libel practice	20–30 years' libel practice	More plaintiff work	More defence work	Even plaintiff and defence work
39	SC			•			•
40	SC		•			•	
41	S	•				•	
42	B		•				•
43	S					•	
44	SC		•				•
45	SC		•				•
46	B		•				•
47	SC			•			•
48	B		•				•

Note: The numbers continue from the 38 London interviewees.

S–Solicitor; B–Barrister; SC–Senior Counsel or Queen's Counsel. (Both the titles of SC and QC are in use in Sydney, but for simplicity and to promote anonymity only one abbreviation is used.)

November 2000 (see Table 5.1).[14] The interviewees included the judge in charge of the Supreme Court's Defamation List, leading barristers, and solicitors from prominent Sydney defamation practices. Interviewees were approached after searching the Supreme Court files and consulting listing services such as *The Legal 500*.[15] As in London, a further 16 interviews were conducted in Sydney in 2003, examining issues about meaning and qualified privilege.[16] The findings about qualified privilege are discussed in Chapter 7. For reasons of simplicity, however, the 2003 interviews are not drawn on in detail in this chapter. But it is worth emphasising the general point that the later interviews supported the findings discussed here and that, in broad terms, the findings can be understood as relating to the larger group of 26 interviews.

Defamation was a sizable part of every interviewee's practice, but for most it formed approximately half their work. For none of the Sydney practitioners was it over 70 per cent of their work. This suggests Sydney has less concentrated

[14] Two interviewees were women.

[15] See <www.icclaw.com>.

[16] Four of the 2003 interviewees also had been interviewed in 2000.

practices than existed in England, where approximately two-thirds of interviewees reported defamation law as more than 70 per cent of their practice (although that appears to have reduced with defamation claims lessening markedly under the *Civil Procedure Rules*). The vast majority of Sydney interviewees had between 10 and 20 years' defamation experience. And a similar majority reported acting approximately equally for plaintiffs and defendants, with the remainder mainly acting for defendant media companies. Each interview lasted approximately one hour. Almost all interviews were audiotape recorded and later transcribed. For one interview, handwritten notes were taken during the meeting in accordance with the interviewee's preference. As for the London interviews, interviewees are referred to by number along with their professional role: solicitor (S), barrister (B) or Senior Counsel or Queen's Counsel (SC).[17] Again, quotations are direct transcriptions from interviews. As described in Chapter 4, the semi-structured interviews proceeded through five areas: the interviewee's background, plaintiff pleading of meaning, defence pleading of meaning, the trial stage and law reform.

II INFORMATION FROM THE COURT FILES

The court files, and judgments relating to them, reveal material about the style of pleading and challenges to imputations, the degree of specificity needed in pleading, defence pleading of meaning and the stage of a dispute at which meaning is decided. This Part discusses general information about these matters from the files, before illustrating significant issues by referring more closely to five files. The files suggest that:

(a) Plaintiffs usually plead multiple imputations, often covering a range of seriousness.

(b) Pre-trial challenges to imputations, or repleading after negotiation, occurs in nearly one in two cases. (But the complexities of NSW law would allow even more challenges to be made.)

(c) Challenges often become very detailed about the form in which an imputation is pleaded and, unlike in England, challenges are reasonably common when plaintiffs plead general imputations.

(d) Defence pleadings related to meaning are rare, with truth being pleaded in nearly one in six defences, contextual truth being pleaded in one in eight defences, and comment being pleaded in one in five defences.

(e) There is a marked contrast between technical interlocutory challenges to imputations and the discussion of meaning in 7A hearings.

(f) Splitting the tribunal of fact under 7A has increased defendants' concerns about imputations that may be ambiguous, which would tend to encourage even more pre-trial fights about meaning.

[17] The judge is referred to as SC to avoid identification and to reflect prior experience.

Table 5.2 – NSW Court File Imputations

Number of Imputations	1	2	3	4	5	>5
Number of Files	2	15	14	13	17	15

A General information

Three points can be made by reference to the entire sample of NSW files that relate to the number of imputations pleaded, pre-trial challenges to imputations and defence pleadings relevant to meaning. First, for the purpose of considering the number of imputations pleaded, each newspaper article, radio broadcast or similar act of publishing material can be treated as a separate 'publication' (with publication not being used in its technical defamation law sense). On that basis, the 68 files dealt with 76 publications, in relation to which 312 imputations were pleaded. There was a range of one to 13 imputations pleaded for each publication, a mean of 4.1 imputations per publication, and a median of 4. Table 5.2 shows the spread of imputations pleaded.

It was quite common for three, four, five or more imputations to be pleaded. This certainly appears to be higher than in England, although direct comparison is impossible given the lack of similar English court records for the period. But it clearly accords with comments from the London barrister who had NSW experience that fewer meanings are pleaded in England (discussed in Part II of Chapter 4).

Second, in relation to pre-trial hearings, many files showed one or more substantial hearings about the pleaded meanings. The hearings are commonly identified as 'form and capacity' hearings, with 'form' referring to the form of the pleading (such as a lack of specificity) and 'capacity' referring to the capability of the pleaded imputation to arise from the publication or for it to be defamatory. Twenty-six of the 68 files showed a substantial hearing about meaning, and of those 26 there were multiple hearings in eight files (with five involving a Court of Appeal hearing).[18] In 22 of the 26 files, the hearing resulted in a change to the pleadings.[19] In another six files the pleaded meanings were changed without any hearing, with correspondence on file suggesting the changes followed negotiation between the parties. And in a further 22 files, pleaded meanings were not challenged even though a challenge would have been possible: in two of these 22 files, a challenge had been foreshadowed in correspondence on file, but the matter settled before any hearing occurred. In the remaining 14 of the total 68 files, no challenge was made and none appeared to be possible. The success

[18] Three files from these eight were consolidated into one case at a later point in the period under study.

[19] Of the remaining four files, in three the challenge to the pleading completely failed, but in one file it succeeded entirely because the publication had no capacity to convey a defamatory meaning.

rate in obtaining *changes* to pleaded imputations appears to be very high. And the 26 challenges, plus 6 negotiated changes to imputations without formal challenge, amounts to attacks on imputations in almost every second case. Challenges nearly always included a capacity argument, or that the publication was not capable of conveying the pleading imputation. These arguments rarely succeeded. But challenges to a pleaded imputation's form also were very common. In particular, the argument was made that the words chosen in the pleading did not attribute an act or condition to the plaintiff in a specific and unambiguous manner.

Third, in earlier chapters the importance of meaning was raised in relation to the defences of truth and comment. In the NSW files, defences of truth and comment were quite rare. A defence of any sort was filed in 34 of the 68 files. Truth was pleaded in just six files, and comment was pleaded in only seven files. In a mere four files were contextual imputations pleaded. By way of contrast, the s 22 defence of qualified privilege was pleaded in 29 of the 34 defences. This accords with the NSW Law Reform Commission's suggestion that the statutory qualified privilege defence under s 22 of the *Defamation Act 1974* (NSW) is pleaded frequently, often without realistic hope of success.[20] It should be noted, however, that the practice was emerging during 1999 and 2000 of defendants pleading a substantial defence only after a 7A hearing. This probably happened in some of the 26 files that remained open in December 2000 – the end of the period of court file analysis. And later case law suggests defendants began to plead more contextual imputations when filing defences after 7A hearings had occurred.[21]

The files also suggest figures about three further issues: the rate of settlements and trials within the two- to three-year period that the files had been open by the end of 2000, the time until settlement or judgment is obtained in NSW defamation matters and the length of hearings. First, out of the 68 files, 34 had settled without a 7A hearing and 12 had progressed to a 7A hearing by the end of 2000. Of those 12 files, two saw verdicts for the defendant at the 7A hearing, one progressed to a judge-alone hearing on the remaining issues, one settled, and eight files remained open. So 50 per cent of the files settled without a 7A hearing and approximately 18 per cent went to a 7A hearing. But the great majority of the files that went to 7A hearings remained open, meaning approximately 56 per cent of files had settled before or after a 7A hearing or obtained judgment. Second, matters took approximately 16 months to reach final disposal via a settlement or judgment. The figures ranged between two and 28 months, with a mean of 15.1 months and a median of between 16 and 17. Third, only one trial had proceeded to a judge-alone hearing by the end of 2000, which ran for five days (after an earlier two-day 7A hearing).[22] The 7A hearings ranged between one and three days, generally running for less than two full days.

---

[20] NSW Law Reform Commission (1993) [4.13] citing the empirical work by Sourdin (1990).

[21] See below, Part III, C.

[22] The five-day figure does not include a later hearing at which judgment was delivered.

B Examples from the files

Five files are used here to illustrate pre-trial and trial disputes about meaning. At times quite detailed descriptions are provided about the incidents – the peculiarities of NSW practice are shown through the minutiae of litigation. The examples consider: form and capacity challenges, especially the need for precision in drafting imputations; 7A hearings and the contrast they display to more technical pre-trial stages; the range of meanings plaintiffs tend to plead; and the effect of splitting the tribunal of fact under the 7A process.

1 Form and capacity challenges

As mentioned above, form and capacity challenges were common in NSW files. *Harvey v John Fairfax Publications*[23] illustrates a partially successful form and capacity challenge. The *Sydney Morning Herald* published an article about John Harvey on 20 September 1997 headed 'The Man Who Sank Elle'. In over 2,000 words, the article detailed some of Harvey's past business activities. The plaintiff pleaded five imputations – all were challenged unsuccessfully with capacity arguments, while three also were challenged on form. This resulted in two relatively minor changes being made to the imputations' form, although the changes may not have been insignificant at trial. The example shows how imputations are not necessarily read in ways to avoid technical challenges.

Consider this passage from the article:

> Ian Lumsden, general manager of the local Yass Shire Council says that Harvey was running about 1000 turkeys in a paddock adjacent to the hotel and 'it became a health issue because the residents got upset about the feathers blowing everywhere and turkeys . . . getting into the creek'. The council took him to court and 'we must have won because the turkeys disappeared'.[24]

The plaintiff pleaded an imputation in the form: 'the plaintiff, in his operation of a farm, placed public health at risk in so serious manner as to warrant him being sued by the local council'. The imputation alleged a *serious* health risk, and measured the degree of seriousness only by saying the risk warranted council action. The defendant attacked the use of 'serious' and said that councils may take action over 'relatively trivial matters',[25] so taking action was not a specific measure of seriousness. Bell J agreed this made the imputation ambiguous, which could lead to confusion about its meaning at trial. The imputation needed to be repleaded. She said the article could mean the plaintiff placed public health at risk in operating a farm, and the plaintiff was given leave to replead the imputation.[26] That is, 'serious' would have to go.

---

[23] [2000] NSWSC 337.

[24] *Ibid* [3] (Bell J).

[25] *Ibid* [4].

[26] *Ibid* [8]–[9].

Another imputation related principally to the following passage in the article:

> The turkeys, too, returned to rear their ugly heads. Hooper says that Harvey was in continual dispute with local tradespeople in the Yass area, and on one occasion a supplier obtained a garnish on his wages over some unpaid-for turkey feed.
>
> 'He had all sorts of excuses – the feed was not delivered; it was wet; it was full of weevils; he wasn't going to pay – but at the end of the day we convinced him it wouldn't look too good if it got into the media, and it was quietly settled.'[27]

The plaintiff pleaded this imputation: 'the plaintiff was a dishonest businessman who refused to pay his just debts'. The *capacity* challenge to this imputation is noteworthy. The defendant argued this was a general imputation being 'squeezed out of a specific incident'.[28] The argument was rejected by Bell J, who said the general imputation was capable of arising, in the whole article's context. Notably, this sort of imputation seems less likely to be challenged in England. A broader, general plea by a claimant would be seen to allow greater scope to introduce defence evidence in justification, which even if it failed to establish a defence could be used to mitigate damages. The imputation's *form* also was challenged. The defendant succeeded in arguing that it contained two imputations combined into one, that is, being a dishonest businessperson and refusing to pay one's debts.[29] It was held that each must be pleaded separately, although Bell J doubted the first one's capacity to arise. Thus a repleading could be expected in these terms: 'the plaintiff dishonestly refused to pay his just debts'.

What has been achieved by these changes? The first imputation has been reduced in seriousness. The plaintiff cannot plead that public health was at *serious* risk. This could be thought to affect the scope of damages. Perhaps it also could affect the viability of any justification defence. But more seems to have resulted from challenging the second imputation. The technicality of NSW's approach can be seen in how the court did not read the imputation, in the context of the publication, as saying the plaintiff is dishonest in business *only* in having refused to pay debts. The imputation was seen to raise a general allegation of dishonesty in business, and the defendant wanted to remove that general allegation. As to the case's later progress, none of the imputations (in an amended statement of claim) were found to be conveyed at a 7A hearing in August 2001. But the Court of Appeal ordered a new trial in relation to just one imputation, the first imputation considered above: 'That the plaintiff, in his operation of a farm, endangered public health.'[30] And the plaintiff's later attempt to plead 10 imputations for the second 7A hearing was rejected.[31]

---

[27] *Ibid* [24].

[28] *Ibid* [26].

[29] *Ibid* [29].

[30] *Harvey* [2003] NSWCA 70.

[31] *Harvey* [2004] NSWSC 188.

The files contained many other examples of challenges to the form of imputations, often to make them less general. Examples included successful challenges to simple pleas that the plaintiff was 'corrupt', 'greedy', or 'a sub-standard pharmacist' without the imputation containing any explanatory context or limitation. But the files also showed instances where challenges to such 'weasel words'[32] were not pursued. For example, imputations with the following bare words were not challenged: that the plaintiff was 'anti-social', 'a procrastinator', 'greedy', 'a Mafia godfather', or 'conducted himself in a disgraceful manner'. There appears to have been no deliberate tactical decision not to challenge these imputations in order to help the defence. Defence pleas of truth or comment were almost entirely absent from these files, even though all of them had defences pleaded. Truth was not pleaded in any of the files, and comment was raised in only one of those files by one defendant. (The second defendant omitted comment from an otherwise equivalent defence.) Generally, these files involved smaller law firms that did not appear elsewhere in the sample (suggesting they did not act frequently in defamation matters) and the files displayed little activity, often settling or being dismissed by the court after long periods of inactivity. Overall, however, the files suggest that challenges to general imputations are reasonably common, especially for actively fought cases.

2 *Pre-trial and 7A hearings compared*

Extensive challenges occurred in *Randwick Labor Club v Amalgamated Television Services*. The Randwick Labor Club was linked to a major political party, the Australian Labor Party (ALP), which at that time formed the NSW Government. As is common enough in NSW, the club was licensed to operate poker machines and they were a substantial source of revenue. The club and its directors sued after a TV news item suggested the club was being used as a Labor 'slush fund'. This is the transcript of the news item. Ann Sanders was the studio newsreader, Adam Walters was a news reporter, and Richard Bull was the NSW opposition gaming minister:

Ann Sanders:	A Sydney Club run by senior Labor Party figures may be charged with breaching licensing laws 13,000 times. The astonishing figure is being investigated by detectives who raided the Randwick Labor Club.
Adam Walters:	(Camera shots of Club from outside) It is not just another poker machine palace, it's as close as it gets to the New South Wales ALP's inner sanctum but the Labor Party's back rooms have been gate-crashed by the police investigating more than 13,000 alleged breaches of the *Liquor and Licensing Act*.

[32] See Chapter 4, Part III, B.

	(Single camera shot of photograph of all board members)
	(Close up camera shot of certain board members with names printed underneath)
	The Club's board reads like who's who of Labor Party number crunchers including right-wing power broker and former Upper House President, John Johnno Johnson and senior ALP strategist, Ken Murray.
Richard Bull:	If these alleged 13,000 breaches are to be found, then these Directors are going to have to . . . mount a . . . answer to a please explain.
Adam Walters:	The alleged breaches relate mainly to irregularities in record keeping and book work. Senior police have confirmed the Club continues to undergo audits and other checks by detectives from the Licensing Enforcement Agency.
	(Camera shots of NSW Premier [that is, political leader] Bob Carr meeting patrons)
	The Club's patrons include Premier Bob Carr – seen here revelling in his election victory at what's become the traditional venue for ALP celebrations.
	(Camera shots of documents)
	Official documents on election funding show that between November 1991 and January 1995 the Club donated $125,000.00 to the Labor Party.
Richard Bull:	It is obviously their slush fund Club in the eastern suburbs. This is in Bob Carr's heartland.
Adam Walters:	Adam Walters – Sydney Nightly News.[33]

The club and seven of its directors pleaded that six or seven meanings were conveyed in relation to each plaintiff. Two imputations are noteworthy here and both illustrate the need for specificity in NSW. The first imputation was originally in this form for the plaintiff directors: 'that each of the [plaintiffs] was a Director of a Club which was a slush fund Club for the Labor Party'.[34] It was challenged in an interlocutory hearing before Levine J.[35] The defence successfully argued the imputation did not attribute to the directors any knowledge of a slush fund, and

33 *Randwick Labor Club v Amalgamated Television Services* [1999] NSWSC 880, schedule A (ellipses in original).

34 *Ibid* [5], [6].

35 *Randwick Labor Club* (Unreported, NSW SC, Levine J, 12 June 1998) (also BC9804489).

so it lacked specificity. The plaintiffs were given leave to replead, which they did in this form: 'The plaintiff was a director of the [Club] whilst knowing it to be a slush fund Club for the Labor Party.' The second imputation was originally in this form: 'that each of the . . . plaintiffs . . . had concealed the activities of the Club as a slush fund Club for the Labor Party and had been found out in respect thereof'.[36] An argument about the imputation concerned the plaintiffs allegedly 'being found out' in respect of concealing the slush fund. This was imprecise in not explaining *who* had found them out. Levine J struck out the imputation with leave to replead. The imputation was changed to the form, 'The plaintiff as a director of the Randwick Labor Club was caught out by the police whilst trying to conceal a secret slush fund of tainted money which the Club had accumulated for the use of the Labor Party.'[37]

After an amended statement of claim was filed, another challenge on form and capacity was made.[38] The second of the above imputations was dealt with simply. It was capable of being conveyed by the publication and satisfactory in form. It more clearly identified the situation in which the plaintiff was alleged to have been caught out, and by whom. But the first imputation was challenged strongly. This time argument focussed on the words *slush fund*. The term, which the publication itself used, was challenged as being imprecise. The *Macquarie Dictionary* was used to illustrate the range of meaning in the words *slush fund* as a 'fund for use in campaign propaganda or the like, especially secretly or illicitly, as in bribery'. The defendant argued the term *could* be used to connote secret and unlawful activities, but *need not* refer to either secret or unlawful actions. Because there is a wide range in seriousness between an openly operated fund and a secret and illegal one, the imputation was argued to be ambiguous. The defendant sought an order for the plaintiff to specify how the term was being used. Levine J, however, rejected the argument and explained: 'To my mind "slush fund" is quite an uncomplicated expression particularly as used in this matter complained of.'[39] This sort of challenge echoes the dispute in *Drummoyne Municipal Council v Australian Broadcasting Corporation*[40] and illustrates something that also was raised in interviews. It appears that such challenges are increasingly unlikely to succeed under current Defamation List practice when the allegedly ambiguous word is used in the publication itself.[41]

Thus the matter proceeded to a 7A hearing on 29 and 30 March 2000 before Abadee J and a four-member jury. Very little evidence is given in 7A hearings. The

---

[36] *Ibid.*

[37] *Randwick Labor Club* [1999] NSWSC 880, [20] (Levine J). Equivalent wording was used for the plaintiff club: [19].

[38] *Ibid.*

[39] *Ibid* [24].

[40] (1990) 21 NSWLR 135.

[41] See eg *Bass v TCN Channel Nine* [2000] NSWSC 270 and *Dix Gardiner v Strathfield Municipal Council* [2003] NSWSC 597. In each case, publications used the word 'shonky' and a pleading in those terms was allowed.

jury reads, hears or views a record of the publication, hears addresses from the plaintiff's counsel and the defendant's counsel,[42] and a summing-up from the judge. The procedure often takes a day of court time, or just a little more. In *Randwick Labor Club*, the defence argued the pleaded imputations were strained – that is, the reasonable viewer would not have perceived imputations as serious as the plaintiffs' pleadings. For example, the publication's statement about bookkeeping irregularities would not be taken to mean the plaintiffs were deliberately dishonest.[43] The defendant also emphasised that the broadcast included words from a political opponent of the Labor Party. An opposition parliamentarian, Richard Bull, used the words *slush fund* and the defence argued a reasonable viewer would interpret this as a meaningless 'cheap political shot'.[44] The jury, after three hours' deliberation, found only partly in favour of the plaintiffs, which suggests some agreement with defence arguments about unreasonable meanings having been pleaded. For example, the first imputation was found to be conveyed and defamatory: the publication did allege that plaintiff directors knew the club to be a slush fund club for the Labor Party. But the second imputation was found to not be conveyed: the publication did not allege the plaintiffs were caught out by police while they tried to conceal a secret slush fund.

What emerges from reading the trial transcript? Most simply, it suggests a striking sense of difference; difference from the law as doctrine. The difference concerns what the jury is told, in what order, and the transience of oral delivery. None of this should be surprising: it is a classic realisation of empirical research into law – but it is worth emphasising, particularly in relation to differences between trial and pre-trial stages. At trial, the law is less precise; it is approximated – at least within the room left by precedential decisions. A lot of defamation law's arcane detail is absent. That detail exists in pre-trial hearings when parties argue about imputations' form and capacity, in hearings that involve only professional legal actors. But in the 7A jury hearing, defamation law is made comparatively plain. And it is not just that the issue in *Randwick Labor Club* was uncontroversial, so that a 'vague' description was given to the jury and each party was satisfied with it. In this case, the parties repeatedly contested defamatory meaning. The difference evident in the transcript also concerns what is not said. For example, the jury is not told at the outset what its role is in the trial; not told that law sets up a particular test for it to decide what the broadcast means; not explicitly told that other questions in the case, such as defences, may be argued later to other legal actors. Instead, the jury is told at the end that its answers do not resolve all issues in the case. It is quite a contrast to the closely fought interlocutory battles about form and capacity. Of course, there is no reason to think this difference is peculiar to NSW. A similar style of difference could be

[42] This is the common order of addresses. *John Fairfax Publications v Rivkin* (2003) 201 ALR 77 confirms the order of addresses (and any reply) is a matter for the trial judge's discretion.

[43] Transcript of Proceedings, *Randwick Labor Club v Amalgamated Television Services* (NSW SC, Abadee J and jury, 29 March 2000) 28–29 (T Hughes QC for defendant).

[44] *Ibid* 27–28.

expected in England and Victoria. In NSW, however, it is likely to be more pronounced owing both to the technicality of pre-trial disputes and the brevity of the 7A hearing.

The transcript also is noteworthy for what the jury was told about the plaintiff being tied to its imputations. The trial judge's summing-up merely referred to these words on the jury questionnaire – '(or imputations which do not differ in substance from them)' – and continued:

> A plaintiff is not bound by the precise wording of the imputations which are put forward and which you have seen and which you will see again when you read the questionnaire in the jury room.
>
> It is sufficient for a plaintiff . . . if you find that the ordinary viewer would have understood the matter complained of, namely the broadcast . . . as conveying an imputation which is not substantially different or different in substance from what has been pleaded or, more accurately, relied on by the plaintiff in respect of each of every one of the imputations that have been asserted. So this is the explanation, members of the jury, for the inclusion of the words: '(or imputations which do not differ in substance from them)'.[45]

This suggests the basis of the NSW action – the pleaded imputation – remained the focus. The jury was told that it could find pleaded imputations were conveyed or imputations 'which do not differ in substance'. But the jury was not told what amounts to a difference in substance under NSW law. Instead the jury was asked about the following imputations in relation to each plaintiff director:

> Has the [plaintiff director] established that the broadcast complained of (of 5 June 1997) conveyed any of the following imputations (or imputations which do not differ in substance from them) to ordinary reasonable viewers and, if so, which:
>
> (a) the [plaintiff] was a director of Randwick Labor Club whilst knowing it to be a slush fund Club for the Labor Party?
>
> (b) the [plaintiff] by virtue of being a director of Randwick Labor Club was involved in the falsification of the records and books of the Club as part of its activities as a slush fund Club for the Labor Party?
>
> (c) the [plaintiff's] conduct as a director of the Randwick Labor Club was such as to warrant the [plaintiff] being reasonably suspected of being involved in the Club committing a large number of serious licensing offences?
>
> (d) the [plaintiff] as a director of the Randwick Labor Club was caught out by the police whilst trying to conceal a secret slush fund of tainted money which the Club had accumulated for the use of the Labor Party?
>
> (e) the [plaintiff] as a director of the Randwick Labor Club had been involved in the donation of $125,000 of tainted money to the Labor Party?[46]

---

[45] *Ibid* (30 March 2000) 13–14.

[46] The jury questions and answers are at *ibid* 30–46.

Given the range of imputations that were presented to the jury, each of which differed in substance, it is plausible that the jury focussed on each imputation exactly as pleaded and gave the concept of not differing in substance little weight. This issue is returned to in Part III in relation to the defence of substantial truth. The range and precision of meanings also contrasts strongly with English lawyers' descriptions of pleading in Chapter 4, as does *Rivkin v John Fairfax Publications*, which is discussion below.

Later in 2000, the case proceeded to a judgment on damages. Although qualified privilege at common law and under s 22 of the *Defamation Act 1974* (NSW) had been pleaded, they were withdrawn five days before the hearing. The defence called no evidence, while the plaintiff directors all gave evidence and relied on a number of other witnesses and documentary material. James J awarded damages totalling $635,657, including interest.[47] The award reportedly amounted to $1 per viewer.[48]

The *Randwick* file illustrates two things for the purposes of this book. First, it shows a contrast between technical interlocutory challenges to meanings and a far less precise jury hearing. And, as part of that, it illustrates how juries can be told little about what 'not different in substance' would mean for their deliberations. Second, it suggests a hard fought litigation style, where pleading points were taken pre-trial even though *no* defence would end up being run. The pre-trial challenges did not seriously raise the possibility of the broadcast being incapable of defaming. They could not have ended the case, nor it seems have meaningfully affected a defence because no defences could be offered for the broadcast.

3 Pleaded meanings' range and specificity

The file for *Rivkin v John Fairfax Publications* illustrates two aspects of NSW practice. It shows how a range of meanings tends to be pleaded in NSW. And it is an even stronger example than *Randwick Labor Club* of the extent that pleading battles can reach when parties fight every point, particularly in relation to what often are called 'weasel words' or the '*Drummoyne* point'.[49] The case concerned a high-profile Sydney stockbroker, Rene Rivkin. Articles published in the *Sydney Morning Herald* and the *Australian Financial Review* concerned, among other things, some of Rivkin's business dealings and the death of a model, Caroline Byrne. The articles were headed 'It's a Bad Business', 'Caroline's World and the Rivkin Link' and 'Boyfriend Denies Killing Model'.[50] The articles were seen by Rivkin as attacking three areas of his reputation: they attacked his abilities in business; criticised the conduct of his sexual life, especially in relation to a male

[47] *Randwick Labor Club* [2000] NSWSC 906 and [2000] NSWSC 1098 in which the plaintiffs were awarded costs on a party-to-party basis.

[48] Good (2000).

[49] See below, fns 61 and 62 and accompanying text.

[50] The articles are reproduced at *Rivkin v John Fairfax Publications* (Unreported, NSW SC, Levine J, 17 July 1998) Annexure A, B and C.

employee called Gordon Wood; and they suggested a connection between Rivkin and the possible homicide of Caroline Byrne, who was Wood's partner.[51] Many of Rivkin's pleaded imputations were challenged in interlocutory hearings. The issues were dealt with by Levine J in two interlocutory judgments in 1998, the first of which ran to 56 pages.[52] The publisher succeeded in only a few of its arguments and went to the Court of Appeal, so in total the file involved three hearings about meaning before a 7A trial. The two noteworthy areas of dispute – the range of meanings pleaded and the extent of interlocutory fights – are considered in terms of each of these interlocutory judgments.

The first area of dispute can be illustrated by these two pairs of imputations:

> That in May 1995 the Australian Securities Commission *had reason to suspect* that the Plaintiff had engaged in unlawful conduct in connection with the affairs of Offset Alpine Press Group.
>
> That in May 1995 the Australian Securities Commission *suspected* that the Plaintiff had engaged in unlawful conduct in connection with the affairs of Offset Alpine Press Group.
>
> That the late Caroline Byrne *had reason to suspect* that the Plaintiff had involved Gordon Wood in unsavoury business dealings connected with the affairs of Offset Alpine Press Group.
>
> That the late Caroline Byrne *suspected* that the plaintiff had involved Gordon Wood in unsavoury business dealings connected with the affairs of Offset Alpine Press Group.[53]

These imputations' wording differs as to whether the Australian Securities Commission (ASC) and the deceased woman *suspected* or *had reason to suspect* something about the plaintiff. The defendant argued each pair of imputations did not differ in substance.

Levine J addressed this issue at length.[54] Drawing in particular on *Sergi v Australian Broadcasting Commission*,[55] he first considered the situation where an entity in a relation of authority towards some person holds a suspicion about that person. In that situation, the reasonable recipient of the publication would think the authority had reasons for its suspicion. Thus, there would be no difference in substance in pleading an authority like the ASC 'suspected' and 'had reason to suspect' something. Levine J then examined the situation for an individual rather than a public authority. The defendant said pleading a 'bare suspicion' by an individual, without asserting the individual had any grounds for the suspicion, could not be defamatory. In that situation 'a reasonable person would have no basis for concluding anything as to the quality or basis of the suspicion and

[51] *Ibid*.

[52] *Ibid*; *Rivkin* (Unreported, NSW SC, Levine J, 18 September 1998).

[53] *Rivkin* (Unreported, NSW SC, Levine J, 17 July 1998) (also BC9803236, 2) (emphasis added).

[54] *Ibid* (also BC9803236, 5–12).

[55] [1983] 2 NSWLR 669.

would just be simply left to "speculate"'.[56] The only exception would be where there was some relation between the individual holding the 'bare suspicion' and the person being suspected, such that the individual could be said to be 'an authority'. An example discussed by the judge and defence counsel concerned a wife who suspected her husband of adultery. The defence said the wife could be called an authority and the situation would meet its test.[57] Levine J agreed that such a bare suspicion could be defamatory, but explained the law differently. He did not accept that a relationship of authority was always necessary:

> [W]hy, one might ask, does the holder of the suspicion have to be a person in authority before the imputation can be held to be capable of being defamatory? If a person is suspected of some misconduct by his/her 'peers' or one of them, might that not be sufficient? . . . I am of the view that if the publication refers to the conduct attributed to the plaintiff and the suspicion about it held by someone else and that there is *something about the relationship between that person vis-a-vis the plaintiff, that gives some cogency or weight to the suspicion* held by that person that might well be sufficient on a capacity argument.[58]

Because Byrne's boyfriend was Gordon Wood, there was 'something about the relationship' which meant pleading that Byrne had a mere suspicion about sexual activity between Wood and Rivkin could be defamatory. And it would differ in substance to pleading that Byrne held a reasonable suspicion about the same thing.[59] This meant a number of imputations related to Byrne and her father could be pleaded both in terms of suspicion and reasonable suspicion.

A second area of dispute concerned a number of imputations in this form:

> That the plaintiff was a person criminally liable in respect of the murder of the late Caroline Byrne.[60]

Argument centred on the use of the words 'criminally liable in respect of'. It was alleged this lacked precision and did not specify the way in which 'criminally liable' was to be understood. This affected how it could be defended; for example, would it include remote forms of liability for Byrne's death? This argument about making the nature and degree of connection clear in the imputation is often called the '*Drummoyne* point', after the case of *Drummoyne Municipal Council v Australian Broadcasting Corporation*.[61] The concept of 'weasel words' also is used to describe words that fail to make clear how they are being

---

[56] *Rivkin* (Unreported, NSW SC, Levine J, 17 July 1998) (also BC9803236, 12).

[57] *Ibid* (also BC9803236, 17–18).

[58] *Ibid* (also BC9803236, 30) (emphasis added).

[59] *Ibid* (also BC9803236, 30–31).

[60] *Ibid* (also BC9803236, 3).

[61] (1990) 21 NSWLR 135. It also could be sourced to *Feros v West Sydney Radio* (Unreported, NSW CA, Moffitt P, Samuels, Reynolds JJA, 22 June 1982) 3–4 (Samuels JA, Moffitt P and Reynolds JA agreed).

[62] See, eg *Amalgamated Television Services v Marsden* (1998) 43 NSWLR 158, 163 (Hunt CJ at CL).

used in imputations.[62] In *Drummoyne*, Gleeson CJ addressed the issue in these terms: 'The requirement upon a plaintiff cannot go beyond doing the best that can reasonably be done in the circumstances.'[63] Here the plaintiff succeeded in arguing that the content of the publications invited suspicion on the part of a reasonable reader, much in the style referred to by the Privy Council in *Jones v Skelton*.[64] And while various theories about Byrne's death were put forward in the publications, when read reasonably the theories were 'incapable of providing the clarification or precision to plead an imputation' that went further than alleging the plaintiff was 'criminally liable' in respect of the death.[65] The second interlocutory hearing raised form and capacity arguments in relation to an amended statement of claim.[66] Arguments continued over imputations that the plaintiff was criminally liable in respect of Byrne's death. For example, imputations that the *defendant* suspected or had reason to suspect the plaintiff was criminally liable were held incapable of arising. Nothing in a normal newspaper article – perhaps unlike an editorial – would suggest the defendant itself held these suspicions.[67]

Although it had succeeded in part, the defendant sought to appeal the two judgments of Levine J. But the summons for leave to appeal was dismissed, with the Court of Appeal rejecting yet another argument about 'criminally liable'.[68] In seeking leave to appeal, the defendant argued the imputations were ambiguous because they used the words 'criminally liable *in respect of*' rather than 'criminal liable *for*' the death of Byrne. The words 'in respect of' arguably included remote forms of liability (such as harbouring Byrne's killer after the event) and thus could be ambiguous at trial. Handley JA rejected this and said the imputation as pleaded would exclude remote forms of liability. In any event, the plaintiff's counsel accepted that 'criminal liability in respect of' meant Rivkin had pushed Byrne over the cliff at which she died, had been present and aided or abetted the offence, or had procured it through prior conduct.[69]

The appellate decision in *Rivkin* also is legally significant for ending the previous liberal approach to interlocutory defamation appeals.[70] In the past, the Court of Appeal usually granted leave to appeal interlocutory form and capacity decisions. But in *Rivkin* it said:

> This Court has hitherto been liberal in granting leave to appeal . . . because all questions of fact including damages had to be decided at the trial by a jury. An erroneous decision at first instance that particular imputations were

[63] *Drummoyne* (1990) 21 NSWLR 135, 137 (Gleeson CJ).

[64] [1963] 1 WLR 1362; see also *Lewis v Daily Telegraph* [1963] 1 QB 340, 374 (Pearce LJ).

[65] *Rivkin* (Unreported, NSW SC, Levine J, 17 July 1998) (also BC9803236, 34–35).

[66] The first hearing had given the plaintiff leave to file an amended statement of claim, subject to certain conditions.

[67] *Rivkin* (Unreported, NSW SC, Levine J, 18 September 1998) (also BC9804778, 4).

[68] *John Fairfax Publications v Rivkin* [1999] NSWCA 164.

[69] *Ibid* [5], [7].

[70] See also Kenyon (2000).

> capable of a defamatory meaning or were capable of arising, if allowed to stand, normally made a new trial inevitable if the jury awarded damages for that imputation and their verdict was challenged on appeal.[71]

The 7A reforms have changed this situation and interlocutory decisions about pleaded meanings can stand until trial. Appellate courts need not interfere so readily pre-trial because many issues have been withdrawn from juries, and appellate courts can correct errors by trial judges.[72] Instead, the ordinary strict approach will be followed for appellate interference with interlocutory orders.[73]

Thus the matter went forward to a 7A hearing during April 2001. In the end, 17 imputations went to the jury in relation to the three articles. All were rejected by the jury, which was most surprising for Rivkin, who earlier had commented: 'If the ordinary reasonable reader doesn't find for me they are immoral.'[74] The defence primarily argued that the imputations were not conveyed: that it was only minds avid for scandal that would understand such meanings.[75] And it appears the jury agreed. Rivkin later appealed against the verdict as being unreasonable and achieved some success in both the NSW Court of Appeal and the High Court.[76] A retrial was ordered with respect to five imputations.[77]

The *Rivkin* file illustrates how a range of meanings can be pleaded and that the requirements for each imputation to differ in substance do not at all mean that pleading is similar to England's, where 'unless the article clearly raises several matters that are distinct, unless it's like that, the claimant will tend to pick one meaning that's clear and sharp, damaging and memorable and sue on it'.[78] Rivkin also shows the extent to which pleading battles can extend. And it is notable in legal terms for reducing the likelihood of future appeals on these matters before 7A hearings.

4 *The split tribunal of fact*

The *Murphy v Nationwide News* file also illustrates how specificity is fought over in NSW and the extent of possible battles. The pleading dispute did not concern a word from the publication, like 'slush fund' in *Randwick Labor Club*. Rather, the

---

[71] *Rivkin* [1999] NSWCA 164, [13] (Handley JA, Sheller JA and Brownie AJA agreed).

[72] *Ibid* [15].

[73] See *The Will of Gilbert* (1946) 46 SR (NSW) 318, 323.

[74] Anonymous (2001).

[75] The defence also argued, at least for one of the imputations, that it would not be defamatory even if it was conveyed. This was an allegation of homosexual intercourse between the married Rivkin and his employee Gordon Wood. On the issue of allegations of homosexuality, see McNamara (2001).

[76] *Rivkin* [2002] NSWCA 87; *Rivkin* (2003) 201 ALR 77.

[77] Subsequently, a consent judgment for the defendant was entered in relation to the retrial: see *Rivkin* [2004] NSWSC 671.

[78] 22S and see Chapter 4, Part II, C.

parties fought about the word 'shyster', which the plaintiff introduced into the pleadings. *Murphy* also is important for illustrating one way in which battles about specificity appear to have gained significance since 7A commenced. This is because 7A splits the tribunal of fact: the jury determines whether the plaintiff's imputations are conveyed and defamatory, while the judge determines everything else. Under 7A, any room for argument about an *imputation*'s meaning greatly concerns defendants because judges may interpret imputations differently from juries. These concerns encourage more pre-trial fights.

A pre-trial hearing in *Murphy* included these submissions from counsel about *shyster*:

Defence Barrister:	The first problem is the use of the word 'shyster'. What does it mean? One can perhaps understand the use of that word . . . if it was the word used in the matter complained of but it is not.
Plaintiff Barrister:	Your Honour 'shyster' is a good word. It is a word that ordinary people will understand. It has a history. . . . The definition really comes down to being someone who is sharp . . . a lawyer engaged in sharp practice. There is no ambiguity.[79]

Actual events in the case cast doubt on whether the jury so easily understood the word, but in any event *shyster* was a major and repeated point of dispute. The case arose from a very short article in a business gossip-style column in *The Daily Telegraph*, headed 'Lots in a Name':

> It seems there's not enough room for two Chris Murphys in Sydney.
>
> After inquiring about former INXS manager Chris Murphy's new natural foods investment, Consolidated Food Australia, *The Daily Telegraph* received a breathless call from his office.
>
> Murphy the businessman, said his staffer, should be referred to as CM Murphy to prevent him being confused with 'celebrity' criminal lawyer Chris Murphy.
>
> It seems that CM, who also owns 60 per cent of radio station 2SM, has, in the past, been mistaken for solicitor Murphy, better known for getting drug dealers and advertising guru John Singleton off criminal charges.
>
> The lawyer reckons you have to earn the name Chris Murphy.
>
> 'He made a fortune out of a rock band and never sung a note,' said the lawyer, who also represented rugby league bad boys Scott Wilson and Mark Geyer.
>
> 'I have to sing for my supper, I have to stand up in court each day and it is damned hard work.'

[79] Transcript of Proceedings, *Murphy v Nationwide News* (NSW SC, Levine J, 11 June 1998) 4, 8 (B McClintock SC for plaintiff; G Reynolds for defendant).

> But relations are apparently cordial.
>
> 'I actually met CM once and he seemed like a thoroughly decent bloke,' the lawyer said.[80]

The article was accompanied by photographs of each Chris Murphy.

Only two imputations were pleaded by the plaintiff lawyer:

> that the plaintiff was a solicitor notorious for obtaining acquittals of guilty drug dealers thus hampering the enforcement of the law;
>
> that the plaintiff was a shyster who deserved to be ridiculed by the defendant's snide reference to him.[81]

These imputations, however, began a long interlocutory battle at first instance and appellate levels. In his initial judgment, Levine J agreed with the defendant that 'hampering the enforcement of the law' was imprecise and could not be conveyed by article. The first imputation was later changed to 'the plaintiff was a solicitor notorious for obtaining acquittals of guilty drug dealers.' This overcame the problems of ambiguity and capacity. The second imputation is of more interest here. Levine J held the latter part of the imputation – 'deserved to be ridiculed by the defendant's snide reference to him' – merely said the plaintiff had been defamed, as well as rolling up two separate points in one imputation. It did not attribute any act or condition to the plaintiff, so those words should be removed from the pleading. There also was debate about the word 'shyster'. Levine J succinctly said:

> I do not accept [the defence's] assertion that there is uncertainty arising from the word 'shyster'. Whilst I am of the view that the mere fact that a word according to a dictionary can have varied meanings, does not establish ambiguity, I am content to take what is said of the word 'shyster' in the *Macquarie Dictionary* namely 'a lawyer who uses unprofessional or questionable methods'.[82]

Debates about 'shyster' did not end there. Abadee J dismissed an application to strike out an amended statement of claim, which had been filed in accordance with the reasons of Levine J.[83] The defendant then went to the Court of Appeal,[84] which delivered judgment just two weeks before its ruling in *Rivkin* narrowed the scope for appeal.[85] Meagher JA focussed on the first imputation and held it could

80 *Murphy v Nationwide News* (Unreported, NSW SC, Levine J, 10 July 1998) (also BC9803232, 2).

81 *Ibid* (also BC9803232, 2–3).

82 *Ibid* (also BC9803232, 6). There has been English argument about the term shyster, although it was far less involved. It related more to what evidence could be admissible in relation to the term due to an argued difference in the term's meaning in New York compared with England: *Lewis v King* [2004] EWCA Civ 1329.

83 *Murphy* (Unreported, NSW SC, Abadee J, 24 July 1998).

84 *Nationwide News v Murphy* (1999) Aust Torts Reports ¶81-506.

85 See above, fns 70–73 and accompanying text.

be defamatory to say a lawyer was notorious for obtaining acquittals of guilty drug dealers. Sheller JA focussed on the second imputation and, noting how 'shyster' was defined in the *Macquarie Dictionary*,[86] said the word 'has a meaning distinct and certain enough to satisfy the requirements of specificity'.[87] Sheppard AJA, however, disagreed. He said 'shyster' has a range of meanings:

> The word 'shyster' is defined in the *Oxford English Dictionary* (1989) to mean a lawyer who practises in an unprofessional or tricky manner; especially one who haunts the prisons and lower courts to prey on petty criminals. . . . Examples of usages given in the dictionary include reference to a prisoner who must wait 'next day for the visits of the "shyster" lawyers – a set of turkey-buzzards whose touch is pollution and whose breath is pestilence'. In the *Shorter Oxford Dictionary* a 'shyster lawyer' is defined as being one who defends drug dealers and takes payment in cocaine. . . .
>
> [T]he words are plainly capable of being defamatory. The difficulty is the satisfactory formulation of the imputations. The only point I make is that it seems undesirable to leave to the jury . . . a word which is of uncertain meaning as an essential part of an imputation.[88]

Thus, Sheppard AJA would have ordered the removal of 'shyster'. In the result, the appeal was dismissed, with Meagher JA being taken to agree with Sheller JA (and the first-instance decisions) in relation to both imputations, although Meagher JA did not directly address 'shyster' in his judgment.

Debate about the appellate judgment arose at the start of the 7A hearing in February 2000.[89] Approximately an hour was spent considering 'shyster' yet again. Counsel for the plaintiff said he would give the imputation a gloss if required:

> Shyster is an ordinary English word and [the jury] will know what the word means. . . . A lawyer who uses unprofessional questionable and sneaky methods is the gloss I would give it if I give it a gloss. Also to suggest in any way that it is ambiguous is incorrect.[90]

Opposing counsel responded that the jury may decide the imputation is conveyed and defamatory on some meaning unknown to the parties. Thus the defendant would not know on what basis to defend publication.[91] The trial judge, James J, concluded that he was bound by the Court of Appeal, which he said had decided 'if a shyster is taken as meaning a lawyer who uses unprofessional or questionable methods, the imputation is not lacking in specificity'.[92] After all

---

[86] Levine J made the same reference; see above, fn 82 and accompanying text. *Murphy* (1999) Aust Torts Reports ¶81-506, [13] (Sheller JA).

[87] *Ibid* [21] (Sheller JA).

[88] *Ibid* [25]–[27] (Sheppard AJA).

[89] See *Murphy* (Unreported, NSW SC, James J, 16 February 2000).

[90] Transcript of Proceedings, *Murphy v Nationwide News* (NSW SC, James J and jury, 16 February 2000) 6–7 (McClintock SC for defendant).

[91] *Ibid* 7.

[92] *Ibid* 11.

these hearings and exchanges about such a short article, counsel addressed the jury in the 7A hearing. Ironically, for this reader at least, the plaintiff's counsel explained concepts like 'imputations' and the 'ordinary reader' to the jury and continued: 'I hope I am clear. Lawyers get mesmerised by the technicality of words'.[93] In the end, the jury found for the plaintiff on both imputations, although they did request a dictionary during their deliberations, which was refused.[94] The transcript suggests that counsel and judge believed the request concerned the word 'shyster'. There is one later judgment in relation to directions over a proposed qualified privilege defence,[95] and the case settled shortly before the rest of the trial was due to be heard (in March 2001), with no information about the terms being publicly available.

This battle about shyster illustrates how imputations' specificity has gained even greater importance under the 7A process, introduced two decades after the *Defamation Act 1974* (NSW). Under it, the tribunal of fact that determines whether the plaintiff's imputations are conveyed and defamatory, is separate from the tribunal of fact that determines issues relevant to defences and remedies. This means defendants are even more concerned about any room for argument about an imputation's meaning. Otherwise, for example, there may be a difference between the meaning the jury finds and the meaning the judge requires in order to prove truth. In *Murphy*, the defendants appeared concerned as to how they could demonstrate the truth of the word 'shyster'. This concern with defences and meaning is a striking difference to England and is returned to in the interview material in Part III.

In this Part, NSW court files and judgments have been discussed to show how: plaintiffs usually plead multiple imputations; pre-trial challenges to imputations are common (often focusing closely on an imputation's form and challenging any general imputations that plaintiffs have pleaded); defence pleadings related to meaning are rare (although it is noted how that may have changed subsequently, below in Part III, C); there is a contrast between technical interlocutory meaning challenges and discussion of meaning in 7A hearings; and splitting the tribunal of fact under 7A accentuates the attention that defendants place on plaintiffs' imputations.

III MATERIAL FROM INTERVIEWS

Seven topics are drawn from the interviews, concerning: the Defamation List in the Supreme Court; the cause of action under s 9 of the *Defamation Act 1974* (NSW); justification defences; comment defences; 7A trials; reform; and the test for what is defamatory.

---

93 *Ibid* 25.

94 *Murphy* [2000] NSWSC 1251, [168] (James J).

95 *Murphy* [2000] NSWSC 813.

A The defamation list

Many interviewees volunteered comments about how Defamation List judges have influenced NSW litigation practice. While other judges hear some defamation matters, both in the regular defamation call-overs and at trial, the List judge was seen as particularly important. A change in personnel was reported to have changed the style of analysis somewhat.[96] The general response was that Hunt J, who headed the Defamation List for many years from its inception in the late 1970s, encouraged major technical development in NSW defamation law.[97] However, at the same time, attempts to define everything into 'absolutely precise meanings'[98] – suggesting perhaps an overly 'fine eye'[99] or at least a very skilful 'wordsmith'[100] – were criticised.[101] Similarly, for example, it was suggested that no one else really understood the idea of an inference on an inference, or even the differences between implications and inferences.[102] For this book's comparative investigation of law and practice, these sorts of comments are useful in emphasising how the style of a specialist judge can influence practice substantially. In NSW, this appears to have been one – but far from the only – factor in the detailed attention given to imputations.

In comparison, there was a 'quantum shift'[103] under Levine J who headed the Defamation List from the early 1990s for approximately 10 years. (Nicholas J became the Defamation List judge in the beginning of 2004.[104]) Interviewees emphasised changes in the period since early 2000 when the List was taken 'by the scruff of the neck'.[105] The change in personnel was reported to have lessened the technicality of form and capacity judgments,[106] and may have reduced the impetus to such frequent interlocutory meaning disputes.[107] 'Trench warfare about form and capacity'[108] continues – but it is less intensive – as judges dispose of arguments 'more efficiently'.[109] All this means the 'inevitable'[110] disputes about form and capacity may be reined in.

---

[96] Eg 41S, 43S.

[97] Eg 45SC, 40SC, 44SC.

[98] 39SC.

[99] 40SC.

[100] 41S.

[101] 39SC, 40SC, 41S, 44SC, 45SC.

[102] 40SC; see Chapter 2, Part III, B.

[103] 41S.

[104] Anonymous (2003).

[105] *Ibid.*

[106] Eg 40SC, 43S.

[107] 39SC; similar comments were made by 41S.

[108] 42B.

[109] *Ibid.*

[110] 47SC.

Two points are notable about this material. First, the List Judge's style appears to have a substantial impact on the approach to meaning taken in litigation – particularly in relation to pre-trial form and capacity applications. This may occur wherever specialist judges are used – in relation to this book's empirical work that happens to varying degrees everywhere except in the US. But it illustrates the need for contextualised knowledge about law's operation when analysing formal law. Second, a high degree of complexity and technicality as regards meaning was seen to have developed in NSW. And while it appears to have been reduced somewhat, the question remains as to whether aspects of the NSW approach supports greater complexity than needed under the common law. The interviews suggest how the two outstanding peculiarities of NSW law – s 9 and the 7A procedure – do just this.

B The cause of action under s 9

Interviewees saw pleaded meaning as centrally important in litigation. A degree of complexity was expected because the pleaded imputation, not the publication itself, is the cause of action under s 9 of the *Defamation Act 1974* (NSW). Echoing the court file material, interviewees said s 9 underlay much of the complexity as regards meaning.[111] As one very experienced barrister commented 'if you get a mob of lawyers for 20 years exercising themselves over the conveying of meaning, then they will create year-by-year, layer upon layer of rules and artificiality'.[112] A tension was recognised between the approach's technicality and the security of (eventually) knowing just what the case is about – namely, the plaintiff's pleaded imputations.[113] One solicitor commented: 'the situation in NSW can be, obviously, dwelling in the realms of pedantry. But, at least you know where you stand.'[114]

It was surprising, however, that only a minority of interviewees strongly supported the NSW system. This was a clear contrast to English and Victorian interviewees' comments about their own jurisdictions. Some did see the NSW approach as 'inherently sound'[115] and better 'simply because everyone knows what the case is about – and you can make decisions based on it'.[116] But there was openness to returning to the common law cause of action,[117] or at least simplifying pleading requirements.[118] Problems with s 9 were described well by a very experienced interviewee:

---

[111] Eg 39SC, 40SC, 45SC, 46B.

[112] 45SC.

[113] Eg 39SC, 40SC, 41S.

[114] 41S; other interviewees also used the term *pedantry* without being prompted: 45SC, 46B.

[115] 40SC.

[116] 44SC.

[117] Eg 39SC, 45SC, 46B.

[118] 47SC.

> In NSW, the cause of action is the imputation. I have no objection to that as a mechanism in principle. Unfortunately, some time ago by reason of judgments particularly of the Court of Appeal, the imputation . . . became highly technical in form with an obsessional regard to whether or not it precisely states the act or condition . . . [This development] has led to a situation where the focus has been placed on the imputation *detached completely* from the publication said to carry it. That is the great flaw.[119]

This detaching of imputations from the publication *may* allow plaintiffs more easily to plead imputations that cannot be defended by truth, comment or contextual truth, in part because they are imputations that publishers could not have intended and did not envisage when publishing.

C Defences related to meaning: truth, contextual truth, Lucas-Box, Polly Peck

Court files suggest that truth pleas are rare. This accords with interview comments on how plaintiffs seek to plead meanings that cannot be defended by truth. For example, it becomes 'a competition to see who can draft the tightest imputation, so that it makes it the hardest for a defendant to justify'.[120] Plaintiff lawyers plead imputations that the defence cannot justify – capable but 'far out' meanings, which the jury can be persuaded are conveyed.[121] The imputations are precise and 'full of detail'[122] and under NSW law and practice that limits the availability of a truth defence. It appears the defence has trouble defending such imputations because a narrow approach is taken to the concept of 'substantial truth'. One interviewee explained:

> [I]t has deflected the defence from its true role – that is, substantial truth plus public interest. I take the view that the drafters of the legislation must have meant originally that so long as you get the gist of the imputation justified, then you ought to be able to succeed. But that is not the trend. . . . [It is] very hard to persuade . . . judges that substantial truth means imputation, main gist, no detail. That's a kind of peculiar NSW problem. . . . [T]he latitude to the court to find substantial truth is much greater [at common law] than it is with the concept of the imputation as the cause of action.[123]

The NSW legislative response is the defence of contextual truth. Under it, the defendant may plead one or more contextual imputations. The contextual imputations must arise in addition to the plaintiff's imputations; be proved true and to have been published in the public interest; and, because of the circumstances making the contextual imputations true, the plaintiff's imputations must cause no further reputational harm. The court files revealed that contextual imputations are

[119] *Ibid*, emphasis in original.

[120] 41S; similar 39SC, 40SC, 43S.

[121] 48B.

[122] 46B.

[123] *Ibid.*

pleaded very rarely.[124] Interviewees also said contextual truth rarely succeeds at trial.[125] However, it should be noted that with the development of 7A practice contextual truth defences appear to have become more common since the fieldwork was conducted.[126] Under the 7A process, there is an added complication because the jury does not assess contextual imputations. At the time of the interviews it was unclear how judges would deal with contextual imputations, beyond the common historical approach of considering whether their substantial truth – that is 'the facts, matters and circumstances said to establish the truth of the contextual imputation'[127] – would be capable of outweighing the plaintiff's imputation.

The contextual truth defence, however, was still seen to affect litigation – it regulates plaintiffs' conduct so they do not sue only on lesser meanings.[128] Instead, plaintiffs plead serious meanings from a publication. The defence also was seen to prompt settlement.[129] If contextual truth would allow defendants to adduce discreditable evidence against plaintiffs, settlement might ensue. To that end, it was suggested defendants' contextual imputations tend to be framed more widely than plaintiffs' imputations.[130] As was seen in England with Lucas-Box defences, a more general imputation would give a greater range of material to draw on for justification and can assist the defendant.

Interviewees supported the idea of contextual imputations, as this solicitor's comments illustrate:

> I think contextual imputations are very useful. . . . [The defence] does allow defendants to at least try to overcome this issue with the pleading of imputations in NSW, which is that when you're pleading for a plaintiff . . . you *do* carefully frame the imputations so they can't be justified. . . . I think it's in the interests of justice really that people aren't getting large verdicts on a technicality. And I think that's what the contextual truth defence does in practice.[131]

Of course, avoiding 'verdicts on technicalities' is what Lucas-Box and Polly Peck pleading seek to achieve as well. And it remains to be argued whether they

[124] Contextual truth was pleaded in only four of the 68 files (in 34 of which defences had been filed); see above, Part II, A.

[125] 41S, 44SC.

[126] See NSW decisions related to the contextual truth defence, such as *John Fairfax Publications v Jones* [2004] NSWCA 205; *West v Nationwide News t/as Cumberland Newspaper Group* [2003] NSWSC 505; *Cotter v John Fairfax Publications* [2003] NSWSC 503; *Saint v John Fairfax Publications* [2003] NSWSC 580; *Tucker v Echo Publications* [2003] NSWSC 554; *Purcell v Cruising Yacht Club of Australia* [2003] NSWSC 245; *Dennison v Refshauge* [2003] NSWSC 78.

[127] *John Fairfax Publications v Blake* (2001) NSWLR 541, [5] (Spigelman CJ, Rolfe AJA agreed).

[128] 40SC, 41S; similar 39SC.

[129] 43S, 48B.

[130] 45SC.

[131] 43S, emphasis in original.

achieve the objective better than contextual truth. Interviewees also supported contextual truth for regulating pleading so that higher meanings are those sued on, and it does appear to do this. But the fieldwork suggests a greater problem is how plaintiffs attempt to plead detailed and somewhat extreme meanings *and* how they often succeed. Then, with NSW's imputation-centred approach, the battleground is shifted to an imputation *detached* almost completely from the publication. It is unclear how contextual truth seeks to address that situation, which brings us to Lucas-Box and Polly Peck.

Court files suggest exactly the same imputations are often pleaded in a contextual truth defence for NSW publication, and in a Lucas-Box or Polly Peck justification defence for Victorian publication. The small number of examples from NSW can be increased by the similar pleading practice shown in the Victorian files (see Part III of Chapter 6). This practice *may* follow from some ACT case law such as *Woodger v Federal Capital Press of Australia*,[132] but interviewees generally did not support that approach.[133] The better view is that the defences operate differently, as discussed in Part I of Chapter 3. Although some interviewees were aware of this,[134] others appeared to misunderstand the effect of Lucas-Box and Polly Peck, even if they also criticised *Woodger*. For example, one experienced barrister suggested:

> I think conceptually Lucas-Box has a lot of problems with it because if [the publication] conveys the plaintiff's sting then it's defamatory and it's indefensible. If it conveys the defendant's sting and the plaintiff isn't complaining about it [Lucas-Box doesn't offer a defence].[135]

The comments offer a strong contrast to those of the English lawyers discussed in Chapter 4 who said it was impossible to imagine running litigation without Lucas-Box. The comments also reflect NSW's imputation-centred approach.[136] Although the interviewee used the term *sting*, the comments appear to address the situation of two imputations being conveyed at once. That is, the plaintiff's imputation is conveyed, and the defendant's different imputation also is conveyed. The point of a Lucas-Box plea is to allow the defendant to argue that the plaintiff's 'sting' is *not* conveyed. Instead, a different, usually lesser meaning is conveyed. And the Lucas-Box plea clarifies what that different meaning is – which accords with long-term trends in pleading meaning. So Lucas-Box is not about two discrete meanings that

[132] (1992) 107 ACTR 1, 23 and 26 (Miles CJ).

[133] 45SC, 46B.

[134] Eg 46B.

[135] 39SC.

[136] Similar comments came from a barrister who – echoing Brennan CJ and McHugh J in *Chakravarti v Advertiser Newspapers* (1998) 193 CLR 519, [8] – suggested Lucas-Box pleading must cause problems in practice and argued that specific jury questions were preferable to the general verdicts traditionally sought at common law (which is an understanding that also can be seen to be influenced by NSW's imputation-centred approach): 48B.

are conveyed by a publication, but about clarifying the dispute between the parties about a publication's meaning.

Such disputes about meaning routinely exist in NSW, but they are not dealt with in the pleadings. Defendants rarely plead contextual imputations, and have no scope to plead Lucas-Box or Polly Peck in relation to NSW publications. Yet, at 7A hearings, juries may well face the same issue they would at common law, as the third of this chapter's opening quotations illustrates. That is, the plaintiff would say the publication conveys a meaning of, for example, guilt while the defendant says it only raises questions about guilt. Such an argument would probably be run under a Lucas-Box plea in England, presuming the defendant could lead evidence to show the lesser Lucas Box meaning was true. But in NSW, the difference does not appear in the pleadings and the 7A hearing does not give the jury evidence related to the truth of any defence meaning:

> Bear in mind [Lucas-Box] is a jury trial, and to play that out in front of a jury is a very different proposition to running a technical 7A case about whether it's this meaning or that meaning. [The full jury trial is] a very different thing, because you're then rehearsing the merits of each side. . . . This is what we say it means and this is the evidence as to why it's true. That creates a very different view in the jury's mind.[137]

But 7A hearings do resemble the common law in how disputes about meaning are of such similar styles in the two hearings. Just as the 7A hearing concerns meaning, a full trial with a Lucas-Box plea is 'about whether it's this meaning or that meaning'.

D Defences related to meaning: comment

The files also suggest that comment is a very rare defence.[138] Indeed, one interviewee explained that meaning is such an important issue in practice because truth is really the only defence concerned with the publication's meaning. In 14 years of defamation work, this interviewee had only pleaded comment once, in a 'rubbishy case'.[139] But interviewees' ideas about comment were noteworthy also for another reason. The existing literature has investigated NSW's comment defence.[140] Without prompting, many Sydney practitioners echoed concerns similar to those raised in the literature.[141] This is so, even though the NSW Court of Appeal has confirmed its approach to the defence,[142] which requires comment to meet the *pleaded imputation* rather than the *publication* as a

[137] 45SC.

[138] Comment was pleaded in seven of the 68 files (in 34 of which defences had been filed); see above, Part II, A.

[139] 48B.

[140] Eg Rares (2004); Kenyon (1996); George (1990).

[141] Eg 39SC, 40SC, 44SC, 45SC, 47SC.

[142] *New South Wales Aboriginal Land Council v Perkins* (1998) 45 NSWLR 340.

whole. This in turn means the defendant must have intended to convey the imputation in question. But as suggested above, 'almost invariably a plaintiff will work out a meaning that does get conveyed that nobody could possibly have intended'.[143] These factors mean that comment is where NSW's approach under s 9 'works the harshest'.[144] The defence is in a 'complete mess'[145] and defendants are 'frightened'[146] of trying to use it. In any event, they rarely get an opportunity because plaintiffs 'will never plead an imputation that could possibly look like a comment, so you can never have a comment defence in what should obviously be a comment case – like an editorial'.[147]

Truth and comment defences appear to be good examples of the effects of *detaching* imputations from the publication. Too great a scope exists for the plaintiff to plead imputations that cannot be defended in an appropriate way, defendants are limited in the way they can argue for alternative meanings, and a narrow approach is taken to substantial truth. And while some practitioners approve of the contextual truth defence for addressing these problems, it seems that Lucas-Box and Polly Peck are likely to better accommodate a fight between 'this meaning or that meaning'.

E The 7A trial, judge and jury roles

The 7A trial procedure was seen to have exacerbated the effects of s 9. It was very clear that 7A trials were generally unsupported. 7A was described as 'wrongheaded',[148] 'ludicrous',[149] a 'disaster' and 'garbage',[150] 'absurd'[151] and one of the 'silliest efforts' at NSW law reform.[152] While it does appear to be 'neat in theory',[153] practice has been problematic. Difficulties flow from the hearing's brevity and the jury's lack of context for its task.[154] For example,

> the jury comes cold to the question and it doesn't have the context in a true sense of what . . . this fight's all about. And it's asked . . . an almost disembodied technical question . . . which it will answer and then have no idea on what impact that will have on the merits of the case.[155]

---

143 39SC.

144 40SC.

145 44SC.

146 47SC.

147 40SC.

148 39SC.

149 40SC.

150 44SC.

151 47SC.

152 45SC.

153 42B.

154 40SC, 42B.

155 45SC.

Of course, this sort of 'disembodied' decision could be seen as according more closely with the legal tests for defamatory meaning, which meant 7A did have some support. It means 'the case is fought on the right issue . . . [The jury's] decision is not coloured by evidence following in the trial.'[156] Support for the 7A process also emphasised the speed and relatively low cost to get the matter before a jury,[157] and the encouragement to settle offered by the process.[158] 'Defendants very quickly have to face up to whether they've got to defend the case. . . . A quick 7A has the *great* benefit that it sets the goalposts for settlement'.[159] The 7A process was even seen as a 'form of summary procedure'[160] under which the whole case could be over within six months of commencing proceedings. Interviewees who were critical of 7A still recognised it can prompt settlement if plaintiffs succeed on some imputations,[161] while a plaintiff loss means the defendant obtains judgment.[162]

Yet the 7A process was generally criticised. One strand of criticism related to the legislation's failure to allow the jury to deal with any defence contextual imputations.[163] Under 7A, even determining questions of meaning is split between two tribunals of fact. This splitting of judge and jury formed another broader strand of criticism. The *same* tribunal deciding meaning and, for example, truth was seen to be preferable,[164] even if that was a judge.[165] Generally, however, interviewees supported a greater jury role in defamation.[166] A particular concern with splitting the tribunal of fact was ambiguity in pleaded imputations. As is clear from the file material in Part II, an imputation may have a range of meaning, and perhaps be dealt with at trial by the plaintiff placing a gloss on its wording. Defence lawyers also raised concerns in interviews that defending an imputation's truth is more difficult under 7A:[167]

> Plaintiffs plead as high imputations as they can, and seek to include words in there which . . . will prevent the defendant from justifying . . . [so] arguments with meaning are absolutely crucial. The judge will have to decide justification later . . . [and] will take a technical approach to something which the jury has not taken a technical approach to. So you really have to get rid of the things . . . before they get to the jury.[168]

---

156 46B.

157 42B, 43S.

158 41S, 43S.

159 46B emphasis in original.

160 41S.

161 42B, 47SC.

162 Eg *Samsun v Wily* [2000] NSWSC 281.

163 40SC, 44SC, 45SC, 47SC.

164 44SC, 45SC.

165 40SC.

166 45SC, 46B.

167 Eg 43S; similar 44SC, 45SC.

168 43S.

As this quote suggests, there was little support for the greater judicial role that now exists in NSW under the 7A process. Respondents tended to support juries deciding all factual matters.[169] Juries were seen to be better protectors of free speech through allowing defendants to win on community understandings of the merits of cases.[170] In effect, juries apply something like a reasonableness test to the defendant's conduct (and thereby overcome limitations in the scope of defamation defences). It was suggested the media often has erred in its investigating, writing or publishing in cases that reach trial.

> And when there's an error – if jury take the view that you shouldn't make the error, they will punish the defendant. . . . But if the jury says well it's fair enough, that was not something that mattered [the defendant will win].[171]

Judges, in comparison, are tied to legal rules and cannot be so forgiving of errors. Juries also were seen to encourage relative simplicity in the law,[172] echoing comments from English interviews. But this investigation of NSW practice suggests 7A's split tribunals of fact combine poorly with NSW's focus on imputations and its narrow approach to defences.

F Reform

The 2000 interviews were conducted when the High Court decision of *John Pfeiffer v Rogerson*[173] and its effects on choice of law in multistate defamation were promoting reform considerations among NSW specialists.[174] *Pfeiffer* was seen as a possible catalyst for uniformity in Australian defamation law,[175] although its practical effect on pleading and trials remained unclear.[176] But the suggested direction for reform was interesting for this book, namely, a possible return to the common law basis for the NSW cause of action[177] or at least a simplification of pleading requirements under s 9.[178] For example, one experienced barrister commented:

> Although I'd always thought [the NSW approach] was a good idea . . . in light of the development of the common law over 20 or more years of pleading rules or so on – it seems to me to make our statutory cause of action redundant. . . .

---

169 Eg 39SC, 44SC, 45SC.

170 39SC, who offered the example of *Wran v Macquarie Broadcasting Holdings* (Unreported, NSW SC, Clarke J and jury, 21 March 1986).

171 39SC.

172 44SC, 45SC.

173 (2000) 203 CLR 503; see generally Collins (2001b).

174 The NSW Bar Association Defamation Working Group was planning a submission to the NSW Attorney General about the issue in the months after the interviews. A submission was made in 2001: NSW Bar Association (2001) 46–47. Subsequent reform efforts are discussed in Chapter 10, Part I, E.

175 Eg 46B.

176 41S.

177 Eg 39SC, 45SC; similar 46B.

178 47SC.

> There's a series of cases in England and they start to discuss the need to plead meanings. . . . And the judge will say particularise it if there's any possible doubt about it. And there always is. Then you've got to the stage when you'll ask yourself what is the contribution of this statutory cause of action?[179]

It is notable that only in NSW did interviewees make comments so critical of their jurisdiction's approach, while other aspects of that approach, especially 7A trials and s 9, suggest the value in the common law. These comments also have interest given the subsequent renewal of long-standing efforts to achieve uniformity in Australian defamation law, which are examined in Chapter 10.

Interviewees also offered some support for a fast-track remedy, although doubts were expressed about how quickly any legal remedy could operate in practice:

> These corrections which you could apply for as a supposedly quick fix – anyone who has any experience with litigation knows that's just utterly absurd. They can't be quick unless you can get it done in a week or two.[180]

Negotiating prompt media corrections was seen as the best remedy for plaintiffs – the one that would most directly address their harm – and it was suggested that corrections had become more frequent since the early 1990s.[181] Overall, while concerns over access to law[182] and the public and litigant costs of trials were seen as important,[183] there was little hope for more prompt legal remedies of the sort raised by the NSW Law Reform Commission in its 1995 report.[184]

G The test for what is defamatory

As has been suggested in Chapter 4, this is a less significant issue in practice than disputes about meaning. It is notable, however, that subsequent to the interviews there have been numerous appeals against jury decisions in 7A hearings that particular imputations are not defamatory.[185] In terms of the test's wording, the term *right thinking* appeared to have currency in practice, both in interviews with defamation specialists[186] and in transcripts of 7A hearings. But the term also was criticised by some interviewees, being seen as 'artificial' and no longer helpful to explain the jury's role.[187] In any event, it was suggested that juries don't take the right-thinking person test to mean more than a direction to think objectively, to 'put aside their prejudices'.[188]

---

179 45SC; similar 39SC.

180 39SC; similar 42B, 47SC.

181 39SC, 40SC; similar 42B.

182 42B.

183 39SC, 47SC.

184 NSW Law Reform Commission (1995) but its aims were endorsed by some: eg 41S.

185 See Chapter 10, Part I, C.

186 Eg 41S, 43S.

187 47SC.

188 43S.

IV CONCLUSION

Three points are particularly noteworthy from this chapter's analysis of NSW court files and practitioner interviews. First, the high degree of specificity sought in pleaded imputations under s 9 of the *Defamation Act 1974* (NSW) and the related challenges to imputations' form appear to be a significant part of litigation practice. Second, NSW defendants rarely plead meaning in the form of contextual imputations, nor do they often plead truth and comment defences in response to plaintiffs' multiple imputations. While recent case law suggests that contextual imputations have become slightly more frequent since the fieldwork under the influence of the 7A process, it does not appear that truth or comment defences have increased. The fieldwork suggests how NSW litigation practice does not allow the parties' differences about meaning to be dealt with through pleading defences, which appears to be connected with the rate of pleading challenges. Third, the jury's limited role under the 7A procedure has accentuated these peculiarities about NSW's imputation-centred approach. Overall, the level of complexity that has arisen under ss 9 and 7A of the NSW Act may not be desirable, and it differs markedly from presentation of the issues before juries in 7A hearings. After an examination of the Victorian situation in the next chapter, Chapters 7 and 8 address matters of qualified privilege and US law, before Chapters 9 and 10 evaluate the comparative treatment of meaning in England, Australia and the US – as well as the implications of developments in qualified privilege and the US law – and examine recent case law developments in England and Australia.

– 6 –

MEANING: VICTORIAN DEFAMATION PRACTICE

> [W]e are actually a bit more robust in Victoria because people say, well, you'll go to the jury, you'll put something to the jury. And provided you're within the range of your meanings it's a matter for the jury anyway.[1]

> Your number one tactic [when acting for a plaintiff] is to get a trial date as quickly as possible. Because nothing is so unsettling for a defendant as a trial date, because the game's over.[2]

This chapter reports on fieldwork investigating how a publication's meaning is dealt with in Victorian defamation litigation. Far more questions about meaning are left until trial in Victoria than in NSW, as the first of the opening quotation suggests. Interlocutory hearings occur much less frequently in Victoria. The common law basis of the cause of action, together with Victorian pleading and litigation practices, mean more of the *detail* of meaning is left to the jury. This is not to suggest that none of the law's complexities, set out in earlier chapters, exist in Victorian practice. As the second opening quotation explains, plaintiffs (perhaps in particular) see that complexity and it is not surprising they like getting to trial. At trial 'the game's over'. But the court files and interviews examined in this chapter suggest the Victorian game is quite different to NSW, and they demonstrate how Victorian litigation proceeds without nearly so many interlocutory hearings about meaning.

This chapter discusses the four matters that are familiar from earlier chapters: the way a party is bound to a pleaded meaning; the degree of specificity required in a pleaded meaning; whether, and how, defence meanings are pleaded and dealt with in litigation; and the stage of a dispute at which differences between the parties about meaning are considered. In the rest of the chapter, material from Victorian practice is presented about these issues. The fieldwork in Melbourne involved analysing court files for cases issued in 1998 and interviewing specialist defamation practitioners. Each research site is outlined in Part I, before court files are discussed in Part II, and interviews are reported in Part III. In Part IV, some brief conclusions are made, before the focus turns to qualified privilege and the US law, in Chapters 7 and 8, and the implications of the legal analysis and fieldwork are examined in Chapters 9 and 10.

---

[1] Interviewed lawyer 56SC. Interviewees are identified by number and role, see below, Part I, B.

[2] Interviewed lawyer 50B.

Six points emerge in this chapter about Victorian practice. First, plaintiffs tend to plead a greater number of meanings than in NSW and England, and it appears the Victorian law against repetitive pleadings is not applied rigorously. Second, the form of pleaded imputations is rarely an issue pre-trial and challenges are uncommon. Because each imputation is not a separate cause of action, successful defence challenges often would have less effect than in NSW. Third, parties are not held particularly close to their pleaded meanings. In part, this occurs because juries are asked *general* questions; they are normally not given questionnaires repeating each pleaded imputation. Victorian trials keep publications before juries; the approach is not imputation-centred. Significantly, however, case law developments following *David Syme v Hore-Lacy*[3] suggest this has changed somewhat since the fieldwork. The implications of those developments are explored in Chapter 9. Fourth, defendants virtually never agree with plaintiffs' imputations, and commonly plead Lucas-Box meanings. Thus differences between the parties on meaning are set out reasonably clearly in Victorian pleadings through the combination of plaintiff and defence meanings. Fifth, justification and fair comment are far more common defence pleas than in NSW. Defendants are not unreasonably precluded from raising them, which may be the case in NSW. Sixth, all these factors mean the issue of meaning is left largely until trial; that is, meaning is left for the jury. And the jury's traditional role at trial – far broader than under NSW's 7A procedure – increases what the opening quotation would suggest is a 'robust' approach to meaning.

I RESEARCH SAMPLES AND METHODS

A Court files for defamation claims

Victorian defamation litigation is common in both the Supreme Court and the County Court, Victoria's intermediate court. Both courts' Registries are open to the public, and Registry managers greatly assisted the fieldwork by granting access to the files without cost.[4] As noted in Part III, lawyers raised few differences between the two Victorian courts – except for suggesting that a greater variety of judges heard County Court matters, some of whom had little defamation experience. But in any event, the interviews suggested Victorian practice could be understood through the combination of these courts. At several points in this Part, it is indicated where figures for each court have been combined.

Registry records show that 22 defamation cases, and one injurious falsehood claim, were issued in the Victorian Supreme Court during 1998. Registry officials were confident their system of computerised records identified almost every defamation file. One notable difference from NSW is that four defamation files, plus the injurious falsehood file, contained generally endorsed writs; that is, they had no statement of claim. Thus no meanings were pleaded, and in every

---

3 [2000] 1 VR 667.

4 See the appendix for a full list of the people who assisted with the research.

instance, the claims later settled or were dismissed due to inactivity with no pleading of imputations taking place. The files may support arguments that 'stop writs' are used by some plaintiffs, at least when courts' case management procedures do not make them impractical. Stop or gagging writs have been a concern in the law reform literature; for example, it has been reported that only a quarter of ACT actions that were initiated between 1985 and 1988 proceeded beyond issuing a writ or an appearance by the defence.[5] However, more active case management by all Australian courts suggests that such concerns are probably historical rather than continuing. Those five files offered no other useful information for this project and are not commented on further, which means that 18 Supreme Court files were examined in detail.

Forty-six defamation cases were issued in the County Court's Melbourne Registry during 1998.[6] Computerised records and court diaries were used to identify cases, and should have found almost every defamation file. The files included only one generally endorsed writ, for which a statement of claim was served promptly, and it is included in this chapter's discussion.

In total, 64 court files were consulted at length during 2000 and 2001, comprising 18 Supreme Court files (excluding the generally endorsed writs) and 46 County Court files. Information was taken from them for the period ending 31 December 2000. All cases had been issued two to three years earlier and had been through common interlocutory activity. Only three of the Supreme Court files and five of the County Court files remained open at the end of 2000.[7] Information from the files was extracted into word-processed documents, and photocopies were taken of relevant pleadings. The information was combined with judgments and trial transcripts, but it should be noted that transcripts were not taken of all County Court hearings, unlike the general practice in the Victorian and NSW Supreme Courts.[8] In any event, the records mean that a detailed picture of pleading practices and challenges could be built up.

B Interviews with specialist lawyers

To supplement the court records, eight interviews were conducted in Melbourne with specialist defamation solicitors and barristers between August and October

[5] Community Law Reform Committee of the ACT (1995) [167]; which concerned the Committee: [177]–[178]; see also Law Reform Commission of Western Australia (1979) [2.5] and [20.6].

[6] An additional three defamation files were issued in Melbourne, but transferred to regional courts, and are not considered in this sample.

[7] The three Supreme Court files had all been transferred to the County Court late in the period under research. No judgments became available for the open files during 2001.

[8] Judgments were obtained from lawyers, court files and online sources: eg the Australasian Legal Information Institute site <www.austlii.edu.au> and commercial services such as LexisNexis Australia <www.lexisnexis.com.au>.

Table 6.1 – Melbourne Interviewee Sample

Interviewee	Subject	5–10 years' libel practice	10–20 years' libel practice	20–30 years' libel practice	Mainly plaintiff work	Mainly defence work	Even plaintiff and defence work
49	SC		•				•
50	B		•			•	
51	S		•			•	
52	SC			•		•	
53	S		•			•	
54	S		•				•
55	B	•					•
56	SC		•			•	

Note: The numbers continue from the 38 interviewees in London and 10 in Sydney.
S – Solicitor; B – Barrister; SC – Senior Counsel or Queen's Counsel. (Both the titles of SC and QC are in use in Melbourne, but for simplicity and to promote anonymity only one abbreviation is used.)

2000 (see Table 6.1).[9] Interviewees were approached after searching court files and consulting listing services such as *The Legal 500*.[10] The interviews' style matched that discussed for England in Part I of Chapter 4. As with London and Sydney, a further 11 Melbourne interviews were conducted in 2003.[11] They examined issues about meaning and qualified privilege; the results concerning qualified privilege are discussed in Chapter 7. For reasons of space, however, the 2003 interviews are not drawn on in detail in this chapter – beyond emphasising the general point that the findings discussed here were supported in general terms by the full set of 19 Victorian interviews.

Defamation was a sizable part of every interviewee's practice, but for most it formed approximately half their work. As in Sydney, defamation practices appear to be less concentrated than in England, although that quality of London practices appears to have lessened since the fieldwork. The vast majority of Melbourne interviewees had between 10 and 20 years' experience in defamation law. Most interviewees worked mainly for media defendants, while others reported doing approximately equal work for plaintiffs and defendants.

[9] Only one interviewee was a woman.

[10] See <www.icclaw.com>; the former Legal Profiles also was consulted: <www.legalprofiles.com.au>.

[11] Four of the 2003 interviews were with people who also had been interviewed in 2000.

II INFORMATION FROM THE COURT FILES

The court files and judgments relating to them reveal material about the style of pleading and challenges, the degree of specificity needed in pleading, defence pleading of meaning and the stage of a dispute at which meaning is dealt with. This Part discusses general information from the files before illustrating significant issues by referring to four files in more detail. The Victorian files from the two courts suggest that:

(a) Plaintiffs usually plead multiple imputations, often repetitive and imprecise ones.

(b) Defendants quite rarely challenge repetitive or imprecise pleadings, at least until trial.

(c) Pre-trial challenges to imputations, or repleading after negotiation, occurs in less than one in 10 cases.

(d) Defence pleadings related to meaning are common – and double the rate of NSW. It appears that justification of the plaintiff's meanings is pleaded in one in four defences, Lucas-Box meanings in one in three defences, and fair comment in more than two in five defences.

(e) The combination of plaintiff pleading and Lucas-Box defences sets out the area of dispute between the parties on meaning, which then is left largely for the tribunal of fact to evaluate. That tribunal is frequently a jury, and it appears to be directed to the publication more than the pleaded imputations.

A General information

1 *Supreme Court files*

The small number of Supreme Court files means information drawn from them should be treated with more caution than the larger samples from the County Court and from NSW. But three points can be made concerning the number of imputations pleaded, pre-trial challenges to imputations, and defence pleadings relevant to meaning. First, for the purpose of considering the number of imputations pleaded, as in Chapter 5, each act of publishing material can be treated non-technically as a separate 'publication'. On that basis, the 18 files dealt with 25 publications, in relation to which 104 imputations were pleaded. There was a range of two to 11 imputations pleaded for each publication, a mean of 4.2 imputations per publication, and a median of 4. The table sets out the spread of imputations pleaded.

Table 6.2 – Victorian Supreme Court File Imputations

Number of Imputations	1	2	3	4	5	>5
Number of Files	0	6	6	4	5	4

Two, three, four, five or more imputations were all quite commonly pleaded. Little difference is suggested from NSW as to the number of imputations pleaded, until the County Court files are considered as well, which is done below.

The second issue was an obvious difference from NSW. There were far fewer pre-trial hearings about meaning. Although there is a Major Torts List in the Supreme Court for handling defamation claims, many pleadings suggested there were differences between the parties about meaning that were not addressed in court before trial or settlement. Only two of the 18 files showed any hearing about meaning, with one of them involving multiple hearings (it had a hearing before a Master and an appeal to the Major Torts List judge[12]). In both these files, the hearing resulted in a change to the pleading. In only two other files were the pleaded meanings changed without a hearing, apparently after negotiation between the parties. But in another 12 files, pleaded meanings were not challenged even though a challenge would have been possible. In NSW there were challenges or negotiated changes to imputations in almost every second case. In the Victorian Supreme Court, the figure was two in nine.

Third, in earlier chapters the importance of meaning was raised in relation to defences. In the Victorian files, defences of justification and fair comment were not as rare as in NSW. A defence was filed in 15 of the 18 Supreme Court files. Justification of the plaintiff's imputations was pleaded in only two files, but Lucas-Box or Polly Peck pleas were made in seven files (which invariably were described as Polly Peck pleas in the files and overwhelmingly took the form of Lucas-Box pleas in this book's terminology) and fair comment was pleaded in seven files.[13] The NSW figures related to 34 defences for 69 files and comprised truth in six files, contextual truth in four files, and comment in seven files. Thus, in the Victorian Supreme Court these 'meaning defences' were pleaded 16 times within 15 defences, while in NSW they were pleaded only 17 times in 34 defences.

2 *County Court files*

The same three points can be addressed by reference to the sample of 46 Victorian County Court files. First, the 46 files dealt with 60 publications, in relation to which 340 imputations were pleaded. There was a range of zero to 18 imputations pleaded for each publication, a mean of 5.7 imputations per publication, and a median of 5. The file with no imputations pleaded involved the rare situation where the publication was plain on its face – it said the plaintiff had raped the defendant. In effect a single meaning was alleged, which is how the file is counted in the following table showing the spread of imputations pleaded.

Between three and five imputations were commonly pleaded, but almost half the files had more imputations. And those with very large numbers of imputations were rarely challenged. Combining the Victorian Supreme and

[12] The Court of Appeal was involved with no pre-trial meaning disputes.

[13] In the Victorian Supreme Court, qualified privilege was pleaded in five files and *Lange* qualified privilege was pleaded in seven files.

Table 6.3 – Victorian County Court File Imputations

Number of Imputations	1	2	3	4	5	6	7	8	9	>11
Number of Files	2	4	16	4	12	4	6	3	2	7

County Court figures also suggests more imputations were pleaded than in NSW – the Victorian mean is 5.2 and the median is 5, while the NSW figures are a mean of 4.1 and a median of 4.

As in the Victorian Supreme Court, there appeared to be few pre-trial hearings about meaning in the Defamation Division of the County Court Damages List. Only seven files were noteworthy. Two files had been transferred from the Supreme Court, where the pleaded imputations had been through various changes.[14] A minor change also occurred in the County Court in one of these files, apparently after correspondence between the parties. Three other files involved minor changes to imputations; one probably after correspondence between the parties and in two files the plaintiff added one or more extra meanings when an amended statement of claim was being filed for other purposes. A sixth file involved repleading natural and ordinary meanings as legal innuendo meanings, possibly at the plaintiff's own instigation. And a seventh file involved extensive hearings not about the pleaded meanings, but about exactly what publications were alleged to have occurred in a slander case. (A similar tactic appeared from another file in which vague and repetitive meanings where not challenged in pre-trial hearings, but there were two challenges alleging the plaintiff had failed to identify the publications clearly enough.) More extensive battles occurred in the List with regard to discovery and interrogatories, while differences between the parties on meaning appear to have been left until settlement or trial. Thus, five files saw changed meanings, but it seems inappropriate to count three of these when comparing the County Court files with other courts. This is because three files involved repleadings that appear to have been instigated by the plaintiff which did not narrow the meanings at all: one file involved popular innuendoes that were repleaded as legal innuendoes and two files saw extra meanings added at the plaintiff's instigation. None of these three files involved repleading after negotiation, and only two files saw changed meanings in any sense comparable to the other courts examined in this research. In another 28 files, pleaded meanings were not challenged even though a challenge would have been possible. In NSW there were challenges or negotiated changes to imputations in almost every second case. In the Victorian Supreme Court, the figure was two in nine. In the County Court, the figure was one in 23. This does not entirely match comments from Victorian interviews that suggested meanings often were addressed at List hearings. But County Court files record few formal results from such considerations. Even if the records are incomplete on this issue – and there is no reason to think they are – it suggests a marked difference to NSW litigation

[14] These files were issued in the Supreme Court before 1998, so they were not within the sample of Supreme Court files analysed in this chapter.

practice.[15] The combined figure for changes to meanings in Victoria is six in 64 files, or under one in 10.

The third matter concerns meaning and the defences of justification and fair comment. In the County Court files, these defences were not as rare as in NSW. A defence was filed in 42 of the 46 files. Justification of the plaintiff's imputations was pleaded in 12 files, while Lucas-Box pleas were made in 12 files and fair comment was pleaded in 18.[16] Thus, in the Victorian County Court these 'meaning defences' were pleaded 40 times in 42 defences (or on combined figures for both Victorian courts, they were pleaded 56 times in 57 defences), while in NSW they arose 17 times in 34 defences.

The combined figures for the two Victorian courts on these defences strongly contrast with those for NSW. In Victoria, justification of the plaintiff's meanings is pleaded in one in four defences, Lucas-Box meanings in one in three defences and fair comment in more than two in five defences. The NSW rates discussed in Chapter 5 are approximately half these figures: truth is pleaded in less than one in six defences, contextual truth is pleaded in one in eight defences and comment is pleaded in one in five defences.

The files also suggest figures about three further issues: the rate of settlements and trials within the two- to three-year period that the files had been open by the end of 2000; the time until settlement or judgment is obtained in Victorian defamation matters; and the length of jury hearings. First, out of the 64 Victorian files, 46 had settled and 11 had been to trial by the end of 2000; that is, approximately 72 per cent settled and 17 per cent went to trial. Second, matters took approximately 11 months to reach final disposal via a settlement or trial judgment. The figures varied little between the Supreme and County Courts, and ranged between one and 28 months, with a mean of 11.1 months and a median of 11. Third, the number of trials was very small. Only 11 matters went to trial in the two courts, and some of these only concerned damages (with one not being contested even on that issue). But it is worth noting that the hearings only ranged between one and eight days and included full-jury trials of three, five, six and eight days. Two matters are worth noting in comparison to the NSW figures on these issues, discussed in Chapter 5. The median time until disposal was 11 months in Victoria and between 16 and 17 months in NSW. And in Victoria, 87 per cent of files had been disposed of by the end of 2000, while in NSW the figure was only 56 per cent.

B Examples from the files

Files are used here to illustrate pre-trial and trial treatment of meaning. First, the combination of plaintiff and defence pleadings set out the area of dispute in

[15] It also is worth noting that if imputations were more regularly considered at hearings, then many imputations must have been allowed to stand (ie, in at least some of the 28 files in which challenges appeared to be open), which could have been subjected to successful challenge in NSW.

[16] General forms of qualified privilege were pleaded in 27 files and *Lange* qualified privilege was pleaded in eight files.

relation to meaning, which then was left until trial; for example, 'high' imputations that had been pleaded by plaintiffs were not necessarily challenged. Second, even where files contained imprecise plaintiff pleadings – which many files did – they tended not to be challenged, but were responded to with Lucas-Box pleas. Third, challenges *were* taken at times and a great degree of specificity could be sought. But the common law approach appeared to discourage frequent challenges. Fourth, trial transcripts suggested two notable points: challenges to pleaded meanings that had not been raised earlier would be raised at trial and the jury is kept close to the publication rather than just to the pleaded imputations.

1 Setting out meaning: plaintiff pleadings and Lucas-Box defences

Often the combination of plaintiff and defence pleadings set out a dispute on meaning that was left until trial, as illustrated by *Danby v Amalgamated Television Services*. It related to a television news item that reported a parliamentarian's wife had obtained an interim domestic violence restraining order against him. The broadcast included these words:

Newsreader's intro:	Cheryl Kernot has been urged to intervene in a dispute over an ALP candidate accused of domestic violence. In a leaked letter, Labor women say the Party cannot afford to ignore the allegations.
Milne voice-over:	Cheryl Kernot has always been a strong campaigner against domestic violence. It was a bonus when she defected to the ALP. She's now running in the Brisbane seat of Dickson, where the Liberal MP, Tony Smith, has been accused of domestic violence and frequenting a brothel. Now, though, there are allegations that one of Labor's own, Michael Danby, has also engaged in domestic violence. Mr Danby, a prominent ALP right-winger, is running in the safe seat of Melbourne Ports, despite being the subject of an interim domestic violence restraining order from his wife. Now the Labor women of Melbourne Ports are appealing to Ms Kernot to help them have Mr Danby's preselection overturned. In this leaked letter, they've written to Ms Kernot saying, 'we wonder how you feel about tackling Tony Smith on this issue, with the knowledge your own Party has endorsed a candidate who has been accused of similar behaviour'.
Milne piece to camera:	The ALP women have put Ms Kernot in a potentially embarrassing position. Labor will find it difficult to exploit Tony Smith's record on alleged domestic violence unless Ms Kernot speaks out against Mr Danby. . . .[17]

[17] *Michael Danby v Amalgamated Television Services* (No 4846 of 1998) Statement of Claim. The reporter was Glenn Milne, while the newsreader is not identified on file.

The plaintiff pleaded two imputations:

(a) the plaintiff had engaged in domestic violence;

(b) [the plaintiff] had committed improper acts similar to the act of which the Liberal MP Tony Smith had been accused, including domestic violence and frequenting a brothel.[18]

The defendants denied these imputations. They also pleaded that the second one was vague and embarrassing, but no challenge was heard pre-trial. The defendants also set out Lucas-Box meanings for Victoria,[19] in these terms:

(a) they say further that in its ordinary and natural meaning the program meant and was understood to mean that:

- the plaintiff had been accused of engaging in domestic violence;
- there were reasonable grounds to suspect that the plaintiff had engaged in domestic violence;
- the plaintiff had been the subject of an interim intervention order sought by his wife.[20]

Various particulars of truth were supplied. The plaintiff attacked the pleading as embarrassing and disclosing no defence.[21] Again no hearing occurred. The defendant later filed an amended defence in which it persisted with these Lucas-Box meanings and added an alternative defence justifying the plaintiff's meanings.[22]

What happened with these pleadings? In NSW, one might expect the plaintiff's first imputation to have been challenged as lacking specificity. It may well have survived because the publication itself used the words 'domestic violence' and it would seem that no greater specificity was possible. That is, the publication is just the sort that was referred to by Gleeson CJ in *Drummoyne v Australian Broadcasting Corporation*, when he described how:

> The requirement upon a plaintiff cannot go beyond doing the best that can reasonably be done in the circumstances. . . . [T]he degree of specificity with which it is appropriate to require [the plaintiff] to formulate the defamatory imputation will need to be related to the nature and content of the defamatory matter.[23]

The imputation could also be challenged on capacity grounds: the plaintiff's pleading arguably is 'high' in stating that the meaning of *engaging in* domestic

[18] *Ibid*.

[19] *Ibid*: the Lucas-Box meanings also were pleaded for South Australia in the same paragraph, and separately for Western Australia, Tasmania, Queensland, the ACT and the Northern Territory.

[20] *Ibid* Defence.

[21] *Ibid* Reply.

[22] *Ibid* Amended Defence.

[23] *Drummoyne Municipal Council v Australian Broadcasting Corpn* (1990) 21 NSWLR 135, 137 (Gleeson CJ).

violence actually arises rather than a lesser meaning of suspicion of domestic violence. In NSW, one would expect pre-trial hearings to debate whether the broadcast would be capable of conveying guilt or merely reasonable suspicion of guilt of domestic violence, while in England discussion would be likely to encompass the three levels of guilt, suspicion or grounds to investigate (which are discussed in Chapters 2 and 3). One also could expect the plaintiff's second imputation to be challenged in NSW – as to its specificity because it combines two allegations in one imputation, and also as to its capacity to arise. Also, in NSW if the Lucas-Box plea was repeated as a contextual truth defence, it would be successfully challenged because the defence imputations are not more serious than the plaintiff's ones, as required by s 16 of the *Defamation Act 1974*. Actually, in this file exactly the same meanings were pleaded as contextual imputations in relation to NSW; this happened in the files whenever NSW publication was at issue and a Lucas-Box plea had been made.[24] And in this case, no such challenges took place. There were several interlocutory hearings about further and better particulars, interrogatories and so forth, and the matter proceeded to trial before O'Bryan J without a jury in October 1999.[25] But even without challenges, it was clear from the pleadings that a major issue between the parties was about *engaged* or *suspected of engaging* in domestic violence.

The trial transcript shows that the plaintiff abandoned its second imputation at the outset.[26] After viewing a video of the broadcast, the judge asked why the plaintiff said the meaning was 'engaged in domestic violence' rather than there being a 'rumour' of this.[27] Counsel relied on textbook discussions of how repeating rumours can convey more substantial meanings. The plaintiff's counsel later returned briefly to the Lucas-Box plea in terms of whether it was open on Victorian law.[28] During most of the second day, the plaintiff gave evidence and the defence persisted in its justification plea through cross-examining the plaintiff about alleged violence. Up to that point, there had been little discussion of the parties' differing meanings. Presumably, more explicit comments would have been made in closing addresses. The case, however, settled at the start of the third day, with an apology read in open court and the defendants agreeing to pay the

---

[24] Also, in two files defendants pleaded that 'contextual imputations' arose without pleading any Lucas-Box defence and without identifying the imputations. These defendants were not required to identify the contextual imputations as they would be in NSW: *National Tax and Accountants' Association v Australian Society of Certified Practising Accountants* (No 4320 of 1998); *Agnes Pali v Faye Harris* (No 1116 of 1998).

[25] The trial was delayed slightly owing to Family Court proceedings involving the plaintiff and his wife.

[26] Transcript of Proceedings, *Michael Danby v Amalgamated Television Services* (Vic SC, Trial before O'Bryan J, 27 October 1999) 1. The defendant also sought to add further particulars to its justification defence in relation to an alleged assault.

[27] *Ibid* 28.

[28] *Ibid* 45. The hearing occurred at a time when Lucas-Box pleading had an uncertain status in Victorian law; ie after *Chakravarti v Advertiser Newspapers* (1998) 193 CLR 519 and cases such as *Carrey v ACP Publishing* [1999] 1 VR 875, but before *David Syme v Hore-Lacy* [2000] 1 VR 667. See further Chapters 2, 3 and 9.

plaintiff's costs on a party-to-party basis.[29] What is interesting for the purposes of this book is the way in which *Danby* illustrates how a difference between the parties as to meaning was made fairly clear in the pleadings (through the plaintiff's pleading and the Lucas-Box defence) but this difference provoked no pre-trial hearings and raised little discussion during two days of a judge-alone trial.

The same tendency is illustrated by *Armstrong v Gillespie*, which involved a dispute among union officials. Various publications concerned the plaintiff union official's alleged misappropriation of funds. Pleaded meanings included that 'the plaintiff was dishonest' and 'the plaintiff had misused union funds'.[30] The defendant denied all the plaintiff's imputations and set up Lucas-Box pleas, similar to this one:

> (a) the Plaintiff engaged in financial impropriety in respect of union funds;
>
> (b) the Plaintiff misappropriated union funds;
>
> (c) the Plaintiff refused to allow the third Defendant to inspect the financial records of the union as was his right according to union rules, despite serious allegations of financial impropriety and misappropriation having been made against the Plaintiff;
>
> (d) the conduct of the Plaintiff in relation to financial impropriety and misappropriation of union funds was serious enough to warrant investigation by branch trustees and a report of such investigation being made to the membership of the union.[31]

The file remained open at the end of the fieldwork period, but the combination of plaintiff and defence pleadings, with the absence of hearings about meaning, suggests again how the focus in Victoria is on the publication – and pleadings are considered in the context of that publication. It is not an imputation-centred approach. Thus, there is not the extent of battles over form and capacity that exists in NSW. And less precise plaintiff imputations, such as the plaintiff is 'dishonest', cause no difficulty *in the context of* the publication and a Lucas-Box plea.

2 *Imprecise plaintiff pleadings and Lucas-Box defences*

Many files contained imprecise plaintiff pleadings, which tended not to be challenged. For example, in County Court files that were open for at least

---

[29] The text of the apology included:

> It is acknowledged by [the defendants] that [the plaintiff] vehemently denies the allegations made against him . . . [and] denies having ever engaged in any acts of domestic violence. [The defendants] unreservedly acknowledge that no allegation of domestic violence has ever been established against [the plaintiff] . . . in any court or otherwise.

[30] *Jan Armstrong v Danny Gillespie* (No 7424 of 1998) Statement of Claim.

[31] *Ibid* Defence.

14 months before any settlement occurred, there were no challenges to bare imputations that the plaintiff was 'dishonest' and 'unscrupulous',[32] an 'unethical person' and 'dishonest person',[33] 'a thief' and liar,[34] 'has acted against the interests of depositors' in a wine bank,[35] 'dishonest person',[36] 'dishonourable' and 'not to be trusted'.[37] In only a few files were similar allegations pleaded in a more specified form: for example, a pleading that the plaintiff real estate agent 'acted dishonestly by falsely maintaining that a genuine purchaser existed'.[38] Quite often, these imprecise pleas were responded to with Lucas-Box defences. The plaintiff's meanings were not challenged in a hearing, but the difference between the parties on meaning was made clear through a Lucas-Box plea. The difference was then left until the matter reached trial or settled.

The Lucas-Box pleas were quite commonly more specific than the plaintiff's meanings. For example, *Taylor v The Herald & Weekly Times* concerned a newspaper article about a volunteer helicopter surf-rescue squad, headed 'Rescue Squad is "too risky"'. The plaintiff pleaded imputations that the plaintiff:

(a) was too old to safely fly the helicopter;

(b) was an incompetent helicopter pilot;

(d) could not navigate or properly navigate the helicopter;

(e) conducted dangerous and unsafe aerial manoeuvres in the helicopter;

(f) piloted the helicopter whilst its rotor blades were in a dangerous and unsafe condition.[39]

The defendant responded with a Lucas-Box plea in these terms:

(a) the plaintiff piloted the helicopter in April 1994 when it crashed into Port Phillip Bay while not carrying life jackets and was thereby so piloted in disregard for the safety of passengers;

(b) the plaintiff piloted the helicopter after a rescue near Port Campbell January 1990 in a way that he became lost, and the helicopter was dangerously low on fuel upon its return to Sorrento;

(c) the plaintiff engaged in the practice of "hedgehopping" [which was described in the article];

---

[32] *Leo Ryan v Wayne Harris* (No 0027 of 1998) Statement of Claim; similarly, 'dishonest' was not challenged in the eight months before settlement in the file of *Chen Mingliang v The Tide Chinese Newspaper* (No 4530 of 1998) Statement of Claim.

[33] *Henry Drazak v Anthony Latessa* (No 0633 of 1998) Statement of Claim.

[34] *Jenny Tsoumeas v Amazzon Brunswick* (No 3941 of 1998) Statement of Claim; similarly, 'thief' was not challenged in *Richard McDonnell v Helen Kerr* (No 3639 of 1998) Statement of Claim.

[35] *Wine Bank Australia v Craig Nodder* (No 4988 of 1998) Statement of Claim.

[36] *Brian Everard v Public Transport Corpn* (No 5111 of 1998) Statement of Claim.

[37] *Alfred Zion v Max Cooper* (No 5363 of 1998) Statement of Claim.

[38] *Keith Beresford v Mark Sutherland* (No 1839 of 1998) Statement of Claim.

[39] *Bruce Taylor v Herald & Weekly Times* (No 0598 of 1998) Statement of Claim.

(d) the plaintiff released a crew member from a static line suspended from the helicopter whilst the crew member was still hanging above the ground, whereby the crew member fell and injured his foot;

(e) the plaintiff piloted the helicopter in December 1996 from Cape Schanck golf course to Moorabbin while its rotor blades were in a dangerous and unsafe condition.[40]

The matter was set down for jury trial without any challenge to these pleadings, but settled before trial. Again, imputations that one would expect to be challenged in NSW were left unchallenged, and surely part of the reason is that the defence could respond with Lucas-Box pleas.

3 *Challenges seeking precision*

Only two Supreme Court files did see challenges. *Nixon v Random House* shows that similar detail to NSW on pleading *can* be sought, although the files overall suggest it rarely is sought. In *Nixon v Random House*, a former director of the University of Melbourne student counselling service sued a book publisher and editor about a chapter in the book *Bodyjamming: Sexual Harassment, Feminism and Public Life*.[41] In part, the book concerned a complaint by two female students from a residential college associated with the University of Melbourne that the college's master had sexually harassed and indecently assaulted them. The master subsequently was acquitted of indecent assault charges. Those matters received very wide media attention in Australia, and the book at issue was a response to some of the coverage. The chapter in question in *Nixon v Random House* was written by one of the complainants in the sexual offence case who was identified in the book only as 'XX'.[42] The plaintiff pleaded these imputations arose from the chapter:

(a) the plaintiff's task was to completely shut down complaints of sexual harassment brought by students against the master . . .;

(b) the plaintiff made use of her position as conciliator to try to shut down the complaints and discourage the complainants from taking their complaints further;

(c) the plaintiff, whilst engaging in the task of conciliation, had wrongly accused one complainant of lying;

(d) the plaintiff wrongly and incompetently recommended that [the master] remain in his position;

(e) the plaintiff handled the complaints of sexual harassment in an unprofessional and biased manner;

---

[40] *Ibid* Defence.

[41] Mead (1997).

[42] Jenna Mead, the second defendant who edited the book, is incorrectly identified as the chapter's author in *Nixon v Random House Australia* [1999] VSC 393. Mead also is mistakenly identified as one of the complainants in relation to the sexual harassment matters.

(f) the plaintiff, in acting as a conciliator, failed to act in accordance with the guidelines of the University of Melbourne guaranteeing confidentiality to complainants in sexual harassment matters;

(g) the plaintiff breached her own undertaking of confidentiality to the complainants in a sexual harassment conciliation;

(h) in order to further her own career, the plaintiff improperly made use of confidential matters revealed to her in a conciliation session.[43]

The defendant admitted the imputations in (f) and (g) were conveyed, denied the other meanings, and set out a Lucas-Box plea:

(a) the Plaintiff had so conducted herself as to cause a complainant to believe that the Plaintiff's key task may have been to completely shut the complaints down;

(b) the Plaintiff handled the complaints of sexual harassment badly in that she adopted a confrontationalist manner rather than one which facilitated the conciliation of the complaints.[44]

Exactly the same meanings were pleaded as contextual imputations in relation to publication of the book in NSW.

The pleadings saw two interlocutory hearings. The first was before Evans M on 15 July 1999.[45] The plaintiff agreed to replead paragraphs (c), (d) and (h) of the statement of claim at the hearing. They were changed to remove the possible ambiguity in the words *wrongly* and *improperly* – classic 'weasel words' in NSW terminology. The imputations became:

(c) the plaintiff, whilst engaging in the task of conciliation, had *breached her duties as a conciliator in that she had* accused one complainant of lying *in order to pressure the complainants to withdraw their complaints;*

(d) the plaintiff *in recommending that [the master] remain in his position did so wrongly and dishonestly in that, rather than conducting a fair and impartial conciliation process, she was merely following the instructions of the Vice Chancellor of the University of Melbourne, to whom she directly reported, whose object was to support the master by discrediting the complainants;*

(h) in order to further her own career, the plaintiff improperly made use of confidential matters revealed to her in a conciliation session *in that she breached both university guidelines guaranteeing confidentiality and her own undertaking to that effect.*[46]

The changes brought a similar degree of specificity to the imputations as normally would be required in NSW. Evans M also struck out the first paragraph

[43] *Susan Nixon v Random House and Jenna Mead* (No 5553 of 1998) Statement of Claim.

[44] *Ibid* Defence.

[45] *Nixon* (Unreported, Vic SC, Evans M, 25 June 1999).

[46] *Susan Nixon v Random House and Jenna Mead* (No 5553 of 1998) Amended Statement of Claim. At the hearing before Evans M, the plaintiff had proposed to use the words 'doing the bidding of her boss' in paragraph (d). The defendant successfully objected to this, so the amended imputation became more specific.

of the defendants' Lucas-Box plea, which the defence appealed against unsuccessfully.[47]

A trial before judge and jury commenced on 29 May 2000. On the first morning, the defence sought a suppression order covering both complainants from the earlier sexual offence trial, who would be witnesses in the defamation trial. Suppression of media reporting of the case was refused.[48] It appears this led to settlement, which was announced that day before the jury was empanelled. *Nixon*, and the one other case with a broadly equivalent meaning dispute,[49] highlights how rare such interlocutory skirmishes are in Victoria. A similar degree of precision to NSW can be sought, and Victorian judges may be persuaded by NSW judgments about meaning notwithstanding that state's peculiar statutory cause of action. But, the general Victorian practice appears to be *not* to make such challenges.

4 *Challenges at trial and meaning before the jury*

It appears that challenges to meaning that are not raised pre-trial will be raised at trial in Victoria. *Kennett v Nationwide News* concerned a newspaper article published one day after the then Victorian premier – the state's political leader – and his wife announced their separation.[50] *The Australian* ran a feature article, headed 'A House Divided', which examined stresses facing the couple in public life. The plaintiff pleaded four imputations:

(a) the Plaintiff, whilst living with his wife Felicity, was sexually involved with other women;

(b) the Plaintiff, whilst living with his wife Felicity, betrayed her by having sexual relations with [one named woman];

(c) the Plaintiff, whilst living with his wife Felicity, betrayed her by having sexual relations with [a second named woman];

(d) the Plaintiff lied by falsely denying that he was sexually involved with [the two women].[51]

The defendant denied these meanings, and denied the article was capable of being defamatory, but pleaded no substantive defence. Thus the case was particularly focussed on meaning. There were no interlocutory hearings about meaning. Interlocutory hearings were concerned with discovery, interrogatories and so forth.

At the trial, a jury of six found against the plaintiff: the article did not defame him. In legal terms, it discussed the rumours without conveying their truth. So how was meaning argued about at the trial? The case ran for five days, with the

[47] *Nixon* [1999] VSC 393.

[48] *Nixon* (2000) 2 VR 523.

[49] *May Wan Khor v Nationwide News* (No 6596 of 1998).

[50] They later reconciled.

[51] *Jeffrey Kennett v Nationwide News* (No 4292 of 1998) Statement of Claim.

defence calling no evidence. The parties explained the legal rules about meaning in a fairly traditional manner, but spent relatively little time on it. Much of the court time was taken up with plaintiff witnesses on damages, and counsel addressing the jury about damages. The transcript also shows that the plaintiff's counsel went through the article at some length with the jury,[52] emphasising its 'dominant theme': 'There are a lot of references to rumours, and speculations and accusations and rumours, and rumours and rumours and rumours.'[53] The approach is shown in this passage from the transcript, in which counsel is quoting from the article:

> 'Speculation about the state of the Kennett marriage' – here is this favourite word, *The Australian* just loves this word – 'Speculation about the state of the Kennett marriage peaked early in 1995 when rumours' – that is the other word most loved by *The Australian* newspaper in this article – 'rumours swept through Melbourne, that it was in deep trouble. So intense was the speculation that Mr Kennett was drawn into a response, telling the *Sydney Morning Herald*, "I have heard that I have been separated in recent times, which I find interesting, but I think that simply came because we moved out of our house for six months while we were having renovations and we were living in East Melbourne. We have been married for 22 years. Yes, I am aware of those rumours. Where do they come from? But they have no substance."'[54]

The defence argued the plaintiff's meanings did not arise – that is, the publication did *not* convey that the rumours were true. The defendant also sought to have the plaintiff's fourth imputation removed from the jury, saying,

> And I am not just relying on the fact that Mr Kennett was unable to [infer the meaning] when I gave him an opportunity [in cross-examination[55]]. In my submission, his inability to do so was because nobody could do so. . . . I suppose it was gratuitous what I said about the plaintiff's inability to do it. It just demonstrates our point. I mean, of all people you would have expected, if anyone could have found it, Mr Kennett could.[56]

The defence had never sought to have that meaning ruled out earlier:[57] the challenge was left until trial. In response, the plaintiff argued that the meaning was open because of these words in the article: 'Two of those Mr Kennett has persistently been linked with, despite their denials' are the two named women.[58] The plaintiff said 'their' denials could include the plaintiff. The trial judge agreed and the matter was left to the jury.[59]

---

52 Transcript of Proceedings, *Jeffrey Kennett v Nationwide News* (Vic SC, trial before Ashley J and jury, 4 March 1999) 18–28.

53 *Ibid* 19.

54 *Ibid* 23.

55 *Ibid* 110–12.

56 *Ibid* (5 March 1999) 217–18.

57 *Ibid* (9 March 1999) 344.

58 *Ibid* 344–45.

59 *Ibid* 347–48.

The plaintiff did not address meaning at great length during the trial. For example, the plaintiff's closing address to the jury only very briefly commented on meaning:

> Now, members of the jury, in this case you will have no difficulty answering those questions and I ask you to have a look at those questions now if I can. See that first question: 'Was the article defamatory?' Of course it was defamatory. It was defamatory because it said of a man of high reputation that he was sexually involved with these other women.[60]

That is all the plaintiff mentioned about meaning in the address, which ran for almost one full day in court. The defence said a little more about meaning, while focussing attention on damages. The defence said it was for the jury to decide meaning, under an objective test, but argued the article meant only that there were persistent, untrue rumours.

> This article does not say that Jeff Kennett has been unfaithful to his wife. It says his wife has been subjected to pressure. One of those pressure points is unfounded persistent rumours, even though they are denied. That is what this article says. And that is not defamatory, and that is nothing like what the plaintiff says it says. And that is really the end of the case. And it is of no importance that Mr Kennett thinks it means something different. He is wrong: and the answer to question 1, therefore, should be 'No' . . .
>
> Now, if I had more courage than brains I would sit down now because really that is the start and finish of the case. 'No' to question 1, and that [is] the end of it.[61]

Not surprisingly, defence counsel did not stop there, but continued to consider damages at length.

The judge also was quite brief on issues of defamatory meaning. But it is noteworthy that he effectively directed the jury to consider the four imputations pleaded. In his address, Ashley J repeated the pleaded imputations and noted the jury might find that some, but not others, of the imputations were conveyed.[62] His approach followed from how the parties had presented their cases. While it might appear similar to NSW, it remained substantially different because of the style of questions left to the jury, which were in the form recommended by *Barclay v Cox*.[63] The jury questions were:

Question 1	Was the article published by the defendant on 29 January 1998 defamatory of the plaintiff?
Question 2	If yes to question 1, in what total sum do you assess the plaintiff's damages? $ . . . . . .

[60] *Ibid* (10 March 1999) 419 (J Ruskin QC for the plaintiff).

[61] *Ibid* 451–53 (J Sher QC for the defendant).

[62] *Ibid* (11 March 1999) 501.

[63] [1968] VR 664, 666 (Winneke CJ, Pape, Adam JJ).

Question 3 Of the amount set out in answer to question 2, what sum, if any, was awarded for exemplary damages? $......[64]

The jury considered their verdict for slightly less than one hour, and simply answered 'no' to the first question. The *Kennett* case illustrates how challenges may be left until trial, and also suggests the flexibility that the jury has on meaning in Victoria. The question they have to answer is general. They do not appear to be addressed at length about it. And their attention seems to be directed more strongly to the publication than to the pleaded imputations.

III MATERIAL FROM INTERVIEWS

As in England and NSW, Victorian interviewees saw meaning as important:

> [Meanings] shape the proceeding, even in Victoria where we're not bound by the imputations as in NSW they still shape the proceedings.[65]

> [Meaning] is *really* where the focus is though. It's where we spend most of our time.[66]

The triumvirate of meaning, truth and fair comment was what 'it really comes down to' in media cases.[67] But as the following discussion suggests, the way it shapes proceedings is different in Victoria. Eight topics are examined here related to court lists, pleadings and the common law cause of action, justification defences, fair comment, the roles of judge and jury, other approaches to meaning, reform possibilities and the test for what conveyed meanings are defamatory.

A Court lists

Many interviewees emphasised the two Victorian Lists' influence on litigation.[68] The use of specialist judges was widely supported,[69] while nothing significant was mentioned about individual judicial styles. But an important aspect that differs from NSW is the use of masters,[70] and non-list judges in interlocutory stages.[71] Some interlocutory hearings would not be conducted by

[64] The questions had been discussed by judge and counsel near the trial's end: *ibid* 349–50 and 374; see also *Jeffrey Kennett v Nationwide News* (No 4292 of 1998) Jury Questionnaire.

[65] 56SC.

[66] 55B; similar comments were made by 49SC.

[67] 55B.

[68] 49SC.

[69] 52SC, 53S; similar 50B.

[70] 51S, 55B.

[71] 54S.

the specialist judge,[72] and a listing master – not the specialist judge – would set a trial date.[73] Lawyers thought specialist judges generally applied the law better, and felt lawyers sometimes 'got lost in the shuffle' between judge and master.[74] For example, when a case was ready for trial, the specialist judge would send it to the listing master. But parties, particularly defendants, could make new applications before the master to avoid a trial date being set. In this way the media had 'happy hunting days' to delay trials.[75] This appeared to be a continuation of practices that pre-date judge-managed lists when the 'obvious tactic' was 'to delay a case as long as possible'.[76]

B Pleadings, challenges and the common law cause of action

Many interviewees distinguished the Victorian situation from NSW's statutory cause of action.[77] Both it and the 7A trial procedure were viewed with scepticism. The NSW situation was seen as 'extraordinary'[78] and 'ridiculous',[79] while the degree of precision required was labelled very counterproductive and 'completely artificial':[80]

> The only thing it's productive of is interlocutory pleading summonses and that's a denial of justice, because it delays the cases.[81]

Challenges to form and capacity were seen as being less frequent than in NSW, primarily because of Victoria's common law cause of action based on the publication rather than the pleaded imputation.[82] Distinctions between implications, inferences and speculation are not referred to in Victoria.[83] And there is less concern about weasel words.[84] But it was suggested the classic weasel word plea of *corrupt* would be challenged, although it might survive depending on what master or judge heard the challenge.[85]

Although the number of pleaded imputations is comparatively high in Victoria, interviewees suggested that a multiplicity of slightly different

---

72 51S, 55B.

73 55B.

74 51S.

75 54S.

76 53S.

77 49SC, 50B, 52SC, 54S, 56SC.

78 49SC, 54S.

79 50B.

80 53S; similar 56SC.

81 50B.

82 49SC, 54S, 55B.

83 52SC, 54S.

84 54S, 56SC.

85 50B, 55B.

imputations is 'unhelpful to the trier of fact'[86] and experienced practitioners will limit the number.[87] Simplicity was seen as a key aim:

> If you can't get a simple defamatory imputation out of it, leave it alone. . . . [A simple meaning is] just like a shining light, right throughout the darkness. In other words, just keep it simple.[88]

Victorian pleading disputes were seen by several interviewees to arise when inexperienced pleaders drew statements of claim.[89] They will be challenged sometimes for 'legitimate legal reasons' because of evidential implications, but also for tactical 'commercial' reasons – to pressure the plaintiff by increasing the cost of litigation.[90]

Defendants are more likely to challenge meanings than plaintiffs. Echoing the second of this chapter's opening quotations, another interviewee commented:

> [Disputes about meaning] are a favoured tactic of defendants. It's not often that you will see a plaintiff arguing about meanings. Indeed, it's not often that you'll see a well-advised plaintiff arguing about anything. I take the view that the plaintiff's best interests are served by going as quickly as possible to trial, even if that means sacrificing some niceties about discovery or even niceties about pleadings.[91]

Other responses also suggested that a common approach in Victoria was for plaintiffs to avoid challenging aspects of a defence case in order to reach trial as quickly as possible: 'I would never pick a fight with a defendant' about Lucas-Box meanings 'unless it was absolutely essential'.[92] For defendants, interviewees offered mixed responses. Some suggested that challenges were fairly common,[93] which appears to be more than the files indicate. But others suggested that *meaning* challenges were not always taken by the defence pre-trial. Victorian practitioners thought plaintiff meanings often survive challenge,[94] which can boost plaintiffs' confidence and help clarify their case – and neither of these effects would please defendants:

> [T]here's a great hesitancy in trying to knock out, or have a go at the meanings, unless it's a lay down misère that all of them are going to go, because the last thing we want to do is . . . help the plaintiff define what [it is] doing in relation to [the] imputations.[95]

---

[86] 51S.

[87] 49SC, 54S, 56SC.

[88] 54S.

[89] 51S, 53S; similar 54S.

[90] 53S; similar 55B.

[91] 56SC.

[92] 50B.

[93] 49SC, 52SC, 55B; similar 56SC.

[94] 50B, 53S.

[95] 54S.

Unless all the meanings will be struck out, it can be better to wait until trial.[96] In any event, all the issues can be raised at trial even if they have not been raised earlier.[97]

An issue that was difficult for interviewees to address concerned the difference in how parties may be held to their meanings. As discussed in Chapter 5, the NSW law states that parties are held to the imputation pleaded or one not substantially different. But under NSW practice, the jury is asked about the specific imputations pleaded in a questionnaire, and it appears the jury may well focus on exactly those meanings. After *David Syme v Hore-Lacy*,[98] Victorian law says parties need to present cases that accord with their pleadings, but it remains open to juries to find a lesser and not substantially different meaning was conveyed. Interviewees could only suggest that there is a difference of degree from NSW in how parties are held to their pleaded meanings.[99] One experienced barrister suggested the judge will probably say something like, 'you might think that the meanings chosen by the parties are the ones you should really concentrate on, as a matter of fairness', and therefore 'it may be a pretty close call' as to whether there is a difference from that in NSW.[100] In the *Kennett* case, discussed in Part II, the trial judge came close to saying just that. But perhaps the difference really is suggested by the style of general jury questions in Victoria, which also is illustrated by the *Kennett* trial.

C Defences related to meaning: Lucas-Box, Polly Peck, contextual imputations

The terms Lucas-Box and Polly Peck pleadings are not distinguished in Victorian practice.[101] 'Practitioners *never* say Lucas-Box.'[102] But as explained in earlier chapters, Lucas-Box pleading is the more common form of the defence and it seems valuable for Australian practice to identify the distinction consistently and clearly, so the term Lucas-Box is used in this chapter. Many interviewees disagreed with the High Court minority judgment in *Chakravarti v Advertiser Newspapers*,[103] seeing it as being very influenced by the NSW approach.[104] Instead, they supported Lucas-Box pleading because it allowed defendants to

---

96 53S.

97 *Roux v Australian Broadcasting Commission* [1992] 2 VR 577, 581–82 (Byrne J); *Carrey* [1999] 1 VR 875.

98 [2000] 1 VR 667.

99 49SC, 56SC.

100 49SC. The interviewee was referring to the approach of the trial judge in *Gumina v Williams;* see appellate report *Gumina v Williams (No 2)* (1990) 3 WAR 351.

101 52SC, 56SC; similar 49SC, 50B, 51S, 54S.

102 56SC.

103 (1998) 193 CLR 519.

104 Eg 49SC, 50B, 56SC.

avoid the 'straightjacket' of plaintiffs' pleadings.[105] Lucas-Box is the common law's benefit:

> [L]ibel law is about what the true meaning of the article is in the eyes of the tribunal of fact and I think if you're going to bring a libel action, you should be prepared to bring it courageously, and you shouldn't be permitted to narrow your meaning, so if on a bad day the jury accepted that meaning, the defendant has its hands tied.[106]

Lucas-Box pleas were seen as being very common – almost a 'reflex'[107] and something that 'always arises in practice'[108] – owing to truth's utility as a defence. 'Practicality suggests the best defence in a libel action is truth.'[109] It is a defence that appeals to juries,[110] and one that is tactically powerful against plaintiffs pre-trial because the evidence admissible to support the plea may encourage plaintiffs to settle.[111]

The pleas are a 'tremendous weapon' for the defence,[112] and this also was acknowledged as raising some concerns:

> [Lucas-Box can be a problem] because it creates the basis for defendants to waste time and cost. I'm concerned about any potential, even though I mostly act for defendants, for defendants to prevent matters coming to trial and having the true dispute resolved.[113]

Just as discussed in *Chakravarti*,[114] the question about Lucas-Box is its appropriateness as a plea:

> Defendants will always strive to plead a meaning which is defamatory . . . that they can justify, in circumstances where they can't possibly justify the imputations pleaded by the plaintiff. Now is that a misuse? I don't know.[115]

This book argues such pleading need not be a misuse, but can be an appropriate response to the circumstances. The same experienced barrister noted the defence will try Lucas-Box 'in circumstances where they can't possibly justify the imputations pleaded by the plaintiff' – and the problem suggested about the NSW approach from court files and interviews is that it allows plaintiffs to plead such imputations too easily. That is, plaintiffs understandably will seek to craft imputations that are very difficult to defend – and the NSW research suggests

[105] 51S; similar 49SC.

[106] 49SC.

[107] 51S.

[108] 52SC.

[109] 49SC.

[110] 49SC, 51S, 55B.

[111] 49SC, 51S; similar 53S, 54S.

[112] 51S; similar 55B.

[113] 56SC.

[114] *Chakravarti* (1998) 193 CLR 519, and see Chapter 3, Part I, K.

[115] 52SC.

this will happen all the more if the parties effectively are held to the plaintiff's meanings. As another barrister suggested,

> We do lots of Polly Peck down here. Defendants love them.... Typically when you've got a newspaper article or something which is wide-ranging and it has a go at someone on all sorts of levels. And the plaintiff's been a bit selective about what they've sued on, which happens all the time.[116]

So while the minority approach in *Chakravarti*[117] would create a fairly simple legal rule – and it *could* be supported on that basis[118] – it is not necessarily the most appropriate response. One interviewee who was ambivalent on this issue, noted:

> I mean in terms of the simplicity of it, I'm not so sure that the Brennan and McHugh approach isn't to be preferred you see. It just cuts away the potential for these kind of rather artificial disputes.[119]

The question of where the rhetorical and pejorative label of 'artificial' should be placed when comparing the NSW and common law approaches will be returned to in Chapters 9 and 10.

With regard to contextual imputations, interviewees emphasised how Lucas-Box pleas were often stated in the same form as contextual imputations – indeed one experienced barrister noted that he had not seen them done differently,[120] and the Victorian court files support this observation. But the lawyers were quite aware that this did not accord with the law. At trial, parties invariably agree to run on one state's defence – in Victoria, the common law Lucas-Box defence not NSW's contextual truth.[121] For many years, multistate issues rarely have arisen before a jury, apart from on the question of damages. But notable examples dealing with multiple states' defences exist from judge-alone cases.[122] The judge's greater role in NSW under the 7A process has seen the consideration of interstate defences increase since the fieldwork.

D Defences related to meaning: fair comment

Interviewees supported common law fair comment in comparison to NSW's defence, primarily for the same reasons that NSW interviewees criticised their comment defence. That is, the NSW defence is almost impossible to run because it must meet the plaintiff's *imputations*. NSW plaintiffs will plead imputations that are not in the form of comments, and strive for imputations that the publisher did not intend. Those problems are avoided in Victoria, with

---

116 55B.

117 *Chakravarti* (1998) 193 CLR 519.

118 52SC, 55B, 56SC.

119 56SC.

120 52SC.

121 52SC, 55B, 56SC.

122 Eg *Gorton v Australian Broadcasting Commission* (1973) 1 ACTR 6; *Renouf v Federal Capital Press of Australia* (1977) 17 ACTR 35.

defendants at least allowed to run fair comment defences to *publications* rather than imputations.[123] This situation has changed somewhat since the fieldwork, due to cases like *Anderson v Nationwide News*, which is discussed in Chapter 9.[124] Although the Victorian law strictly requires all the facts underlying fair comment be proved true, interviewees suggested that juries would take a reasonably flexible approach.[125] In effect, the focus would move to proving the substantial truth of most facts.[126] And defendants would rely on free speech arguments to say they were entitled to publish their opinions on the basis of on those facts.[127]

One other noteworthy point about fair comment, which also may increase the plea's popularity in Victoria, was raised in interviews as well as being suggested by the files. For a justification defence of any type, the defence needs to make clear the meaning that it will seek to prove true. But for a fair comment defence, Victoria still allows the rolled-up plea, which means plaintiffs are not entitled to particulars of what the defence argues is comment and what is fact.[128] However, defendants now need to identify the substance of what is allegedly comment.[129] Court files suggest the plea is common, being pleaded more than twice as often as 'standard' fair comment. This difference from justification is incongruous. While greater requirements have been placed on defendants when pleading justification, they have not been placed on defendants to plead the underlying facts for fair comment. To a degree, 'the plaintiff is ambushed' when faced with a rolled-up plea.[130] However, the plea provoked little disquiet from interviewees, and appears to remain accepted.

E Judge and jury roles

No interviewees supported reducing the jury role. Two prime reasons could be seen for supporting the jury. First, it provides community input to litigation practice, which is particularly suited to defamation.[131] In part, this was acknowledged as a flexible response to the merits of a case, as perceived by the jury, rather than a technically correct legal decision:

[123] 52SC.

[124] (2001) 3 VR 619; see Chapter 9, Part IV, A.

[125] 49SC, 55B.

[126] 55B.

[127] 49SC.

[128] See eg Gillooly (1998) 145–46. The plea fell into disuse in England under the former *Rules of the Supreme Court 1965* (Eng) Ord 82 r 3(2); in England now see *Civil Procedure Rules 1998* (Eng) 53 PD 2.6. Similarly, it is unavailable under NSW court rules: *Supreme Court Rules 1970* (NSW) Pt 67; note, at the time of writing, the *Uniform Civil Procedure Rules* (NSW) did not contain specific provisions for defamation: see Chapter 1, Part I, C.

[129] See *Fletcher v POS Solutions Australia* [2004] VSC 507, [33]–[36] (Ashley J) and the discussion in Chapter 9, Part IV, A, about *Anderson v Nationwide News* (2001) 3 VR 619. See also *Watt v Herald & Weekly Times* [1997] Aust Defamation Reports [52,085].

[130] 49SC.

[131] 49SC; similar 52SC, 53S, 55B.

> [A] community verdict might take into account whether they think in all the circumstances the case is worthy. And I don't see that's a factor that shouldn't be taken into account.[132]

Second, and as in NSW, there were strong suggestions that juries simplified trials.[133] The presence of juries tended to limit the number of meanings that were pleaded, or were persisted with: 'particularly' in jury trials plaintiffs want to focus on only a few 'big meanings'.[134] And more generally than just in relation to meaning, trials need to be presented in a simple manner:

> [M]y experience at trial is that all of [the legal nicety] washes away and you have your real dispute, particularly in front of a jury. And the degree of detail that people exhaust themselves on, in these interlocutory stages, *vanishes*. . . . Juries are a wonderful discipline to counsel because you have to devise a way to conduct the litigation in such a way that you will not lose the interest of the jury . . . that will enable them to understand what the dispute is about, and will enable them to deliberate in some sensible way.[135]

> If a defamation case goes for more than three or four days, the jury will lose interest. . . . [B]oth plaintiffs and defendants will strive to make the case as short as possible and get to the point.[136]

This tendency would not be surprising in jury trials in other areas of law. Interestingly, however, an experienced barrister suggested simplification at trials *was* more pronounced in defamation than in other legal areas.[137] Defamation law's particular complexities mean counsel strive to make things simple.

F Other approaches to meaning

The jury deciding meaning at the end of a full trial was seen to be a very different situation than the 7A procedure.[138] While something like the approaches in *Radio 2UE Sydney v Parker*[139] or *Marks & Spencer v Granada Television*[140] could be tried in Victoria, interviewees suggested neither party would support it.[141] Deciding meaning at the outset was seen as arguing 'in a sterile environment'.[142] Plaintiffs would want the jury to hear all their case:

132 49SC.

133 49SC, 50B, 56SC.

134 49SC.

135 56SC.

136 50B.

137 56SC.

138 49SC, 53S, 54S.

139 (1992) 29 NSWLR 448. See Chapter 2, Part III, C.

140 (Unreported, Popplewell J, QBD, 23 February 1998).

141 50B, 52SC; similar 56SC.

142 50B.

> You'd want the plaintiff sobbing in the box; you'd want the wife or the husband coming in; you'd want the kids sobbing in the box. You'd want the whole panoply of the drama of the defamation trial in front of the jury.[143]

But interviewees raised a significant difference from the approach that was tried in *Parker* and *Marks & Spencer*. In Victoria, the jury probably would be asked only 'Is the publication defamatory?'[144] That is, the jury would not be asked to pick between each party's meaning. This accords with the style of questions used at the end of current trials, as shown in Part II. Interviewees thought that sort of question meant the approach would rarely be valuable. It would only have use when there was substantial argument about whether a publication conveyed any defamatory meaning at all. 'In long, convoluted cases [the *Parker* approach] is a good idea, because it might save an awful lot of time and money'[145] but not in the 'ordinary' case.[146] In addition, the approach's acceptance in Victoria remains an open question. Interviewees suggested the approach has been prepared in several cases,[147] but it appears that it has never been used.[148] Although the matter was not raised in the Court of Appeal's judgments in *Oakley v 3AW Southern Cross Radio*,[149] the issue was mentioned by counsel. One of the judges, however, reportedly thought the *Parker* approach was 'ridiculous' and 'preposterous'.[150] Overall it was not surprising that, given general approval of Victoria's ordinary approach to meaning, interviewees showed little support for other approaches to meaning.

G Reform

The question of some fast-track procedure to dispose of defamation cases received a mixed response from interviewees. They differed as to whether access to law was a peculiary important problem in the area of defamation – and as in England, it appeared that solicitors were more likely than barristers to say that worthy plaintiffs are unable to pursue claims.[151] The strongest doubt about reform raised by respondents concerned whether any feasible system could be implemented.[152] There were concerns that a limited damages approach like England's ss 8–10 of the *Defamation Act 1996* would still be expensive for plaintiffs to litigate.[153] The media would continue to 'dig their heels in and do

[143] 52SC.

[144] 50B, 55B, 56SC.

[145] 52SC; similar 54S, 56SC.

[146] 53S.

[147] 52SC, 55B.

[148] 52SC.

[149] [1999] VSCA 96.

[150] 52SC.

[151] Eg 53S, 54S; cf 52SC.

[152] 51S, 52SC.

[153] 50B.

everything that's humanly possible to ensure that they're not perceived as an easy target'.[154] Interviewees also raised concerns about court-ordered apologies arguably infringing media free speech.[155] But if fast-track remedies were limited to capped damages, some interviewees suggested the media would benefit through disposing of claims cheaply,[156] or that these sorts of reform proposals were really media-driven.[157] The difficulty of assessing the present system also was noted, with one experienced barrister suggesting:

> To my knowledge, [defamation claims] settle on the basis that, in quite a few cases, the plaintiff gets some money. Now that's something that's occurring under the present system. And measuring efficiency of defamation dispute resolution at the global level . . . is not to be undertaken by looking at the extremely small sample that ends up at a trial with counsel going all the way to final address.[158]

H The test for what is defamatory

As in earlier chapters, the question of whether a publication conveys a *defamatory* meaning can be dealt with briefly. The Victorian material supports the research from England and NSW. Interviewees tended to see the standard as objective,[159] or at least that the test would consider the majority view of what is appropriate behaviour.[160] While, strictly, these two approaches differ, interviewees emphasised how in practice one 'can always find another way of putting something that gets around the problem' of whether the meaning conveyed by the publication is *defamatory*.[161] The term *right-thinking person* will be used, but perhaps by way of 'lip-service'[162] for the trial judge's benefit more than in order to convey any particular concept to the jury.[163] This also was seen in the *Kennett* trial, where Ashley J said if one or more of the meanings were made out, the jury would need to decide whether they were defamatory:

> The plaintiff must satisfy you that by reference to general community standards the imputations . . . were likely to injure [the plaintiff's] reputation, or, to put it another way, that they would tend to lower [the plaintiff] in the estimation of right thinking people. . . . You do not have to be told what are

154 54S.

155 51S, 53S.

156 55B.

157 49SC.

158 56SC.

159 Eg 50B, 55B. 56SC gave a detailed example of how it would not be possible to argue a 'community segment' version of the test, which is the US approach to 'defamatory'; see Chapter 8 and below, fn 165.

160 Eg 51S.

161 51S.

162 *Ibid*.

163 54S.

> general community standards. Your accumulated experience of life will tell you what those standards are. They will tell you the effect of any imputation that you find established on right-thinking people.[164]

So while *right-thinking* is used, it is unclear that it has the normative connotations that have been debated in the literature.[165]

IV CONCLUSION

Three important points emerge from this chapter's analysis of Victorian court files and practitioner interviews. First, plaintiffs often plead more imputations than in England and NSW, but challenges by defendants are uncommon, especially in relation to the form of plaintiffs' imputations. Second, defendants commonly plead Lucas-Box meanings (which results in the parties' differences on meaning being set out reasonably clearly in the pleadings) and defendants plead defences of justification and fair comment far more frequently than in NSW. Third, after those pleadings the issue of meaning largely is left until trial, so meaning is left for the tribunal of fact – which is a jury in many instances – and the general questions given to juries makes the approach not an imputation-centred one. The implications of how meaning is dealt with in defamation law and practice are discussed in Chapters 9 and 10, after examining qualified privilege in England and Australia in Chapter 7 and, in relation to issues of meaning and public interest speech, US defamation law and practice in Chapter 8.

164 Transcript of Proceedings, *Jeffrey Kennett v Nationwide News* (Vic SC, trial before Ashley J and jury, 11 March 1999) 505–506.

165 See eg McNamara (2001); Trindade (1999); Cottrell (1998); Lidsky (1996); Watterson (1993); Note (1949).

– 7 –

QUALIFIED PRIVILEGE: ENGLISH AND AUSTRALIAN LAW AND PRACTICE

I INTRODUCTION

Earlier chapters have concentrated on one of the central issues most often at stake in defamation disputes – the role that a publication's meaning plays in defamation law and litigation practice. This chapter moves to the book's second main theme and examines ways in which political and public interest speech is protected by qualified privilege in England and Australia. It focuses on the scope and strength of recently developed qualified privilege defences in each country and considers the practicality of litigating qualified privilege claims. Chapter 8 then examines US defamation law as it has developed in the 40 years since *New York Times v Sullivan*,[1] in relation to both this book's themes – issues connected with a publication's meaning and the protection of public interest speech.[2]

A Traditional defamation law and 1990s developments

Defamation law traditionally has imposed liability on many defendants who cannot prove the truth of their publications. This follows in part from defamation law's unusual burden of proof for a civil action. Defamation claimants or plaintiffs need to prove three things: publication, identification and defamatory meaning.[3] They need not prove that publishers were at fault, nor that publications were false. In addition, once published material about the claimant or plaintiff is shown to be defamatory, general damages are presumed. The presumption of general damages and the need for most defendants to prove truth are key aspects in the idea of defamation law's chilling effect.[4] As earlier chapters have examined in detail, truth is central for defendant publishers because the primary defences of justification and fair comment require a publication's factual basis to be proved true. While truth need not be shown for the other major

[1] 376 US 254 (1964).

[2] The chapter updates and expands two earlier publications: Kenyon (2004b, 2005).

[3] See eg Price and Duodu (2004) [1.01]–[1.04].

[4] The presumption of damages has received wide criticism: see eg Barendt (1999); Fleming (1978).

defences of absolute and qualified privilege, these defences have traditionally applied to few media publications beyond fair reports of court proceedings or parliaments.

The frequent need to prove truth is something that Australian and English developments in qualified privilege have sought to address. Since the mid-1990s, extended forms of qualified privilege have developed in each country, with the central cases being *Reynolds v Times Newspapers*[5] and *Lange v Australian Broadcasting Corporation*.[6] (Broadly similar changes have occurred in New Zealand and some other comparable legal jurisdictions.[7]) In doctrinal terms, the defences certainly appear to protect more political or public interest speech than traditional defamation law. *Reynolds* privilege, for example, seeks to protect defamatory material of public importance that defendants have published responsibly, irrespective of the material's truth or falsity.[8] In this, *Reynolds* privilege attaches to *publications* to the world at large, rather than to *occasions* in the traditional sense.[9] *Reynolds* can be seen as 'conceptually, a different species of qualified privilege' from the traditional duty-interest defence,[10] or at least as a substantial expansion of the circumstances in which the defence can be satisfied.[11] *Lange* also has been described as making 'fundamental changes' to privilege's 'conceptual foundations'.[12] Under *Lange*, privilege has become a 'relatively egalitarian' defence that promotes '"free" discussion . . . in which all citizens, so long as they act "reasonably", may participate on equal terms, rather than with some enjoying the status of "privileged publishers"'.[13] While the doctrinal changes do appear substantial, the terms '*Reynolds* privilege' and '*Lange* privilege' are used here for clarity and brevity rather than to suggest any *complete* separation from traditional qualified privilege. This terminology also accords with case law references to the defences.[14]

---

5 [2001] 2 AC 127.

6 (1997) 189 CLR 520.

7 In relation to the New Zealand developments in *Lange v Atkinson* [2000] 3 NZLR 385, see eg Burrows and Cheer (2005) 89–98; Gillooly (2004) 129–39; Tobin (2003). Also see Stone and Williams (2000).

8 See *Loutchansky v Times Newspapers (No 2)* [2002] QB 783.

9 *Kearns v General Council of the Bar* [2003] 1 WLR 1357, 1358 (Simon Brown LJ, Mantell and Keane LJJ agreed).

10 Price and Duodu (2004) [13.01].

11 Eg *Jameel v Wall Street Journal Europe SPRL (No 2)* [2004] EMLR 11.

12 Chesterman (2000) 106.

13 *Ibid* 109.

14 Eg *Jameel v WSJ* [2005] EWCA Civ 74; *McCartan Turkington Breen v Times Newspapers* [2001] 2 AC 277; *Amalgamated Television Services v Marsden* [2002] NSWCA 419, [1161] (Beazley, Giles, Santow JJA); *John Fairfax & Sons v Vilo* (2001) 52 NSWLR 373, [111] (Heydon JA). In *John Fairfax Publications v O'Shane* [2005] NSWCA 164, [251] (Young CJ in Eq) noted that referring to the '*Lange* principle' is shorthand for common law qualified privilege.

B Chapter outline

This chapter examines whether the English and Australian legal developments do offer accessible defences for media publications. It combines case law analysis with qualitative investigation of defamation litigation in each country. The research suggests that *Reynolds* is far more likely to reduce any chilling effect on the media than *Lange*, but difficult issues of litigation practice remain for both defences and important questions about the strength of *Reynolds* privilege in different fact situations remain unclear. Part II briefly outlines the traditionally limited protection offered by qualified privilege to media publications, before examining recent case law. It explains how the two new defences differ doctrinally, both in scope and in strength. *Reynolds* privilege is comparatively broad and flexible: it appears to offer the media meaningful benefits over Australia's *Lange* developments, even if primarily for non-tabloid investigative publications. And it *may* develop to support wider commentary and public debate. *Reynolds* at least has that potential. *Lange* privilege is comparatively narrow in its focus on political communication. More significantly, however, *Lange* privilege is weak. As with the long-standing statutory privilege under s 22 of the *Defamation Act 1974* (NSW), it appears likely that publishers will have trouble demonstrating to courts' satisfaction that they acted reasonably. Doctrinal analysis set out in Part II also suggests that judge and jury roles are problematic under both the English and Australian defences.

Part III examines defamation lawyers' perspectives on the defences, obtained in interviews with 50 leading practitioners in London, Melbourne and Sydney. The interviews suggest that *Reynolds* privilege is supported in England, despite uncertainties about its future development and its litigation practicality. *Reynolds* also appears to be affecting the media's pre-publication conduct and encouraging what may be seen by some observers as more balanced reporting. That is, media practices may be changing to meet the *Reynolds* factors, arguably against the common perceptions of the media's own commercial interests.[15] In Australia, *Lange* privilege appears to be a barely useable defence, primarily due to the reasonableness requirement – however ironic that may sound. Practitioners suggest revising the defence, with preferable models offered by *Reynolds* or an expanded duty-interest privilege in the style of the earlier Australian approach under *Theophanous v Herald & Weekly Times*.[16] The fieldwork also suggests that privilege defences need to allocate judge and jury roles carefully. Otherwise, the greater protection of some types of speech, which appears to have been sought by the English and Australian developments in qualified privilege, will be undercut substantially in practice.

---

[15] Cf Schilling (2000) 49 who doubted such changes would happen under *Reynolds*. Of course, the research discussed in this chapter only suggests that changes in media practices may be happening – its focus remains on the law and litigation practice; see also Weaver et al (2006) Chapters 8 and 9.

[16] (1994) 182 CLR 104. The *Theophanous* approach is examined below in Part II, D, 2.

II DEVELOPMENTS IN QUALIFIED PRIVILEGE

A The traditional defence

Defamation law has long recognised various categories of qualified privilege, which have been said to exist for the 'common convenience and welfare of society'.[17] Qualified privilege has been available where publishers were under a legal, social or moral duty, or they acted to protect an interest *and* recipients had a corresponding duty or interest.[18] Distinctions also have been drawn between communications in established or non-established relationships, but commentary suggests the concepts of 'duty' and 'interest' (rather than 'relationship') continue to have utility.[19] The principles of duty and interest commonly have been stated at this 'very high level of abstraction and generality' and can 'never be catalogued and rendered exact'.[20] Shared duties or interests could exist for material published to small audiences,[21] but widespread publications were likely to see the defence fail.[22] (The media also might be able to rely on an ancillary or derivative protection, for example, if it published one person's reply to an attack by another.[23]) But, while qualified privilege has long existed for fair reports of parliamentary and court proceedings, the defence has not generally protected media publications of political or public interest as such.[24] Established occasions of privilege can be criticised in many ways, not least for their historical class bases.[25] Qualified privilege did not protect media publications about suspected corruption; instead, alleged malfeasance had to be reported to what courts regarded as proper authorities. Nor did privilege protect publications that reasonably were believed to be true. However, while the traditional defence was narrow, it was strong because only malice would defeat publications that were made on, and relevant to, a privileged occasion. In both England and Australia, however, qualified privilege developed during the 1990s and the reformed qualified privilege defences appear to have changed this situation. This chapter concentrates on *Reynolds* and *Lange* privileges, but it is worth noting another 1990s development in England and Australia, which meant that elected governing bodies, like local authorities or local councils, could not sue in

17 *Toogood v Spyring* (1834) 1 Cr M & R 181, 193; 149 ER 1044, 1050 (Parke B).

18 *Adam v Ward* [1917] AC 309, 334 (Lord Atkinson).

19 Cf *Kearns* [2003] 1 WLR 1357; Milmo and Rogers (2004) [14.8].

20 *Bashford v Information Australia (Newsletters)* (2004) 204 ALR 193, [10] (Gleeson CJ, Hayne and Heydon JJ), in part quoting *London Association for the Protection of Trade v Greenlands* [1916] 2 AC 15.

21 *Chapman v Ellesmere* [1932] 2 KB 431.

22 *Braddock v Bevins* [1948] 1 KB 580.

23 See eg *Bass v TCN Channel Nine* (2003) 60 NSWLR 251.

24 *See eg Wason v Walter* (1868) LR 4 QB 73; *Curry v Walter* (1796) 1 Bos & P 525; 126 ER 1046. For a re-examination of the history of qualified privilege and wide publications, see Dent (2005).

25 See eg Robertson and Nicol (2002) 73–75; Chesterman (2000) 89–91.

defamation. Although the decisions of *Derbyshire CC v Times Newspapers* in England and *Ballina Shire Council v Ringland* in Australia barred suits by such bodies, the individual council officers still could sue personally if they were identified by a defamatory publication about the council.[26] The rationale for barring suits, however, appears closely related to the later developments in *Reynolds* and *Lange* privilege. In *Derbyshire*, for example, Lord Keith said,

> [There is] no public interest favouring the right of organs of government, whether central or local, to sue for libel. . . . It is contrary to the public interest because . . . such actions would place an undesirable fetter on freedom of speech.[27]

Before examining those later changes, it is worth noting some points about defences for fair reports that are available in many jurisdictions under common law or statute, and defences of qualified protection that exist under the defamation codes in Queensland and Tasmania.

Some jurisdictions have significant statutory fair report defences.[28] For protection as a fair report, publications must be presented as reports; it is not sufficient for court or parliamentary proceedings merely to be the source of information in a publication.[29] Some defences require the publication of reasonable replies (where they are sought by potential claimants or plaintiffs) that explain the original report.[30] In any event, reports are not protected so far as they encompass wider discussion or debate about the events in court or parliament.[31] Thus, defamation law has imposed liability on many media defendants who cannot prove such publications to be true. And in this way, the law appears to focus more on protecting reputation than promoting wide debate about public interest issues. Even though statutes in some jurisdictions have created more occasions of absolute or qualified privilege that can protect media publications, they are far from comprehensive and, within Australia in particular, they vary significantly.[32] In England and NSW – more so than in Victoria – statute has extended protection to more media reports, including reports of at least some public meetings.[33] The protection does not apply to statements made on such

[26] *Derbyshire CC v Times Newspapers* [1993] AC 534; *Ballina Shire Council v Ringland* (1994) 33 NSWLR 680; see also *New South Wales Aboriginal Land Council v Jones* (1998) 43 NSWLR 300. The bar on actions has been extended to political parties in England: *Goldsmith v Bhoyrul* [1998] QB 459. See further, Weaver et al (2006) 94–99.

[27] *Derbyshire* [1993] AC 534, 549.

[28] See eg *DA 1996* (UK) s 15, sch 1; *DA 1974* (NSW) ss 24, 25, sch 2. For a detailed English examination of the protection offered to reports of local government inquiries, see Law Commission (England and Wales) (2004).

[29] *Eg Rogers v Nationwide News* (2003) 216 CLR 327, [18] (Gleeson CJ and Gummow J).

[30] See eg Kenyon (1999).

[31] See eg *Cornwall v Rowan* (2004) 90 SASR 269, [597]–[599].

[32] See eg Milmo and Rogers (2004) [13.35]–[13.48] and Chapter 15; Gillooly (1998) Chapters 10, 11 and 12.

[33] *DA 1996* (UK) s 15 and sch 1; *DA 1974* (NSW) ss 24, 25 and sch 2.

occasions but may be available to reports of those statements. Significantly, in *McCartan Turkington Breen v Times Newspapers* the House of Lords held that reports of media conferences can be defended under the statutory protection for fair reports of public meetings; that is, media conferences can amount to public meetings for the purposes of the defence.[34] Lord Bingham emphasised that a 'modern participatory democracy' needs media that is 'free, active, professional and inquiring'[35] and the statutory protection for fair reports could extend to reports that were drawn from media releases issued at, but not explicitly discussed during, media conferences. But the traditional less expansive approach to qualified privilege does not sit comfortably with commonplace, even if idealised, concepts about the media's role as a fourth estate in liberal democracies.[36] Nor does the approach fit well with valuing inclusive public debate about social, economic and technological transformations.[37]

B Australian code defences

An important difference in Australian approaches to privilege also should be noted.[38] The code states of Queensland and Tasmania offer what appears to be far wider, and probably also stronger, protection for many publications made in good faith 'for the public good' under their defences of qualified protection.[39] However, questions about the code defence are not examined in detail in this chapter because the key case law developments in England and Australia, and the far earlier changes in the US that are considered in Chapter 8, offer what should be fruitful avenues for comparison across the jurisdictions. The code provisions are substantially equivalent to NSW defamation law between 1958 and 1974 – when the State operated under the *Defamation Act 1958* (NSW) – but the received wisdom appears to be that the NSW qualified protection provisions were unworkable. For example, in a review that preceded the *Defamation Act 1974* (NSW), the State's Law Reform Commission found the 1958 Act had 'not been a

---

[34] *McCartan* [2001] 2 AC 277, 290–93 (Lord Bingham, Lords Hoffman, Millett and Cooke agreed), 296–98 (Lord Steyn, Lord Cooke agreed).

[35] *Ibid* 290–91 (Lord Bingham). The case has not received Australian consideration, beyond its relevance to statutory interpretation outside the area of defamation law: *Hore v Albury Radio Taxis Co-Operative Society* (2002) 56 NSWLR 210.

[36] These ideas retain great purchase for practising journalists; see eg Schultz (1998).

[37] Eg Kenyon (2001) 540–44.

[38] Also worth further examination is the ACT defence of non-negligent publication under s 134 of the *Civil Law (Wrongs) Act 2002* (ACT), which has not received judicial interpretation: see, generally, Collins (2001c). Note: The defamation provisions have been moved into this Act and renumbered since they were introduced in the *DA 2001* (ACT).

[39] *DA 1889* (Qld) s 16(1); *DA 1957* (Tas) s 16(1); see Butler and Rodrick (2004) 86–92. In Queensland, from 1899 to 1995, most defamation law was found in the state's *Criminal Code 1889*. In 1995, the provisions were transferred to the *DA 1889* (Qld): Gillooly (1998) 14 and its note 74.

satisfactory attempt at codification' and reported 'formidable difficulties' with the provisions, including those for qualified protection.[40]

Australia certainly has notorious defamation cases that have become ensnared in the complexity of the code provisions' wording. High-profile disputes like the *Bellino* litigation suggest the code defence is difficult to operate and offers an unhelpful number of appeal points to determined litigants.[41] The media publication at issue in *Bellino* was of major public importance. It commonly is seen as the catalyst for several events: holding an official inquiry into police corruption in Queensland that led to substantial efforts to reform the state police force[42]; jailing the then Queensland police commissioner (that is, the state's most senior police officer)[43]; and significantly contributing to the electoral defeat of a long-standing state government. But during all the years between 1987 and 1999, the program's main journalist Chris Masters and the Australian Broadcasting Corporation's lawyers were involved in defending the program in a series of hearings, including several levels of appeal and retrial. The main defence at every stage was the qualified protection offered under Queensland's defamation code. At almost every stage, the media succeeded in the defence, yet the litigation continued. The general story was of undoubted public importance, but the legal costs to defend it would have amounted to millions of dollars. It does not seem unfair to suggest that defamation law – and the code defence – was complicit in 'one of the most relentless attacks on good journalism' in Australia.[44]

But the general effects of the code defence are difficult to assess from contemporary case law, given the defence's absence from the law of Australia's most frequent defamation jurisdictions: NSW and Victoria. And it is worthwhile noting that the code provisions may not *now* pose the peculiar difficulties for litigation practice that commonly are believed to exist. It is interesting – if of limited generalisability[45] – that a handful of expert Queensland defamation lawyers all offered supportive interpretations about the scope and strength of the code defence of qualified protection during separate interviews in 2003 and 2004. Their comments included: qualified protection is 'very strong' and 'robust', it is the media's 'bread and butter' defence in Queensland and it is more than plausible to argue it as a defence for most media publications – certainly more so

[40] NSW Law Reform Commission (1971) [14].

[41] In particular, *see Bellino v Australian Broadcasting Corpn* (1996) 185 CLR 183; *Bellino* (1998) Aust Torts Reports ¶81–479; and the journalist's relevant book publications: Masters (1992) Chapter 3 'The Moonlight State' 43; Masters (2002) especially 'Introduction: The X–Files of News' 1, and 'Battle Fatigue' 193.

[42] See Queensland, Fitzgerald Inquiry (1989); Queensland, Criminal Justice Commission (1997).

[43] Sir Terence Lewis was sentenced to 14 years' imprisonment on multiple corruption charges in August 1991.

[44] Ackland (1999).

[45] In particular, information from these few key informants cannot be combined with extensive material from court files, as was possible for the examination in Chapters 5 and 6 of NSW and Victorian practice relevant to a publication's meaning.

than *Lange* privilege and the NSW statutory privilege under s 22 of the *Defamation Act 1974* (NSW).[46] This suggests that *Bellino* may be a poor example for understanding general practice under the code defence. (It may be a similar situation to US defamation litigation, discussed in Chapter 8, which differs in how complex it *can be* and how complex it *is* in its usual operation.) Combined with the substantial body of case law that includes notable High Court decisions on the provisions,[47] perhaps the problems that were encountered in Sydney during the 1960s under its code defence are better understood as being exacerbations caused by aggressive litigation practices.[48] These could be controlled to a stronger degree by the more active judicial supervision of litigation that now exists. So the defence should be considered to be another option for protecting speech on public issues, which *perhaps* does not pose great difficulties in the usual sort of claim. Even so, the code would appear to suffer from difficult divisions in role between judge and jury – the same issue that is explored in detail for *Reynolds* and *Lange* privilege in this chapter.

C England – Reynolds privilege

1 *Background*

Reynolds arose after *The Sunday Times* published a story in its London edition criticising Albert Reynolds, who had recently resigned as Ireland's Taoiseach, or Prime Minister.[49] Reynolds had played a major role in the Northern Ireland peace process, and his resignation was significant throughout the UK. The story was headed 'Goodbye Gombeen Man: Why a Fib Too Far Proved Fatal for the Political Career of Ireland's Peacemaker and Mr Fixit'. It accused Reynolds of misleading party colleagues and the Dáil, or parliament. But the story omitted the explanation that Reynolds had made to the Dáil. In contrast, a longer report published that was in *The Sunday's Times*' Irish edition suggested his conduct was accidental and that he was 'the hapless victim of circumstance'.[50] At trial, the jury rejected a defence of truth, found the publisher had not been actuated by malice, and awarded no damages. The judge substituted an amount of one penny for the award, having found that no qualified privilege defence applied. A retrial was

---

[46] The interviewees were two very experienced solicitors and three barristers (two of whom were senior counsel). They were interviewed in person between August 2003 and January 2004 in Brisbane, and all interviews were audio recorded and transcribed. While their comments supported the qualified protection provisions, there were some relatively minor criticisms of the difficulty in succeeding on the defence in the few matters that reach trial.

[47] Eg *Australian Consolidated Press v Uren* (1966) 117 CLR 185; *Calwell v Ipec* (1975) 135 CLR 321.

[48] See eg *Motel Holdings v Bulletin Newspaper* (1963) 63 SR (NSW) 208, 218 (Wallace J); *Justin v Associated Newspapers* [1967] 1 NSWR 61, 71 (Wallace P).

[49] Ruddock and Burns (1994).

[50] Loveland (2000b) 356.

ordered by the Court of Appeal due to the trial judge's jury directions.[51] Before then, however, the House of Lords had to determine whether qualified privilege could be argued at retrial. In its 1999 decision, the House of Lords held that the duty-interest requirement for privilege could be satisfied by media publications that the public had a right to know in all the circumstances.[52] This was a major development, making *Reynolds* the 'most important' recent privilege decision,[53] 'an important and potentially far-reaching reform'[54] and 'a marked liberalisation'[55] in the law – although it is notable that some commentators suggested English judges were merely 'tiptoeing towards free speech',[56] particularly in comparison to US law. The tension between an innovative approach to protecting speech and caution about whether the circumstances of specific investigations are sufficient to publish particular defamatory allegations can be seen in subsequent cases[57] – and the longer-term shape of *Reynolds* privilege remains somewhat open, especially in terms of how particular fact combinations will be analysed.[58] The focus of this chapter, however, is on comparing the English and Australian defences. And for that purpose, the expansive aspects of the *Reynolds* developments stand out.

2 *Not a privilege for political speech*

Reynolds sought to recalibrate the legal balance between reputation and free speech through altering the scope and strength of defamation law's defences.[59] But the House of Lords did not provide as strong a change as the media had sought: its decision rejected a generic privilege for political material in order to maintain what it saw as adequate protection for reputation.[60] This followed the rejection by earlier law reform reports of a defence for public interest statements believed to be true and published with reasonable care, notably by the Faulks Committee.[61] A qualified privilege for all political material was thought by the House of Lords to protect too strongly the wrong type of speech. Protection

---

[51] *Reynolds v Times Newspapers* [1998] 3 All ER 961.

[52] *Reynolds* [2001] 2 AC 127, 195.

[53] Shillito and Barendt (2000) 391, 407.

[54] Loveland (2001) 233.

[55] Williams (2000) 754.

[56] Robertson (1999) cited in Loveland (2000c) 356–57.

[57] *Eg Jameel v WSJ* [2004] EMLR 11 and in the Court of Appeal [2005] EWCA Civ 74. In May 2005, the House of Lords granted permission to appeal.

[58] See *Miller v Associated Newspapers* [2004] EMLR 33, [33] (Eady J).

[59] The potential for different remedies to achieve a new balance between reputation and free speech has been less attractive to judges, even though there has been long-standing encouragement for this reform path: see eg Fleming (1978).

[60] *Reynolds* [2001] 2 AC 127, 200 and 204 (Lord Nicholls), 217 (Lord Cooke agreeing), 237 (Lord Hobhouse agreeing), 210–11 (Lord Steyn), 234–35 (Lord Hope).

[61] Faulks Committee (1975) 53–55.

would be too strong because, influenced by the *European Convention on Human Rights and Fundamental Freedoms*,[62] journalists' confidential sources are very strongly protected in England. This makes it 'virtually impossible' to prove malice to defeat qualified privilege.[63] In addition, the wrong speech would be protected in that a political defence would be too narrow. Instead, the defence should focus on the public interest qualities of publications. While political speech is an important example of protected material,[64] *Reynolds* privilege is defined by a test of *public*, rather than political, interest assessed in light of all the circumstances in which the defamatory allegations were made.[65]

3 *The Reynolds factors*

The House of Lords in *Reynolds* required multiple factors to be considered when deciding whether defendants have established privilege, with Lord Nicholls listing 10 illustrative factors:

> 1. The seriousness of the allegation. The more serious the charge, the more the public is misinformed and the individual harmed, if the allegation is not true. 2. The nature of the information, and the extent to which the subject matter is a matter of public concern. 3. The source of the information. Some informants have no direct knowledge of the events. Some have their own axes to grind, or are being paid for their stories. 4. The steps taken to verify the information. 5. The status of the information. The allegation may have already been the subject of an investigation which commands respect. 6. The urgency of the matter. News is often a perishable commodity. 7. Whether comment was sought from the [claimant, who] may have information others do not possess or have not disclosed. An approach to the [claimant] will not always be necessary. 8. Whether the article contained the gist of the [claimant's] side of the story. 9. The tone of the article. A newspaper can raise queries or call for an investigation. It need not adopt allegations as statements of fact. 10. The circumstances of the publication, including the timing.[66]

These factors mean that a court will need to consider matters about the publication – including its public importance, urgency and overall tone and whether it included the claimant's position – as well as matters about the information's source, such as steps taken by the publisher or another relevant body in verification. The House of Lords' flexible approach was widely preferred

[62] Opened for signature 4 November 1950, 213 UNTS 221 (entered into force 3 June 1952).

[63] Shillito and Barendt (2000) 408. See also Loveland (2000c) 351; Mitchell (2000) 115; *Gaddafi v Telegraph Group* [2000] EMLR 431.

[64] See Loveland (2001) 233.

[65] See eg *Jameel v WSJ* [2004] EMLR 11, [31] (Eady J).

[66] *Reynolds* [2001] 2 AC 127, 205.

to that of the Court of Appeal,[67] which gave great weight to whether the information had an 'authoritative' source such as a government media release.

Although the House of Lords confirmed that a wider qualified privilege defence existed in law, a majority said the *Sunday Times* could not rely on it at retrial. In particular, this was because the publisher had failed to put Reynolds' side of the story when making serious allegations of political misconduct.[68] Even so, a passage near the end of Lord Nicholls' speech suggests the defence should be useful to the media:

> Above all, the court should have particular regard to the importance of freedom of expression. The press discharges vital functions as a bloodhound as well as a watchdog. The court should be slow to conclude that a publication was not in the public interest and, therefore, the public had no right to know, especially when the information is in the field of political discussion. *Any lingering doubts should be resolved in favour of publication.*[69]

4 *Applications of Reynolds privilege*

Commentators quickly suggested that courts would treat the *Reynolds* factors as a 'checklist'[70] or 'the standard template'.[71] Courts have done this, while maintaining that the factors are illustrative (rather than mandatory) within the law's attempt to protect 'responsible' journalism. Five case law examples suggest that *Reynolds* privilege may not protect sensational and repeated publications, publications that use unreliable sources, publications made without claimants having been contacted (at least where publication is held not to be urgent), and publications that present suspicion as fact. But the examples also show the defence's potential to develop broader protection for reporting allegations that are being made by others, at times without even attempting to verify the allegations.[72]

First, in *Grobbelaar v News Group Newspapers*,[73] the defence failed, in particular, because of the publications' sensational style. *Grobbelaar* concerned allegations about a goalkeeper taking bribes in relation to professional football matches. The newspaper defendant had videotapes that it believed proved the publications' truth. But the jury found for the claimant and awarded £85,000 in damages. The

---

[67] This was criticised by several commentators: eg Shillito and Barendt (2000) 409; Williams (2000).

[68] *Reynolds* [2001] 2 AC 127, 206 (Lord Nicholls), 217 (Lord Cooke agreeing), 237 (Lord Hobhouse agreeing); cf 216–17 (Lord Steyn), 237 (Lord Hope).

[69] *Ibid* 205 (emphasis added).

[70] Shillito and Barendt (2000) 410.

[71] Williams (2000) 753. See also Baker (2002a); and the detailed consideration of each factor in Robertson and Nicol (2002) 130–33.

[72] For further consideration, see Weaver et al (2006) 99–111.

[73] [2001] 2 All ER 437. Similar concerns with a publication's sensational style can be seen in *Galloway v Telegraph Group* [2005] EMLR 7.

trial judge rejected *Reynolds* privilege. This element of the decision was sustained on appeal, with the Court of Appeal going through the 10 *Reynolds* factors in detail.[74] (On further appeal to the House of Lords, damages were reduced to £1.[75]) The *Reynolds* defence failed although the bribery allegations were of great public interest. A key reason appears to have been the repeated and sensational publications. For example, Simon Brown LJ said,

> What seem to me to be the critical considerations . . . [are the] massive and relentless coverage of the story over seven separate daily issues of *The Sun*, generally across several pages. . . . [F]ar from . . . raising questions or calling for an investigation they asserted . . . Grobbelaar's guilt in the most unequivocal terms.[76]

It could appear, as the media lawyer Sarah Thomas has suggested, that the publisher 'was penalised by the court for being a tabloid newspaper'.[77] But some commentators supported the decision for its understanding of journalistic practices, suggesting the reasoning 'demonstrate[s] not only judicious balance, but a sound grasp of the way in which contemporary tabloid journalism is produced and published.'[78] This issue, and the courts' approach to popular media forms, may prove to be an enduring and controversial aspect of how journalists' conduct is judged under *Reynolds*. The apparent legal aversion to popular media suggests there would be value in exploring the changing roles of celebrity in contemporary cultures and the implications for law's approach to different media forms.[79]

Second, *Reynolds* privilege failed in *James Gilbert v MGN*[80] because the media used unreliable sources, failed to ask the claimants about the charge that was made in the publications, faced no particular urgency in publishing the material and presented the matters as fact rather than allegations. Thus, the media failed to meet standards of responsible journalism. Similar points can be seen in other cases. Failing to ask a potential claimant about serious charges also was fatal in *Armstrong v Times Newspapers* and *Galloway v Telegraph Group*,[81] while in *Jameel v Wall Street Journal Europe SPRL (No 2)* allegations that the claimants were associated with, and previously had provided funds to, Al-Qaeda were not established to a degree that warranted publication in a form that identified the

[74] [2001] 2 All ER 437, 445–50 (Simon Brown LJ), 465 (Thorpe LJ), 483–85 (Jonathan Parker LJ). Note, this aspect of the decision was not challenged in the House of Lords: [2002] 1 WLR 3024.

[75] [2002] 1 WLR 3024.

[76] [2001] 2 All ER 437, 447.

[77] Thomas (2002).

[78] Robertshaw (2001) 927.

[79] See eg Turner (2004); Couldry (2003); Thompson (2000).

[80] [2000] EMLR 680. The publications concerned child labour being used by the claimant's subcontractors and the claimant failing to investigate the situation.

[81] *Armstrong v Times Newspapers* [2004] EWHC 2928; *Galloway* [2005] EMLR 7.

individuals allegedly involved.[82] Relying on the concept of urgency is quite understandable as an element of the defence. But it raises important concerns that urgency will be evaluated with hindsight rather than from the perspective of publishers who must draw on their own skill and experience to decide whether delaying a story is likely to produce more information about a claimant's version of events.[83] However such aspects of editorial judgment may be treated under *Reynolds* privilege, it is notable the defence did not fail in *Grobbelaar* and *James Gilbert* because of the publications' subjects. Bribery in professional football and child labour in manufacturing were clearly important matters that could be protected under *Reynolds*. As Roy Baker has noted, such matters 'are stock-in-trade for journalists, typical of stories of business misconduct and . . . consumer journalism, that occupy the news daily'.[84] These cases illustrate how the scope of *Reynolds* privilege is broad and, as appears below, it is significantly wider than *Lange*.

Third, the new qualified privilege defence succeeded in *GKR Karate (UK) v Yorkshire Post Newspapers*.[85] In *GKR Karate*, a regional newspaper criticised a company that taught karate (without directly naming the company) in relation to its business practices and the quality of its instructors. The publications suggested the company may have placed profit before student safety. The defence succeeded because the newspaper's local readership included people who needed to be warned about the matter, only one restrained article was published and an apparently reliable source was relied on.[86] *GKR Karate* was novel for determining qualified privilege as a preliminary issue. This procedure was approved on appeal in light of the *Civil Procedure Rules'* case management objectives, discussed in Chapter 1.[87] However, early determination of an issue like qualified privilege lies within the trial judge's discretion; it is not a common practice. It was suitable in *GKR Karate* because there was limited dispute about the facts that were relevant to whether qualified privilege would be available. It is not clear whether such early determination would often be feasible. The same situation applies for more traditional qualified privilege cases.[88]

Fourth, the Privy Council applied the *Reynolds* defence in *Bonnick v Morris*.[89] When dealing with a Jamaican newspaper article that criticised the managing director of a government-owned business, the Privy Council emphasised that standards of responsible journalism should be applied in a practical manner.

---

82 [2005] EWCA Civ 74, [78]–[81] (Lord Phillips MR for Eng CA).

83 Eg Cram (2004) 149.

84 Baker (2002a) 91–92.

85 [2000] EMLR 410.

86 *Ibid* [45].

87 [2000] 2 All ER 931, [12]–[13] and [24] (May LJ, Tuckey LJ agreed); see Chapter 1, Part I, C.

88 Eg *MacIntyre v Phillips* [2003] EMLR 9, [35] (Brooke LJ, Dyson LJ and Wall J agreed); *Halford v Chief Constable of Hampshire Constabulary* [2003] EWCA Civ 102.

89 [2003] 1 AC 300.

Conduct need not be judged in relation to the meaning that a publication is found to have conveyed. If a range of meanings is arguable, and the publisher reasonably thought another meaning was conveyed, the publication may have been responsible. The approach considers conduct more than meaning:

> To be meaningful this standard of conduct must be applied in a practical and flexible manner. . . . [A] journalist should not be penalised for making a wrong decision on a question of meaning on which people might reasonably take different views.[90]

This means it may be necessary for the defendant to plead the meaning it believed was conveyed.[91] This flexible consideration of meaning has similarities with the statutory defence for reasonable publication under s 22 of the *Defamation Act 1974* (NSW).[92] It also has similarities with malice for more traditional qualified privilege in England, in which a publisher's honesty usually would be judged by considering the meaning intended by the publisher, not just the meaning found to have been conveyed by the publication.[93] And it is interesting to note this flexible approach to meaning in light of the ninth *Reynolds* factor about the publication's tone. Even before *Bonnick v Morris*, Geoffrey Robertson and Andrew Nicol had suggested this factor would allow rumours and allegations to be reported and inquiries called for.[94] While *Bonnick v Morris* has been treated cautiously in some later judgments,[95] its approach should be followed where the defendant's meaning is a plausible one.

Fifth, the significance of a publication's tone when reporting allegations also is underlined by *Al-Fagih v H H Saudi Research & Marketing UK*.[96] The case concerned a political dispute within part of the Saudi Arabian community that was opposed to the Saudi royal family. The defendant newspaper published a series of articles about the ongoing dispute. Allegations that one party to the dispute made against another were published without any attempt to verify them. In *Al-Fagih*, the Court of Appeal emphasised the fact that allegations were being made was of public importance in itself and properly could be reported. While the repetition rule applies to the defence of justification (as discussed in Chapter 3) it does not limit qualified privilege in the same manner. The repetition rule does not mean that 'an unadopted allegation' must be 'treated in the same way as an allegation asserted to be true'.[97] The decision is important for holding that some neutral reportage can be protected under *Reynolds*. But a publication that does not take a neutral position in relation to allegations that it reports may

---

[90] *Ibid* [24].

[91] *Jameel v WSJ* [2005] EWCA Civ 74, [26]–[29] (Lord Phillips MR for Eng CA).

[92] See *Morgan v John Fairfax & Sons (No 2)* (1991) 23 NSWLR 374.

[93] Eg *Halford* [2003] EWCA Civ 102, [42]–[45] (Simon Brown LJ).

[94] Robertson and Nicol (2002) 132.

[95] Eg *Jameel v WSJ* [2005] EWCA Civ 74, [90]–[97] (Lord Phillips MR for Eng CA).

[96] [2002] EMLR 13.

[97] *Ibid* 231 (Simon Brown LJ).

not see the reportage argument succeed.[98] The Court of Appeal has since noted that reportage may apply more widely than to political disputes. Simon Brown LJ said:

> I am certainly prepared to recognise that the approach adopted in *Al-Fagih* may need to be taken further still – rather than perhaps confined merely to the reporting of statements (attributed and unadopted) by both sides to a political dispute.[99]

All these cases illustrate the flexibility and potentially far-reaching effects of the English approach. While it must be acknowledged that media defendants have failed on *Reynolds* privilege in almost all the cases, that may reflect how the defence can be argued for even in inopportune cases.[100] However, failure also may follow from the caution that is evident in some judgments' application of the *Reynolds* factors. In any event, and certainly in comparison to Australia's *Lange* privilege, the reasoning in the decisions does not suggest that *Reynolds* privilege is narrow in its scope, nor necessarily weak in its strength.

5 *Litigating Reynolds privilege*

Litigating claims of *Reynolds* privilege may be difficult, particularly in relation to judge and jury roles.[101] Defamation law traditionally seeks a relatively simple division of roles under which judges determine whether occasions of publication are privileged, while juries decide if publications were affected by malice. Although there can be complications in judges deciding if a publication's content is *relevant* to privileged occasions,[102] these complications do not arise as a matter of course, nor do they usually depend on disputed facts. However, the *Reynolds* factors encompass matters that traditionally are dealt with under malice.[103] Many disputed facts could be relevant to the *Reynolds* factors, with juries needing to determine each of the primary facts before judges decide whether occasions are privileged. (And these jury questions should be framed to seek 'yes' or 'no' answers.[104]) Beyond raising issues for pleading,[105] this could lead to very complex

[98] Eg *Galloway* [2005] EMLR 7.

[99] *Mark v Associated Newspapers* [2002] EMLR 38, [35] (Simon Brown LJ, Mummery and Dyson LJJ agreed). A differently constituted Court of Appeal has referred to *Al-Fagih* with apparent approval: *Loutchansky (No 2)* [2002] QB 783, [22], [34] and [39] (Lord Phillips MR for Eng CA). See also *Al Misnad v Azzaman* [2003] EWHC 1783.

[100] See *Miller* [2004] EMLR 33, [33] (Eady J).

[101] Shillito and Barendt (2000) 411.

[102] See eg *Bashford* (2004) 204 ALR 193, 201 (Gleeson CJ, Hayne and Heydon JJ), 247 (Kirby J), cf 203 (McHugh J); *El Azzi v Nationwide News* [2005] NSWSC 247, [44]–[56] (Levine J).

[103] Eg *Jameel v WSJ* [2005] EWCA Civ 74, [26]–[28] (Lord Phillips MR for Eng CA).

[104] *Jameel v WSJ* [2004] EMLR 11, [5] (Eady J). The questions from that trial, including seven related to *Reynolds* privilege, were set out on appeal: [2005] EWCA Civ 74, [40] (Lord Phillips MR for Eng CA).

[105] Eg *Jameel v WSJ* [2005] EWCA Civ 74, [18] and [31] (Lord Phillips MR for Eng CA).

jury questionnaires as in *Loutchansky v Times Newspapers (No 4)* where the jury was set an 'examination paper'.[106] Some have suggested this will reduce the jury's role. Paul Mitchell, for example, has noted,

> Now that it is clear that judges can take into account so many factors when deciding if the occasion is privileged, there is a greater chance of privilege being withdrawn from the jury altogether. Where defences of privilege do go before a jury it is unlikely that there will be evidence of malice: if there had been such evidence (for instance, in the tone of the language . . .), the judge would probably have held that there was no occasion of qualified privilege to start with. . . . [T]he judge's decision either way is likely to be decisive.[107]

Certainly, *Reynolds* can be seen to blur the distinction between qualified privilege and malice.[108] And in *Loutchansky*, the Court of Appeal said the privilege now attaches to the publication more than to the occasion, which leaves little independent scope for malice.[109] But the jury's role will be increased in another aspect, if it needs to determine the potentially large number of factual matters in dispute under *Reynolds* privilege. Eady J has commented that in cases in which *Reynolds* is argued,

> It is now almost inevitable that . . . the jury will be asked to answer a series of questions in order for the court to arrive at the necessary factual substratum upon which to base the ruling. The questions will be directed no doubt largely to establishing the raw data for answering those of the ten non-exhaustive tests identified by Lord Nicholls in *Reynolds* . . . as may be relevant to the case in hand.[110]

Under this approach, judges retain significant powers to interpret and apply those jury answers, with '[a]ny value judgments, and to a large extent also any inferences to be drawn from the raw data' reserved for judges.[111]

The division of roles could make trial by judge alone more likely. For example, in *Gregson v Channel Four Television*,[112] Morland J ruled the jury would deal with meaning, but the rest of the case would be tried by judge alone because of the complex matters relevant to qualified privilege.[113] That decision was appealed unsuccessfully. As mentioned in Chapter 2, jury trials for defamation in England are required unless trial would involve 'prolonged examination of

[106] [2001] EMLR 38, [35] (Gray J).

[107] Mitchell (2000) 117.

[108] Spilsbury (2000) 46; Loveland (2003) 179.

[109] *Loutchansky (No 2)* [2002] QB 783, [33] (Lord Phillips MR for Eng CA).

[110] *Jameel v WSJ* [2004] EMLR 11, [4] (Eady J).

[111] *Ibid.*

[112] [2002] EWCA Civ 941.

[113] The division occurred because Morland J already had expressed an opinion about meaning. This meant there would have been a delay while a different judge was allocated, if the entire case was to be tried by judge alone. There appears to have been no mention of *Marks & Spencer v Granada Television* (Unreported, QBD, Popplewell J, 23 February 1998); see Chapter 2, Part III, C.

documents or accounts or any scientific or local investigation which cannot conveniently be made with a jury'.[114] The changes under *Reynolds* in relation to malice were important in this instance, with Morland J stating,

> [T]he factor which militates most strongly in favour of trial by judge alone is the number of primary detailed facts still in dispute on which the jury would have to be asked to make unanimous findings. The claimants have lodged 12 proposed questions and the defendants have lodged 48 proposed questions.[115]

On appeal, Waller LJ noted 'the very fact that there is a debate as to what questions should be put to the jury when *Reynolds* privilege is in issue'[116] would be another factor supporting trial by judge alone. As David Price has suggested, this is 'potentially a very significant decision',[117] and it has some similarity to NSW practice discussed in Chapter 5. In *Jameel v Wall Street Journal Europe SPRL (No 2)*, the Court of Appeal noted,

> The division between the role of the judge and that of the jury when *Reynolds* privilege is in issue is not an easy one; indeed it is open to question whether jury trial is desirable at all in such a case.[118]

It should be noted, however, that some reports of *Reynolds* privilege cases do not suggest great difficulty at trial, which could follow from the particular facts that are in dispute in those cases. For example, Jonathan Coad has discussed *English v Hastie Publishing*,[119] in which Gray J considered the 10 *Reynolds* factors and asked the jury questions about steps that the defendant journalist argued he had taken. The jury rejected six of the seven steps, leading Gray J to rule that qualified privilege was unavailable.[120] The degree to which the division of judge and jury roles will cause complications at trial remains an important area for research, but the potential for unhelpful complexity appears to exist. In any event, the existing cases suggest that *GKR Karate*'s early resolution of the issue may not be common.

Overall, *Reynolds* privilege is broad, not being limited to political publications. With strong protection for journalists' sources, and some later cases demonstrating a flexible approach to meaning and the recognition of a form of neutral reportage, *Reynolds* privilege appears to offer journalists meaningful benefits, while also requiring journalistic conduct of a kind that will satisfy later judicial examination. These changes mean that English protection for matters of political and public interest appears to have been strengthened, at least for the classic investigative reporting that courts envisage.

---

[114] *Supreme Court Act 1981*, c 54, s 69; and see Chapter 2, Part I, F.

[115] [2002] EWCA Civ 941, [19] (Waller LJ, Robert Walker LJ agreed).

[116] *Ibid* [21].

[117] Price (2002).

[118] [2005] EWCA Civ 74, [70] (Lord Phillips MR for Eng CA).

[119] (Unreported, Gray J, QBD, 31 January 2002).

[120] Coad (2002).

D Australia – Lange privilege

1 *Background*

A broader common law privilege defence that is available to the media also developed in Australia during the 1990s. The Australian changes were influenced by the implied constitutional protection for political communication that the High Court has discussed in a series of cases from 1992, which was noted in Chapter 1. The Australian Constitution has no express protection for speech, but the text and structure of the Constitution creates an implied protection for political communication. The protection limits the ability of the legislature to restrict speech about government or political matters. Restrictions must be appropriate in serving a legitimate and that the legislation pursues. In a similar fashion, the common law is affected by the implied protection for political communication.[121]

2 *The first stage: Theophanous and two privilege defences*

The Australian developments can be divided into two main stages. The first concerns the 1994 *Theophanous* decision.[122] It created two defences for publications about political and government matters: a *constitutional* defence and a *common law* defence. The constitutional defence could apply where defendants were unaware that publications were false, had not published recklessly without caring about truth or falsity and publication was reasonable in the circumstances.[123] *Theophanous* also expanded common law qualified privilege to cover media publications about political or government matters. For such publications, defendants need not meet the constitutional defence's reasonableness requirement. The expanded common law privilege was defeated only by malice, making it the most significant development for publishers in *Theophanous*.

The majority judgments in *Theophanous* also suggested that political communication was wide in scope and came close to encompassing all communication about 'public affairs'. The *Theophanous* joint judgment referred approvingly to the use by Mason CJ of the term *public affairs* in the earlier *Australian Capital Television v Commonwealth*.[124] Political communication included speech about governments, politicians, candidates, public officers, political and public bodies and people whose activities were matters of political debate, such

[121] The literature on the Australian constitutional protection for speech is extensive; see eg Stone (2005); Meagher (2004); Lindell (2003); Williams (1999); Cass (1994) 179.

[122] *Theophanous v Herald & Weekly Times* (1994) 182 CLR 104; see also *Stephens v Western Australian Newspapers* (1994) 182 CLR 211. For an examination of the *Theophanous* defence and subsequent developments, see Butler and Rodrick (2004) 77–82; Gillooly (1998) 188–96; Walker (2000) 207–28.

[123] *Theophanous* (1994) 182 CLR 104, 140 (Mason CJ, Toohey and Gaudron JJ).

[124] *Ibid* 122–3 citing (1992) 177 CLR 106, 138–40.

as trade union leaders and political commentators.[125] The majority cited Eric Barendt to describe *political speech* as 'all speech relevant to the development of public opinion on the whole range of issues which an intelligent citizen should think about'.[126] With a common law privilege defence that could only be defeated by malice, *Theophanous* suggested that many public interest matters would be protected far more than previously: it appeared to be a wide and strong defence.

3 *The second stage: Lange privilege*

But the *Theophanous* defences did not survive. The High Court's divisions in *Theophanous* and related cases led it to reconsider matters. The 1997 *Lange* decision forms the second and current stage of Australian developments. *Lange* concerned a leading Australian current affairs television program, *Four Corners*, which has been produced since 1962 and commonly is seen as the most significant program for major investigative reporting on Australian television. The program criticised the conduct of the New Zealand Prime Minister, David Lange. Lange pleaded the program meant he was unfit to hold public office,[127] and the High Court heard a pre-trial challenge to the availability of the *Theophanous* defences. In a rare unanimous judgment, the High Court solidly established the existence of the implied protection for political communication and refashioned the way in which it affects defamation law. The judgment combined elements of the constitutional and common law *Theophanous* defences into a single, new form of extended qualified privilege.

The High Court confirmed that political communication could give rise to an occasion of privilege:

> [E]ach member of the Australian community has an interest in disseminating and receiving information, opinions and arguments concerning government and political matters that affect the people of Australia. The duty to disseminate such information is simply the correlative of the interest in receiving it. The common convenience and welfare of Australian society are advanced by discussion – the giving and receiving of information – about government and political matters.[128]

This means *Lange* privilege can apply to widespread publications about political and government matters. The High Court, however, said that widespread publication made it appropriate to require defendants to establish their conduct in publishing was *reasonable*. In general, defendants must establish they had reasonable grounds to believe publications were true, did not believe they were false, and had made proper inquiries to verify the publications. In addition,

---

[125] *Ibid* 124.

[126] *Ibid* citing Barendt (1985) 152. See now Barendt (2005) 161–62.

[127] *Lange v Australian Broadcasting Corpn* (1997) 189 CLR 520, 521.

[128] *Ibid* 571.

defendants must have sought and published a response from the potential plaintiff, except where that was not practical or necessary.[129] While these tests sound simple enough, other Australian experience – particularly under s 22 of the *Defamation Act 1974* (NSW) – suggests that reasonableness may be very difficult for the media to establish to courts' satisfaction. This is explored further below, after reviewing the scope of *Lange* privilege.

4 *Lange privilege and the scope of political communication*

The scope of political communication protected by the constitution appears to have become relatively narrow under *Lange*. This point remains contentious and important for future decisions.[130] In earlier judgments about the issue, the majorities of divided High Court benches took a fairly broad approach to the scope of protection. As mentioned above, the majority judgments in *Theophanous v Herald & Weekly Times* suggested that political communication extended to discussion of the 'conduct, policies or fitness for office' of governments, political and public bodies, public officers and people seeking public office. This wide view of 'political' took it close to a concept of 'public affairs'. Now, however, political communication may be limited to information that is relevant to electors' decisions about voting. That is, the concept may be 'exhausted by political publications . . . which are calculated to influence choices',[131] which is the very limitation that was denied in earlier judgments. For example, perhaps most criticism of judicial officers – who are appointed not elected in Australia – will not come within the implied protection.[132] Some judgments have suggested that the argument to apply *Lange* privilege to defamatory statements about judges 'is devoid of merit'.[133] Criticism calling for a judge's *dismissal* may come within the protection,[134] but maybe not criticism related merely to an individual case.[135] The privilege may, 'in certain circumstances, extend to matters relating to [court] activities or officers'; perhaps, for example, for 'comments pertaining to the fitness of an officer of the judicial arm of government'.[136] Thus, *Lange*

[129] *Ibid* 574.

[130] See eg Chesterman (2000); Meagher (2004).

[131] *Theophanous* (1994) 182 CLR 104, 124 (Mason CJ, Toohey and Gaudron JJ).

[132] *Herald & Weekly Times v Popovic* (2003) 9 VR 1, [6] and [9]–[10] (Winneke ACJ), [498]–[500] and [504] (Warren AJA), cf [247]–[251] (Gillard AJA).

[133] *O'Shane* [2005] NSWCA 164, [139] (Ipp JA). See also [95]–[97] (Giles AJ) (discussing arguments for an analogous privilege in ways that suggest *Lange* privilege would not apply), [304] (Young CJ in Eq); and at trial *O'Shane* (2004) Aust Torts Reports 81–733, [187]–[196] (Smart AJ).

[134] *Popovic* (2003) 9 VR 1, [6] and [9]–[10] (Winneke ACJ), [247]–[251] (Gillard AJA), cf [498]–[500] and [504] (Warren AJA). This is because dismissing a judge would involve parliamentary action.

[135] *Ibid* [6] and [9]–[10] (Winneke ACJ).

[136] *Peek v Channel Seven Adelaide* (2004) 90 SASR 522, [64]–[66] (Gray J).

privilege may include politics only 'in an electoral sense'[137] or in relation to the executive and legislature.[138] The defence appears to be narrower and weaker than earlier Australian approaches and, although the judgments are far from consistent,[139] later cases suggest the *Lange* defence is less encompassing than *Reynolds*.

The comparatively narrow scope of political communication is one important reason for the relative dearth of subsequent case law on *Lange* privilege: many media publications in which publishers might seek to argue their conduct was reasonable are not 'political' publications in the required sense. Case law examples suggest that while *Lange* privilege may include some discussion of public administration, it is in no way a general public interest defence and it will rarely encompass discussion of commercial issues. However, courts continue to suggest the defence should not be interpreted narrowly,[140] and the scope of *Lange* privilege is likely to remain unclear and contentious for some time.

Discussion of public administration may often be within the defence's scope. One example is offered by *Chapman v Conservation Council of South Australia*.[141] This was one case in a long, hard-fought bridge development, which became an issue of national public concern over several years.[142] In *Chapman*, *Lange* privilege was held not to apply to publications alleging that property developers threatened to sue residents who opposed the bridge development. This was so even when the publications were couched in terms of free speech and of misusing the legal process to silence opposition.[143] Other publications concerned with the development, however, were potentially within *Lange*'s scope. These publications suggested the developers had engaged in 'token' consultation with indigenous groups. Such consultation was less than required by the statutory planning process, and the administration of that planning process could come within the scope of political communication.[144]

---

137 *Popovic* (2003) 9 VR 1, [504] (Warren AJA).

138 See eg discussion in *Cornwall* (2004) 90 SASR 269, [614]–[624].

139 See eg the differing approaches to political discussion in *Coleman v Power* (2004) 209 ALR 182. Other examples exist of wider approaches being taken to political communication: eg, in a context outside defamation, *Australian Broadcasting Corpn v Lenah Game Meats* (2001) 208 CLR 199, 281–82 (Kirby J).

140 See eg *Cornwall* (2004) 90 SASR 269, [614].

141 (2003) 87 SASR 62.

142 For general background to the development, see eg Simons (2003) or brief backgrounds provided in Graycar and Morgan (2002) 81–83 and the Full Court: (2003) 87 SASR 62, [178]–[215] (Besanko J).

143 *Chapman v Conservation Council of South Australia* (2003) 87 SASR 62, [16]–[18] (Doyle CJ), [294]–[296] (Besanko J), cf [148] (Gray J). This publication also exceeded the defence's scope at trial, even when the concept of Strategic Lawsuits Against Public Participation (SLAPPs) was raised in the publication: (2002) 82 SASR 449, [287]–[297] (Williams J). For background to SLAPPs, see Chapter 8, Part I, F, and eg Smolla (2004) [9.107]–[9.109]; Walters (2003); Kenyon (2001) 524, 530–32.

144 *Chapman* (2003) 87 SASR 62, [28] (Doyle CJ), [143]–[148] (Gray J), [358] (Besanko J).

In addition, a number of interlocutory decisions support the idea that *Lange* privilege will apply to at least some discussion about public administration. For example, it could apply to discussion about the enforcement of taxation laws;[145] the exercise of ministerial powers in relation to the environment;[146] a state government minister allegedly misleading an inquiry (which was not focussed on the minister's official conduct);[147] how the principal of a government-funded school handled complaints, including those from the education department;[148] or public prosecutors' performance of their duties.[149] Of course, the defence not being ruled out in these interlocutory examples remains far from establishing that *Lange* privilege has this breadth. The *Lange* defence also may extend to discussion of a person's suitability for a board whose membership is appointed by the executive and which has a supervisory role over state police.[150]

The *Lange* defence, however, does not encompass all public interest matters.[151] Publications concerning the corporate sector, whether non-profit entities or for-profit companies, can be expected to fall outside the scope of *Lange*. For example, in *NRMA v John Fairfax Publications*,[152] material about aspiring candidates for a corporate board was beyond *Lange* even if the candidates were former politicians. In *John Fairfax & Sons v Vilo*,[153] publications about a public company director allegedly leaving Australia when the corporate regulator was investigating the company's affairs was outside *Lange*. And in *Orion Pet Products v RSPCA (Vic)*,[154] criticism of a company that made electric dog collars also was beyond *Lange*'s scope. In the last instance, suggestions that the government should take action against the company were held to be only a small part of the publication and failed to bring the criticism within *Lange* privilege: 'The *Lange* defence does not give carte blanche to defame another merely because the statements which are said to be defamatory form part of the background to a campaign for legislative change.'[155]

In addition, discussion of matters with commercial significance may not come within *Lange*'s scope even if it occurs in a context that appears to be political – such as where elected members of a local council (ie, a local government body) discuss a property development at council meeting. In one decision, the discussion concerned development approval that the plaintiff had obtained on appeal

145 *Archer v Channel Seven Perth* [2002] WASC 160.

146 *Buddhist Society of Western Australia v Bristile* [2000] WASCA 210.

147 *Shave v West Australian Newspapers* [2003] WASC 83.

148 *Searle v West Australian Newspapers* [2004] WASC 11.

149 *Cock v Hughes* [2002] WASC 108.

150 *Marsden* [2002] NSWCA 419, [1149] (Beazley, Giles, Santow JJA). But in obiter comments the court expressed doubt as to whether *Lange* did have this breadth: [1162].

151 Eg *ibid* [1160]; *Cornwall* (2004) 90 SASR 269, [623] and [627].

152 [2002] NSWSC 563. See also *Gutnick v Dow Jones (No 2)* [2003] VSC 79, [43] (Bongiorno J).

153 (2001) 52 NSWLR 373.

154 (2002) 120 FCR 191.

155 *Ibid* [276].

against the wishes of the council, the degree to which various development conditions had been complied with, and the effects of the development on local residents. The discussion was held to fall outside the scope of *Lange*:

> [B]y no stretch of the imagination, could the discussion at the Council meeting properly be described as a debate or discussion about 'government or political matters'. . . . [T]he councillors were expressing their concerns, not about matters of policy or government, but about what they perceived to be the flouting by the plaintiff of the terms of the development consent, and their opposition to the development consent that had been granted by the Land and Environment Court.[156]

These examples may make it surprising that courts often have stated the *Lange* defence should not be given a narrow scope.[157] In any event, the cases suggest that success in *Lange* privilege may be found to exist primarily for a relatively narrow range of publications, namely, discussion about political candidates[158] or the actions of elected representatives – although at least some private individuals, who do not hold official or government positions, may be defamed without liability when discussing political matters.[159]

5 *Lange, reasonableness and the NSW s 22 defence*

Under *Lange*, publishers must establish that their conduct was reasonable. This raises another important reason for suspecting that *Lange* privilege may not protect many publications. That reason is the history of a wider statutory form of qualified privilege in NSW under s 22 of that state's *Defamation Act 1974*. Analysing the provision may gain much wider relevance in Australia if uniform Defamation Bills, which are discussed in Chapter 10, are enacted. This is because the proposed uniform law includes a statutory privilege defence very like s 22 (see Chapter 10, Part II, C). The current provision, which applies in addition to the common law in NSW, looks wide in its terms:

> Where, in respect of matter published to any person:
>
> (a) the recipient has an interest or apparent interest in having information on some subject,

---

[156] *West v Nationwide News t/as Cumberland Newspaper Group* [2003] NSWSC 505, [135] (Simpson J).

[157] *Eg Popovic* (2003) 9 VR 1, [8] (Winneke ACJ), [244] (Gillard AJA); *Cornwall* (2004) 90 SASR 269, [614].

[158] See *Featherston v Tully (No 2)* (2002) 83 SASR 347; *Brander v Ryan* (2000) 78 SASR 234; *Price v Hesse* [2002] VSC 149.

[159] *Cornwall* (2004) 90 SASR 269, [623]–[629]; cf the trial decision which had suggested that criticisms from a public review panel about the administration of a women's refuge were outside *Lange's* scope. The publications dealt with the capability of the organisation's staff, but concerned a 'small' organisation 'which was not a government institution. . . . The allegations concerned private individuals . . . not individuals holding high office who were employed in the public sector': *Rowan v Cornwall (No 5)* (2002) 82 SASR 152, [553] (Debelle J).

(b) the matter is published to the recipient in the course of giving . . . information on that subject and

(c) the conduct of the publisher in publishing that matter is reasonable in the circumstances,

there is a defence of qualified privilege.

The third element, reasonable conduct in publishing, is the important one in most instances and has clear similarities to *Lange*. The High Court considered *Lange* on the basis of NSW law, and held that the law would unreasonably burden political discussion if not for s 22. This meant the common law required the expanded privilege set out in *Lange* in order to meet the constitutional protection for political communication.[160]

Reasonableness under s 22, however, has been restrictively interpreted by the courts in an approach that 'effectively negates the availability' of the defence.[161] Under s 22, it has become necessary for most defendants to establish their honest belief in the publication's truth.[162] Defendants also must establish that the 'manner and extent of publication did not exceed what was reasonably required', that they made reasonable inquiries to check sources, and that their conclusions 'followed logically, fairly and reasonably' from what their inquiries revealed.[163] These appear to be onerous requirements given the way s 22 has been applied. They are far more than is required for the common law defence of fair comment, for example, where opinion can be exaggerated, prejudiced or obstinate.[164] The s 22 defence is very hard to establish if the facts underlying the publication are not true and 'proper' inquiries were not made before publication.[165] The defence appears to be commonly pleaded, but has succeeded in very few cases since it was introduced in the 1974 Act.[166]

An issue that *Lange* left unresolved is whether defendants need to establish their belief in a publication's truth, or merely reasonable grounds to believe in its truth. Academic commentary favours the latter approach, which differs from how s 22 has been interpreted and is said to make *Lange* privilege more widely available.[167] Case law has not yet dealt explicitly with this possible difference

160 (1997) 189 CLR 520, 573–75.

161 Rares (2004) 47.

162 See *Morgan* (1991) 23 NSWLR 374, which makes clear that the belief must relate to the meaning that the publisher intended.

163 *Ibid* 388 (Hunt AJA).

164 See Chapter 2 and eg *Merivale v Carson* (1887) 20 QBD 275, 281 (Lord Esher MR), 283–84 (Bowen LJ).

165 See eg Walker (1998a) 21.

166 See *Pinniger v John Fairfax & Sons* (1979) 26 ALR 55; *Barbaro v Amalgamated Television Services* (1989) 20 NSWLR 493; *Bowin Designs v Vincent Joyce* [1996] 1070 FCA 1 (Unreported, Lindgren J, 6 December 1996); *Lear v Malter* (Unreported, Donovan AJ, NSWSC, 14 March 1997); *Millane v Nationwide News t/as Cumberland Newspaper Group* [2004] NSWSC 853. In addition, the defence was set aside on appeal in *Evatt v Nationwide News* [1999] NSWCA 99.

167 See eg Walker (1998a) 28.

between the *Lange* and s 22 defences. But recent cases have noted that reasonableness under *Lange*, as well as under s 22, should not be inflexible. The criteria of reasonableness should be adaptable: 'Reasonableness is not a concept that can be subjected to inflexible categorization.'[168] The factors listed in *Lange* are not 'principles of law', nor 'essential elements in the proof of the defence'.[169] They are 'not to be treated as . . . a statutory provision'.[170] It can be reasonable not to seek a response before publication in certain circumstances, for example, where the subjects of a publication were 'making ample use of the media' to convey their points of view.[171] But failing to meet any one of the factors in *Lange* would 'in most cases prove fatal'.[172] Overall, however, courts' interpretation of reasonableness appears to track the s 22 approach closely,[173] notwithstanding the different basis to the NSW action where each pleaded imputation is a separate cause of action.[174]

Additions were made to s 22 in 2002 after a report by the NSW Attorney-General's Task Force on Defamation Law Reform.[175] It examined the factors set out in *Reynolds* and noted that no factor requires publishers to show they believe in the publications' truth. It recommended amending s 22 of the *Defamation Act 1974* (NSW) to similar effect:

> [T]he 'reasonableness requirement' in s 22 should have attached to it a statutory set of factors to be considered by a court in determining whether the publication is protected by qualified privilege. Such a list ought to make clear to decision makers that it is not necessary for a publisher who wishes to invoke qualified privilege to prove that they had objective grounds for believing in the truth of the matter published.[176]

This led to the introduction of an inclusive list of factors in s 22(2A) which set out the flexible approach that should be taken to reasonableness:

> In determining . . . whether the conduct of the publisher . . . is reasonable in the circumstances, a court may take into account the following matters and such other matters as the court considers relevant:

---

[168] *Rogers* (2003) 216 CLR 327, [30] (Gleeson CJ and Gummow J).

[169] *Popovic* (2003) 9 VR 1, [92] and [197] (Gillard AJA).

[170] *Cornwall* (2004) 90 SASR 269, [661].

[171] *Chapman* (2003) 87 SASR 62, [361] (Besanko J), [29] (Doyle CJ agreeing), [149] (Gray J). See also *Brander* (2000) 78 SASR 234, [113] and [119]–[121] (Lander J, Prior and Bleby JJ agreed); *Popovic* (2003) 9 VR 1, [213]–[218] (Gillard AJA), [453] (Warren AJA agreed); *O'Shane* (2004) Aust Torts Reports ¶81–733, [204] (Smart AJ); *Cock v Hughes* [2002] WASC 263, [42] (McLure J); *Mickelberg v 6PR Southern Cross Radio* [2003] WASC 209, [52]–[62] (Newnes M); *Cornwall* (2004) 90 SASR 269, [630]–[638].

[172] *Popovic* (2003) 9 VR 1, [92] (Gillard AJA).

[173] *O'Shane* [2005] NSWCA 164, [308] (Young CJ in Eq) citing Kenyon (2004b) 418–19.

[174] At times, courts have recognised the different cause of action means s 22 decisions may deserve limited influence in relation to the common law defence: see eg *Popovic* (2003) 9 VR 1, [201] (Gillard AJA).

[175] NSW Attorney–General's Task Force on Defamation Law Reform (2002) 28.

[176] *Ibid* 29.

(a) the extent to which the matter published is of public concern,
(b) the extent to which the matter published concerns the performance of the public functions or activities of the person,
(c) the seriousness of any defamatory imputation carried by the matter published,
(d) the extent to which the matter published distinguishes between suspicions, allegations and proven facts,
(e) whether it was necessary in the circumstances for the matter published to be published expeditiously,
(f) the sources of the information in the matter published and the integrity of those sources,
(g) whether the matter published contained the substance of the person's side of the story and, if not, whether a reasonable attempt was made by the publisher to obtain and publish a response from the person,
(h) any other steps taken to verify the information in the matter published.

As yet, it is unclear that these additions to s 22 have changed case law interpretations – similar matters were always open for consideration by courts under s 22. And there have not been specific cases on the amended provisions.[177]

6 *Lange privilege and malice*

Although there will be little room to consider malice beyond the question of reasonableness, malice remains a separate element that defeats *Lange* privilege. In *Lange*, the High Court stated that desiring to cause political harm to an opponent would not constitute malice.[178] That is a central role for political speech, so targeting a political opponent does not mean malice is established.[179] (But such targeting outside politics would suggest the improper purpose required for malice.[180]) Similarly, campaigns about public issues may seek to influence public opinion to apply pressure to one side of a dispute without that constituting malice[181] – although the subjects of such campaigns may often be outside the scope of *Lange* privilege. Subsequent to *Lange*, the High Court has emphasised that the publisher having a dominantly improper purpose is the fundamental issue for malice in relation to qualified privilege; a lack of honest

[177] Eg *O'Shane* [2005] NSWCA 164, [223] (Young CJ in Eq) noting the amended s 22(2A) did not apply to the 1999 publication that was at issue.

[178] *Lange* (1997) 189 CLR 520, 574; and see eg *Brander* (2000) 78 SASR 234, [127] (Lander J, Prior and Bleby JJ agreed).

[179] *Roberts v Bass* (2002) 212 CLR 1.

[180] *Marsden* [2002] NSWCA 419, [1239] (Beazley, Giles, Santow JJA).

[181] Eg *Chapman* (2003) 87 SASR 62, [22]–[24] (Doyle CJ), [163] (Gray J), [310] (Besanko J).

belief in the publication is not a distinct ground of malice in relation to qualified privilege in Australia.[182]

7 *Litigating Lange privilege*

There also is an issue for *Lange* privilege about the division of roles at trial where a jury is used. It would appear that the jury rules on questions of primary fact that are relevant to the defence; for example, it may need to be asked a series of questions about whether certain inquiries were made and, if so, what they revealed. The judge then rules on whether the defence is made out as a matter of law. Although practices at trials have varied, the Victorian Court of Appeal has unanimously endorsed this approach.[183] Thus *Lange* is most likely to follow the traditional judge and jury roles, which are reflected in the English developments under *Reynolds*, discussed above. But the multiple and diverse issues that can be relevant to whether a publisher's conduct was reasonable suggest that complexities often will exist in matters reaching trial.

E Comparing the English and Australian law

The developed English and Australian privilege defences have been analysed above in terms of their scope, strength and trial practicality. The points are summarised here before examining reports of litigation practice from interviews with defamation lawyers. English cases suggest the value of a broad privilege defence that is not limited to an institutional concept of politics.[184] In addition, English cases apply a reasonably wide variety of factors in assessing publishers' conduct, and appear to apply them quite flexibly. In particular, *Bonnick v Morris* illustrates the value of a non-technical approach to a publication's meaning for the privilege defence.[185] The English approach to publications' tone is another notable example,[186] although it is one that favours non-tabloid publications. In comparison, the Australian approach under *Lange* privilege is narrow – it is not a public interest defence and rarely encompasses speech about commercial issues. *Lange* privilege also appears to be weak because of the requirement for publication to be proved reasonable. Reasonableness under *Lange*, however, may be a more achievable standard than under s 22, depending on whether defendants will be required to establish their belief in the truth of the publication under *Lange* (and whether s 22 is reinterpreted in light of the *Reynolds*-style factors that have been added to it). In any event, neither *Lange* nor s 22 offers the

182 *Roberts* (2002) 212 CLR 1. English cases have not taken this approach: eg *Halford* [2003] EWCA Civ 102.

183 *Popovic* (2003) 9 VR 1, [13] (Winneke ACJ), [104] and [116]–[117] (Gillard AJA), [509] (Warren AJA).

184 See NSW Attorney-General's Task Force on Defamation Law Reform (2002) 20–23.

185 *Bonnick v Morris* [2003] 1 AC 300.

186 *Al-Fagih v H H Saudi Research & Marketing UK* [2002] EMLR 13.

strength of protection offered by *Theophanous* common law privilege. In terms of litigation practicality, *Theophanous* common law privilege, like traditional qualified privilege, offers a reasonably clear division between judge and jury roles. The jury addresses malice without needing to answer an 'examination paper' of questions about disputed events. It appears that such examination papers may arise under both *Reynolds* and *Lange* privileges, which may undercut the benefits aimed for in developing the defences. Next, qualitative material about litigation practice is examined in relation to these issues about the defences' scope, strength and practicality in litigation.

III ENGLISH AND AUSTRALIAN PRACTICE

A Fieldwork

To investigate these qualified privilege defences (*Reynolds*, *Lange* and s 22) in action, interviews were conducted with 50 defamation practitioners in England, NSW and Victoria. Two were conducted in December 2002 and the rest in 2003. The 23 London interviewees comprised specialist defamation judges, barristers from two leading defamation chambers, solicitors with substantial defamation practices and in-house lawyers for media companies.[187] In Australia, 27 defamation practitioners were interviewed from the two largest defamation jurisdictions, NSW and Victoria.[188] They included a specialist judge and leading defamation barristers, solicitors and in-house lawyers. Defamation formed the major part of most interviewees' practices, often being a sizeable majority. As noted in earlier chapters, the concentrated media law practices that exist in each country mean the interviewees represent a good cross-section of lawyers, with significant involvement in defamation.

Each interview lasted approximately one hour, with all except two being audio recorded and transcribed.[189] Transcriptions were analysed according to the legal issues discussed, with major areas concerning each defence's scope, strength and effects in litigation. Quotations are direct transcriptions from interviews, with only minimal changes made to interviewees' words for clarity and readability. To protect interviewees' confidentiality, no quotation is identified with a named interviewee. Instead, interviewees are referred to by number, along

[187] All English interviews were conducted in May 2003. They are identified here as 57–79. Five interviewees were women, and all interviews were conducted separately except for two pairs: 72 and 73, and 74 and 75.

[188] There were 16 interviewees from NSW and 11 from Victoria. Two Australian interviews were conducted in December 2002 (96 and 97), with all the others occurring in June and July 2003. The interviewees are identified here as 80 to 95 from NSW, and 96 to 106 from Victoria. Five interviewees were women, and all interviews were conducted separately, except for 101 and 102.

[189] Handwritten notes were made at two interviews: once due to background noise preventing audio-recording, and once to accord with the interviewee's wishes.

with their professional role: solicitor (S), barrister (B), Queen's Counsel (QC) or Senior Counsel (SC).[190] All those who assisted in relation to the interviews are sincerely thanked.[191]

Obtaining this sample of experienced defamation lawyers means a sizeable minority of interviewees acted predominantly for the media, for example, in solicitors' firms retained by media companies to give pre-publication and litigation-related legal advice. However, a diverse group of experienced lawyers was sought, and the most common background for interviewees was to do significant amounts of work for defamation claimants or plaintiffs and for defamation defendants. Only a small minority of the 50 interviewees did more work for defamation claimants or plaintiffs. However, no direct relationship was apparent between interviewees' professional backgrounds and their views about defamation law and litigation.[192] This means it would be misleading to treat interviewees primarily as advocates for, or against, the media. As with earlier chapters, the 50 interviews dealt with here generated a very large amount of material, but offered the most accessible and viable source of empirical information.[193]

B English interviews

Three broad, related issues are discussed here from the 2003 interviews with London practitioners. First, despite uncertainties about its future development, *Reynolds* privilege is supported and is affecting pre-publication legal advice and media conduct. Second, particular concerns exist about each party's position, related to the focus on media conduct under *Reynolds* privilege. Third, the division between judge and jury roles is problematic at trial, but may be difficult for trial judges to improve.

First, *Reynolds* overwhelmingly is seen as significant. It offers a comparatively strong defence for media publications. There is uncertainty about how it will develop and how its multiple factors will apply in any litigated case. Two factors, however, are seen as central to the defence: whether the publisher attempted to contact the subjects of potential publications and what sort of tone or balance publications adopt. These factors mean that *Reynolds* privilege appears to alter

---

[190] Judges are identified as QC or SC, reflecting their prior roles.

[191] See the appendix for a full list of people who assisted with interviews.

[192] Eg one strong comment within the Australian interviews was that *Lange* had not improved the position of publishers (see below, fn 274), while in England many interviewees suggested that *Reynolds* had improved the media's position (see below, fns 198–201 and accompanying text). In Australia, the 13 responses came from seven lawyers who predominantly did media defence work, one lawyer who conducted more plaintiff work, and five lawyers with roughly even practices. In England, the 16 responses came from six lawyers with predominantly media practices, three lawyers with mainly claimant practices, and seven lawyers with roughly equal practices.

[193] The interview transcriptions drawn on in this chapter totalled 400,000 words. As noted in earlier chapters, they dealt with many aspects of defamation law and practice, see eg Chapter 4, Part I.

Table 7.1 – English and Australian Interviewee Sample

Interviewee	Subject	5–10 years' libel work	10–20 years' libel work	20–30 years' libel work	>30 years' libel work	More claimant or plaintiff work	More defence work	Even work for each party
57	S			•			•	
58	S		•			•		
59	S		•					•
60	QC				•			•
61	QC			•			•	
62	B	•					•	
63	QC			•				•
64	B	•						•
65	B	•						•
66	B	•				•		
67	S		•				•	
68	B		•					•
69	QC				•			•
70	S		•				•	
71	QC				•			•
72	S		•				•	
73	S	•					•	
74	S			•				•
75	S	•						•
76	QC				•	•		
77	QC			•				•
78	S			•			•	
79	S			•			•	
80	SC		•			•		
81	SC			•				•
82	B			•			•	

(Continued)

Table 7.1 – Continued

Interviewee	Subject	5–10 years' libel work	10–20 years' libel work	20–30 years' libel work	>30 years' libel work	More claimant or plaintiff work	More defence work	Even work for each party
83	B		•					•
84	SC				•			•
85	S	•					•	•
86	S		•				•	
87	S		•				•	
88	S		•				•	
89	SC			•				•
90	S		•				•	
91	S	•					•	
92	S			•			•	
93	S			•			•	
94	S	•					•	
95	S			•			•	
96	S	•					•	
97	S			•			•	
98	B	•						•
99	B							•
100	S		•					•
101	S		•				•	
102	S		•				•	
103	SC			•			•	
104	B			•				•
105	SC			•		•		
106	B	•						•

Note: S – solicitor (any English solicitor-advocates are identified here as S); B – barrister; QC – Queen's Counsel (used for English interviewees); SC – Senior Counsel (used for Australian interviewees).

the media's pre-publication conduct. Not surprisingly, London interviewees described *Reynolds* as important.[194] It offers a 'whole new defence' that is arguable in almost all media cases.[195] The development is 'revolutionary'[196] and a 'massive change'.[197] It is a 'significant improvement' for the media,[198] as it provides a useable, or even strong, defence.[199] For some interviewees, initial doubts or disappointments have given way: 'I remember the first time I read *Reynolds* thinking that this is all rather a disappointment. . . . [B]ut gradually re-reading it, one began to see its potential and the actual results have been really very considerable.'[200] More cautious responses still saw the potential in *Reynolds* for a 'very useful defence'.[201]

While some interviewees suggested that *Reynolds*' flexibility had value,[202] a major area of criticism was its uncertainty and unpredictability.[203] An experienced barrister commented: 'I think the problem with *Reynolds* in practice is that it is a "sniff test". Does it have a bad smell about it or does the judge feel warm about it?'[204] How will courts balance publications' public interest qualities, the potential harm to subjects' reputations, and defendants' conduct before publication? It is difficult to predict how any particular situation will be interpreted in light of the relevant factors:

> Things like how urgent was it? Was it really necessary to publish this? How far do you have to check it in the heat of the moment? . . . [It is] very difficult to say [and] newspapers rather take a punt.[205]

---

194 Almost all interviews emphasised the decision's importance: 57S, 58S, 59S, 60QC, 61QC, 64B, 65B, 67S, 68B, 70S, 72S, 73S, 74S, 75S, 77QC, 78S. Along with some of these respondents, other interviewees suggested that *Reynolds* will develop significance over time (63QC, 66B) while 76QC suggested that it was too early to tell whether it would achieve the desirable strengthening of qualified privilege. 62B emphasised the defence's unpredictability, with which 71QC agreed (while noting it has led to innovative subsequent decisions). 69QC supported a qualified privilege defence for media publications but believed that the traditional duty-interest style of qualified privilege, expanded to include at least some media publications, would be far preferable.

195 67S; similar 58S, 62B, 66B, 75S, 77QC. However, many respondents noted the differing positions of broadsheet and tabloid newspapers: eg 72S, 73S, 78S. Others also noted the importance of deciding whether to plead *Reynolds* in any particular case because of the way it alters a trial's focus: 68B, 72S, 76QC, 79S.

196 57S.

197 64B.

198 59S, 61QC; similar 58S, 64B, 70S, 72S, 75S, 78S.

199 57S, 60QC, 73S, 77QC, 78S.

200 60QC; similar 57S.

201 65B; similar 63QC, 66B, 76QC.

202 57S, 59S, 65B.

203 58S, 60QC, 61QC, 62B, 63QC, 66B, 67S, 69QC, 71QC, 72S, 76QC, 77QC, 78S.

204 61QC. Others commented on the power the approach gives judges: 64B, 70S, 74S, 79S.

205 67S.

It is difficult to predict whether some publications will be found to have 'the right calibre of public interest'[206] or how the degree of public interest relates to the required level of investigation.[207] Yet the checklist should not be 'rigid'[208] – 'fluidity' is wanted, rather than having the 10 factors 'set in stone'.[209] While subsequent decisions have clarified somewhat the defence's scope and strength,[210] *Reynolds*' uncertainty – its 'inherently case-by-case' analysis – not surprisingly is expected to continue.[211]

Of the 10 *Reynolds* factors, however, two were more influential for interviewees: contacting the subject of a publication[212] and carefully considering the publication's tone or balance.[213] Notwithstanding comments about the defence's uncertainty in litigation, these two factors were seen as particularly important and also were reported as being central to changing pre-publication conduct. Speaking to the subject and publishing a response is seen as 'the litmus test',[214] although it is 'not clear how much time you should give them to respond'.[215] At the least, the defence is very likely to fail if there has been no attempt to contact the subject.[216] Not attempting to make contact 'is such a moronic failure, you're almost holed below the water line'.[217] In theory, perhaps *Reynolds* should not affect what is published, 'because a newspaper . . . ought not ever have published unless it had taken reasonable care and honestly believed that what it was saying was true'.[218] However, the way in which tone is 'critically important' changes this position.[219] Interviewees suggested that *Reynolds* assists the media to raise more allegations or suspicions,[220] and to publish more public interest or whistle-blowing stories.[221] At the same time, it encourages what may

---

206 76QC.

207 63QC.

208 65B; similar 73S.

209 67S.

210 58S, 67S.

211 77QC; similar 67S.

212 57S, 59S, 60QC, 61QC, 63QC, 64B, 68B, 72S, 73S, 75S, 78S.

213 58S, 63QC, 64B, 68B, 70S, 72S, 73S, 75S, 78S.

214 61QC.

215 72S. The courts' attitude to urgency also was raised as a matter needing clarification: 66B, 68B, 70S, 73S.

216 Attempting contact is necessary if not sufficient: 63QC.

217 68B.

218 77QC.

219 78S; similar 63QC, 72S, 75S.

220 58S (due to the tone factor), 64B, 72S. 63QC also noted the reportage line of cases. 'Reportage' refers to *Al-Fagih* and related decisions: above, Part II, C, 4. Other interviewees saw the decision in *Al-Fagih* as 'altogether odd' (57S; similar 65B), or at least a distinct development beyond what would have been expected with *Reynolds* (63QC, 64B); cf 77QC, who strongly endorsed the development.

221 59S, 72S, 73S, 75S, 78S.

be seen as more balanced reporting – publications are more likely to include subjects' points of view.[222] Before *Reynolds*, 'if you had a story which was clearly defamatory, but you had a pretty good source there would be little point in publishing it in a balanced way. So you'd simply go for it'.[223] But now publishers are likely to consider *Reynolds* and moderate the tone of publications. Television journalism in particular 'will be well served by *Reynolds*' because its longer lead times mean that everyone involved can work to 'the *Reynolds* program'.[224] (It is notable in relation to *Reynolds* privilege that television has long been subject to detailed codes in relation to news and current affairs programming.[225]) These comments suggest that *Reynolds* is affecting media conduct, with publishers exercising greater care when they research and write stories.[226]

Second, concerns were expressed about each party's position under *Reynolds*. Claimants face particular difficulties because they lack knowledge of many *Reynolds* factors.[227] Most often, claimants will know only whether they were approached for comment before publication. They will not know what research journalists have undertaken, so claimants will be less able to predict the general strength of a *Reynolds* defence. This differs from other defences that involve truth or a clear occasion of privilege, such as reporting parliamentary debates. Correspondence between the parties, often referring explicitly to *Reynolds'* factors, may help clarify the position for claimants.[228] In addition, *Reynolds*, which 'spotlights the newspaper', can make claimants feel that their interests have been overlooked.[229] One interviewee stated that '[c]lients do not really care whether the journalists were ethical or not; they care that a falsehood has been stated about them',[230] and several interviewees suggested claimants would like to seek declarations of falsity under *Reynolds*.[231] For claimants, the uncertain 'shadow of *Reynolds*'[232] deters claims and encourages settlements.[233] *Reynolds* is 'very

---

222 57S, 59S, 60QC, 61QC, 63QC, 64B, 68B, 72S, 73S, 75S, 78S.

223 64B.

224 68B; similar 72S.

225 See Ofcom (Office of Communications), *Ofcom Broadcasting Code* (London: Ofcom, 2005) and the former Independent Television Commission, *ITC Programme Code* (London: ITC, January 2002); see <www.ofcom.org.uk>.

226 57S, 58S, 59S, 60QC, 64B, 67S, 70S, 78S. While solicitors and in-house media lawyers reported that pre-publication practices were changing, and that uncertainty was not a problem at that stage, an experienced barrister thought difficulties in predicting how a judge might apply the *Reynolds* factors also would exist at the pre-publication stage.

227 60QC, 62B, 63QC, 77QC.

228 75S. Similarly, 58S noted claimants are able to judge the content of publications, if not any underlying investigation, which is important in assessing their position.

229 67S; similar 57S, 60QC, 66B, 76QC, 77QC.

230 77QC.

231 57S, 58S, 60QC.

232 77QC.

233 58S (there is a 'chilling effect' on claimants), 63QC, 68B, 71QC, 77QC.

expensive to defeat',[234] with 'almost no claimant [being] confident of victory, and therefore reasonable settlements for reasonable awards, or indeed for apologies and costs, are becoming [more] common'.[235]

The position of defendants also drew concerns. As for claimants, the costs of trying the defence were raised: 'even in the case of a newspaper article, and a relatively short one at that, you can have a four-week trial involving a lot of detailed factual issues and a number of legal issues and vast expense and an enormous amount of time.'[236] Other respondents, however, noted that publications could involve comparatively small amounts of background material. The information sources and documentary evidence held prior to publication were 'finite',[237] although the amount varied between 'very little' and 'massive'.[238] Justification, by way of contrast, can draw on a far wider range of material, and may be a more unwieldy defence.[239] Concerns also were raised about focusing on publishers' conduct:[240] 'for defendants, the *Reynolds* defence is a bit of a Trojan horse because it changes the dynamics of the trial. If you run a *Reynolds* defence alone the trial will turn into a trial of your journalists.'[241] Journalists' motives and actions will be scrutinised more closely than has been routine, notwithstanding the issues that historically have arisen on malice.[242] There is a 'much less benign atmosphere for media defendants than was expected',[243] and the evaluation of journalists' conduct by courts 'can be very painful'.[244] Interviewees were unsure whether courts could fully understand the pressures associated with daily news production:[245] 'If you're a newspaper on a 24 hour turnaround . . . you're not going to be able to do all the things that they want you to do'.[246] It was suggested that the views of judges and journalists about standards differ markedly: 'the highest level of journalistic endeavour' achieved in the media is 'miles short of where the court sets the lowest standard for journalistic endeavour'.[247]

---

[234] 62B.

[235] 77QC; similar 63QC.

[236] 63QC; similar 62B, 64B, 66B.

[237] 67S; similar 58S, 75S, 78S.

[238] 62B; similar 67S.

[239] 66B, 67S.

[240] 59S, 61QC, 62B, 63QC, 68B, 73S, 76QC, 77QC, 79S.

[241] 68B; similar 73S, 79S.

[242] 59S, 61QC, 62B.

[243] 76QC; similar 61QC, 63QC, 77QC.

[244] 76QC.

[245] 70S, 73S.

[246] 72S.

[247] 68B.

Third, interviewees strongly criticised the division between judge and jury,[248] emphasising the complexity of the *Reynolds* defence in practice.[249] Its 'odd dichotomy'[250] of roles creates a 'bad system'.[251] An experienced barrister stated: 'I can't imagine a more clumsy and unsatisfactory way of determining an issue.'[252] Practitioners thought that courts had been 'blind to the practical consequences of simply saying the jury can find the primary facts'.[253] The key difficulty appears to be the number of factual determinations juries may need to make under *Reynolds*.[254] A trial can end with 'twenty questions for the jury, all on tiny bits of fact about who said what, what was the journalist told, and did the journalist phone twice to check or only once?'[255] Asking the jury to address many detailed questions is 'completely different from how juries have always been regarded' in English defamation and subverts their traditional role of delivering general verdicts.[256] At a trial's outset, it is unclear what questions the jury will need to answer. Specific questions emerge from evidence: 'If anyone . . . tried to forecast in advance what questions they would [need] to have decided, it would [be] folly.'[257] These complexities mean that 'if you asked the jury afterwards to explain what was going on [with] qualified privilege, [jury members] wouldn't have a . . . clue'.[258] To the 'bemused' jury,[259] the questions must appear 'slightly irrelevant and thoroughly trivial'.[260] Through such specific questions, juries will seek to deal with a more general issue: should publishers succeed in the defence? As one interviewee suggested: 'I'm not sure that's very satisfactory at all, because embedded in the long list of factual questions which the jury [is] going to answer is always the ultimate question: Was this behaviour responsible?'[261] In its allocation of judge and jury roles, *Reynolds* is 'totally unsatisfactory'.[262] It makes the jury's role far more difficult, if not 'almost impossible'.[263]

These views led to suggestions either to increase the jury's role on qualified privilege or to sideline it. Some respondents suggested that the jury 'should be

248 60QC, 62B, 64B, 65B, 67S, 68B, 69QC, 72S, 76QC, 77QC, 78S.

249 60QC, 62B, 64B, 65B, 67S, 69QC, 78S.

250 67S.

251 78S.

252 69QC.

253 60QC; similar 62B 68B, 71QC, 77QC.

254 60QC, 62B, 64B, 65B, 77QC.

255 64B; similar 68B, who had planned to ask a particular jury 40 questions.

256 64B; similar 69QC.

257 60QC.

258 70S.

259 78S.

260 69QC; similar 67S, 70S, 77QC.

261 76QC.

262 69QC.

263 68B; similar 65B, 66B.

asked general questions. Do you find for the claimant or the defendant? . . . I think this intermediate idea of asking them a huge taxonomy of different questions is just unsatisfactory and counterproductive'.[264] Other interviewees suggested that early judicial rulings on privilege would be valuable.[265] But such rulings require that no factual issues be in dispute. This is difficult to achieve given the range of factors that can be relevant to *Reynolds* privilege. Defendants may decide 'to concede facts' to seek a summary ruling.[266] Some interviewees suggested removing juries entirely, or removing them in relation to qualified privilege: 'I think the simple answer to all this is that we should get rid of the juries'.[267] But many aspects of this book, particularly the chapters related to meaning, would doubt the value of such a change. Other respondents made a related point that *Reynolds* privilege makes more sense in judge-only trials[268] and that this change may be happening, to a degree, through judicial rulings that cases can be tried conveniently without juries.[269] Interviewees also suggested that the jury is being sidelined in that judges have room to decide whether *Reynolds* privilege succeeds by interpreting jury answers[270] – sometimes because of the inconsistency of the jury's answers.[271]

Overall, although the *Reynolds* defence is seen as having difficulties at trial, London practitioners describe the developments as 'sensible'[272] and 'evidently justifiable'.[273] While it may be the case that lawyers' apparent enthusiasm for many aspects of *Reynolds* changes, depending on future judgments, the contrast is likely to remain striking compared with the Australian situation discussed in the next Section.

C Australian interviews

Four issues from Australian interviews are discussed here. First, *Lange* privilege is not seen as a useable defence. Its reasonableness requirement, which almost all practitioners equate with the defence under s 22 of the *Defamation Act 1974* (NSW), is the primary reason for this failing. Second, notwithstanding its legal weaknesses, *Lange* appears to have reduced suits by politicians. Third, the roles of judge and jury under *Lange* are seen as problematic, echoing concerns from England. Fourth, most interviewees suggested that *Lange* needs review, with

264 65B; similar 60QC, 76QC.
265 61QC, 62B, 65B, 77QC.
266 61QC.
267 65B; similar 68B, 72S, 78S.
268 76QC, 77QC.
269 60QC, 76QC, 77QC; and see Chapter 2, Part I.
270 57S, 64B, 74S, 78S.
271 69QC.
272 58S, 59S, 78S; similar 57S, 61QC, 65B, 70S.
273 77QC; similar 73S, 76QC.

Reynolds being seen as a preferable approach and the *Theophanous* form of common law privilege also receiving substantial support.

First, in marked contrast to the English situation under *Reynolds*, Australian interviewees suggested that *Lange* has not improved the position of publishers.[274] While *Lange* privilege allows defendants to raise more arguments, it 'was quite clearly constructed to be . . . in results, pro-plaintiff'.[275] Judges have suggested that political discussion requires greater protection, but *Lange* has not achieved this 'at all'.[276] The media has attempted to 'stretch the boundaries'[277] of the defence. Where stories have a political 'slant'[278] or a 'hint'[279] of politics, *Lange* will be pleaded.[280] Judges, however, retain 'the discretion to knock things out on what seem to be fairly technical grounds'.[281] For example, the interpretation of political and government matters in *Popovic v Herald & Weekly Times*[282] that excluded much criticism of judges was not supported,[283] with a wider scope to the defence being preferred.[284]

While *Lange* privilege's scope raised some concerns, interviewees more strongly criticised the reasonableness requirement. Its restrictive interpretation was seen as a key failing in the defence.[285] Under *Lange* 'you walk straight into reasonableness'.[286] As discussed above, the test appears to be interpreted restrictively.[287] Reasonableness 'is the stumbling block and will always be the stumbling block'.[288] It is the 'killer'[289] that one 'always come[s] back to'[290]:

274 80SC, 81SC, 87S, 89SC, 90S, 91S, 92S, 94S, 95S, 98B, 100S, 103SC, 106B. There were only two more supportive views: 'I see the *Lange* defence as a very important defence for publishers, a very practical defence in terms of what it allows to be published': 96S; and *Lange* 'has been very positive for the media': 97S.

275 89SC; similar 103SC, 106B.

276 106B.

277 90S; similar 84SC, 106B.

278 106B.

279 103SC.

280 93S, 103SC. It is pleaded 'more often than not' by the media: 99B. One barrister went further to suggest that 'in almost all media cases involving public figures . . . *Lange* generally has a run': 89SC.

281 99B; similar 85S.

282 [2002] VSC 174. See also *Popovic* (2003) 9 VR 1. And see above, Part II, D, 4.

283 96S, 97S, 100S, 103SC (*Popovic* is 'bizarre'), 104B, 106B.

284 90S, 96S, 97S, 100S, 103SC, 104B, 106B.

285 81SC, 84SC, 85S, 86S, 87S, 89SC, 91S, 92S, 93S, 94S, 95S, 99B, 100S, 101S, 102S, 103SC, 106B.

286 94S.

287 See above, Part II, D, 5.

288 84SC; similar 86S: 'People regard the reasonableness test as too high to be jumped over and frankly judges pretty much make it too high to be jumped over'.

289 103SC.

290 93S; similar 103SC.

> Why should a defendant have the added burden of reasonableness when the High Court [judges] are trying to espouse a principle that in political speech there should be more freedom. In fact, there's less freedom because defendant publishers can never or hardly ever get up to that standard of reasonableness.[291]

A related point was raised about s 22 of the *Defamation Act 1974* (NSW). *Lange* privilege is seen to have done little in NSW because it is seen as merely a subset of the s 22 defence.[292] *Lange* is believed to operate, within the area of political communication, in *effectively* the same restrictive manner as s 22. As noted above, academic commentary and law reform documents suggest differences between the *Lange* and s 22 defences.[293] Under s 22 publishers must virtually always believe publications to be true, while under *Lange* it appears that they only need reasonable grounds to believe publications to be true. Notably, however, many interviewees did not see this distinction as having any practical importance.[294] It is 'too fine' to change arguments at trial,[295] except in very rare cases. A small minority of respondents suggested or hoped that a different approach would emerge for *Lange* reasonableness,[296] or even that reasonableness under s 22 would be interpreted less strictly to meet constitutional requirements for political communication.[297] But the overwhelming impression was that reasonableness, under *Lange* or s 22, remains a *very* difficult hurdle. As discussed above in Part II, s 22 was amended in 2002 and now includes an inclusive list of factors that can be considered in relation to reasonableness. Interviewees, however, suggested these changes added little or nothing to the law.[298] The list of factors is 'insulting'[299] and 'an absolute waste of time'.[300] It merely re-expresses what courts have always been able to do.[301]

Although comparatively narrow in scope and weak in strength, *Lange* privilege appears to have one effect like *Reynolds*: it encourages the media to seek comment.[302] *Lange* privilege 'brings into sharp focus what was done before the publication, and . . . the need to provide the opportunity for comment'.[303] The

---

[291] 103SC.

[292] 80SC, 81SC, 82B, 83B, 84SC, 89SC, 90S, 91S, 92S, 93S, 94S, 95S, 104B.

[293] See eg Walker (1998a); NSW Attorney-General's Task Force on Defamation Law Reform (2002) 219.

[294] 81SC, 82B, 90S, 91S, 92S, 94S, 99B.

[295] 99B; similar 90S.

[296] 85S, 88S. Others expressed far less confident hopes for such a change: 87S, 95S.

[297] 101S.

[298] 81SC, 84SC, 89SC, 91S, 93S, 95S ('unless judges decide to interpret [reasonableness differently]').

[299] 91S.

[300] 89SC.

[301] 93S.

[302] 88S, 91S, 96S, 100S.

[303] 102S; similar 87S, 88S, 97S, 101S, 103SC.

attention paid to investigation is good,[304] and not seeking comment would most probably cause the defence to fail.[305] To a degree this has clarified journalists' responsibilities,[306] but interviewees were concerned about uncertainty in the concept of reasonableness[307] as well as the narrowness of *Lange*'s scope.[308] Journalists need some clear benchmarks,[309] applied with flexibility in the context of each publication.[310] The law, however, sets out 'a suggested way that things are to happen, in relation to publications . . . generally. . . . [W]hat is reasonable in the circumstances is never looked at. . . . There is no differentiation for the circumstances.'[311]

Second, notwithstanding their limited impact on the formal law, *Lange* and the preceding High Court decisions have reduced suits by politicians and related figures.[312] These decisions also have lowered the costs of settlement.[313] The 'spectre' of *Lange* privilege dissuades lawsuits.[314] *Lange* has given politicians 'pause to stop'[315] – politicians now appear to have a 'generic belief' that they cannot sue.[316] This reported shift in litigation patterns may explain why 'almost every barrister and judge in the country' believes *Lange* has not changed anything in substance, but 'almost every journalist in the country thinks it has'.[317]

Third, Australian interviewees echoed concerns from England about judge and jury roles. Doctrinal orthodoxy might suggest that the roles under *Lange* should resemble those under *Reynolds*; namely, where there is a jury, the jury would resolve disputed facts while judges would determine whether occasions of publication are privileged. When interviews were conducted, Australian case law had not yet examined the division of roles in any detail.[318] At least one jury had been asked the general question: Was this publication reasonable?[319] It had not been asked to answer questions about the underlying factual matters. Interviewees supported this approach, generally strongly.[320] It was seen as a jury question in

[304] 84SC, 90S, 96S, 101S.

[305] 98B, 105SC.

[306] 88S.

[307] 91S, 99B, 100S, 105SC, 106B.

[308] See above, fn 284.

[309] 91S.

[310] 98B.

[311] 94S.

[312] 87S, 91S, 93S, 97S, 98B, 99B, 100S, 103SC, 105SC.

[313] 97S, 98B, 101S.

[314] 93S.

[315] 105SC.

[316] 91S; similar 98B, 99B, 100S.

[317] 86S.

[318] See now *Popovic* (2003) 9 VR 1.

[319] See eg *Popovic* [2002] VSC 174.

[320] 96S, 99B, 100S, 103SC, 105SC, 106B. It was contrasted by some interviewees with the NSW s 22 defence where reasonableness is an issue for the judge: eg 103SC.

principle,[321] and one of great importance:[322] 'whether something is reasonable or not is quintessentially a jury question. Juries have grappled with that question always'.[323] If the jury deals with reasonableness, it need not provide answers to a potentially complex series of questions on specific factual matters.[324] As in England, practitioners supported juries having a *general* role in addressing reasonableness.

Fourth, *Lange* privilege had little support overall, apart from dissuading some political plaintiffs: 'when you actually get to trial . . . *Lange*'s hopeless, completely hopeless, about as hopeless as you can possibly get and still be a defence'.[325] It is 'a bit of a disaster'.[326] Some interviewees did suggest that *Lange* may have more effect in time,[327] with reasonableness being interpreted less restrictively.[328] Most interviewees, however, suggested that *Lange* should be reviewed.[329] 'We have all been waiting for the High Court to really take *Lange* to the next stage in saying "well clearly it's been set too high, the benchmark" and we should have known that in the first place'.[330] Australian interviewees gave far more support to *Reynolds*.[331] The 'very different',[332] 'strong'[333] and 'sensible'[334] defence 'has provided a better basis for evolution of doctrine than *Lange*'.[335]

> We really need to look at this in the context of *Reynolds* and whether there should be a broad based public interest privilege defence. . . . Is there a role for it in Australia in terms of lowering the benchmark for reasonableness [and] widening the ambit outside politics?[336]

---

321 100S, 103SC, 104B, 106B.

322 105SC, 106B.

323 106B.

324 105SC.

325 98B.

326 95S.

327 86S.

328 85S, 88S, 98B, 101S (who could see the arguments extending to s 22).

329 Eg 81SC, 84SC, 85S, 86S, 87S, 90S, 91S, 92S, 95S, 96S, 97S, 98B, 99B, 100S, 101S, 103SC, 104B, 106B. Only four interviewees offered any notable support for the current law on privilege: 80SC, 82B and 83B approved of s 22, while 105SC suggested that *Lange* struck a happier balance between parties than the common law qualified privilege defence under *Theophanous*.

330 91S.

331 84SC, 86S, 91S, 92S, 97S, 98B, 106B. One solicitor suggested that 'the outcome is pretty much the same' under both defences: 101S.

332 98B.

333 92S.

334 106B.

335 84SC; similar 86S.

336 91S.

In any event, the application of *Lange* privilege could be developed. Although the current High Court may not be 'minded to expand' the defence's scope,[337] reasonableness need not be overly restrictive: *Lange* privilege could be applied far more like *Reynolds* while remaining unchanged in terms of law.[338]

An alternative development that some interviewees raised would be an expanded duty-interest style of qualified privilege for media publications.[339] This existed for political publications under the *Theophanous* common law qualified privilege.[340] These lawyers saw the reasonableness requirement of *Lange* privilege as 'wrong in principle',[341] compared with the traditional privilege defence that would only be defeated by malice. Such a duty-interest style of defence would give the jury a clearer role and place defendant publishers in a much stronger position. Without such changes, truth will remain the vital defence,[342] and the aim of *Lange* privilege to reduce the chill of defamation law appears unlikely to be achieved.

Overall, *Lange* privilege was seen to offer only the smallest improvement on the traditional common law defence, and none on NSW's s 22 privilege. *Lange* was not described with anything like the support that English practitioners offered for *Reynolds*, even allowing for the qualifications they had about *Reynolds'* predictability and trial practicality. There was much support for reforming Australian *Lange* and s 22 privileges, or at least substantially developing their application.

IV CONCLUSION

This chapter has reviewed some of the more significant ways in which the traditionally limited qualified privilege defences have developed since the mid-1990s in English and Australian law. Unlike many traditional forms of qualified privilege, the *Reynolds* and *Lange* privileges are available to media publications and protect at least some speech about public or political matters. The chapter's legal analysis and interviews with practitioners suggest the English defence is *comparatively* wide and strong, and it has greater support from the profession than Australia's *Lange* privilege or the s 22 defence in NSW. As well as its apparently narrow political focus, *Lange* appears to be weak in the protection it offers. Weakness of protection also appears to be a key problem under s 22, which recent statutory reforms have not affected to date. But *Lange* does appear to have

337 91S; similar 101S. Another participant suggested that 'the High Court [is] champing at the bit to have another go at it': 92S.

338 98B.

339 85S, 91S, 92S, 95S, 100S, 101S, 103SC, 106B. Some interviewees, however, did not support such a 'massive change': 80SC; similar 105SC.

340 See above, Part II, D, 2.

341 103SC.

342 81SC, 87S, 98B, 99B, 105SC.

encouraged more diverse reporting, in the limited sense of encouraging publications to include subjects' points of view. It is worth repeating that a statutory privilege for reasonable publication, like s 22, may be enacted in proposed uniform Australian defamation law. (Uniform Defamation Bills are discussed in Chapter 10.) If the proposals do become law, *Lange*'s apparently narrow scope may be of reduced significance because the statutory defence would not be limited to government and political matters. Potentially, it would cover publication on any subject matter. However questions about the strength of the statutory privilege, in particular, then would become a key issue facing Australian courts. And what *should be* required for publication to be reasonable could be expected to receive further judicial attention. *Reynolds* privilege appears to have had greater effect on media conduct through the wide range of factors that are clearly relevant to the defence and the comparatively achievable standard that appears to be required of publishers. Importantly, English practitioners suggested that the media can publish more allegations and stories of public interest under *Reynolds*. The application of *Reynolds* to varied fact situations remains unclear, but the defence may grow to support a more diverse range of public debate. The legal analysis and empirical research reported here also underlined particular difficulties for litigation practice that may follow from the division of judge and jury roles in relation to *Reynolds* and *Lange* privilege. These and related factors are returned to in Chapter 10, after US defamation law and practice is explored in the next chapter and conclusion are drawn about Lucas-Box and Polly Peck pleading in Chapter 9.

– 8 –

US DEFAMATION LAW AND PRACTICE

> [W]e have no such fixing at the beginning of the defamatory meaning. . . . The [English] practice seems to . . . tell the lawyers what the potential range of meanings are. . . . In the US you don't ever really have a definition.[1]
>
> It's not that the journalists are any better [in the US] but there is a better opportunity to do good journalism here. . . . You leave it with the journalists who actually know what they're doing. . . . I think the problem with the Commonwealth system is there is no reward and no protection for doing your job well. . . . [T]here is in a limited sense with *Reynolds*, in a limited sense with *Lange* . . . [but] mistakes are inevitable in journalism. . . . Especially when you have this whole meaning issue, mistakes are inevitable after the fact because they decide you meant to say something different. . . . [A]mbiguity should not be a firing offence.[2]

Earlier chapters compared aspects of the law most relevant to each side in defamation litigation under English and Australian law. They investigated legal doctrine and litigation practice to appreciate more about how speech is dealt with under each country's defamation law – in relation to defamatory meaning and its most closely allied defences and in relation to developments in qualified privilege. US constitutional approaches since *New York Times v Sullivan*[3] offer obvious possibilities for comparison with English and Australian qualified privilege defences. There also is value in exploring the very different ways in which meaning, falsity and opinion are dealt with under US law. Comparing the US and non-US situations, however, is not straightforward. US defamation law is complex and varied – it encompasses issues of federal and state constitutional law and state common law.[4] While many aspects of its traditional defamation law 'are *theoretically* subject to constitutional attack',[5] the Supreme Court has avoided commenting on them.[6] The

[1] Interviewed lawyer 116. Interviewees are identified by number; see below, Part II, A.

[2] Interviewed lawyer 119.

[3] 376 US 254 (1964).

[4] The US has no federal common law: *Erie Railroad v Tompkins*, 304 US 64 (1938); and the Supreme Court does not determine matters of state tort law. For a detailed examination of the interaction of US constitutional and tort law see Anderson (2004).

[5] Smolla (2004) [13.26] (emphasis in original).

[6] Compared to England and Australia, the lack of final appellate defamation decisions in the US since the early 1990s is notable, *Tory v Cochran*, 2005 US Lexis 4347 notwithstanding.

result is that: 'Simple statements about the law of libel and slander should . . . be approached with caution.' Constitutional and common law issues mean 'things are rarely simple'.[7]

The combination of constitutional doctrine and varied state common law makes it less feasible to analyse US defamation law as closely as has been done for England and Australia. The United States' less concentrated defamation litigation also affects what empirical research is viable. Therefore, this chapter provides an outline of important constitutional aspects of US defamation law in Part I and then more closely examines several of the differences that have most significance for comparative analysis. The interview sample and method are described in Part II, while general observations about US defamation litigation are offered in Part III. Then, in Part IV, more specific matters about meaning and the *Sullivan* rules are considered. These include issues about meaning, pleading, substantial truth, mitigation, discovery and pre-trial motions. As for England and Australia, the analysis draws on interviews with leading defamation practitioners as well as an examination of the law.

I OUTLINE OF US DEFAMATION LAW

A Traditional law to the *Sullivan* rules

Before 1964, US defamation law broadly resembled the English approach to defamation. There were differences in the US law: for example, a community-segment test was common for deciding what is defamatory.[8] Given the relative insignificance in English and Australian practice of the test for what is defamatory – notwithstanding recent NSW difficulties under the 7A process[9] – the possible effects of the less restrictive US test are left to one side here. Other differences before 1964 included the approach to fair comment, which often was conceptualised as a form of qualified or conditional privilege.[10] In addition, in some but not all states fair comment allowed far greater protection for speech about matters of public interest.[11] But the law broadly accorded with English and Australian approaches – plaintiffs needed to show that defendants published material about them that would harm their reputation. No proof was required of the publisher's fault or the material's falsity. It remains true that many aspects of US defamation law reflect the traditional common law position. For example, definitions of defamatory material involve concepts such as harming reputation, lowering a person in the estimation of others, or deterring people from associating

[7] Sack (1999) [2.1.4].

[8] See eg *Peck v Tribune*, 214 US 185, 190 (Holmes J) (1909); Lidsky (1996).

[9] See Chapter 10, Part I, C, 3.

[10] See eg Keeton (1984) 831–32. There are similarities in the historical treatment of fair comment under English common law, see eg Dent (2005); Mitchell (2005).

[11] See eg *Press Co v Stewart*, 199 Pa 584 (1888); *Coleman v MacLennan*, 98 Pac 281, 287 (1908); Loveland (2000a).

with the person.[12] The term *innuendo* is used in the US to refer to a legal innuendo meaning that is dependant on material extrinsic to the publication.[13] There also are substantial similarities between US, English and Australian defences for fair reports of court proceedings and similar bodies, even though US constitutional changes largely supersede qualified privilege in media cases. Notwithstanding the constitutional overlay, it could be noted that US protection for reports can be broader than traditional English and Australian approaches; for example, the *Second Restatement of Torts* provides absolute privilege for, among other things, reports of public meetings about matters of public concern.[14] This is somewhat similar to, but stronger than, the House of Lords' decision in *McCartan Turkington Breen v Times Newspapers* that reports of media conferences can be defended under the statutory qualified privilege for fair reports of public meetings.[15]

While many US, English and Australian defamation rules are similar, substantial developments in US law since *New York Times v Sullivan*[16] mean any resemblance with traditional English and Australian approaches may be 'largely superficial'.[17] Many elements of US defamation law look similar to English and Australian law, but the overall effect differs. Existing literature provides detailed examination of key Supreme Court cases and the reasoning used within them.[18] Here, those decisions' effects are outlined to describe six main aspects of the US approach to defamation law. They are related to public plaintiffs; private plaintiffs; the treatment of opinion; state and federal courts; interlocutory hearings and appeals; and judges, juries and post-trial appellate review.

B Public plaintiffs

The US approach to defamation usefully can be called the *Sullivan* rules to emphasise that it is not a public figure *defence*; rather, it is a set of particular burdens that the First Amendment places on some defamation *plaintiffs*.[19] The

[12] See American Law Institute, *Second Restatement of Torts* (1977) §559. Broadly equivalent definitions exist under state law.

[13] See eg Sack (1999) [2.4.5]. See also Chapter 2, Part I.

[14] American Law Institute, *Second Restatement of Torts* (1977) §611. For specific examination of the US fair report privilege, see Elder (1988).

[15] *McCartan Turkington Breen v Times Newspapers* [2001] 2 AC 277, 290–93 (Lord Bingham, Lords Hoffman, Millett and Cooke agreed), 296–98 (Lord Steyn, Lord Cooke agreed); and see Chapter 7, Part II, A.

[16] 376 US 254 (1964). For a detailed examination of *Sullivan*, see Lewis (1991).

[17] Anderson (2003) 721.

[18] See eg Sack (1999) Chapter 1; Smolla (2004) Chapters 2 and 3; Weaver et al (2006) Chapter 3. For outlines of defamation law in every US jurisdiction, see Media Law Resource Center (2004a), while a useful overview is provided by American Law Institute, *Second Restatement of Torts* (1977) §§558–623. (ALI restatements, compiled by academics and practitioners, are persuasive legal authority and have been adopted by some states in law reform.)

[19] Chesterman (2000) 155.

relevant parts of the First Amendment to the US Constitution read: 'Congress shall make no law . . . abridging the freedom of speech, or of the press, or the right of the people peaceably to assemble, and to petition the Government for a redress of grievances.' Since the *Sullivan* decision these words have created an approach to defamation law that differs significantly from English and Australian law.

Under the *Sullivan* rules, US law distinguishes between different categories of defamation plaintiff. Plaintiffs who are public officials or public figures face far greater burdens than under traditional common law. Public plaintiffs must prove the usual elements of publication, identification and defamatory meaning. But they also must establish with 'convincing clarity' that the publication was made with 'actual malice'. Actual malice is a term of art under US law, which requires plaintiffs to establish that defendants published material knowing it to be false, or with reckless disregard as to its falsity.[20] There is no comprehensive test of what amounts to reckless disregard, but it requires a 'high degree of awareness' of the material's 'probable falsity'.[21] Or, as described in *St Amant v Thompson*, it needs 'sufficient evidence to permit the conclusion that the defendant in fact entertained serious doubts' about the publication's truth.[22] In addition, public plaintiffs must demonstrate actual malice with convincing clarity, which is a standard of proof substantially higher than the usual civil standard.[23] Because of the First Amendment issues involved, whether a litigant is a public or private plaintiff is seen as a question of law for the judge to decide.[24] It is worth noting that the term *actual malice* causes confusion in some US litigation, especially when both common law malice and actual malice are relevant; for example, in some private plaintiff cases where claims are put forward for presumed or punitive damages.[25] And the Supreme Court has noted the term may confuse juries.[26] It may be better to use the term *constitutional malice* for comparative purposes to distinguish actual malice from malice under English and Australian law. However, given its US ubiquity, the term *actual malice* is used in this book.

The *Sullivan* decision established these rules for public officials and explicitly aimed to enlarge the legal space for discussion and debate about government. The Supreme Court held that the traditional defence of truth insufficiently protected speech: a 'rule compelling the critic of official conduct to guarantee the truth of all [its] factual assertions' inevitably leads to self-censorship.[27] The *Sullivan* rules changed the burden of proof to support the 'profound national commitment to the principle that debate on public issues should be uninhibited, robust and wide-open'.[28]

---

[20] *New York Times v Sullivan*, 376 US 254, 279–80 (1964).

[21] *Garrison v Louisiana*, 379 US 64, 74 (1964).

[22] 390 US 727, 731 (1968).

[23] *Sullivan*, 376 US 254, 270 (1964).

[24] Eg *Rosenblatt v Baer*, 383 US 75, 88 (1966).

[25] See eg *Schafer v Time*, 142 F 3d 1361 (11th Cir, 1998).

[26] *Masson v New Yorker Magazine*, 501 US 496 (1991).

[27] *Sullivan*, 376 US 254, 277 (1964).

[28] *Ibid* 270. See also *Rosenblatt*, 383 US 75 (1966).

The *Sullivan* rules were extended to public figures in *Curtis Publishing v Butts*,[29] with Warren CJ commenting:

> [A]lthough they are not subject to the restraints of the political process, 'public figures', like 'public officials', often play an influential role in ordering society. . . . Our citizenry has a legitimate and substantial interest in the conduct of such persons, and freedom of the press to engage in uninhibited debate about their involvement in public issues and events is as crucial as it is in the case of 'public officials'.[30]

After the 1971 decision in *Rosenbloom v Metromedia*,[31] it appeared the constitutional approach might go further to encompass speech about all public events and matters of public or general concern. But moving from a focus on the plaintiff's public status to considering the publication's subject matter never achieved a clear Supreme Court majority. Instead, the plaintiff status approach was confirmed in the 1974 decision of *Gertz v Robert Welch*.[32]

While the *Sullivan* rules create national requirements for public plaintiffs, the rules' scope has not been clearly set by the Supreme Court. This means that states vary in their approach to classifying who is, or is not, a public plaintiff. In relation to public officials, all elected officials, candidates and appointed officials of some seniority will come within the *Sullivan* rules. Whether lower-level officials are included varies across the states. For example, all police officers appear to be covered in some states,[33] while only officers of a higher rank would be subject to *Sullivan* in some states.[34] Who qualifies as public figures differs even more between states. In New York a 'prominent' business person was held to be a public figure,[35] while in New Jersey the sole owner of a construction company that only carried out public contracts was not necessarily a public figure.[36] There also are variations in how case law recognises three categories of public figures – all-purpose public figures, limited-purpose public figures and, the much rarer, involuntary public figures.[37]

As well as concerns about classifying plaintiffs, determining actual malice has been controversial. One notable case determined whether altering quotations can amount to actual malice. In *Masson v New Yorker Magazine*,[38] the

[29] 388 US 130 (1967); see also *Greenbelt Cooperative Publishing v Bresler*, 398 US 6 (1971).

[30] *Curtis Publishing v Butts*, 388 US 130, 164 (1967).

[31] 403 US 29 (1971).

[32] 418 US 323 (1974). However, the concept of public concern remains relevant for private plaintiffs, see *Dun & Bradstreet v Greenmoss Builders*, 472 US 749 (1985).

[33] Eg in California, *Gomes v Fried*, 136 Cal App 3d 924 (1982), and in Massachusetts, *Rotkiewicz v Sadowsky*, 730 NE 2d 985 (2000).

[34] Eg a state trooper was held not to be a public figure in Louisiana: *Trentecosta v Beck*, 703 So 2d 552 (1997).

[35] *James v Gannett Co*, 40 NY 2d 415 (1976).

[36] *Schiavone Construction Co v Time*, 847 F 2d 1069 (3rd Cir, 1988).

[37] See eg Calvert and Richards (2002).

[38] 501 US 496 (1991).

Supreme Court considered interview quotations that had been altered by a journalist. Deliberately altering quotations could amount to actual malice only if the alterations caused 'material change' in the meaning that publications conveyed.[39] Defendants then would be taken to know they were publishing falsehoods. However, if a publisher 'alters a speaker's words but effects no material change in meaning . . . the speaker suffers no injury to reputation that is compensable as a defamation'.[40] More extensive concerns have been raised about the complexity of the actual malice standard in trials.[41] These concerns are examined in Chapter 10, in light of the US empirical material that is discussed below in Parts III and IV.

Although some disquiet was expressed about the *Sullivan* rules in Supreme Court decisions after 1964 – the constitutional approach was considered open to revision even in the mid-1980s[42] – *Sullivan* is now an 'absolutely settled law'[43] and its 'unchallenged authority . . . is crystal clear'.[44] Thus, in the US, all public plaintiffs are subject to the requirements of actual malice.

C Private plaintiffs

The US Constitution's effect on private plaintiffs – those who are neither public officials nor public figures – was examined by the Supreme Court most closely in *Gertz v Robert Welch*.[45] The decision established that private plaintiffs must prove some degree of fault when suing the media about matters of public concern. The degree of fault required of publishers – either negligence or a higher standard – is a matter for state law. *Gertz* also established that damages for private plaintiffs can only compensate 'actual injury' unless plaintiffs prove actual malice. Actual injury, however, is not just the proved economic loss that must be shown if plaintiffs seek special damages. It includes damage to reputation and mental distress, but excludes presumed and punitive damages.

It also is clear that private plaintiffs suing the media over matters of public concern must establish falsity, as well as fault.[46] But private plaintiffs suing over matters that are not of public concern do not need to meet the federal constitutional requirements.[47] They could face just the traditional common law rules, depending on state law. This 'constriction of constitutional standards'[48] has

---

39 *Ibid* 516–17 (Kennedy J for SC, White and Scalia JJ dissented in part).

40 *Ibid* 528.

41 See eg Murchison et al (1994); Gilles (1998); Chesterman (2000).

42 Eg Matheson (1987) 218.

43 Smolla (2004) [6.14], who notes the judgment of Rehnquist CJ in *Hustler Magazine v Falwell*, 485 US 46 (1988), is particularly important in this regard.

44 Epstein (1999) 515.

45 418 US 323 (1974).

46 *Philadelphia Newspapers v Hepps*, 475 US 767, 777 (1986).

47 *Dun & Bradstreet*, 472 US 749 (1985).

48 Sack (1999) [1.2.7].

had little effect on media publications because courts overwhelmingly treat media content as being of public concern. For example, it has been suggested that varied lower court decisions on public concern mean 'the only plausible explanation for some "private concern" cases not being considered "public concern" cases is that the defamatory material did not appear in the news media'[49] and that 'almost by definition' the category of public concern 'could include most subjects found newsworthy by professional journalists'.[50] Even so, the Supreme Court has offered little definitional guidance and the category remains underdefined.[51] It also should be noted that the Supreme Court has criticised distinguishing media and non-media defendants (in *Dun & Bradstreet v Greenmoss Builders*[52]), and it appears that the *Hepps* requirements about falsity are 'routinely' applied to all private plaintiffs by US courts.[53] In addition, private plaintiff defamation claims appear to be more common in some non-media areas in the US than in England or Australia. Claims related to employment are a notable example, receiving chapter-length coverage in a leading US defamation treatise.[54] Given the prominence of media defendants in English and Australian law, and the relevance of media publications to policy debates about defamation law in all three countries, these non-media aspects of US defamation law are left aside here.

States apply various standards to private plaintiffs. The most common is a negligence standard, in accordance with *Gertz*.[55] But New York – the country's third most populous state and a significant site for the media industry – applies a gross negligence standard to private plaintiffs under the *Chapadeau* decision.[56] The *Chapadeau* standard applies where publications 'arguably' come 'within the sphere of legitimate public concern' and relate to 'matters warranting public exposition'.[57] It requires plaintiffs to establish that publishers 'acted in a grossly irresponsible manner without due consideration for the standards of information gathering and dissemination ordinarily followed by responsible parties'.[58] States can also impose an actual malice requirement on private defamation plaintiffs, as Indiana does for matters of public concern.[59]

---

49 Drechsel (1990) 15.

50 Mitchell (2004) 442.

51 Post (1990) 668; Stern (2000).

52 472 US 749, 783–84 (1985).

53 Eg Sack (1999) [3.3.2.2].

54 Smolla (2004) Chapter 15. Such claims appear to be much less common in England and Australia, although they are far from unknown: eg *Orford v Ramsi Eletronics* [2004] EWCA Civ 809.

55 Eg in California, *Brown v Kelly Broadcasting Co*, 48 Cal 3d 711 (1989), and in Massachusetts, *Stone v Essex County Newspapers*, 367 Mass 849 (1975); see Smolla (2004) [3.30].

56 *Chapadeau v Utica Observer-Dispatch*, 38 NY 2d 196 (1975).

57 *Ibid* 199.

58 *Ibid*. The civil standard of proof applies.

59 See eg *Journal-Gazette v Bandido's*, 712 NE 2d 446 (1999); Smolla (2004) [3.31].

The result of these rules is that public plaintiffs must meet the actual malice standards, while almost all private plaintiffs suing the media will need to establish that the published defamatory allegations are false and that the media was at fault in publishing them – at least to a standard of negligence, but perhaps to a higher standard such as gross negligence.

D The treatment of opinion

How to treat publication of opinion has been 'a persistent problem' in US law.[60] The judgment of Powell J in *Gertz v Robert Welch* famously states:

> We begin with the common ground. Under the First Amendment there is no such thing as a false idea. However pernicious an opinion may seem, we depend for its correction not on the conscience of judges and juries but on the competition of other ideas. But there is no constitutional value in false statements of fact. Neither the intentional lie nor the careless error materially advances society's interest in 'uninhibited, robust, and wide-open' debate on public issues.[61]

This appears to create a complete constitutional protection for publishing opinion,[62] which was the approach adopted in the vast majority of courts over subsequent years.[63] In *Milkovich v Lorain Journal*,[64] however, the Supreme Court re-expressed the constitutional requirements and held that defamation actions must involve statements of fact that are capable of being proved false.[65] This decision can be related to the earlier *Philadelphia Newspapers v Hepps*; it protects media publications about matters of public concern which contain no statement that can be proved false.[66] Many statements of opinion do not convey such factual imputations, so they are not actionable under US law. Closely related to this approach to opinion, publications cannot be sued over if they are merely rhetorical hyperbole,[67] or parodies that would not be understood to convey factual allegations.[68] As Rodney Smolla has noted,[69] *Milkovich* changed the terminology from 'fact or opinion' to 'fact or non-fact', but it did not change in substance the protection for opinion:

> [I]t would misread *Milkovich* . . . to treat the case as opening the door to defamation actions based upon what most courts had come to treat as

---

[60] Sack (1999) [1.8].

[61] 418 US 323, 339–40 (1974) (footnote omitted).

[62] See eg American Law Institute, *Second Restatement of Torts* (1977) §566.

[63] Eg Sack (1999) [4.2].

[64] 497 US 1 (1990).

[65] *Ibid* 19–20.

[66] 475 US 767 (1986); see eg Sack (1999) [1.8].

[67] Eg *Greenbelt*, 398 US 6 (1970); see also *Old Dominion Branch No 496, National Association of Letter Carriers v Austin*, 418 US 264 (1974).

[68] *Hustler*, 485 US 46 (1988).

[69] Smolla (2004) [6.2]; see also Sack (1999) [4.2].

> constitutionally protected 'opinion.' 'Opinion' by any other name is still free speech: statements not subject to objective proof, including statements of imaginative expression, rhetorical hyperbole, and emotional caricature are still immune under the First Amendment.[70]

For example, a newspaper publication described a lawyer in these terms: 'history reveals that he will say or do just about anything to win, typically at the expense of the truth'.[71] The statement was opinion. In context, the 'collection of opinions, colorfully expressed' made the publication 'simply . . . rhetorical hyperbole'. The description of the lawyer was 'not provably true or false' because 'no core of objective evidence' could exist in relation to it.[72] While similar material *may* be defensible under the common law defence of fair comment,[73] the breadth of US protection for opinion – and the role of pre-trial determinations on the issue, which are considered below – means the US approach goes beyond English and Australian opinion defences. The US approach 'clothe[s] the use of epithets, insults, name-calling, and hyperbole with virtually impenetrable' protection.[74]

E State and federal courts

The US has both state and federal courts. Depending on the parties that are involved, it is possible for defamation cases to proceed in either court system. The state tribunals are of general jurisdiction and include trial, intermediate and supreme courts. The highest court in most states is its Supreme Court. But in New York, trials are held in the state's Supreme Court, intermediate appeals in its Appellate Division and the highest state court is the New York Court of Appeals. Most states exercise jurisdiction over defamation defendants from outside the state if the publication has targeted the state in question.[75] While issues remain about which state's law will be applied,[76] it will be the law of a single state: American defamation law applies a single publication rule. The rule means that only one cause of action exists for 'any single publication . . . such as any one edition or issue of a newspapers or book or magazine . . . or any one broadcast over radio or television'.[77] In comparison, if Australian plaintiffs sue over

[70] Smolla (2004) [6.21]. While aiming to clarify the earlier *Gertz* decision, *Milkovich* generated great controversy as to its effects on the treatment of opinion: see eg Sowle (1994); Eversole (1998).

[71] *Cochran v NYP Holdings*, 58 F Supp 2d 1113, 1115 (1998).

[72] *Ibid* 1124, affirmed on appeal, 210 F 3d 1036 (9th Cir, 2000).

[73] On this issue, comparisons could be investigated between US and non-US approaches to opinion in light of the US concepts of 'pure' opinion (where a publication also contains facts related to the opinion) and 'mixed' opinion (in which the publication does not disclose the facts on which the opinion is based): see eg Smolla (2004) [6.29]–[6.31].

[74] Sack (1999) [2.4.7].

[75] Eg *Calder v Jones*, 465 US 783 (1984); Smolla (2004) [12.9]–[12.24].

[76] See eg Smolla (2004) [12.25]–[12.41]; Pielemeier (2003).

[77] American Law Institute, *Uniform Single Publication Act*; see eg Smolla (2004) [4.93].

publication in multiple states, the varying state and territory laws – notable aspects of which were discussed in earlier chapters – come into play in the litigation. (As discussed in Chapter 10, this is one of the elements that would change under Australian uniform defamation laws.)

Federal courts include District Courts and Courts of Appeal, which are divided into circuits in different regions of the country.[78] Federal courts' jurisdiction is limited and, in general terms, encompasses matters in which the US is a party, matters that involve the federal Constitution or federal statutes and matters that involve litigants from different states.[79] The last category is the most important one for defamation – it applies in many media cases. Where a federal case involves parties from different states, the court is said to be 'sitting in diversity'.[80] When sitting in diversity, federal courts apply state rather than federal law, but apply federal procedural rules.[81] Because corporations are deemed to be citizens of both the state in which they are incorporated and the state of their principal place of business,[82] corporations often have dual citizenship. This means that many media defamation actions can be brought in federal as well as state courts. It also is possible for defendants to shift civil actions from state to federal courts, where the action could originally have been brought federally.[83]

F Interlocutory hearings and appeals

The usual steps in US defamation litigation are similar in state and federal courts: pleadings, pre-trial motions and discovery, and trial. Two interlocutory motions are particularly important in defamation: motions to dismiss and motions for summary judgment.[84] A third class of motion has great significance in California: motions to strike defamation claims under the state's legislation against 'SLAPP' suits or strategic lawsuits against public participation. First, a motion to dismiss for failing to state a sufficient legal claim – which in some states is still called a demurrer[85] – occurs more frequently in defamation than in most actions. Motions can argue matters such as the publication not identifying the plaintiff, being protected by a clear privilege or limitations period, not being capable of

---

[78] As well as the 11 Circuits, there is a Court of Appeals for the District of Columbia and another that hears matters such as patent disputes.

[79] See eg Friedenthal et al (1999) Chapter 2.

[80] Diversity jurisdiction is available only for matters involving at least $50,000.

[81] As to which state's law is applied where publications cover multiple states, see eg Smolla (2004) [12.25]–[12.40].

[82] See eg Friedenthal et al (1999) 33–36.

[83] See eg Smolla (2004) [12.43]. The reverse move, from federal to state court, is not open. In relation to defamation appeals to the US Supreme Court and the importance of separating state and federal grounds for decision within lower courts, see Smolla (2004) [13.29].

[84] It also is possible at trial to seek judgment as a directed verdict or judgment notwithstanding a jury verdict: see below, Part I, G.

[85] Sack (1999) [16.2].

conveying defamatory meanings, or not being capable of conveying factual allegations; that is, the publication merely is opinion. Any of these arguments can dispose of claims at the outset.

The second important interlocutory motion is one for summary judgment. The motion is difficult to obtain where facts are in dispute. Disputed facts, however, are material only if they could affect a trial's result.[86] In defamation, defendants can seek summary judgment by arguing that public plaintiffs will be unable to prove actual malice with convincing clarity at trial because of certain undisputed facts, even if other facts remain in dispute at the summary judgment stage. As Robert Sack notes, 'After discovery, it is often clear . . . that whatever the defendant's faults, "actual malice" . . . is not among them.'[87] Motions for summary judgment in defamation commonly are made after discovery, which in the US includes the deposition process and is far more extensive than English disclosure or Australian discovery.[88] While summary judgment has been hard to obtain in many types of case, in defamation 'the observation that summary judgment seems to be the rule, not the exception, reflects experience'.[89] A significant reason for summary judgment's prevalence in defamation is the Supreme Court decision in *Anderson v Liberty Lobby*.[90] *Anderson* established that, under federal procedural rules, public plaintiffs need to show actual malice with convincing clarity at the summary judgment stage not just at trial.[91] It should be noted that there have been debates about whether summary judgment in defamation is preferred as a matter of First Amendment policy, is simply more common in defamation because of the applicable legal standards, or (in the least common view) actually is disfavoured because the legal standards focus on the defendant's state of mind.[92] It is clear, however, that the burdens facing US plaintiffs at the pre-trial stage are very different than in England and Australia and they facilitate, in practice, the disposal of many more claims.

A third type of pre-trial motion arises under anti-SLAPP legislation. The label of SLAPP traditionally refers to suits brought by corporate or public sector entities to silence criticism and debate about their activities. George Pring and Penelope Canan, who developed the concept, investigated a wide variety of behaviour that led to suits against individuals or activist groups, such as participating in demonstrations, seeking signatures for petitions, or reporting breaches of environmental regulation.[93] The concept of SLAPPs has become

[86] *Anderson v Liberty Lobby*, 477 US 242, 248 (1986).

[87] Sack (1999) [16.3].

[88] See eg Jolowicz (2000) 41–45.

[89] Sack (1999) [16.3] (footnote omitted).

[90] 477 US 242 (1986).

[91] Cf the earlier Supreme Court observation, in *Hutchinson v Proxmire*, 443 US 111, 120 and its note 9 (1979) that determining actual malice 'does not readily lend itself to summary disposition'.

[92] See eg Sack (1999) [16.3]; Smolla (2004) [12.69]–[12.75]; Matheson (1987); Gilles (1998).

[93] See Pring and Canan (1996); Pring (1989); Canan and Pring (1988); Pring and Canan (1988).

identified with corporations suing individual activists or environmental groups, and has been used analogously for many cases where the parties have differing resources. Some commentators argue the label is applicable to a wider group of 'relentless' litigants, and others would extend it to all cases involving matters of public concern.[94] Anti-SLAPP statutes exist in some US states, often giving defendants particular procedural protections. Californian legislation is important for defamation because, perhaps appearing incongruous to non-US readers, it has been applied to media defendants in defamation suits. The legislation 'is to be construed broadly' and covers any conduct 'in furtherance of the constitutional right of . . . free speech in connection with a public issue or an issue of public interest'.[95] It provides that such actions are subject to special motions to strike, unless plaintiffs establish that they have a probability of prevailing in their claims. Media defendants can use the procedure against defamation suits over media reports about matters of public concern.[96] Media entities are 'among the main beneficiaries'[97] of this 'potent weapon'[98] for defendants.

Under California's anti-SLAPP legislation, motions to strike must be issued within 60 days of complaints being filed, unless courts grant leave for later filing. Discovery is substantially limited in state courts once a motion to strike has been issued, which can make it harder for plaintiffs to demonstrate a reasonable probability of prevailing in their suit. For public defamation plaintiffs, 'truncated' discovery 'can be an onerous burden' when they face the hurdle of actual malice.[99] Significantly, if a motion to strike is granted, defendants are entitled to recover their legal fees. Such fee shifting is extremely rare in US defamation litigation. The Californian anti-SLAPP provisions can apply in federal courts, but the Ninth Circuit Court of Appeals has held that the legislation's limitations on discovery conflict with federal procedural rules. This means the Californian provisions cannot be applied in the same way to limit discovery in federal court when plaintiffs face a motion to strike.[100] In general, the anti-SLAPP legislation that exists in some other states is narrower and does not apply to media defendants in defamation suits.[101]

---

[94] Kumar (1997); Cosentino (1993).

[95] *Californian Civil Procedure Code* §§425.16 and 425.17. For a detailed review of the provisions see Tate (2000), and for a brief commentary on reforms effective from 1 January 2004 see Media Law Resource Center (2004a) 295–97. The reforms aimed to curb abuse of the anti-SLAPP provisions in non-media litigation: see *Californian Civil Procedure Code* §425.17(d)(1).

[96] *Lafayette Morehouse v Chronicle Publishing*, 37 Cal App 4th 855 (1995).

[97] Smolla (2004) [12.24.50].

[98] Sack (1999) [16.2.2].

[99] Smolla (2004) [12.54.50].

[100] *Metabolife Intern v Wornick*, 264 F 3d 832 (9th Cir, 2001); cf the earlier *US ex rel Newsham v Lockheed Missiles and Space*, 190 F 3d 963 (9th Cir, 1999).

[101] For detail about anti-SLAPP legislation in those states in which it exists, see Media Law Resource Center (2004a).

It also is worth noting the approach to appeals from interlocutory rulings on motions to dismiss, motions for summary judgment and motions to strike. If such a motion is *granted*, the losing party can appeal. But most US states take a different approach where motions for dismissal or summary judgment are *refused*. Under the final judgment rule, appeals are possible only after a final judgment that 'ends the litigation on the merits'.[102] This applies in most states, so interlocutory orders generally cannot be appealed, although they can be reviewed in a post-trial appeal. (In comparison, England controls the appeals process by requiring permission to appeal to be obtained in almost all types of case.[103]) Statutory and case law exceptions exist to the final judgment rule, but most have little relevance for defamation claims. Some states, however, do have broader statutory exceptions or more flexible approaches to what amounts to a final judgment.[104] Also, some states will consider writs of mandamus or prohibition to challenge interlocutory orders beyond the very limited scope for such claims in federal courts.[105] Even so, pre-trial appeals do not play a substantial role in federal courts or the courts of many states. But three states must be noted that are significant in terms of defamation law and practice. First, New York allows interlocutory appeals in civil actions generally and, second, Texas allows appeals against denials of summary judgment in media cases.[106] Third, decisions in motions to strike under anti-SLAPP legislation can be appealed immediately in Californian state courts.[107] Overall, interlocutory appeals appear to be rare in most US courts, but common in defamation claims in state courts in the three most populous states of California, Texas and New York.

Other research into defamation could be reviewed briefly in light of this factor about appeals. Some research suggests that pre-trial appeals are very common in defamation.[108] Two factors may be relevant to such findings: First, three significant states do have interlocutory appeals. Second, such analyses may combine the apparently quite different incidence of appeals when pre-trial motions are *granted* and when they are *refused*. Consistent with that interpretation, other reports suggest far lower rates of defendant appeals at summary judgment stage; for example, 332 plaintiff appeals from grants of summary judgment between 1990 and 1999, compared with 67 defendant appeals.[109]

---

102 *Caitlin v US*, 324 US 229, 233 (1945); see eg Friedenthal et al (1999) 600–618.

103 See eg Andrews (2003) 901–3.

104 For detail about appeals in each state, see Media Law Resource Center (2004a).

105 See eg Friedenthal et al (1999) 615–18.

106 *New York Civil Practice Law and Rules* §5701; *Texas Civil Practice and Remedies Code* §51.014(6); and see Media Law Resource Center (2004a) 993–94.

107 See *Californian Civil Procedure Code* §425.16(g); Media Law Resource Center (2004a) 294–97.

108 Eg Bezanson et al (1987) 129–33.

109 Libel Defense Resource Center (2001) 4, 16 and 20.

G Judges, juries and post-trial appellate review

Compared with England and Australia, juries have a far more prominent role in most US tort litigation, and appellate courts are more deferential to jury verdicts.[110] The Seventh Amendment to the US Constitution provides for a right to jury trial for all claims above $20, and most state constitutions provide similar rights.[111] The size of juries varies across the states, with six-member juries having been endorsed by the Supreme Court. But the situation with regard to the jury's prominence differs for defamation. Arguably, defamation juries are less significant in the US because so many defamation cases are disposed of at interlocutory stages.[112] This is partly due to the Supreme Court decision in *Anderson v Liberty Lobby*.[113] Its requirement for public plaintiffs to show actual malice with convincing clarity in order to avoid summary judgment was 'a crucial victory for the press'.[114] In addition, the *Sullivan* rules' clear and convincing evidence standard greatly increases the importance of appellate review of any trial decisions in public plaintiff defamation cases. Under *Sullivan*, appellate courts must review the facts that were found at trial to ensure that constitutional standards have been met; the facts relevant to actual malice will be particularly significant.[115] This independent review has been described as de novo review of 'constitutional facts':

> [A]n appellate court has an obligation to 'make an independent examination of the whole record' in order to make sure that 'the judgment does not constitute a forbidden intrusion on the field of free expression'.[116]

There are theoretical and practical tensions in how a judge should reconcile independent review with traditional deference to jury findings – particularly in relation to issues of witness credibility.[117] In any event, the importance of appellate oversight in defamation exceeds that in England and Australia. A key element of the US approach to defamation is this 'distinctly intrusive form of judicial supervision'.[118] As David Anderson suggests, merely requiring plaintiffs to prove falsity and fault may not have substantially altered the US law:

> What assured a decisive break with the English tradition was the court's demonstrated willingness to supervise the administration of state libel law, to

---

110 See eg Davies (2002).

111 *Colgrove v Battin*, 413 US 149 (1973); see Friedenthal et al (1999) 545–47.

112 Eg Logan (2001) 509–12.

113 477 US 242 (1986).

114 Calvert (1996) 45.

115 *Sullivan*, 376 US 254, 285 (1964). In relation to pre-trial appeals, see above fns 102–108 and accompanying text.

116 *Bose Corpn v Consumers Union of United States*, 466 US 485, 499 (1984) quoting the *Sullivan* decision.

117 See eg Sack (1999) [16.5.5]; Matheson (1987) 271–84.

118 Chesterman (2000) 165.

> make sure that the preference for 'wide open, robust debate' was observed in practice as well as in theory.[119]

Similar considerations apply to seeking a directed verdict at trial or a judgment notwithstanding the verdict. These post-trial motions are 'inextricably intertwined'[120] with independent review and are far more frequent and influential in US practice than in England or Australia.[121] Given the low percentage of defamation cases that reach trial, however, it is not surprising that these motions were not given a prominent role in the interviews discussed in Part II. As well as liability issues, the post-trial motions often involve challenges to damages awards. While remedies are probably the most important aspect of English, Australian and US defamation not examined closely in this book, it is important to note the potentially far higher damages awards in the US. Their quantum can run to many millions of dollars. For example, figures from the Media Law Resource Center (MLRC)[122] suggest there have been at least 10 defamation judgments against the media of more than $25 million (in 2003 dollar values).[123] High awards, however, are very unlikely to be upheld and the dangers to large media defendants appear to be less serious than suggested in some earlier academic literature. Anderson, for example, explains that 'from 1980 through 2000, the total amount of final libel judgments against media was less than $21 million' and emphases that this figure 'is 0.01 per cent of the media revenues for *one year*'.[124] The $21 million figure represented an average award of approximately $260,000. While this is not a small sum, within English or Australian comparisons it needs to be assessed in light of the US approach to legal fees under which fee shifting is very rare.[125]

II INTERVIEW SAMPLE AND METHOD

A The sample of lawyers interviewed

Given the high number of US jurisdictions and the dispersed nature of defamation litigation against the media, interviewing lawyers was the most viable empirical method in the US. The American context suggests that alternatives such as

[119] Anderson (2003) 725.

[120] Smolla (2004) [12.82], and see [12.78]–[12.82].

[121] See eg Logan (2001) 516.

[122] The Media Law Resource Center was called the Libel Defense Resource Center (LDRC) before 2003. For simplicity, MLRC is used in the text to refer to the organisation under both names. It is a non-profit information and research organisation funded primarily by media companies and media lawyers; see <www.medialaw.org>.

[123] Media Law Resource Center (2004b) 68.

[124] Anderson (2002) 484 and its note 298 (emphasis in original). Anderson based his analysis on LDRC figures. Logan (2001) provides a similar analysis; as do Weaver et al (2006) Chapter 9. For more recent figures, see Media Law Resource Center (2004b) 17.

[125] See above, fns 99 and 100 and accompanying text, and below, Part III, F.

observing court hearings or accessing court files would not be practical because the material would be too widely dispersed in location and time. During 2003, interviews were conducted with 24 specialist defamation attorneys.[126] As well as litigation experience, several interviewees had backgrounds in academic teaching and research. Very usefully for comparative purposes, some interviewees also had experience in English or Australian defamation litigation. The MLRC provided contact details for many of the interviewees as being lawyers with extensive defamation experience. Others, including lawyers with plaintiff experience, were contacted on the recommendation of interviewees.

As Table 8.1 indicates, the sample included lawyers with very extensive experience. Defamation was an important part of every interviewee's practice, and in many cases advising about defamation and related legal actions formed a majority of their work. The interviewees' experience with defamation ranged from five to more than 30 years, with most having between 10 and 30 years' experience. However, in a marked difference to English and Australian interviews, all but four of the US interviewees had acted only for media defendants, never for defamation plaintiffs against the media. In part, this is because very few US lawyers are experienced in representing defamation plaintiffs. And those with substantial experience, such as lawyers who have acted for major corporate or celebrity plaintiffs, appear not to be representative of most defamation litigation. The typical US defamation plaintiff's lawyer has not acted in any other defamation dispute. It appears to be a classic instance of 'repeat player' media lawyers facing inexperienced plaintiff lawyers.[127] In part, this situation reflects the fused US legal profession. There is no equivalent to the leading English and Australian barristers who regularly argue both sides of defamation law.[128] In addition, US media defendants appear to offer no work to lawyers who act for defamation plaintiffs.[129] The distinction between plaintiff and defendant lawyers is 'nearly religious',[130] with media lawyers not wanting to make 'bad law'[131] in the form of decisions that harm the media's general interests. One defence lawyer did note that describing all defamation suits as unwarranted attacks on free speech 'undervalues the other side of the balance, the reputational interest'.[132] But interviewees, even those who acted for defamation *plaintiffs*, more

[126] Three interviewees were women. See the appendix for a full list of people who assisted with the research. The US interviews were conducted during April and May 2003, except for the final three interviewees, who were seen in January 2004 by a colleague from the University of Melbourne, Tim Marjoribanks, as part of our related research into defamation law and news production practices.

[127] 108; similar 107, 111, 112, 114, 118, 122, 123, 124, 125, 127; see eg Galanter (1974).

[128] The English bar remains very small in number and exhibits a cohesion distinct from US lawyers. See the useful overviews of the bar (and US attorneys and English solicitors) in the 1980s study: Atiyah and Summers (1987) 360–75.

[129] Eg 114; similar 116, 118.

[130] 113.

[131] 118.

[132] 107.

Table 8.1 – US Interviewee Sample

Interviewee	5–10 years libel work	10–20 years libel work	20–30 years libel work	>30 years libel work	Any plaintiff work	Only defence work
107		•				•
108		•			•	
109			•			•
110	•					•
111			•			•
112		•				•
113		•				•
114	•				•	
115			•			•
116			•		•	
117				•		•
118				•		•
119		•				•
120	•					•
121			•		•	
122			•			•
123				•		•
124		•				•
125		•				•
126	•					•
127		•				•
128		•				•
129			•			•
130	•					•

Note: The interview numbers continue from the English and Australian interviewees. No letters are used (such as 'B' for barrister) because all interviewees worked as attorneys, rather than in one branch of the divided professions in England and Australia.

commonly emphasised the importance of the First Amendment protections for speech.

The degree to which these interviews represent defamation practice is less easy to determine than for the English and Australian samples. The interviews offer useful information from experienced US defamation lawyers who do not appear atypical in terms of US defamation practice. While the number of interviewees is not large, the relative number of defamation litigators appears to be smaller in the US than in England and Australia, because of the rates of litigation and less extensive pre-publication advice.[133] And while the sample is unbalanced in terms of plaintiff litigators, that appears to reflect the prevalence of experienced defamation lawyers. The number of media defence interviewees – and, importantly, the way in which they could be seen as advocating media viewpoints in a qualitatively different way than English and Australian lawyers[134] – needs to be remembered when interpreting the interview material, as does the overriding limitations of a relatively small number of interviews without substantial documentary sources being used. That said, the sample does suggest how experienced US defamation lawyers discuss and understand their practice, and the interviews highlight some important differences for any comparative examination of US, English and Australian defamation law.

B The interviews' style and content

Each interview lasted approximately one hour. Almost all interviews were audiotape recorded and later transcribed.[135] As in earlier chapters, quotations are direct transcriptions from interviews. The semi-structured interviews proceeded through these main areas – meaning and pleading, substantial truth, pre-trial motions and discovery, actual malice and burdens of proof – in addition to offering interviewees opportunities to comment on other issues they thought significant. The interview material is discussed in the next two parts. General matters about US defamation litigation are considered in Part III, before Part IV examines more specific aspects relevant to meaning and the *Sullivan* rules.

III GENERAL OBSERVATIONS ABOUT US DEFAMATION LITIGATION

The interviews, and other published material, suggest six matters about the context of US defamation litigation. They concern the rates of defamation claims, the spread of litigation expertise, multiple causes of action, the importance of pre-trial motions, preferences for state or federal courts, and legal fees and settlement.

---

133 See below, Part III, A; Marjoribanks and Kenyon (2003).

134 Cf eg Chapter 7, Part III, A.

135 The transcripts totalled approximately 215,000 words. Handwritten notes were taken during two interviews: once due to high levels of background noise and once for the sole telephone interview reported in this book.

A The number of claims against the media

It is commonly thought that US rates of defamation litigation against the media are far lower than in England and Australia. While that generalisation appears to be true, particularly in relation to Australia, it is interesting to note how existing research suggests the rates of claim in each country may not be so markedly different. The greatest caveat to any discussion of this issue is that the figures obtainable in relation to US defamation claims are far less precise than for England or Australia. Annual rates of defamation suits against all types of defendant can be estimated at one claim per 295,000 people in England, as discussed in Chapter 4.[136] Such statistics about civil litigation are less well reported in Australia.[137] However, figures from NSW and Victorian court files in Chapters 5 and 6, coupled with those states' dominance in Australian defamation litigation, suggest that perhaps 170 claims are filed nationally each year. Using a national population figure of 20 million would produce a rate of one claim per 120,000 people in Australia.[138]

As earlier chapters indicate, the majority of English and Australian actions involve media defendants. If between 60 per cent and 75 per cent of the claims involve the media, the rates of defamation suits against the media would lie within the approximate range of one claim per 400,000 to 500,000 people in England and one claim per 160,000 to 200,000 people in Australia. It is worth noting that Australian court files suggest the rates of suits against the media may well be higher than the 60 per cent lower estimate that has been applied here.

Estimates of the rate of US defamation claims against the media can be drawn from existing research. But, as is made clear below, the figures are less accurate than the estimates for England and Australia. One thing that can be noted from the above figures is the approximate number of defamation claims needed for the US to reach the English and Australian rates. The US media would need to be the subject of between 600 and 750 defamation actions per year to reach the estimated English rate, and between 1,500 and 1,850 claims annually to reach the Australian rate.[139] The MLRC have examined actions against media defendants related to media content. For example, media and insurer members of the organisation reported that 340 actions were filed against them in US courts during 2001.[140] Of these actions, 245 involved a defamation claim and the rate of suits appears to have

---

[136] See Chapter 4, Part II, A.

[137] Eg Opeskin (2001) [246]–[248].

[138] These figures differ only slightly from those estimated by Roy Baker of one claim per 200,000 people in England and Wales and one claim per 128,000 people in Australia: (2003). As Chapter 4 suggests, the English figure now appears lower than the 265 annual claims that would be needed for a rate of one claim per 200,000 people.

[139] These figures use an estimated 2005 US population figure of 295 million people.

[140] Libel Defense Resource Center (2002). A small number of claims were excluded from this total by the LDRC: see 11–12.

been similar during the later 1990s.[141] The MLRC has extensive membership from US media companies and media defence lawyers.[142] This suggests that its analyses involve a good cross-section of the types of defamation claims against the media. The MLRC report, however, emphasises that its figures are drawn from a subset of the US media.[143] And it is difficult to estimate what portion of total media defamation claims is represented by the figure of 245. Consider four possibilities. If the figure was taken to represent all defamation claims against the media, there would be approximately one claim per 1.1 million people (using a population estimate of 280 million people for 2001). If the figure represents 75 per cent of all defamation claims against the media, there would be 326 claims per year, or approximately one claim per 860,000 people. If the figure is half of the annual claims, there would be approximately 490 claims per year, or one claim per 570,000 people. And if the figure represents only 25 per cent of annual claims, there would be approximately 980 claims each year, or one claim per 285,000 people. One thing these figures suggest is that the lower limit to the rate of claims is a little under one claim per million people annually. That is certainly far lower than English or Australian rates, but the range of possible figures suggests that the actual US rate may not be as far below the English rate as usually is suggested.

Other MLRC research also illustrates the difficulty in determining US litigation rates in this area. Using the specialist Media Law Reporter and the legal database Westlaw, the MLRC has investigated motions to dismiss, summary judgment motions and trials in defamation claims against the media. The MLRC identified 317 motions to dismiss, 659 summary judgment motions, and 184 trials in media defamation claims during the 10 years from 1991 to 2000.[144] Allowing for slight duplication within the cases in the MLRC reports – for example, if some matters in which summary judgment was rejected continued to trial – the figures show that more than 850 actions against the media involved judgments worthy of reporting during the decade, at least to the specialist audience of those report series. Of course, the difficult question is what percentage of total claims is represented by these 85 cases per year? Only some decisions would appear in the sources used by the MLRC, but the specialist nature of the Media Law Reporter suggests it may well not be an extremely low percentage of all cases – unlike, for example, the situation that could be expected for reporting more routine civil claims. In addition, interviews with US litigators suggest motions to dismiss and

---

[141] *Ibid* 18 and its Table 4. The 2001 figure is similar to the average of 254 defamation claims per year from the three years 1996–1998, for which LDRC figures also are reported: *ibid*.

[142] The membership is listed at the MLRC site: <www.medialaw.org>. As well as many media companies, members includes groups such as the American Society of Newspaper Editors, Association of American Publishers, California Newspapers Publishers Association, Investigative Reporters and Editors, Magazine Publishers of America, National Association of Broadcasters, New York Press Association and Newspaper Association of America.

[143] Libel Defense Resource Center (2002) 10–11.

[144] Media Law Resource Center (2004b) 17; Libel Defense Resource Center (2001) 4.

summary judgment motions are *very* common and that few media defamation cases would not involve one of those motions or a trial.[145] However, it appears that US courts often may reject motions summarily without providing written decisions. And it also is clear that some cases are not pursued by plaintiffs and end without any formal court proceeding, while other cases settle. Taking these factors into consideration, the MLRC figures clearly need to be treated cautiously. However, they do suggest a range of possible litigation rates. If the MLRC figures for cases reaching pre-trial or trial decisions represent only one in 10 defamation actions against the media, there would be an annual rate of claims against the media of approximately *one claim per 300,000 people* (using a population estimate of 260 million across the decade). However, if the MLRC figures represent one in two actions against the media, the rate would be *one claim per 1.5 million people.* This seems unlikely – it is higher than the notional 'limit' figure that was arrived at from the MLRC complainant studies, above. But it is notable that the figures again suggest the rate of US media defamation claims may not be so much less than in England (although the Australian rates still appear to be substantially higher). This brief analysis should not suggest that the US rates are equivalent to the other countries. They most probably are lower – actually far lower – than England and Australia, but these figures from existing research suggest more research may be warranted into the comparative rates of claim.

B Expertise in defamation litigation

As noted above, defamation law expertise is not evenly spread between plaintiffs and defendants.[146] Interviewees recognised that media defendants have 'a distinct advantage' in this situation,[147] especially because of the detailed and complex law that exists under the *Sullivan* rules:[148]

> [I]n the United States . . . there has historically been a big differential between the expertise of the defence bar and the plaintiffs' bar. . . . It would not be unusual for a plaintiff's lawyer, in most places in the country, to be handling their first or their second libel suit and they don't know the doctrine that well.[149]

---

145 See below, fns 158–161 and accompanying text. Contrary to these comments, one interviewee suggested that 'probably several thousand' libel suits are filed annually in the US: 119. However, many of the suits 'die early on' – they are just 'filed to make a point and they disappear': *ibid*. Even if this far higher estimate of *initial* suits has some accuracy, it could be noted the interviewees also emphasised the very high number of cases that quickly become inactive. The Australian court files, examined in Chapters 5 and 6, suggest very low rates of inactive defamation files, and England should have a very low rate under the *Civil Procedure Rules 1998* (Eng).

146 See above, fn 127 and accompanying text.

147 109; similar 107, 111, 112, 116, 118, 122, 123, 124, 125. A plaintiff lawyer also noted that media defence offered a 'good learning curve' to plaintiff lawyers: 114.

148 109; similar 116, 118, 123, 125.

149 108; similar 118.

However, the situation may not differ from England and Australia as much as the quotations imply. Interviewees also suggested that plaintiffs with the resources to pay lawyers directly – rather than use contingency fees – were very different opponents and their lawyers would have defamation expertise.[150] Defence expertise also is relevant in another way. The US does not use specialist defamation judges – unlike English and much Australian litigation. This means it is common for only the defence lawyer to have detailed knowledge of the effects of *Sullivan*, *Gertz* and the relevant state authorities.[151] This aspect of defence expertise is particularly important given the weight that the US rules place on the judge's role in pre-trial motions.[152]

C Multiple causes of action

US practice differs notably from England and Australia in the prevalence of multiple causes of action in suits against the media. Defamation claims commonly are combined with claims related to privacy or newsgathering torts.[153] '[W]e expect to see four or five or more torts asserted in a complaint. . . . [T]hat is now common.'[154] While multiple actions are common, the issue is left aside here because non-defamation claims do not appear influential in most litigation. For example, defendants may note in their pre-trial motions that 'all the other claims are just as frivolous' as the defamation claim, and that 'if the defamation claim falls, all the others fall'.[155] The focus of defendants and judges 'overwhelmingly' appears to be on the defamation elements of the claims.[156] That said, there remain serious issues about how the actions will develop and, in particular, how constitutional protections will apply to newsgathering.[157]

D Pre-trial motions not trials

US defamation practice centres on motions to dismiss and motions for summary judgment, as well as the related discovery process. There is 'a great emphasis on motions to dismiss or, failing that and more commonly, on summary

150 Eg 118, 119, 129.

151 114 (judges are often led by defence counsel), 116 ('you want . . . to . . . educate the judge really early on the special character' of defamation), 123, 124; although 121 noted that, sometimes, defendants would want to avoid educating the plaintiff's lawyer too early in the litigation about the obligations of each party.

152 115; similar 116.

153 108 (multiple actions have exploded), 109 ('very much in vogue'), 110, 112 ('not at all unusual'), 113 (very common), 116 (expect multiple actions 'more and more'), 117, 118, 123, 124, 126 (very common); see eg Gilles (2000).

154 123.

155 118; similar 109, 115, 116, 123.

156 118.

157 124; similar 117, 121. There also can be concerns about how plaintiffs may try to develop these actions during the discovery process: 116.

judgment'.[158] Media defendants expect to take one or the other of these motions in every case.[159] Thus, even the most experienced media lawyers had seen very few defamation cases go to trial; for example, only two or three trials in almost 40 years of defamation and related practice,[160] or no defamation trials after being 'pretty much a full time libel defence lawyer for more than ten years'.[161] The role of pre-trial motions is examined further below in Part IV.

E Preferred courts

As outlined above, many media defamation cases could be heard in state or federal courts.[162] In general, interviewees expressed a preference for federal courts,[163] although that depended on the state in question. The preference was particularly one of defence lawyers – for the media defendant 'there is almost a knee jerk reaction or wish to move things into federal jurisdiction if one can'.[164] This was related to various differences between the courts: the consistently high calibre of federal judges and their associates, federal judges being appointed with tenure, federal courts' greater resources and the larger regions from which federal jury pools are drawn.[165] State courts, in comparison, are 'deprived of virtually every resource'.[166] Where preferences were expressed for state courts (eg, in relation to New York[167]) this often depended on interlocutory appeals being available as of right. Overall, however, it would be fair to consider the federal-state issue as a relatively minor one in terms of English and Australian comparison. As one interviewee summarised the effects of the issues about federal and state courts, the 'profound difference is between places that have the First Amendment and places that do not'.[168]

F Legal fees and settlement

Lawyer's fees in US defamation litigation differ in two notable ways from the traditional English and Australian approach. First, each US litigant generally

158 117.

159 113, 117, 122, 124.

160 118. Similarly, 109 had run two trials in 23 years of media defence work and 115 had only one matter go to trial in just over 100 defamation actions over approximately 25 years of media work.

161 113; similar 114, 124, 125, 126, 127. These figures reflect the analysis of the MLRC, which found an average of approximately 26 trials per year during the 1980s, 23 trials per year during the 1990s, and only 12.5 trials per year in the early years of the 2000s: Media Law Resource Center (2004b) 2.

162 See above, Part I, E.

163 Eg 109, 111 (although depends on particular case), 112, 117 (although less concerned that used to be), 120; cf 124 (New York state courts are the first preference).

164 120.

165 112, 117, 118, 120, 127; similar 126.

166 127.

167 109, 111, 124.

168 113.

pays its own legal fees. The winning party does not recover fees from the other side.[169] (California's anti-SLAPP legislation – discussed above in Part I, F – is probably the most relevant situation in which defendants are likely to recover legal fees in defamation actions.) Second, plaintiffs can run litigation under a contingency fee agreement so that fees are due only if the case concludes successfully for the plaintiff – the fees are paid out of a percentage of the award or settlement.[170] While England has seen significant moves towards this sort of approach under conditional fee agreements,[171] the US situation is long-standing and appears to be far more prevalent.

Interviewees generally estimated that a high percentage of individual plaintiffs run cases on contingency fee agreements.[172] Findings from the Iowa Libel Research Project suggest the practice in defamation is long-standing as well as commonplace. In the 1980s, researchers conducted telephone interviews with 164 plaintiffs who had pursued defamation cases against the media. The Iowa Project found that up to 86 per cent of plaintiffs had full or partial contingency fee arrangements.[173] While several interviewees said it was difficult to know,[174] it appears to be 'highly unusual'[175] for non-corporate plaintiffs to pay lawyers hourly fees. Even so, a plaintiff's lawyer suggested that defamation cases are not taken on a contingency basis for financial rewards:

> [Defamation is] not the kind of case that you would ever take for money. . . . The odds are against you. . . . You can only do one . . . a year. . . . This was my case. But . . . if [the plaintiff] does win . . . I think it will really help [the plaintiff] forever. It's worth it, definitely worth it for me.[176]

Defence lawyers also suggested that plaintiff lawyers operating with contingency fees would find it difficult to make defamation cases economically viable.[177] Not surprisingly, interviewees, particularly defence counsel, expressed frustration in their inability to recover legal fees from the other side:

---

169 It has been noted that such arrangements do not provide financial disincentives to defamation actions: see eg Bezanson et al (1987) 149–50.

170 For differing research into US litigation and contingency fees in general, see eg Brickman (2003); Kritzer (2002); Yeazell (2001).

171 See Chapter 4, Part IV, A, and Chapter 10, Part I, D.

172 108 (perhaps 95 per cent), 111 (most), 112 ('I can't recall a defamation case where [the] p[laintiff] wasn't on contingency fee; it's highly unusual'), 115 ('vast majority'), 117 ('almost every individual plaintiff'), 118 ('they are all [on them] in my experience').

173 Bezanson et al (1987) 69–72 and appendix A. The 164 plaintiffs were drawn from the 323 cases that were reported between May 1980 and April 1984 in the *Media Law Reporter* and the LDRC's 50 State Survey.

174 122, 124, 125.

175 112.

176 114.

177 115, 118, 122, 126.

> [W]inning is . . . not really winning, because what does it mean to . . . spen[d] a million dollars over three years to win? To defend a story that was right from the beginning?[178]

Reasons to settle were suggested for both sides. The difficulties facing US defamation plaintiffs mean lawyers may decide to 'walk away' from cases fairly early in litigation.[179] And legal fees, particularly those associated with discovery and depositions, can encourage defendants to settle. At least certain types of media outlet – probably smaller media companies and non-newspaper defendants – make some settlement decisions based on the commercial costs of litigation.[180]

> The percentages [of media defendants that do not settle on principle compared with those who approach settlement commercially] has definitely changed over the last 20 years. . . . It was easy to say . . . we'll fight to the death when there really was no cost in doing that. When there's a real tangible cost just for fighting the fight, it becomes much more difficult.[181]

But compared to other actions, settlement appears to be significantly less common in defamation.[182] Plaintiff and defence lawyers commented that settlement would be more likely when the media had made a clear error.[183] Interviewees did not report that insurance had any direct influence on settlement decisions. But adequate defamation insurance was seen as an essential element of any media company's operations:

> [T]ypically media companies have libel insurance that protects them. [Even for smaller companies] having insurance is not a luxury, it's really the ability to defend the integrity of your business.[184]

The scale of potential damages under US defamation law makes such comments unsurprising.

IV ISSUES ABOUT MEANING AND THE *SULLIVAN* RULES

Earlier chapters suggested the way in which defamation law deals with publications' meaning is a central aspect of English and Australian litigation. Issues connected with meaning also are important in the US, but they arise quite differently. Four points were suggested by the interviews, concerning meaning's

---

178 113; similar 118, 121.

179 118.

180 107, 108, 109, 110, 111, 112, 115, 117, 118, 120, 123, 124, 126, 130.

181 109; similar 118, 123, 124; cf 125 (commercial pressures are not having any greater influence on settlement, from a lawyer who represented quite large media interests).

182 108, 109, 111, 115 (very rare), 116, 123.

183 111, 113, 114, 115, 116, 125 (needs extraordinary fact situation), 128 (error would be the only situation in which settlement would be considered).

184 113; similar 107.

relationship to pleading, implications, substantial truth, and mitigation. The interviews also raised matters about litigation under the *Sullivan* rules, particularly in relation to pre-trial motions and discovery. And they addressed several disparate matters about litigation under *Sullivan*, including the approach of focussing on the plaintiff's status, the concept of actual injury and the burden of proving falsity.

A Meaning and pleading

Pleading practice and disputes about pleaded meanings are not significant in US defamation litigation. Defamation plaintiffs generally need to set out the precise words published, but not identify the defamatory meaning conveyed by the publication with great particularity.[185] As to the way that defamation pleading operates, one interviewee commented:

> [L]awyers in this country, and judges, have totally lost why it is we have these pleadings . . . in the first place, and what they're supposed to do. . . . Here the view is [that pleadings are] a pain in the neck formality and all of this law has grown up about how pleadings are to be liberally construed. . . . So you rarely get a sense of what the plaintiff is actually complaining about.[186]

Similarly, academic texts often consider the issue of whether published words need to be pleaded verbatim and do not discuss pleading in any detail in the sense done for England and Australia.[187]

In some states, plaintiffs must seek a retraction before issuing a defamation claim. Some such provisions apply only to suits against the media, or against elements of the traditional print and broadcast media.[188] Retraction statutes generally require notifying the media promptly in writing about alleged defamations, while limiting the damages that are recoverable if retractions are not sought (or after retractions have been published). Such requests can entail a greater degree of specificity in identifying the allegedly false and defamatory statement.[189] In addition, defendants can seek more definite statements from plaintiffs to identify exactly which false facts are being complained about,[190] but pleading defamatory meaning with precision is not central to defamation practice:

> [P]laintiffs are obliged under the law of just about every state to [say] with specificity what statement it is that injures their reputation. It's amazing the

[185] Eg 118 (the plaintiff just needs to quote the article; usually the meaning is pretty clear), 120, 121, 123; similar 124.

[186] 109.

[187] Eg Sack (1999) [2.4.13]. Smolla (2004) [12.47] also notes the 'verbatim' issue, and in [12.48] mentions the need to 'sufficiently state the defamatory meaning (express or implied) on which the cause of action is based'.

[188] Eg *Californian Civil Code* §48(a); Media Law Resource Center (2004a) provides details for each state.

[189] 125, 127.

[190] 108, 115, 116, 121.

> number of plaintiffs who hold out . . . and refrain from doing so until absolutely compelled by the court at the pain of dismissal. And even then they'll say, 'Well it's the totality of the statement, so there's not a single one of these statements that would be defamatory but . . . when taken together . . . they have defamatory meanings'.[191]

Lawyers with English or Australian experience emphasised that pleading in US defamation practice is different. In this chapter's first opening quotation, one lawyer with English experience noted how the US has 'no such fixing at the beginning [of litigation] of defamatory meaning' and that 'you don't ever really have a definition' in the US approach.[192] Other interviewees stated that there is 'a huge difference between the importance of pleadings in the US and in the Commonwealth',[193] with pleadings being '*much* less important' in US defamation.[194] Courts will examine meaning 'irrespective of' the pleadings and US plaintiffs are not nearly as tied to any pleaded meanings as are English and Australian plaintiffs.[195] US practice does not focus on what interviewees saw as the English and Australian tendency to *rewrite* publications through the pleadings:

> [It is] very disturbing to an American ear . . . that the judge is basically rewriting the story to meet the meaning that [the judge] thinks is suitable [given the judge's] feelings about the reporters and everybody else. . . . I find it outrageous. It offends the heck out of me. . . . The [English] system is so focused on rewriting and both sides are indulging in . . . saying what the thing is, so that you almost have nothing to do with the story you wrote, it has something to do with the legal necessity of the case.[196]

> I understand there's a good rationale for this, which is . . . tell us what it means. But the problem is you're not really saying in those pleadings what the journalist intended to say [or] what you think [it means]. It's what you can persuade a judge the article reasonably meant . . . and that is utterly absurd.[197]

As both these quotations suggest, interviewees with comparative experience had some awareness of how pleaded meanings drive English and Australian litigation. The English and Australian approach 'shapes the discovery, trial, the whole thing. It is completely the cart before the horse.'[198] This is one of the most significant aspects about US defamation in comparison with England and Australia: pleaded meanings do not shape litigation to anything near the same degree. This is not to suggest that meaning has no importance in US practice. As one interviewee noted: 'even though the glamour in American defamation law

191 120.

192 116.

193 119.

194 123.

195 123; similar 121.

196 116.

197 119.

198 119.

[is] the First Amendment defences . . . a giant part of almost all significant American defamation cases turns on defamatory meaning'.[199] The concern, however, is with whether publications are capable of conveying actionable meanings at all, more than the precise wording that has been pleaded for such meanings. One result of this is that questions about meaning are conceptualised as being related to issues such as 'libel by implication' and substantial truth, which are considered in the next two Sections.

A separate issue related to meaning, which has been controversial in the US, can be noted in passing. It involves the concepts of 'slander per se' and 'libel per se'. Sack provides a useful overview, including this brief explanation:

> [T]he term 'slander per se' has to do with the nature of the charges made [as it does in English and Australian law], while the term 'libel per se', in most [US] jurisdictions, relates to whether the statement is injurious to reputation on its face.[200]

Statements that are libellous per se are defamatory without the addition of extrinsic material. Where extrinsic material is needed to convey defamatory allegations, the publication can be referred to as 'libel per quod' and most states require plaintiffs to plead special damages for 'per quod' libels. While '[n]o concept in the law of defamation has created more confusion' in the US,[201] the issue did not appear to be a major concern in interviews. But the complex doctrine did give media defendants opportunities to claim that inexperienced plaintiffs' lawyers must plead more than is actually required; for example, that 'libel per se' requires plaintiffs to plead special damages unless the alleged defamation relates to one of the four categories of 'slander per se'.

B Meaning and implication

A significant strand in US defamation literature concerns what is called 'libel by implication'. States vary as to how ready they are to accept implication arguments. Most states will allow it where the implication 'flow[s] logically as a matter of common sense, in some significant way, from what is said'.[202] Interviewees described the approach to implications as, doctrinally, 'a mess' with room for constitutional development.[203] But defence arguments of substantial truth often would limit the impact of any alleged implication.[204]

English and Australian lawyers may find it difficult to identify quite what is at stake in the US idea of libel by implication. Publications' literal meanings are very rarely the subject of suit in England and Australia. Instead, the implications

[199] 108; similar 116.

[200] Sack (1999) [2.8.1] and see generally [2.8].

[201] *Ibid* [2.8.1].

[202] 108; similar 112.

[203] 118; similar 117.

[204] 110; similar 108, 125.

that ordinary recipients take from publications are central to most litigation; that is, implications are conceptualised as being an ordinary part of meaning in English and Australian law. Similarly, at least one US interviewee recognised the issue as being merely an aspect of the general approach to meaning:

> I don't view the libel by implication problem as being a real separate problem. All the [uproar is about] how can it possibly be that we can be sued for something that the article doesn't even say . . . to which my response is that that concept is just one of defamatory meaning and it's been around forever.[205]

But another aspect of US law, which often is related to libel by implication, does appear to differ from English and Australian law. That is, US law is more ready to allow actions to be based on allegedly defamatory headlines.[206] Notable cases, however, have focussed on 'headline' statements published on the cover of publications that were not necessarily counteracted by the content of articles many pages away from the cover.[207] While the US approach to headlines does seem more flexible, this situation is somewhat different than cases such as *Charleston v News Group Newspapers*,[208] which was mentioned in Part III of Chapter 2.

There certainly are questions about how implied meanings should be dealt with under the actual malice standard: how can defendants be taken to believe they were publishing falsities, or to be reckless as to falsity, when defendants did not believe they were making the particular allegations at all? One way in which the situation can arise is where publications' explicit facts cannot be proved false, but plaintiffs argue that false and defamatory meanings are implied by the publications, perhaps because other true facts are omitted. In such contexts, there have been arguments that, under the *Sullivan* rules, defendants must have been aware that any defamatory implication was false.[209] Not surprisingly, media defence lawyers endorsed arguments for an 'awareness of meaning' standard in interviews.[210] For example, one litigator commented: 'You ought to be protecting libel by implication. The stuff you're really getting at under American law is the intentional falsehood. That really is the paradigm.'[211] In any event, unintended meanings can be dangerous for defendants. Interviewees suggested that simply denying that unintended meanings were conveyed by publications may hamper arguments against the meanings' falsity, unless the denials were handled with care.[212]

---

205 121.

206 See eg King (2003).

207 Eg *Condit v National Enquirer*, 248 F Supp 2d 945 (2002); *Kaelin v Globe Communications*, 162 F 3d 1036 (9th Cir, 1998). See generally, Smolla (2004) [4.25]–[4.29].

208 [1995] 2 AC 65.

209 For a discussion of the issues, see eg Calvert (1996) and (1995a); Dienes and Levine (1993); Franklin and Bussel (1984). Case law varies, but for an example applying an awareness of meaning standard, see *Dodds v American Broadcasting Co*, 145 F 3d 1053 (9th Cir, 1998).

210 Eg 109, 115, 117, 123.

211 117.

212 116; similar 108, 112.

The uncertainty as to how implications will be dealt with under the *Sullivan* rules encourages media lawyers to focus on ambiguities in any pre-publication review.[213] This does not necessarily entail softening a publication's tone, which may be the common result for concerns with ambiguity in England and Australia. Consider, for example, English interviewees' comments about the tone factor's effect under *Reynolds* privilege.[214] As one barrister noted, clearly defamatory stories with 'a pretty good source' may not have been published 'in a balanced way' – instead, the media would 'simply go for it'.[215] Under *Reynolds*, however, publishers are likely to moderate the tone of their publications. In the US, it appears that factual allegations may be made more specific and more damning, and humorous comments may be made more extreme:

> [I]t's really all about making sure that implications are specific enough or if they're vague, that they're vague in a way over the top sort of way. . . . [D]ry senses of humour are not as constitutionally protected in this country as . . . stupid slapstick.[216]

C Meaning and substantial truth

Falsity is a central aspect of US defamation practice; for example, even private plaintiffs need to prove falsity when media publications address matters of public concern.[217] Under this test, public concern is a 'very broad standard' and few media cases 'fall below that radar screen'.[218] If media defendants can show the substantial truth of the allegations in question, plaintiffs' actions will fail. US cases describe the defence of substantial truth in similar terms to England and Australia. In *Masson v New Yorker Magazine*, for example, the Supreme Court described the issue as whether the publication 'would have a different effect on the mind of the reader from that which the pleaded truth would have produced'.[219] Interviews, however, suggested substantial truth is a more flexible concept.[220] Substantial truth is 'very important . . . [I]t means that the target isn't as small. . . . [T]he justification target isn't that small here, it's broader' than in England, which is a 'big difference'.[221] The breadth of substantial truth appears to be related to the lack of specificity required of plaintiffs in relation to meaning. In addition, where plaintiffs need to prove actual malice, defendants can argue they did not know a particular allegation was false and were not reckless as to falsity

---

[213] 119, 126; similar 109.

[214] See Chapter 7, Part III, B.

[215] 64B.

[216] 126; similar 119.

[217] See above, fn 46 and accompanying text.

[218] 108.

[219] 501 US 496, 517 (1991), quoting Sack (1999) see [3.7].

[220] 110, 111, 116, 117, 118.

[221] 116 (comparing US practice to restrictions on the justification defence in English litigation in which the lawyer had been involved).

because of what they knew to be true about the plaintiff.[222] In that regard, it was interesting that interviewees suggested errors such as those in the *Sullivan* advertisement would be defended successfully as a matter of substantial truth under current practice.[223] Interviewees' general responses about substantial truth accord with comments by Anderson when comparing US and English defamation:

> While the English courts require defendants to establish the precise truth of the defamatory accusation, the American courts usually accept a rough approximation. For example, evidence showing that the plaintiff, a journalist, had fabricated one story was held sufficient to preclude liability for a statement that the journalist had been fired for repeatedly fabricating stories.[224]

D Meaning and mitigation

The US approach to substantial truth underscores the way in which meaning is *not* closely related to mitigation under US law and practice. In England and Australia, evidence that the publication's allegations are true can mitigate damages, even where the evidence does not fully defend a publication. But the evidence that can be admitted is controlled largely by pleaded meanings, which makes defence pleading of meaning so important especially in England and Victoria. In NSW, mitigation is influenced substantially by the plaintiff's pleaded imputations – and not by any contextual imputations pleaded by the defence – which may increase the importance of pre-trial challenges to the plaintiff's imputations.[225] US defendants appear far more able to bring in damaging information about plaintiffs. Courts accept this evidence for various reasons, in particular those related to whether the defendant had the requisite degree of fault, whether the publication was substantially true and whether the false and defamatory allegation caused damage to the plaintiff's reputation. Defendants will 'learn everything' about the plaintiff's life, and 'all the bad things' that plaintiffs have done will come out in the litigation.[226] As Smolla notes:

> [E]ven if the defamatory statement is proven to be false, evidence that the plaintiff already has a bad reputation is admissible in mitigation of damages. . . .

---

[222] 116, 117.

[223] Eg 117. Errors included stating that police had 'ringed' a campus (an exaggeration), and protesters sang 'My Country, 'Tis of Thee' rather than the US national anthem. Some commentary suggests problems in the *Sullivan* trial decision followed poor application of defamation law, rather than resulting from flaws in the traditional law: eg Epstein (1999) 514: The Supreme Court 'made no real showing of how the traditional rules, fairly applied, posed any serious threat to the freedom of speech and political debate'. Another example concerns identification: that aspect of the trial decision was considered explicitly in *Sullivan*, 376 US 254, 292 (Brennan J) (1964): an 'impersonal attack on governmental operations' cannot be 'a libel of an official responsible for those operations'.

[224] Anderson (2003) 722–23 referring to *Shihab v Express-News*, 604 SW 2d 204 (1980).

[225] See Chapter 3, Part I, B.

[226] 108.

> If the defendant chooses to be aggressive in its pursuit of discovery . . . the plaintiff's life may become an open book.[227]

Under traditional US law, evidence is not admissible of specific acts that are unrelated to the publication. However, federal rules suggest that evidence of previous discreditable acts may be admissible. The argument follows from r 405(b) of the Federal Rules of Evidence which states that if a person's 'character . . . is an essential element of a charge, claim or defense, proof may . . . be made of specific instances of that person's conduct'. For example, when a magazine publication accused a plaintiff of being a traitor to the US who had leaked information that led to the bombing of an international passenger flight, the rule allowed defence cross-examination of the plaintiff about matters including a criminal conviction, breach of parole conditions, drink driving convictions, offences related to cheques and tax returns, and failing to pay child support.[228] Whether this federal rule applies or not, opinion evidence about the plaintiff's reputation for earlier discreditable acts will be admitted in defamation cases, subject to the usual controls for relevance and prejudice.[229]

The wider admissibility of discreditable evidence, and lesser importance of pleaded meanings, can also be seen in others aspects of US law related to its treatment of meaning, such as the 'libel proof plaintiff' and 'incremental harm' doctrines that have been accepted by some courts. Under the first doctrine, previous actions might have made the plaintiff 'libel proof' or immune to further reputational damage from defamatory publications.[230] The second doctrine measures the incremental harm inflicted by the allegations being sued over, compared with any harm from the rest of the publication. If the extra harm is nominal, no action can be maintained.[231] Incremental harm has been accepted under some state law,[232] but it is not an aspect of federal constitutional law.[233] In addition to these detailed elements of the US approach, Sack draws on a variety of case law to suggest the defence has greater room if it can argue the publication misreported the plaintiff's situation:

> Although proof that a plaintiff committed a wrongful act different from that alleged in the offending communication will not establish truth, it will be admissible in mitigation to demonstrate that had the truth been published . . . the plaintiff's reputation would also have been injured.[234]

---

227 Smolla (2004) [13.17].

228 See *Schafer*, 142 F 3d 1361 (11th Cir, 1998), and discussion in Sack (1999) [10.5.5.2].

229 Eg Smolla (2004) [9.60].

230 See eg *ibid* [9.61]; Note (1985).

231 See Sack (1999) [2.4.18] for a useful example considering substantial truth, libel proof plaintiffs and incremental harm, drawn from *Bressler v Fortune Magazine*, 971 F 2d 1126 (6th Cir, 1992).

232 Eg *Masson*, 895 F 2d 1535 (9th Cir, 1989); *Simmons Ford v Consumers Union*, 516 F Supp 742 (1981).

233 *Masson*, 501 US 496 (1991).

234 Sack (1999) [10.5.5.1] (citations omitted).

E Motions to dismiss

In relation to the *Sullivan* rules, interviews raised several matters connected with litigation practice. The first concerned motions to dismiss. They are an important pre-trial step in US defamation litigation, and are 'crucial' in distinguishing US practice.[235] Interviewees suggested that motions to dismiss are made frequently,[236] and often succeed.[237] These responses are not surprising and, in broad terms, accord with earlier research into defamation litigation.[238] Motions usually are based on written submissions, although they also may involve speaking motions in support of the submissions. Motions to dismiss do not require discovery, which makes them a relatively cheap step for defendants to take. This is an important point to note: it can distinguish motions to dismiss from much commentary about the complexity and expense of summary judgment. As well as their good success rate in disposing of cases, motions are attractive because, in most states, they delay other steps such as discovery.[239]

F Discovery and depositions

The discovery process is particularly significant in US defamation litigation, and differs from English and Australian practices. Academic literature and notable cases have highlighted the potential to investigate media production processes in minute detail during discovery.[240] The most notorious example is the case of *Herbert v Lando*,[241] in which depositions were taken from a journalist on 26 occasions during one year and produced nearly 3,000 pages of transcripts.[242] The interviews offered a somewhat different picture of the *usual* media defamation case. Four matters are noteworthy.

First, while discovery could be very extensive with regard to fault, particularly in relation to actual malice,[243] it varies substantially depending on the issues in

---

[235] 116.

[236] 108 (would expect 'a motion to dismiss or a motion for summary judgment, or both'), 109 ('almost always' challenge), 111 (far more likely than in other actions), 112 (in at least one-third of matters), 115 (file one-third of time), 116 (in New York, the tendency is to try 'an immediate motion to dismiss'), 117 (motion to dismiss or motion for summary judgment tried in every case), 121 (taken 'more often than not'), 122 (motion to dismiss or motion for summary judgment before discovery made 'in three quarters of cases, maybe higher'), 123 (tried in a significant percentage of cases), 124 (more now than 10 years ago), 129 (used especially in cases based on official documents).

[237] 109 ('almost always' succeed), 111 (far more likely than in other cases), 121 (succeed 'more often than not'), 122 (very high success rate), 124 (estimate one in four of own actions has a winning motion to dismiss).

[238] Eg Bezanson et al (1987) 129–34.

[239] 109.

[240] See eg Chesterman (2000) 161–62; Gilles (1998) 1768.

[241] 441 US 153 (1978).

[242] *Ibid* 176 and its note 25.

[243] 117, 122, 127; similar 129.

dispute and the parties' wills and resources: 'It depends on . . . the complexity of the plaintiff's claim and I think also the plaintiff's commitment.'[244] Second, it appears that plaintiffs often do not take extensive depositions due to the expense involved. The expense of oral depositions is well recognised and probably is their 'chief drawback'.[245] In interviews, a plaintiff's lawyer reported that a recent defamation case took 120 hours of work to get through the depositions stage, which was a substantial investment by a small firm operating on contingency fees.[246] Other interviewees suggested that plaintiffs often do not take extensive depositions because of the cost, which many lawyers are unable or unwilling to fund:

> [The problem for plaintiffs] is that depositions cost money and [for] a plaintiff who has a lawyer on a contingency . . . an all day deposition, put aside the lawyer's time, the transcript could be $1,000. [Lawyers] are very reluctant to advance that kind of money. . . . So they don't usually take [depositions].[247]

Third, taking depositions in defamation cases was described as a particular skill, which inexperienced defamation lawyers could find difficult.[248] This is not surprising, given the style of US depositions. (It is worth noting that US law in general appears to be less hostile to wide-ranging discovery – to what are called fishing expeditions in English and Australian procedure.[249]) Depositions allow lawyers to 'confront and question any person' – not just parties but also, for example, likely witnesses – about 'the subject matter of the case'.[250] Answers must be sworn or affirmed and the process recorded. Often the deponent signs a transcript of the proceedings. As this description suggests, depositions should not be equated with interrogatories. Interrogatories can only be directed to the opposing party and, in effect, will 'be answered by the lawyer[s]'.[251] Depositions are far more powerful. In particular, defendants can seek admissions on issues that will support summary judgment motions.[252] A very experienced media lawyer commented: 'I can take a deposition of a plaintiff for two days or three days and have . . . one exchange that wins the case.'[253] Inexperienced plaintiff defamation lawyers would appear unlikely to use the process as effectively.

Fourth, the depositions process can be 'very useful'[254] for defendants in ways that go beyond the parties' frequently different resources and levels of

---

244 117; similar 125.

245 Friedenthal et al (1999) 408.

246 114. The time included related motions to compel discovery of particular documents.

247 118.

248 Eg 118. Many interviewees reported they often face plaintiffs' lawyers who are running their first defamation case: see above, fn 127 and accompanying text.

249 Eg Hauser (1994).

250 Friedenthal et al (1999) 407.

251 123; similar 116.

252 117.

253 118. Note, since 2000 Federal court rules limit deposition of any person to one day unless otherwise agreed or ordered: r 30(d)(2).

254 118.

defamation law experience. Depositions can encompass wide issues about plaintiffs' reputations, on which they will be questioned at length in the process's unrestrained environment.[255] One interviewee commented: 'Once you put reputation at issue, there's very little that the defendant isn't entitled to ask about [in depositions]'.[256] Another interviewee emphasised the strategic power of this aspect of the discovery process:

> This is the first time that the plaintiff is exposed to the reality that this is not a free ride; this is not a walk in the park. [The plaintiff is] going to be asked some very tough questions and we're going to find the holes in the story . . . and any of the bad things: [Was the plaintiff] ever arrested? [Was the plaintiff] ever fired? . . . [Y]ou're allowed to ask all those questions.[257]

This is one way in which depositions can be used by defendants to force settlement,[258] or to establish defence arguments for summary judgment.[259]

> [The] goal . . . is to obtain as much corroboration as possible for the proposition that the reporter honestly believed his or her story to be true, or at least had no subjective belief that it might be false.[260]

In addition, defendants can strengthen their position if they can use the depositions process to show plaintiffs how an error came to be made in the publication, and that the error would not meet the fault standards applicable to the case.[261]

Those four matters support the idea that discovery can be extremely expensive and complex,[262] particularly if many staff are involved in a media publication's editorial team.[263] Concerns also exist about the burdens imposed on discovery by digital communications, such as email.[264] However, the opportunity for great complexity and expense does not mean it eventuates in all media defamation cases. It is 'probably true' that *Herbert v Lando* is atypical: there are very few public plaintiffs who have the resources for such extensive discovery.[265] And interviewees certainly saw the process as varying significantly in scope and complexity depending on the case.[266] Examining summary judgment in the next Section does suggest that discovery often is extensive, but probably to a lesser degree than some high-profile defamation disputes imply.

[255] 111, 118, 121, 123; similar 122.

[256] 113.

[257] 118.

[258] 111; similar 129.

[259] 112, 118, 124, 129; similar 120.

[260] 124.

[261] 129.

[262] 113, 114, 117, 118, 121, 122, 123, 127.

[263] 124.

[264] Eg 121 (journalists 'live by email'), 123, 124.

[265] 121; similar 114, 117.

[266] See above, fns 243 and 244 and accompanying text.

Two final points are relevant to discovery's costs. Discovery can be sequenced – that is, parties can seek orders that discovery is limited to particular issues such as fault (if fault is likely to be a key argument for summary judgment).[267] And judicial oversight to limit excessive depositions, which has been developed in federal courts, could be used more widely to focus depositions on central issues.[268]

G Motions for summary judgment

Summary judgment is the second common pre-trial motion in US media defamation cases, and it is another key element in understanding the law.[269] Some motions can be relatively simple – if they can be brought on the basis of few documents and without taking extensive depositions. But getting to the stage of summary judgment was reported to be very labour-intensive,[270] particularly when defending investigative stories on the basis of the defendant's newsgathering and state of mind: '[if] you have major investigative pieces . . . you're talking . . . hundreds of thousands of documents and depositions and private investigators'.[271]

> [T]o get to the summary judgment stage you have to go through a lot of discovery and if the case is complicated, that can be time consuming and expensive. I guess any defence that turned on state of mind is going to end up being a little mini trial.[272]

While it may resemble a 'mini-trial', summary judgment differs from trial hearings in significant ways. In particular, the issues are legal not factual so the hearing does not involve live testimony or issues of credibility.[273]

Summary judgment motions usually argue about whether the requisite level of fault could be established at trial. As mentioned above, in Part I, an important reason for summary judgment's high profile in defamation is *Anderson v Liberty Lobby*, which, under federal procedural rules, requires public plaintiffs to show actual malice with convincing clarity at the summary judgment stage and not just at trial.[274] Even so, it is difficult for defendants to succeed on the issue of falsity alone – although substantial truth could be argued more successfully.[275] It is more

---

[267] Eg 113. The Supreme Court has recognised this power; eg *Herbert v Lando*, 441 US 153 (1978).

[268] 123; similar 122; and see above, fn 253.

[269] 117.

[270] 109, 113, 114, 115, 116, 119. Some interviewees also noted that far from every case reaches the summary judgment stage: 122, 125.

[271] 109; similar 113, 116 (the process can involve every journalist and editor who worked on the item).

[272] 115.

[273] 109, 120.

[274] 477 US 242 (1986).

[275] Eg from particular information that the plaintiff admits is true: 115; similar 122.

common for falsity to be argued in conjunction with arguments on fault, particularly actual malice or gross negligence.[276]

H Motions to strike

In California, the media routinely responds to defamation actions with motions to strike under the state's anti-SLAPP legislation.[277] Defence lawyers emphasised three powerful effects. First, discovery is stopped once motions to strike are issued, unless plaintiffs obtain judicial orders allowing discovery. Second, where motions to strike are denied, the decision can be appealed immediately by defendants in state courts. Third, successful defendants recover legal fees.[278] It was suggested that these effects have changed defamation practice more than anything else in California.[279] As well as having high success rates, media defendants also saw the process as deterring potential plaintiffs:

> [W]hen we get a demand . . . we automatically fire off a response letter which educates the potential plaintiff about the fact that we will . . . bring a SLAPP motion [if they sue] and the burden will be on them to prove their case and if they can't [prove it] at an early stage, then they're going to pay our attorney's fees. . . . I think [all] that's a huge deterrent.[280]

I Actual malice and the plaintiff's status

To this point, describing the US interviews has centred on issues about meaning and mitigation, as well as pre-trial motions and discovery. Three further matters are noteworthy, beginning with the US focus on the plaintiff's status. In general, the actual malice requirement was widely supported by interviewees, which is not surprising given the general position of the First Amendment in US law, and the prevalence of media defence lawyers among interviewees. But it is notable that even plaintiff lawyers did not criticise actual malice, at least in its application to important public officials. For example, consider these comments about political publications from a defamation lawyer who acted for plaintiffs, largely on a pro bono basis:

> [B]ecause there's public discourse, [*Sullivan* is] something that we really want out there. We really don't want to stifle that. . . . But then when you start getting down through the . . . levels, there seems to me there should be less and less [protection].[281]

---

276 108, 109, 111, 113, 115, 118, 121, 122, 123.

277 Eg 116, 120, 126, 127.

278 Eg 126, 127.

279 127.

280 126.

281 114.

This interviewee did suggest the 'focus should be on public discourse' rather than the plaintiff's status. That was a less common, although not solitary, view in interviews.[282] Interviewees suggested that the approach of dividing public and private figures was a 'good distinction' that 'works well' and should not be changed 'at all'.[283] It 'makes perfect sense' with its 'unspoken rationale' concerning 'access to the media' and the idea that 'public figures, because they so often do have the ability to fight back' through speech, 'should essentially be required to do so'.[284]

Other interviewees, however, preferred the idea in *Rosenbloom v Metromedia* of applying the *Sullivan* rules to all matters of public concern – that is, in newsworthy stories about important subjects, actual malice should be required from all plaintiffs.[285] Their comments resembled concerns raised outside the US about the focus on the plaintiff's status rather than the publication's subject matter. Michael Chesterman, for example, described how the public figure rules include people who have notoriety for reasons other than exercising public power, but miss at least some 'highly influential' people who exercise power in the private sector.[286] Similarly, interviewees commented:

> [O]ne of the problems I have with [the plaintiff status approach] is that it does lead to strange results when you focus on someone's notoriety . . . rather than the contribution to the public debate. . . . [O]ften . . . there are very important things that contribute to the public debate that don't get reported as fully as they might because some lawyer has said to the editor, well none of these people are public figures.[287]

> If the purpose of the constitutional defence is to protect . . . the freedom to talk about certain categories of things because they're important to society and how it functions . . . [the approach] maybe isn't broad enough.[288]

With regard to applying the distinction between public and private plaintiffs, interviewees generally saw courts as working reasonably well,[289] despite the undoubted complexity in states' detailed and varied rules for classifying plaintiffs.[290] The general approach was endorsed, although the position of corporations was raised.[291] While larger corporations appear to be rare

[282] Eg cf 113 (less comfortable in judges deciding what is a matter of public concern than deciding the plaintiff's public or private status).

[283] 123.

[284] 124.

[285] 115; similar 107, 117, 122; see 403 US 29, 44–45 (Brennan J) (1971).

[286] Chesterman (2000) 160–61.

[287] 117.

[288] 122; similar 107.

[289] 108, 112, 113, 122, 123; similar 119, 124, 127.

[290] See eg the extensive discussion of courts' approaches to public figures in Smolla (2004) Chapter 2.

[291] Eg 119 emphasised that publicly held corporations automatically should be public figures.

defamation plaintiffs[292] – a few high-profile cases notwithstanding[293] – defence lawyers raised concerns about smaller corporations. They might be classified as private plaintiffs but have greater resources than many individual plaintiffs,[294] which can change markedly the defamation expertise of the lawyers acting for them.

J Actual injury

Under *Gertz v Robert Welch*,[295] private plaintiffs can only recover damages for 'actual injury' unless they prove actual malice. Actual injury, however, includes damage to reputation and mental distress as well as any economic loss. Interviewees generally saw the actual injury standard as carrying little weight in litigation[296] – unless inexperienced plaintiffs' lawyers omitted to bring forward necessary evidence of injury.[297] That is, actual injury is not 'a load-bearing mechanism' in US defamation law.[298] One limitation related to actual injury could be the requirement in most states – but not as matter of federal constitutional law – for plaintiffs to show reputational harm before they can give evidence of their personal anguish.[299] Interviewees, however, generally thought it was not difficult to find recipients to testify that publications made them think less of plaintiffs,[300] although this was one area in the interviews with notable dissenting views.[301] Once reputational evidence is presented, the plaintiff can simply say 'I felt hurt'.[302] Plaintiffs make strong tactical use of the opportunity – one very experienced litigator commented: 'I've never seen a plaintiff . . . who didn't cry on the stand.'[303]

One effect that the actual injury requirement may have lies in the greater willingness of US courts to hear causation arguments in defamation. Interviewees noted that, because damages are not presumed under *Gertz* unless actual malice is shown, defendants' causation arguments carry weight.[304] This distinguishes the

292 107, 112, 113, 118, 122; cf 124 corporate plaintiffs in general have 'become an enormous concern in recent years' and 129.

293 Eg *Bose Corporation*, 466 US 485 (1984); *Philip Morris v American Broadcasting Co*, 36 Va Cir 1 (1995).

294 107, 113, 126; similar 111, 116.

295 418 US 323 (1974).

296 108, 109, 113, 114, 115, 118, 121, 125.

297 109 ('more than occasionally' a plaintiff's lawyer has not realised the obligation exists).

298 108.

299 See eg Smolla (2004) [9.24]–[9.29]; and generally Anderson (2004).

300 Eg 109; similar 108.

301 Eg 117; similar 123.

302 115.

303 121. In addition, the actual injury requirement was not seen as significant because so few cases get to trial: 118.

304 116, 121. See eg Anderson (1984).

US position from English and Australian law: actual injury means 'more in America than it does in England where the instruction on presumed damages is such that . . . the plaintiff has no duty to call witnesses'.[305] Under the US approach, defendants can bring in wider evidence to counter the plaintiff's evidence that the publication caused reputational harm. This relates to the examination of mitigation earlier in Part IV of this chapter. In the US, evidence of 'other types of reputational things that are close [to the publication] but not exact that would never [be admitted] in England' can be used by defendants.[306]

K Burden of proving falsity

Responses to whether the burden of proving falsity mattered were interesting for their variations. Some interviewees initially suggested that requiring plaintiffs to prove falsity was a significant change from traditional law,[307] and that falsity is a 'core principle' under the First Amendment.[308] After further consideration, however, many of these interviewees suggested the burden does not affect many cases,[309] or has not affected any of their own litigation.[310] That is, interviewees suggested the shift in burden should make a difference for 'principled reasons':[311]

> [Y]ou shouldn't even be in the court unless you can prove that the statement is false and that burden should never change . . . otherwise it condones censorship . . . of truthful statements.[312]

However, the shift in the burden of proving falsity did not appear to have significance in litigation – rather, the requirement to prove fault is the primary change:

> [T]he truth-falsity issue, which one would have thought perhaps in a logical construct drives the train, is . . . once the fault standard was established, an afterthought. . . . [T]he fault standard is what drives it.[313]

In accordance with such conclusions, the most common view from interviewees was that placing the burden of proving falsity on plaintiffs did not change litigation greatly.[314] Fault is the more important element in most situations. Plaintiffs will provide some evidence of falsity – perhaps just their own testimony.[315] While that

---

305 121.

306 121.

307 108, 109, 113, 118, 122, 125, 127.

308 127; similar 123.

309 108, 109, 118, 120, 127.

310 125, 127.

311 127.

312 *Ibid.*

313 117.

314 112, 115, 116, 117, 120, 121, 124, 127.

315 124; similar 122.

evidence may not be believed, the practical burden at trial remains on the defence:[316]

> [U]ltimately if you have a trial . . . I don't think its going to be an effective defence . . . to say they haven't proven falsity. . . . I think . . . the jury is going to be looking to you to prove the truth.[317]

If the overall effect of the burden may be slight, there were ways in which it was seen as important. The plaintiff having the burden of proving falsity clearly is a central element of the protection of opinion after *Milkovich*.[318] The burden also could be significant pre-trial as a 'screening mechanism' to assist judges in dismissing weak defamation claims.[319] Even where clear and convincing evidence is required of falsity as well as fault – which it is in some states – the burden of proving falsity is more relevant to judicial decisions, whether before or after trial.[320] In these contexts, it is more common for truth to be part of, but not the primary line in, defence arguments.[321] Falsity may be used to reinforce an argument on fault: 'I don't think anybody pins it on truth. You pin it on fault.'[322]

V CONCLUSION

This chapter has outlined central aspects of US defamation law and practice, concentrating on issues particularly relevant to a publication's meaning and the approach to litigation under the *Sullivan* rules. The chapter has explained that US defamation law classifies claimants into public or private plaintiffs – an approach that appears to have broad support from lawyers. Private plaintiffs need to prove that media publishers acted with fault in publishing false and defamatory allegations of fact. Public plaintiffs need to prove publishers had actual malice – that is, knowledge of falsity or reckless disregard of falsity – with clear and convincing evidence. This is a higher than usual standard of proof, which makes appellate review more intrusive in US defamation practice. In addition, the focus on factual falsity means opinion is treated differently than in England and Australia – only opinions that convey false and defamatory facts are actionable under US defamation law.

In relation to meaning, earlier chapters described how English and Australian claimants or plaintiffs can seek to shape litigation by pleading a particular specific and damaging meaning. If defendants are not allowed to respond with

[316] 112, 119, 120, 124.

[317] 112.

[318] While only 127 raised this explicitly about the burden, interviewees' comments about opinion often related to the burden's effect.

[319] 108; similar 116, 123.

[320] 116, 121; similar 115. Some interviewees did suggest the burden's impact is greatest at trial, but because so few cases reach trial this also make the burden not particularly significant: 109, 123.

[321] 124.

[322] 118.

different meanings – for example by using the English style of Lucas-Box plea – or cannot successfully challenge the other parties' pleaded meanings pre-trial, then defendants will have to prove claimants' or plaintiffs' meanings are true, and defendants will face relatively severe limits on introducing other evidence to mitigate damages. US plaintiffs do not appear to have anything like the same ability to influence the area of dispute in defamation cases. The law requires them to concentrate on defamatory factual allegations that can be proved false and it seems at least some courts will be less ready to accept arguments about meanings being implied by publications. Meaning in US practice appears to focus on explicit factual allegations and obvious implications – at least in comparison with England and Australia. In any event, US defendants will be able to argue that wider discreditable information about the plaintiff which can be proved true is relevant to issues of fault, substantial truth and damage.

In relation to litigation under the *Sullivan* rules, the chapter has discussed the centrality of motions to dismiss and motions for summary judgment. Motions to dismiss can be relatively simple to prepare, while summary judgment motions may be far from simple. In large part, this depends on the extent and complexity of discovery, which understandably varies with the facts in issue. But it also is important to emphasise that it varies depending on the plaintiff's resources and experience. And defence media lawyers have far more experience than most plaintiff lawyers and judges who are involved in US defamation litigation. The chapter suggests the potential complexities of US defamation litigation are very real, but also that they may occur less frequently in ordinary cases against the media than suggested in some previous analysis. Implications from many of these findings are discussed further in Chapter 10.

– 9 –

LUCAS-BOX AND POLLY PECK IN AUSTRALIA

> It seems to me that it's almost inevitable that at some point in any defamation action, you will have debates about the meanings on which the battle lines are to be drawn. And it is . . . the function of the profession, and if need be the parliaments, to seek to simplify as much as possible where those battlegrounds ought to be.[1]

Earlier chapters have examined the defamation law and litigation practice in England, NSW and Victoria in relation to how law decides where battles about meaning are to be set. They also have detailed the development of qualified privilege defences in England and Australia that, in different ways, can protect some public speech and they have considered the very different US situation for both defamatory meaning and protecting speech. In the final two chapters, the project's concerns are brought together in several broad issues for defamation law and litigation practice. This chapter focuses on issues concerned with meaning in England and Australia. In earlier chapters, four related areas have been raised as significant with regard to meaning: the way a party is bound to a pleaded meaning, the degree of specificity required in a pleaded meaning, how defence meanings are pleaded and dealt with in litigation and the stage of a dispute at which differences between the parties about meaning are dealt with. This chapter takes up those themes by addressing one of the most significant issues to emerge from the comparative investigation of defamation law and litigation practice in the three countries – Lucas-Box and Polly Peck pleading. In particular, it discusses how Lucas-Box and Polly Peck pleading should be understood in Australian common law jurisdictions and examines the implications of changes since *David Syme v Hore-Lacy*.[2] Lucas-Box and Polly Peck pleading are well-accepted parts of English law and litigation practice. But since the comments of Brennan CJ and McHugh J in *Chakravarti v Advertiser Newspapers*,[3] the pleas' status in Australian common law jurisdictions has been doubted. Although no High Court majority has made comments against the *Polly Peck* decision, some state courts have sought to follow Brennan CJ and McHugh J – notably the influential later decision of the Victorian Court of Appeal in *Hore-Lacy*. Under it and subsequent Victorian, Western Australian and South Australian decisions, Lucas-Box and Polly Peck pleading have survived only in a

[1] Interview 39SC (from NSW).

[2] [2000] 1 VR 667.

[3] (1998) 193 CLR 519; see Chapter 2, Part III, H, and Chapter 3, Part I, K.

modified form. However, the modifications adopted by *Hore-Lacy* and later cases pose great, if inadvertent, dangers to the fair and efficient trial of defamation disputes in Australia. The argument in simple terms – if perhaps also in unexpected terms for readers unfamiliar with the operation of English Lucas-Box pleading – is that such defence pleading is a central way in which the law can seek as much as possible to make the parties' battles about meaning relatively simple and equitable and, in turn, simplify the litigation process in defamation.

The developments are examined here in four parts. First, in Part I it is suggested that the *Chakravarti* judgments should be interpreted to maintain some flexibility about issues of meaning, and the judgment of Brennan CJ and McHugh J need not be closely linked with the case's other judgments. The comments of Brennan CJ and McHugh J are analysed in doctrinal terms more closely in Part II. Their judgment suggests an unusual understanding of Lucas-Box and Polly Peck pleading, which need not follow from the precedents they use. In Part III, the empirical research most relevant to meaning in this project (which has been examined at length in Chapters 4 to 6) is summarised in order to underscore some of the important differences that can be expected to flow from changing Lucas-Box and Polly Peck pleading. Then Part IV examines subsequent Australian state judgments that modify the defence pleas, which are contrasted with some English examples to underline the Australian differences. The research underlying this chapter suggests that the trend evident in the Australian decisions should be reviewed. And the preferable approach to defence meanings should become a major focus for Australian courts if planned uniform defamation law is introduced. (The uniform Defamation Bills are discussed in Chapter 10.) If that happens, NSW courts in particular will have a clean slate on which to consider the matters discussed at length in this chapter. Much of the chapter's case law analysis is lengthy and detailed in order to make clear which aspects of the decisions are supported by the empirical material and which are not. While the aims of the Australian courts in these decisions are understandable, the empirical evidence makes them appear misguided. The chapter argues that legal changes under *Chakravarti* fail to 'simplify as much as possible where those battlegrounds ought to be' – in the words of this chapter's opening quotation. The changes under *Hore-Lacy* and related cases increase the attention that is placed on pleaded imputations, which moves Australian common law quite some way towards an imputation-centred approach like NSW. This will fail to achieve the valuable aims that are being pursued in the cases since *Chakravarti*. While the chapter is the most Australian-focussed of the book, it also offers a study of wider significance about how overtly similar laws can diverge substantially once the combination of doctrine and practice is appreciated. That is something that readers from any of the countries examined in this book – and from other common law jurisdictions – should gain from what may appear a dauntingly close investigation of Australian cases. The chapter illustrates how, for comparative analysis, the detail of practice matters.

As a final introductory point, it is notable that in Chapters 9 and 10 significant findings arise in relation to NSW's imputation-centred approach. The research discussed in earlier chapters suggests the NSW approach inappropriately limits defendants' ability to respond to claims, shifts attention further towards the imputations at the expense of other issues and encourages more pre-trial disputes about meaning. In this, the research offers support for judicial criticism of the NSW statutory regime, such as comments by Kirby and Levine JJ.[4] In *Chakravarti*, for example, Kirby J suggested the NSW situation makes interlocutory processes more complex and means attention may be deflected from the publication onto debates about the pleaded imputations.[5] A concern raised by the cases examined in this chapter is that the criticism may now apply to other Australian jurisdictions. This would be particularly ironic, given widespread Australian recognition of the value in moving away from the NSW imputation-centred approach in any national uniform defamation law.[6] As discussed in Chapter 10, the research supports such a change – it suggests great strengths in basing the cause of action on the publication rather than the plaintiff's pleaded imputations. At the same time, as this chapter makes clear, Australian case law appears to be in danger of turning the publication-based cause of action into something quite like the NSW approach.

I THE *CHAKRAVARTI* JUDGMENTS

All the High Court judges in *Chakravarti* said plaintiffs could be bound to pleaded meanings, but plaintiffs would be able to depart from them if defendants would not be prejudiced. It is worth emphasising that the judgments concerned a plaintiff who had pleaded a popular innuendo of being guilty of civil or criminal misconduct relating to financial transactions. The plaintiff later sought to rely on an imputation of suspicion of the same misconduct.[7] Judicial discussion in *Chakravarti* and subsequent cases may have been influenced by a concern that allowing plaintiffs to succeed on non-pleaded meanings could prejudice defendants. Courts, for example, have spoken of avoiding the 'need' for the defendant to plead alternative meanings.[8] But this research suggests that, because parties will almost always disagree about meaning, the legal changes under *Chakravarti* will allow plaintiffs to shift the battle to particular pleaded imputations and will prejudice defendants by limiting their ability to defend alternative meanings. In doing this it will create incentives for each party – which have not been expressly addressed in Australian judgments – that tell against the prompt, proportionate and appropriate disposal of defamation claims.

---

[4] Eg *ibid* [139] (Kirby J); *Hughes v Seven Network* (Unreported, NSW SC, Levine J, 13 November 1998) (BC9806166).

[5] *Chakravarti v Advertiser Newspapers* (1998) 193 CLR 519, [139] (Kirby J) and see Chapter 2, Part III, H.

[6] Proposals for uniform defamation law across Australian jurisdictions are discussed in Chapter 10, Part I, E.

[7] In the end, the High Court found most of the plaintiffs' pleaded imputations were conveyed: see Kenyon (1999) 12–14.

[8] *David Syme v Hore-Lacy* [2000] 1 VR 667, [3] (Ormiston JA), similar [54] (Charles JA).

Each judgment in *Chakravarti* considered how plaintiffs would be bound and, consequently, what meanings defendants could seek to justify. Brennan CJ and McHugh J suggested 'a different nuance of meaning from the meaning pleaded' or perhaps a less serious meaning could go to the jury if that is not unfair to the defendant.[9] Support for the 'nuance of meaning' approach was found in English and Australian cases,[10] including NSW although greater restrictions could be expected under its imputation-centred approach. Thus, Brennan CJ and McHugh J described how a plaintiff was confined to pleaded meanings:

> A plaintiff who pleads a false innuendo thereby confines the meanings relied on. The plaintiff cannot then seek a verdict on a *different meaning* which so *alters the substance of the meaning pleaded* that the defendant would have been entitled to *plead a different issue*, to *adduce different evidence* or to *conduct the case on a different basis*.[11]

If being able to plead a different issue, use different evidence, or conduct the case on a different basis involves a meaning of different substance, then little departure can be possible from the plaintiff's pleading. The whole approach appears close to the NSW situation, as was suggested in Australian interviews.[12]

Gaudron and Gummow JJ said that plaintiffs could succeed on meanings 'comprehended in' the statement of claim, less injurious meanings or simply variants of pleaded meanings.[13] Prejudice to the defendant would be the limiting factor. But 'substantially different' meanings or those focussing on 'some different factual basis' could cause problems.[14] Gaudron and Gummow JJ added a significant point for practice. They said the question of whether defendants might be disadvantaged – and plaintiffs bound to pleaded meanings – should be 'answered having regard to all the circumstances of the case, including the material which is said to be defamatory and the issues in the trial, and not just simply by reference to the pleadings.'[15] While this was quite possible in the *Chakravarti* appeal, which occurred after a full trial, under existing practice the issue would often arise on the pleadings pre-trial. The subsequent case law, examined below in Part IV, illustrates how difficult it could be to answer the question 'having regard to all the circumstances of the case' if attention focuses heavily on the plaintiffs' pleaded imputations, especially pre-trial. The research suggests that this important concern of Gaudron and Gummow JJ will be met better by Lucas-Box pleading. The general approach of Gaudron and Gummow JJ is less stringent than Brennan CJ and McHugh J: they

---

[9] *Chakravarti* (1998) 193 CLR 519, [20]–[24].

[10] Eg *Slim v Daily Telegraph* [1968] 2 QB 157, 185 (Salmon LJ); *Hadzel v De Waldorf* (1970) 16 FLR 174, 182 (Fox J); *Prichard v Krantz* (1984) 37 SASR 379, 386 (King CJ, Millhouse and Prior JJ); *Taylor v Jecks* (1993) 10 WAR 309, 317–18; *Crampton v Nugawela* (1996) 41 NSWLR 176, 183 (Mahoney ACJ).

[11] *Chakravarti* (1998) 193 CLR 519, [19] (emphasis added).

[12] In Victoria: 44SC, 45B, 51SC; and NSW: 43B.

[13] *Chakravarti* (1998) 193 CLR 519, [60].

[14] *Ibid.*

[15] *Ibid.*

appear to support Lucas-Box pleading,[16] and see the rules about meaning as concerning 'fair and efficient practice'.[17] These points, along with their concern to evaluate meaning issues by drawing on more than the pleadings, makes their judgment appear closer to that of Kirby J. And, importantly, their judgment does not support ruling out *defence* meanings pre-trial on the basis of their relationship to *plaintiff* meanings; a wider context is necessary. As will be made clear below, the better context for ruling out either plaintiff or defendant meanings simply is the test of whether the meaning in question is capable of arising from the publication.

Like Gaudron and Gummow JJ,[18] Kirby J emphasised that pleading rules serve the fair determination of disputes, but implied that greater movement from pleaded meanings could be possible. Kirby J said that more serious meanings will include less serious ones, but not of a substantially different kind, and 'nuances or shades of meaning' would pose no problems at all.[19] His approach should be understood in light of his strong criticism of the NSW situation, and his belief that the common law should not follow the NSW focus on pleaded imputations.[20]

The *Chakravarti* judgments have been interpreted as meaning that plaintiffs can succeed on – and defendants can seek to defend by justification or fair comment – only meanings that are not substantially different from nor more serious than the plaintiff's pleaded meanings.[21] But this may be too narrow an interpretation. Instead, the starting points should be the aim to avoid prejudice to either party and to promote fair and efficient practice. And it must be recognised that each party will seek to gain advantages under the law's approach to meaning. If the case is centred on the plaintiff's pleaded meanings, plaintiffs will gain unwarranted ability to limit the dispute to imputations that have been crafted specifically to prevent them being defended. NSW practice provides ample evidence of how that is possible, and of the dangers posed to the very cause of action by the resulting interlocutory battles. NSW interviews suggested that plaintiffs' imputations are 'full of detail'[22] so they cannot be defended by truth. As Levine J remarked, without alterations in practice to overcome its complexities, the tort of defamation is in danger of dying in NSW.[23] However, if there are no restrictions on defendants' meanings, they will seek to introduce wider and more damaging material and courts rightly have been concerned about the scope and complexity of trials. But prejudice should not be assumed to arise whenever a party departs from its pleaded meanings. And the 'substantially different meaning' of Gaudron and Gummow JJ, or the meaning 'of a substantially different kind' of Kirby J – that is, the meaning which would not be allowed – should not be as narrowly drawn as it is in NSW.

[16] Eg they cite *Lucas-Box v News Group Newspapers* without any criticism: *ibid* [52] and [56], and cite a large number of Australian and English cases since *Polly Peck v Trelford*: [52].

[17] *Ibid* [56].

[18] *Ibid* [56]–[60].

[19] *Ibid* [139].

[20] *Ibid* [149].

[21] See below, Part I, C.

[22] 46B; see also 39SC, 40SC, 41S, 43S, 48B; Chapter 10, Part I, A.

[23] Levine (1999) [16]; see Chapter 10, Part I.

What the empirical material and analysis of cases suggest is that Australian courts should reconsider the way in which a plaintiff is held to pleaded meanings in defamation. Before and at trial, the focus should remain on the publication and the allegations it conveys, not on the precise detail of any imputation pleaded by the plaintiff. Plaintiffs no doubt should be constrained from relying on distinct *allegations* that they have not complained about: Chapter 2's example about a newspaper article that reports matters related to tax returns and another person's disappearance could illustrate such distinct allegations.[24] Beyond that, however, care is needed. The test for each party's meaning should be whether the meaning is capable of arising from the publication – the publication, not the imputation, should be the focus. These issues are returned to after examining the doctrinal support for the comments of Brennan CJ and McHugh J.

II THE JUDGMENT OF BRENNAN CJ AND McHUGH J

The judgment of Brennan CJ and McHugh J states that Polly Peck pleading is contrary to normal pleading practices, and suggests it must cause difficulties in practice for the defence to raise meanings that are not part of the plaintiff's case.[25] It is easy to understand why such criticisms might be made – Lucas Box and Polly Peck pleas *are* unusual in terms of civil litigation and they *do* appear to contravene usual pleading practice. However, the English interviews in particular suggest the pleas work extremely well in the jurisdiction in which they are most used: remember that lawyers described Lucas-Box pleading as 'absolutely vital'.[26] The English experience greatly lessens any concerns about the practical effect of allowing defendants to plead meanings. But the judgment in *Chakravarti* also can be analysed in terms of doctrine and precedent. The comments of Brennan CJ and McHugh J in *Chakravarti* suggest an unusual understanding of the *Polly Peck* decision, and the precedents they rely on could support varied interpretations.

Brennan CJ and McHugh J regard *Polly Peck*'s 'fundamental' defect to be allowing 'severable' defamatory parts of a publication to be linked and their meanings subsumed in a common sting; that is, a common meaning at a higher level of abstraction.[27] They illustrate the defect to suggest that it would be wrong to treat allegations of a criminal conviction and defrauding shareholders as having a common sting:

> [A] defendant cannot take a part of an article that wrongly alleges that the plaintiff has convictions for dishonesty and a part that imputes that the plaintiff has defrauded shareholders, assert that the article means that the plaintiff is

[24] See Chapter 2, Parts I, A, and III, H.

[25] *Chakravarti* (1998) 193 CLR 519, [8] and see Chapter 2, Part III, H.

[26] 24QC; similar 22S; and see Chapter 4, Part III, D.

[27] *Chakravarti* (1998) 193 CLR 519, [11].

> dishonest, and then justify that meaning, perhaps by proving that the plaintiff had in fact defrauded the shareholders.[28]

They continue: 'Yet this is the sort of finding that must result from applying the central proposition of *Polly Peck*.'[29] But a common sting need not be found in their example. The presumably severable parts in their example – criminal conviction and defrauding shareholders – may not be subject to a Polly Peck plea at all. Instead, their example may resemble an *impermissible* Polly Peck plea, although that would depend on the actual publication in question.

Their use of precedent also can be questioned. Brennan CJ and McHugh J approvingly quote from the earlier decisions of *Bremridge v Latimer*,[30] *Watkin v Hall*[31] and *Templeton v Jones*.[32] O'Connor LJ discussed these cases at length in *Polly Peck*, explicitly disapproving relevant aspects of the *Bremridge* and *Watkin* decisions.[33] Brennan CJ and McHugh J, however, do not address the explanation of O'Connor LJ.[34] As Charles JA suggested in *Hore-Lacy*, one can doubt 'how much assistance is really to be gained by minute scrutiny of decisions on defamation practice in the nineteenth century'.[35] Similarly, in *Burstein v Times Newspapers* May LJ mentioned concerns about applying pre-*Judicature Act* cases, especially since the introduction of the *Civil Procedure Rules*.[36] But Brennan CJ and McHugh J draw on 19th century case law – and those decisions must remain an important issue – so it seems appropriate to consider the cases. And, contrary to the comments in *Chakravarti*, analysing the cases suggests they can support Lucas-Box and Polly Peck pleading. Overall, however, the more compelling arguments probably arise from contemporary case law and practice, which is reviewed in Parts III and IV.

A *Bremridge v Latimer*

It now appears ironic that Byles J in *Bremridge v Latimer* suggested the decision would be 'a very useful one to those who have the conduct of the pleadings in actions of libel.'[37] The 1864 decision in *Bremridge* has been anything but that. Two points are relevant here – whether and how the plaintiff was bound to its pleaded

28 *Ibid.*

29 *Ibid.*

30 (1864) 12 WR 878.

31 (1868) LR 3 QB 396.

32 [1984] 1 NZLR 448.

33 *Polly Peck v Trelford* [1986] QB 1000, 1032 (O'Connor LJ, Robert Goff and Nourse LJJ agreed).

34 It also is possible that they may not have referred to all three reports of *Bremridge v Latimer*, which O'Connor LJ noted as being necessary for a full understanding. Only the report at (1864) 12 WR 878 is cited; the reports at 10 LT 816 and 4 NR 285 are not cited in *Chakravarti*. O'Connor provides a synthesised version of the facts and holdings in *Bremridge* at *Polly Peck* [1986] QB 1000, 1021–23 (O'Connor LJ, Robert Goff and Nourse LJJ agreed).

35 *Hore-Lacy* [2000] 1 VR 667, [55].

36 [2001] 1 WLR 579, [24].

37 (1864) 12 WR 878.

meaning, and whether the plaintiff was seeking to limit the dispute through editing the publication in its pleadings. *Bremridge v Latimer* concerned a political candidate, who previously had been an election agent for a parliamentarian called Hodgson. A newspaper article 'charged the plaintiff with being kicked out of the House of Commons for bribery, and with the base desertion of his old client and benefactor, Hodgson.'[38] The plaintiff pleaded certain passages from the article, from which words about having been convicted of bribery were deleted. And the plaintiff pleaded this innuendo:

> [T]hat Hodgson had been ignominiously flouted and sent off with scorn and contumely by the plaintiff at the last-mentioned election, and the plaintiff had basely deserted Hodgson and refused to act as his agent, or to render him any assistance or support at such election, because Hodgson had then become impoverished in his circumstances.[39]

The defendant quoted the whole article in its defence, and pleaded that it contained words referring to the plaintiff as a 'briber', which the plaintiff had omitted in order to alter the article's meaning.[40] It is worth that emphasising words about bribery were in the very passages the plaintiff relied on, but the plaintiff's pleading omitted the words when it reproduced the passages.

The Court of Common Pleas decided the publication made two distinct charges: bribery and desertion. This meant, in contemporary terminology, the defence could not prove the truth of a distinct charge of which the plaintiff did not complain. Willes J, however, initially doubted whether two charges arose, admitting: 'I thought that the libel might not, perhaps, involve two distinct charges of misconduct, but that these charges might be so connected together as to form one.'[41] At its most narrow, then, *Bremridge v Latimer* says nothing unusual in relation to contemporary Lucas-Box or Polly Peck practice.

But the decision is unclear as to whether plaintiffs were held to pleaded innuendoes. It was noted in Part III of Chapter 2 that, before the *Common Law Procedure Act (CLPA) 1852*,[42] very technical pleading rules existed for defamation which required prefatory averments for any non-literal meanings to which the plaintiff was held. The situation changed after 1852 and the practice developed of pleading extravagant innuendoes. In *Bremridge v Latimer*, Erle CJ suggested that plaintiffs were not held to pleaded innuendoes under the *CLPA 1852*:

> Under s 61 . . . a plt. is entitled to a verdict if the words complained of are libellous, although they do not bear out the innuendo, and if the words are not libellous they cannot be made so by an innuendo; but the section does not enable the deft. to impute another meaning to [the] words from that set out in the innuendo and then to justify them.[43]

---

[38] *Ibid* 4 NR 285, 286; 10 LT 816, 816.

[39] *Ibid* 4 NR 285, 286.

[40] *Ibid* 4 NR 285, 286; 10 LT 816, 816.

[41] *Ibid* 12 WR 878, 879; similar in 4 NR 285, 287; 10 LT 816, 816.

[42] 15 & 16 Vict, c 76.

[43] (1864) 10 LT 816, 816.

The first part of this quotation suggests that plaintiffs are not bound to pleaded innuendoes – if words are defamatory without the plea, plaintiffs can succeed on non-pleaded meanings. The second part of the quotation *may* say that defendants cannot justify any non-pleaded meanings, but in the circumstances of the case it may refer merely to defendants' inability to raise separate and distinct meanings from those that plaintiffs complain about.

In the New Reports version of *Bremridge v Latimer*, however, a distinction appears to be drawn between what would now be called popular and legal innuendoes, with the suggestion that plaintiffs are not held to popular innuendoes while being held to legal ones. Erle CJ is reported as saying:

> Where the declaration has an innuendo which does not show a libel, but the words are actionable without it, there the plaintiff is entitled to succeed; and I fully agree with my brother Willes, that if the innuendo impute what is actionable, and the words do not bear that out, the defendant must succeed under the general issue.[44]

The suggestion appears to be that plaintiffs can succeed without relying on pleaded innuendoes unless the innuendoes 'impute what is actionable', in which case plaintiffs would be held to their pleas. Similarly in the Weekly Reporter, Erle CJ is reported as saying:

> Where there is an *innuendo*, although without it the words are actionable, and the plaintiff does not prove the *innuendo*, [the plaintiff] may still be entitled to succeed, and, upon this subject, I entirely agree with what has been said by my brother Willes.[45]

The third report of the decision also suggests that Erle CJ fully agreed with Willes J about this.[46] But Willes J appeared to suggest plaintiffs were bound to pleaded innuendoes, whereas Erle CJ appears to have suggested plaintiffs were only sometimes bound. Only the Weekly Reporter gives any information about these comments by Willes J. He noted that before the *CLPA 1852*,

> where the *innuendo* could be supported, the plaintiff was bound by it. Now, the words of the 61st section, which provide 'that, where the words or matter set forth with or without the alleged meaning show a cause of action, the declaration shall be sufficient' make no difference in the old laws of pleading and evidence. *The plaintiff must always sustain the cause of action of which [the plaintiff] has complained, and not abandon it by an allegation that certain words would have been actionable if the declaration had been framed in a different manner.*[47]

Overall, the judgments suggest that if plaintiffs are *bound* to pleaded meanings, defendants cannot raise *any* other meanings, and even if plaintiffs are *not bound* to pleaded meanings, defendants cannot raise *separate and distinct* meanings. The

[44] *Ibid* 4 NR 285, 287.

[45] *Ibid* 12 WR 878, 879 (emphasis in original).

[46] *Ibid* 12 WR 878, 879.

[47] *Ibid* 12 WR 878, 879 (emphasis added to final sentence).

later decision in *Watkin v Hall*[48] made clear that plaintiffs actually were not bound to pleaded meanings under the *CLPA 1852*, which suggests that *Bremridge v Latimer* need no longer be seen as particularly significant. It merely states that defendants cannot raise separate and distinct meanings to those that plaintiffs complain about.

The second point to consider about *Bremridge v Latimer* is the idea of plaintiffs trying to limit artificially the field of dispute about meaning. In *Polly Peck*, O'Connor LJ saw *Bremridge* as directly raising this issue:

> I do not think that a plaintiff is permitted to use a blue pencil upon words published . . . so as to change their meaning and then prevent the defendant from justifying the words in their unexpurgated form. It seems to me that this is exactly what the plaintiff in *Bremridge v Latimer* succeeded in doing.[49]

O'Connor LJ emphasises this issue because the plaintiff's pleading in *Bremridge* omitted particular words from the publication. For example, the article stated:

> Hodgson, who was his client and representative for so many years, did not get very generous treatment from him in the day of his adversity. Hodgson had spent £80,000 in and on the borough. Bremridge, the convicted briber, was his agent, and when Hodgson's money was all spent . . . he was ignominiously flouted and sent off with scorn and contumely.[50]

The plaintiff's pleading omitted the words 'the convicted briber' when quoting the passage. The judgments in *Bremridge* decided the article made two distinct charges, although Willes J clearly had initial doubts.[51] It would appear that O'Connor LJ, in contrast, thought that removing the words altered the passage's meaning. At the least he thought it arguable that a jury 'might well have concluded that the passage as published . . . meant that Bremridge was a corrupt, unreliable, heartless man unfit to be a Member of Parliament' as opposed to the plaintiff's innuendo.[52]

Neither of these aspects of the *Bremridge* judgments – whether and how the plaintiff was held to its pleading, and the concept of changing the field of dispute – is addressed in *Chakravarti*. But closely analysing *Bremridge* makes it far harder to see the case as inconsistent with the law after *Polly Peck*.[53] While no reading of the various reports of *Bremridge* is unproblematic, the decision may only say that defendants cannot raise meanings in justification that relate to separate and distinct allegations.

B *Watkin v Hall*

In 1868, four years after the *Bremridge* decision, *Watkin v Hall* concerned the repetition of a rumour and whether the defendant could justify the publication

---

48 (1868) LR 3 QB 396 (QB) and see below, fns 54 and 56 and accompanying text.

49 *Polly Peck* [1986] QB 1000, 1023 (O'Connor LJ, Robert Goff and Nourse LJJ agreed).

50 Quoted in *ibid* 1022.

51 See above, fn 41 and accompanying text.

52 *Polly Peck* [1986] QB 1000, 1023 (O'Connor LJ, Robert Goff and Nourse LJJ agreed).

53 *Ibid*.

by proving the rumour existed.[54] Blackburn J said the *CLPA 1852* meant that plaintiffs were not bound to pleaded meanings:

> [A] declaration containing one count for libel or slander, with an innuendo that the words were used in a particular meaning, shall be taken as if there were two counts, one with the innuendo and one without the innuendo; and if the plaintiff proves either, it is sufficient. It follows, then, that the defendant may plead a justification as to the words with the meaning in the innuendo, and also as to them without the meaning.[55]

Note how this suggests the defendant can raise a different meaning in justification. Immediately after this extract, Blackburn J said he agreed with *Bremridge v Latimer* but suggested it dealt with a different issue:

> I think the decision in *Bremridge* . . . correct, because in that case a portion of a newspaper article being set forth in the declaration, with an innuendo, the defendant endeavoured to show that if the whole article was taken, the plaintiff would have had a different cause of action, and [the defendant] sought in [pleading], to set out the whole article, and, so, to justify it as true in fact. That was a matter utterly irrelevant to the question at issue, whether he had published the libel charged in the declaration.[56]

It seems that *Bremridge v Latimer* was taken to concern the question of defendants trying to plead separate and distinct meanings – which is not the same as what is currently called Lucas-Box and Polly Peck pleading. *Watkin v Hall* appears far closer to suggesting that, where plaintiffs are not bound to their pleading, defendants can plead justification to any meanings on which plaintiffs could succeed. That is what is now called Lucas-Box and Polly Peck pleading. *Watkin v Hall* clearly separates the issue of what meaning arises from a charge and the defendant's inability to defend one charge by justifying a separate and distinct one. In this way, it does not appear to be close to the judgment of Brennan CJ and McHugh J.

C *Templeton v Jones*

Certainly, there may be a question as to the appropriateness of analysing imputations as having a common sting; that is, the availability of a Polly Peck plea on particular facts can be contentious. *Templeton v Jones*, the third case relied on by Brennan CJ and McHugh J, illustrates this. The publication contained an allegation of hating 'bureaucrats, civil servants, politicians, women, Jews and professionals' and also used a wider description, the 'politics of hatred',[57] which apparently was intended to cover a general attitude. The plaintiff only complained about allegedly hating Jews. A general meaning was held incapable of arising by Cooke J for the New

---

[54] (1868) LR 3 QB 396 (QB).

[55] *Ibid* 402. Similarly Lush J at 403 said: 'It is not enough to say, that the plaintiff has failed in placing upon [the published words] the meaning . . . intended by the innuendo, if the words which the defendant did use are capable of another meaning which renders them actionable.'

[56] *Ibid* 402.

[57] [1984] 1 NZLR 448, 450 (Cooke J for NZ CA).

Zealand Court of Appeal. Only distinct imputations were capable of arising, so no evidence of general hatred could be adduced. But Cooke J noted the 'principle does not apply if the words are not severable in that there are not distinct charges but in substance only one', which suggests the case need not affect the earlier decisions.[58] It merely is controversial on its facts as to whether the publication should have been understood only to make separate allegations.

Analysing the cases suggests that in *Bremridge v Latimer* the plaintiff *may* have limited the 'battlefield', which was possible because the plaintiff was held to its plea. By the time of *Watkin v Hall*, however, plaintiffs were not held to their pleaded innuendo meanings and it would seem that defendants could justify any meaning that could arise. On that analysis, *Templeton v Jones* appears as just another, and perhaps a dubious, application of the idea of separate and distinct charges. *Polly Peck* criticised *Templeton v Jones* in this way and suggested the allegations were capable of conveying a common sting.[59] O'Connor LJ approved an earlier test suggested by Bridge LJ:

> Is this a case where the sting lies in the totality of the allegations in the defendants' article . . . a case where the plaintiffs are seeking artificially to limit the area of debate by choosing a part only of that total libel as their battleground?[60]

The court in *Polly Peck* agreed that the plaintiff should not be able to limit the field of dispute. The defendant could look to the whole publication and – leaving aside separate and distinct meanings – the defendant could seek to justify any meaning capable of arising from the publication.

As a separate matter, it has been suggested that the comments of Brennan CJ and McHugh J may not extend to the requirement after the *Lucas-Box* decision for defendants to make clear the meanings they seek to justify.[61] As explained in earlier chapters, the term Polly Peck as it generally is used in Australia can be seen to have two elements: justifying different meanings in general and justifying common stings, or what are called Lucas-Box and Polly Peck pleas in this book. The comments of Brennan CJ and McHugh J may not apply to Lucas-Box pleading equivalently to common sting pleas. If even a small range of meanings exists, defendants may need to make clear the meanings they seek to justify. This would equate to the way in which plaintiffs must make their meanings clear in setting out their claims. Brennan CJ and McHugh J discuss at some length this need for clarity from plaintiffs.[62] The corresponding need for defence clarity

---

[58] *Ibid* 452. That is so even though it may not accord with some New Zealand understandings of *Templeton v Jones*. For a useful NZ analysis of the decision and its influence on later case law and statutory interpretations, see Burrows and Cheer (2005) 148–52.

[59] *Polly Peck* [1986] QB 1000, 1030 (O'Connor LJ, Robert Goff and Nourse LJJ agreed).

[60] *Stonor v Daily Telegraph* (Unreported, Eng CA, Cairns, Bridge LJJ, 19 July 1976) quoted in *ibid* 1028–30.

[61] Eg *Hore-Lacy* [2000] 1 VR 667, [20] (Ormiston JA), [58] (Charles JA); Kenyon (1999) 20.

[62] *Chakravarti* (1998) 193 CLR 519, [14]–[19].

could apply to lesser meanings that may be found within plaintiffs' pleaded meanings or, more broadly, to Lucas-Box meanings properly understood. The criticisms Brennan CJ and McHugh J made of the idea of a common sting may remain separate to this issue. Brennan CJ and McHugh J do not comment greatly on English case law since *Lucas-Box* and *Polly Peck* nor on the reasons for which it developed. The English approach aims to limit plaintiffs' ability to restrict the meanings presented to juries – while also limiting defendants to meanings that are capable of arising from publications – and thus it seeks to deal effectively with the almost inevitable difference between the parties about meaning.

To this point, two matters have been argued. First, the *Chakravarti* decision – especially the judgments of Gaudron, Gummow and Kirby JJ – should be seen to restrict meaning less than may be suggested by the judgment of Brennan CJ and McHugh J. Second, the comments of Brennan CJ and McHugh J can be criticised in doctrinal terms. While their starting point is not surprising – defamation pleading does not appear to accord with normal civil pleading – the understanding of Lucas-Box and Polly Peck pleading in the judgment seems unusual and it need not follow from the precedents they rely on. The treatment of meaning in defamation is, and should be, different than in many other areas of law. As Ormiston JA noted in *Hore-Lacy*: 'certain rules of pleading and practice in defamation actions . . . in a number of respects . . . have required an approach different from that applicable to other proceedings'.[63] Admittedly, close analysis of the historical precedents is inconclusive – which is not surprising given the age of the nineteenth-century decisions and the varied reports of *Bremridge v Latimer*. But it is significant that those cases can be seen to *support* Lucas-Box and Polly Peck pleading. Now two further matters can be considered: what does the empirical research in relation to meaning suggest for this issue; and what has happened to the scope of Lucas-Box and Polly Peck pleas in subsequent Australian cases?

III IMPLICATIONS FROM THE EMPIRICAL RESEARCH

If Lucas-Box and Polly Peck pleas are not available for justification and comment defences, it appears likely that even greater interlocutory activity will occur, and Australian common law jurisdictions will move an appreciable distance towards NSW practice – as Michael Gillooly noted soon after the *Chakravarti* decision itself.[64] To appreciate what this implies, it is useful to summarise the empirical findings from the largely common law jurisdictions of England and Victoria, and the mainly statutory jurisdiction of NSW. In relation to English practice, Chapter 4 suggests that each side tends to plead relatively few meanings, and the specificity of pleas is rarely an issue. Parties almost always argue that different meanings arise from a publication before a jury at trial; defamation trials generally use juries, and jury determinations of meaning at a trial's start are rare, notwithstanding the precedent offered by *Marks & Spencer v Granada Television*.[65] Lucas-Box pleading is normal

[63] *Hore-Lacy* [2000] 1 VR 667, [23].

[64] Gillooly (1999) 193.

practice, and it is seen as a necessary and useful part of litigation. While it developed quite separately from court rules, Lucas-Box pleading is now supported directly by the *Civil Procedure Rules*.[66] Justification of a defence meaning and its relevance for mitigation of damages are where meaning becomes central in English litigation. The research found no support for the view that defence meanings must cause problems in practice, although some interviewees said care was necessary in applying the principle of Polly Peck pleading[67] – depending on the publication in question – as opposed to Lucas-Box pleas, which were seen as essential to good practice.[68]

For NSW, Chapter 5 suggests that plaintiffs usually plead multiple meanings at varied levels of seriousness. The form of pleaded imputations is often an issue pre-trial, and challenges to their specificity are common. As plaintiffs are bound to their pleaded imputations, there is no room for defendants to respond with Lucas-Box or Polly Peck meanings, and there are only limited circumstances in which contextual imputations can arise. This accentuates plaintiffs' ability to shape their imputations into particular wordings that are capable of arising, but incapable of being defended. Thus defendants' attention is directed toward interlocutory hearings to challenge plaintiffs' imputations. The research suggests this pre-trial battleground has been intensified by the operation of defences in NSW. Defences related to truth and opinion appear to have become tightly focussed on plaintiffs' imputations and made less accessible as a result. Thus defendants' disagreements with plaintiffs' meanings can be dealt with realistically only pre-trial – and interlocutory battles attacking plaintiffs' pleaded imputations can be seen to operate as a major form of 'defence'. In addition, the jury's confined role under the 7A procedure has accentuated these peculiarities of NSW. For all these reasons, the whole approach can be described as imputation-centred.

For Victoria, the research reported in Chapter 6, which largely concerned the situation before *Chakravarti*'s interpretation in *Hore-Lacy*,[69] suggests that plaintiffs plead more meanings than in NSW and England, with repetitive pleadings often not being challenged. The form of pleaded imputations is rarely an issue pre-trial, parties are not held particularly close to their pleaded meanings, and juries are not asked specific questions about each pleaded imputation. Defendants virtually never agree with plaintiffs' imputations, and Lucas-Box pleas are fairly common. The combination of plaintiff and defence pleadings means differences between the parties about meaning are usually set out fairly clearly. Justification and fair comment are far more common pleadings than the corresponding NSW defences. It seems that defendants are not unreasonably precluded from raising them, which well may be the situation in NSW because of its imputation-centred approach. All these factors result in meaning predominantly being left until trial, left for the jury, and focussed upon the publication.

65 (Unreported, QBD, Popplewell J, 23 February 1998).

66 *Civil Procedure Rules* Pt 53 PD 2.5.

67 Eg 6QC, 15B, 24QC, 25S.

68 Eg 1B, 3S, 6QC, 16B, 17S, 18B, 19S, 20S, 21S, 30S.

69 *Chakravarti* (1998) 193 CLR 519; *Hore-Lacy* [2000] 1 VR 667.

Figures from NSW and Victorian court files also are notable. They suggest how changes to pleaded meanings are far more common in NSW, defence pleadings relevant to meaning are far less common and rates of trial and settlement differ. First, with regard to amending pleadings, in NSW there were challenges or negotiated changes to imputations in almost every second case. In Victoria, changes occurred in just under one in 10 cases. Second, with regard to defences, in NSW truth was pleaded in less than one in six defences, contextual truth in one in eight defences, and comment in one in five defences. (Contextual truth pleas appear to have increased subsequently under 7A, although the defence appears rarely likely to succeed.) Victoria saw approximately double these rates of pleading: justification of the plaintiff's meanings was pleaded in one in four defences, Lucas-Box meanings in one in three defences, and fair comment in more than two in five defences. Third, Victoria saw a greater percentage of cases settle more quickly or be disposed of at trial than in NSW. In Victoria, nearly 90 per cent of files had been disposed of by the end of 2000, while in NSW less than 60 per cent had been completed. And while the figures on the length of hearings related to only a small number of files, the Victorian trials did not run for any significant amount longer than NSW matters. On the information available from the files, it does not appear that the cost to the public of the Victorian approach exceeds that of NSW. Indeed, the public cost would appear to be less, given the lower number of interlocutory challenges and quicker disposal of claims in Victoria.[70]

As is discussed further below, the changes under *Chakravarti*, *Hore-Lacy* and related cases move Australian common law towards NSW in terms of increasing the attention given to imputations. Of course, a jurisdiction's pleading and litigation practice will not be changed immediately by the modification of Lucas-Box and Polly Peck pleading. But the move towards NSW increases the opportunities for – and the value in – fighting about meaning, without simplifying litigation practice more generally. In this way, changes promoted by the obiter comments in *Chakravarti* appear counterproductive to the fair litigation of defamation disputes. Comparative empirical research suggests they should be reconsidered.

IV MODIFICATION OF LUCAS-BOX AND POLLY PECK

Some Australian decisions have followed Brennan CJ and McHugh J in *Chakravarti* and changed the availability of Lucas-Box and Polly Peck pleas. Such defence pleas of meaning have been doubted and rejected in the ACT.[71] In Queensland, the Court of Appeal ruled that what it called Polly Peck pleading was not available as

[70] Michael Chesterman and David Barrett have raised the important matter of the costs to public resources of defamation litigation, as well as the costs to the parties: Chesterman (2000) 170; Barrett (1986).

[71] Polly Peck pleas were doubted in *Steiner Wilson & Webster t/as Abbey Bridal v Amalgamated Television Services* (1999) Aust Torts Reports ¶81-537, [200] (Crispin J) and rejected in *Kelly v Nationwide News* (1998) 147 FLR 410, [32]–[33] (Gallop ACJ). See also Kenyon (1999).

a matter of law in *Robinson v Laws*.[72] While the High Court refused leave to appeal from that decision, it said the case was not suitable for considering the availability of defence pleading in Queensland.[73] In any event, the Queensland analysis largely can be left aside here because, under its defamation code, that state's cause of action is centred on the imputation in a similar manner to NSW.[74]

It is worth investigating subsequent decisions in other Australian states that have modified the pleas' availability. While many cases are examined in this Part, four cases are of central importance: *David Syme v Hore-Lacy*,[75] *Anderson v Nationwide News*,[76] *Herald & Weekly Times v Popovic*[77] and *Nationwide News v Moodie*.[78] These cases show that Australian common law defamation jurisdictions now limit defence pleas of justification and fair comment to meanings that are not substantially different nor more injurious than plaintiffs' pleaded meanings. There are at least two points of debate within the decisions. One concerns what meanings come within the requirement of being 'not substantially different'. The cases are reviewed to explain that meanings such as being *guilty* or being *suspected* of some discreditable conduct should be seen as not substantially different and be permissible pleas under decisions like *Hore-Lacy*. The second point arises because a majority of the Victorian Court of Appeal in *Popovic* explicitly did not follow the comments of Brennan CJ and McHugh J in relation to Polly Peck pleas, and applied a test that does not appear completely consistent with the approach in *Hore-Lacy* – it actually appears to be a preferable test on the basis of the empirical research. Beyond these two points, the research suggests the *Hore-Lacy* approach, which is imputation-focussed, does not approach defence meanings in the most useful way. Courts should focus on the publication and ask whether the defence meanings are capable of arising from it (and ask whether they are not separate and distinct allegations from what the plaintiff complains about). Similarly, plaintiffs should not be held as closely to their pleaded imputations as some of the comments in *Chakravarti* suggest.

A Victorian decisions

1 *David Syme v Hore-Lacy*

One of the most influential decisions since *Chakravarti* has been *David Syme v Hore-Lacy*.[79] A football club president sued a newspaper over an article that

---

[72] [2003] 1 Qd R 81.

[73] Transcript of Proceedings, *Laws v Robinson* (HC Leave Hearing, Gleeson CJ, McHugh, Callinan JJ, 19 March 2002). It noted the imputations had been bad in terms of their form.

[74] See *Bellino v Australian Broadcasting Corpn* (1996) 185 CLR 183, 230 (Dawson, McHugh and Gummow JJ); 237 (Gaudron J) approving *Pervan v North Queensland Newspaper Co* (1993) 178 CLR 309, 333 (McHugh J).

[75] [2000] 1 VR 667.

[76] (2001) 3 VR 619.

[77] (2003) 9 VR 1.

[78] (2003) 28 WAR 314.

[79] [2000] 1 VR 667.

concerned media interviews he gave about a possible club merger or takeover.[80] In its decision, the court narrowed the range of meanings that could be included within any pleaded imputation. The judgments of Ormiston and Charles JJA are particularly noteworthy. Ormiston JA read the *Chakravarti* judgments, excluding the comments of Brennan CJ and McHugh J, as stating that plaintiffs would be held closely to pleaded meanings:

> [I]n other words, the jury will have to be told that they cannot find for the plaintiff unless they agree with . . . one of the meanings put forward on behalf of the plaintiff, or unless the meaning they would give the publication was only a nuance or variant, not substantially different or more serious from that proposed by the plaintiff.[81]

This in turn would mean that a defendant could not 'plead or rely on a meaning other than one which *is* not more serious and otherwise is not substantially different'[82] than the plaintiff's meaning.

Charles JA noted that, in *Chakravarti*, Gaudron and Gummow JJ did not appear to disapprove of[83] – and Kirby J approved of[84] – the Victorian decision in *National Mutual Life Association of Australasia v GTV Corporation*.[85] The *National Mutual Life Association* case held that pleadings do not confine the meanings that are open to juries. Charles JA then examined how *Chakravarti* suggested that plaintiffs would be confined to their pleaded meanings; that is, departure would be allowed only if defendants would not be prejudiced. Charles JA concluded:

> The position then remains that at trial neither the plaintiff nor the defendants should be permitted to raise . . . a meaning substantially different from, or more injurious than, the meanings alleged by the plaintiff.[86]

Earlier, he had suggested:

> Whether the meaning was substantially different would presumably be tested by asking whether the defendant would have been entitled to plead a different issue, adduce different evidence or conduct the case on a different basis (Brennan CJ and McHugh J in *Chakravarti*) or possibly whether the justification would be substantially different (Gaudron and Gummow JJ).[87]

These tests set out in the Victorian Court of Appeal, particularly the ones drawn from Brennan CJ and McHugh J, appear to be quite strict and may be overly conservative, given the analysis in Parts I, II and III above. In any event, the

---

80 *Ibid* [25]–[26] (Charles JA).

81 *Ibid* [21].

82 *Ibid* [22] (emphasis in original).

83 *Chakravarti* (1998) 193 CLR 519, [54]–[58].

84 *Ibid* [139].

85 [1989] VR 747, 768; see also *Barclay v Cox* [1968] VR 664.

86 *Hore-Lacy* [2000] 1 VR 667, [63].

87 *Ibid* [52] (footnotes omitted).

Hore-Lacy position is that defence meanings cannot be substantially different or more injurious than plaintiff meanings.

A question about the *Hore-Lacy* approach is what meanings come within the concept of 'not substantially different'? Little guidance is provided by the facts of *Hore-Lacy*. The plaintiff had pleaded meanings including:

> (a) the plaintiff had told lies concerning the Fitzroy Football Club's financial situation during the radio and television interviews referred to;
>
> (b) the plaintiff had treated members of the Fitzroy Football Club who attended at their annual general meeting as credulous dupes or fools;
>
> (c) the plaintiff had lied to the members of the Fitzroy Football Club who attended at the annual general meeting . . .
>
> (f) the plaintiff had been guilty of sharp practice in obtaining proxies from shareholders of the Fitzroy Football Club.[88]

The defendants at first avoided pleading the alternative meaning that they sought to justify, instead providing particulars on which they would rely. But, in line with *Lucas-Box v News Group Newspapers*,[89] the defendants were required to make clear the meaning they would defend and pleaded two imputations:

> (a) the plaintiff had told lies in statements made by the plaintiff broadcast on radio and television in the previous week when he denied a report in [the Melbourne-based newspaper] *The Age* that the financial jig was up with the Fitzroy Football Club;
>
> (b) the plaintiff had misled members of the Fitzroy Football Club who attended the annual general meeting.[90]

Not surprisingly, the two parties' meanings were found to be similar and the Lucas-Box plea was allowed to stand.[91] It is hard to see substantial differences between the pleas – except that the defence plea seems narrower and suggests fewer discreditable matters arose from the publication.

But a significant point about 'not substantially different' emerges from the judgment of Ormiston JA. That is, imputations of guilt and suspicion do not appear to be substantially different for the purposes of defence pleas under *Hore-Lacy*. Ormiston JA said:

> [M]any articles in the press . . . are devised on the 'no smoke without fire' premise, so that many allegations take a form which might be construed . . . as alleging highly improper activity though on detailed analysis . . . the allegation would appear less serious. It is this sort of case which might go to the jury with the plaintiff pleading imputations of high impropriety and the defendant asserting . . . less serious peccadillos which it wished to justify. The

[88] *Ibid* [27] (Charles JA).

[89] [1986] 1 WLR 147; see Chapter 3, Part I, K.

[90] *Hore-Lacy* [2000] 1 VR 667, [31] (Charles JA).

[91] *Ibid* [23] (Ormiston JA), [62] (Charles JA).

> 'smoke' could therefore be justified but it would remain for the jury . . . to decide whether the imputation was still one of 'fire'.[92]

The distinction between 'smoke' and 'fire' echoes the words of Lord Devlin in *Lewis v Daily Telegraph*, which addressed the distinction between suspicion and guilt: 'It is not . . . correct to say as a matter of law that a statement of suspicion imputes guilt. It can be said as a matter of practice that it very often does so'. People who want 'to talk at large about smoke may have to pick [their] words very carefully' if they want 'to exclude the suggestion that there is also a fire'.[93] Thus guilt and suspicion are not substantially different meanings for the purposes of *Hore-Lacy* – or, at the least, they should not be treated as being substantially different. It will be seen below, however, that some later decisions have differed from this approach. Three further points can be made about the passage from Ormiston JA. First, a similar result on guilt or suspicion was arrived at in *Chakravarti*, although that may have followed primarily from how the trial was run. The parties in *Chakravarti* clearly raised questions of guilt and suspicion between their two cases, so the High Court held that the defendant could not be prejudiced if the plaintiff relied on a non-pleaded meaning of suspicion. Second, this common law position – it also applies under the English approach to three levels of meaning[94] – differs from NSW, where imputations of guilt and suspicion are treated as substantially different and must be separately pleaded.[95] Third, there is another very important point made by Ormiston JA in this passage: many publications, and certainly many media publications, are capable of varied interpretations. That truism of defamation law is a central reason why defamation cases should not be diverted onto the plaintiff's pleaded meanings alone, but should remain focussed on the publication in issue.

2 *Anderson v Nationwide News*

The subsequent Victorian case of *Anderson v Nationwide News* applied the *Hore-Lacy* changes to fair comment.[96] In *Anderson*, the chief executive of a major company, BHP, sued over a newspaper article that was headed 'When bullies talk, it's time to walk'. The plaintiff pleaded the article meant that he had promoted, supported and contrived the merger of BHP and another resource company, Billiton plc, and breached his duty to BHP and its shareholders 'for the ulterior purpose of enabling him and his wife to return to live in the United States earlier than what otherwise would have been the case'.[97] This sort of meaning seemed plausible, as extracts from the article illustrate:

---

[92] *Ibid* [22].

[93] *Lewis v Daily Telegraph* [1964] AC 234, 285 (Lord Devlin).

[94] See Chapters 2 and 3, and eg *Windsor v Boycott* (Unreported, QBD, Eady J, 9 May 2001) in which suspicion of guilt was described as 'a less serious charge on the scale of gravity where actual guilt occupies the top rung of the ladder' (no pinpoint reference available).

[95] Eg *Hepburn v TCN Channel Nine* [1984] 1 NSWLR 386, 397–98 (Hunt J).

[96] (2001) 3 VR 619.

[97] *Ibid* [2].

> BHP shareholders should be aware that the main reason they are gathering . . . to vote on the disguised takeover of their company by South Africa's Billiton Plc is because Kathy, the wife of BHP chief executive Paul Anderson, detests Australia and loathes Australians.
>
> She wants to go back to the US and live in the mansion she and her husband are building in New England. . . .
>
> His wife wanted him out of Australia. Clearly, the pressure was irresistible.[98]

The defence, however, sought to justify these meanings:

> (a) the plaintiff was promoting and supporting a merger of Billiton and BHP on terms which did not favour BHP or its shareholders;
>
> (b) the plaintiff was promoting and supporting a merger of Billiton and BHP on terms which were not as favourable as they should have been to BHP and its shareholders.[99]

Ashley J said the justification plea was 'outside the permissible limits' of *Hore-Lacy*.[100] The plaintiff would not be entitled to a verdict on the defence meanings – if they were the meanings conveyed by the publication – because acting for ulterior motives was a substantially different meaning than acting against shareholders' interests.[101]

Ashley J also considered the defence of fair comment. Like justification, it was argued to be limited to meanings that are not substantially different nor more serious than the plaintiff's meanings. Ashley J agreed:

> [W]here a plaintiff sues on an entire article, alleging that it bears a particular defamatory meaning (not necessarily the only defamatory meaning of the article) a defence of fair comment is untenable unless it pertains specifically to the defamatory meaning pleaded – or a permissible variation thereof.[102]

Ashley J discussed fair comment and the way in which 'congruency' is needed between the plaintiff's pleaded meaning and the defence. He took the term congruency from NSW cases, although the peculiar statutory basis of the NSW defence suggests the term may not deserve an influential role elsewhere.[103] (Outside NSW, congruency should be understood merely as referring to the

---

[98] Rolph (2002).

[99] *Anderson v Nationwide News* (2001) 3 VR 619, [3] (Ashley J).

[100] *Ibid* [13].

[101] *Ibid* [18]. The plea was allowed to stand in so far as it told the plaintiff what the defence would argue the publication's meaning was at trial: [19]–[20].

[102] *Ibid* [33].

[103] See eg *New South Wales Aboriginal Land Council v Perkins* (1998) 45 NSWLR 340; Rares (2004, 2002); Kenyon (1996). Note, although the High Court has refused leave to appeal when the NSW approach was sought to be challenged, it has not endorsed the existing approach, instead saying the case was not a suitable vehicle for such arguments: Transcript of Proceedings, *Radio 2UE Sydney v Goldsworthy* (HC Leave Application, Gleeson CJ, Kirby J, 6 April 2001).

allegation made in the publication which the plaintiff complains about; that is, the term is equivalent to saying that a separate and distinct allegation cannot be raised in a fair comment defence.) Ashley J said:

> It is true that, in Victoria, regardless of how many meanings are conveyed . . . only one cause of action arises . . . But I do not consider that it follows . . . there is congruency if a defence of fair comment addresses a severable defamatory meaning of the publication which is not relied upon by the plaintiff. So to conclude would be to ignore the fact that nowadays a plaintiff is in general bound by the meanings which [the plaintiff] attributes to a publication.[104]

Thus, Ashley J said the defence could not raise a separate and distinct meaning by way of fair comment – which is unproblematic in terms of the law before or after *Chakravarti* – and he also said the way a plaintiff is bound to its pleaded meanings limits the range of possible fair comment pleas. This is not surprising after *Hore-Lacy*, but it is an important change. Again, it is a shift from the publication to the pleaded imputation. Under the judgment of Ashley J, a fair comment plea can be struck out if it relates to a meaning that is substantially different from the plaintiff's plea.[105] This will restrict the availability of fair comment and raise some of the difficulties that are experienced in NSW, where interviews suggested the statutory approach 'works the harshest'.[106]

Before examining the third of the four significant decisions in this Part, another aspect of the *Anderson* decision is worth addressing. Ashley J discussed at some length the unreported English Court of Appeal judgment in *Lloyd v Express Newspapers*.[107] While *Lloyd* probably is consistent with the idea that a distinct charge cannot be raised by way of fair comment, it less clearly supports the rest of his judgment. As the English Court of Appeal has suggested in *Cruise v Express Newspapers*, the effect of *Lloyd* is opaque.[108] *Lloyd* was a case where an article arguably contained separate stings – one related to the plaintiff's work as a television weather presenter and the other concerning her personal life. In her pleadings, the plaintiff reproduced passages from the publication dealing with both aspects, but only pleaded meanings related to her professional life, such as:

> (a) the plaintiff is an unqualified, unintelligent and unprofessional weather-girl who hasn't the wit or brains to present the weather except by repeating parrot-fashion a science she does not understand;

[104] *Anderson* (2001) 3 VR 619, [76] (Ashley J).

[105] *Ibid* [84].

[106] 35SC; similar criticisms were raised by 34SC, 39SC, 40SC, 42SC; see Chapter 5, Part III, D.

[107] [1997] EWCA Civ 1319. In *Anderson*, the case is referred to as *Sian Lloyd v Express Newspapers*, but the title used in *Cruise v Express Newspapers* [1999] QB 931 is adopted here, which also accords with Kirwan and Masters (2002).

[108] *Cruise* [1999] QB 931, 954 (Brooke LJ, Stuart-Smith LJ and Sir John Knox agreed).

(b) in the circumstances, the plaintiff is incapable of presenting the weather properly and ought to be dismissed.[109]

The defendant pleaded different meanings by way of fair comment; for example, that the plaintiff:

(1) is a smug, self-satisfied, jumped-up, comic and silly little drip;

(2) has got the sort of face you want to crush a custard pie into;

(3) looks and sounds on her television weather broadcasts like a witless airhead who does not understand anything about the weather; . . .

(7) is no more than a two-timing cheat who gives the impression of loving the drama of having two boyfriends at once and who appears intent on milking the situation for all the publicity she can get irrespective of the pain caused to them.[110]

Most significantly for present purposes, this defence plea was allowed to stand. The plaintiff failed to limit the action to her professional life. Lord Bingham MR said:

> It is of course true that the meanings pleaded by the plaintiff do relate solely to her professional life, but it must be clear that the defendants are not limited in the meaning which they plead to those asserted by the plaintiff. They are entitled – if, indeed, they are not bound – to plead what they say is the meaning of the words complained of, which they have done so.[111]

This is the orthodox English position – and it is worth emphasising – defendants are not limited to the meanings that claimants plead and defendants must plead *the* meaning of the publication that they seek to justify.[112] In *Lloyd*, it is not entirely clear whether the meanings that related to the plaintiff's personal life were seen as separate and distinct meanings or not – but, given the result, they cannot have been completely distinct. Lord Bingham MR, however, made both these comments:

> It seems to me that this is a case in which, on the view which I prefer, the article does contain separate stings: one relating to the plaintiff's professional life, and one to her personal life. . .
>
> In my judgment therefore the judge was wrong to treat this as a case in which there were separable defamatory meanings of which the plaintiff had complained of only one.[113]

---

[109] *Lloyd v Express Newspapers* [1997] EWCA Civ 1319 (no pinpoint reference available) (Lord Bingham MR; Peter Gibson and Phillips LJJ agreed).

[110] *Ibid.*

[111] *Ibid.* Paragraph 6 of the defence was struck out as being incapable of being comment, but the remainder was approved by the Court of Appeal.

[112] Unless they choose to justify only the claimant's meaning.

[113] *Ibid.*

If the second of these quotations more accurately explains the position of the Court of Appeal in *Lloyd v Express Newspapers* – and it is much easier to reconcile with the result[114] – then it is hard to see how the parties' disputes about meaning so differed in *Lloyd* and in *Anderson* that fair comment could go forward in *Lloyd* but not in *Anderson*. In any event, Ashley J concluded in *Anderson*:

> All in all, the position concerning fair comment set out in *Polly Peck*, as understood in *Sian Lloyd*, appears to be consistent with the way in which the common law concerning defamation has developed in this country.[115]

However, the research undertaken for this book demonstrates that English claimants are not held to pleaded meanings in the way stated by *Hore-Lacy*, which means defendants can argue that publications are fair comment in any meanings that are capable of arising – except where defendants would be seeking to draw on separate and distinct charges.

As a separate matter, it should be noted that Ashley J said the English decision of *Control Risks v New English Library*[116] required defendants to state the 'substance of the comment' that they seek to defend.[117] He said this does not entail defendants stating the meanings in which they say publications are fair comment, although that 'will presumably coincide with or relate closely to' the defence meanings.[118] This position resembles the need for clarity about the meanings that defendants seek to defend by justification, as explained in Chapter 3,[119] and it accords with English practice.

Fair comment also was considered in a later interlocutory judgment in *Anderson v Nationwide News* by Bongiorno J.[120] The judgment again says the defence is limited after *Hore-Lacy*. Bongiorno J concluded the plaintiff's meaning concerned 'an ulterior motive' while the fair comment defence would go 'only to a lack of business judgment'. Thus, the defence was ruled out.[121] As well as moving matters quite close to the NSW position, the *pre-trial* determination in *Anderson* is a long way from the comments of Gaudron and Gummow JJ in *Chakravarti* that the issue of whether defendants might be disadvantaged (and thus whether plaintiffs might be bound to pleaded

[114] That is, the first quotation appears to have omitted the word *not* between the words *does* and *contain*. And it should read 'the article does not contain separate stings: one relating to the plaintiff's professional life, and one to her personal life'.

[115] *Anderson* (2001) 3 VR 619, [81] (Ashley J).

[116] [1990] 1 WLR 183.

[117] *Anderson* (2001) 3 VR 619, [58] (Ashley J).

[118] *Ibid* [62].

[119] See Chapter 3, Part I, K; *Prager v Times Newspapers* [1988] 1 WLR 77, 91 (Nicholls LJ).

[120] *Anderson v Nationwide News (No 2)* (2002) 3 VR 639.

[121] *Ibid* [14]. It also could be noted that Bongiorno J refers to the '"sting" of the libel alleged by the plaintiff' in terms of the particular meaning that is alleged, which differs to the term's common English usage in the sense of the charge or allegation that a publication conveys.

meanings) should be 'answered having regard to all the circumstances of the case, including . . . the issues in the trial, and not just simply by reference to the pleadings'.[122]

3 *Herald & Weekly Times v Popovic*

The Victorian Court of Appeal has commented further on defence pleading of meaning in *Herald & Weekly Times v Popovic*.[123] The case is important for providing one of the most clear and detailed analyses of the law on defamatory meaning in Australia and it is notable for its coverage of the *Lucas-Box* decision.[124] *Popovic* comes very close to setting out what this research suggests is the best practice with regards to meaning in defamation litigation. However, there are certain points at which it differs – generally through not explaining fully the English practice that is being adapted in Australia.

The plaintiff in *Popovic*, Victoria's deputy chief magistrate, sued over a newspaper article that criticised the handling of certain cases by her and a colleague. It misdescribed the events in various ways, and ended by asking: 'why should we employ them for a day longer?'[125] The plaintiff pleaded meanings that she: had subverted the law by prejudging a criminal prosecution for arson that she was presiding over; had bullied a police prosecutor in that case; and had so misconducted herself in that case 'and on at least one other occasion (when she hugged two drug traffickers she let go free) that her removal from office as a magistrate was warranted'.[126] Along with arguments about *Lange* privilege and fair reports, the defence pleaded three Lucas-Box imputations; namely, that the plaintiff:

> (a) had prejudged the case then before her by indicating that if she were the presiding magistrate she would find the charges proven and then dismiss them without knowing the facts of the case;
>
> (b) had bullied the police prosecutor . . . by accusing him of repeatedly arguing with her and then warning him . . . when he was attempting to put the . . . case for proceeding with the prosecution;
>
> (c) conducted herself inappropriately as a judicial officer by indicating during the course of the hearing . . . an antipathy towards the Indonesian Consulate (whose flag had allegedly been burned by the accused) by querying whether it was the Indonesian Consulate that was pushing the prosecution by commenting that it would be cheaper to buy a new flag and . . . showed sympathy for the accused whom she said were presumably young people some of whom she said had worked in a voluntary capacity in East Timor.[127]

[122] *Chakravarti* (1998) 193 CLR 519, [60].

[123] (2003) 9 VR 1.

[124] See especially the judgment of Gillard AJA with whom Warren AJA agreed on these matters: *ibid* [274]–[355] (Gillard AJA), [453]–[454] (Warren AJA).

[125] The article is reproduced in *ibid* 106 (annexure A).

[126] *Ibid* [31] (Gillard AJA).

[127] *Ibid* [32].

These pleadings make clear that one of the important differences between the parties' meanings concerned whether the article said the magistrate had *presided over* an arson prosecution or whether she had been involved in a *pre-trial hearing* about the case. The latter was the true situation.

As one of the most detailed Australian examinations of pleading in defamation, it is useful to consider closely the comments of Gillard AJA. And it should be noted that Warren AJA agreed with Gillard AJA on all these issues about meaning and justification.[128] There are six points to examine about the judgment, which concern: first, the tribunal of fact is not tied to either party's pleaded meanings; second, Lucas-Box and Polly Peck pleas differ from each other and defence pleas of meaning are necessary for good defamation practice; third, a Lucas-Box meaning is not exactly the meaning which the defendant contends that the publication actually bears; fourth, the criticisms of McHugh CJ and Brennan J concerned Polly Peck not Lucas-Box meanings; fifth, some aspects of a Polly Peck plea differ from the explanation in *Popovic*; and sixth, two judges in *Popovic* apply what should be seen as the best test for evaluating defence pleas – and this appears to differ from the *Hore-Lacy* approach, although that issue is not addressed directly in *Popovic*. Overall, there is much in the judgment that should be drawn on by Australian courts in terms of meaning and defamation law and practice.

First, Gillard AJA was clear that the jury determines the publication's meaning, not merely whether the plaintiff's pleaded imputations are conveyed. This extract puts the matter well and usefully reviews the law discussed in Chapters 2 and 3:

> What the words mean and whether they are defamatory of the plaintiff are questions of fact for the jury. The practice which is now invariably followed in defamation cases is for a plaintiff to plead the imputations relied upon. In the course of the trial, counsel and the judge will have carefully considered the imputations relied upon, there may be amendments, and the jury will be told ... how the case on the alleged imputations is being put by the parties. By the time the jury retires ... [it] will have a very good understanding of how the case is being put ... Nevertheless, the questions are for the jury and they are not strictly bound by the way each party puts their case on the defamatory imputations.[129]

This means where defence meanings have been pleaded, the jury could 'conclude that the article is defamatory . . . in the meanings put forward by the publisher or the plaintiff or a combination of both'.[130]

Second, Gillard AJA reviews *Lucas-Box, Polly Peck* and related English decisions and usefully distinguishes between the two situations of Lucas-Box meanings and common sting meanings.[131] He also emphasises that English practice does

[128] *Ibid* [453].

[129] *Ibid* [284]; see also [308]. Both passages cite *Barclay v Cox* [1968] VR 664; *Lucas-Box v News Group Newspapers* [1986] 1 WLR 147 and *Chakravarti* (1998) 193 CLR 519.

[130] *Ibid* [284].

[131] *Ibid* [300] and [310]–[318].

not allow defendants to defend a publication by proving the truth of a distinct and separate allegation about which the claimant does not complain.[132] English practice gives room to defendants to raise different meanings, but not about separate and distinct allegations. Gillard AJA also explains how fair litigation practice requires Lucas-Box pleading:

> [T]he words expressing the defamatory imputation relied upon by the plaintiff may not accord with what the jury . . . find as the defamatory imputation. It follows, in my opinion, it is just and fair that the defendant should . . . be able to plead [the defendant's own] version of the defamatory imputations and plead justification in those meanings.[133]

In a slightly earlier passage, Gillard AJA commented:

> [A] plaintiff's legal practitioner may through ignorance, a misunderstanding of the language, carelessness, or seeking to confine the plaintiff's case within narrow limits or for some other reason, plead . . . imputations which are inadequate or in some way do not properly or fully convey the true defamatory meaning of the words complained of. Common sense and justice demands that the defendant be permitted to plead the true imputation conveyed by the words complained of and in that meaning prove that they are true and correct. Also fairness and justice require that the defendant . . . apprise the plaintiff of the defamatory imputations sought to be justified. . . . Under the modern practice the plaintiff pleads the imputations. It is necessary to do justice that the defendant plead the imputations, if they are different, which [the defendant] intends to justify. Of course the imputations must be confined to the words actually complained of by the plaintiff subject to context.[134]

These statements accord almost perfectly with what practice should be as regards meaning in defamation law. The key points are that each side should set out the meaning that is being argued, the meanings must be capable of arising on the publication, and the meanings must not relate to separate and distinct allegations. Defence meanings, if challenged on their capacity to arise from the publication, are not evaluated in light of the plaintiff's imputations but in light of the publication in context. In relation to the first sentence in the second passage reproduced above, it is worth noting that evidence from English and Australian practice would emphasise that plaintiffs' imputations will be shaped carefully by their lawyers. Empirical research suggests this will be the case especially if plaintiffs are held fairly closely to those imputations.

The third point to note about the judgment also concerns the above statements. The second of the passages may elide an important distinction within Lucas-Box pleas that was set out in Chapter 3 and is repeated here for convenience; namely, the distinction

> between (a) the meaning of the words complained of for which the defendant contends (. . . the defendant is not obliged to plead that meaning) and (b) the

[132] *Ibid* [309].

[133] *Ibid*.

[134] *Ibid* [303].

> meaning of the words which, if it is the true meaning of those words, the defendant will seek to justify (that is the meaning which the defendant must now spell out sufficiently . . .).[135]

Thus, the defendant need not set out 'the true imputation conveyed by the words' but should set out the meaning that, if found to be the publication's meaning by the jury, the defendant will prove to be substantially true. It is quite possible for the defendant to plead that the publication is not defamatory and also plead, in the alternative, that if the publication is defamatory and has the meaning set out in the defendant's own plea, that meaning is true. (Of course, difficult forensic choices may remain as to whether both these arguments should be presented to the tribunal of fact, but that is a separate issue – one which appears to have been significant in *Popovic*.) This apparently small difference is important because it leads Gillard AJA to suggest that the defendant must establish the truth of every imputation that it has pleaded, rather than establish the truth of all the meanings that the jury finds actually to have been conveyed. For example, at one point Gillard AJA says:

> The publisher, by pleading its own imputations, is keeping all its eggs in one basket . . . [T]he defence fails unless the jury find that each defamatory imputation relied upon by the publisher is true.[136]

This suggests the defendant is bound to its meaning plea. While the defendant may be restrained from departing from its plea in presenting its case (depending on matters of prejudice to the plaintiff and trial management), the jury is not constrained to the meanings pleaded by the plaintiff or defendant. As Gillard AJA notes elsewhere in the judgment – for example, see the first point made above – the jury may decide that the publication's meaning is some mix of the plaintiff and defendant meanings. Then, if a defendant had pleaded justification to the plaintiff's imputations and, in the alternative, had made a Lucas-Box plea, the jury might agree that truth had been established for all the imputations it found to have been conveyed. Other examples are possible, such as where: the plaintiff sets out four imputations; the defendant sets out three Lucas-Box imputations; the jury says the meaning of the publication is captured by two of the defence imputations and none of the other plaintiff or defendant meanings and those two imputations are true. In such a case, the defence should not fail because its third Lucas-Box imputation is not proved to be true.

Although this analysis may well appear pedantic, it is aimed at avoiding the commonplace concern in defamation litigation of attention shifting from the publication to focus too closely on the pleaded imputations. There are substantial dangers in defamation practice that issues of meaning will move from the publication and its ordinary recipients to the pleaded imputations and the craft of lawyers. It is true that each party's imputations set out the case to be presented: their pleadings will inform the court and the other side of their case. But issues of

135 *Prager* [1988] 1 WLR 77, 91 (Nicholls LJ).

136 *Herald & Weekly Times v Popovic* (2003) 9 VR 1, [287].

meaning – and the defences most related to meaning – are dealt with best if they are left to the tribunal of fact in a comparatively flexible form. That gives the tribunal room to perform its particularly important role in relation to determining meaning. As noted in Chapter 1, defamation actions usually are centred on the meaning of words, which 'is probably the most important single factor' and 'is of cardinal significance'.[137] And it is the approach of leaving meaning to the jury in as simple a form as possible – with suitable judicial supervision as to issues of capacity and trial practicality – which disciplines both sides' lawyers to present their cases in terms of meanings that are plausible and to contain all their arguments to what is most needed for a fair determination of the dispute.

The fourth matter arising from *Popovic* is similar to an interpretation set out earlier in this chapter: Gillard AJA said the criticisms made by Brennan CJ and McHugh J in *Chakravarti* addressed common sting meanings rather than all defence meanings.[138] And Gillard AJA doubted the example of a common sting meaning that they offered. As argued above in Part II, Gillard AJA suggested the two allegations about criminal conviction and defrauding shareholders may not convey a common sting at all. Rather they appear to be separate and distinct.[139] However, and most significantly, Gillard AJA did not accept the criticisms of Polly Peck pleading made by Brennan CJ and McHugh J. Following Levine J in *Whelan v John Fairfax Publications*[140] (which is mentioned below) Gillard AJA held the defence plea to be a proper part of defamation law.[141] Where it is capable of arising from a publication, which may need careful consideration in individual cases, a common sting plea is a necessary element of defamation law.

Fifth, notwithstanding his support for common sting pleas Gillard AJA provided an unusual explanation of their operation. He appeared to suggest that where an article refers to two incidents which have a common sting,

> it is not open to the defendants . . . to justify the common sting by selectively narrowing the plea to some but not all examples of alleged misconduct found in the article . . . If the defendants wish to justify the common sting, namely, that she had behaved inappropriately, they were bound to plead and prove the truth of all examples in the article which were described to support that conclusion.[142]

However, Polly Peck pleading allows just that: as illustrated by *Khashoggi v IPC Magazines*, which Gillard AJA refers to earlier and also is discussed in Chapter 3.[143] In short, proving some of the imputations true justifies all the imputations where they have a common sting. In *Khashoggi v IPC Magazines* allegations of

---

[137] Faulks Committee (1975) 22; see Chapter 1, Part I.

[138] *Popovic* (2003) 9 VR 1, [319].

[139] *Ibid* [319]–[320].

[140] (2002) 56 NSWLR 89.

[141] *Popovic* (2003) 9 VR 1, [302].

[142] *Ibid* [350].

[143] *Ibid* [321]–[322]; see Chapter 3, Part I, K.

separate acts of adultery arguably had a common sting of adulterous promiscuity.[144] Therefore, even if one allegation of adultery mentioned in the article could not be proved true, the defence would be arguable if there was evidence to prove the common sting true.

Sixth, only Winneke ACJ directly addressed the *Hore-Lacy* approach – that is, defence meanings cannot be substantially different nor more injurious than the plaintiff's imputations. He said that it provided another reason for the justification defence to fail on the facts of *Popovic*. Winneke ACJ noted that the plaintiff's imputations said the article meant 'she was engaged in presiding over a criminal prosecution for arson' – rather being involved than a pre-trial hearing about the case – and that is what gave substance to the plaintiff's imputations of 'bias' and 'inappropriate conduct'.[145] He continued:

> The meanings pleaded by the defendants deliberately steered clear of this aspect of the meanings pleaded by the plaintiff. That fact, in itself, renders the defendants' meanings substantially different from those pleaded by the plaintiff.[146]

Thus, for Winneke ACJ the defence meanings were impermissible under *Hore-Lacy*. However, the other two judges in *Popovic* did not address *Hore-Lacy* directly. Instead, Gillard AJA (with whom Warren AJA agreed on these six issues) applied what should be seen as the best test in relation to assessing defence pleas of meaning – a test that appears to differ from *Hore-Lacy*. It is to evaluate a defence pleading in terms of whether the meaning is capable of arising from the publication in question:

> The learned trial judge, in considering whether the issue should be left to the jury, considers whether the words complained of are capable of bearing the defamatory meaning pleaded by the defendants. In performing that function, the judge will . . . [take] into account that the average reader is not naive, tends to read between the lines, is more ready to find an implication than a lawyer and to indulge in an amount of loose thinking. . . . The trial judge should approach the task, stepping into the shoes of the average reader, and not subject the article to a strict legal interpretation.[147]

It is true that this test may not have been seen as differing from *Hore-Lacy* – that would explain the lack of reference to the decision on this issue. It might be suggested, for example, that this judicial determination only arises after defence meanings have passed the *Hore-Lacy* test, which, apart from anything else, would suggest the *Hore-Lacy* test is quite broad. However, that suggestion does not sit easily with the emphasis that is placed on the jury not being bound, nor on the whole examination of meaning in the judgment. The different focus of the test set out by Gillard AJA – the publication interpreted in context, not the plaintiff's pleaded imputations – is a vital shift. And the conclusion of Gillard AJA, at least, is stated clearly in those terms: it 'would not have been open to the judge to leave

[144] [1986] 1 WLR 1412.

[145] *Popovic* (2003) 9 VR 1, [21].

[146] *Ibid*.

[147] *Ibid* [333].

the [defence] imputation to the jury. It is a selective piece of pleading. It omits some very important facts which are clearly stated in the article'.[148] That is, the defence meaning is not capable of arising from the publication. If the defence meaning should have been ruled out in *Popovic*, this is the reason on which the action should have been taken, not the approach of *Hore-Lacy*. Of course, it will remain the case that the defendant will be unable to justify one allegation by proving that a separate and distinct allegation in the publication is true (as explained in the second point above).

4 Other Victorian cases

There are two points to be made about two subsequent Victorian cases: *Gutnick v Dow Jones (No 4)*[149] and *Fletcher v Pos Solutions Australia*.[150] First, they illustrate the way in which meanings now appear to be confined in Victorian practice. Second, they do not relate easily to the statements of Gillard and Warren AJJA in *Popovic* about meaning being an issue for the tribunal of fact and – because plaintiff lawyers may plead imputations which 'do not properly or fully convey the true defamatory meaning of the words complained of'[151] – that fairness demands the defendant should be able to plead its own version of the words' meaning and seek to justify it. This relates to the issue described in *Polly Peck* of plaintiffs trying to limit artificially the field of dispute about meaning.[152] This second point is not surprising, because in *Chakravarti* all judges focussed on possible disadvantage to the defendant if the plaintiff is allowed to depart from pleaded meanings. Comparative research into practice suggests that is an important but insufficient question. Defendants may be disadvantaged if they are not allowed to depart from plaintiffs' meanings. The issue should be to ensure that each party has an equivalent opportunity to present its case based on the words complained of.

The dispute in *Gutnick v Dow Jones* is well known internationally for the earlier High Court decision that established the defendant publisher could be sued in Victoria in relation to an internet publication originating from the US.[153] However, a later judgment in the dispute – the final judgment before the matter settled – is a useful example of how the *Hore-Lacy* approach can confine meanings.[154] In *Gutnick*, the plaintiff pleaded imputations related to being guilty of certain conduct. The defence sought to plead imputations that the meanings were at the levels of reasonable suspicion and reason to investigate, not at the level of guilt. In *Gutnick*, this difference between guilt and suspicion (or guilt and reason to investigate) was held not to be open under *Hore-Lacy*. That is, the

---

148 *Ibid* [335].

149 (2004) Aust Torts Reports ¶81-748.

150 [2004] VSC 507.

151 *Popovic* (2003) 9 VR 1, [303].

152 *Polly Peck* [1986] QB 1000.

153 *Dow Jones v Gutnick* (2002) 210 CLR 575; see eg Collins (2003); Garnett (2003).

154 *Gutnick v Dow Jones (No 4)* (2004) Aust Torts Reports ¶81-748.

defence plea was ruled out not because the article was incapable of conveying the defence meanings, but because the plaintiff had chosen to pitch meanings at the level of guilt. So much does this result differ from English Lucas-Box practice that it is worthwhile to set out the imputations. The plaintiff pleaded that he:

(a) was a customer of [a person] who had recently been in prison for tax evasion and money laundering; and
(b) was the biggest customer of [the person] who had recently been in prison for tax evasion and money laundering; and
(c) was masquerading as a reputable citizen when he was, in fact, a tax evader who had laundered large amounts of money through [the person]; and
(d) had bought [the person's] silence so as to conceal his identity as one of the customers of [the person] who had recently been in prison for tax evasion and money laundering.[155]

The relevant defence pleas were:

(a) the plaintiff was reasonably suspected by prosecutors and investigators of having been a money laundering customer of [the person] who had recently been in prison for tax evasion and money laundering;
(b) there was reason to investigate whether the plaintiff was a money laundering customer of [the person] who had recently been in prison for tax evasion and money laundering;
(c) there was reason to investigate whether the plaintiff had bought [the person's] silence in order to conceal his involvement as a money laundering customer of [the person] who had recently been in prison for tax evasion and money laundering.[156]

Bongiorno J held that it was 'sufficient to examine and apply the principle in *Hore-Lacy* to the proposed imputations to conclude that they do not meet the imputations pleaded by the plaintiff nor are they permissible variants of those imputations'.[157] He considered significant English cases on guilt and suspicion – such as *Lewis v Daily Telegraph* and *Stern v Piper* – and held they established that meanings of guilt and suspicion are substantially different.[158] In addition, he noted the comments of Ormiston JA in *Hore-Lacy*,[159] which suggest that allegations of 'smoke' or 'fire' – suspicion or guilt – are permissible pleas under *Hore-Lacy*. But in *Gutnick* it was held that the plaintiff would need to establish its meaning of guilt and could not succeed if the jury believed the publication's meaning was lesser. Bongiorno J commented: 'As the cases to which I have

155 *Ibid* [5] (Bongiorno J).
156 *Ibid*.
157 *Ibid* [7].
158 *Ibid* [8]–[10] referring to eg *Lewis* [1964] AC 234; *Stern v Piper* [1997] QB 123.
159 *Ibid* [10].

referred make clear, whilst both allegations might be libellous they are not variants of each other as that term is used in *Hore-Lacy*.'[160] While this is true of the way that some Victorian decisions have interpreted *Hore-Lacy*, it is worth emphasising one point. The English cases about different levels of meaning do not operate in any manner like that. The type of defence argument rejected in cases such as *Gutnick* is a standard response to English defamation claimants and is supported as an important part of practice by litigators.

Similarly, in *Fletcher v Pos Solutions Australia* a defence meaning was ruled out, with the defendants being held very closely to the plaintiffs' pleaded meanings.[161] In effect, the individual plaintiff's meanings concerned lying about the reliability of a competing business product, while the defence plea was that plaintiff had made untrue statements about the product.[162] Ashley J commented that 'There is a distinct difference between factual inaccuracy and lying inaccuracy in things written and said.'[163] The defence plea was disallowed. Again, it remains to be seen how this interpretation of *Hore-Lacy* sits with comments such as those of Gillard AJA in *Popovic* about the tribunal of fact's role in determining meaning.[164] It is useful to note that these cases have not considered whether the defence plea was arguable on the basis of the publications; that is, on the basis of the words complained of. And, this makes it not surprising that there was no express consideration of how plaintiffs may direct meaning to an unwarranted degree – a degree that evidence from practice suggests is unlikely to promote prompt, proportionate or appropriate defamation litigation.

B Western Australian decisions

1 *First-instance examples*

For some time after *Hore-Lacy*, Western Australian decisions varied in their approach to defence pleading. A series of first-instance decisions in Western Australia approved Lucas-Box and Polly Peck pleading and appeared to follow the modifications under *Hore-Lacy*, although some retained a more flexible approach and implicitly or explicitly criticised *Hore-Lacy*. Several decisions are

---

160 *Ibid* [12].

161 [2004] VSC 507.

162 *Ibid* [12] and [20].

163 *Ibid* [21].

164 See above Part IV, A, 3. *Popovic* is not mentioned in the decision in *Gutnick (No 4)* (2004) Aust Torts Reports ¶81-748.

165 Reference also could be made to *Brown v Marron* [2001] WASC 100; *Wallis v Wallis* [2001] WASC 134. See also *Reynolds v Nationwide News* [2001] WASC 90, [23] (Hasluck J), which suggests an even stricter approach (although it has not been applied subsequently) because it treated a 'milder and less specific assertion' as a substantially different meaning. As discussed above, in Part IV, A, this does appear to be the same approach as some Victorian decisions, eg *Gutnick (No 4)* (2004) Aust Torts Reports ¶81-748.

used here to illustrate the situation.[165] Then the analysis shifts to the fourth central case for this Chapter's discussion of Lucas-Box and Polly Peck in Australia – the Western Australian Full Court's subsequent decision in *Nationwide News v Moodie*.[166]

In *Jackson v ACP Publishing*, a magazine and daily newspaper published articles criticising a religious group called the Exclusive Brethren, with headings such as 'Aussie Sect Has Our Kid' and 'Death of a Friend Leads to Breakaway'.[167] The plaintiffs pleaded a range of meanings, including:

> (i) The plaintiffs were cruel to children with disabilities; . . .
> (iv) The plaintiffs discriminated against persons with disabilities;
> (v) The plaintiffs discriminated against the parents of persons with disabilities;
> (vi) The plaintiffs were uncaring or indifferent towards persons with disabilities.[168]

The plaintiffs originally pleaded two more imputations. After the plaintiffs deleted them in an amendment, the defendant magazine sought to justify those imputations in a Lucas-Box plea as being the article's only imputations:

> (a) the plaintiffs were insensitive to the needs of others; and
> (b) the plaintiffs were unchristian.[169]

Similarly, the defendant newspaper tried to re-introduce and justify imputations about the plaintiffs being 'inhuman' or 'insensitive to the needs of others'.[170] These imputations were broader than those of the plaintiffs. The plaintiffs presumably realised wider evidence could be admissible in relation to such meanings and wanted to avoid facing such material. Anderson J said:

> By contending . . . the words truly mean that the plaintiffs are 'insensitive' and 'unchristian', the defendants plainly seek to shift the factual inquiry into a completely different and much wider area than is covered by the plaintiffs' claim.[171]

He noted the defence was the type identified as a Lucas-Box plea in this book.[172] Anderson J reviewed the Australian case law, and approved of *Hore-Lacy* in concluding:

> [T]he imputations pleaded by the plaintiffs are confined to specific matters; namely, the plaintiffs alleged treatment of, and attitude towards, disabled children and their parents. . . . [T]he wider meanings contained in the . . .

166 (2003) 28 WAR 314.

167 [2001] WASC 121, [3] and [38] (Anderson J).

168 *Ibid* [4].

169 *Ibid* [6].

170 *Ibid* [42].

171 *Ibid* [14]–[15].

172 *Ibid* [20].

> defence are not meanings which would be fairly open to the tribunal of fact . . . because they are substantially different from the meanings complained of by the plaintiffs.[173]

However, differences from *Hore-Lacy* are suggested by a later hearing in the case. The defendants sought to argue that each publication had a common sting in the same terms as their rejected Lucas-Box pleas. Anderson J accepted that some common sting pleas were open:

> Arguably, the imputations contended for by the plaintiffs . . . namely, that the plaintiffs are cruel to and discriminate against children with disabilities and their parents, have to them the same sting as an imputation that the plaintiffs are inhuman.[174]

This suggests the allowable degree of difference varies between Lucas-Box and Polly Peck pleas, although why this should be so is not explored. In any event, *Jackson v ACP Publishing* may be a more flexible approach than many Victorian decisions and is closer to the approach in *Popovic*.[175]

One reason for the differences from Victoria may be the view that *Hore-Lacy*, and in particular the judgment of Ormiston JA, too narrowly reads *Chakravarti*. McLure J has made this point repeatedly. In *Vitale v Bednall*, she emphasised that the position of Ormiston JA in *Hore-Lacy* 'appears to be very close' to that of Brennan CJ and McHugh J in *Chakravarti*.[176] And in *Moir v Flint*,[177] McLure J disagreed with the reasoning of Ashley J in *Anderson v Nationwide News* about fair comment.[178] McLure J noted that the defence 'is applied by reference to the meanings in which the words would be understood'.[179] But because the plaintiff is not held to its pleaded meanings, the defence can be raised in relation to any capable meaning. Thus she noted:

> Notwithstanding the test of fair comment is by reference to the imputations, it is accepted in common law jurisdictions that the pleading of the defence of fair comment is by reference to the words complained of.[180]

---

[173] *Ibid* [34].

[174] *Jackson v ACP Publishing* [2002] WASC 5, [20] (Anderson J).

[175] It also could be noted that Anderson J discussed some of this common sting argument in terms of contextual imputations: eg *ibid* [15]. He cited the NSW defence's requirements as explained by Hunt J in *Hepburn* [1984] 1 NSWLR 386, 399 which have no necessary relevance to the common law: [23]. In any event, he made no reference to the statutory basis in NSW, or the cases on how it compares to the common law. See Chapter 3, Part I, J.

[176] [2001] WASC 278, [41] (McLure J). See also *Cock v Hughes* [2002] WASC 263, [8]–[10] (McLure J).

[177] [2002] WASC 48.

[178] See above, Part IV, A, 2.

[179] *Moir v Flint* [2002] WASC 48, [24] (McLure J) citing Neill and Rampton (1983) [13.32].

[180] *Ibid* [25].

Again, McLure J suggested the statement of Ormiston JA in *Hore-Lacy* may be too narrow.[181] In any event, a lesser defence meaning on the same subject matter would not be ruled out, which was the situation in *Moir v Flint* because both sides were arguing about the plaintiff's allegedly deceptive dealings in relation to a newspaper interview.[182]

It also should be noted that a differing view of the *Anderson v Nationwide News* litigation[183] has been expressed in Western Australia in *Cock v Hughes*.[184] In that case, the general approach in *Anderson* was endorsed by Hasluck J, at least as to defendants needing to state the substance of the comment in their pleading when that was required for clarity.[185] However, this should not be seen to endorse the narrowing of possible defence pleas that *Anderson* achieved because Hasluck J suggested his ruling did not limit the meanings open to defendants to argue.[186]

2 *Nationwide News v Moodie*

After first-instance decisions such as those above, the issue reached the Western Australian Full Court in *Nationwide News v Moodie* where a majority adopted the general approach of *Hore-Lacy*.[187] That is, a plaintiff's case cannot go to the jury on meanings that are substantially different or more injurious than the plaintiff's pleaded meanings. Defence pleadings are limited to the same degree.[188] In *Moodie*, McLure J did not adopt the reasoning of the majority, again emphasising that the approach of Ormiston JA in *Hore-Lacy* may be too narrow. However, she did not need to determine the exact test to be applied to defence meanings because the defence meanings were open in this instance on any of the approaches.[189] There are two significant points about the decision in *Moodie* for this chapter. First, the defence meanings that were allowed here – on the *Hore-Lacy* approach – are important to note, but it is crucial to appreciate that their availability depended on the manner in which the plaintiff pleaded its case. Second, and not surprisingly in light of earlier decisions, the judgments do not appear to appreciate the significance of Lucas-Box pleas – to defendants and to the fair and efficient processing of defamation claims.

---

[181] *Ibid* [28].

[182] *Ibid* [15]–[17].

[183] See above, Part IV, A, 2.

[184] [2002] WASC 108; cf [2002] WASC 263, [8]–[10] (McLure J).

[185] [2002] WASC 108, [45] (Hasluck J).

[186] *Ibid* [46].

[187] (2003) 28 WAR 314, [11]–[13] (Anderson J), [57]–[60] (Steytler J).

[188] *Ibid* [58]–[59]. In the majority, however, Steytler J explicitly referred to the lack of a clear High Court majority on the issue and noted the situation remained dependant on further guidance.

[189] *Ibid* [94].

The factual background is relevant to the first issue about whether defence meanings could go forward. The plaintiff in *Moodie* was a hospital administrator who sued over two newspaper articles. One was headed 'Chief a "Toecutter"' and concerned the plaintiff being stood down as a public hospital chief executive. It included statements that the plaintiff 'was accused of running a mafia-style operation before resigning from his last job in NSW' and that his management style was 'roundly criticised as secretive and abrasive'. The second article contained more about a NSW parliamentary inquiry including the statement that: 'Medical professionals spoke of a "wall of silence", a lack of public consultation, morale in hospitals at an all-time low, communication problems and severe budget cut-backs.'[190] The plaintiff pleaded meanings including:

> (c) that the plaintiff acted as a mafioso in performing his duties as chief of [the relevant NSW health service] . . .
>
> (d) that the plaintiff acts as a mafioso in performing his duties as chief executive of the [NSW health service and the Western Australian hospitals] using mafia tactics to enforce his policy . . .
>
> (h) that the plaintiff is a dishonest, ruthless mafioso style executive.[191]

The defence meanings at issue were:

> 7.1 The plaintiff in performing his duties as Chief Executive Officer of the [NSW health service and the Western Australian hospitals] was dictatorial and secretive in his management style . . .
>
> 7.2 The plaintiff in performing his duties as Chief Executive Officer of the Hospitals was dictatorial and secretive in his management style.[192]

At first instance, Hasluck J held the defence meanings to be impermissible because they differed substantially from the plaintiff's meanings:

> An assertion that a person is acting in the manner of the mafia would surely convey to an ordinary reader that the person is acting in breach of the law or . . . conforms to the practices of a group that stands outside . . . the law . . . [T]his is significantly different from an assertion that a person is acting in an overbearing or secretive manner. In the present case, the tenor of the words complained of are far stronger than the meanings sought to be relied upon by the defendant.[193]

Although the issue does not appear to have received attention in the Full Court, this passage suggests two bases for the decision of Hasluck J. The first

[190] *Ibid* [23]–[25] (Steytler J) provides some details about the publications.

[191] *Ibid* [26]–[27]. It could be noted how far these meanings are from the US approach to hyperbole, discussed in Chapter 8. Comparisons also could be made to European case law that has emphasised the need to allow room for journalistic exaggeration and provocation: eg *Radio France v France* (2005) 40 EHRR 29.

[192] *Ibid* [30].

[193] *Moodie v Nationwide News* [2002] WASC 246, [29] (Hasluck J).

one – and the explicit reason relied on – is that the defence imputations did not meet the *Hore-Lacy* test because they differed substantially from the plaintiff's meanings. But a second reason is implicit in the passage's final sentence; namely, a determination that the defence meaning was not capable of arising on the publications in question. While the Full Court clearly differed from that interpretation of the publications, its decision was based on the first reason. It unanimously held that the defence meanings came within the *Hore-Lacy* test. They were meanings not substantially different from the plaintiff's meanings and comprehended within those meanings in the context of the publications.[194] This suggests a wider approach than some Victorian decisions discussed above – and it also more clearly accords with the approach to matters like guilt or suspicion in *Hore-Lacy*. In addition, the second basis mentioned by Hasluck J is interesting to note because that approach is what this book's research suggests should be adopted in Australia in terms of defence pleading: the scope of justification should not be limited by the plaintiff's pleading – apart from distinct allegations about which the plaintiff does not complain – but it should be limited by the 'meanings which the words are reasonably capable of bearing'.[195]

Another aspect of the allowed meanings is crucial to appreciate. The decision of Steytler J, in particular, appears to have been influenced by the way in which the plaintiff pleaded its case. He noted that:

> It is quite plain, from the two articles, and indeed from the pleaded imputations themselves, that the references to 'mafioso' and 'mafia tactics' refer exclusively to the [plaintiff's] management style. In those circumstances, and given that ordinary people might understand the pleaded imputations in different ways, it seems to me that it is open to the [defendant] to plead, and to seek to justify, imputations to the effect that the [plaintiff], in performing his duties, was dictatorial and secretive in his management style. . . .
>
> I should add that the situation might well have been different had the [plaintiff] chosen to plead its imputations with more precision, at least if the pleaded imputations were to the effect contended for in oral argument, being imputations, only, of unlawful or criminal conduct.[196]

It is worth examining what decision would be likely, on the basis of this passage, if the plaintiff had pleaded a more specific imputation such as one limited to criminal conduct. It can be expected that such an imputation would be capable of arising – the test for capacity is not and should not be a strict one (as is explored in Chapter 10). At the same time, however, the publication and its ordinary recipients would not have changed. The defence meaning about dictatorial and secretive management still would be capable of arising from the

[194] *Nationwide News v Moodie* (2003) 28 WAR 314, [20] (Anderson J), [64] (Steytler J), [94] (McLure J).

[195] Milmo and Rogers (2004) [11.14].

[196] *Moodie* (2003) 28 WAR 314, [63]–[64].

publication – and it does not concern a separate and distinct allegation. The ground of battle, however, would have been shifted substantially by such a change in plaintiff pleading.

This passage from Steytler J raises the second aspect of *Nationwide News v Moodie* that is notable for the purposes of this book. It involves a central concern that defence pleading of meaning addresses; namely, claimants or plaintiffs unreasonably restricting the scope of dispute. With regard to this issue, the judgments may not appreciate the significance of Lucas-Box pleas to defendants and to good defamation litigation practice. (The same comments could be made of the other decisions on this issue – including *Chakravarti* itself and *Hore-Lacy* and some commentary that, in light of this project's comparative empirical research, focuses too heavily on rules applicable in other areas of civil law.[197]) It bears repeating that parties will differ, in almost every case, about quite what meaning is conveyed by a publication. In part that is for tactical reasons, and in part it follows from the varied interpretations that almost all publications can be subject to by their recipients. The approach adopted by the majority in *Moodie* runs a very real danger of being unfair to defendants and harmful to litigation practice. This is because restricting the ability of plaintiffs to succeed on meanings that differ from what they have pleaded also gives plaintiffs the ability to restrict the scope of the dispute to the meanings they have pleaded. That moves the law a long way towards the NSW approach. It will give plaintiffs far greater reason to plead imputations that are incapable of being defended because of the specific form of words chosen. This can be seen in the passage from Steytler J that is quoted above: if the plaintiff in *Moodie* had pleaded imputations that were only in terms of 'unlawful or criminal conduct', it seems the defence would not have been able to respond with imputations about secretive and dictatorial management. At trial, it would have been able to argue only that the plaintiff's meaning was not conveyed. That shifts the dispute from the substance

[197] See eg Morris (2000) especially 767–70. The article is concerned with Lucas-Box pleading, not common sting pleading. It is not surprising that Morris promotes what appears logical for defamation pleading, but his position is not supported by this project's evidence from litigation practice in England, NSW and Victoria. The vital issues of plaintiffs shaping the litigation, and the effects that has on defamation litigation, need further consideration. The 'oppression' (769) that is possible in defamation goes not only one way, and empirical evidence from English and Australian jurisdictions is of great importance for appreciating the ways in which oppression can arise. It should be noted, however, that depending on the breadth of 'not substantially different' meanings, the approach that Morris suggests could operate somewhat similarly to English Lucas-Box practice. Cases subsequent to the Morris article, which say more about 'not substantially different', are addressed in the current Part of this chapter. But, as argued in this chapter, the limitation should relate to *allegations* about which the plaintiff complains, not to *meanings* that are 'not substantially different'. However, the suggestion from Morris for defendants to request plaintiffs to disclaim any reliance on meanings they otherwise would seek to plead in a Lucas-Box defence would seem useful – even if plaintiffs refused such concessions – especially given the subsequent changes in Australian law under the *Hore-Lacy* approach.

of the publication to the imputations. The defence meaning would remain a probable interpretation of the publications – it may well be what a jury would find to be the single meaning that ordinary recipients would have taken from the articles. Thus, both meanings would be capable of being conveyed and not relate to distinct and separate allegations – the plaintiff would have been taking a 'blue pencil' to the publications if those passages about secretive and abrasive management were removed[198] – and that is why it was good that the defence plea was allowed in *Moodie*. But the fact that the defence plea met the test in *Hore-Lacy* is incidental. The court should remain focussed on the publication and not be diverted into an approach that may be dominated by pleaded imputations. While in some instances there may be concerns about the scope of material that could be admissible to defend a particular meaning, they should be addressed otherwise than through the test for permissible meaning pleas (as is explored further in Chapter 10).

On the *Hore-Lacy* approach, while defendants could choose to argue only that the plaintiff's imputations do not arise, evidence from practice strongly suggests they will have greater recourse to interlocutory battles and the 'sterile' technicality of defamation practice will be increased, not lessened.[199] Instead, the touchstone should be the publication itself and the meanings that are capable of being conveyed by it. To suggest simply that defence meanings which are different to plaintiff meanings will raise false issues risks not appreciating the effect that artfully crafted imputations can have on an entire claim. In this, good defamation practice may well be different from some other civil actions. That, however, is the evidence from empirical research and it reflects the particular role of meaning in English and Australian defamation law and practice – a role remarkably different to the US practice described in Chapter 8.

It is notable that McLure J came close to stating this position in *Moodie* in emphasising that the extent to which a plaintiff could depart from pleaded meanings 'would be dictated in large measure by the formulation of the defendant's [Lucas-Box] imputations'.[200] She explained that the *Chakravarti* judgments use the concept of unfairness in a trial as a reason to restrict plaintiffs from departing from pleaded imputations which then also restricts defendants. McLure J noted that the *Chakravarti* judgments do not use the concept of disadvantage in relation to the converse issue: namely, allowing defendants greater room to depart from pleaded meanings.[201] It is interesting that this is the point at which McLure J states there is no need to decide exactly which test is the correct one to apply to defence meanings, because the defence meanings in

---

198 See *Polly Peck* [1986] QB 1000, 1023 (O'Connor LJ, Robert Goff and Nourse LJJ agreed).

199 Levine (2001). Levine used the adjective about NSW practice. The analysis in this chapter suggests there are dangers the 'sterile' aspects of NSW defamation litigation will be encouraged elsewhere.

200 *Moodie* (2003) 28 WAR 314, [93].

201 *Ibid* [94].

Moodie are open on any of the tests. McLure J has suggested, however, the point that results from holding plaintiffs to pleaded imputations – that is, unfairness to defendants and to the efficient disposal of defamation claims.[202]

C Other Australian decisions

The cases examined above set out the most important issues about Lucas-Box and Polly Peck in Australia. However, it is worth mentioning some other decisions briefly here. South Australia also has adopted the approach of *Hore-Lacy*. The leading decisions is *Advertiser-News Weekend Publishing v Manock*, in which Doyle CJ with the agreement of Vanstone and White JJ went further and agreed with the comments of Brennan CJ and McHugh J in *Chakravarti*.[203] One passage is worth quoting at length:

> In my respectful opinion the observations of Brennan CJ and McHugh J are supported by practical considerations. The approach that they take is conducive to the fair conduct of a trial. I agree with them that under the law as stated in *Polly Peck* it appears open to a defendant to plead and justify meanings that differ from the meaning on which the plaintiff relies, resulting in the introduction of evidence that will increase the length of the trial, may tend to cloud the issues, and may work to the unfair prejudice of the plaintiff . . .
>
> For these reasons, as a matter or principle, as a matter of fairness and having regard to the public interest in the efficient conduct of a trial, the law as stated by O'Connor LJ in *Polly Peck* should not be applied in this State.[204]

While these statements may appear perfectly understandable in terms of most civil litigation – and they contain some important points for defamation practice – they are not supported by the evidence of Australian and English practice that is detailed at length in this and earlier chapters. That evidence suggests the approach taken in cases like *Hore-Lacy*, *Nationwide News v Moodie*, and this decision of *Advertiser-News v Manock* will promote neither fairness to the parties nor the public interest in efficient defamation trials. It is true that some Lucas-Box and Polly Peck pleas need to be controlled, to avoid unwarranted trial length, clouding of issues or prejudice to the plaintiff – as Doyle CJ notes. But that

202 Further Western Australian decisions could be considered, including *Fogarty v Nationwide News* [2005] WASC 2, which applied *Moodie* to fair comment: the defence must identify the substance of the opinion that is being defended, which must not differ substantially from the plaintiff's imputations. See also *Bell-a-Bike Rottnest v Automotive, Food, Metals, Engineering Printing and Kindred Industries Union of Workers* [2003] WASC 51, [18]–[20] (Hasluck J); *Bond v John Fairfax Publications* [2002] WASC 130, [15]–[20] (Hasluck J); *Anderson v Ah Kit* [2004] WASC 194.

203 [2005] SASC 82, [75]–[82] (Doyle CJ, Vanstone and White JJ agreed). See also *Selecta Homes & Building v Advertiser-Weekend Publishing* (2001) SASR 451; *Sullivan v South Australian Water Corpn* [2004] SASC 138, [8]–[17] (Burley J).

204 *Advertiser-News Weekend Publishing v Manock* [2005] SASC 82, [80] and [82] (Doyle CJ, Vanstone and White JJ agreed).

control should not be exercised on the basis of the plaintiff's pleaded imputations. It should be done on the basis of the meanings that are capable of arising from the publication – which each party should have a fair opportunity to present to the tribunal of fact – and on the basis of good case management practices (which were the points listed by O'Connor LJ in *Polly Peck* and are explored further in Chapter 10).[205] The alternative approach displayed in the reasoning of *Advertiser-News v Manock* and the other Australian cases leaves unconstrained the plaintiff's tactical interests in limiting the scope of battle away from many shades of capable meaning. Just as defendants may seek to convert 'a modest and narrow claim . . . into a wide-ranging expansive and extensive inquiry',[206] plaintiffs will seek to limit the ability of defendants to argue the substance of the publications in issue.[207]

Two brief points are worth noting about NSW decisions since *Chakravarti* and *Hore-Lacy*. First, additional complications flow from the 7A process in NSW, which means that Lucas-Box pleading has no room to operate in NSW even in relation to interstate publications. As *John Fairfax Publications v Jones* makes clear the parties are bound by the jury finding at the 7A hearing that one or more of the plaintiff's imputations were conveyed, so Lucas-Box cannot be argued.[208] Second, NSW courts have made statements broadly similar to the criticisms by McLure J in Western Australia of *Chakravarti* and subsequent cases. For example, in *Whelan v John Fairfax Publications*, Levine J doubted *Chakravarti* and followed the orthodox English approach.[209]

D English examples

The Australian situation outlined above differs from England. Lesser meanings that *Hore-Lacy* suggests would be allowed also would be available in England – namely those of suspicion where guilt has been pleaded – although some other Australian decisions suggest this difference in meanings is impermissible. In any event, in England different meanings also would be available, depending always on the publication, not on the pleaded imputations. Two English cases illustrate how Lucas-Box meanings operate to allow a plaintiff and defendant to present

[205] *Polly Peck* [1986] QB 1000, 1021 (O'Connor LJ, Robert Goff and Nourse LJJ agreed).

[206] *Woodger v Federal Capital Press of Australia* (1992) 107 ACTR 1, 21 (Miles CJ).

[207] In terms of South Australian decisions, reference also could be made to *Bass v Roberts and Case* [2000] SADC 35, [276] (Judge Lowrie) and *Roberts v Bass* (2000) 78 SASR 302. In the most relevant appellate judgment, Williams J said the Lucas-Box pleas failed on the facts, but also said he would restrict Lucas-Box and Polly Peck pleas to cases in which the plaintiff 'has chosen to ignore part of the publication so as to alter its true meaning': [16]. The High Court appeal (*Roberts v Bass* (2002) 212 CLR 1) dealt with other issues, primarily qualified privilege and malice.

[208] [2004] NSWCA 205, [80]–[82] (Hodgson JA), [115] (Ipp JA agreed).

[209] (2002) 56 NSWLR 89, [47]–[50] which also noted the criticisms made by Hedigan J in *Carrey v ACP Publishing* [1999] 1 VR 875. See also *Sydney Refractive Surgery Centre v Beaumont* [2002] NSWSC 638, [44]–[52] (Simpson J).

more substantially different meanings to the jury. It is important to appreciate the scope of this variation and to remember how the empirical research described in Chapter 4 shows that English lawyers – whichever parties they commonly represent in defamation disputes – see Lucas-Box as central to good litigation practice as do the *Civil Procedure Rules*.[210]

Bennett v Guardian Newspapers was a consolidated action by five police officers who sued over articles in *The Guardian* newspaper.[211] The articles concerned a police anti-corruption investigation called Operation Jackpot and referred to eight unnamed officers from Stoke Newington police station. The articles said the officers had been transferred to other stations after allegations of police corruption related to drugs. The plaintiffs pleaded that the articles meant:

> [That each plaintiff] had been involved in drug dealing and in 'planting' drugs on suspects; and that he had in particular
>
> (1) offered immunity from prosecution to drug dealers in exchange for money;
> (2) given protection to drug dealers who were working on their behalf;
> (3) charged drug users with possessing smaller amounts of drugs than they were arrested with;
> (4) offered drugs as a reward to potential witnesses in a murder inquiry; and
> (5) beaten a suspect in a police van, and then planted drugs in his car and fabricated evidence in an unsuccessful attempt to convict him.[212]

But the newspaper only sought to justify this meaning:

> That [each plaintiff] had been transferred from Stoke Newington police station following allegations of police corruption and/or misconduct, which allegations were being investigated as part of the anti-corruption investigation, Operation Jackpot.[213]

The Court of Appeal said the newspaper's meaning could be 'fairly described as "minimalist"',[214] with the newspaper clearly not seeking to justify the plaintiffs' meanings of actual involvement in corruption. Neither side pleaded a lesser meaning of suspicion, although the plaintiffs were allowed to advance that lesser meaning in the closing speech to the jury. The point for present purposes, however, is that the defence plea was allowed and what Australian courts would probably call substantially different meanings were presented to the jury. They did not concern separate and distinct allegations and both meanings were *capable* of arising from the publications: it was quite arguable in what way, if at all, the unnamed officers were related to the allegations about drugs.

---

210 See above, fns 66–68 and accompanying text.

211 [1998] EWCA Civ 1178.

212 *Ibid* (no pinpoint references available).

213 *Ibid*.

214 *Ibid*.

Another example is provided by *Loveless v Earl*.[215] The defendant financial services company published a letter about terminating the plaintiff's employment. The letter was ambiguous. The plaintiff pleaded the imputation that he had been sacked for illegally offering investment services in breach of relevant financial legislation. The Court of Appeal allowed the defendants to plead a Lucas-Box meaning that the plaintiff had been guilty of different misconduct warranting the termination of his employment. This misconduct included, for example, making false statements in an application to remortgage a house. Again, it is noteworthy that the factual basis relied on for the defence plea would be quite different to that relevant to the plaintiff's meanings. But the two parties' meanings did not concern separate and distinct allegations – rather there was a dispute about the meaning which arose and both parties' meanings were capable of arising as *the* meaning of the publication.

The English situation also differs in relation to Polly Peck meanings. Common sting meanings may be more serious meanings, rather than the less serious meanings required under *Hore-Lacy*. (However, less serious meanings are by far the most common pleading for Lucas-Box meanings.) The English situation can be illustrated by *Khashoggi v IPC Magazines*.[216] In that case, a publication that alleged a number of separate acts of adultery was held capable of conveying a common sting of adulterous promiscuity. Sir John Donaldson MR noted that it arguably was 'not more defamatory to have an extra-marital affair with one person rather than another', at least in the circumstances of that case.[217] But nothing is suggested in *Khashoggi* about the common sting meaning *needing* to be of lesser seriousness than the plaintiff's imputations. It seems that an allegation of promiscuous infidelity often would be more serious than a single allegation of infidelity, so common sting meanings often would be more serious than a plaintiff's meaning. After *Hore-Lacy*, however, a *Khashoggi*-style common sting meaning would appear to be unavailable in Victoria and other Australian jurisdictions which have adopted that approach.

E Australia and Polly Peck

In relation to common sting meanings – rather than Lucas-Box meanings – one further English example can be offered about Polly Peck pleading that could be useful for Australian courts faced with arguments about common sting pleas. As noted already, determining whether a common sting is arguable may be difficult on the facts of a particular case.[218] The English case of *Haslam v Times Newspapers* may offer Australian courts a useful explication of allowable Polly Peck – rather than Lucas-Box – pleas. In *Haslam*, Gray J stated:

> The question whether there is a common sting is plainly fact sensitive, but it appears to me that it will generally be relevant to take into account whether

[215] [1999] EMLR 530.

[216] [1986] 1 WLR 1412.

[217] *Ibid* 1417.

[218] See eg Chapter 4, Part III, D.

> the imputations bear on the same or a closely related sector of the claimant's reputation; whether there is some link or connection between the imputations; whether the imputations share common features, and so on. It may, in addition, be appropriate to pose the question . . . whether the publisher can legitimately claim to have included the imputation not complained of by the claimant because it was material to the imputation of which the claimant did complain. Another possibly helpful test is to pose the question whether the imputation not complained of is in any way probative of the imputation which is the subject of complaint.[219]

So, in relation to Polly Peck pleas, Australian courts may find it useful to consider the sectors of reputation addressed by the imputations, the connection between the imputations, common features to the imputations, and whether the defence meaning is material to or probative of the plaintiff's meaning. But this style of analysis is not required in relation to Lucas-Box pleas. For Lucas-Box, and issues of case management more generally, recent comments from English and NSW cases that are outlined in Chapter 10 easily could be drawn upon.

V CONCLUSION

It is unlikely that any of the above English justification pleas would be allowed in many Australian jurisdictions now. Current precedents suggest a defendant would be allowed to plead the different meaning only to make clear why it denied the plaintiff's meaning.[220] Evidence supporting the defence meaning's truth would not be admissible. This project's research into litigation practice suggests that defendants are unlikely merely to deny the plaintiff's meaning: for example, the *Kennett v Nationwide News* trial discussed in Chapter 6 was a rare situation where the defendant simply denied the plaintiff's meaning.[221] Instead, greater interlocutory activity is likely, with practice becoming more technical and more removed from the publication. In addition, the review of approaches demonstrates why defendants should be able to raise a Lucas-Box plea: 'Far from raising a false issue, it directs attention to the very essence of the dispute.'[222]

This chapter has engaged closely with Australian case law and drawn on the comparative legal analysis and empirical research that has been set out earlier in the book. It has done this to examine how Lucas-Box and Polly Peck pleading are dealt with under Australian law, and to suggest particular ways in which the approach should change. The analysis suggests that defence pleading of meaning should be assessed on the basis of the publication in question – not on the basis of

[219] *Haslam v Times Newspapers* (Unreported, QBD, Gray J, 15 November 2001) (no pinpoint references available).

[220] See eg above fn 101.

[221] (Unreported, Vic SC, Ashley J and jury, 11 March 1999) and see Chapter 6, Part II, B.

[222] Gillooly (1999) 193.

the plaintiff's pleaded imputations – and, so long as the defence plea does not concern a separate and distinct allegation, the plea should be open under Lucas-Box and Polly Peck. That is the way in which defamation law most successfully can seek to simplify battles over meaning and to focus litigation on the substance of the publications in question. It will serve the goal of defamation litigation that is – within the law's admittedly limited terms – cost-effective, equitable, practical and timely.

– 10 –

COMPARATIVE DEFAMATION LAW AND PRACTICE

> The tort of defamation is intended to provide a remedy for a person whose reputation has indefensibly been injured. . . . It boils down to determining what the publication means. Or it should. The amount of . . . time, let alone litigants' resources, expended profligately in the determination of what words, sentences and phrases mean is positively scandalous.[1]

> Although I'd always thought [the NSW approach] was a good idea. . . . [But] in light of the development of the common law over 20 or more years of pleading rules or so on – it seems to me to make our statutory cause of action redundant. . . . [Y]ou've got to the stage when you'll ask yourself what is the contribution of this statutory cause of action?[2]

This book has examined defamation law and practice in England and Australia in relation to issues of meaning and qualified privilege, and has discussed the quite different US approach to defamation and speech. In relation to meaning in England and Australia, four related areas have been focussed on: how parties are bound to pleaded meanings, the degree of specificity required in pleaded meanings, how defence meanings are pleaded and considered in litigation and the stage of disputes at which differences on meaning are dealt with. With regard to *Reynolds* and *Lange* privileges,[3] the strength, scope and trial practicality of each defence has been examined. And for the US, the combination of federal and state defamation law has been examined, especially in its relevance to media publications. Some of the issues most connected with meaning – Lucas-Box and Polly Peck pleading – have been examined closely in Chapter 9. That is an area in which this book's combination of doctrinal and empirical research has produced detailed arguments about the law. The analysis has relevance to Australia, in particular, and to England both in terms of defence pleas and any consideration of Australian precedents about meaning. This chapter discusses other matters related to the treatment of a publication's meaning in defamation. It also examines issues related to *Reynolds* and *Lange* privilege and to US defamation law. In these areas, the chapter discusses implications from the research set out in earlier chapters. The overriding aim has been to inquire about important elements of defamation law and litigation practice in England,

---

[1] Levine (1999) [12].

[2] Interview 45SC (from NSW).

[3] *Reynolds v Times Newspapers* [2001] 2 AC 127; *Lange v Australian Broadcasting Corpn* (1997) 189 CLR 520.

Australia and the US – and, through that, to provide a basis for other comparative consideration, whether scholarly or professional, of defamation in these countries.

Part I of this chapter examines implications of the research for England and Australia in relation to meaning – beyond the issues of Lucas-Box and Polly Peck addressed in Chapter 9. NSW is a particular focus, because of its unusual cause of action and limited jury trial. What, if any, changes to NSW practice appear desirable and possible under the current law? What, if any, legislative reforms are suggested for NSW? And, at least as importantly, what does the NSW experience suggest for England and Victoria? As this chapter's opening quotations suggest, NSW law may have the most to learn about simplifying meaning: developments since the *Defamation Act 1974* (NSW) was enacted mean the common law now deals comparatively well with issues of meaning. And as noted at the start of Chapter 9, the research suggests that the NSW approach limits the ability of defendants to respond to claims, shifts attention towards the imputations over other issues, and encourages pre-trial meaning disputes – all of which offers support for judicial criticism of the NSW statutory regime.[4] But the analysis in Part I also emphasises the value in developing case management practices for dealing with issues of meaning in defamation. Important English examples exist under the *Civil Procedure Rules*, which could be very influential under NSW's changed procedural regime with its *Civil Procedure Act 2005*. But English decisions preceding the *Civil Procedure Rules* could be drawn on more generally in Australia. Part I also examines the implications of 2004 and 2005 proposals for uniform national defamation law in Australia – proposals that, at the time of writing, had reached broad state agreement about the terms for new law and one state, South Australia, had the Defamation Bill 2005 before its parliament. The crucial point to appreciate about such uniform defamation law is that almost every issue addressed in this book related to meaning, justification, opinion defences and qualified privilege would remain relevant under the changes. If Australia finally does lose its distinctive variation in defamation law – it is a particular issue because Australian courts do not adopt a US-style single publication rule when plaintiffs sue over material published in multiple states – the book's detailed analysis of what the law and practice has been should be valuable for English and US lawyers, as well as Australian readers when faced with issues of how best to understand and develop their systems.

In Part II, the chapter examines some of the research's implications about *Reynolds* and *Lange* privileges, as well as the defence under s 22 of the *Defamation Act 1974* (NSW). The defences' scope, strength and litigation practicality are examined, as are ways of developing the Australian law in light of the empirical material discussed in Chapter 7. The comparative material about privilege could be particularly useful under proposals for uniform Australian defamation law. Then, in Part III, the chapter sets out five points

[4] See eg *Lange* (1997) 189 CLR 520, 578 (Kirby J); *Hughes v Seven Network* (Unreported, NSW SC, Levine J, 13 November 1998) (BC9806166).

about the US position, with the aim of clarifying some issues that appear relevant for both US and non-US comparative analysis: the very different way in which meaning arises; the steps through which most media-related defamation cases proceed; the usual expertise of lawyers and judges; the US focus on the status of the plaintiff far more than the subject matter of the publication; and the way that the complexity of US litigation *may* be less than suggested in some of the prior research. Overall, the material provides the background for US readers to appreciate how issues about meaning, justification, opinion and privilege operate in England and Australia – under a very different procedural regime to the US – and for English and Australian readers to appreciate that the US law in its operation involves far more than the *Sullivan* rules, as important a doctrinal difference as they are from English and Australian law.

One further point must be emphasised at the outset. The chapter criticises certain aspects of NSW law and some of the justifications given for it in the literature. This result was not expected when research began. The wealth of NSW judgments and its detailed statutory provisions were expected to offer valuable material for other jurisdictions. Undoubtedly this is true, in part. But it appears the common law may offer valuable lessons for improving defamation law and litigation, especially for efforts within a relatively traditional framework; for example, one that does not require plaintiffs to prove falsity. The 1995 Report of the NSW Law Reform Commission remains the most significant Australian or English proposal for substantial reform of that kind.[5] But such change has not been taken up in more recent Australian reform efforts. Some of the Law Reform Commission's comments relevant to meaning, however, *are* important for this research, and they are analysed in Part I. In particular, questions are raised about the imputation-based cause of action and the limited jury role, and it is argued that reasons offered for the law deserve re-examination.

I COMPARATIVE LESSONS ABOUT MEANING

Beyond the significant issue of Lucas-Box and Polly Peck pleas, which has been examined closely in Chapter 9, what lessons related to meaning are suggested for each jurisdiction from this research? What changes, if any, to NSW practice appear desirable and possible under the current law? What legislative reforms, if any, are suggested by the research for NSW – in terms of the imputation-based cause of action and the jury's role? What does the NSW experience suggest for England and Victoria? And what can be said of the planned uniform defamation law in Australia and of changes to civil procedure in NSW? These related areas are addressed in Sections A to E.

[5] NSW Law Reform Commission (1995).

A Changes in NSW practice

The view that NSW defamation litigation is unnecessarily complex with regard to meaning largely is supported by this research, as is described in Chapter 9's summary of the interview and court file research on meaning.[6] The research also suggests a weakness in the sophisticated doctrinal analysis undertaken by Hunt J over many years in the NSW Defamation List. His judgments undoubtedly can form the basis of innovative legal arguments – an example is offered in the description in Chapter 2 of the possible relevance to *conveyed* meaning of a publisher's *intended* meaning.[7] And his contribution through the case law, especially on interlocutory matters, rightly is seen as substantial. He is a 'doyen of defamation judges' whose judgments 'did much to demystify and elucidate the law of defamation both in NSW and elsewhere'.[8] But the judgments also appear to have played a significant role in complicating the law on meaning and focussing unwarranted attention on imputations – in many regards, of course, these developments understandably built on the imputation-based cause of action in defamation in NSW. But if the complexities are not overcome, it may be true that the tort of defamation 'will be dead, the remedy will be dead, the rights will be dead'.[9] Three areas for change are raised by the research in relation to NSW practice under the *Defamation Act 1974* (NSW), concerning the precision required in pleading imputations, the operation of the Defamation List, especially in relation to pre-trial hearings, and the treatment of 'substantial' for the defences of truth and contextual truth.

As the interviews suggested, a change in judicial personnel appears to have modified some of the strictness of the law on specificity. This has extended to the NSW Court of Appeal, where a notable example is the decision in *Greek Herald v Nikolopoulos*.[10] Although the court split over a principle about specificity, the majority view has been applied in NSW subsequently to dismiss pre-trial challenges to imputations.[11] The case suggests that a change of emphasis has occurred in the Defamation List at least since 2002, which the findings of this research would strongly support.

In *Greek Herald v Nikolopoulos*, the directors of a soccer club sued a newspaper over a number of articles. They pleaded imputations including:

(c) the plaintiffs lied to members of the Canterbury Marrickville Olympic Soccer Football Club;

(d) the plaintiffs hid from members of the Canterbury Marrickville Olympic Soccer Football Club a more advantageous offer for the sale of the Club's property.[12]

---

6 See Chapter 9, Part III.

7 See Chapter 2, Part III, E.

8 Gillooly (1998) 52 and its note 125.

9 Levine (1999) [16]; see also Kenyon (2000) 100.

10 (2002) 54 NSWLR 165.

11 See below, fns 22–24 and accompanying text.

12 (2002) 54 NSWLR 165, [34] (Young CJ in Eq).

During the 7A hearing, the defendants sought a direction for the jury to consider whether each imputation was defamatory by examining it *in isolation*. The defendants accepted that, when deciding whether imputations are conveyed, imputations can be examined in the context of the publication. But the defendants argued s 9 made context irrelevant for deciding whether imputations are defamatory. Counsel submitted:

> [W]hen one assesses whether [imputation (c)] is defamatory, one looks just at those words, and does not import into them . . . what the lie was about, which one knows from the article, why the lie was told, of which the plaintiffs assert one version in earlier imputations. . . . [It] would be wrong for [the jury] to import anything about the lie at all from the article. All they know is, as it is drafted, the plaintiffs lied to the members of the club. . . . They do not know why, or with what result or intent.[13]

At the 7A trial, Dowd J rejected this submission and said:

> [T]he imputations can only be looked at in the light of the context, the jury cannot divorce its mind . . . as an ordinary reasonable reader, from the whole of the article, because it is an impression that they are looking at. . . . [If counsel's] contention is correct . . . it would oblige prolix and unnecessary complex questions which would unnecessarily fetter the jury in the difficult task they have.[14]

The jury held the above two imputations were conveyed, but found that only imputation (c) was defamatory.

An appeal rejected equivalent defence arguments, and provided a passage that appears very useful for improving NSW defamation practice. Mason P, with agreement from Wood CJ at CL, stated:

> The pleader's task is to capture the essence of the specific matters imputed in relation to the plaintiff. Necessarily there will be questions of degree and 'if a problem arises, the solution will usually be found in considerations of practical justice rather than philology' (per Gleeson CJ in *Drummoyne* . . .). In this as in other areas, pleadings serve the ends of justice: they must not be permitted to assume an independent self-referential function. The pleaded imputation . . . is not a straitjacket, although the rules of procedural fairness place limits upon judge and jury's capacity to enlarge the issues. . . .
>
> These considerations point to the broader issue of principle. Words, a fortiori words not found in the text, are necessarily to be read in context. This is a basic tenet of literary and legal construction. . . . Holmes J reminds us that:
>
>> A word is not a crystal, transparent and unchanged, it is the skin of a living thought and may vary greatly in color and content according to the circumstances and the time in which it is used.[15]

---

[13] *Ibid* [9] (Mason P).

[14] *Ibid* [10].

[15] *Ibid* [18]–[21] quoting Holmes J in *Towne v Eisner* 254 US 418, 425 (1918) (citations omitted).

Thus, the argument of the defendants 'may befit a philosophy seminar' but was 'so divorced from the reality of the true dispute between the litigants as to be a wasteful perversion of justice.'[16] The extent to which this differs from the older NSW approach is suggested by the third judgment. Young CJ in Eq agreed there should be no new trial, but based this on the defendants' delay in raising the pleading argument.[17] He differed substantially in his reasoning and said the statutory cause of action in NSW required imputations to be pleaded with precision and their defamatory quality to be assessed on their own terms, divorced from the context of the publication and unlike the common law.[18]

Two points about *Greek Herald v Nikolopoulos* are significant here. First, Mason P quoted extensively from the NSW Law Reform Commission's 1971 report in evaluating the defence arguments.[19] This attention to the original aims of introducing s 9 is welcome, and the general issue is explored below in Section B. Second, Mason P stated:

> The principle which I would uphold . . . must not become the passport to sloppy or ambiguous pleading of imputations. It is . . . incumbent on the parties to thrash out the true issues at the pre-trial stages. If a pleaded imputation lacks a sting or if the sting has multiple barbs, then the plaintiff should be challenged to clarify the pleaded imputation.[20]

As can be seen in contemporary English judgments discussed below, the court is seeking a balance between simplifying issues before trial and avoiding time-consuming hearings.[21] The judgment of Mason P was quickly applied in the Defamation List and his emphasis on 'practical justice' provided a simple method of rejecting some challenges to imputations' form. For example, challenges to imputations such as the plaintiff 'is anti-social because he kept objectionable rubbish on his property' and 'has attempted to frustrate' orders of the local council were rejected by explicitly examining the imputations in the context of the publications and quoting most of the above passage from Mason P.[22] That is, the imputations did not lack specificity when understood in the context of the publications. Similarly, an imputation alleging that the plaintiff was 'volatile' was not imprecise in the context of the publication in question.[23] And a challenge to

---

[16] *Ibid* [23].

[17] *Ibid* [39]–[40].

[18] *Ibid* [44]–[46] and [52] summarising and then endorsing counsel's submissions.

[19] *Ibid* [14], quoting NSW Law Reform Commission (1971) [44]–[51].

[20] *Ibid* [28].

[21] See below, Part II, D, 3.

[22] *Justelius v Michael Southern and Associates* [2002] NSWSC 348, [21], [42]–[43] and [48] (Levine J), although another challenge succeeded in relation to the imputation: 'By failing to clean up his property the Plaintiff encouraged local vandals.' Levine J agreed that the imputation may 'refer to a "*static*" state of affairs or an active role on the part of the plaintiff' (emphasis in original), but actually ruled the imputation out on capacity grounds: [26].

[23] *Cohen v Sir Moses Montefiore Jewish Homes* [2003] NSWSC 502, [22] and [84] (Simpson J).

an imputation that plaintiffs 'acted perversely in finding [a rugby player] guilty of striking another player' was rejected by emphasising that context can be used to reinforce the 'lay' meaning of a word contained in an imputation.[24] The *Greek Herald* decision also has been relied on to rule that an imputation is incapable of being defamatory,[25] in determining whether pleaded imputations differ in substance,[26] and when deciding whether an imputation relates to a matter of public interest.[27] The statements made in *Greek Herald v Nikolopoulos* have become an orthodox and frequent reference.[28] Levine J explained the approach in these terms:

> *Nikolopoulos* does not in any way derogate from the requirement of proper pleading as propounded by Gleeson CJ in *Drummoyne*. . . . In my view *Nikolopoulos* . . . recognises the good sense and reality that imputations simply cannot be viewed, in terms of both form, that is, on a pleading basis, or on capacity, in the abstract. Recourse can, and good sense demands that it must be, had to that which generates the grievance namely the matter complained of which has been published.[29]

This response to pleading challenges relies on a strong reading of the comments of Gleeson CJ in *Drummoyne*, which are referred to in the passage from *Greek Herald* quoted above. In *Drummoyne*, Gleeson CJ said:

> Almost any attribution of an act or condition to a person is capable of both further refinement and further generalisation. In any given case a judgment needs to be made as to the degree of particularity or generality which is appropriate . . . and as to what constitutes the necessary specificity. If a problem arises, the solution will be usually found in considerations of practical justice rather than philology. . . . [T]he question is ordinarily one to be resolved by considerations of practical justice in the circumstances of the particular case, rather than considerations of the possibility of linguistic refinement.[30]

---

[24] *Hall v Gould* [2002] NSWSC 359, [3] and [8]–[9] (Levine J). A similar challenge to an imputation alleging the plaintiffs acted corruptly (with some additional details pleaded) also was rejected by relying on the context of the publication: [13].

[25] *Kriss v John Fairfax Publications* [2003] NSWSC 319.

[26] *Hill v Westfield* [2003] NSWSC 437, [8]–[9] (Simpson J).

[27] *Millane v Nationwide News t/as Cumberland Newspaper Group* [2004] NSWSC 853, [118]–[119] (Hoeben J).

[28] Eg *Saffron v John Fairfax Publications* [2004] NSWCA 254; *Gorman v Barber* [2004] NSWCA 402. It is noteworthy that similar arguments in support of a publication's context under the NSW approach have been made by Kirby J: *John Fairfax Publications v Rivkin* (2003) 201 ALR 77, [123]–[124].

[29] *Obeid v John Fairfax Publications* [2003] NSWSC 563, [11] (Levine J); see also *Kelly v John Fairfax Publications* [2003] NSWSC 586 [41] (Levine J); cf *Ezzo v Grille* [2004] NSWSC 522 [18]–[20] and [31] (Levine J), which should be understood to reflect the ambiguities that still can arise in relation to imputations that the plaintiff 'caused' some state of affairs – ambiguities that may not be resolved by a publication's context.

[30] *Drummoyne Municipal Council v Australian Broadcasting Corpn* (1990) 21 NSWLR 135, 137–138 (Gleeson CJ).

Gleeson CJ then said he was in agreement with the test that Hunt J enunciated in *Whelan v John Fairfax & Sons*: the issue that must be decided in each case is 'whether there is likely to be confusion either at the pleading stage or at the trial in relation to the meaning for which the plaintiff contends'.[31] While the empirical research suggests the *application* of this test in NSW has not focussed necessarily on whether confusion is likely – and it may have paid too much attention to pleaded imputations separated from their publications – the judgments since *Greek Herald v Nikolopoulos* appear to be taking a broader approach. In particular, where publications themselves use words that may be ambiguous, it appears that challenges to imputations will be more difficult. Pleaders probably will be held to have been as specific as warranted in the circumstances of the publication in question.[32] Thus, it may be less a situation of 'sloppy or ambiguous pleading' being endorsed,[33] than overly technical challenges to imputations being rejected. There is an apparent desire to connect imputations more closely with publications and partially answer criticisms of NSW's technicality. Such an approach should be influential elsewhere – whether in the Australian code states or common law jurisdictions in England, Australia and other countries with similar approaches to defamation.

In addition to the concept of 'specificity', the above cases relate to a second area for change under NSW law: the Defamation List's operation. This also can be related to the significant changes to civil procedure in NSW from mid-2005. Earlier changes are examined here before noting the *Civil Procedure Act 2005* (NSW). The aim to simplify pre-trial processes and discourage repeated pleading challenges has been evident for some years. For example, in 1999 Levine J suggested the Defamation List would change. He said that, under the 7A process, the Defamation List would primarily be concerned with capacity issues. Only in the 'clearest of cases' would the jury's decision be pre-empted. In many cases, once capacity has been determined, 'to put it starkly' a party may 'view the opponent's case as pleaded and particularised as "if that's the best they can do let's get on with this litigation at trial"'.[34]

Since then, a new Practice Note and amendments to the Supreme Court rules formalised changes aimed at lessening the number of interlocutory hearings. Levine J extra-judicially described the aims of these changes in a procedural overview for practitioners.[35] He noted the Defamation List had been preoccupied with 'sterile' arguments about meaning:

> The Defamation List seemed to be an arena in which plaintiffs and defendants appeared to be competing for non-existent prizes in drafting, point-taking,

---

31 (1988) 12 NSWLR 148, 155 (Hunt J).

32 Eg *Strasberg v Westfield Ltd (t/a Westfield Hornsby)* [2002] NSWSC 340, [20] (Levine J) in relation to the words 'provocative manner'; *Halkane v John Fairfax Publications* [2002] NSWSC 341, [17] (Levine J) in relation to the plaintiff being 'connected to the underworld'.

33 See above, fn 20 and accompanying text.

34 *Warren v Nationwide News* [1999] NSWSC 446. See also discussion in Kenyon (2000).

35 Levine (2001).

> nit-picking and the loss of sight of the objective of the remedy being pursued. The number of actions litigated at trial was disproportionately low compared to the resources of the Court expended upon the resolution of 'arguments'.[36]

In response to this history, the Practice Note sought to contain pre-trial hearings to two occasions. First, there should be one hearing to deal with all issues prior to the 7A trial, which usually addresses form and capacity issues. Second, where the plaintiff succeeds at the 7A stage, there should be one later hearing to deal with all issues prior to a judge determining defences and remedies in a final hearing. The changed rules required parties to fully particularise their case to disclose all issues in the pleadings,[37] exchange notices in relation to disputes,[38] and related matters. It is not clear to what degree the objectives have been met: that is, whether all issues to be resolved are listed and argued on one of these two occasions. But these efforts to reform the operation of defamation litigation are significant, and this model of driving the matter to trial should be encouraged. Again, there are similarities to English developments, considered below.[39] In addition, the efforts should find great resonance with the general changes to civil litigation in NSW under the *Civil Procedure Act 2005* (NSW).[40] The Act offers a further opportunity to simplify defamation litigation (which is discussed below in Section D).

A third area for possible NSW change under current law arises both from the interviews and the comparative lack of truth pleas in NSW files. It concerns the scope given to the concept 'substantial'. As noted in Part III of Chapter 9, truth appears to be pleaded in NSW in less than one in six defences, and contextual truth in one in eight defences. In Victoria, justification of the plaintiff's meanings appears to be pleaded in one in four defences and Lucas-Box meanings in one in three defences. The interviews suggested that this arises, in part, because plaintiffs plead imputations that are 'full of detail',[41] which cannot be defended by truth. It is 'a competition to see who can draft the tightest imputation' that will be the hardest to justify.[42] It also appeared that defendants had difficulty because a narrow approach is taken to the idea of 'substantial truth' and it is 'very hard to persuade juries or judges that substantial truth means imputation, main gist, no detail.'[43]

---

[36] *Ibid* (no pinpoint references available).

[37] *Supreme Court Rules 1970* (NSW) Pt 67 r 12; and see reference to *Uniform Civil Procedure Rules* (NSW) Chapter 1, Part I, C.

[38] *Ibid* r 12A.

[39] See below, Part I, D, 3.

[40] See Chapter 1, Part I.

[41] 46B.

[42] 41S; similar 39SC, 40SC, 43S, 48B.

[43] 46B. See generally Chapter 5, Part III, C. The quote could be contrasted with the comments of Eady J in *Turcu v News Group Newspapers* [2005] EWHC 799, [108]–[109], which suggests a somewhat broader approach that can be linked to European case law and the need to allow 'a degree of exaggeration' in publishing matters of fact not just opinion. Compared with NSW, it also is notable that justification was made out on the defendant's Lucas-Box meaning: [112]

In light of this, it could be noted that introducing the statutory provision defining substantial truth was not intended to change the common law approach.[44] In its 1971 report, the NSW Law Reform Commission said its aim merely was to affirm *Sutherland v Stopes*,[45] and reject any earlier idea that there was a rigid rule about proving truth:

> The subsection is a statutory affirmation of what Lord Shaw said in *Sutherland v Stopes*. . . . 'If I write that the defendant on March 6 took a saddle from my stable and sold it the next day and pocketed the money all without notice to me . . . and if the facts truly are . . . the defendant did not take the saddle from the stable but from the harness room, and that [the defendant] did not sell it the next day but a week afterwards, but . . . did, without my knowledge or consent, sell my saddle . . . and pocketed the proceeds, then the whole sting of the libel may be justifiably affirmed . . . notwithstanding these errors in detail.'[46]

Judges could emphasise this intent in relation to the concept of substantial truth for the NSW defences, given their role under the 7A process in determining all matters of defence.

These three areas of development appear worthwhile, but the scope for NSW change is limited overall and consideration of legislative amendment also seems warranted – even if long-standing moves (which are examined below in Section E) fail to achieve uniform defamation law in Australia. Two possible changes relevant to meaning particularly stand out. They concern the imputation-based cause of action and the limited jury role. These are two elements that most distinguish NSW from the common law. Each area of possible change is considered next. It is notable that both state and federal uniform defamation law plans would change both these areas – which this research would strongly support.

B Possible changes to NSW legislation: the imputation-based cause of action

This book has suggested through doctrinal analysis and empirical research that the imputation-based cause of action in NSW may be an important source of complexity in NSW defamation litigation.[47] But the imputation-based cause of action has been supported repeatedly by the NSW Law Reform Commission. This project's NSW interviews, however, suggested there was some openness to returning to the common law cause of action,[48] or at least simplifying pleading.[49]

---

44 *DA 1974* (NSW) s 7(2).

45 [1925] AC 47.

46 NSW Law Reform Commission (1971) appendix D [31]; quoting *Sutherland v Stopes* [1925] AC 47, 79.

47 This section draws on Kenyon (2004a).

48 Eg 39SC, 45SC, 46B.

49 47SC.

Similar sentiments appear in a 2001 submission to the NSW Attorney General by the defamation working party of the NSW Bar Association,[50] which argued for the publication to give rise to the cause of action, as at common law. And more recent reform proposals have seen the common law cause of action endorsed, at least for the purpose of achieving national uniformity.[51] Even so, the Law Reform Commission's support for the imputation-based cause of action could suggest that moving to the common law cause of action is not an ideal development. But a close examination of the background of the Law Reform Commission publications relevant to the cause of action suggests they should not hamper its reconsideration at all. This section begins by noting an ACT response to the NSW cause of action. The section's main focus, however, is to investigate the origins of the NSW approach and to argue they did not concern the matters of specificity that subsequently have been offered as important reasons for s 9. In addition, the 1990s NSW literature does not appear to have appreciated the considerable development in the common law as regards defamation pleading.

1 *Australian Capital Territory Community Law Reform Committee*

Some judicial criticism of the NSW approach – in focussing attention on imputations more than publications, and making interlocutory processes more complex – has already been mentioned.[52] Criticism also exists within law reform literature and, in particular, the 1995 report of the Community Law Reform Committee of the ACT.[53] It examined procedural and substantive reforms in light of early-1990s moves towards uniformity in Australian defamation law by Queensland, NSW and Victoria.[54] The Committee recommended a statutory cause of action, but it would be one based on the publication not the imputations:

> [T]he approach in the New South Wales Act tends to encourage barren semantic speculation about the effect of defamatory matter which results in interminable interlocutory skirmishes. The Committee agrees that 'imputations' are properly dealt with by way of particulars and should not give rise to separate causes of action.[55]

The Committee thought defamation cases were prone to interlocutory fights and said '[a]necdotal evidence tends to suggest that many of these are often frivolous

[50] NSW Bar Association (2001) 46–47. The abolition of 7A also was recommended, and amendments to the *District Court Act (DCA) 1973* (NSW) were called for to provide a right to jury trial equivalent to the Supreme Court: see now *DCA 1973* (NSW) s 76B. Membership of the defamation working party is listed at 13.

[51] See below, Part I, E.

[52] See eg above, fn 4 and accompanying text.

[53] Community Law Reform Committee of the ACT (1995).

[54] See below, Part I, E.

[55] Community Law Reform Committee of the ACT (1995) [57].

or misconceived'.[56] The qualitative research underlying this book provides more evidence to support these concerns. And the ACT model of a statutory cause of action that is not based on imputations could be worthwhile for any future NSW reforms or for moves towards uniformity across Australian jurisdictions – if there was not a more substantial move towards the common law basis for the action.

2 NSW Law Reform Commission: 1968 working paper

In its very first working paper,[57] the NSW Law Reform Commission itself was wary of focussing too closely on imputations. This is shown in at least two ways. First, common law plaintiffs then were not required to plead popular innuendo meanings, although in 1964 Lord Devlin in *Lewis v Daily Telegraph* had suggested that such pleading was good practice.[58] The Commission said requiring plaintiffs to plead popular innuendoes and making them bound to the pleadings 'might lead to technicality and rigidity, since "false" innuendoes are not in the nature of things finite in number and perfectly distinct'.[59] Second, when discussing justification the Commission made it clear that the parties may differ as to a publication's meaning. The example of *Lewis v Daily Telegraph* was raised,[60] which is a classic situation of a 'guilt or suspicion' kind of difference between the parties. The Commission suggested that defendants should be able to justify their own meanings (if they also established public interest). The Commission suggested this statutory wording could be appropriate:

> In an action for defamation a defence of justification [requiring public interest] . . . shall not fail, where the words in the sense in which they would reasonably be understood are true, merely because a defamatory inference not shown to be true might be drawn from the true state of affairs to which the words refer, whether reasonably or not.[61]

To a degree, this implies the defendant has argued for the reasonable meaning, and it is not clear how the plaintiff's meaning also would arise under the legal test, although the wording does suggest the plaintiff's defamatory meaning reasonably could be drawn from the publication as well and left undefended. What is noteworthy, however, is the Commission's clear concern about defendants being limited in their ability to respond to plaintiffs' meanings. Coupled with the Commission's concerns about possible technicality and rigidity through being bound to pleaded imputations, it suggests a very different point of view than subsequent publications by the Law Reform Commission. The 1968 proposals were tentative and the Commission later changed its position.

56 *Ibid* [167] and its note 111.

57 NSW Law Reform Commission (1968).

58 [1964] AC 234, 280–81 (Lord Devlin).

59 NSW Law Reform Commission (1968) appendix D [286].

60 *Ibid* [180]; [1964] AC 234.

61 *Ibid* [181].

But later publications may not address closely enough these issues of technicality, rigidity and defendants being limited in their ability to respond to plaintiffs' cases.

3 *NSW Law Reform Commission: 1971 report*

The current NSW approach can be seen first in the Law Reform Commission's 1971 report.[62] The Commission suggested there were 'difficult' and 'unserviceable' distinctions between whether one or multiple causes of action arose in relation to a particular publication. It said the 'purpose of s 9 is to put the matter on a rational basis and to meet the difficulties which inhere in the multiplicity of causes of action.'[63] In part, these difficulties were seen to arise when material was published to many people or was published in several jurisdictions. But the Commission also considered there was a 'related problem of a multiplicity of causes of action by reason of a multiplicity of defamatory imputations conveyed by means of a single report, article, speech or other matter.'[64] The Commission said a legal innuendo certainly creates a separate cause of action, but suggested that doubts existed as to whether popular innuendoes create separate causes of action.[65] It said this gave rise to complexities and uncertainties.[66] However, this appears to be a problem of little practical significance, as the Australian Law Reform Commission has noted.[67] A plaintiff simply could plead a meaning as both a legal innuendo and a popular innuendo in the alternative. This can be seen in the example the Commission discussed. Is it common knowledge or not that Casanova can mean 'libertine'? That would affect whether the meaning could arise as a popular or legal innuendo. The Commission said:

> The meaning of any communication depends in part on what is in the mind of the recipient. To make the existence of a separate cause of action depend on whether extraneous facts are common knowledge or not is bad because to do so is to found a distinction on something inherently unascertainable.

The Commission appears to be saying that 'the mind of the recipient' cannot be known and thus meaning, in any absolute sense, is neither ascertainable nor predictable. This is unexceptionable, as case law and secondary references to the artificiality of meaning for defamation suggest.[68] The Commission continued:

> We think that the solution most likely to promote an analysis which will lead to just results, is to provide that a person defamed has a separate cause of

[62] NSW Law Reform Commission (1971).

[63] *Ibid* appendix D [36].

[64] *Ibid* [41].

[65] *Ibid* [42]–[46].

[66] *Ibid* [47].

[67] Australian Law Reform Commission (1979) [90].

[68] Eg Fleming (1998) 587; see Chapter 2, Part III, D.

> action for each defamatory imputation published [about that person] and for each person to whom the publication is made.[69]

Whether this is true or not, it is notable that no concern about *specificity* was connected with introducing s 9. The Commission was discussing multiple causes of action, not the clarity with which a case is made. And the Commission considered the defects of existing NSW law to centre on conflicts of law, prolixity of pleadings in relation to multiple imputations, reaching verdicts on multiple causes of action and assessing damages.[70] Nothing was mentioned about procedure and specificity as such.

Two further points are important. First, justification was discussed without canvassing the change from the 1968 working paper. Justification was treated as involving only the plaintiff's imputations and no concern was raised about defendants being limited in their ability to respond to plaintiffs' cases.[71] Second, the proposed court rules said each imputation should be specified:

> At present, in the common case of defamation by words, the plaintiff must, as a rule, specify in [the] declaration the words complained of. . . . If [the plaintiff] relies on a false innuendo [the plaintiff] may, but need not, specify the false innuendo in [the] declaration. . . . Under [s 9], each defamatory imputation would support a separate cause of action. It is therefore appropriate that each defamatory imputation should be specified in the statement of claim.[72]

The report was followed by the creation, in the *Defamation Act 1974* (NSW), of a statutory cause of action based on the imputation pleaded by the plaintiff. It is important to note that there is nothing in this explanation to suggest the requirements for each pleaded imputation would differ from the common law – 'specify' appears to be used equivalently for both regimes. And while, at that time, a common law plaintiff *may* have pleaded popular innuendoes, that pleading now *must* be done in all but the exceptional case.

4 NSW Law Reform Commission: 1990s publications

The Law Reform Commission's 1993 discussion paper and 1995 report on defamation may dismiss the common law too quickly, especially given the above background, the existing judicial criticisms of technicality in NSW practice, and this project's empirical research. Two aspects of the 1990s publications can be criticised. First, the original reasons for recommending s 9 have not been addressed clearly. Second, the Commission's description of the common law may be misleading. At the least, these criticisms suggest the justifications offered for the NSW position are insufficient and more evidence would be needed if the cause of action was *not* to be changed.

---

[69] NSW Law Reform Commission (1971) appendix D, [49].

[70] *Ibid* [51]–[56].

[71] *Ibid* [61]–[72].

[72] *Ibid* [319].

The Commission's 1993 discussion paper contains the following about s 9:

> This provision was designed to overcome the 'difficult' and 'unserviceable' distinctions, and 'areas of doubt', arising at common law regarding the cause of action in defamation.
>
> Given that the pleaded imputations constitute the case which the defendant must answer, they must be pleaded with sufficient precision to define the issues. . . .
>
> There has been an 'unfortunate furore' in the case law over the level of precision required when pleading imputations, although this now appears to have been resolved.[73]

An extra-judicial paper by Hunt J was cited to support the apparent resolution of that 'furore', although – as is clear from this and earlier chapters – the matter has not disappeared from NSW cases.[74] But this passage also fails to make clear that the initial recommendation for s 9 apparently had nothing to do with precision and specificity, as those terms subsequently have been used in NSW. In addition, the passage is incorrect if it is taken to suggest that, in 1971, the Commission was concerned about the parties' meanings being clear and specific. Those were not the 'difficult' and 'unserviceable' distinctions raised in 1971 at all.

In relation to the common law, the Commission's 1993 discussion paper said:

> In jurisdictions such as Victoria and England, in circumstances in which the meaning of the words is not clear, the plaintiff *may* plead the meanings which they are alleged to convey. However, the jury is not restricted to those meanings and must decide for itself what meanings the words in fact convey.
>
> The defendant may allege that the words convey a different set of meanings, which again may or may not be accepted by the jury. This means that the defendant may establish defences based on an *entirely different set of meanings* to that pleaded by the plaintiff. The issues to be contested are thus not defined until after the trial has started.[75]

This passage appears misleading in suggesting that common law plaintiffs *may* plead imputations, when in almost every case they *must* plead them. And this has been the situation for as long as the *Defamation Act 1974* (NSW) has existed (as discussed in Part III of Chapter 2). It also could mislead in suggesting that common law defendants can pursue 'an entirely different set of meanings', when only meanings capable of arising from a publication (and meanings that are not separate and distinct from the plaintiff's meanings) can be argued for under Lucas-Box or Polly Peck pleas. The Commission further described the common law:

> A defendant is able to lead evidence that a less serious meaning to that pleaded by the plaintiff was conveyed, and . . . was true. This allows

[73] NSW Law Reform Commission (1993) [4.33]–[4.35].

[74] Hunt (1991) 1, 11–12; and see eg *Marsden v Amalgamated Television Services* [2001] NSWSC 510, [5030] (Levine J). Also see above Part I, A.

[75] NSW Law Reform Commission (1993) [4.37]–[4.38] (emphasis added).

> defendants to use the unfair tactic of leading evidence that they 'almost got it right', which may influence the jury to reduce the damages.
>
> Additionally, the common law approach leads to the waste of much expensive court time. At the conclusion of evidence, a bargaining process often takes place between opposing counsel and the judge to decide which meanings can be left to the jury.[76]

But the defence response described in the first paragraph is not necessarily unfair at all (and this book's research would doubt that time is generally wasted at trial). They are complex questions, as the book has sought to show through considering the parties' legal position as to pleading and litigation practice evidenced by court documents and practitioners' understandings. If defamation remedies are meant to address harm to reputation, the common law approach seems preferable. In any event, the above conclusion of the Commission is less plausible if the common law is understood accurately. And the change from 1968 is marked: then, the Commission expressed serious concern about defendants being limited in their ability to respond to plaintiffs' arguments about meaning.[77] As this book's research demonstrates, this remains a serious concern throughout English and Australian jurisdictions.

The Law Reform Commission's 1995 report contains a similar analysis of the common law. For example, the 1971 recommendations were said to 'promote just results and to overcome both areas of doubt and unserviceable distinctions in the common law' in a manner which could imply that specificity was a concern in 1971.[78] And again it was suggested that common law plaintiffs *may* plead, rather than *must* plead, popular innuendoes and that defendants may allege different sets of meanings:[79]

> The inefficiencies of the common law system include . . . letting the defendant establish defences which are only relevant to the imputations for which it contends and which are never going to be accepted. . . . [T]he Commission also regards as unacceptable the fact that the defendant is able to put before the jury material which is *wholly irrelevant* to the plaintiff's complaint.[80]

The Commission then cited *Polly Peck* as 'an eloquent indictment of the common law system'.[81] In giving a further reference to *Woodger v Federal Capital Press of Australia*,[82] the Commission clearly is referring to both elements of *Polly Peck*, or what are called Lucas-Box and Polly Peck pleas in this book. But this project's empirical research into practice shows that English lawyers would be very

---

[76] *Ibid* [4.40]–[4.41] (footnote omitted). See also *NRMA Insurance v Amalgamated Television Services* (1989) Aust Defamation Reports [50,055].

[77] See above, fn 61 and accompanying text.

[78] NSW Law Reform Commission (1995) [4.2].

[79] *Ibid* [4.3].

[80] *Ibid* [4.4] (emphasis added).

[81] *Ibid* and its note 6; *Polly Peck v Trelford* [1986] QB 1000.

[82] *Ibid*; (1992) 107 ACTR 1, 23–24 (Miles CJ), which describes the defence pleas as two forms of Polly Peck pleading; see Chapter 3, Part I, K.

surprised to hear the common law allows defendants 'to put before the jury material which is *wholly irrelevant* to the plaintiff's complaint'. That is neither the intention nor effect of the common law on defence pleading. In addition, the Commission's suggestion that defendants can justify meanings 'which are never going to be accepted' is not correct in terms of Lucas-Box and Polly Peck pleading. Defence meanings are only allowed to go forward under those pleas if they are capable of arising from the publication; thus it is perfectly possible for the defence pleadings to be *the* meanings that a publication conveys, which is why the whole approach is warranted. While it may appear plausible that greater uncertainty about a publication's meaning exists under the common law and that this increases the cost of litigation, NSW defamation actions appear to occupy more court time pre-trial than in Victoria, and do not appear to be disposed of any more quickly at trial – and much of the NSW court time is concerned with issues of meaning.[83]

The Law Reform Commission concluded its consideration of the basis of the cause of action in these terms:

> Although one submission . . . expressed concern about a trend towards 'increased technicality concerning imputations', there was general support for retaining imputations as the basis of the cause of action. The . . . savings in costs and delay achieved by the precision of carefully pleaded imputations . . . far outweigh any appearance of technicality. . . .
>
> The procedure also has the practical effect that, once the plaintiff's imputation has been accepted, there is usually no real defence to it (the plaintiff having selected the imputation for that purpose). Alternatively, if the plaintiff's imputation has not been accepted, there is no time wasted on the defences pleaded to it.[84]

Two further important points can be made about these conclusions. First, the apparently general support for s 9 noted by the Commission may have been weaker at the time of this project's interviews. At the least, concerns with technicality were evident in some interviews,[85] as they had been in the 'one submission' to the Commission.[86] And those concerns have appeared in subsequent reform publications.[87] Second, the Commission itself suggests a potential unfairness to defendants under the NSW approach: plaintiffs will select imputations to plead that offer 'no real defence'. Again, the contrast with 1968 is striking. Evaluation of this area of defamation law really needs to consider how the law contains *each party's* understandable tactical ambitions in relation to meaning.

---

83 See Chapter 9, Part III.

84 NSW Law Reform Commission (1995) [4.5]–[4.6] (notes omitted).

85 Eg 39SC, 40SC, 41S, 45SC, 46B, 47SC; see also above, fn 50.

86 It was the Young Lawyer's submission, and Judith Gibson is listed as its author: NSW Law Reform Commission (1995) appendix 2. She was appointed a District Court judge from 21 May 2001, giving her an important role in the development of NSW defamation law.

87 Eg NSW Attorney-General's Task Force on Defamation Law Reform (2002) 37.

This review of the origins of s 9 and the more recent justifications that have been offered for it suggests that the historical preference for the imputation-based cause of action in NSW is misplaced. Comments by the NSW Law Reform Commission in the 1990s should not be thought to hamper any change to a cause of action based on the publication. And the comparative empirical work of this project further calls into question the Commission's position. The imputation-based cause of action may not just be 'redundant', as the chapter's second opening quotation suggests, it may be one element that significantly complicates NSW defamation litigation.[88] That has significant implications for other jurisdictions in relation to how NSW precedents are used.

C Possible changes to NSW legislation: the limited jury role

The interviews discussed in Chapter 5 very clearly suggested the 7A process was not supported by many practitioners.[89] Among other descriptions, it was called 'wrongheaded',[90] 'garbage',[91] 'ludicrous',[92] and 'absurd'.[93] Into what context can these criticisms be placed? Two points are important initially. First, worthwhile aims can be seen in the section's introduction; namely, to avoid complexities at trial and simplify and shorten proceedings.[94] These understandable concerns also can be seen in earlier NSW cases that allowed jury determination of meaning at the start of full trials,[95] and in the independent English developments in *Marks & Spencer v Granada Television*.[96] Second, the 7A reforms were less dramatic than those canvassed in the Law Reform Commission's 1993 discussion paper. The Commission suggested in 1993 that splitting aspects of defences between judge and jury added to trials' complexity, especially given the use of jury questionnaires.[97] This led the Commission to canvas the possibility of trial by

[88] It also is worth nothing that Roy Baker's Australian research on the third-person effect (discussed in Chapter 1, Part II, B) suggests the effect might encourage more damaging meanings to be found to be conveyed: Baker (2004) 21–24. Where the parties effectively are held to the plaintiff's pleaded imputations, as in NSW, it seems likely that any such effect would be greater.

[89] See also above, fn 50.

[90] 39SC.

[91] 44SC.

[92] 40SC.

[93] 47SC.

[94] Eg parliamentary debates suggest that an aim of introducing 7A was to avoid complexity at trial: NSW, *Parliamentary Debates*, Legislative Council, 22 November 1994, 5742 (J P Hannaford, Attorney General). There also were suggestions that an independent MP had a particular interest in defamation reform, which the government was interested to support, at least in part, for unconnected political reasons: eg 5843 (Elisabeth Kirkby).

[95] Eg *Radio 2UE Sydney v Parker* (1992) 29 NSWLR 448 and see Chapter 2, Part III, C.

[96] (Unreported, QBD, Popplewell J, 23 February 1998).

[97] NSW Law Reform Commission (1993) [4.5]–[4.6].

judge alone, which it suggested would help matters reach trial more quickly, and create less need for new trials after successful appeals.[98] Against this background, the *Defamation (Amendment) Act 1994* introduced the 7A process and reduced the jury's role without removing it entirely.[99] Research, however, suggests how accurate it is to describe the 7A process as 'generally an unhappy mechanism' in practice.[100] The research raises queries about the reforms in two areas: separating the roles of judge and jury and promoting simplicity.

1 *Judge and jury roles*

The 7A process was intended to separate more clearly the roles of judge and jury by removing defences from the jury. In effect, the section assumes plaintiffs can plead imputations that have no ambiguity – as the entire NSW approach does, to a substantial degree – so an imputation found by a jury will be understood in exactly the same way by the judge. However, that could encourage more formal interpretation of imputations and prompt defendants to challenge more imputations. Comments from NSW interviews support this interpretation and suggest that defending an imputation's truth is more difficult under 7A and arguments about meaning are crucial:

> The judge will have to decide justification later . . . [and] will take a technical approach to something which the jury has not taken a technical approach to. So you really have to get rid of the things . . . before they get to the jury.[101]

In comparison, parliamentary debates when the 7A process was introduced contain various speeches endorsing the limited jury role proposed by the Bill, for example:

> The bill will *maintain the presence of a jury to determine the most important questions of the defamation action*, such as whether the imputations alleged are contained in the material, and whether they are defamatory. It is fitting that such questions be considered by a range of people chosen from the general public, the peers of the plaintiff and the defendant.[102]

If public input into questions of meaning is supported, however, it should extend at least to contextual imputations. Under 7A, contextual imputations are determined by the judge, although the legislative materials provide no reason for this division. And beyond that issue, this research strongly suggests that the jury's role should extend to the defences having most connection with

---

[98] *Ibid* [4.13].

[99] The Bill also included provisions to make truth a defence without requiring a public interest element, but these were removed in amendments.

[100] *El-Azzi v Nationwide News* [2004] NSWSC 929, [8] (Levine J).

[101] 43S; similar 44SC and 45SC; see Chapter 5, Part III, E.

[102] NSW, *Parliamentary Debates*, Legislative Council, 22 November 1994, 5841 (J M Samios) (emphasis added).

meaning: truth, contextual truth and comment. That is, if one wants to 'maintain the presence of the jury to determine the most important questions' about meaning, it may not be helpful to divide these questions about imputations and defences between jury and judge. (Similarly, a limited jury role in relation to extended forms of qualified privilege – even if it resembles the traditional qualified privilege role – appears unhelpful, as discussed below in Part II.)

2 *Promoting simplicity*

Arguments that reducing the jury's role will allow trials to be conducted more quickly sound appealing; they accord with some of my own previous writings on defamation.[103] But the fieldwork in this project suggests that may not be the effect in practice. Juries may be powerful forces for simplicity because lawyers must present cases in a manner that is appropriate to the jury. In all jurisdictions, comments in interviews suggested this important influence of juries; for example:

> [A]t trial . . . all of [the legal nicety] washes away and you have your real dispute, particularly in front of a jury. And the degree of detail that people exhaust themselves on, in these interlocutory stages, *vanishes*. . . . Juries are a wonderful discipline to counsel because you have to . . . conduct the litigation in such a way that you will not lose the interest of the jury . . . that will enable them to understand what the dispute is about, and will enable them to deliberate in some sensible way.[104]

It is possible at least – and this book's research would suggest it is probable – that regular judge-alone trials on defamation defences would allow more complexity to develop in legal arguments and would lengthen trials. As an experienced NSW barrister noted, this is exactly what may have happened with s 9 and the law about specificity: 'If you get a mob of lawyers for 20 years exercising themselves over the conveying of meaning, then they will create year-by-year, layer upon layer of rules and artificiality.'[105]

Supporters of the 7A process could vary the 'simplicity' argument to say the 7A process encourages settlements. But the fieldwork samples did not show a high rate of settlement after 7A hearings.[106] And the high rate of post-7A appeals, mentioned below, also must be noted. Even if 7A was found to encourage settlement, this research suggests caution. For example, one could wonder at the

---

103 Kenyon (2000).

104 56SC (emphasis in original); similar 1B, 49SC, 50B.

105 45SC; and see Chapter 5, Part III, B. A separate but related concern could be the length of time before written reasons might be provided by a judge, in comparison to the comparative speed of jury deliberations.

106 From 10 7A hearings at which plaintiffs succeeded, only one settled. One proceeded to a judge-alone trial and eight remained open at the end of 2000; see above Part I, E.

range of imputations pleaded in each jurisdiction. Is it really the case that NSW defendants should be able to plead truth and comment so much less than the corresponding Victorian defences?[107] It could be suggested that NSW imputations are more specific – which generally appears to be the case – and so defences are controlled more appropriately. But the interview material does not support that position. There is an understandable tendency for plaintiffs in all jurisdictions to seek to craft imputations that cannot be defended. This is a key reason for allowing defence meanings to be pleaded – as in current English law. Of course, the same 'optimistic view'[108] about meanings can be expected of defendants in raising Lucas-Box or Polly Peck pleas. As has already been suggested in relation to defence pleading, *both* parties understandably will be ambitious about pleading.[109] Allowing both parties to face the jury with meanings that are capable of arising from the publication seems the most appropriate course. And not allowing the parties that chance appears to increase pre-trial challenges – as the figures from NSW suggest.

3 *Discussion of 7A*

Overall, the research suggests that it may not be beneficial to split the tribunal of fact because questions of meaning can arise in relation to so many aspects of a trial. If roles are split, two alternatives seem probable: binding plaintiffs to their pleaded imputations, as in NSW, or allowing juries to determine imputations themselves, which occurred in *Marks & Spencer v Granada Television*.[110] As the NSW Law Reform Commission's 1968 comments suggest, there is a danger of technicality and rigidity in binding plaintiffs to pleaded popular innuendo meanings that 'are not in the nature of things finite in number and perfectly distinct.'[111] And the English interviews pointed out difficulties in allowing juries to construct imputations.[112] Overall, the interviews and court transcripts strongly suggest the value in making the jury the tribunal of fact, rather than a judge alone. In addition, what appears to be the high rate of successful appeals against jury findings in 7A hearings suggests weaknesses in a limited jury role.[113] This may remain problematic even following the High Court's 2003 decision in *John*

[107] See Chapter 9, Part III.

[108] Milmo and Rogers (2004) [11.16].

[109] See eg Chapter 3, Part I, B.

[110] (Unreported, QBD, Popplewell J, 23 February 1998).

[111] NSW Law Reform Commission (1968) [286].

[112] See eg Chapter 4, Part III, F.

[113] Eg *Gorman* [2004] NSWCA 402; *Harvey v John Fairfax Publications* [2003] NSWCA 70 and see Chapter 5, Part II, B; *Rivkin* [2002] NSWCA 87 and (2003) 201 ALR 77; *Pavy v John Fairfax Publications* [2002] NSWCA 46; *Buck v Jones* [2002] NSWCA 8; *Mularczyk v John Fairfax Publications* [2001] NSWCA 467; *Cinevest v Yirandi Productions* (2001) Aust Torts Reports ¶81-610. This rate of successful appeals also suggests that more appeals are likely to be brought, even if not all succeed: eg *Sarma v Federal Capital Press of Australia* [2002] NSWCA 93.

Fairfax Publications v Rivkin, which underscored the respect to be paid to defamation jury verdicts – for an appeal to succeed, the challenged decision must be one that 'no reasonable jury could reach'.[114]

The aim of simplicity and a workable trial is very valuable in relation to defamatory meaning. And, for meaning to be dealt with well, at least some defences need to be jury matters. But the NSW Law Reform Commission's concern that leaving defences to juries can create complexity at trial is important to acknowledge. That in turn may suggest the law on all *defences* is an area to simplify. In any event, it is important to note that the question of what tribunal should determine damages can remain a separate consideration. Determining damages, while they exist as the primary remedy,[115] may be an area in which trials can be simplified by giving judges a greater role without shifting the battle onto more pre-trial hearings.

These suggestions should not be taken to imply that a few straightforward judgments or legislative amendments will bring NSW litigation close to common law jurisdictions. This research illustrates that no simple cause-and-effect relationship should be thought to exist between doctrinal law and its application in litigation. For example, repealing s 9 is unlikely to transform NSW pleading practice into exactly the Victorian or English approach. But changes may influence practitioners and move NSW practice in the direction of what appears to be useful in the common law; for example, the way in which the parties' pleadings often set out the area of dispute on meaning which can then be left until trial, the way imprecise pleadings need not be challenged pre-trial but can be responded to with Lucas-Box pleas and so forth.[116] These issues also are important to examine in relation to long-standing efforts to achieve uniformity in Australian defamation law, which is discussed below after considering the project's further implications for England and Australia.

D Further implications for the common law: England and Australia

Probably the most important lessons for the common law's treatment of meaning were discussed in Chapter 9: Lucas-Box and Polly Peck pleading. In short, less technicality is preferable when dealing with meaning in defamation and it appears useful not to seek precision to the degree that has happened in NSW. In 1971, the NSW Law Reform Commission suggested that the common law – and

114 *Rivkin* (2003) 201 ALR 77, [179] and [185] (Callinan J). See generally Rolph (2003). At least some later challenges in NSW have been rejected: *Beran v John Fairfax Publications* [2004] NSWCA 107; *Maitland v Nationwide News* [2004] NSWCA 155; *Pavy* [2004] NSWCA 177; *Australian Broadcasting Corpn v Reading* [2004] NSWCA 411, which also illustrates further difficulties that can arise in the 7A process where jury answers are unclear. In addition leave to appeal against jury decisions in the 7A process has been refused in cases such as *Saffron* [2004] NSWCA 254; *Nationwide News v Carmichael* [2005] NSWCA 56.

115 Cf eg Barendt (1999); Chesterman (2000) 180–91.

116 See eg Chapter 6, Part IV.

particularly the defence of fair comment – displayed 'a tendency, noted both here and in England, to an over-refinement of doctrine'.[117] This research suggests it is now NSW defamation law that displays an over-refinement of doctrine, and not merely in relation to comment. Thus the primary lessons for the common law are to understand the roles of ss 9 and 7A in the NSW legislation and the litigation practices that exist under them. In particular, efforts to draw on NSW case law should be very carefully evaluated in all other jurisdictions, and courts should keep in mind how the peculiarities of ss 9 and 7A mean that some of the fine distinctions made in NSW law need not be applied elsewhere. Such care has not always been apparent in Australian judgments and English commentary, in particular, but simple statements such as that of Gillard J in *Waters v Western Australian Newspapers* are a useful reference: 'One must be very careful in quoting any New South Wales decision in this area, for the very obvious reason that in New South Wales, the imputation is a cause of action.'[118]

For example, the law on implications, inferences and speculation in NSW does not appear to be a major element of practice.[119] NSW interviews suggested that practitioners did not understand any unproblematic difference between implications and inferences, or when a meaning depends on drawing an inference on an inference.[120] And nothing in the NSW fieldwork suggested that these tests could be explained well to a jury. It is unclear what the terms add to the practicality of litigation. Instead, arguments about implications, inferences and speculation should be seen as part of the 'saraband'[121] of pre-trial arguments about pleading – something that appears markedly different to the presentation of cases at trial, even in NSW.[122] The distinctions between inferences, implications and speculation may be too fine and context-specific to be useful for the common law. Beyond these general points, several areas are worth examining in relation to the common law, relating to *Marks & Spencer v Granada Television*,[123] the early disposal of claims, case management, conditional fee agreements and opinion.

1 The trial stage for determining meaning: Marks & Spencer and 7A

As described in Chapters 2 and 4,[124] the decision in *Marks & Spencer* was seen as important when it was delivered – especially after it was approvingly cited by

[117] NSW Law Reform Commission (1971) [34].

[118] [2004] VSC 124, [38].

[119] Notwithstanding cases such as *Marsden* (1998) 43 NSWLR 158, 167 (Hunt CJ at CL; Mason P and Handley JA agreed) and its affirmation by *TCN Channel 9 v Antoniadis* (1998) 44 NSWLR 682; see also Chapter 2, Part III, B.

[120] See Chapter 5, Part III, B.

[121] *Morrell v International Thomson Publishing* [1989] 3 All ER 733, 734 (May LJ).

[122] See eg Chapter 5, Part II, B and discussion of *Randwick Labor Club v Amalgamated Television Services* (NSW SC, Abadee J and jury, 29–30 March 2000).

[123] (Unreported, QBD, Popplewell J, 23 February 1998).

[124] See Chapter 2, Part III, C and Chapter 4, Part III, F.

Hirst LJ in *Shah v Standard Chartered Bank*.[125] The decision, however, has not proved to be a watershed. This largely may be due to the other methods for early disposal that now exist under the *Civil Procedure Rules* and *Defamation Act 1996*, which are discussed below. But concerns about the *Marks & Spencer* approach and mitigation also have been raised (see Part III of Chapter 4). So an initial point is made here about mitigation, before generally analysing the stage at which meaning is determined.

A slightly more flexible approach to mitigation evidence was set out in *Burstein v Times Newspapers*,[126] as noted in Part I of Chapter 3. Evidence will be admissible about matters of 'directly relevant background context' to the publication.[127] If such context evidence was admitted liberally, defendants' concerns about allowing an early jury determination of meaning could be substantially lessened. But cases since *Burstein* suggest that context evidence will be controlled carefully, notwithstanding some submissions by counsel that the decision is revolutionary.[128]

Even if greater change develops for mitigation evidence, an important concern will remain about the *Marks & Spencer* approach; namely, allowing the jury to determine its own meaning. (Similar issues about juries determining meaning can arise in relation to qualified privilege, as *Jameel v Wall Street Journal Europe SPRL (No 2)* illustrates.[129]) This concern suggests that calls could emerge to adopt something resembling NSW's 7A process. In such a proposal, introducing an imputation-based statutory cause of action could be considered to make the model workable, or the law amended so that claimants are held to their pleaded meanings. Such changes should not be thought particularly likely, but they are worth examining in light of the NSW court material and interviews, which suggested ss 9 and 7A underlay much of the state's complexity about meaning.[130]

---

[125] [1999] QB 241, 265–66 approving *Marks & Spencer v Granada Television* (Unreported, QBD, Popplewell J, 23 February 1998); see Shillito and Barendt (1999) 370, 373 who suggested the case 'may be a very significant development'.

[126] [2001] 1 WLR 579.

[127] *Ibid* 598 (May LJ, Sir Christopher Slade and Aldous LJ agreed).

[128] Eg *Burstein* was described as 'radical and innovative' by counsel in *Berezovsky v Forbes* [2001] EMLR 45, [15] (Sedley LJ for Eng CA); but see eg *MacIntyre v Chief Constable of Kent* (Unreported, QBD, Gray J, 1 February 2002); *Windsor v Boycott* (Unreported, QBD, Eady J, 9 May 2001).

[129] [2005] EWCA Civ 74, [84]; also see [94] (Lord Phillips MR for Eng CA). (In May 2005, the House of Lords granted permission to appeal in this case.) In *Jameel*, the jury was not asked 'to define precisely the gravity of the defamatory meaning of the article' that it found conveyed, which the Court of Appeal endorsed: the 'precise nature of the defamatory sting' was not capable of affecting the result with regard to *Reynolds* privilege in this case. Comparative research suggests the jury should not be asked for a meaning where that is possible and, where the level of meaning is significant, it should be dealt with in terms of the 'three levels' approach used in England: see Chapter 2, Part I, J.

[130] Eg 39SC, 40SC, 45SC, 46B; and see above, fn 105.

That material offers substantial evidence against England making imputations the cause of action or holding claimants to pleaded imputations. Parties would be likely to pay greater attention to pleaded imputations under such changes, increasing pre-trial activity and counteracting any benefits of quicker trials. The research suggests that jury trials have significant strengths, especially in avoiding an 'over-refinement' of doctrine on specificity and pleading. Rather than looking to 7A, the research supports Patrick Milmo's suggestion to require juries to choose between claimants' and defendants' meanings, if the *Marks & Spencer* approach is pursued at all.[131] Such an approach may remain suitable for occasional cases, where there is no issue on liability apart from meaning.[132] But it seems that such cases will be rare and the general English approach to meaning is preferable. Concerns exist with any detailed jury questionnaires about meaning, in that they can move the trial's focus from the publication to the pleaded imputations. In any event, the rare cases like *Marks & Spencer* also may suit early disposal, which is examined next.

2 *Early disposal: Civil Procedure Rules and Defamation Act 1996*

Two avenues exist for early disposal of defamation claims in England: summary judgment under Pt 24 of the *Civil Procedure Rules* and the *Defamation Act's* summary disposal provisions in ss 8–10. It also is worth noting the offer of amends procedure under the *Defamation Act 1996*. Part 24 allows for summary judgment to be granted in any type of proceeding,[133] when a party has 'no real prospect' of success in relation to a claim (or an issue within a claim) and there is no other compelling reason for trial.[134] It thus appears to apply normal summary judgment procedures to defamation, unlike the traditional English position.[135] But case law has shown that it only will be available in certain situations: effectively, it is limited to questions within the judge's role because of the right to a jury trial for defamation under s 69 of the *Supreme Court Act 1981*. Thus, to be suitable for summary judgment, all questions must be able to be disposed of by the judge and there can be no issue of fact that could properly be left to a jury.[136] This still allows for 'a fair degree of judicial creativity',[137] particularly in light of the *Civil Procedure Rules'* overriding objective to deal justly with disputes in proportion to the amount, importance and complexity of the issues and with

[131] Milmo (1998) 656. The meanings could be pleaded with the flexibility that currently exists.

[132] Eg *Kennett v Nationwide News* (Unreported, Vic SC, Ashley J and jury, 11 March 1999) and see Chapter 6, Part II, B.

[133] *Civil Procedure Rules 1998* (Eng) (*CPR*) r 24.3.

[134] *CPR* rr 24.3 and 24.2.

[135] See Chapter 2, Part III, A.

[136] *Safeway Stores v Tate* [2001] QB 1120; *Alexander v Arts Council of Wales* [2001] 1 WLR 1840; *Spencer v Sillitoe* [2003] EMLR 10.

[137] Price and Duodu (2004) [29.06].

consideration of the parties' relative positions.[138] Summary judgment could be available for some meaning disputes, such as for publications incapable of being defamatory.[139] But a more common use probably will relate to qualified privilege, where relevant facts are not disputed or any case of malice is weak.[140]

The specific summary disposal provisions of the *Defamation Act 1996* set out an alternative that is available, at least where a party seeks to dispose of the entire claim.[141] The process provides for a judge-alone hearing, in which the claimant's case can be dismissed 'if it appears to the court that it has no realistic prospect of success and there is no reason why it should be tried'.[142] Alternatively, the claimant can be granted summary relief if it appears that no defence has a realistic prospect of success and there is no other reason for a trial.[143] The 'no realistic prospect of success' test under the *Defamation Act 1996* is equivalent to the Pt 24 test of 'no real prospect' of succeeding.[144] The claimant's summary relief can comprise four elements: damages up to £10,000, a declaration of the defamatory publication's falsity, an order the defendant publish a correction and apology and an order restraining further publication.[145] Unless the claimant has sought summary disposal, the court must be satisfied these remedies offer sufficient compensation.[146] If the parties cannot agree on the terms for a correction and apology, the court can order the defendant to publish a summary of its judgment.[147] The legislation sets out non-exclusive factors that the court must consider when deciding if a trial is warranted.[148] These include the extent of any conflict of evidence and the seriousness of the alleged defamation. It is worth noting that, because no evidence is admissible on natural and ordinary meanings, courts could grant summary disposal when parties disagree about a publication's meanings.

As mentioned in Chapter 4, the summary disposal provisions came into force in April 2000, well after most of the *Defamation Act* and only just before the initials English interviews.[149] Subsequent cases have shown that claimants can

---

138 *CPR* Pt 1.

139 *Alexander* [2001] 1 WLR 1840; Price and Duodu (2004) [29.25].

140 Eg *Regan v Taylor* [2000] EMLR 549, which was decided on the first day of the *CPR*'s operation; *Adoko v Lewis* [2002] EWHC 848.

141 A party must choose whether to seek an order under *CPR* Pt 24 or *DA 1996* (UK) s 8: *CPR* 53.2. The summary disposal provisions' origins are discussed in *James Gilbert v MGN* [2000] EMLR 680, 684 (Eady LJ).

142 *DA 1996* (UK) s 8(2).

143 *Ibid* s 8(3).

144 Eg *Mosley v Focus Magazin Verlag* [2001] EWCA Civ 1030.

145 *DA 1996* s 9(1).

146 *Ibid* s 8(3).

147 *Ibid* s 9(2); see also *CPR* 53 PD 5.3.

148 *Ibid* s 8(4); *James Gilbert* [2000] EMLR 680, 683 (Eady LJ).

149 See Chapter 4, Part IV, A.

choose to limit damages to £10,000,[150] and defendants can abandon defences for the purpose of summary disposal.[151] Both these decisions can remove hurdles that would weigh heavily against granting summary relief: the limited compensation that is available and the conflicts of evidence that could require jury trial. In addition, defendants may succeed where publications have no real prospect of being found defamatory or of identifying claimants.[152] But it appears unlikely that any apology will be ordered where defendants maintain their belief in the publication's truth.[153] The provisions would be interesting for Australian consideration, as they show some resemblance to the declaration of falsity proposed by the NSW Law Reform Commission,[154] and English courts have recognised that the speed of summary disposal may justify lower damages awards. A solicitor suspected of being a vindictive liar by a publication, for example, was awarded £5,000 even when the claimant argued that more than the £10,000 limit was required.[155] However, this sort of situation may not be particularly common. What appears most important for this book in the summary judgment and summary disposal provisions is the influence of the *Civil Procedure Rules'* overriding objectives and the more active case management that English courts have adopted under it, which is explored in the next section. Given the *Civil Procedure Act 2005* (NSW), there is great scope for NSW courts to adapt elements of the English experience under the *Civil Procedure Rules*.

One further point is noteworthy about these two avenues for early disposal in England. The specific statutory basis of the *Defamation Act 1996* provisions may mean that summary disposal is available more readily than summary judgment under Pt 24. For example, in *Gillick v Brook Advisory Centres*,[156] Gray J determined that a publication was not defamatory, rather than making the more traditional determination of whether defamatory meanings were capable of arising from the publication (although that occurred without argument[157]). An ability to determine the actual meaning of words may be inconsistent with appellate decisions about the summary judgment provisions.[158] But the separate provisions

[150] *Loutchansky v Times Newspapers (No 2)* [2002] QB 783, [88]–[101] (Lord Phillips MR for Eng CA); *James Gilbert* [2000] EMLR 680, 703 (Eady LJ).

[151] *Milne v Telegraph Group* [2001] EMLR 30, 771 (Sir Oliver Popplewell).

[152] See, respectively, *Gillick v Brook Advisory Centres* (Unreported, QBD, Gray J, 12 March 2002); *Mosley* [2001] EWCA Civ 1030.

[153] *Loutchansky (No 2)* [2002] QB 783, [100] (Lord Phillips MR for Eng CA).

[154] NSW Law Reform Commission (1995) [2.16]–[2.20].

[155] *Milne* [2001] EMLR 30, 770 and 776 (Sir Oliver Popplewell). But summary disposal was refused in *Burstein v Times Newspapers* [2001] 1 WLR 579; it seems largely because the £10,000 limit was seen as too low, although a jury later awarded only £8,000.

[156] (Unreported, QBD, Gray J, 12 March 2002).

[157] *Ferguson v Associated Newspapers* (Unreported, QBD, Gray J, 15 March 2002).

[158] Price and Duodu (2004) [29.06], citing *Alexander* [2001] 1 WLR 1840; but cf [29.25] where the ability to determine meaning under *DA 1996* ss 8–10, is noted without criticism.

under ss 8–10 of the *Defamation Act 1996* do appear to support judges dealing with cases that turn on meaning in a summary fashion, especially where appropriate damages would fall within the £10,000 limit of the provisions.[159]

In relation to summary procedures, it also is worth examining the offer of amends process. The provisions under ss 2–4 of the *Defamation Act 1996* (UK), which have operated since early 2000, appear to be vastly more popular than the historical provisions under the 1952 Act.[160] The changed climate under the *Civil Procedure Rules* and the influence of other summary approaches in defamation appear to have been significant in this. Under the process, an offer is to make a 'suitable correction' and 'sufficient apology', to publish them in a reasonable and practical manner, and to pay such compensation and costs as are agreed or determined.[161] If the parties do not agree to a sum under the process, damages are assessed by a judge; under this process, the damages appear to have been reduced significantly.[162] In terms of one of this book's themes, it is noteworthy that offers can be qualified to relate to particular meanings.[163] But more significant overall is the strong defence that is given when a claimant rejects an offer of amends. To defeat the defence, claimants must establish that publishers knew or had reason to believe three things: the material identified them, it conveyed a defamatory meaning and that meaning was false.[164] It appears that 'reason to believe' will not be easy to establish and it amounts to a requirement of recklessness.[165] It also seems that offers will be rejected only rarely – in part because of the courts' approach – which means it may be some time before a useful comparison could be made between the requirements of proving actual malice under the *Sullivan* rules and the requirements for defeating an offer of amends.[166]

Provisions similar to the earlier English law applied in NSW under ss 36–45 of the *Defamation Act 1974* (NSW). From 25 August 2003, they were replaced by ss 9A to 9G, which, as yet, appear to have been little used.[167] While offering an apparently strong defence, the sections require the offer to have been made as soon as was practical after the defendant became aware the matter was (or might

---

[159] A useful discussion exists in *Ferguson* (Unreported, QBD, Gray J, 15 March 2002).

[160] *DA 1952* (UK) s 4.

[161] *DA 1996* (UK) s 2(4).

[162] See eg *Nail v News Group Newspapers* [2005] EMLR 12; *Cleese v Clark* [2004] EMLR 3; *Turner v News Group Newspapers* [2005] EWHC 892.

[163] *DA 1996* (UK) s 2(2).

[164] *Ibid* s 4(3).

[165] See eg *Milne v Express Newspapers* [2004] EMLR 24.

[166] In England, discovery may be ordered of journalists' notes to assist a claimant decide whether to accept an offer: *Rigg v Associated Newspapers* [2004] EMLR 4. The *CPRs*' concerns with the proportionate allocation of resources suggests this will not develop into the complex discovery process that has been seen in some US litigation; see below, Part III, E and see the *Rigg* decision: [25] (Gray J).

[167] The same applies to the ACT provisions: *Civil Law (Wrongs) Act 2002* (ACT) ss 116–122.

be) defamatory, the publisher to remain ready to perform the offer any time until trial and the offer to have been reasonable in all the circumstances.[168] Broadly similar provisions to NSW exist in Australia's uniform defamation proposals (other aspects of which are discussed below), but the English model with its strong judicial interpretation remains worthy of Australian consideration.

3 *Case management and 'generosity' as to capable meanings*

As discussed in Chapter 1, the *Civil Procedure Rules'* overriding objective is to deal justly with disputes in a manner that is proportionate to the issues' importance and complexity, and taking account of the parties' relative financial positions.[169] Courts have wide powers of case management to further this aim, including power under r 3.1(2), to:

> (i) direct a separate trial of any issue . . .
> (k) exclude an issue from consideration . . .
> (m) take any other step or make any other order for the purpose of managing the case and furthering the overriding objective.

Courts also have power 'to exclude evidence that would otherwise be admissible' under r 32.1(2). Even before the introduction of the *Civil Procedure Rules*, the Court of Appeal clearly had concerns about libel litigation. In *Bennett v News Group Newspapers*, Robert Walker LJ for the Court of Appeal said:

> In libel actions tried with a jury (more perhaps than in civil litigation of any other kind) there is a balance to be struck between two objectives which are often difficult to reconcile, although each in itself is desirable. On the one hand, there is a need to clear the decks before the jury trial begins, in order to reduce . . . the risks of delay, misunderstanding and confusion if hopeless or near-hopeless issues are raised and addressed in the evidence placed before the jury. On the other hand, there is also a need to discourage time-consuming and expensive interlocutory applications which may sometimes have the tactical objective of wearing down the other side's determination and resources, and . . . may seriously delay the eventual trial.[170]

Seeking a balance between simplifying issues and avoiding time-consuming hearings is something that resonates with all the jurisdictions considered in this research. And it is significant how English courts have sought to address this concern by taking on greater case management. If this attitude continues, the complexities seen in NSW practice are unlikely to develop. This book offers substantial support to the *Civil Procedure Rules'* approach and underlines how tighter control (such as control of meaning and its pleading) is not always

168 *DA 1974* (NSW) s 9G.

169 *CPR* 1; see Chapter 1, Part I.

170 [2002] EMLR 39, [13].

productive. In short, more pre-trial pleading hearings should be avoided unless they are likely to shorten the time before cases are finalised.[171]

In the *GKR Karate* decision, for example, the Court of Appeal approved using Pt 24 to determine qualified privilege's availability at the start of a jury trial, and stated:

> Libel cases had historically been notoriously long drawn out and expensive. They were especially amenable to the culture of the new procedural code, needing new and imaginative case management to achieve what had hitherto often not been achieved.[172]

And in *McPhilemy v Times Newspapers*, May LJ discussed the *Civil Procedure Rules'* objectives and stated:

> As with all actions, libel actions should, by proper case management, be confined within manageable and economic bounds. They should not descend into uncontrolled and wide-ranging investigations akin to public inquiries, where that is not necessary to determine the real issues between the parties. The court will . . . strive to manage the case so as to minimise the burden on litigants of slender means. This includes excluding all peripheral material which is not essential to the just determination of the real issues between the parties, and whose examination would be disproportionate to its importance to those issues. It does not . . . extend in this case to excluding potentially important evidence, which is central to a legitimate substantial defence.[173]

The desire to exclude all 'peripheral material which is not essential to the just determination of the real issues' and 'whose examination would be disproportionate' has been applied subsequently.[174] The distinction between such peripheral material and important evidence that is central to legitimate defences appears to be a useful reference for courts in delimiting, among other things, the scope of arguments about meaning and the evidence to be considered for justification and opinion defences.[175]

---

[171] Eg Gray J has cautioned against making such preliminary determinations if they are likely to be appealed: *MacIntyre* (Unreported, QBD, Gray J, 1 February 2002) [26]–[27].

[172] *GKR Karate (UK) v Yorkshire Post Newspapers* [2000] 2 All ER 931, [13] (May LJ, Tuckey LJ agreed).

[173] [1999] 3 All ER 775, 791 (May LJ, Lord Woolf MR and Judge LJ agreed). There also were suggestions that less detailed pleadings would be required, with greater reliance being placed on witness statements: 788–89 (May LJ), 792–93 (Lord Woolf MR); see also *Berezovsky* [2001] EMLR 45, [20] (Sedley LJ for Eng CA).

[174] Eg *Tancic v Times Newspapers* (Unreported, Eng CA, Brooke, Hale LJJ, 7 December 1999); *Schellenberg v British Broadcasting Corpn* [2000] EMLR 296, 310 (Eady J); *Mahon v Rahn (No 2)* [2000] EMLR 873, 908 (Brooke LJ, Mantell and Laws LJJ agreed); *Cook v News Group Newspapers* [2002] EWHC 1070(QB).

[175] See also *Burstein* [2001] 1 WLR 579, [41]–[42] and [47] (May LJ, Sir Christopher Slade and Aldous LJ agreed); *Carlton Communications v News Group Newspapers* [2002] EMLR 16, [30]–[33] (Latham LJ, Mantell LJ agreed); and the much earlier, but long neglected, 1988 Court of Appeal decision, *United States Tobacco International v British Broadcasting Corpn* [1998] EMLR 816.

In a similar vein, English courts have discouraged appeals on pre-trial rulings about meaning, at least where a meaning is not ruled out.[176] An important and connected development has emphasised the difficulty in having a meaning ruled incapable of arising from a publication. In *Berezovsky v Forbes*, the Court of Appeal stated:

> [A]scertaining the range of legitimate meanings ... [is] a matter of impression ... not of what the words mean but of what a jury could sensibly think they meant. Such an exercise is an *exercise in generosity, not in parsimony*.[177]

The requirement for generosity not parsimony also applies to defendants' meanings.[178] The approach should further discourage pleading battles, and instead push disputes towards trial. Coupled with the courts' developing case management practices under the *Civil Procedure Rules*, this suggests meaning will be made reasonably clear by the parties' statements of case and then largely left until trial. As discussed in Chapter 6,[179] this is the approach that appeared useful in Victoria – although there also could be important benefits for Australian jurisdictions in a *Civil Procedure Rules*' style of case management. (An obvious example is NSW with its *Civil Procedure Act 2005*, which is examined briefly below.)

In all these ways, the English defamation courts appear to be implementing the *Civil Procedure Rules*' aims with some vigour. The observations of Sedley LJ in July 1999, soon after the rules began operation, are being followed through. In a failed defence appeal on capacity, Sedley LJ said:

> [D]efamation practitioners may do well to accustom themselves to the fact that the wind of change in civil procedure is blowing on them as it blows on everybody else. The kind of pleading issue ... run before us today is now history. It is perfectly plain what this case is about. What it requires is trial or settlement, not interlocutory jockeying for forensic advantage.[180]

None of this is to say that English law and practice relevant to meaning has been completely revolutionised. But the courts' attitude in seeking a balance between simplifying issues pre-trial and avoiding unnecessary hearings – which existed even before the *Civil Procedure Rules*, and appears broadly similar to recent NSW judicial statements[181] – should be strongly supported.[182]

---

176 *Geenty v Channel Four Television Corpn* [1998] EMLR 524, 532 (Hirst LJ, Millett and Brooke LJJ agreed) explaining *Hinduja v Asia TV* [1998] EMLR 516, and see Chapter 2, Part III, A.

177 [2001] EMLR 45, [16] (Sedley LJ for Eng CA) (emphasis added).

178 *Haslam v Times Newspapers* (Unreported, QBD, Gray J, 15 November 2001).

179 See Chapter 6, Part II, B.

180 *Dwek v Macmillan Publishers* [2000] EMLR 284, 294 (Sedley LJ), see also 288 (May LJ); see also *Wallis v Valentine* [2003] EMLR 8.

181 See above, Part II, A.

182 The English courts also appear to be taking a stronger approach under the *CPRs* to the potential misuse of defamation proceedings, see eg *Dow Jones v Jameel* [2005] EWCA Civ 75 in which the apparently small number of recipients to an online publication saw an abuse of process argument succeed: the cost of litigating would be out of all proportion to any damage suffered by the claimant.

4 *Conditional fee agreements*

Conditional fee agreements were mentioned briefly in Chapter 4,[183] where it was noted their use has been controversial. Known as CFAs, the agreements allow lawyers to recover a success fee in addition to their usual legal fees. While the success fee can be up to 100 per cent of the usual fees (although the frequency of that high rate in defamation claims remains for investigation), it is important to note that it cannot be a percentage of any award as is commonplace with contingency fees in the US. CFAs are used far more commonly by claimants than defendants in England. Claimants also can seek after the event insurance to cover the risk of needing to pay the defendants' costs if claimants lose.[184] If such coverage is obtained, claimants face no further financial risk – although their lawyers will receive no payment unless a claim succeeds. If coverage is not obtained and claimants do not have assets, defendants will not be able to recover their costs if they defeat the claim. But defendants still face having to pay higher costs if the claim succeeds.

In *Musa King v Telegraph Group*, the Court of Appeal recognised the dangers this situation can pose to speech. In that case, the parties agreed that the claimant was unlikely to recover more than £150,000 in damages at the most, the claimant's solicitors estimated their costs to be nearly £360,000 before any uplift was applied and the defendants estimated their own costs would be similar.[185] Brooke LJ noted: 'Something seems to have gone seriously wrong.'[186] The conduct of the claimants' solicitors in that case was criticised strongly – it appeared likely to inflame the dispute and deter settlement, contrary to the whole approach of the *Civil Procedure Rules*. What is not yet clear is the degree to which such conduct will be common, and the effects it will have on different categories of defendants.[187]

It appears that the most likely avenue for defendants will be to seek an order capping costs at a very early stage of the dispute, an order that would be inclusive of any uplift in legal fees.[188] The use of such costs powers was endorsed clearly by the Court of Appeal in *Musa King* in relation to defamation claims brought without after the event insurance.[189] CFAs are likely to warrant further investigation after greater experience of their operation in relation to defamation:

---

183 See Chapter 4, Part IV, A. Useful overviews are provided by Price and Duodu (2004) [34.18]–[34.25]; Department for Constitutional Affairs (2004b) [33]–[49].

184 It is possible for the insurance fee to be recovered from the other side if the insured party wins; fees are reported to be approximately 20 per cent of the sum insured (ie the estimated costs of the other side); and it is possible to insure the insurance premium: see Price and Duodu (2004) [34.21].

185 [2004] EMLR 23, [56] (Brooke L, Jonathan Parker and Maurice Kay LJJ agreed).

186 *Ibid* [57].

187 Eg existing research has identified varied effects of defamation law on different media defendants: see Chapter 1, Part II, C.

188 See eg Anonymous (2005), which reports what appears to be the first cost-capping order in a CFA defamation case (*Matadeen v Associated Newspapers*).

189 *Ibid* [87]–[106] (although an order was not made in the particular case because it had not been sought in the initial hearing). See also *Pedder v News Group Newspapers* [2004] EMLR 19; *Armstrong v Times Newspapers* [2004] EWHC 2928, [111]–[117] (Eady J).

when used with costs being kept in proportion, whether by the lawyers involved or by court orders, the arguments that CFAs improve access to law appear strong. And the agreements are available to defendants, which could be significant for protecting the speech of those with less financial resources.[190] Equally significant, however, is the general attitude of the English courts to keeping costs in proportion and their more active case management under the *Civil Procedure Rules*.

5 *Opinion*

A final area to note in relation to England concerns the opinion defence of fair comment. Arguments that European case law should change the legal approach to meaning, particularly in relation to the distinction between fact and comment,[191] so far have been rejected. In *Berezovsky v Forbes*, counsel argued:

> [T]he meaning of meaning in defamation actions has itself been altered by the Human Rights Act 1998 . . . and [must] be reoriented towards the enlargement of press freedom. . . . An article written ethically and honestly is now to be judged not by making nice distinctions of pleaded meaning but according to a broad judgment whether, having regard to those true facts and fair comments which the article contains, it is necessary in a democratic society to restrict the journal's freedom of expression by making its publisher and editor liable for its inaccuracies.[192]

The Court of Appeal firmly rejected this, stating that defences of comment and privilege provided the necessary protection for speech containing exaggeration or error.[193] The general approach to meaning was appropriate. As this extract implies, fair comment is seen as a significant defence for free speech. Case law has long said as much, and English courts can be expected to maintain that fair comment already pays necessary attention to free speech.[194] There may be greater readiness, however, to classify material as comment in individual cases. That would be a useful development and, coupled with s 6 of the *Defamation Act 1952*,[195] it offers a substantial improvement on the Australian position for defending opinion. In any event, one important point about the defence can be made from this project's research. Fair comment under the *Human Rights Act 1998* should not be tied to the claimant's meanings – and the developments in Australian cases such as *Anderson* should not be applied in England.[196] The key element should be the commentator's honest belief in the comment sought to be made, as English cases have stated.[197]

---

190 Use by defendants might offer some analogies to anti-SLAPP legislation in the US: see Chapter 8, Part I, F.

191 A detailed review of the English approach in this context is provided by Young (2000).

192 [2001] EMLR 45, [8] (Sedley LJ for Eng CA).

193 *Ibid* [12].

194 Eg *Branson v Bower* [2002] QB 737, [11] (Eady J).

195 See Chapter 3, Part II, D.

196 *Anderson v Nationwide News* (2001) 3 VR 619 and see Chapter 9, Part IV, A, 2.

197 *Branson* [2002] QB 737, [23]–[28] (Eady J); see also *Field v Local Sunday Newspapers (North)* [2002] EWHC 336.

6 *Case management for Australia*

The strong case management that appears to be evolving in England and the somewhat similar moves under NSW case law also offer suggestions for wider Australian adoption. Preferences already exist in Victorian judgments about such matters, and this research suggests they should be further developed in Australia. For example, in the *Carrey* decision, Hedigan J had to determine whether a defence meaning was capable of arising from the publication:

> What is of importance is to determine whether or not the imputation . . . that the plaintiff was "psychologically unstable" is reasonably open to . . . the jury. I do not take the view that the determination of that issue cannot include consideration of some of the practical consequences of leaving it [to the jury], such as the expansion of the matrix of evidence to lengths that make the trial likely to be over-long, over-expensive and dominated by irrelevances. As such, it is likely to be unfair.[198]

The recent English examples discussed above suggest that defamation is particularly suited to such considerations about evidence and fairness.

The common law position in Victoria might temper, but need not exclude, such approaches. In *Bell v Kingsbay (No 2)*, for example, Gillard J emphasised that a publication's meaning remains a question for the tribunal of fact and is not to be tied specifically to the pleaded imputations.[199] He also said courts should be slow to strike out meanings as being incapable and such meaning challenges should be discouraged.[200] And he offered similar criticisms of the technicality of NSW practice as Kirby J.[201] This research strongly suggests the general position articulated by Gillard J should be encouraged in the Victorian law – as Chapter 9 makes clear. But courts also have case management responsibilities, which are reflected in general court rules and appear to be of particular importance in defamation.[202] It should not be thought that the recent English cases discussed above rest purely on the *Civil Procedure Rules*. Those rules certainly have been significant in prompting careful attention being given to defamation practice. However, such attention in England pre-dates the civil procedure reforms and – most importantly for Australian purposes – it was exercised under traditional court rules, with English courts referring to the 'fourth principle' set out by O'Connor LJ in *Polly Peck*:

> [T]he trial of the action should concern itself with the essential issues and the evidence relevant thereto and that public policy and the interest of the parties

[198] *Carrey v ACP Publishing* [1999] 1 VR 875, 882–83 (Hedigan J).

[199] [2001] VSC 498, [22]–[23] (Gillard J).

[200] *Ibid* [26]–[27].

[201] *Ibid* [25] and [28], as Gillard J noted, citing *Chakravarti v Advertiser Newspapers* (1998) 193 CLR 519, [139]. It also is noteworthy that Gillard J expressed obiter doubt as to whether defendants should be limited to less serious meanings than pleaded by the plaintiff: [56].

[202] However, it should be noted that general Australian attitudes may be somewhat less receptive than in England; see eg *Queensland v JL Holdings* (1997) 189 CLR 146.

> require that the trial should be kept strictly to the issues necessary for a fair determination of the dispute between the parties.[203]

In addition, at least some Australian jurisdictions are making notable changes in relation to their civil procedure and moving closer to the *Civil Procedure Rules*. In particular, the *Civil Procedure Act 2005* in NSW offers the possibility for meaningful developments – perhaps depending finally on the attitude of the High Court.[204] Section 56 of the Act prescribes an overriding purpose to 'facilitate the just, quick and cheap resolution of the real issues in the proceedings'. This does not differ greatly from earlier provisions in NSW, but the Act sets out in greater detail how case management considerations should influence the overriding purpose. In addition, procedures should be implemented so that legal costs will be proportionate to the claim:

> In any proceedings, the practice and procedure of the court should be implemented with the object of resolving the issues between the parties in such a way that the cost to the parties is proportionate to the importance and complexity of the subject-matter in dispute.[205]

This resonates closely with the objectives of England's *Civil Procedure Rules* and – drawing on English experience – NSW courts could bring about substantial developments in the handling of defamation disputes. And like English concerns that existed about defamation litigation before the *Civil Procedure Rules*,[206] NSW judges have sought to improve case management markedly over recent years. Interviews and case law suggests that, within the limits of the imputation-based cause of action and the 7A process, much has been achieved. That trajectory could well be continued under the *Civil Procedure Act 2005* (NSW).[207]

E Uniform Australian defamation law and meaning

The research discussed in this book also raises implications for long-standing moves towards uniformity in Australian defamation law.[208] Here, a brief

[203] *Polly Peck* [1986] QB 1000, 1021 (O'Connor LJ, Robert Goff and Nourse LJJ agreed); see eg *United States Tobacco* [1998] EMLR 816.

[204] See *Queensland v JL Holdings* (1997) 189 CLR 146.

[205] *Civil Procedure Act 2005* (NSW) s 60.

[206] See eg *DA 1996* (UK) ss 8–10.

[207] The new statutory basis for the *UCPR* (NSW) suggests that greater development may occur than under some other Australian changes, such as Queensland's *Uniform Civil Procedure Rules 1999*.

[208] See eg Community Law Reform Committee of the ACT (1995) 103–105; NSW Law Reform Commission (1995) [1.14]–[1.20]. The idea of uniformity certainly was supported as early as NSW Law Reform Commission (1968) [296], while the ACT's Community Law Reform Committee goes so far to suggest that efforts have existed in Australia for 'more than 150 years': 103.

outline is provided of earlier reform efforts, before some issues relevant to meaning are discussed. (Aspects of the proposals relevant to privilege are addressed below in Part II.)

1 *Past uniformity efforts in Australia*

Failed efforts towards uniformity in Australian defamation law have been considerable, especially during the 1980s and early 1990s. Those wanting to undertake detailed analysis probably should commence with Australian Law Reform Commission's 1979 report, *Unfair Publication: Defamation and Privacy*.[209] It still offers a 'most comprehensive and persuasive blueprint for the reform of defamation'[210] and has been particularly influential in commonwealth reform proposals during 2004 and 2005. The ALRC report led to an Exposure Draft Defamation Bill 1983 (Cth), which was circulated but did not proceed. Differences between the commonwealth, states and territories over defences, as well as media opposition to court-ordered correction statements and related remedies, appear to have been influential in stalling the Bill.[211] Work on reform continued during the 1980s and the Attorneys-General of NSW, Queensland and Victoria issued two joint discussion papers on defamation in 1990 and 1991.[212] Defamation Bills based on these efforts were introduced into the parliaments of NSW, Queensland and Victoria during 1991 and 1992. The Bills were uniform to a substantial but not complete degree. However, none of the Bills passed. Elections intervened in Queensland and Victoria, while in NSW the parliamentary legislation committee recommended referring defamation law reform to the NSW Law Reform Commission.[213] That reference led to the Commission's 1995 report, which also appears to have received influential opposition. Australia's Standing Committee of Attorneys-General removed uniform defamation law from its agenda in 1998, but the issue did not entirely

[209] Australian Law Reform Commission (1979). It followed a 1976 constitutional convention in Hobart that recommended referring powers to the commonwealth in order to achieve uniform defamation law: [47].

[210] Walker (1994) 71.

[211] Exposure Draft Defamation Bill 1983 (Cth) cll 18–21; and see Attorneys-General of NSW, Queensland and Victoria (1990) 5.

[212] Attorneys-General of NSW, Queensland and Victoria (1991, 1990).

[213] The Defamation Bill 1991 (NSW) was introduced on 14 November 1991, and re-introduced after an election as the Defamation Bill 1992 on 25 February 1992. In Victoria, the Defamation Bill (1991) also was introduced on 14 November 1991, but was not pursued after a change of government. In Queensland, a Draft Bill was tabled on 14 November 1991 and introduced into the Legislative Assembly as the Defamation Bill 1992 on 10 March 1992. Walker (1994) 71 notes a Draft Bill also was tabled in the ACT. A background to the Bills' development is provided in the NSW second reading speech: *Hansard* (14 Nov 1991) 4583; and for an overview of the failure of the NSW, Queensland and Victorian efforts, see Community Law Reform Committee of the ACT (1995) 103–105.

disappear, with calls for reform continuing.[214] Uniform defamation law returned to prominence from late 2003.[215]

Against that background, this project suggests the early-1990s model in Queensland, Victoria and NSW should not be followed in its plan for a statutory cause of action based on the plaintiff's pleaded imputations.[216] There is little in the published material about the early-1990s proposals about why the statutory basis was then preferred. One could expect that reasons would be given similar to those in the NSW Law Reform Commission's 1995 report. But as argued above,[217] those reasons deserve re-examination. As well as an imputation-based cause of action, the 1991 and 1992 bills proposed abolishing common law justification and replacing it with defences similar to NSW's truth and contextual truth.[218] But the situation for comment would have varied between jurisdictions. It appears that NSW would have retained its existing statutory defence, while the Victorian Bill was silent as to comment and would have maintained the common law defence. Given the concerns that remain about the utility of the NSW approach, which requires the comment defence to be directed to the imputations,[219] it is unfortunate that the Victorian Bill did not clarify how the common law defence was expected to operate with a statutory cause of action. It probably would have experienced many of the NSW difficulties, if the Victorian cause of action became the plaintiff's pleaded imputation.

It could be noted that earlier reform proposals generally focused on the preferable defamation law for the particular state or territory in question, with individual jurisdictions perhaps optimistically suggesting their proposals may provide a basis for national uniformity. (An important exception is the ALRC report with its national scope.) For example, the 2002 report of the NSW Attorney-General's Task Force on Defamation Law Reform stated:

> While this report can only have any direct impact on NSW law . . . these proposals could form the basis for discussion . . . with a view to a further attempt to bring about national reform.[220]

Similar sentiments exist in documents from the Attorneys-General of NSW, Queensland and Victoria,[221] the NSW Law Reform Commission[222] and two

[214] Eg Williams (1998); Australian Press Council (1998).

[215] See eg Shiel (2003).

[216] Eg Defamation Bill 1992 (Vic) cll 7, 8. See Attorneys-General of NSW, Queensland and Victoria (1991, 1990).

[217] See above, Part I, B.

[218] Eg Defamation Bill 1992 (Vic) cll 19–21.

[219] *New South Wales Aboriginal Land Council v Perkins* (1998) 45 NSWLR 340; and see Chapter 5, Part III, D.

[220] NSW Attorney-General's Task Force on Defamation Law Reform (2002) 37, see also recommendation 18 at 38.

[221] Attorneys-General of NSW, Queensland and Victoria (1990) 4.

[222] NSW Law Reform Commission (1995).

Western Australian reports.[223] This history makes the moves for uniformity in 2004 and 2005 particularly interesting. While clearly influenced by the *Defamation Act 1974* (NSW) and the 1979 ALRC report,[224] the proposals drew on them and the experience of NSW practice in a sophisticated manner. The resulting proposals, particularly the state proposal, avoid some of the worst complications of Australian defamation law.

2 *Uniformity and multistate publications*

The difficulty of defamation litigation over material published in multiple states has not been prominent in recent calls for uniformity. But the complexities raised by *John Pfeiffer v Rogerson* meant that uniformity was seen to have renewed importance during the NSW interviews reported in Chapter 5.[225] After *John Pfeiffer*, courts must apply the substantive law of the place in which the tort occurred; so for publications in multiple states, multiple laws must be applied at trial. For publications in NSW and Victoria, for example, this means that different defences must be applied, such as could arise in relation to common law and statutory justification defences, NSW's contextual truth and the common law's Lucas-Box or Polly Peck pleas. While there has been some consideration of differing state laws as to assessing defamation damages since *John Pfeiffer*,[226] courts have tended to avoid addressing multiple approaches to a publication's meaning and the associated defences.[227] But it has not been unknown for a more complex jury questionnaire to be used, with the jury being asked directly about different defences in various jurisdictions.[228] The more common approach appears to be illustrated by the *Marsden* litigation, in which the defendant pleaded truth and contextual truth in NSW and what were described as 'cognate defences' for the other jurisdictions. That is, the defendant pleaded equivalent words to the contextual imputations as alternative meanings in common law jurisdictions.[229] Levine J described these pleadings and stated:

> The characterisation of the 'contextual imputations' or alternative 'meanings' pleaded in respect of other States or Territories will be dealt with if the occasion arises separately to consider those pleadings. Clearly the starting

[223] Law Reform Commission of Western Australia (1979) [10]; Western Australia (2003) 68; cf Law Reform Committee of South Australia (1972), which only mentioned uniformity briefly, in relation to 'foreign' (ie interstate) publications: 5.

[224] See eg Sexton (2004).

[225] (2000) 203 CLR 503; see generally Collins (2001b); and Chapter 5, Part III, F.

[226] Especially in relation to the availability of exemplary damages: eg *Randwick Labor Club* [2000] NSWSC 906, [190] (James J); *Marsden* [2001] NSWSC 510, [4915]–[4917] and [5252] (Levine J).

[227] Eg *Lee v Kim* [2002] NSWSC 353, [25] (Levine J); *National Roads and Motorists Association v Nine Network Australia* [2002] ACTSC 37, [6] (Connolly M).

[228] Eg *Bass v McDonald (No 8)* [2001] NSWSC 1033, [1]–[5] (Sperling J).

[229] *Marsden* [2001] NSWSC 510, [105]–[110] (Levine J).

point is the determination of the defences under the New South Wales legislation.[230]

Levine J found the evidence failed to establish truth and contextual truth in relation to NSW; there was no additional evidence offered for other jurisdictions and so he did not have to consider different statutory and common law approaches to justification.[231] (Levine J did note that defence pleading of meaning related to other jurisdictions had not 'been assisted in terms of its stability let alone uniformity, in the light of the differing approaches adopted' in Queensland, West Australian and Victorian cases[232] – referring to the issues addressed at length in Chapter 9.) Even so, *Pfeiffer* clearly underlines the value in uniformity to assist with the actual litigation of defamation disputes.

3 2004 and 2005 proposals in general

Writing in the first half of 2005, it seemed moderately likely that uniform Australian defamation law would arrive within the next year: the law might lose its diversity across the states – which has been an 'outstanding characteristic' of the Australian situation.[233] Of course, the history described above also suggests reform is far from certain. At the time of writing there were two proposals: one from the states and territories and the other from the commonwealth government. They are referred to here as the state and commonwealth proposals. General information was available about the proposals following discussion papers released in 2004 (along with submissions, some public, made by lawyers, media organisations and others).[234]

A general difference between the proposals should be noted first: the commonwealth proposal would not apply to all defamation actions. Commonwealth legislative power is limited under the Australian Constitution. No express head of power exists for defamation law, and the commonwealth proposal would encompass, in general terms, only publications that are made across state borders, by corporations, when using postal or telephonic services or in the electronic media.[235] Within its scope, the commonwealth legislation would override state law. But it would not encompass many non-media publications that occur within a state's boundaries – such as statements at local meetings, pamphlets produced and distributed by individuals and so forth. Clearly this would leave great complexities for some defamation claims. State legislative

---

230 *Ibid* [111].

231 *Ibid* [2907]–[2916].

232 *Ibid* citing *Robinson v Laws* [2003] 1 Qd R 81; *Reynolds v Nationwide News* [2001] WASC 90; and *David Syme v Hore-Lacy* [2000] 1 VR 667.

233 Tilbury (1998) 244.

234 For background see Attorney-General's Department (Australia) (2004a, 2004b); SCAG Working Group of State and Territory Officers (2004). (SCAG stands for Standing Committee of Attorneys-General.)

235 Attorney-General's Department (Australia) (2004b) 40.

power is not limited in this way, and the state proposal would apply to all actions. The states and territories released a model Bill in November 2004 – referred to here as the Model Defamation Provisions – and each state and territory parliament was expected to introduce equivalent legislation during 2005, which would apply to actions concerning publications made after 1 January 2006.[236] Media reports also suggested that an intergovernmental agreement would be signed between the states to ensure that later amendments were agreed to and passed by all states.[237] However, that timetable may be optimistic as South Australia was the only state to have introduced the Defamation Bill 2005 by the end of May 2005.

After media reports in April 2005, it appeared that only three significant areas of difference existed between the states and the commonwealth over uniform defamation.[238] The commonwealth maintained that if these differences were not addressed, it would proceed with legislation.[239] (Many of the details of such legislation remained to be determined at the time of writing: the 2004 commonwealth proposal included some draft sections but not a complete Bill.[240]) The differences between the states and commonwealth concerned corporate plaintiffs, the availability of juries and whether courts could issue correction notices. First, the state proposal would restrict the ability of most corporations to sue – only some small corporations and non-profit corporations that were not governmental or public authorities could sue in defamation.[241] The commonwealth would not restrict any categories of plaintiff, apart from maintaining the restrictions that exist at common law since *Ballina Shire Council v Ringland* in relation to elected governing bodies.[242]

Second, the availability of juries would be left to state and territory law under the state proposal. It was one of several areas where variation could remain between states.[243] The Model Defamation Provisions would allow either party to elect to have a jury in states that use civil juries, subject to that being disallowed where the trial would require 'prolonged examination of records' or 'any technical, scientific or other issue that cannot be conveniently considered and resolved by a jury'.[244] (South Australia uses no civil juries, and they are not used

236 Defamation Bill 2005 (SA) (SA Bill 2005) cl 2 and sch 1, Pt 6; Model Defamation Provisions ss 2, 49 (Model DP).

237 Eg Merritt (2005).

238 Earlier differences included whether actions could relate to deceased plaintiffs.

239 Eg King (2005).

240 Attorney-General's Department (Australia) (2004b) 41–49.

241 SA Bill 2005 cl 9; Model DP s 9. Small corporations are those employing less than 10 people (and not related to other corporate bodies). A similar provision was previously introduced in NSW: *DA 1974* (NSW) s 8A.

242 Attorney-General's Department (Australia) (2004b) 38–39; see (1994) 33 NSWLR 680 and Chapter 7, Part II, A. On the issue of whether corporations should be able to sue, see eg Herzfeld (2005); Patfield (1994).

243 Variation was also envisaged in relation to some states possibly adding to the occasions of absolute privilege or material protected as reports of public documents or proceedings of public concern: Model DP ss 27, 28, 29.

244 Model DP s 21; see eg for England *Supreme Court Act 1981* s 69.

in practice in the ACT or Northern Territory.[245]) Where a jury was used, it would determine all issues in the plaintiff's and defendant's cases apart from damages and any defences that the general law reserves to judges.[246] The commonwealth proposal expressed itself in similar terms in relation to the role of judge and jury – with judges determining remedies.[247] But media reports in 2005 suggested the federal Attorney-General sought all jurisdictions to offer juries as a vital element of uniform defamation law.[248] Third, the commonwealth proposal would create alternative remedies. As well as damages, remedies would include rights of reply against news media[249] and court-issued correction orders,[250] and the commonwealth proposals would seek to encourage apologies that would mitigate damages.[251] No draft provisions were released for these measures; remedies were discussed only in general terms in the commonwealth proposal, so it is not possible to address them closely here. In any event, the merit and practicality of such remedies is not directly related to the interview and court file material investigated in this project. But it is worth noting that the research suggests the English offer of amends and summary disposal provisions (discussed above) offer useful models for consideration. It also is useful that, in discussing the value of summary judgment procedures in defamation, the commonwealth proposal referred to Pt 24 of England's *Civil Procedure Rules*.[252]

In addition to those differences between the state and commonwealth proposals, there is a fourth distinction that could be the most significant one: the commonwealth proposal would codify defamation law and end reliance on the common law. So far as the research underlying this project touches on that issue, it would strongly support retaining the common law. And it could be noted that the commonwealth did not maintain that codification was a key difference in its 2005 statements.[253] The commonwealth proposals released during 2004 did suggest greater differences: for example requiring a version of

---

245 The South Australian position dates from the 1870s, see eg Balkin and Davis (2004) [18.9]; cf Attorney-General's Department (Australia) (2004b) 28.

246 Model DP s 22.

247 Attorney-General's Department (Australia) (2004b) 29. The commonwealth proposal also would send all appeals to the Federal Court, rather than state appellate courts: 27.

248 Eg King (2005).

249 See Attorney-General's Department (Australia) (2004b) 32, which notes that news media could be defined in various ways in legislation, and refers to the definition under *Defamation Act 1992* (NZ) s 2, where news medium is defined as a medium for 'dissemination, to the public or a section of the public, or news, or observation on the news, or advertisements'.

250 Correction orders could be issued only on completion of a trial: Attorney-General's Department (Australia) (2004b) 34.

251 See *ibid* 33–34: apologies that were 'full and complete', published 'at the earliest opportunity' and 'of substantially similar prominence to the original' publication would only mitigate damages – they would not bar actions.

252 *Ibid* 30.

253 See eg King (2005).

public interest to be shown as part of a justification defence, and creating a statutory definition of 'defamatory imputation' that would extend to matters that harmed reputation in the estimation of 'a substantial and reputable section of the public'.[254] Given statements from the federal Attorney-General that suggested only the first three points discussed above were crucial – and subsequent media reports that the federal Attorney-General might not insist even on those three matters[255] – only particularly pertinent differences between the proposals are mentioned below when they are examined in relation to the treatment of a publication's meaning.

4 2004 and 2005 proposals most relevant to meaning

Even though differences existed between the state and commonwealth proposals, in terms of this book's concerns there were notable areas of agreement. In particular, each based the cause of action on the publication, and neither supported continuing NSW's 7A process. As the discussion about NSW law and practice earlier in this chapter makes clear, the research underlying this book strongly support such changes to Australian defamation law. Elements of the state proposal are discussed here, with some reference being made to the commonwealth proposal.

The state proposal based the cause of action on the publication of defamatory matter, which was defined to include media publications, letters, spoken words, and 'any other thing by means of which something may be communicated to a person'.[256] It also preserved the general law on defamation, except where expressly or impliedly changing that law.[257] In relation to defences, it is important to note that the scope of defences under the general law would not be limited:

> A defence under [this Act] is additional to any other defence or exclusion of liability available to the defendant apart from this Act (including under the general law) and does of itself vitiate, limit or abrogate any other defence or exclusion of liability.[258]

The defence of justification would accord with the common law – substantial truth would suffice and public interest (or public benefit) would not need to be shown in addition to truth.[259] There also would be a statutory defence of contextual truth, similar to the NSW defence:

---

[254] For a detailed analysis of the probable effects of such a proposal, see Baker (2004). The definition also would extend to material affecting a person's occupation or financial standing, in a similar style to the Australia code states; see Chapter 2, Part II.

[255] Eg Pelly (2005).

[256] SA Bill 2005 cll 4 and 8; Model DP ss 4 and 8.

[257] SA Bill 2005 cl 6; Model DP s 6.

[258] SA Bill 2005 cl 22; Model DP s 24.

[259] SA Bill 2005 cl 23; Model DP s 25.

> It is a defence to the publication of defamatory matter if the defendant proves that:
>
> (a) the matter carried, in addition to the defamatory imputations of which the plaintiff complains, one or more other imputations (contextual imputations) that are substantially true, and
>
> (b) the defamatory imputations do not further harm the reputation of the plaintiff because of the substantial truth of the contextual imputations.[260]

As explained in Chapter 3, the defence of contextual truth is quite distinct to Lucas-Box and Polly Peck, being closer in lineage and effect to the extended justification defence under s 5 of the *Defamation Act 1952* (UK).[261] Because the proposal bases the cause of action on the published matter and does not abrogate general law defences, all the issues concerning Lucas-Box and Polly Peck would remain for Australian law. As will be clear from Chapter 9, this research strongly supports that position. It also means that the issues about Lucas-Box and Polly Peck pleading considered in Chapter 9 would be relevant to all Australian jurisdictions.[262] They would likely be an important matter for judicial consideration under the new law.

In relation to matters of opinion, there would be a statutory defence of honest opinion under the state proposal, which would read:

> It is a defence to the publication of defamatory matter if the defendant proves that:
>
> (a) the matter was an expression of opinion of the defendant rather than a statement of fact, and
>
> (b) the opinion related to a matter of public interest, and
>
> (c) the opinion is based on proper material.[263]

In an equivalent style to the defence under the *Defamation Act 1974* (NSW), the proposal would deal clearly with the opinion of employees, agents and third parties.[264] The defences also would deal well with an issue broadly equivalent to malice at common law: the defences would be defeated if plaintiffs showed that

---

[260] SA Bill 2005 cl 24; Model DP s 26. A similar defence headed 'Not defamatory in context' was contained in the commonwealth proposal: Attorney-General's Department (Australia) (2004b) 44.

[261] See Chapter 3, Part 1, K.

[262] The same would be true of the commonwealth proposal, except that justification defences would require a statutory version of public interest to be shown in addition to substantial truth: Attorney-General's Department (Australia) (2004b) 41–44. But the commonwealth did not mention the public interest requirement as being crucial in April 2005; see eg King (2005).

[263] SA Bill 2005 cl 29(1); Model DP s 31(1).

[264] SA Bill 2005 cl 29(2) and (3); Model DP s 31(2) and (3).

defendants did not honestly hold the opinion, or did not believe it was honestly held by an employee or agent, or had reasonable grounds to believe it was not honestly held by a third party commentator.[265] The defences extend beyond material that is true in two notable ways. First, 'proper material' would be defined in these terms:

> (4) For the purposes of this section, an opinion is based on proper material if it is based on material that
>
> (a) is substantially true, or
>
> (b) was published on an occasion of absolute or qualified privilege (whether under this Act or at general law), or
>
> (c) was published on an occasion that attracted the protection of defence under this section or [the sections relating to public documents or proceedings of public concern].[266]

Second, not every fact on which opinion was based would need to be proved substantially true. The defence could succeed 'if the opinion might reasonably be based on such of the material as is proper material'.[267] This aspect is drawn from the 1974 NSW Act which requires the comment to represent 'an opinion which might reasonably be based on that material to the extent to which it is proper material'.[268] As in NSW, the state proposals' reasonableness requirement may be interpreted more restrictively than the extended defence under s 6 of the *Defamation Act 1952* (UK) which focuses on whether the opinion is capable of being a commentator's honest opinion based on those facts that have been proved true.[269]

In broad terms, the commonwealth proposal for honest opinion was similar to the state proposal. It focussed on whether the published matter expressed opinions that were the genuine opinion of the relevant author, but did not extend to the situation where only some facts could be proved true.[270] The commonwealth proposal differed in offering guidance about when something should be treated as opinion. It stated that regard should be had to:

> (a) the extent to which it can be verified or proved; and

[265] SA Bill 2005 cl 29(4); Model DP s 31(4).

[266] SA Bill 2005 cl 29(5); Model DP s 31(5).

[267] SA Bill 2005 cl 29(6); Model DP s 31(6).

[268] *DA 1974* (NSW) s 30(3); see eg *John Fairfax Publications v O'Shane* [2005] NSWCA 164.

[269] See Chapter 3, Part II, D.

[270] Attorney-General's Department (Australia) (2004b) 44–45. It could be contrasted with the earlier commonwealth proposal, which would have required opinions to be those that a 'reasonable' person could hold on the relevant facts: see Attorney-General's Department (Australia) (2004a) 3.

(b) the context in which it was published and, in particular, whether that context would have the effect that it is likely to be understood as opinion, rhetoric or hyperbole; and

(c) its language and, in particular, whether cautionary or qualifying language was used or a disclaimer was published together with the matter.[271]

Although this would not necessarily differ from the approach that Australian (and English) courts already take to the issue, the reference to rhetoric and hyperbole is interesting and could move courts' interpretation somewhat closer to the US approach discussed in Chapter 8.

There is one aspect of the state proposal for opinion that could be particularly important for it to achieve the objectives claimed for the reforms; namely, to provide 'defences relating to the publication of matter that expresses an opinion that is honestly held by its maker.'[272] The defences relate to published defamatory *matter*, not the plaintiff's pleaded *imputations*, unlike the somewhat similar NSW statutory defence.[273] When the cause of action is the published matter, as it is in both the state and commonwealth proposals, defences of honest opinion should relate to the *allegation* in the publication of which complaint is made. But there is no warrant for tying the defences to the plaintiff's pleaded *imputations*. The NSW defence has caused great problems in practice,[274] and this aspect of the state proposal should improve significantly the workability of the defences. The focus on the published matter also means that all the issues considered in this and earlier chapters about defence meanings and opinion defences would be relevant for Australian litigation. (It could be noted that the commonwealth proposal focussed on the published matter, not the plaintiff's imputations, so all issues of defence pleading of meaning discussed in Chapter 9 also would be relevant under it).

Some comments about remedies were made in the general discussion of the proposals above. But there also are matters to note about damages – one of which is relevant to the treatment of meaning in practice. The Model Defamation Provisions would limit general damages, in most situations, to $250,000, while the commonwealth proposal would not limit damages.[275] The commonwealth proposal, however, would abrogate the rule in *Scott v Sampson* and evidence of specific misconduct by the plaintiff – relevant to the aspect of reputation at issue – would be admissible.[276] There also could be significant – although difficult to predict – effects from judges rather than juries determining damages in terms of

[271] Attorney-General's Department (Australia) (2004b) 45.

[272] See eg South Australian second reading speech: Hansard (2 March 2005) 1834–40.

[273] *DA 1974* (NSW) ss 29–35.

[274] See Chapter 5, Part III, D; and eg Rares (2004, 2002); Kenyon (1996).

[275] See SA Bill 2005 cl 33; Model DP s 35; Attorney-General's Department (Australia) (2004b) 34–36.

[276] Attorney-General's Department (Australia) (2004b) 36–37.

the links between pleaded meanings and mitigation that were raised by the research set out in Chapters 2–6.

II REYNOLDS AND LANGE PRIVILEGE

Developments in English and Australian privilege defences were examined in Chapter 7. This part discusses some issues related to the law and practice discussed there, and examines Australian proposals for uniform defamation law in relation to privilege.

A Scope, strength and litigation practicality

It has been suggested, in a detailed and useful comparison of *Reynolds* and *Lange*, that both Australian and English courts gave the media what it 'had sought for decades' by 'significantly' extending privilege's application 'to stories of public importance appearing in the mass media'.[277] The empirical research discussed in Chapter 7 suggests that may be true for the English developments under *Reynolds* – or at least the potential exists for *Reynolds* to develop in that way – but the analysis may have been too optimistic about the Australian changes: reasonableness under *Lange* is 'more onerous' for defendants than responsibility is under *Reynolds*.[278] *Lange* appears not to have improved the position of publishers to any significant degree. It has not reduced the apparent chill of defamation law, apart perhaps from reducing suits by politicians. *Lange* is 'completely hopeless'[279] as a defence and, if anything, it is 'constructed to be . . . in results, pro-plaintiff'.[280] But *Lange* does appear to have encouraged more diverse reporting, in the limited sense of encouraging publications to include subjects' points of view.

As set out in Chapter 7, *Reynolds* privilege appears to have greater effects through the wide range of factors that clearly have relevance. It is significant that English interviewees suggested the media can raise more allegations and stories of public interest under *Reynolds*. This follows from the approach of English courts to a publication's tone. But tone remains a problematic factor for tabloid newspapers,[281] which do not produce 'the sort of journalism [that] judges want to read'.[282] *Grobbelaar v News Group Newspapers*, for example, may suggest that

[277] Baker (2002a) 88.

[278] See Chesterman (2000) 104.

[279] 98B.

[280] 89SC; similar 103SC, 106B.

[281] 59S, 64B, 70S, 72S, 73S, 78S, 79S. 61QC commented that *Reynolds* itself suggested a 'transformed' judicial attitude to tabloids, although later cases have seen a 'slipping back' against tabloid styles of presentation.

[282] 70S.

publishers will be penalised for tabloid approaches.[283] Overall, the English courts' approach to tone is innovative, particularly in relation to reportage and the degree to which publications distinguish suspicions and allegations of fact. It may grow to support a far more diverse range of public debate. However, the position remains dependant on further case law: the strength of *Reynolds* privilege in different fact situations remains unclear. These matters about tone and reportage do not arise explicitly under *Lange* and have been little considered in Australia.[284] The research suggests, however, that Australian courts should take a wide range of factors as relevant to *Lange* reasonableness, and should apply those factors flexibly.

Reynolds and *Lange* can change the shape of the litigation so that its focus is placed closely on the publisher's conduct: a *Reynolds* defence, for example, will turn the litigation 'into a trial of your journalists.'[285] Interviewees raised concerns about the cost of litigating the defence – even a short article could underlie 'a four week trial involving a lot of detailed factual . . . and . . . legal issues and vast expense'.[286] But respondents appeared to vary about the likelihood of that situation eventuating, and some suggested that other defences could pose similar complexities in terms of the scale of material involved. This shift in focus under the privilege defences increases the significance of many aspects of a defendant's conduct, including the media production process. But it *may* not pose the difficulties in litigation that have been seen, at least at times, under the US *Sullivan* rules. A simple reason may be the different style and scope of US discovery and depositions. The deposition process and lower judicial aversion to exploratory discovery may set the US apart, although the evaluations of publishers' conduct in England and Australia may be a matter to reconsider once more *Reynolds* and *Lange* cases have occurred.

However, the problems in seeking jury responses to multiple, detailed questions may thwart many of the benefits sought through the doctrinal changes. In England, the division in roles was strongly criticised, while in Australia there was strong support for asking juries a general question about whether publication was reasonable.[287] Subsequent Australian case law is against that approach,[288] but the research reported in Chapter 7 suggests benefits if reasonableness under *Lange* and responsibility under *Reynolds* were determined by the jury. To do otherwise could make trials difficult to run and undermine protection for discussion of

[283] [2001] 2 All ER 437; see Chapter 7, Part II, C, 4.

[284] Tone, however, was expressly considered in *Rowan v Cornwall (No 5)* (2002) 82 SASR 152. In addition, the way in which *Lange* privilege may protect comment is an underdeveloped area in Australia: see Baker (2002b); Rares (2002).

[285] 68B; similar 73S, 79S.

[286] 63QC; similar 62B, 64B, 66B.

[287] See Chapter 7, Part III, B and C.

[288] *Herald & Weekly Times v Popovic* (2003) 9 VR 1.

matters of political or public importance. Another response to the interview material could be to advocate judge-only trials for defamation. But the research into meaning discussed in this book suggests that jury trial can simplify defamation litigation. Most Australian courts, in jurisdictions where defamation juries are available, could have some flexibility to use the jury in a *general* role of assessing reasonableness.[289] The research suggests the courts should take that opportunity. English trial courts may have more difficulty with the clearly established practices and direct judicial statements about judge and jury roles under *Reynolds*,[290] but the probable benefits in another approach seem equally clear. If English law cannot move directly to having the jury determine the responsibility or otherwise of publication, courts will need to contain the complexities posed by lengthy jury questions, without unnecessarily limiting the defence. Appellate courts should not be 'blind to the practical consequences' of judge and jury roles in moving to simplify those roles.[291]

B Developing Lange and s 22?

Doctrinal and empirical research points towards a broader and stronger Australian defence – one that is neither limited to a narrow version of political communication nor requires an onerous standard of reasonableness. First, it appears that *Lange* privilege should be broader. A broader Australian defence is supported by many factors, including the diverse range of publications that can seek protection under *Reynolds* privilege,[292] the criticism of *Lange*'s narrow scope in interviews[293] and existing academic literature.[294] As Lord Cooke said in *Reynolds* itself:

> It is doubtful whether the . . . new defence could sensibly be confined to political discussion. There are other public figures who exercise great practical power over the lives of people or great influence in the formation of public opinion or as role models. [Their] power or influence may indeed exceed that of most politicians. The rights and interests of citizens in democracies are not restricted to the casting of votes. Matters other than those pertaining to government and politics may be just as important in the community; and they may have as strong a claim to be free of restraints on freedom of speech.[295]

The High Court has noted that it is possible for the common law defence under *Lange* to be broader than the constitutional protection for political

[289] Victorian trial courts remain bound by Popovic (2003) 9 VR 1.

[290] See Chapter 7, Part II, C.

[291] 60QC.

[292] See Chapter 7, Part II, C.

[293] See Chapter 7, Part III, C.

[294] See eg Chesterman (2000) 99; Baker (2002a); Kenyon (2001).

[295] *Reynolds* [2001] 2 AC 127, 220.

communication.[296] While the defence's scope has not been approached in this way in the cases,[297] the development appears to be open and useful. Existing hesitancy by appellate courts need not dispose of the issue,[298] and *Reynolds* could be drawn on to develop *Lange* privilege. There appears to be no reason not to mention the factors set out in *Reynolds*. Uniform defamation law in Australia also would have relevance to the issue of scope (which is explored below in Section C).

Second, it appears that *Lange* privilege should be stronger. The difficult task of meeting the reasonableness requirement was one of the clearest concerns seen through the interview research.[299] Again, *Reynolds* offers useful material – and there are benefits offered by the empirical research in showing this where some doctrinal analyses have suggested the reverse.[300] Given the way that Australian courts have emphasised the flexibility in the *Lange* requirement of reasonableness, and the list of factors in s 22(2A) of the NSW statutory privilege defence, again the *Reynolds* factors would appear to be a useful source to draw on. While the English experience with *Reynolds* suggests an approach that is far less definite than the US situation discussed in Chapter 8, *Reynolds* is broader and may well be stronger than the Australian situation. Yet, in general terms the legal and media environments in England and Australia share some notable similarities.

With regard to how developments may be promoted, recent comments by two members of the High Court are noteworthy. In *Rogers v Nationwide News*, Gleeson CJ and Gummow J stated that 'reasonableness is not a concept that can be subjected to inflexible categorisation'[301] immediately before discussing the need for greater consideration of the circumstances of news production:

> In the respondent's written submissions, reference was made, without elaboration, to 'the circumstances in which daily newspapers are published'. It may be enlightening if . . . courts were given more evidence as to those circumstances. . . . Where, as here, serious errors are made, and attributed to 'the circumstances in which daily newspapers are published', a court would be in a better position to judge the reasonableness of the publisher's conduct if it were told exactly what those circumstances were, why they prevailed, and how they contributed to the error.[302]

---

[296] *Lange* (1997) 189 CLR 520, 571.

[297] Although it should be noted that the defamation defence clearly applies to all political matters (eg whether related to state or federal issues), which may differ from the effect of the constitutional implication outside defamation: see eg Lindell (2003) 202ff.

[298] See eg *Marsden* [2002] NSWCA 419, [1168]–[1170] (Beazley, Giles and Santow JJA).

[299] See Chapter 7, Part III, C.

[300] See eg the detailed, comparative study by Amponsah (2004) 143–46. While there is much of interest in such analyses, they probably deserve development in light of empirical material of the sort set out here.

[301] *Rogers v Nationwide News* (2003) 216 CLR 327, [30].

[302] Ibid [31].

Defendants 'need to condescend to greater particularity when seeking to persuade a court that their conduct has been reasonable'.[303] The judges, however, did note that reasonableness is not just what is commercially reasonable for publishers. And their invitation suggests that if the media can draw on empirically rich material about what is reasonable conduct in publication, perhaps the courts' approach could be revised. While this book offers some material, it focuses on comparative law and litigation practice. More relevant may be research into news production practices and media content under differing defamation laws.[304]

Similar concerns can be seen in the history of Australian developments to qualified privilege. In *Lange* and related cases, the High Court developed the law in light of changed social circumstances. A common reference has been to this statement of McHugh J in *Stephens v Western Australian Newspapers*:

> [T]he quality of life and the freedom of the ordinary individual in Australia are highly dependent on the exercise of functions and powers vested in public representatives and officials by a vast legal and bureaucratic apparatus funded by public moneys. How, when, why and where those functions and powers are or are not exercised are matters that are of real and legitimate interest to every member of the community. Information concerning the exercise of those functions and powers is of vital concern to the community. So is the performance of the public representatives and officials who are invested with them. It follows . . . that the general public has a legitimate interest in receiving information concerning matters relevant to the exercise of public functions and powers vested in public representatives and officials.[305]

Even if the focus remains on political and public officials – which this passage most easily relates to[306] – it appears that the Australian law may not have changed in an effective manner when the English experiences with *Reynolds* and other empirical research into media content are considered. While the legal analysis and empirical material would suggest developing *Lange* privilege, it should be noted that such change may not be imminent. Comments in *John Fairfax Publications v O'Shane* in the NSW Court of Appeal can serve as just one illustration.[307] Young CJ in Eq reviewed *Lange* privilege cases and suggested that *Lange* probably is the 'high water mark' with regard to the scope of the privilege,[308] and that there is a 'flavour' about the cases that *Lange* privilege has 'got to the stage of "this far and no further."'[309] Even so, the Australian defences, under *Lange* and s 22, remain flexible and courts do have the ability to develop

303 Ibid [32].

304 See eg Weaver et al (2006); Marjoribanks and Kenyon (2003); Dent and Kenyon (2004).

305 *Stephens v Western Australian Newspapers* (1994) 182 CLR 211, 264.

306 Eg *Popovic* (2003) 9 VR 1, [244] (Gillard AJA).

307 [2005] NSWCA 164.

308 *Ibid* [304].

309 *Ibid* [281].

them in light of changed social and media conditions. And uniform Australian defamation law may be a key influence for any such development. If a statutory defence styled on s 22 of the *Defamation Act 1974* (NSW) operates Australia-wide, there will be many more cases in which the defence can be argued because it will not have the apparently narrow political focus of *Lange*.

C Australian uniform defamation law and privilege?

The 2004 and 2005 proposals for uniform defamation law in Australia have been outlined above,[310] where issues most relevant to meaning were considered. Uniform defamation law also would affect privilege. In general terms, and allowing for the different basis to the cause of action under the *Defamation Act 1974* (NSW), privilege defences would resemble the NSW position. Under the state proposal for uniformity, broad defences would exist for publishing material drawn from public documents – which would include documents issued for public information by governments of any country or their officers, employees or agencies – and for fair reports of proceedings of public concern – which would include public meetings related to matters of public interest held in Australia. These would be defeated only if the plaintiff proved that the material 'was not published honestly for the information of the public or the advancement of education'.[311] These defences would bring welcome uniformity to an area of Australian law that has varied greatly across jurisdictions and would allow close consideration of the House of Lords decision in *McCartan Turkington Breen v Times Newspapers*.[312] As discussed in Chapter 7, the *McCartan* decision means that reports of at least some media conferences can be defended under the statutory protection for fair reports of public meetings.

In relation to qualified privilege, the state proposal would create a statutory defence in virtually identical terms to s 22 of the *Defamation Act 1974* (NSW). The provision would include a list of factors relevant to assessing the reasonableness of publication:

> (3) In determining . . . whether the conduct of the defendant in publishing matter about a person is reasonable in the circumstances, a court may take into account:
>
> (a) the extent to which the matter published is of public interest, and
>
> (b) the extent to which the matter published relates to the performance of the public functions or activities of the person, and
>
> (c) the seriousness of any defamatory imputation carried by the matter published, and

310 See above, Part I, E.

311 SA Bill 2005 cll 26, 27; Model DP ss 28, 29. The commonwealth proposal also extended to documents issued for public information by governments of any country or their officers, employees or agencies, but did not deal with pubic meetings: Attorney-General's Department (Australia) (2004b) 47–49.

312 *McCartan Turkington Breen v Times Newspapers* [2001] 2 AC 277; see Chapter 7, Part II, A.

(d) the extent to which the matter published distinguishes between suspicions, allegations and proven facts, and

(e) whether it was in the public interest in the circumstances for the matter published to be published expeditiously, and

(f) the nature of the business environment in which the defendant operates, and

(g) the sources of the information in the matter published and the integrity of those sources, and

(h) whether the matter published contained the substance of the person's side of the story and, if not, whether a reasonable attempt was made by the defendant to obtain and publish a response from the person, and

(i) any other steps taken to verify the information in the matter published, and

(j) any other circumstances that the court considers relevant.[313]

The provision also would state explicitly that malice defeats the privilege and that the matter being published for reward is not enough to defeat it. The list of factors has two differences from the list in s 22(2A) in NSW. First, the NSW provision asks whether it was 'necessary' in the circumstances for the matter to be published expeditiously, while the Model Defamation Provisions ask whether such publication was in the public interest in the circumstances. Second, the state proposal adds a factor about the business environment in which the defendant operates. While both these changes could be expected to support a more flexible approach to the defence, either provision – the proposal or the NSW law under s 22(2A) – gives courts substantial ability to determine whether publications were reasonable. A similar argument could be made about the commonwealth proposal: although its wording was more restrictive than the provision under s 22(2A) of the *Defamation Act 1974* (NSW),[314] courts would retain wide ability to interpret reasonableness under

---

[313] Model DP s 30; SA Bill 2005 cl 28.

[314] The Commonwealth proposal listed these factors:

(a) whether the matter relates to a subject of public interest;

(b) the seriousness of the defamatory imputations conveyed by the matter;

(c) whether the defendant took adequate steps to check the accuracy of any facts conveyed by the matter;

(d) whether the defendant believed that any facts conveyed by the matter were untrue;

(e) whether the defendant gave the plaintiff adequate opportunity to comment on the matter before publishing it;

(f) whether the matter and any matter published together with it provides balanced information about the plaintiff's perspective on the subject the matter addresses;

(g) the manner of publication;

(h) the language of the matter;

(i) the number of persons to whom the matter was published.

the inclusive commonwealth list. Overall, the proposals are important for two reasons in particular. They are not limited to matters of political communication – as *Lange* privilege is – and they would allow significant recourse to English decisions under *Reynolds*. The first aspect – changing the scope of protection – would be a marked alteration in the Australian law and could lead to many more cases in which the privilege defence would be argued. The second aspect – recourse to *Reynolds* – is open under existing law, but may be promoted by the statutory lists.

Given widespread support for *Reynolds* by Australian interviewees, s 22(2A) in NSW and its equivalent provisions in the uniform proposals may offer very useful bases for arguments to revise reasonableness. For example, the NSW legislation explicitly refers to 'the extent to which the matter published distinguishes between suspicions, allegations and proven facts'.[315] This could support arguments drawing on the English reportage cases. And since the defence is not limited to *Lange* privilege's political communication, the arguments should be open in many cases. While *Sullivan* may be thought of as the alternative that haunts the English and Australian law on privilege, there is another doctrinal option that more readily may have influence. That would be a qualified privilege defence for political or public interest speech that is only defeated by malice. The common law privilege under *Theophanous v Herald & Weekly Times* offers an example.[316] To date, provisions of similar strength have been proposed in Australia but not enacted. For example, two out of four members of a 2002 review for the NSW Attorney-General recommended introducing a statutory privilege for a broad range of political material that would be subject only to malice, but the recommendation did not appear in the subsequent Bill.[317] This is an area where further case law may clarify whether the aims of the English and Australian 1990s decisions to reduce defamation law's burden of proving truth can be met under *Reynolds* and *Lange* privilege.[318] In any event, if privilege defences are to allow diverse speech and reduce any chill from defamation law, English and Australian courts would do well to remain 'slow to conclude that a publication [is] not in the public interest' and resolve doubts 'in favour of publication'.[319]

---

[315] *DA 1974* (NSW) s 22(2A)(d).

[316] (1994) 182 CLR 104. See Chapter 7, Part II, D.

[317] NSW Attorney-General's Task Force on Defamation Law Reform (2002) 31–32, which offers just one illustration that removing the reasonableness requirement may be difficult to achieve. The empirical research suggests that changes like that may be reasonably significant, but not to the level suggested by the comments of Callinan J in *Australian Broadcasting Corpn v Lenah Game Meats* (2001) 208 CLR 199, [340] (Callinan J); cf [193]–[194] and [213] (Kirby J).

[318] See eg Spilsbury (2000) 46–7, who suggests that judges should determine privileged occasions according to whether publications have public interest content, and that juries should deal with the circumstances of publication in terms of malice.

[319] *Reynolds* [2001] 2 AC 127, 205.

III US DEFAMATION LAW AND PRACTICE

This part sets out five broad points about the US position. It aims to clarify some issues that appear most relevant in comparative evaluations of US and non-US defamation. The points concern: the very different way in which meaning arises; the steps through which most media-related defamation cases proceed; the usual expertise of plaintiff and defendant lawyers and judges; the US focus on the status of the plaintiff over the publication's subject matter, unlike the *Reynolds* and *Lange* developments; and the way that the complexity of US litigation *may* be less than suggested in some of the prior research, at least in the common media-related defamation case. Overall, the material cautions against simple comparisons between US and English or Australian defamation law. Rather, the research set out in earlier chapters provides background for US readers to appreciate how issues about meaning, justification, opinion and privilege operate in England and Australia – under a very different procedural regime. It also should help English and Australian readers remember that the US law involves far more than the *Sullivan* rules, as important a difference as they are from English and Australian defamation law. Part III concludes with some observations about areas for future US and comparative research.

A Meaning in US defamation

The first point arising from this book's analysis of law and practice concerns the very different way in which issues of meaning arise in US defamation. English and Australian claimants and plaintiffs can seek to shape defamation litigation through their pleaded meanings. This appears to be particularly true in NSW and, increasingly, it may be the position in other Australian states under the alterations to Lucas-Box pleading that have been criticised in Chapter 9. For US plaintiffs, the situation seems very different and it is worth noting briefly matters concerned with opinion, implications, pleading, substantial truth and mitigation. For opinion to be actionable, US law requires it to convey factual matters that can be proved false. In effect, if not explicit doctrine, the US position maintains that 'there is no such thing as a false idea'.[320] And the US law overall appears less ready to accept arguments about publications implying particular meanings. Meaning appears to be more a matter of explicit statements and comparatively straightforward implications, at least in the usual case. In addition, pleading does not appear to be an important aspect of US practice with regard to meaning. While the precise publication must be set out – as it must under English and Australian law – it appears that US plaintiffs avoid being specific about meaning, certainly in comparison with English, Australian and especially NSW practice. The US focus is placed more on false facts stated in the publication or relatively obvious implications. To US lawyers, English and Australian laws appear to rewrite publications through pleading and pre-trial disputes about meaning. In

[320] 418 US 323, 339 (Powell J) (1974).

relation to the lesser concern with meaning in the US, it is interesting to note early-1990s research by Brian Murchison and colleagues about the journalistic behaviours at issue in more than 400 actual malice cases. In descending frequencies of between 29 and 23 per cent of the cases analysed in the Murchison research, plaintiffs raised issues about the media: failing to verify information from a source, using 'unclear writing', failing to accurately summarise information and failing 'to investigate adequately the information in the story'.[321] While 'unclear writing' is listed as one of the most common factors here, it was not a factor that was significant in the cases' results:

> [D]espite the large number of cases in which the clarity of the media's writing was at issue, there is not a single case in the study in which this behavior alone was cited as proof that the defendant had acted recklessly.[322]

It also appeared not to be important when unclear writing was argued to be present in combination with other factors. This suggests that US defamation litigation – at least for public plaintiffs – focuses on other issues more than the specifics of meaning in the way that is usual in English and Australian litigation.

The approach to truth also appears to differ in US practice, beyond the changed burden of proof. The relative lack of US concern with pleaded meanings – probably coupled with plaintiffs' need to prove falsity – appears to underlie a greater flexibility in the defence of substantial truth. The justification target appears 'broader' than in England or Australia.[323] Mitigation is another significant element for understanding meaning in US defamation, with the admission of damaging information about plaintiffs appearing to be less restricted and far less tied to any pleaded meanings than in England and Australia. Discreditable information about the plaintiff that can be proved true often will be relevant and admissible on issues of fault – particularly when actual malice is the standard – as well as issues of substantial truth and damage. All these differences about meaning may help make clear for US readers the particular issues that will be most valuable to take from the detailed examination in Chapters 2 to 6 of the law and practice relevant to meaning in England, Victoria and NSW. And it may help them appreciate the significant implications of the differing ways in which English and Australian jurisdictions deal with defence pleading of meaning. For example, the Victorian decision in the *Gutnick* litigation, which is discussed in Chapter 9,[324] limited the ability of the defendant to respond to the publication in a way that would not occur in England, let alone the US. In effect, the defendant was tied to the particular level at which the plaintiff pleaded the alleged meaning of the publication: because the plaintiff pleaded imputations about being guilty of certain conduct, the defence could not plead meanings at the levels of reasonable suspicion or reason to investigate the

---

321 Murchison et al (1994) 29.

322 *Ibid.*

323 116; see Chapter 8, Part IV, C.

324 See Chapter 9, Part IV, A; *Gutnick v Dow Jones (No 4)* (2004) Aust Torts Reports ¶81-748.

plaintiff about that conduct. As well as criticising this approach – primarily for its effects on litigation practice – the discussion of Lucas-Box pleading in Chapter 9 underlines how at least some Australian decisions differ from the English position, which is one way that English law appears to offer markedly more protection for speech than some current Australian law.

B Defamation litigation's usual steps

In comparing US and non-US defamation law and practice it is important to appreciate the steps through which most media-related defamation cases proceed. On one level, these steps – pleading, pre-trial hearings, trial and appeal – appear similar in all the countries dealt with in this book. However, they differ in practice in many ways, as earlier chapters discuss. For the US, motions to dismiss and motions for summary judgment have a central role in litigation. They are far more important in *ending* cases than the pre-trial meaning disputes that are common in England and Australia. Those disputes, however, are central to shaping the relative positions of the parties in a dispute and, it would seem, in influencing settlement decisions. Another important difference in US practice is the differing breadth and style of discovery, which includes depositions. Typical defamation practices are considered further below in Section E, but it is interesting that US interviews suggested great variation may exist in relation to the extent of discovery in different defamation cases, and that this is influenced to a significant degree by the parties' resources.

C Lawyers' experience

In many US cases, only defence lawyers appear to have substantial experience in defamation. Neither plaintiff lawyers nor judges regularly act in defamation. Although US law relies more on written argument from lawyers than is common in English and Australian trials, defamation experience would remain a substantial difference in terms of how the technicality of US defamation rules – with their combination of federal and state constitutional law and state common law – can be deployed in cases. The different US system for funding civil litigation also appears to be related to the differing levels of experience in the lawyers who usually are available to each side in US defamation claims.[325]

D Plaintiff status not subject matter

The fourth point is an obvious element of the US doctrine, but probably worth emphasis. The US law classifies plaintiffs more than it provides particular defences for speech that is thought deserving of protection. England and Australia, in comparison, have maintained defences for particular types of speech – whether related to truth or opinion, the absolute privilege for speech in courts and

[325] Impacts of the differing costs rules are considered further in Weaver et al (2006).

parliaments, or the common law and statutory protection for fair reports and other forms of qualified privilege. Since the mid-1990s, however, England and Australia have developed broader protections for some speech of public or political interest. England, in particular, appears to be tackling the treatment of public interest speech with a similar scope to the temporary and tentative US law under *Rosenbloom v Metromedia*.[326] Even so, the English and Australian defences appear to be markedly weaker than the US law. And the Australian position under *Lange* certainly is narrower in its focus on political – and perhaps primarily electoral – speech. But comparison remains difficult considering how recently, in the law's terms, the English and Australian changes occurred. There has not yet been the four decades of case law experience that the US has seen since *New York Times v Sullivan*.[327]

E Common complexity?

The research also has implications for some of the existing commentary on US defamation law and litigation. In short, the law may be less complex in the usual case than some of the literature could be taken to suggest. This would appear to be only a difference of degree, and is one of the areas that further research into defamation decisions – considered below – could help illuminate. Here, three notable analyses of US defamation law and procedure are examined briefly. They raise, in particular, concerns with discovery, appellate review and the costs of litigation.

In the later 1980s, Scott Matheson analysed procedural rules in defamation cases under *Sullivan*.[328] Matheson raised concerns about the discovery process and the role of appellate review, among other things, and argued that US liability standards may deserve revision because of the difficulties they pose in litigation. At the least, courts should supervise carefully the procedural aspects of public plaintiff defamation cases. Matheson's work is valuable for raising arguments for doctrinal reform on the basis of procedure's interaction with the formal law. Much of what is discussed in this book suggests the value in carefully examining the interaction of law and litigation practice, particularly when drawing on comparative legal approaches.

A basic concern in his analysis was that the aims of *Sullivan* to protect speech could be undermined by the complexity and expense of litigation. The US standards are difficult to litigate: actual malice and lesser fault standards mean the editorial processes of media defendants must be evaluated. That, in turn, means information related to the media's news production processes is an important part of the discovery and deposition process. For Matheson this pointed 'to a serious conflict between the free expression values the standard is intended to serve and the procedural consequences of its implementation'.[329] His

[326] 403 US 29 (1971); see Chapter 8, Part I, B.

[327] 376 US 254 (1964).

[328] Matheson (1987).

[329] *Ibid* 233.

concerns with discovery extended beyond issues of intrusion and cost to questions about the ambiguity of some discovered information for litigation's fact-finding process. For example, Matheson referred to the *Tavoulareas* litigation[330] and the disputes that could be seen across multiple judgments in the case about whether an internal memorandum of the defendant provided evidence of actual malice:

> The Peterson memorandum was part of an editorial process designed to produce deliberation and accuracy. Those with access to greater information received her memorandum, responded to it, and made editorial decisions. The memorandum was unquestionably discoverable after *Herbert*. *Tavoulareas* stands as 'sound reason to believe that editorial exchanges are . . . subject to distortion and . . . recurring misunderstandings'.[331]

After this study raising problems of cost, intrusion and unreliability, in the early 1990s researchers in the Iowa Libel Research Project analysed the ways in which US judges have created norms for journalism in relation to research, writing and editing stories under the actual malice standard. From analysing a substantial number of decisions, Brian Murchison and his co-authors found that:

> [T]he promise of *Sullivan* remains unfulfilled. Libel litigation has not disappeared. The specter of unpredictable litigation and large libel judgments has been replaced by the certainty of legal costs that make the judgment in *Sullivan* pale in comparison. While the incidence of judgments against the press is very low, as *Sullivan* promised, the cost to the press of obtaining favorable judgments is crushing.[332]

It is important to note the researchers realised that US rates of defamation litigation might have been falling.[333] Subsequent research generally supports that view.[334] While the Iowa Project researchers doubted the *Sullivan* rules were playing a significant role in any reduction in suits, the interviews reported in Chapter 8 suggest that *Sullivan* should be seen as an important factor – along with the greater defamation experience of US defence lawyers and subsequent decisions like *Anderson v Liberty Lobby* (much of the influence of that decision would be subsequent to the Murchison study, which dealt with cases up to 1990).[335] It also is noteworthy that the research found most actual malice arguments concern recklessness with regard to truth or falsity – not publishing a known falsity.[336] Only in 10 per cent of the cases studied did plaintiffs 'attempt

---

330 See eg *Tavoulareas v Washington Post*, 567 F Supp 651 (1983); *Tavoulareas v Piro*, 759 F 2d 90 (DC Cir, 1985); 763 F 2d 1472 (DC Cir, 1985).

331 Matheson (1987) 251 and its note 202, quoting *Herbert v Lando*, 441 US 153, 174 (1978).

332 Murchison et al (1994) 11.

333 *Ibid* 11 and its note 9: 'While libel lawsuits are often filed, the number of libel trials may be diminishing.'

334 See eg Logan (2001); Anderson (2002); Weaver et al (2006).

335 477 US 242 (1986).

336 Murchison et al (1994) 25–29.

to prove that the media had knowingly published false information'.[337] This is related to what has particular interest here; namely, suggestions the Murchison study offers for future comparative research, which is turned to below.

Susan Gilles conducted another detailed consideration of procedural law relevant to the First Amendment in the late 1990s and found similar problems. She argued the US approach is 'expensive, drawn out, and fails to protect expression effectively'.[338] Again, discovery and its expense were particular concerns: 'Discovery almost always requires extensive court intervention to resolve motions to compel and requests for protective orders.'[339] Her analysis was interesting, in particular, for examining the changing levels of procedural protection during the life of a defamation case:

> This is First Amendment process in the typical libel case: no protections at the initial pleading and discovery stages, but with ever-increasing safeguards from summary judgment through trial to appeal.[340]

Largely drawing on 1980s figures – when disposal of cases may have been more difficult for media defendants than recent figures suggest[341] – Gilles still notes defendants' very high success rates:

> When looked at in combination, the impact of the Court's First Amendment process is striking: between 70% and 80% of all defense motions for summary judgment are granted. Of the suits which remain, plaintiffs lose about a third of them at trial. . . . Studies have repeatedly reported that only 5%, and up to perhaps 10% of plaintiffs who file suit, ever recover.[342]

There is an important caveat to figures like this about summary judgment, which Gilles and others have noted. The rate of successful motions is probably over-estimated in the figures. Similar to the difficulty of determining US rates of defamation litigation against the media, which was discussed in Chapter 8,[343] the figures are based on reported decisions about summary judgment. But when summary judgment is denied, US courts often do not issue reasons.[344] Even so, rates of summary judgment in defamation do appear to be markedly higher than in other tort actions.[345]

---

[337] *Ibid* 28 and its note 85.

[338] Gilles (1998) 1756. She has also criticised the Sullivan rules' possible effects on media content: Marshall and Gilles (1994).

[339] Gilles (1998) 1769.

[340] *Ibid* 1774.

[341] See above, fn 334.

[342] Gilles (1998) 1779 (footnotes omitted).

[343] See Chapter 8, Part III, A.

[344] Gilles (1998) 1774 and its note 74.

[345] *Ibid* noting that US research about the disposition of tort cases found 1.7 per cent ended by summary judgment and citing Smith et al (1995) 3.

All these studies – and similar analysis of the US position by Michael Chesterman in Australia[346] – suggest problems about the discovery and deposition process and the costs associated with it. The interview material set out in Chapter 8 also suggests these issues can be real concerns in running litigation – probably for defendants more than plaintiffs, but not solely for defendants. However, it appears from the interviews that the concerns *may* not be common in the usual media case. Perhaps a crucial point to take from the earlier literature, in light of the research discussed in Chapter 8, involves the way in which extensive intrusion into media processes and associated costs is possible in US defamation litigation. The US law certainly allows that because of the legal standards under *Sullivan* and the US approach to discovery and depositions. However, its prevalence may deserve further research. As well as investigating the substantiality of pre-trial processes in defamation cases, it also would be valuable to consider the role of earlier motions. In particular, motions to dismiss did not appear to be rare from the interviews and often may be relatively simple and inexpensive procedures in US defamation cases.

From her detailed analysis, Gilles recommended some changes to US law. In general, the US and comparative research set out in this book supports those suggestions. As Gilles and other authors state, some of the options already are within courts' powers. For example, courts can sequence the discovery process to limit its cost for all parties and focus it on the issues that, in the circumstances of the particular case, are most likely to be determinative of summary judgment. Gilles' suggestions include making it a constitutional requirement for plaintiffs to plead the exact words of the publication, applying the constitution to sequencing procedural steps like discovery and providing for appeals from denials of summary judgment. US experience with later defamation appeals suggests that many denials of summary judgment would be reversed immediately if an appeal was available. However, the research set out in this book raises concerns about one of her suggestions involving treating actual malice as a question of law. As Gilles notes, the status of the plaintiff already is treated as a legal issue and jury findings on actual malice are subject to independent appellate review.[347] But moving the issue of actual malice to the judge would entail a jury role similar to that under *Reynolds* and *Lange* privilege. Gilles suggests:

> [T]he jury would determine any disputed facts by responses to special interrogatories. For instance, a jury might be asked: Did the reporter lie about what a witness said in an interview, or did an editor change the meaning of the reporter's story? The trial court would then be required to determine if, given these factual findings, these actions constituted actual malice.[348]

[346] Chesterman (2000) Chapter 4.

[347] Eg *Rosenblatt v Baer*, 383 US 75, 88 (1966); *Bose Corpn v Consumers Union of United States*, 466 US 485, 499 (1984); and see Chapter 8, Part I, G.

[348] Gilles (1998) 1805 (footnotes omitted).

English and Australian experience discussed in Chapter 7 suggests that this sort of change to the jury role should be considered carefully. Of course, the legal tests under *Sullivan* are different from the English and Australian privilege defences, and US law already applies a constitutional review standard to this issue. But the comparative research suggests that complex jury questionnaires may not simplify the process of litigating under *Sullivan*.[349] (In any event, the interview research illustrates how rare US defamation trials are in practice.)

It also should be noted that, even if the more extreme examples of discovery and depositions are relatively rare in the US, concerns would remain about the approach. It gives the opportunity for what appears to be oppressive discovery to plaintiffs with substantial resources, and that may pose greater concerns for particular media outlets. At the least, it would seem plausible that smaller book and magazine publishers, for example, could face far greater financial threats from the deposition process.[350] It also is very much an open question how the US rules would operate under English or Australian procedural models. The Californian experience with anti-SLAPP legislation suggests that the risk of paying defence costs could be a major deterrent to potential litigants,[351] but the very different traditions in England and Australia as regards pleading and meaning caution against making simple comparisons about this sort of change.

F Future US and comparative research

There are several ways in which the US material discussed in Chapter 8 could be useful for future research. First, analyses could be undertaken of samples of defamation judgments. As discussed in Chapter 1, earlier researchers have used samples of defamation pre-trial, trial and appellate judgments to investigate aspects of US law and practice.[352] Similar methods could be applied to more recent samples of cases to examine, for example, the role of substantial truth in US approaches to meaning. The US, English and Australian research has suggested a difference in how the concept operates in the US. There is great scope for researchers to investigate this further through case analysis. The descriptions in Chapter 8, for the US, and Chapters 2 to 6, for England and Australia, could provide a useful basis for such efforts. Similar analyses could be conducted about the interpretation of publications in terms of opinion.[353] Second, the material set out there may be related to research about defamation law, media content and media production practices. Media content and production have not been

349 Gilles also raises more general risks associated with reducing the jury role: *ibid* 1807–1808.

350 This would echo concerns about such publishers raised by Barendt et al (1997) 182–86; and Cheer (2005).

351 See Chapter 8, Parts I, F and IV, H.

352 See Chapter 1, Part II, A.

353 See Chapter 8, Part I, D.

considered in any detail in this book owing to the focus on law and litigation practice. But evaluating existing or future work about defamation and the media may be assisted by understanding some of the important differences in defamation litigation that face the media and their legal advisers in each of these countries.[354]

Third, further avenues for research are suggested by drawing on the earlier US research discussed above. For example, Murchison and his co-researchers showed how, in the US,

> courts are engaged in evaluating each step of the journalistic process. The relevance of this conduct is a natural product of . . . *Sullivan*, although it is difficult to believe that the *Sullivan* Court ever imagined the scope of behaviors that would come under scrutiny in applications of the actual malice test.[355]

An issue for comparative investigation concerns which behaviours have most relevance under the *Sullivan* rules and under *Reynolds* and *Lange* privileges (or the similar Australian statutory defences). Compared to the role of tone under *Reynolds* privilege,[356] it is interesting that the Murchison research found US judges to be more restrictive about standards of research than about writing and editing. The focus was more on conduct (and its implications for state of mind) than on tone. This may reflect US concerns about laws directed at the content of speech – which could be traced to the First Amendment and appear particularly strong. It also appears to echo comments from US interviewees about English defamation practice: for example, that English judges 'basically rewrite the story to meet the meaning that [the judge] thinks is suitable', which is 'outrageous'.[357] Conduct no doubt would be important under any of the countries' approaches; however, analysis of cases soon could extend to US decisions under the *Sullivan* rules and English cases involving *Reynolds* privilege – the narrower scope of Australia's *Lange* privilege means it is likely to take noticeably longer for a large enough body of decisions to appear.[358] This work could build on the Murchison study, which concluded that the best media defence in an actual malice case 'is evidence of an adequate investigation of the challenged facts.'[359] Just what US and English courts evaluate as an 'adequate investigation' in particular

[354] See eg Barendt et al (1997); Dent and Kenyon (2004); Weaver et al (2006). Similarly, the work could be related to legal and non-legal literature on roles of the media: eg Morant (2004); Couldry (2003).

[355] Murchison et al (1994) 51 (footnote omitted).

[356] See above, Part II and Chapter 7.

[357] Interviewed lawyer 116.

[358] The uniform defamation proposals may allow more cases to emerge (see above Part II, C).

[359] Murchison et al (1994) 51. Future research could extend to other US fault standards such as negligence and gross negligence. And, like Murchison et al, it would seem valuable to include US decisions on summary judgment motions and similar pre-trial steps: see *ibid* 30 and its note 94.

circumstances could be a valuable area for research, especially when further decisions have appeared under *Reynolds*. That sort of investigation, however, also needs to take into account the general legal and procedural differences that are discussed in this book.

IV CONCLUSION

This book has concentrated on two themes: the treatment of a publication's meaning, and the protection of media speech, in English, Australian and US defamation law and litigation practice. Analysing defamation doctrine and investigating litigation practice has produced findings in many areas. In relation to meaning, the book has argued at length in Chapter 9 against Australian developments about defence pleading of alternative meanings. In this chapter, it has explored areas for change in NSW practice and argued for legislative reform to move NSW closer to the common law on meaning. The analysis has shown why common law courts in England and Australia should carefully consider any use of NSW precedents relevant to meaning. It also has supported contemporary English developments in case management and argued for Australian courts similarly to promote careful case management as well as alter their approaches to meaning. And it has described the very different ways in which issues of meaning play out in US defamation law and practice. In addition, the book has investigated issues related to the protection of public interest speech under *Reynolds* and *Lange* privileges and the *Sullivan* rules, and suggested areas for future comparative research. Overall, it has sought to demonstrate the value in a detailed examination of legal doctrine and litigation practice, drawing on varied sources from the case law, from legal commentary, and from qualitatively focussed empirical research.

It is worth repeating that the book's findings will have great significance for several aspects of the proposed uniform defamation law in Australia. In particular, the findings are important for the basis of the cause of action, defence meanings and the development of qualified privilege. Issues about meaning will remain central under the proposed law. The cause of action will be the publication, which means Lucas-Box and Polly Peck pleading will remain for Australian courts to engage with. As stated at the outset of this chapter, the intention was not to criticise NSW law and practice. The amount of litigation in that state – and historically, the amount that has been reported – has made NSW something of a favourite for many English and Australian defamation commentators. And it meant NSW was expected to offer important lessons for common law jurisdictions. The fieldwork substantially changed that expectation. Instead, what NSW offers are important lessons suggesting how its reforms have not created a litigation environment with advantages for dealing with defamatory meaning in particular, nor defamation in general.

Under the *Defamation Act 1974* in NSW, the battleground may have moved – from the common law's full trial to pre-trial hearings and the 7A process, and also from the publication to the imputations at least somewhat divorced from the publication. Recent NSW moves to address these problems should be supported. Instead of such an imputation-centred approach and extensive pre-trial manoeuvring, it appears preferable to reach trial as quickly as is practical. As noted in Chapter 6, a Victorian plaintiff's primary tactic can be to seek a trial date as soon as possible because then 'the game's over'.[360]

Overall, the strongest conclusion from the research is the value in a wide approach being taken to Lucas-Box pleading. Before the Australian changes examined in Chapter 9, that defence pleading practice had been 'firmly entrenched' in Victoria,[361] for example, and it remains so in England. Interviewed lawyers supported Lucas-Box pleading because it allowed defendants to avoid the 'straightjacket' of claimant or plaintiff pleadings. And that is a key benefit of the approach – it places the parties in equivalent positions with regard to meaning. As a Victorian interviewee suggested: '[I]f you're going to bring a libel action, you should be prepared to bring it courageously, and you shouldn't be permitted to narrow your meaning, so . . . the defendant had its hands tied'.[362] Given the complexity of the meaning of words and the legal tests focused on the hypothetical ordinary recipient, the better legal approach appears to be having flexible, less prescriptive rules about a publication's meaning and about pleading. Thus parties should not be bound closely to their pleaded meanings, great specificity in imputations should not be required and defendants should be able to make Lucas-Box and Polly Peck pleas. The focus should remain, as far as possible, on the publication and the allegations within it that are complained about. In attempting to confine disputes to pleaded imputations, rather than publications, NSW appears to have thrown greater attention onto the pleadings, encouraged more pre-trial disputes about specificity, and limited defendants' ability to plead truth and comment defences. The research has also suggested how, for US defamation lawyers, English and Australian practice seems focussed very closely on meaning.

The more flexible legal approach suggested by the research recognises that a range of meanings almost always is arguable in relation to any publication, and English and Australian defendants will usually want to respond to the other party's claim by arguing a different meaning is conveyed. It has been made clear why this does not arise in the US – and some of the shifts in perspective that are needed for comparative analysis have been clarified. For England and Australia, Lucas-Box and Polly Peck pleas are a practical way of accommodating meaning disputes. They allow an understandable choice to be presented to the tribunal of fact; namely, the publication's meaning is something short, sharp and memorable that claimants or plaintiffs allege to be conveyed. Or the publication's meaning is something usually less serious and often broader that defendants have sought to prove is justified or is their honest opinion. Under this approach, limits to contain trials within workable boundaries can be provided by capacity rulings on

---

360 50B.

361 *Carrey* [1999] 1 VR 875, 885 (Hedigan J).

362 44SC.

whether meanings can arise, by general case management practices and by the discipline imposed on parties through the presence of a jury at a full trial (at least where juries are used). A trial is a peculiar setting in which to determine the meaning of a publication. And the unexpected impression created by the fieldwork is that a full jury hearing has advantages. It places each side in an equivalent position: each can plead any of a number of meanings that are capable of being conveyed by a publication (and do not relate to separate and distinct allegations). But each side will be restrained by knowing its meanings will be evaluated against the other side's meanings by the jury. This may do as much as anything to temper the 'pyramid of insulting paraphrases' that defamation pleaders erect on the words that were published.[363] The approach of allowing each side to present different meanings to the jury in a full hearing – all of which meanings are capable of arising from the allegations in the publication – appears to be a comparatively simple way of dealing with defamatory meaning. And it appears far more preferable to the combination of using an imputation-based cause of action and dividing the fact finding between the judge and jury, as in NSW.

This in turn supports comments by the ALRC made nearly 25 years ago about Australia, which quoted the seventh edition of *Gatley on Libel and Slander* about England to state that problems for defamation existed particularly in relation to procedure:

> Lawyers, in their effort to make the law more precise, have succeeded in making it more technical. . . . Because the law of defamation is at best a reconciliation of opposite interests there is always room for a legal argument at the points of conflict. If these are exposed with too much care, there arise the current grievances – misdirection, appeals, pre-trial skirmishing, increased expense.
>
> There does not seem to be a quick or easy answer to this. What may be needed is an effort of self-abnegation on the part of judges and lawyers and a willingness to leave matters to juries in as simple a form as possible.[364]

Although the word games of defamation have changed, that suggestion for law remains.

[363] *Halford v Chief Constable of Hampshire Constabulary* [2003] EWCA Civ 102, [63] (Sedley LJ): 'libel pleaders never seem content to say that the words in issue mean what they say: a pyramid of insulting paraphrases has to be erected on them', also referring to *Alexander* [2001] 1 WLR 1840, [41] (May LJ).

[364] Australian Law Reform Commission (1979) [72], quoting McEwen and Lewis (1974) vi–vii.

APPENDIX

EMPIRICAL METHODOLOGY AND RESEARCH SAMPLES

This book pursues its comparative investigative of defamation law and litigation practice in part through sociolegal research. This appendix examines its empirical methodology, concentrating on Chapters 4 to 6 as examples.[1] Approaches to empirical work vary greatly, as do researchers' underlying premises. Setting out something about the methodology used allows others to evaluate the project's findings from their own perspectives.[2]

I THE PROJECT HAS TWO TYPES OF EMPIRICAL SOURCE

The empirical research for this project used two sources – court files and interviews with lawyers. These sources appeared likely to provide the sort of information needed in the research, but they also were chosen for quite contingent reasons: one or both of them were relatively easily available in each jurisdiction. The sought information concerned litigation practice: what *happens* at different stages of a dispute. Clearly, written records could provide some of the needed material. The Australian court files, for example, appeared likely to offer information such as what sorts of meanings are pleaded, what interlocutory applications are made and with what result.[3] But a wider context about what happened at different stages of the process also would seem useful. Given the project's questions are framed by legal doctrine, it appeared valuable to hear about the understanding of lawyers who are involved with the doctrine in practice. All those who assisted in relation to these two sources are sincerely thanked.[4]

---

[1] Chapters 4 to 8 include further information about the research methods and each of the samples.

[2] Eg Kirk and Miller (1986) and Seale (1999) emphasise the importance of reporting procedures.

[3] In this, the project ventures beyond the conclusion of the NSW Law Reform Commission (1995) [1.21]. The LRC decided against updating and expanding existing empirical studies and suggested the limited material available would add little to that work. This study, however has shown that gains in comparative analysis can be obtained through a combination of court file, interview and doctrinal research.

[4] Individuals are listed here who assisted with the organisation or provision of interviews in England, Australia and the US, or assisted in relation to accessing transcripts or court files (each is identified with any title held at that time): Caroline Addy, Maureen Ahearne, Adrian Anderson, Ian Angus, Peter Applegarth SC, Kevin Baine, Manuel Barca, Peter Bartlett, John Bennett, Gordon Bishop, David Boddice SC,

Two alternatives to interviews were not pursued: observing litigation and using a questionnaire to survey lawyers. Why not observe behaviour instead of interviewing practitioners? Observation was impractical primarily because litigation activities take place over many months or years in a variety of locations, within and outside courts. Court files and interviews allow actions across a broad range of time and location to be considered. Interviews, for example, can provide information about widely dispersed events:

> [I]nterviewees can recall and summarize a wide range of observations in seconds, which would take weeks and months of observational work to achieve. They can also speak about things that cannot be observed.[5]

A questionnaire delivered by post or email was another alternative.[6] But this appeared to be overly structured and a serious limitation for the project. Less formal interviews seemed better suited to this research. For example, interviews would be more likely to reveal differences in the meanings attached to apparently equivalent terminology in each jurisdiction.[7] In addition, concerns about confidentiality and a low response rate to any questionnaire were likely to be addressed better through interviews.

Alastair Brett, Mal Brooks, Desmond Browne QC, Andrew Buchanan, Bruce Burke, Tom Burke, Godwin Busuttil, Siobhain Butterworth, Peter Carter-Ruck, David Caspersonn, Joanna Cassidy, Norman Chapman, Cindy Christian, Iain Christie, Jonathan Coad, Richard Coleman, Dr Matt Collins, Stephen Collins, Martin Cruddace, Christopher Dale, Sophie Dawson, Jacob Dean, Frank Dehn, Mark Dreyfus QC, Sir David Eady, David Engel, Catrin Evans, Bill Farley, Jeremy Feigelson, Anne Flahvin, George Freeman, Kevin Goering, Penelope Gorman, Sir Charles Gray, Geoff Gronow, Tim Hale SC, Laura Handman, Jon Hart, Dave Heller, Alister Henskens, Natalie Hickey, Will Houghton QC, Anthony Hudson, Christopher Hutchings, Jan Johannes, Nerida Johnston, Merrit Jones, Stephen Jupp, Stuart Karle, David Korzenik, Victor Kovner, Jim Lake, Richard Leder, Justice David Levine RFD, Lee Levine, Adam Liptak, Bruce McClintock, Ruth McColl SC, Findlay McCrae, David McCraw, Jennifer McDermott, Laurence Maher, Michael Martin, Alexandra Marzec, Ann Matheson, Amber Melville-Brown, Patrick Milmo QC, Tom Molomby SC, Patrick Moloney QC, Justine Munsie, Sir Brian Neill, Matthew Nicklin, Leanne Norman, Ken Norwick, Peter O'Donahoo, Stephen O'Meara, Adrienne Page QC, Marcus Partington, Susan Poffley, Richard Potter, David Price, James Price QC, Gary Pruitt, Stav Psonis, Nicholas Pullen, Richard Rampton QC, Steven Rares SC, Guy Reynolds, Dean Ringel, Rhory Robertson, Jeremy Ruskin QC, Joseph Saltalamacchia, Julie Scott-Bayfield, Georgina Schoff, David Schulz, Geoffrey Shaw QC, Richard Shillito, Stephen Shotnes, Michael Skrein, Simon Smith, Rod Smolla, Michael Smyth, Adam Speker, Darien Spence, Doug Spence, Mark Stephens, the Honourable Judge Stott, Paul Sutton, Patrick Swaffer, Nicola Thatcher, Belinda Thompson, Jerianne Timmerman, Terence Tobin QC, Robert Todd, Laura Tyler, David Wachen, Mark Warby QC, Michael Wheelahan, Scott Wheelhouse and Simon Wilson QC.

[5] Seale (1999) 59.

[6] Alternatives such as telephone surveying across international time zones would appear even less feasible.

[7] For a brief discussion of questions about meaning equivalence in comparative research, see May (2001) 213–15. Seale provides an overview of similar concerns about survey research: (1999) 133–35.

While this combination of court file and interview material was available in Australia, it was not possible in England except in the most cursory sense. As is explained in Chapter 4, the style of court records available in Australia did not exist in England. Using other written sources of information was impractical. For example, some legal researchers have sought information about legal practice from lawyers' files. Richard Ingleby's work on divorce lawyers in England is one illustration.[8] Ingleby monitored a range of files at five family law solicitors in various locations in England to investigate what solicitors did during disputes. He was interested in lawyers' out-of-court activity as a process and believed examining files could bring him close to that process in an unobtrusive manner.[9] Defamation law, however, has far fewer practitioners than family law. Access to a range of defamation litigation files was quite unlikely, and less promising than relatively wide-scale interviewing of defamation practitioners.[10]

II THE MECHANICS OF THE FIELDWORK AND INITIAL ANALYSIS

Court files were analysed in Melbourne and Sydney primarily during 2000. Initial contact was made by letter with the Registrar, Prothonotary or Chief Executive Officer for each court.[11] All courts were happy to provide access and waive any fees for searching.[12] This assistance was invaluable for the research. Between five and 10 days was spent in each registry, and a large amount of practical assistance was provided by registry staff in locating files and understanding systems used in internal court documentation. Defamation cases issued during 1998 were identified by manually searching through records of the daily lists of court hearings for defamation hearings held since 1998, and by using computerised records that were available in some courts. The filing systems used in each court mean that almost every defamation case issued during 1998 should have been identified.[13] Files were analysed at the registries, and notes entered

[8] Ingleby (1992).

[9] *Ibid* 13–18.

[10] This conclusion is supported by the reticence some English lawyers and media companies have shown previously in discussing sensitive information about defamation: Barendt et al (1997) 36.

[11] For the NSW SC, the judge then in charge of the defamation list, Justice David Levine, suggested the CEO would be the most appropriate contact and supported my request to access court files.

[12] The NSW access should be noted in particular as NSW court files are not open to public searching (unlike the Victorian Supreme and County Courts). On court file access in Australian jurisdictions see Walker (2000) 463–79. The NSW Supreme Court was happy to provide access, with appropriate undertakings to maintain the confidentiality of matters that have not been discussed in open court.

[13] A few cases involving defamation alongside another claim may have been missed, but court personnel suggested the figure would be very small.

directly onto a computer.[14] The contents of the files were analysed in terms of categories that are relevant to defamatory meaning and arise from legal doctrine.[15] As well, photocopies were taken of certain documents from the court files; for example, pleading documents and the publications at suit.[16] Return visits were made early in 2001 to each registry. Files that had remained open in 2000 were reviewed and any further activity was noted. This allowed a uniform cut-off date to be set for the files of 31 December 2000.

English interviews were conducted in June 2000 and May 2003. Victorian and NSW interviews occurred between August and November 2000, during December 2002, and in June and July 2003. US interviews were conducted in April and May 2003 (with two being conducted in January 2004). Interview subjects generally were approached by letter,[17] and followed up by email, letter or telephone. Almost all interviews were conducted at interviewees' workplaces. Most interviews lasted approximately one hour, although several were shorter or extended to one and a half hours. The interviews were semi-structured and allowed all interviewees to offer general comments.

Almost all interviews were audiotape recorded and later transcribed. In several instances, information was enriched by documentary material being provided. This was particularly important in London, where court records were not available. Examples included pleading documents, files prepared for court and transcripts of hearings. Tapes of the interviews were transcribed in a word-processed form and a physical file was created for each jurisdiction with tapes, transcripts and any further documentary material that had been provided. Rather than a research software program being used,[18] the full transcripts were summarised into a separate word-processed document and coded according to the general legal issues addressed in the interviews. Points made by interviewees were listed under each general area, and illustrative quotations were recorded. This long and detailed process brought about great familiarity with the material, and maintained easy access to interviewees' own words.

Issues of confidentiality and attribution were raised in initial correspondence with potential interviewees, and at the start of each interview. During the interview, interviewees were asked whether they were happy for any quotations from their interviews to be attributed or preferred quotations not to be directly

---

[14] The style of information taken from the files is described further in Chapters 5 and 6.

[15] To build on Edgeworth and Newcity (1992) and Sourdin (1990) a file analysis form was adapted from their work. It covered matters such as party names, date file opened and current file status, parties' occupations, subject matter of publication, imputations pleaded and challenged, pre-trial hearings and settlement or disposal information.

[16] Copies of print publications usually were on file. In many other cases, transcripts of electronic media publications were on file.

[17] Initial contact was by email in a few instances in England and Australia (and more often in the US, where postal or fax details were less obtainable than email).

[18] Eg such as NVivo; a general discussion of software and coding is provided by Seale (2004b) 305.

attributed. Approximately half the interviewees were happy for all material to be attributed to them. Although other interviewees were happy for their participation to be acknowledged, they preferred not to be identified directly with a particular statement. To protect those wishes, no quotation has been identified with a named interviewee in this book. Instead, interviewees are referred to by number, along with their professional role. Quotations used are direct transcriptions from interviews. Only minimal changes have been made to the subjects' own words, the aim being to produce 'clarity and readability'.[19]

III QUALITATIVE AND QUANTITATIVE METHODS

This project draws on qualitative and quantitative research methods, principally semi-structured interviews and content analysis of court files. It is increasingly common to see qualitative and quantitative research as part of a spectrum of information collection methods, rather than necessarily opposed camps of social research.[20] Theoretical questions about ontology and epistemology may differentiate research approaches more importantly and in different ways than the labels of qualitative or quantitative, even if some researchers may suggest the division reflects more than a conventional distinction.[21] In any event, it is common for media research to include both sorts of information. An Australian example within media studies is the work underlying *Fame Games: The Production of Celebrity in Australia*, which included quantitative content analysis of media products and qualitative interviews with industry professionals.[22] Another is provided by *Accounting for Tastes: Australian Everyday Culture*,[23] which examined the distribution of cultural tastes within Australian society. It drew significantly, but not uncritically, on the work of French sociologist Pierre Bourdieu and in particular his book, *Distinction: A Social Critique of the Judgement of Taste*.[24] Although Bourdieu's large body of work, which combines many methods of collection and analysis, may not be commented very frequently by English-language empirical sociologists,[25] their work is applying similar combinations of methods.

---

[19] Ewick and Silbey (1998) 259. As these authors note, that does not mean the quotations seek to achieve any romantic idea of conveying interviewees' 'pure' words: 258.

[20] Eg see Flyvbjerg (2001); Bryman (1998) 138; Silverman (2000); Morrow with Brown (1994) 207–11 (where the 'false dichotomy' between quantitative and qualitative methods is explored).

[21] Eg consider how quantitative and qualitative are used to divide all aspects of the research process in texts like Sarantakos (1998).

[22] Turner et al (2000).

[23] Bennett et al (1999).

[24] (1984).

[25] Eg it is not examined at all in works such as Silverman (2000); Seale (2004a); and Sarantakos (1998). But see eg May (1998) 157.

As David Silverman suggests, at one level many differences between research approaches disappear:

> [T]he days of a great divide between qualitative and quantitative research work have now largely passed. The argument that each of these methodologies is inextricably linked to separate philosophical or theoretical positions . . . is less and less convincing to most practising social researchers.[26]

Many criticisms that have been levelled at qualitative research, particularly problems of reliability and validity, can be raised against quantitative work as well. And all methods can be used without appropriate awareness of their presuppositions and weaknesses. For example, the apparently objective statistics arrived at in some quantitative research can be questioned in various ways, such as the initial choice of categories and the allocation of material to them.[27] Interpreting quantitative material can be seen to involve 'measurement by fiat'; that is, explaining correlations between variables may be based on researchers' values more than on empirical data.[28] The chosen categories are not value-free, and empirical social research cannot escape questions that flow from its own interpretive power. This project clearly leans toward the qualitative in the spectrum of sociological research. It is concerned more with generating knowledge about a particular issue, not testing a hypothesis, and that knowledge is understood to be context- and situation-dependent.[29] Its focus is on how legal rules are enacted in routine practice, which it approaches through extensive fieldwork. But whatever methodological approaches are used, the status of the information needs consideration.

IV THE STATUS OF THE INFORMATION AND ITS ANALYSIS

In what way can extrapolations be drawn from the material?[30] Does the research have what commonly is called reliability and validity?[31] The information drawn from court files and described in Chapters 5 and 6 concerns almost every defamation case issued in three Australian courts during 1998.[32] The information should have a close relationship to elements of litigation practice in these courts; for example, the pleading practice and procedural steps that parties undertake. There is

26 Silverman (2000) 157.

27 Eg see discussion of official statistics in May (2001) 71–87; Silverman (2000) 6.

28 Seale (1999) 120 drawing on Cicourel (1964).

29 See Flyvbjerg (2001) for close analysis of the context-dependent quality of social research.

30 This may be a more useful concept than generalisability: Alasuutari (1995) as Silverman (2000) 110–11 notes.

31 Eg Silverman (2000) 175. For an overview of qualitative approaches to reliability, see Seale (1999) Chapter 10.

32 The Supreme Court of Victoria, the Supreme Court of NSW, and the District Court of NSW, which means the material encompasses the two Australian states with the most defamation litigation.

little to suggest cases issued in that year are atypical, although certain ways in which practice appears to be changing are noted in Chapters 4 to 6 when the material is discussed, and in later chapters that draw on 2003 interviews and more recent case law. (For example, it is noted that since 1998 a sizable minority of NSW litigation appears to have moved to the intermediate District Court level. And more recent changes in the courts' approach to pleading disputes are explored.) Thus, it is claimed that material in the court files has a meaningful connection to current litigation practice. As well, the coding of this material should be fairly reliable, in the sense that moderately consistent categorisation would have been likely if different observers had been used to code material from the files.[33] This is because the coding relied on recognised doctrinal categories in defamation law.

The interview material in Chapters 4 to 6 is somewhat less representative of practice, particularly for Australia, where a smaller number of interviews were conducted. But the Australian interviews merely aim to supplement extensive court file material. They also were updated by 2003 interviews. Among other things, the interview material suggests the tactical reasons for which parties adopt certain approaches to interlocutory steps. In England, many more interviews were conducted and it is suggested the responses are indicative of current English practice. The size of the sample, and the extremely concentrated nature of London defamation litigation practice, means that the material does provide a meaningful image of London libel practice. Given the pool of potential interviewees, the number of interviews is substantial, and the sample is typical of London defamation lawyers.[34] Using recognised legal categories goes some way towards addressing concerns about reliability in the interview material. One could expect that broadly similar material would be found by another researcher or presented by these interviewees at another time. At the same time, the transcription, summarisation and coding method that was adopted aimed to maintain good access to the material – to what people said and the way subjects described the categories.[35]

As well as concerns about reliability, researchers often consider the validity of their empirical material. In this context, validity is understood to be the accurate representation of social phenomena. In the limited context of this legal research, that description could be accepted. That is not to suggest that validity is an unproblematic concept. As Silverman suggests:

> Broadly, many models that underlie qualitative research are simply not compatible with the assumption that 'true' fixes on 'reality' can be obtained separately from particular ways of looking at it. . . . The problem only arises when you use such multiplicity [of datasets] as a way of settling validity questions.[36]

[33] For a discussion of reliability, see eg Seale (1999) 140–58 and Silverman (2000) 175.

[34] McNeill (1990) 14.

[35] Eg see Glassner and Loughlin (1987) 16–17, 24–29, and their concern to maintain access to subjects' words in a project bridging quantitative and qualitative approaches.

[36] Silverman (2000) 177.

But the representations drawn from this material should be meaningful in terms of how legal discourse understands certain legal phenomena involved in defamation litigation.

In addition to remembering the limited *legal* scope of this project, aiming at a comprehensive treatment of the material and including atypical cases improves the research's validity. It addresses a weakness in some qualitative research; namely, its anecdotalism. For example, a researcher can quote a few comments from interviews, without it being apparent how representative the responses are and without contrary examples being considered.[37] In this project, the relatively extensive footnoting allows readers to assess both issues, at least to some degree, by making the depth of response about particular issues more transparent. That is, a simple counting of responses within the material is made relatively transparent to the reader.[38] Naturally, problems remain about interviewees' retrospective reporting of their behaviour. And not every interviewee commented on each issue: the semi-structured interviews allowed respondents a degree of latitude to focus on what they believed to be the most significant matters about defamation law and litigation practice. The interview transcripts record how interviewees responded to questions and represent a narrative construction of their legal practice.[39] But, given the interviews' significant focus on doctrinal questions, it also is suggested this construction has validity within legal discourse: the interviews provide descriptive material about legal doctrine that has value within law. Overall, the material reported here should be assessed with the understanding that where an issue receives many comments, practitioners see the issue as important; where many interviewees hold a particular view, that view is likely to be common among experienced practitioners; and where divergences of views appeared in interviews, they are noted in the reporting.

The interviews did not appear to suffer from some other weaknesses that have been suggested about interview material for two reasons. First, there appeared to be no particular reason for interviewees to misrepresent their activities. The interviews did not focus directly on controversial aspects of interviewees' professional practice. The project does not, for example, investigate ethical behaviour of lawyers in defamation litigation. So while the research involved the socially powerful, they had no particular interest in resisting being researched.[40] Instead, most interviewees appeared very open to the research and viewed it as topical. For example, when many Sydney lawyers were interviewed in 2000 they were considering the implications of a recent High Court case for litigation practice and law reform.[41] This made them particularly interested in the research's comparative aspects. Similar issues existed for interviews conduced subsequently

---

[37] Eg *ibid* 11.

[38] The approach follows eg Silverman (1993) 163 (and see 2001). See generally Seale (1999) Chapter 9.

[39] Eg Holstein and Gubrium (1995); Ingleby (1991) 6–7.

[40] Cf Smigel (1958).

[41] *John Pfeiffer v Rogerson* (2000) 203 CLR 503.

and elsewhere.[42] Second, I shared a degree of professional similarity with interviewees. A 'blending-in' of backgrounds was apparent between interviewer and interviewees.[43] This allowed a useful rapport to be established quickly in the great majority of interviews.[44] Clearly, our engagement with law is quite distinct, in academia and in legal practice. But my knowledge of recent developments in other jurisdictions positioned me as a legal colleague with relative expertise. Many questions about comparative law and practice were asked of me; the interview process was far from one-way. All this may have assisted the taping of interviews to occur without it appearing to inhibit discussions.

If the material can be said to have a substantial degree of reliability, what is the status of the methods of analysis? In this project, a form of content analysis is used to analyse court files. The categories applied to the files arise from legal doctrine, and within the legal system they are uncontroversial. For example, ideas like Lucas-Box pleading and justification[45] are used in analysing the court files, but no particular claim is made for them in this project beyond their legal currency.[46] While these categories do not exist in some sense prior to legal culture, they exist in legal discourse before their interpretation in this study. For the interviews, law again supplies the theoretical scheme for coding the material; that is, the transcripts are coded according to legal issues of doctrine and procedure.[47]

There is a final point to note about this combination of methods and research material. It need not be understood as triangulation.[48] There are limitations in simple approaches to triangulation in social research; that is, in supposing there is an independent definitive version of the social research subject, which can be revealed more clearly by adopting multiple methods.[49] Rather, the context from which the information arises is important to keep in mind any aggregation of the material.[50] At the same time, divergences between interview and court file material can prompt careful analysis, perhaps by exposing different aspects of the litigation process more than validating one information source over the other.

---

[42] Eg US interest in Australian law and practice was heightened at the time of the interviews by the High Court decision in *Dow Jones v Gutnick* (2002) 210 CLR 575.

[43] Eg May (2001) 128.

[44] As well as these factors to encourage rapport, I had lived in London for 12 months several years earlier while completing postgraduate legal study.

[45] See Chapter 3, Part I, K.

[46] The approach differs to common styles of analysis for taped interviews, where categories used in coding transcripts emerge from themes raised by interviewees: eg see Ewick and Silbey's discussion of coding interview transcriptions with lay people about their legal attitudes (1998) 253–54.

[47] With some attention also being paid to non-categorised activities, eg through responses to general questions about other issues that could be relevant to the project; see eg Silverman (2000) 147.

[48] Cf eg Denzin (1970), which he has subsequently developed into a more sophisticated approach (1997).

[49] Eg Seale (1999) 53; Silverman (2000) 98–99; Blaikie (1991) 130–31.

[50] Silverman (2000) 99.

BIBLIOGRAPHY

Abel, Richard L and Lewis, Philip S C (1995), 'Putting Law Back into the Sociology of Lawyers' in Abel and Lewis (eds), *Lawyers in Society: An Overview* (Berkeley: University of California Press)

Ackland, Richard (1999), 'End of a Moonlight Nightmare', *Sydney Morning Herald* (Sydney) (9 July)

Alasuutari, Pertti (1995), *Researching Culture: Qualitative Method and Cultural Studies* (London: Sage)

Anderson, David A (2004), 'First Amendment Limitations on Tort Law' 69 *Brooklyn Law Review* 755

_______ (2003), 'An American Perspective' in Simon Deakin, Angus Johnston and Basil Markesinis, *Markesinis and Deakin's Tort Law* (Oxford: Clarendon Press, 5th ed)

_______ (2002), 'Freedom of the Press' 80 *Texas Law Review* 429

_______ (1984), 'Reputation, Compensation, and Proof' 25 *William and Mary Law Review* 747

Andrews, Neil (2003), *English Civil Procedure: Fundamentals of the New Civil Justice System* (Oxford: Oxford University Press)

Anonymous (2005), 'Associated gets Cost Cap against CFA Claimant with £558,000 Bill' *Media Lawyer*, see <www.medialawyer.press.net>

_______ (2003), 'Henric Nicholas to do both Equity and Defamation' no 151 *Gazette of Law and Journalism*, see <www.lawpress.com.au>

_______ (2001), 'Plaintiff not a Happy Camper: Rene Rivkin loses Defamation Case against Fairfax' no 127 *Gazette of Law and Journalism*, see <www.lawpress.com.au>

Amponsah, Peter N (2004), *Libel Law, Political Criticism and Defamation of Public Figures: The United States, Europe and Australia* (New York: LFB Scholarly Publishing)

Atiyah, P S and Summers, Robert S (1987), *Form and Substance in Anglo-American Law: A Comparative Study of Legal Reasoning, Legal Theory, and Legal Institutions* (Oxford: Clarendon Press)

Attorney-General's Department (Australia) (2004a), *Outline of a Possible National Defamation Law* (Canberra: Attorney-General's Department, March)

_______ (2004b), *Revised Outline of a Possible National Defamation Law* (Canberra: Attorney-General's Department, July)

Attorneys-General of NSW, Queensland and Victoria (1991), *Reform of Defamation Laws: Discussion Paper (No 2)* (Australia)

_______ (1990), *Discussion Paper on Reform of Defamation Law* (Australia)

Austin, John L (1975), *How to do Things with Words* (ed J O Urmson and Marina Sbisà) (Oxford: Clarendon Press)

Australian Law Reform Commission (1979), *Unfair Publication: Defamation and Privacy*, Report 11 (Canberra: Australian Government Publishing Service)

Australian Press Council (1998), *Submission of the Australian Press Council to the Federal, State and Territory Attorneys-General* (Sydney: Australian Press Council, 13 October), see <www.presscouncil.org.au>

Baker, Roy (2004), *Deciding Defamation* (Sydney: National Defamation Research Project/Communications Law Centre)

_______ (2003), 'Defining the Moral Community: The "Ordinary Reasonable Person" in Defamation Law', paper delivered at Communications Research Forum, Canberra (2 October)

_______ (2002a), 'Extending Common Law Qualified Privilege to the Media: A Comparison of the English and Australian Approaches' 7 *Media & Arts Law Review* 87

_______ (2002b), 'Defamatory Comment on the Judiciary: *Lange* Qualified Privilege in *Popovic v Herald & Weekly Times*' 7 *Media & Arts Law Review* 213

Balkin, R P and Davis, J L R (2004), *Law of Torts* (Sydney: LexisNexis Butterworths, 3rd ed)

Barendt, Eric (2005), *Freedom of Speech* (Oxford: Oxford University Press, 2nd ed)

_______ (1999), 'What is the Point of Libel Law?' 52 *Current Legal Problems* 110

_______ (ed) (1996), *Yearbook of Media and Entertainment Law 1996* (Oxford: Oxford University Press)

_______ (1985), *Freedom of Speech* (Oxford: Clarendon Press)

Barendt, Eric M and Firth, Alison (eds) (2000), *Yearbook of Copyright and Media Law 2000* (Oxford: Oxford University Press)

_______ (1999), *Yearbook of Copyright and Media Law 1999* (Oxford: Oxford University Press)

Barendt, Eric; Lustgarten, Laurence; Norrie, Kenneth; and Stephenson, Hugh (1997), *Libel and the Media: The Chilling Effect* (Oxford: Clarendon Press)

Barker, Martin and Petley, Julian (1997), *Ill Effects: The Media/Violence Debate* (London: Routledge)

Barrett, David A (1986), 'Declaratory Judgments for Libel: A Better Alternative' 74 *California Law Review* 847

Bennett, Tony; Emmison, Michael; and Frow, John (1999), *Accounting for Tastes: Australian Everyday Cultures* (Cambridge: Cambridge University Press)

Bezanson, Randall P (1988), 'The Libel Tort Today' 45 *Washington & Lee Law Review* 535

________ (1986), 'The Libel Suit in Retrospect: What Plaintiffs Want and What Plaintiffs Get' 74 *California Law Review* 789

________ (1985), 'Libel Law and the Realities of Litigation: Setting the Record Straight' 71 *Iowa Law Review* 226

Bezanson, Randall P; Cranberg, Gilbert; and Soloski, John (1987), *Libel Law and the Press: Myth and Reality* (New York: Free Press)

Blaikie, Norman (1991), 'A Critique of the Use of Triangulation in Social Research' 25 *Quality and Quantity* 115

Bonnell, Victoria E and Hunt, Lynn (eds) (1999), *Beyond the Cultural Turn: New Directions in the Study of Society and Culture* (Berkeley: University of California Press)

Bourdieu, Pierre (1984), *Distinction: A Social Critique of the Judgement of Taste* (trans Richard Nice) (London: Routledge [1979])

Bow, James and Silver, Ben (1984), 'Effects of *Herbert v Lando* on Small Newspapers and TV Stations' 61 *Journalism Quarterly* 414

Brennan, F G (1975), 'Written Pleadings' 12 *University of Western Australia Law Review* 33

Brennan (Lord) and Blair, William (eds) (2004), *Bullen & Leake & Jacob's Precedents of Pleadings* (London: Sweet & Maxwell, 15th ed)

Brickman, Lester (2003), 'The Market for Contingent Fee-Financed Tort Litigation: Is the Price Competitive?' 25 *Cardozo Law Review* 65

Brown, Malcolm (2002), 'Sydney is the "Defamation Capital of the World"', *Sydney Morning Herald* (Sydney) (23 May)

Brown, Raymond E (1994), *The Law of Defamation in Canada* (Scarborough, Ont: Carswell, 2nd ed)

Bryman, Alan (1998), 'Quantitative and Qualitative Research Strategies in Knowing the Social World' in May and Williams (1998)

Bullen, Edward and Leake, Stephen Martin (1868), *Precedents of Pleadings in Personal Actions in the Superior Courts of Common Law with Notes, and an Appendix of Recent Statutes and General Rules Relating to Pleading* (London: Stevens & Sons, 3rd ed)

Bunker, Matthew D (1992), 'Application of Libel Law Principles by Kansas Editors' 13 *Newspaper Research Journal* 13

Burgess, Robert G (ed) (1982), *Field Research: A Sourcebook and Field Manual* (London: Allen & Unwin)

Burrows, John and Cheer, Ursula (2005), *Media Law in New Zealand* (South Melbourne: Oxford University Press, 5th ed)

Butler, Des (2000), 'Is Polly Peck at Risk of Losing Its Sting?' 5 *Media & Arts Law Review* 259

Butler, Des and Rodrick, Sharon (2004), *Australian Media Law* (Sydney: Lawbook Co, 2nd ed)

Cairns, Bernard (2002), *Australian Civil Procedure* (Sydney: Lawbook Co, 5th ed)

Calvert, Clay (1998), 'The First Amendment and the Third Person: Perceptual Biases of Media Harms and Cries for Government Censorship' 6 *CommLaw Conspectus* 165

_______ (1996), *Constitutionalizing Defamatory Meaning in Libel Law* (Unpublished PhD Thesis, Stanford University)

_______ (1995a), 'Awareness of Meaning in Libel Law: An Interdisciplinary Communication and Law Critique' 16 *Northern Illinois University Law Review* 111

_______ (1995b), 'Harm to Reputation: An Interdisciplinary Approach to the Impact of Denial of Defamatory Allegations' 26 *Pacific Law Journal* 934

Calvert, Clay and Richards, Robert D (2002), 'A Pyrrhic Press Victory: Why Holding Richard Jewell as a Public Figure Is Wrong and Harms Journalism' 22 *Loyola of Los Angeles Entertainment Law Review* 293

Canan, Penelope and Pring, George W (1988), 'Strategic Lawsuits Against Public Participation' 35 *Social Problems* 506

Cass, Deborah Z (1994), 'Through the Looking Glass: The High Court of Australia and the Right to Political Speech' in Tom Campbell and Wojciech Sadurski (eds), *Freedom of Communication* (Aldershot: Dartmouth)

Cassimatis, Anthony E (1994), 'Civil Defamation – The Defence of Fair Comment' 2 *Torts Law Journal* 171

Cheer, Ursula (2005), 'Myths and Realities about the Chilling Effect: The New Zealand Media's Experience of Defamation Law' 13 *Tort Law Journal* 259

Chesterman, Michael (2000), *Freedom of Speech in Australian Law: A Delicate Plant* (Aldershot: Ashgate)

Chesterman, Michael; Chan, Janet; and Hampton, Shelley (2001), *Managing Prejudicial Publicity* (Sydney: Law and Justice Foundation of NSW)

Cicourel, Aaron V (1964), *Method and Measurement in Sociology* (New York: Free Press)

Coad, Jonathan (2002), 'More Light Shed on Reynolds' Defence in First Insurance Industry Libel Trial' 13 *Entertainment Law Review* 90

_______ (2001), '"Pressing Social Need" and Strict Liability in Libel Law' 12 *Entertainment Law Review* 199

Cohen, Jeremy and Gleason, Timothy (1990), *Social Research in Communication and Law* (Newbury Park, CA: Sage)

Cohen, Jeremy and Gunthier, Albert (1987), 'Libel as Communications Phenomena' 9(5) *Communications and the Law* 9

Cohen, Jeremy; Mutz, Diana; Price, Vincent; and Gunthier, Albert (1988), 'Perceived Impact of Defamation: An Experiment on Third-Person Effects' 52 *Public Opinion Quarterly* 161

Collins, Matthew (2005), *The Law of Defamation and the Internet* (Oxford: Oxford University Press, 2nd ed)

_______ (2003), 'Defamation and the Internet after *Dow Jones and Co Inc v Gutnick*' 8 *Media & Arts Law Review* 165

_______ (2001a), *The Law of Defamation and the Internet* (Oxford: Oxford University Press) (also see 2nd ed, 2005)

_______ (2001b), 'Choice of Law in Defamation after *John Pfeiffer Pty Ltd v Rogerson*' 6 *Media & Arts Law Review* 171

_______ (2001c), 'New Defamation Law for the ACT' 6 *Media & Arts Law Review* 335

Community Law Reform Committee of the Australian Capital Territory (1995), *Defamation*, Report 10 (Canberra: Publications and Public Communication)

Cosentino, Victor J (1993), 'Strategic Lawsuit Against Public Participation: An Analysis of the Solutions' 27 *California Western Law Review* 399

Cotterrell, Roger (1994), 'Introduction: The Law and Society Tradition' in Cotterrell (ed), *Law and Society* (Aldershot: Dartmouth)

Cottrell, Jill (1998), 'What Does "Defamatory" Mean? Reflections on *Berkoff v Burchill*' 6 *Tort Law Review* 149

Couldry, Nick (2003), *Media Rituals: A Critical Approach* (London: Routledge)

Cram, Ian (2004), 'Reducing Uncertainty in Libel Law after *Reynolds v Times Newspapers*? *Jameel* and the Unfolding Defence of Qualified Privilege' 15 *Entertainment Law Review* 147

Cranberg, Gilbert (1985), 'Fanning the Fire: The Media's Role in Libel Litigation' 71 *Iowa Law Review* 221

Davies, Martin (2002), 'The Role of Juries in US Torts Cases' 10 *Torts Law Journal* 109

Dent, Chris (2005), '"The Privileged Few" and the Classification of *Henwood v Harrison*: Foucault, Comment and Qualified Privilege' 14 *Griffith Law Review* 34

Dent, Chris and Kenyon, Andrew T (2004), 'Defamation Law's Chilling Effect: A Comparative Content Analysis of Australian and US Newspapers' 9 *Media & Arts Law Review* 89

Denzin, Norman K (1997), *Interpretive Ethnography: Ethnographic Practice for the 21st Century* (Thousand Oaks, CA: Sage)

________ (1970), *The Research Act in Sociology* (London: Butterworths)

Department for Constitutional Affairs (2004a), *Judicial Statistics 2003* (London: DCA); see also Lord Chancellor's Department (below)

________ (2004b), *Making Simple CFAs a Reality*, CP22/04 (London: DCA)

________ (2003), *Judicial Statistics 2002* (London: DCA)

Dewar, John and Parker, Stephen (1999) (with Barbara Tynan and Donna Cooper), *Parenting, Planning and Partnership: The Impact of the New Part VII of the Family Law Act 1975*, Working Paper 3 (Brisbane: Family Law Research Unit, Griffith University)

Dienes, C Thomas and Levine, Lee (1993), 'Implied Libel, Defamatory Meaning and State of Mind: The Promise of *New York Times Co v Sullivan*' 78 *Iowa Law Review* 237

Donson, Fiona (2000), *Legal Intimidation: A SLAPP in the Face of Democracy* (London: Free Association Books)

Drechsel, Robert E (1990), 'Defining "Public Concern" in Defamation Cases since *Dun & Bradstreet v Greenmoss Builders*' 43 *Federal Communications Law Journal* 1

Edgeworth, Brendan and Newcity, Michael (1992), 'Politicians, Defamation Law and the "Public Figure" Defence' 10 *Law in Context* 39

Eekelaar, John and Maclean, Mavis (1990), 'Divorce Law and Empirical Studies – A Reply' 106 *Law Quarterly Review* 621

Elder, David A (1988), *The Fair Report Privilege* (Stoneham, MA: Butterworths)

Epstein, Richard A (1999), *Torts* (Gaithersburg, MD: Aspen Law and Business)

Eversole, M Eric (1998), 'Eight Years after *Milkovich*: Applying a Constitutional Privilege for Opinions under the Wrong Constitution' 31 *Indiana Law Review* 1107

Ewick, Patricia; Kagan, Robert A; and Sarat, Austin (1999), 'Legacies of Legal Realism: Social Science, Social Policy, and the Law' in Ewick, Kagan and Sarat (eds), *Social Science, Social Policy, and the Law* (New York: Russell Sage Foundation)

Ewick, Patricia and Silbey, Susan S (1998), *The Common Place of Law: Stories from Everyday Life* (Chicago: University of Chicago Press)

Fachiri, Alexander P (1925), *Principles and Practice of the Law of Libel and Slander with Suggestions on the Conduct of a Civil Action, Forms and Precedents, and all Statutes Bearing on the Subject, by Hugh Fraser* (London: Butterworth, 6th ed)

Faulks Committee (1975), United Kingdom, *Report of the Committee on Defamation*, Cmnd 5909 (London: HMSO)

Fehlberg, Belinda (1997), *Sexually Transmitted Debt: Surety Experience and English Law* (Oxford: Clarendon Press)

Fitzgerald, Tony (1999), 'Telling the Truth, Laughing' no 92 *Media International Australia* 11

Fleming, John G (1998), *Law of Torts* (North Ryde, NSW: LBC Information Services, 9th ed) (book published posthumously; chapter 25, 'Defamation' revised by Michael Chesterman)

________ (1978), 'Retraction and Reply: Alternative Remedies for Defamation' 12 *University of British Columbia Law Review* 15

________ (1971), *Law of Torts* (Sydney: Law Book Co, 4th ed)

________ (1965), *Law of Torts* (Sydney: Law Book Co, 3rd ed)

Flyvbjerg, Bent (2001), *Making Social Science Matter: Why Social Inquiry Fails and How It Can Succeed Again*, trans Steven Sampson (Cambridge: Cambridge University Press)

Franklin, Marc A (1986), 'A Declaratory Judgment Alternative to Current Libel Law' 74 *California Law Review* 809

________ (1983), 'Good Names and Bad Law: A Critique of Libel Law and a Proposal' 18 *US Federal Law Review* 1

________ (1981), 'Suing Media for Libel: A Litigation Study' [1981] *American Bar Foundation Research Journal* 795

________ (1980), 'Winners and Losers and Why: A Study of Defamation Litigation' [1980] *American Bar Foundation Research Journal* 455

Franklin, Marc A and Bussel, Daniel J (1984), 'The Plaintiff's Burden in Defamation: Awareness and Falsity' 25 *William & Mary Law Review* 825

Friedenthal, Jack H; Kane, Mary Kay; and Miller, Arthur R (1999), *Civil Procedure* (St Paul, MN: West, 3rd ed)

Galanter, Marc (1974), 'Why the "Haves" Come Out Ahead: Speculations on the Limits of Legal Change' 9 *Law and Society Review* 95

Garnett, Richard (2003), '*Dow Jones & Co Inc v Gutnick* – An Adequate Response to Transnational Internet Defamation?' 4 *Melbourne Journal of International Law* 196

George, Patrick T (1990), 'Congruency: Unravelling the Defamation Action' 6 *Australian Bar Review* 124

Gibbons, Thomas (1996), 'Defamation Reconsidered' 16 *Oxford Journal of Legal Studies* 587

Gilles, Susan M (2000), '*Food Lion* as Reform or Revolution: "Publication Damages" and First Amendment Scrutiny' 23 *University of Arkansas at Little Rock Law Review* 37

_______ (1998), 'Taking First Amendment Procedure Seriously: An Analysis of Process in Libel Litigation' 58 *Ohio State Law Journal* 1753

Gillmor, Donald M (1992), *Power, Publicity, and the Abuse of Libel Law* (New York: Oxford University Press)

Gillooly, Michael (2004), *The Third Man: Reform of the Australasian Defamation Defences* (Sydney: Federation Press)

_______ (1999), 'False Innuendoes and the Polly Peck Defence' 7 *Tort Law Review* 189

_______ (1998), *The Law of Defamation in Australia and New Zealand* (Sydney: Federation Press)

Glassner, Barry and Loughlin, Julia (1987), *Drugs in Adolescent Worlds: Burnouts to Straights* (Basingstoke: Macmillan)

Good, Ron (2000), 'Defamation Damages Reach $1 a Viewer' no 120 *Gazette of Law and Journalism*, see <www.lawpress.com.au>

Graycar, Regina and Morgan, Jenny (2002), *The Hidden Gender of Law* (Sydney: Federation Press, 2nd ed)

Grice, H Paul (1975), 'Logic and Conversation' reprinted in *Studies in the Way of Words* (Cambridge, MA: Harvard University Press)

Gunningham, Neil and Johnstone, Richard (1999), *Regulating Workplace Safety: System and Sanctions* (Oxford: Oxford University Press)

Gunthier, Albert C and Mundy, Paul (1993), 'Biased Optimism and the Third-Person Effect' 70 *Journalism Quarterly* 58

Hale, Dennis (2003), 'The Impact of State Prohibitions of Punitive Damages on Libel Litigation: An Empirical Analysis' 5 *Vanderbilt Journal of Entertainment Law & Practice* 96

Handsley, Elizabeth and Davis, Gary (2001), 'Defamation and Satire: *Hanson v Australian Broadcasting Corporation*' 9 *Torts Law Journal* 1

Hansen, Anders; Cottle, Simon; Negrine, Ralph; and Newbold, Chris (1998), *Mass Communication Research Methods* (Basingstoke: Macmillan)

Harkess, Jason (1998), 'A Linguistic Inspection of the Law of Defamation' 8 *Auckland University Law Review* 653

Hauser, Paul (1994), 'Divided by a Common Language', *The Lawyer* (London) (27 September) 24

Heerey, Peter (1987), 'Talking about Defamation: Pleading Defamatory Meaning' 61 *Law Institute Journal* 442

Herzfeld, Perry (2005), 'Corporations, Defamation and General Damages: Back to First Principles' 10 *Media & Arts Law Review* 135

Holdsworth, Sir William (1937), *History of English Law* (London: Sweet & Maxwell, 2nd ed, reprinted 1966)

Holstein, James A and Gubrium, Jaber F (1995), *The Active Interview* (Thousand Oaks, CA: Sage)

Hunt, Justice David A (1991), 'Defamation – Pre-Trial Practice' in J C Gibson (ed), *Aspects of the Law of Defamation in New South Wales* (Sydney: Young Lawyers Section, Law Society of NSW)

Hunter, Jill; Cameron, Camille; and Henning, Terese (2005), *Litigation I: Civil Procedure* (Sydney: LexisNexis Butterworths, 7th ed)

Hunter, Rosemary and Leonard, Alice (1995), *The Outcomes of Conciliation in Sex Discrimination Cases* (Parkville, Vic: Centre for Employment and Labour Relations Law, University of Melbourne)

Ingleby, Richard (1992), *Solicitors and Divorce* (Oxford: Clarendon Press)

________ (1991), *In the Ball Park: Alternative Dispute Resolution and the Courts* (Carlton South, Vic: Australian Institute of Judicial Administration)

Jacob, Sir Jack I H and Goldrein, Iain S (1990), *Pleadings: Principles and Practice* (London: Sweet & Maxwell)

Jennings, Bryant and Thompson, Susan (2002), *Fundamentals of Media Effects* (Boston: McGraw-Hill)

Jensen, Klaus Bruhn (ed) (2002), *A Handbook of Media and Communication Research: Qualitative and Quantitative Methodologies* (London: Routledge)

Jolowicz, John A (2000), *On Civil Procedure* (Cambridge: Cambridge University Press)

Keeton, W Page (ed) (1984), *Prosser and Keeton on the Law of Torts* (St Paul, MN: West, 5th ed)

Kenyon, Andrew T (2005), 'Developments in Qualified Privilege: England, Australia and Ireland?' in Eoin O'Dell (ed), *Freedom of Expression* (Aldershot: Ashgate)

________ (2004a), 'Imputation or Publication: The Cause of Action in Defamation Law' 27 *University of NSW Law Journal* 100

________ (2004b), '*Lange* and *Reynolds* Qualified Privilege: Australian and English Defamation Law and Practice' 28 *Melbourne University Law Review* 406

——— (2001), 'Defamation and Critique: Political Speech and *New York Times v Sullivan* in England and Australia' 25 *Melbourne University Law Review* 522

——— (2000), 'Defamatory Meaning: Pleading and Practice in New South Wales' in Barendt and Firth (2000)

——— (1999), 'Pleading Defamatory Meaning, Fair Report Defences and Damages: *Chakravarti* in the High Court' 7 *Torts Law Journal* 9

——— (1996), 'Defamation, Artistic Criticism and Fair Comment' 18 *Sydney Law Review* 193

Kenyon, Andrew T and Richardson, Megan (eds) (2006), *New Dimensions in Privacy Law: International and Comparative Perspectives* (Cambridge: Cambridge University Press)

King, David (2005), 'Ruddock Warning to States on Libel', *The Australian* (Sydney) (14 April) 4

King, Joseph H Jr (2003), 'Defining the Internal Context for Communications Containing Allegedly Defamatory Headline Language' 71 *University of Cincinnati Law Review* 863

Kirby, Justice Michael D (1977), '"The Purest Treasure"? National Defamation Law Reform in Australia' 8 *Federal Law Review* 113

Kirk, Jerome and Miller, Marc L (1986), *Reliability and Validity in Qualitative Research* (Beverly Hills: Sage)

Kirwan, Lucy and Masters, Jeremy (eds) (2002), *Australian Guide to Legal Citation* (Melbourne: Melbourne University Law Review Association, 2nd ed)

Klar, L N (1979), 'The Defence of "Fair Comment"' 8 *CCLT* 149, cited in Brown (1994) 994–95

Kritzer, Herbert M (2002), 'Seven Dogged Myths Concerning Contingency Fees' 80 *Washington University Law Quarterly* 739

Kumar, J P (1997), '"Fair Game": Leveling the Playing Field in Scientology Litigation' [1997] *The Review of Litigation* 747

Labrunski, Richard E and Pavlik, John V (1985), 'The Legal Environment of Investigative Reporters: A Pilot Study' 6 *Newspaper Research Journal* 13

Lacey, N (1994), 'Socio-Legal Studies: Definitions and Directions' 12 *Socio-Legal Newsletter: The Newsletter of the Socio-Legal Studies Association* 2

Law Commission (England and Wales) (2004), *In the Public Interest: Publication of Local Authority Inquiry Reports*, Report 289 (London: Law Commission)

Law Reform Commission of Western Australia (1979), *Report on Defamation*, Project No 8 Part II (Perth: Law Reform Commission)

Law Reform Committee of South Australia (1972), *Report Relating to the Reform of Libel and Slander*, 15th Report (Adelaide: Government Printer)

Levine, Justice David (2001), 'Defamation Practice: Change and Reform: plus a change . . . ?', speech at University of New South Wales Law School, Continuing Legal Education Conference (16 March)

_______ (1999), 'The Future of Defamation Law' (31 August), for both speeches see <www.lawlink.nsw.gov.au/sc/sc.nsf/pages/speeches_index>

Lewis, Anthony (1991), *Make No Law: The Sullivan Case and the First Amendment* (New York: Random House)

Lewis, Philip (ed) (1981), *Gatley on Libel and Slander* (London: Sweet & Maxwell, 8th ed)

Libel Defense Resource Center (2002), '2001 Complainant Study and Supreme Court Report – 2001 Term' [August 2002] *LDRC Bulletin* 7

_______ (2001), '2001 Summary Judgment Study' [August 2001] *LDRC Bulletin* 4

Lidsky, Lyrissa Barnett (1996), 'Defamation, Reputation, and the Myth of Community' 71 *Washington Law Review* 1

Lindell, Geoffrey (2003), 'The Constitutional and Other Significance of Roberts v Bass – Stephens v West Australian Newspapers Ltd Reinstated?' 14 *Public Law Review* 201

Logan, David A (2001), 'Libel Law in the Trenches: Reflections on Current Data on Libel Litigation' 87 *Virginia Law Review* 503

Lord Chancellor's Department (2002), *Judicial Statistics 2001* (London: LCD) see now Department for Constitutional Affairs (above)

_______ (2001), *Judicial Statistics 2000* (London: LCD)

_______ (2000), *Judicial Statistics 1999* (London: LCD)

_______ (1999), *Judicial Statistics 1998* (London: LCD)

Loveland, Ian (2003), 'The Ongoing Evolution of Reynolds Privilege in Domestic Libel Law' 14 *Entertainment Law Review* 178

_______ (2001), 'Freedom of Political Expression: Who Needs the *Human Rights Act*?' [2001] *Public Law* 233

_______ (2000a), *Political Libels: A Comparative Study* (Oxford: Hart)

_______ (2000b), '*Reynolds v Times Newspapers* in the House of Lords' [2000] *Public Law* 351

_______ (2000c), 'Political Libels – Whose Right Is It Anyway?' 53 *Current Legal Problems* 333

_______ (ed) (1998), *Importing the First Amendment: Freedom of Expression in American, English and European Law* (Oxford: Hart)

McBarnett, Doreen (1981), 'Magistrates' Courts and the Ideology of Justice' 8 *British Journal of Law and Society* 181

McEwen, Sir Robert and Lewis, Philip (1974), *Gatley on Libel and Slander* (London: Sweet & Maxwell, 7th ed)

McGonagle, Marie (ed) (1997), *Law and the Media: Views of Journalists and Lawyers* (Dublin: Round Hall Sweet & Maxwell)

McGraw, David (1991), 'How do Readers Read? Social Science and the Law of Libel' 41 *Catholic University Law Review* 81

McNamara, Lawrence (2001), 'Bigotry, Community and the (In)visibility of Moral Exclusion: Homosexuality and the Capacity to Defame' 6 *Media & Arts Law Review* 271

McNeill, Patrick (1990), *Research Methods* (London: Routledge, 2nd ed)

Macualay, Stewart (1963), 'Non-Contractual Relations in Business: A Preliminary Study' 28 *American Sociological Review* 55

Magnusson, Roger S (2002), *Angels of Death: Exploring the Euthanasia Underground* (Melbourne: Melbourne University Press) (with contributions from Peter H Ballis)

——— (2001), 'Freedom of Speech in Australian Defamation Law: Ridicule, Satire and Other Challenges' 9 *Torts Law Journal* 269

Maher, Laurence W (1993), 'Defamatory Meaning and the Defence of Truth: *Polly Peck* in Australia' 1 *Torts Law Journal* 215

March, John (1647), *Actions for Slander*, cited in Holdsworth (1937) vol viii, 369

Marjoribanks, Timothy and Kenyon, Andrew T (2003), 'Negotiating News: Journalistic Practice and Defamation Law in Australia and the US' 25 *Australian Journalism Review* 31

Marshall, William P and Gilles, Susan (1994), 'The Supreme Court, the First Amendment, and Bad Journalism' [1994] *Supreme Court Review* 169

Mason, Laurie (1995), 'Newspaper as Repeater: An Experiment on Defamation and Third-Person Effect' 72 *Journalism and Mass Communication Quarterly* 610

Masters, Chris (2002), *Not for Publication* (Sydney: ABC Books)

——— (1992), *Inside Story* (Pymble, NSW: Angus & Roberston)

Matheson, Scott M Jr (1987), 'Procedure in Public Person Defamation Cases: The Impact of the First Amendment' 66 *Texas Law Review* 215

May, Tim (2001), *Social Research: Issues, Methods and Process* (Buckingham: Open University Press, 3rd ed)

——— (1998), 'Reflections and Reflexivity' in May and Williams (1998)

May, Tim and Williams, Malcolm (eds) (1998), *Knowing the Social World* (Buckingham: Open University Press)

Mead, Jenna (ed) (1997), *Bodyjamming: Sexual Harassment, Feminism and Public Life* (Milsons Point, NSW: Vintage)

Meagher, Dan (2004), 'What Is "Political Communication"? The Rationale of the Implied Freedom of Political Communication' 28 *Melbourne University Law Review* 438

Media Law Resource Center (ed) (2004a), *Media Libel Law 2004–05: MLRC 50 State Survey* (New York: MLRC)

_______ (2004b) 'MLRC 2004 Report on Trials and Damages' [February 2004] *MLRC Bulletin* 1

Merritt, Chris (2005), 'Horse has Bolted, NSW tells Ruddock', *Australian Financial Review* (Sydney) (11 March) 58

Milmo, Patrick (1998), 'The "Pros" and "Cons" of Preliminary Decision Making' 148 *New Law Journal* 655

Milmo, Patrick and Rogers, W V H (eds) (2004), *Gatley on Libel and Slander* (London: Sweet & Maxwell, 10th ed)

_______ (2002), *Gatley on Libel and Slander: First Supplement to the Ninth Edition* (London: Sweet & Maxwell)

_______ (1998), *Gatley on Libel and Slander* (London: Sweet & Maxwell, 9th ed)

Mitchell, James C (2004), '*Rosenbloom*'s Ghost: How a Discredited Decision Lives On in Libel Law' 40 *Idaho Law Review* 427

Mitchell, Paul (2005), *The Making of the Modern English Law of Defamation* (Oxford: Hart)

_______ (2000), 'Political Qualified Privilege' 11 *King's College Law Journal* 114

_______ (1998), 'Malice in Defamation' 114 *Law Quarterly Review* 639

Morant, Blake D (2004), 'Democracy, Choice, and the Importance of Voice in Contemporary Media' 53 *De Paul Law Review* 943

Morris, Anthony J H (2000), 'Polly Peck Defence: Its Future in Australia' 74 *Australian Law Journal* 760

Morrow, Raymond A with Brown, David D (1994), *Critical Theory and Methodology* (Thousand Oaks, CA: Sage)

Murchison, Brian C; Soloski, John; Bezanson, Randall P; Cranberg, Gilbert; and Wissler, Roselle L (1994), '*Sullivan*'s Paradox: The Emergence of Judicial Standards of Journalism' 73 *North Carolina Law Review* 7

Neill, Sir Brian and Rampton, Richard (1983), *Duncan & Neill on Defamation* (London: Butterworths, 2nd ed)

Neill Committee (1991), Supreme Court Procedure Committee (England and Wales), *Report on Practice and Procedure in Defamation* (London: Supreme Court Procedure Committee)

Newcity, Michael (1991), 'The Sociology of Defamation in Australia and the United States' 26 *Texas International Law Journal* 1

New South Wales Attorney-General's Task Force on Defamation Law Reform (2002), *Defamation Law: Proposals for Reform in NSW* (Sydney: NSW Attorney-General's Department)

New South Wales Bar Association (2001), *Annual Report 2001* (Sydney: NSW Bar Association)

New South Wales Law Reform Commission (2000), *Contempt by Publication*, Discussion Paper 43 (Sydney: NSW Law Reform Commission)

——— (1995), *Defamation*, Report 75 (Sydney: NSW Law Reform Commission)

——— (1993), *Defamation*, Discussion Paper 32 (Sydney: NSW Law Reform Commission)

——— (1971), *Report of the Law Reform Commission on Defamation*, Report 11 (Sydney: Government Printer)

——— (1968), *Defamation*, Working Paper 1 (Sydney: NSW Law Reform Commission)

New Zealand, Committee on Defamation (1977), *Recommendations on the Law of Defamation – Report of the Committee on Defamation* (Wellington: Committee on Defamation)

Nielsen, Laura Beth (2004), *License to Harass: Law, Hierarchy and Offensive Public Speech* (Princeton: Princeton University Press)

Note (1985), 'The Libel-Proof Plaintiff Doctrine' 98 *Harvard Law Review* 1909

——— (1949), 'The Community Segment in Defamation Actions, A Dissenting Essay' 58 *Yale Law Journal* 1387

O'Barr, William M and Conley, John M (1988), 'Lay Expectations of the Civil Justice System' 22 *Law & Society Review* 137

Odgers, W Blake (1929), *Odgers on Libel and Slander (A Digest of the Law of Libel and Slander: And of Actions on the Case for Words Causing Damage, with the Evidence, Procedure, Practice, and Precedents of Pleadings, Both in Civil and Criminal Cases)* (London: Stevens, 6th ed)

Odgers, W Blake and Odgers, Walter Blake (1915), *Bullen and Leake's Precedents of Pleadings* (London: Stevens & Sons, 7th ed)

Opeskin, Brian (2001), *Appellate Courts and the Management of Appeals in Australia* (Carlton: Australian Institute of Judicial Administration)

Paine, Wyatt (1906), *Clerk and Lindsell on Torts* (London: Sweet & Maxwell, 4th ed)

Patfield, Fiona (1994), 'The Origins of a Company's Right to Sue for Defamation' 45 *Northern Ireland Legal Quarterly* 233

Pelly, Michael (2005), 'Defamation Goes National', *Sydney Morning Herald* (Sydney) (20 May) 8

Pether, Penelope (1999), 'Critical Discourse Analysis, Rape Law and the Jury Instruction Simplification Project' 24 *Southern Illinois University Law Journal* 53

Phillips Davison, W W (1983), 'The Third Person Effect in Communication' 47 *Public Opinion Quarterly* 1

Pielemeier, James R (2003), 'Choice of Law for Multistate Defamation – The State of Affairs as Internet Defamation Beckons' 35 *Arizona State Law Journal* 55

Porter Committee (1948), United Kingdom, *Report of the Committee of the Law of Defamation*, Cmd 7536 (London: HMSO)

Post, Robert C (1993), 'Meiklejohn's Mistake: Individual Autonomy and the Reform of Public Discourse' 64 *University of Colorado Law Review* 1109

——— (1990), 'The Constitutional Concept of Public Discourse: Outrageous Opinion, Democratic Deliberation, and *Hustler Magazine v Falwell*' 103 *Harvard Law Review* 601

——— (1986), 'The Social Foundations of Defamation Law: Reputation and the Constitution' 74 *California Law Review* 691

Pound, Roscoe (1915), 'Interests in Personality' 28 *Harvard Law Review* 343 (part 1) and 445 (part 2)

Prescott, Peter (1995), 'Libel and Pornography' 58 *Modern Law Review* 752

Price, David (2005), 'A System of Merit' *Media Lawyer* (8 June) see <www.medialawyer.press.net>

——— (2002), David Price Solicitors and Advocates, *Media Law Newsletter* (July) see <www.lawyers-media.com>.

Price, David and Duodu, Korieh (2004), *Defamation: Law, Procedure and Practice* (London: Sweet & Maxwell, 3rd ed)

Price, Vincent; Huang, Li-Ning; and Tewksbury, David (1997), 'Third Person Effects of News Coverage: Orientations Toward Media' 74 *Journalism & Mass Communication Quarterly* 525

Pring, George W (1989), 'SLAPPs: Strategic Lawsuits Against Public Participation' 7 *Pace Environmental Law Review* 3

Pring, George W and Canan, Penelope (1996), *SLAPPs: Getting Sued for Speaking Out* (Philadelphia: Temple University Press)

——— (1988), 'Studying Strategic Lawsuits Against Public Participation: Mixing Quantitative and Qualitative Approaches' 22 *Law & Society Review* 385

Queensland, Criminal Justice Commission (1997), *Integrity in the Queensland Police Service: Implementation and Impact of the Fitzgerald Inquiry Reform* (Brisbane: Criminal Justice Commission)

Queensland, Fitzgerald Inquiry (1989), Commission of Inquiry into Possible Illegal Activities and Associated Police Misconduct, *Report of Commission of Inquiry* (Brisbane: Commission of Inquiry)

Rares, Steven (2004), 'Can I Say That?' 25 *Australian Bar Review* 45

_______ (2002), 'No Comment: The Lost Defence' 76 *Australian Law Journal* 761

Riffe, Daniel and Freitag, Alan (1997), 'A Content Analysis of Content Analyses: Twenty Five Years of Journalism Quarterly' 74 *Journalism and Mass Communication Quarterly* 515

Robertshaw, Paul (2001), 'The Review Roles of the Court of Appeal: *Grobelaar v News International*' 64 *Modern Law Review* 923

Robertson, Geoffrey (1999), 'Tiptoeing towards Free Speech', *The Guardian* (London) (29 October) 22

Robertson, Geoffrey and Nicol, Andrew (2002), *Media Law* (London: Sweet & Maxwell, 4th ed)

Rojas, Hernando; Shah, Dhavan V; and Faber, Ronald J (1996), 'For the Good of Others: Censorship and the Third-Person Effect' 8 *International Journal of Public Opinion Research* 163

Rolph, David (2003), 'Perverse Jury Verdicts in New South Wales Defamation Trials' 11 *Torts Law Journal* 28

_______ (2002), 'BHP boss torpedoes *The Australian*'s main defence' no 136 *Gazette of Law and Journalism*, see <www.lawpress.com.au>

Ruddock, Alan and Burns, John (1994), 'Goodbye Gombeen Man' *The Sunday Times* (London) (20 November) 19

Sack, Robert D (1999), *Sack on Defamation: Libel, Slander and Related Problems* (New York: PLI Press, 3rd ed) (looseleaf service)

Sarantakos, Sotirios (1998), *Social Research* (Basingstoke: Macmillan, 2nd ed)

Sarat, Austin and Kearns, Thomas R (eds) (1993), *Law in Everyday Life* (Ann Arbor: University of Michigan Press)

SCAG (Standing Committee of Attorneys-General) Working Group of State and Territory Officers (2004), *Proposal for Uniform Defamation Laws* (Sydney: Legislation and Policy Division of NSW Attorney-General's Department, July)

Schauer, Frederick (2005), 'The Exceptional First Amendment' in Michael Ignatieff (ed), *American Exceptionalism and Human Rights* (Princeton: Princeton University Press) 29

_______ (1978), 'Fear, Risk and the First Amendment: Unraveling the "Chilling Effect"' 58 *Boston University Law Review* 685

Schilling, Keith (2000), 'The Americanisation of English Libel Laws' 11 *Entertainment Law Review* 48

Schultz, Julianne (1998), *Reviving the Fourth Estate: Democracy, Accountability and the Media* (Cambridge: Cambridge University Press)

Scott-Bayfield, Julie (1998), 'Defamation Update' 142 *Solicitors Journal* 229

Seale, Clive (ed) (2004a), *Researching Society and Culture* (London: Sage, 2nd ed)

_______ (2004b), 'Coding and Analysing Data' in Seale (2004a)

_______ (1999), *The Quality of Qualitative Research* (London: Sage)

Searle, John R (1979), *Expression and Meaning: Studies in the Theory of Speech Acts* (Cambridge: Cambridge University Press)

_______ (1969), *Speech Acts: An Essay in the Philosophy of Language* (Cambridge: Cambridge University Press)

Sexton, Michael (2004), 'An Erosion of Freedom of Speech?', *The Australian* (Sydney) (22 March)

Shawcross Report (1965), United Kingdom, *Report of a Joint Working Party of Justice and the British Committee of the International Press Institute on the Law and the Press* (London: Stevens & Sons)

Shiel, Fergus (2003), 'Time for Unity on Defamation, says Ruddock', *The Age* (Melbourne) (15 November)

Shillito, Richard (2004), '*King* – CFAs out of Control? 154 *New Law Journal* 856

Shillito, Richard and Barendt, Eric (2000), 'Libel law' in Barendt and Firth (2000)

_______ (1999), 'Libel law' in Barendt and Firth (1999)

_______ (1996), 'Libel law' in Barendt (1996)

Shoemaker, Pamela and Reese, Stephen (1996), *Mediating the Message: Theories of Influence on Mass Media* (White Plains, NY: Longman, 2nd ed)

Silverman, David (2000), *Doing Qualitative Research: A Practical Handbook* (London: Sage)

_______ (1993), *Interpreting Qualitative Data: Methods for Analysing Talk, Text and Interaction* (London: Sage) (see also 2nd ed 2001)

Simons, Margaret (2003), *The Meeting of the Waters: The Hindmarsh Island Affair* (Sydney: Hodder Headline)

Smigel, Erwin (1958), 'Interviewing a Legal Elite: The Wall Street Lawyer' 64 *American Journal of Sociology* 159

Smith, Steven K; De France, Carol J; and Langan, Patrick A (1995), *Tort Cases in Large Counties*, Bureau of Justice Statistics Special Report NCJ-153177 (Washington DC: Bureau of Justice Statistics)

Smolla, Rodney A (2004), *Law of Defamation* (New York: Thomson, 2nd ed) (looseleaf service, 1997, updated to 2004)

Smolla, Rodney A and Gaertner, Michael J (1989), 'The Annenberg Libel Reform Proposal: The Case for Enactment' 31 *William & Mary Law Review* 25

Soloski, John (1985), 'The Study and the Libel Plaintiff: Who Sues for Libel?' 71 *Iowa Law Review* 217

Soloski, John and Bezanson, Randall P (eds) (1992a), *Reforming Libel Law* (New York: Guilford Press)

_______ (1992b), 'A Concluding Note' in Soloski and Bezanson (1992)

Sourdin, Tania (1990), *A Study of Defamation Proceedings Commenced in the New South Wales Supreme Court for the period 1/1/1987 to 31/12/1988* (Sydney: NSW Supreme Court, unpublished)

Sowle, Kathryn Dix (1994), 'A Matter of Opinion: *Milkovich* Four Years Later' 3 *William & Mary Bill of Rights Journal* 467

Spilsbury, Sallie (2000), 'Bloodhounds and Watchdogs – Qualified Privilege, Malice and the Publication of Material in the Public Interest' 11:3 *Entertainment Law Review* 43

Stern, Nat (2004), 'Creating a New Tort for Wrongful Misrepresentation of Character' 53 *Kansas Law Review* 81

_______ (2000), 'Private Concerns of Private Plaintiffs: Revisiting a Problematic Defamation Category' 65 *Missouri Law Review* 597

Stone, Adrienne (2005), 'Australia's Constitutional Rights and the Problem of Interpretive Disagreement' 27 *Sydney Law Review* 29

Stone, Adrienne and Williams, George (2000), 'Freedom of Speech and Defamation: Developments in the Common Law World' 26 *Monash University Law Review* 362

Tate, Kathryn W (2000), 'California's Anti-SLAPP Legislation: A Summary of and Commentary on its Operation and Scope' 33 *Loyola of Los Angeles Law Review* 801

Taylor, Peter (ed) assisted by Brown, Bruce (2005), *Ritchie's Supreme Court Procedure New South Wales* (Sydney: Butterworths/LexisNexis) (looseleaf service, 1984 updated to 2005)

Thomas, Jeffrey E (1999), 'A Pragmatic Approach to Meaning in Defamation Law' 34 *Wake Forest Law Review* 333

Thomas, Sarah (2002), 'Red Devils' *The Guardian* (London) (4 November) Media Guardian 10

Thompson, John B (2000), *Political Scandal: Power and Visibility in the Media Age* (Cambridge: Polity Press)

Tiersma, Peter M (1999), *Legal Language* (Chicago: University of Chicago Press)

________ (1987), 'The Language of Defamation' 66 *Texas Law Review* 303

Tilbury, Michael (1998), 'Uniformity, the Constitution and Australian Defamation Law at the Turn of the Century' in Nicholas J Mullany and Allen M Linden (eds), *Torts Tomorrow: A Tribute to John Fleming* (North Ryde, NSW: LBC Information Services)

Tobin, Rosemary (2003), 'Political Discussion in New Zealand: Cause for Concern?' [2003] *New Zealand Law Review* 215

Tobin, Terence K and Sexton, Michael G (2005), *Australian Defamation Law and Practice* (Sydney: Butterworths/LexisNexis) (looseleaf service, 1995 updated to 2005)

Turner, Graeme (2004), *Understanding Celebrity* (London: Sage)

Turner, Graeme; Bonner, Frances; and Marshall, P David (2000), *Fame Games: The Production of Celebrity in Australia* (Melbourne: Cambridge University Press)

Trindade, F A (1999), 'When Is Matter Considered "Defamatory" by the Courts?' [1999] *Singapore Journal of Legal Studies* 1

Walker, Sally (2000), *Media Law: Commentary and Materials* (Pyrmont Ryde, NSW: LBC Information Services)

________ (1998a), '*Lange v ABC*: The High Court Rethinks the "Constitutionalisation" of Defamation Law' 6 *Torts Law Journal* 9

________ (1998b), 'Civil Defamation' in Lawbook Co, *Laws of Australia*, volume 6 (Sydney: Lawbook Co, current to 31 March, updated by Rupert Burns)

________ (1994), 'The New South Wales Law Reform Commission's Discussion Paper on Defamation' 2 *Torts Law Journal* 69

Walters, Brian (2003), *Slapping on the Writs: Defamation, Developers and Community Activism* (Sydney: UNSW Press)

Watterson, Ray (1993), 'What is Defamatory Today?' 67 *Australian Law Journal* 811

Weaver, Russell L and Bennett, Geoffrey (1993), 'Is the *New York Times* "Actual Malice" Standard Really Necessary? A Comparative Perspective' 53 *Louisiana Law Review* 1153

Weaver, Russell L; Kenyon, Andrew T; Partlett, David F; and Walker, Clive P (2006), *The Right to Speak Ill: Defamation, Reputation and Free Speech* (Durham, NC: Carolina Academic Press)

Western Australia (2003), *Western Australian Defamation Law: Committee Report on Reform to the Law of Defamation in Western Australia* (Perth: Committee)

Williams, Daryl (1998), 'Disappointment at Lack of Action on Defamation', Media Release (Canberra: Attorney-General's Department) (17 April)

Williams, George (1999), *Human Rights under the Australian Constitution* (South Melbourne: Oxford University Press)

Williams, Kevin (2000), 'Defaming Politicians: The Not So Common Law' 63 *Modern Law Review* 748

Williams, Neil J (2005), *Civil Procedure Victoria* (Sydney: Butterworths/ LexisNexis, 3rd ed) (looseleaf service, 1987 updated to 2005)

Wissler, Roselle L; Bezanson, Randall P; Cranberg, Gilbert; Soloski, John; and Murchison, Brian (1992), 'Resolving Libel Out of Court: The Libel Dispute Resolution Program' in Soloski and Bezanson (1992)

Woolf (Lord) (1996), *Access to Justice: Final Report to the Lord Chancellor on the Civil Justice System in England* (London: HMSO)

Yeazell, Stephen C (2001), 'Re-Financing Civil Litigation' 51 *De Paul Law Review* 183

Young, Alison L (2000), 'Fact, Opinion and the Human Rights Act 1998: Does English Law Need to Modify Its Definition of "Statements of Opinion" to Ensure Compliance with Article 10 of the European Convention on Human Rights?' 20 *Oxford Journal of Legal Studies* 89

Young, Alison (1990), *Femininity in Dissent* (London: Routledge)

INDEX

www.ingramcontent.com/pod-product-compliance
Lightning Source LLC
LaVergne TN
LVHW011103300926
849160LV00008B/265
9781844720217